names to grow on

CHOOSING A NAME
YOUR BABY WILL LOVE

by Suelain Moy with the editors of american baby.com

Meredith® Books
1716 Locust Street
Des Moines, Iowa 50309–3023
meredithbooks.com
First Edition.
Printed in the United States of America.
Library of Congress Control Number: 2007904775
ISBN: 978-0-696-23269-0

Front cover photo: Photodisc Photography/Verr
Back cover photo: Joe Polillio

For my parents, Calvin and Shirley Moy,
who gave me life and a name,
and for my son, Otter Lee,
who gave me the courage to forge a new life
and learn many new names.

contents

→ most popular names

2006 Top 100 Boys' Names

1. Jacob		51. Thomas	
2. Michael		52. Cameron	
3. Joshua		53. Connor	
4. Ethan		54. Hunter	
5. Matthew		55. Jason	
6. Daniel		56. Diego	
7. Christopher		57. Aaron	
8. Andrew		58. Owen	
9. Anthony		59. Lucas	
10. William		60. Charles	
11. Joseph		61. Juan	
12. Alexander		62. Luis	
13. David		63. Adrian	
14. Ryan		64. Adam	
15. Noah		65. Julian	
16. James		66. Bryan	
17. Nicholas		67. Alex	
18. Tyler		68. Sean	
19. Logan		69. Nathaniel	
20. John		70. Carlos	
21. Christian		71. Jeremiah	
22. Jonathan		72. Brian	
23. Nathan		73. Hayden	
24. Benjamin		74. Jesus	
25. Samuel		75. Carter	
26. Dylan		76. Sebastian	
27. Brandon		77. Eric	
28. Gabriel		78. Xavier	
29. Elijah		79. Brayden	
30. Aiden		80. Kyle	
31. Angel		81. Ian	
32. Jose		82. Wyatt	
33. Zachary		83. Chase	
34. Caleb		84. Cole	
35. Jack		85. Dominic	
36. Jackson		86. Tristan	
37. Kevin		87. Carson	
38. Gavin		88. Jaden	
39. Mason		89. Miguel	
40. Isaiah		90. Steven	
41. Austin		91. Caden	
42. Evan		92. Kaden	
43. Luke		93. Antonio	
44. Aidan		94. Timothy	
45. Justin		95. Henry	
46. Jordan		96. Alejandro	
47. Robert		97. Blake	
48. Isaac		98. Liam	
49. Landon		99. Richard	
50. Jayden		100. Devin	

2006 Top 100 Girls' Names

1. Emily		51. Jennifer	
2. Emma		52. Avery	
3. Madison		53. Mackenzie	
4. Isabella		54. Zoe	
5. Ava		55. Riley	
6. Abigail		56. Sofia	
7. Olivia		57. Maya	
8. Hannah		58. Kimberly	
9. Sophia		59. Andrea	
10. Samantha		60. Megan	
11. Elizabeth		61. Katelyn	
12. Ashley		62. Gabrielle	
13. Mia		63. Trinity	
14. Alexis		64. Faith	
15. Sarah		65. Evelyn	
16. Natalie		66. Kylie	
17. Grace		67. Brooklyn	
18. Chloe		68. Audrey	
19. Alyssa		69. Leah	
20. Brianna		70. Stephanie	
21. Ella		71. Madeline	
22. Taylor		72. Sara	
23. Anna		73. Jocelyn	
24. Lauren		74. Nicole	
25. Hailey		75. Haley	
26. Kayla		76. Paige	
27. Addison		77. Arianna	
28. Victoria		78. Ariana	
29. Jasmine		79. Vanessa	
30. Savannah		80. Michelle	
31. Julia		81. Mariah	
32. Jessica		82. Amelia	
33. Lily		83. Melanie	
34. Sydney		84. Mary	
35. Morgan		85. Isabelle	
36. Katherine		86. Claire	
37. Destiny		87. Isabel	
38. Lillian		88. Jenna	
39. Alexa		89. Caroline	
40. Alexandra		90. Valeria	
41. Kaitlyn		91. Aaliyah	
42. Kaylee		92. Aubrey	
43. Nevaeh		93. Jada	
44. Brooke		94. Natalia	
45. Makayla		95. Autumn	
46. Allison		96. Rebecca	
47. Maria		97. Jordan	
48. Angelina		98. Gianna	
49. Rachel		99. Jayla	
50. Gabriella		100. Layla	

baby name nation

In a recently conducted americanbaby.com poll, we asked parents:

"HOW DID YOU CHOOSE YOUR BABY'S NAME?"

Family name 21%

Baby book.............................18%

Special Meaning................ 20%

Other 41%

Excuse me, but "Other"?

That got us thinking. What other reason could there possibly be?

And so began our quest, to discover not only what parents were naming their children, but why and how. We wanted to know: What's in a baby name exactly? And this is what we found.

We live in an extraordinary era of baby naming. Parents are exercising their right and freedom to choose. They are pushing, nudging, and advancing the envelope of what's acceptable with each birth certificate and monogrammed blankie. Never have there been so many choices, inspirations, and examples.

Today's parents want names that reflect a child's unique identity and heritage with not just one positive meaning but many, many good vibrations. Names are personal, sacred truths, whether they're inherited, borrowed, or invented.

This is the story of the other baby name book—the guide that puts you in the driver's seat and makes you the baby-naming expert. How do we do this? By giving you all the wisdom, knowledge, and research you'll need and showing you how to apply it in fresh ways. We wouldn't dream of preaching what's proper or cool or perfect. We know that process and decision is way too intimate and important for somebody else to undertake for you. Instead, we provide the tools for you to choose or create a name for your baby that you will love.

There's a lot of time spent waiting for a child, especially if it's your first. And while this can be an anxious period full of worry, it also can be a profoundly sweet and hopeful time. We want you to spend that time wisely. We want you to spend that precious, wondrous time with us.

Accordingly we've packed the book with plenty of useful, practical, and fun information. You'll hear insightful advice and discover whizbang features you wouldn't expect to find elsewhere: rankings that reflect the true popularity of a name, smart-alecky trivia, and interviews with parents. A great deal of our time, devotion, attention, and care went into the creation of this book. We're proud of our baby.

And we're proud of you too. By picking up this book, you are making history. Personal, family-making, babynaming history.

After all, our children are the true celebrities in our lives with starring roles in our family productions. They are celebrated, cooed, photographed, picked up, fussed over, and applauded.

They receive many wardrobe changes and standing ovations in their lifetimes. Entourages of caretakers and admirers follow their every breath, smile, cry, and step. This book is our homespun valentine to them—and to you.

P.S. If you're worried that you'll screw it up, relax. In another recent americanbaby.com poll, we asked:

BE HONEST: DO YOU REGRET GIVING YOUR BABY THE NAME YOU DID?

No, I still love it. 91%

Now that we have a nickname, I like it better. 3%

I'd have chosen something different in hindsight. 6%

That's right. A whopping 91 percent said they still loved the names they chose.

Yes, by the time you put down this book, you will be a baby-naming expert, volunteering your services to every family in the neighborhood.

7

divine inspiration

1,001 WAYS TO ADORE YOUR CHILD

Rapper and R&B singer Lil' Mo is a true believer. That's why she named her daughters God'Iss Love and Heaven Love'on. And she's not the only one. Many parents feel their babies are blessings, naming their progeny Joshua (God is salvation), Theodore (gift of God), Michael or Michelle (Who resembles God?), and John (God is gracious).

As source material the Bible remains one of the most fertile and traditional, a testament to ancient marvels, human endurance, and tests of faith. Bible names consistently make the top-10 lists every year. Many of the names found in the Bible have been so absorbed into the mainstream culture that they no longer carry religious tones or associations. Jacob, Michael, Joshua, and Ethan were the four most popular boys' names in 2006. Of the four, Michael topped the list for 32 years, from 1966 to 1998. Hannah and Abigail both appeared on the top-10 list for girls in 2006.

Still there was something about Mary, the most popular girl's name in the country from 1880 to 1946 and again from 1953 to 1961, that reigned supreme in America and abroad. If you include the

continued on page 10

TIP #1

Make three columns of lists titled HEAVEN, HELL, and PURGATORY. Under HEAVEN write down the names you absolutely adore. HELL is for those you loathe, and PURGATORY represents the names that could be redeemed by a new spelling, circumstance, or variation.

And The Winner Is . . .

If there were a popularity contest for names, Mohammed (worthy of praise) would win with more than 500 variants in the world. The prophet, his followers, and descendants often appear in many Muslim names. Arabic names, such as Kareem (generous) and Kamal (perfect), pay homage to one of the 99 traits attributed to God, or Allah, in the Koran. In America spellings featuring "eem" are favored over the internationally prevalent "im" ending, thanks to basketball star Kareem Abdul-Jabbar. His original name? Ferdinand Lewis Alcindor Jr. The most famous Muhammad in America is former three-time World Heavyweight Champion boxer Muhammad Ali, who changed his name from Cassius Clay Jr. when he became a Muslim.

TRY THIS AT HOME

It's a Miracle! The name Miracle recently entered the ranks of the top 500 girls' names, while Messiah rose to #798 for boys. Faith, Charity, and Hope still burn brightly, and they've been joined by Destiny (#37), Trinity (#63), Genesis (#169), and Serenity (#135).

Heaven Knows

Nevaeh is now a popular girls' choice, thanks to Christian rocker Sonny Sandoval, who reversed the letters in the word "heaven" for his daughter. After Sandoval's appearance on MTV in 2000, the number of newborn Nevaehs rose from eight in 1999 to 5,814 in 2006. At #43, Nevaeh flew past Heaven at #253.

years Mary was ranked #2, she ruled serenely for more than 80 years. Known as Maria in Italy and Spain, Marie in France, and Maura in Ireland, Mary is also hailed as the Madonna in Italy. Among the many appellations honoring Mary are Lourdes, Mercedes, Pilar, Concepción, Soledad, and Dolores.

What This Style Says About You
You want the best for your child, and you are not taking any chances or leaving anything to fate. Parenting is a sacred trust you take very seriously. You want a name that is timeless and enduring; one that can weather and witness many storms, changes, and miracles. Tradition is comforting to you, a source of strength and stability in times of war and peace.

Which of these biblical names do you like best?

Gabriel	43%
Joshua	35%
Joseph	16%
Paul	6%

(TOTAL VOTES: 7,182)

Which of these "virtue" names do you like the best?

Grace	57%
Faith	23%
Hope	11%
Charity	9%

(TOTAL VOTES: 6,749)

TIP #2
Make a pilgrimage to different faiths, myths, and religions. Uma Thurman's name is derived from a Hindu goddess.

CASE HISTORY
Isis Arias, music publicist

"My mother's name is Cynthia, after Artemis, the Greek goddess of the moon. I was named after her because Isis is the Egyptian goddess of the moon. My brothers' names are Nyle—that's Gaelic for Niall, not the river—and Torin. I think our names are dope, and I've grown to love my name although I get very different reactions upon meeting new people. It was interesting when I was growing up—lots of 'Ice, Ice Baby' sung around me when Vanilla Ice's song came out. I've heard every nickname under the sun, including anything with Ice. Lately my closest friends have shortened it to 'Is.' I plan to stick with the goddess line with my daughters too, but that's not for a while yet."

Don't Leave Home Without It

In war-torn Iraq concerned parents create an extra set of identification cards, or *jinsiyas*, for their children to show at neighborhood checkpoints because names associated with Sunni Muslim or Shiite sects can be a dead giveaway. One popular Sunni name, Omar, has even been targeted for assassination by a rival party. Although the price of forged or fake documentation has risen, it's cheaper and safer than a legal name change, which is published in the local newspaper.

Take Me to the River

Before they married, Chris Martin wrote the song "Moses" for Gwyneth Paltrow with the lyrics: "Like Moses has the power of the sea, so you've got power over me . . ." The name had a powerful tug on the actress, who chose to call their son Moses in 2006.

"Moses to me is just such an amazing name. Plus he was born on the holiest Sabbath of the year, which is the Saturday before Passover. And he [our son] was born at Mount Sinai Hospital in New York. And it was my father's Hebrew name."
—Gwyneth Paltrow

A GUIDE TO RECOGNIZING YOUR SAINTS

Expectant mothers facing difficult or unpredictable labors often turn to St. Gerard for help in the delivery room. As a sign of gratitude, many sons have received Gerard as a first or middle name, and numerous maternity wards have been named in honor of the saint as well. Catholic parents who have difficulty conceiving also pray to St. Colette, the patron saint of expectant mothers.

sentimental journey

A NAMING ODYSSEY

Consider your child's name as the coolest of destinations, detours, and discoveries. Intrepid parents take the Route 66 approach to baby naming, finding inspiration in the far-flung and the mundane. Under these circumstances, the ordinary— a city, a hotel, a street—can become extraordinary as a name.

Spin the globe. Flip the atlas. Send and keep postcards. Consult road maps and review trip itineraries. Keep travel diaries

continued on page 14

CASE HISTORY
Colleen Hughes, magazine editor

Colleen Hughes, editor in chief of *Angels on Earth* magazine, has a deep and abiding love for her native Louisiana and its traditions. She believes "that whole sense of physical connection to a place can be kept alive."

"I'm from New Orleans," says the editor. "My daughter's name is Louisiana. For me, Louisiana is the place I call home. It's where my whole family is. We go back two to three times a year to visit because I have big, big family there. It's wonderful to go through the airport and see people's faces light up when they hear her name."

Hughes found the name of her second daughter, Evangeline, in the famous poem by Henry Wadsworth Longfellow. "'Evangeline' is the story of the Acadians, the ancestors of the Cajuns, who fled Nova Scotia and came down into Louisiana," Hughes explains. "It's also a love story between her and Gabriel. It's our *Romeo and Juliet*. When we were in Girl Scouts, we used to go on campouts in Covington and parts of Slidell. In the story we heard, Gabriel goes off on a ship and where Evangeline cried and cried, this beautiful oak tree grew, the Evangeline Oak." She adds of her daughter, "I call Evangeline my Christmas Evie because she was born on Christmas Eve. And she's got red hair."

Love Shack

The Carlyle Hotel is a sweet spot for many celebrities. Ron Howard's twins, Jocelyn Carlyle and Paige Carlyle, were conceived there. The posh New York City hotel is also where Julie Cypher, the former partner of Melissa Etheridge, got a little help from singer and sperm donor David Crosby. The rocker made a special delivery, dropping off his sperm in a paper bag. As Cypher recalls, "I checked in . . . and called David's room. Twenty minutes later he shows up at the door: knock, knock, knock. 'Nice to see you, how are you?' hands me the paper sack . . . and Beckett was conceived, just me in the hotel room. I still have the robe; he should have been named Carlyle."

"For years and years I wanted a baby. I knew I'd have a little girl and I knew I'd name her India . . . It's just an incredibly magical, spiritual place full of history and color and vibrancy. I love the name. And I love the country."
—SARAH MCLACHLAN

TIP #1

Follow your inner compass. If a name sounds right, then stick with it. If it doesn't, chances are it never will.

SKIP TO MY LOU

Dakota Fanning's first name is Hannah. Dakota is the actress' middle name. Younger sis, Elle, also likes to skip her first name, Mary.

of where you visited. Photograph tourist attractions. Remember, "not all who wander are lost." During your odyssey pay special attention to countries, islands, states, rivers, and roads.

What This Style Says About You
You are adventurous and romantic, open to new influences and experiences. Sometimes you feel restless and wonder about what's on the horizon or around the corner. Your freewheeling nature is balanced by a sweet sentimentality. You enjoy collecting souvenirs, photographs, scrapbooks, and mementos of happy times, especially from childhood.

CASE HISTORY: Beautiful Little Girl
Joe and Kierra Parlagreco, parents of Sonoma Rose

Joe and Kierra Parlagreco were sitting in rush hour traffic and arguing about baby names in the car. It was easier to come up with boys' names at first. "My father's name is Joe, and my name is Joe," Joe explains. "Kierra's father's name is Bob, and his father's name is Bob. Kierra wanted Max from *Where the Wild Things Are*, but it didn't go with our Italian last name, so I suggested Maximus from the movie *Gladiator*." Joe Bob, Maximus, and Maximus Joe followed. As for Kierra: "I was tossing out boys' names from soap operas that I had watched in high school. I said, "How about Frisco Jones from *General Hospital*?"

"I said there's no way I'm naming my son Frisco," Joe recalls now. "It's an insult to San Francisco and I'm from San Francisco. Only out-of-towners call it Frisco. Frisco Joe? That's ridiculous." That's when Joe suggested, "But how about Sonoma if it's a girl?"

"I'll always remember that moment," he says. "Immediately both of us knew that was her name. We pulled the car over because we thought it was so cool."

"We both loved it," Kierra says. "Sonoma is one of our favorite places in the world. It's our little slice of heaven." Sonoma met all of their requirements—it sounded musical and went well with their last name. And it was unique and easy to remember.

Kierra points out, "People always remember her name, but not ours." The couple added Rose as a middle name in honor of their grandmothers.

The couple soon discovered that there were few hard facts on the origins of Sonoma and many theories. The definitions ranged from "valley of the moon" (the title of a Jack London novel) to "chief big nose." Kierra's favorite meaning is rooted in the Native American word, *tso*, which means "the most sacred," and *noma*, which signifies "place." "It could be interpreted as the center of the universe," Kierra explains, "which she is for us." Joe, however, has decided that the name is Italian. He declares proudly, "I always say that it means 'beautiful little girl.'"

My Country 'Tis of Thee

Washington state and Washington, D.C. are named after George Washington, the first president of the United States. The city of Madison, Wisconsin, pays tribute to James Madison, the fourth president, who is also known as the Father of the Constitution. (Indeed there are streets in Madison named after each of the 39 signers of the Constitution.) Virginia was named in honor of Queen Elizabeth I, who was hailed as the Virgin Queen in England, and Georgia was named after King George II in 1733.

GO FISH

Mariel Hemingway was named after the Cuban port town of Mariel, where her grandfather, Ernest Hemingway, and her father liked to fish.

TRY THIS AT HOME

Helen Hunt thinks of Hawaii as her home. She wanted her daughter, Makena'lei, to be a real *kamaaina*, or local. In Hawaiian, Makena'lei means "many flowers of heaven."

AmericanBaby.com

Which of these city names for girls do you like best?

Madison	44%
Savannah	25%
Charlotte	12%
Cheyenne	12%
Helena	6%
Olympia	1%

(TOTAL VOTES: 12,383)

Pick the place name that you like best for a boy.

Austin	49%
Camden	26%
Dakota	12%
Brooklyn	5%
Dallas	5%
Boston	3%

(TOTAL VOTES: 6,209)

CASE HISTORY: A Tale of Two Tennessees
Tennessee Hale and Tennessee Bragg Le Porte in California

Tennessee Hale and Tennessee Bragg Le Porte were born a few years apart, grew up within blocks of each other but never bumped into each other. Their mothers marvel over the happy coincidences now, but at times having two Tennessees in the neighborhood was comically confusing. "For six years we didn't know the other family existed," exclaims Polly Le Porte. "I would go into stores on Larchmont Boulevard," Barbara Hale remembers, "and the shopkeepers would say, 'Oh, there's another baby named Tennessee!' and I would say, 'There couldn't be! You must be mixed up.'" Then the girls attended the same tiny private school in Los Angeles and the two families crossed paths. "It was really bizarre when we went to school and found out that there was another Tennessee," Le Porte recalls.

The similarities didn't stop there. "Both their fathers are actors," adds Hale, "and both their fathers are named George." For a while this caused some confusion at school receptions, events, and parties "as to which Tennessee and which George."

Both mothers drew inspiration from their families for their daughters' names. Hale knew immediately that she wanted to honor her father, Claflin Torpey, who was a distant relation of the Claflin sisters, Victoria Claflin Woodhull and Tennessee Claflin. Early suffragettes, the sisters were notorious for their colorful lifestyles and outspoken views on love, marriage, and women's rights. They opened the first women's stock brokerage firm in New York City and published the newspaper *Woodhull & Claflin's Weekly*. Cornelius Vanderbilt was an admirer. "They were ahead of their time and quite beautiful," says Hale. "Victoria ran for president of the United States against Ulysses S. Grant in 1872 with Frederick Douglass as her running mate."

Le Porte, on the other hand, deliberated over her daughter's name. "No name was good enough," she laments. "My first daughter at the age of 40!" She wanted to name her firstborn Beulah Bragg after her mother but was dissuaded by friends. She considered Sullivan, the county where she was born, and Harmony, her father's birth county, before settling on Tennessee, "where all my loved ones were born." Happily enough the name also belonged to a favorite playwright, Tennessee Williams. "I'm always homesick," the actress explains. "I lived in New York City for years and now I live in Los Angeles. I love Tennessee. I think it's a beautiful place, and I wanted to be reminded of it every day."

A Map of the World

Imagine if Angelina Jolie and Brad Pitt had named their children after their countries of birth. Maddox, Zahara, and Shiloh would be known as Cambodia, Ethiopia, and Namibia, while their brother, Pax Thien, would be called Vietnam.

FIRST, MIDDLE NAMES	MEANING	NICKNAME	BIRTH NAME
Maddox Chivan	Beneficent	Mad	Rath Vibol
Zahara Marley	Flower	Zee	Tena Adam
Shiloh Nouvel	Peaceful One	Shy	Shiloh Nouvel
Pax Thien	Peaceful Sky	Pax	Pham Quang

who's done it

Alabama Luella	Travis B
Alexandria Zahra	David Bowie & Iman Abdulmajid
Atlanta Noo	John Taylor & Amanda DeCadenet
Austin	Tommy Lee Jones & Kimberlea Gayle Cloughley
Brooklyn	David & Victoria Beckham
Caledonia	Shawn Colvin & Mario Erwin
Chelsea	Rosie O'Donnell & Kelli Carpenter
Dakota (g)	Melanie Griffith & Don Johnson
Dakota (b)	Melissa Gilbert & Bo Brinkman
Dallas	Fred Durst & Jennifer Rovero
Eden	Marcia Cross & Tom Mahoney
Georgia	Harry Connick Jr. & Jill Goodacre
India	Sarah McLachlan & Ashwin Sood
Indiana (b)	Casey Affleck & Summer Phoenix
Italia	LL Cool J & Simone Johnson
Kenya	Quincy Jones & Nastassja Kinski
Kingston	Gwen Stefani & Gavin Rossdale
London	Slash & Perla Ferrer
Memphis Eve	Bono & Ali Hewson
Milan	Scott Stapp & Jaclyn Nesheiwat
Paris	Pierce Brosnan & Keely Shaye Smith
Rio Kelly	Sean Young & Robert Luhan
Savannah	Marcia Cross & Tom Mahoney
Shiloh	Brad Pitt & Angelina Jolie

namesmithing

INVENTING THE PERFECT NAME

Do you find yourself rhapsodizing over an "R," following the serpentine curves of an "S," or admiring the perfect shape of an "O"? Perhaps you like the way certain letters sound, prefer a hard, kicky "K" over a more civilized "C", or swoon over a tumble of consonants or vowels.

If you find yourself paying rapt attention to your p's and q's and deliberating their placement carefully, this style might suit you to a "T."

Namesmiths are folks who like to hammer out and fashion names. They might rearrange the letters in a name, combine two names to create a new one, or spell a name or word phonetically.

TIP #1

Use exotic letters. Only a handful of girls' names beginning with O, Q, and U are in the top 1,000. U, X, and Y are the least common starters for boys.

Unusual and surprising combinations by spelling or pronunciation are the norm, not the departure.

What This Style Says About You

Individuals who invent their own names often have strong personal preferences. They notice if Scarlet is spelled with one "T" or two. They know what they like and what they don't like. They will try to incorporate current trends or adapt them by playing with letters, syllables, and sounds. They consider names to be personal reflections and works of art.

TRY THIS AT HOME

Spell a name in reverse, such as Semaj for James or Aron for Nora.

Freedom Writers

In the '60s and '70s many African Americans rejected what they saw as their "slave names"—names passed down through generations of families since the time of slavery. As a celebration of individuality and freedom, they chose or invented new names for themselves, often spelled in a unique way. Many also turned to Muslim and African names in a search for greater personal truth and identity. This tradition continues today. Hip-hop artist and musical performer Erykah Badu was formerly known as Erica Abi Wright. "I didn't want to have the slave name any more," Badu explains, "so I changed the spelling of my first name because the 'kah' is Kemetic [ancient Egyptian] for 'the inner self.'"

Dream Girl

Changing one letter can make a dramatic difference in a name. Beyoncé Knowles' first name is derived from her mother's maiden name, Beyincé. You get extra credit for adding or subtracting letters.

HOW SWEET IT IS

The mother of Condoleezza Rice composed her daughter's name from the musical notation con dolcezza, which means "with sweetness" in Italian. It was an apropos beginning for a girl who could read music before learning how to read books and remembers her mother, grandmother, and great-grandmother all playing the piano.

19

CASE HISTORY: FROM ISRAEL TO AMERICA
Daneet Steffens

"Daneet is the feminine of Dan, like Daniela or Danielle, except that it was made up by my parents. My mom is Israeli and 'eet' is the feminine ending for many Israeli names, often spelled with an 'I'—Ronit, Galit, Amit, Dorit— so my parents made up the name and the spelling. I think now there are lots of Danits in Israel, but at the time of my birth in Berkeley in 1963, there was only me, as far as I know.

"Hate may be too strong a word, but as a kid, it's hard to be different, and it was hard having a name that even teachers didn't know how to pronounce. At roll call I'd always know when they got to me because there would be a pause; quite often I'd rush to say it for them.

"Of course, as soon as you are an adult, it suddenly becomes 'unique' and 'beautiful' to other people. I really like that my parents took the time and effort to create something they thought was beautiful for me. It holds a direct key to my identity since I am half American and half Israeli and generally grew up all over the place. When I was living in Israel in first and second grade, I fell on some steps and chipped one of my front teeth; it was capped and stayed that way until I was in my early 20s. Then one New Year's Eve, the cap suddenly fell off and I had a chipped tooth again. I haven't capped it since. It adds a bit of character. I feel the same way about my name."

Backward and Forward

You can read these palindrome names front to back or back to front:

ANNA
AVA
BOB
ELLE
EMME
HANNAH
LIL
OTTO
PIP

YOU SAY POTATO . . .

Variant spellings are emerging on top of the popularity charts. Currently Bryan outranks Brian, Camryn is more favored than Cameron, Blaze wins over Blaise, and Kason is ahead of Cason.

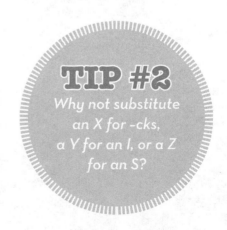

TIP #2

Why not substitute an X for -cks, a Y for an I, or a Z for an S?

The Origins of Oprah

It was an accident at the registrar's office that changed Oprah's name from Orpah to Oprah. "I was named after Orpah in the Bible," explains Winfrey. "My Aunt Ida named me, but she wasn't the person who put the name on the birth certificate, so the "R" and "P" got transposed." Instead of Orpah, after Naomi's daughter-in-law in the book of Ruth, the letters spelled out Oprah. During the beginning of her broadcast career, television producers urged Winfrey to change her name to Susie, but she kept it. Later, when she created her production company, she simply reversed the letters in her first name to spell out Harpo, for Harpo Productions. And when she published her magazine, she chose, simply, *O*.

"I'm a product of the late '60s. My parents were into this harmony thing, and I think that's what I'm about in my disposition and being half black and half white. They believed their love was real. It didn't matter about color. You could mesh and there could be harmony and they wanted their child to be a product of that . . . so they took the first three letters of each name— 'she' and 'mar'—and that's me, baby!"
—SHEMAR MOORE, WHOSE FIRST NAME IS A COMBINATION OF HIS MOTHER'S NAME, MARILYN, AND HIS FATHER'S NAME, SHERROD.

who's done it

Dannielynn (g)	Anna Nicole Smith & Larry Birkhead
D'Lila Star (g)	Sean "Diddy" Combs & Kim Porter
Dekker (b)	Nikki Sixx & Brandi Brandt
Diezel Ky (b)	Toni Braxton & Keri Lewis
Ginel (g)	Ginuwine
Jermajesty (b)	Jermaine Jackson & Alejandra Genevieve Oaziaza
Jourdyn (b)	Jermaine Jackson & Margaret Maldonado
Daniel Julez (b)	Solange Knowles & Daniel Smith
Kaiis (b)	Geena Davis & Reza Jarrahy
Kayah (g)	Ginuwine
Reignbeau (g)	Ving Rhames & Deborah Reed
Seargeoh (b)	Sylvester Stallone & Sasha Czack
Tryumph (g)	Jayson Williams & Tanya Young Williams
Whizdom (g)	Jayson Williams & Tanya Young Williams

SOUND CHECK

The more creative a name is, the more your child has to explain how to spell it and pronounce it correctly. Visualize seeing the name on a birthday cake, a name tag, an invitation, a driver's license, a business card. Can you say it easily or do you need a pronunciation key?

TIP #3

If you can't decide between two names, try combining them.

CASE HISTORY:
SARAH + ELLEN = SARELLE
Sarelle Katzman Scardino, retired school teacher

"Oh, I hated my name when I was growing up. I wasn't happy. I didn't want to be different. I didn't like that kind of attention. Everybody always questioned me about it. They asked me, 'Is it French?' Every year I had a different teacher and I had to explain my name and I didn't want to stand out. Everyone loved it. 'Oh, it's so beautiful!' they would say. My father always called me Suzy. I asked my parents, 'Why didn't you name me Susan?' I was named after my mother's mother. Her Jewish name was Sarela and her English name was Sarah. My parents didn't really understand that it was difficult for me. It's funny, the feelings you have as a child stay with you for a lifetime—and I'm 71. Even to this day, I don't think a week goes by when I don't have a discussion about my name."

CASE HISTORY: COOL COMBO

Tiffany Gibson named her son Jerryaaron

"His name was supposed to be Aaron, but his father wasn't having any of that," she remembers. "His father's name is Jerry Morales, and when I was signing the papers in the hospital, he said, 'That's great. I think you'd better get another piece of paper because that's not happening!' I put the two names together as a compromise. In school the teacher calls our son Jerryaaron. The kids call him Jerryaaron too."

Who's Working It

Erykah Badu, Geena Davis, Leeza Gibbons, Ginuwine, Beyoncé Knowles, Groucho Marx, Julianne Moore, Shemar Moore, Chynna Phillips, Busta Rhymes, Condoleezza Rice, Oprah Winfrey, Malcolm X

Happy En-dings

Parents often focus on the first letter in a child's name, but resourceful mothers and fathers also pay attention to the way a name ends. The most popular first letters for girls' names are A, K, M, and J. For boys, it's J, D, A, and C. While many girls' names end in the feminine "a" and "ella," trendy boys' names conclude with the popular "-en" ending. A quick run down the alphabet shows Aiden, Braden, Branden, Caden, Damien, Hayden, Jaden, Jalen, and Owen—and myriad variations of each. Other fashionable finishers for boys include "er," "on," and "an," as in Asher, Carter, Parker, Tyler, Brandon, Devon, Landon, Donovan, Logan, and Tristan.

where the wild things are

EVERYTHING'S BLOOMING AND ZOOMING

Naming your child is a labor of love that can feel natural, even organic. When you're expecting a baby, all of your senses are heightened. You see life bursting and blossoming around you. Your awareness of the world and connection to it deepens. You notice tiny details. There is a great element of discovery in what you see and do.

Nature names encompass an entire universe of appellations, from the dreamy (flowers, fruits, gemstones, and skies) to the ruggedly flinty (rocks, forests, rivers, mountains, and oceans).

They are indelibly associated with the innocence and idealism of the 1960s, along with the era's decadence and experimentation.

What This Style Says About You
You are inspired by the natural world. Intuitive and observant, you prefer to follow your instincts and do what feels right to you. You like to go with the flow and may find your moods reflected in the weather or the season. Your freedom is important to you, and you may have a strong independent or creative streak.

Who's Working It

Lily Allen, Lake Bell, Wolf Blitzer, Ruby Dee, Scarlett Johansson, Eartha Kitt, Heather Locklear, Stone Phillips, Brooke Shields, Sting, Plum Sykes, Lili Taylor, Amber Valletta, Forest Whitaker, Venus Williams, Tiger Woods

Flower Girls

You could gather a sweet bouquet from all the flower names in the top 1,000 girls' names: Jasmine, Lily, Daisy, Rose, Iris, and Violet. Television actress Poppy Montgomery's original name was Poppy Petal Emma Elizabeth Deveraux Donahue. "My mom, who's British, had this flower fairy book from the 1800s, and she loved it," recalls Montgomery, a native Australian who is one of five sisters with flower names. Her sisters are named Rosie Thorne, Daisy Yellow, Lily Belle, and Marigold Sun.

TRY THIS AT HOME

Raid the kitchen cabinet for the latest herb and spice girls and boys—Cinnamon, Basil, Pepper, Saffron, Sage, Rosemary, and Thyme. Add a little sweetness with Sugar or Honey.

TIP #1

Pair a very traditional name with a more outrageous middle name so your child does not sound like the latest ice cream flavor.

STRANGE FRUIT

Quince, Plum, and Huckleberry are all ripe for the picking now, but from the late 1880s until the early 1900s Orange was the top squeeze for boys, along with Lemon. Both names first rolled into the top 1,000 in the late 1880s. Of the two Orange was often considered the juicier fruit but dropped off the charts in 1901, while Lemon lingered until 1910. "Blind" Lemon Jefferson was a popular blues singer in the 1920s.

"As she came out of my tummy, Bluebell had both arms flung wide in the air as if announcing to the world, 'Hi! I'm here!' She was screaming her head off as though she was shouting, 'Hello, Wembley!' No one else has that name, apart from the Virgin Madonna and the singer whom I love. But what really clinched it for me was my mother telling me that the bluebell is increasingly rare—so it's [a] precious flower, which seems just right for my daughter."

—GERI HALLIWELL, "GINGER SPICE" OF THE SPICE GIRLS
AND THE AUTHOR OF A CHILDREN'S BOOK SERIES ABOUT
A 9-YEAR-OLD NAMED UGENIA LAVENDER

CASE HISTORY: The Bear Necessities
Bear Braumoeller, professor at Harvard, was 14 when his father legally changed his name from Gordon to Bear

"To the Swedes it's not an unusual name because the name Bjorn means 'bear' in Swedish, so they don't bat an eye or think anything unusual about it. I realized awhile ago that it's almost freakish the extent to which no one has made a big deal of it. I certainly haven't felt disadvantaged in any particular way. The only thing is I really have to make a good first impression because people don't forget me. I'm painfully aware of it when I don't.

"My parents had pet names for each other: Poppa Bear and Momma Bear. When I was 3 or 4, my father was a big fan of the Alabama Crimson Tide and Coach Bear Bryant. Because their house was sliding down the hill, they moved to a house on Bear Ridge Road and took that to be a sign. When I was a toddler, I had curly blond hair and the state animal was the California golden bear. I was 14 when we took a family trip to Germany and I needed to get a passport. My father asked me, 'How would you like to get your name changed to Bear?' The only thing my original name, Gordon, ever got me was teasing. The only person who ever called me Gordon was my babysitter. Years later, after my father's death, my mother said something about how he was rather a strange man who 'did things like running around, renaming the children.' I said, 'You mean you didn't know about that?' And she said, 'No!'"

TIP #2

Color me beautiful! Scarlet and Violet are hot hues right now that also sound vintage.

WHAT'S WHITE AND BLACK AND RED ALL OVER?

When they're performing on stage, the White Stripes often stick to three "power" colors: red, white, and black. Lead singer Jack White and supermodel Karen Elson named their daughter Scarlett. White's original name was John Anthony Gillis. When he married bandmate and first wife, Meg White, he unexpectedly took her last name.

AmericanBaby.com

Which of these botanical names do you like best?

Lily	64%
Rose	23%
Daisy	9%
Fern	3%
Petunia	1%

(TOTAL VOTES: 22,496)

Which of these nature names do you like the best?

Skye	37%
Summer	24%
Autumn	24%
Robin	11%
Sandy	4%

(TOTAL VOTES: 10,418)

who's done it

Apple	Gwyneth Paltrow & Chris Martin
Bamboo (b)	Big Boi & Sherlita Patton
Daisy Boo	Naked Chef Jamie Oliver & Juliette Norton
Dusti Raine (g)	Vanilla Ice & Laura Giarritta
Lily	Kate Beckinsale & Michael Sheen
Ocean (b)	Forest Whitaker & Monique Miller
Phoenix Chi (g)	Melanie Brown "Scary Spice" & Jimmy Gulzar
Poppy Honey (g)	Jamie Oliver & Juliette Norton
Puma (g)	Erykah Badu & The D.O.C.
Ruby Sweetheart (g)	Tobey Maguire & Jennifer Meyer
Sierra Sky (g)	Brooke Burke & Dr. Garth Fisher
Speck Wildhorse (b)	John Mellencamp & Elaine Irwin Mellencamp
Storm (b)	Nikki Sixx & Brandi Brandt
Violet (g)	Ben Affleck & Jennifer Garner

vintage
MAKING THE OLD WORLD NEW AGAIN

These charming, old-fashioned, and heirloom-quality names are precious because they speak of tradition and adorn a child with old-world grace and elegance. The names of yesteryear possess a retro glamour. They can be classic and stately or endearingly folksy and humble. A generation gap (or two or three) provides enough distance and nostalgia to appreciate these names anew and render them suitable for revival.

Abigail, Olivia, and Isabella have swept into vogue again, along with more sensible and earthy character builders such as Caleb, Samuel, and Henry.

What This Style Says About You
Authenticity is a form of innovation. Parents who dig these names love a good find and usually don't mind taking the time to excavate them from long-forgotten sources. Like avid antiques collectors and historians, parents dust off these treasures and restore them until they shine with a burnished glow.

TIP #1
Traditional songs such as "Waltzing Matilda" and "Oh, My Darling Clementine" are great source material for names.

IT'S A BIRD, IT'S A PLANE, IT'S KAL . . .
The middle name of Jerry Seinfeld's son, Julian Kal, tips its hat to Seinfeld's father, Kal, and also Seinfeld's hero, Kal-El, better known as Superman.

TRY THIS
AT HOME

Do the Russell Crowe! Give a child a l-o-n-g name like Tennyson and call him by a short, cute nickname like Tenny.

Hollywood's Heyday

Celebrity parents looking for mystique and sophistication can find inspiration in the names of Hollywood legends such as Ava Gardner, Tallulah Bankhead, Greta Garbo, Olivia de Havilland, Jean Harlow, Greer Garson, and Rudolph Valentino. Ava, Tallulah, Greta, Olivia, Greer, Harlow, and Valentino are getting plenty of face time as baby names. Patricia Arquette and Joely Fisher named their daughters Harlow and True Harlow respectively. Coincidentally both actresses made their movie debuts in the 1987 film *Pretty Smart*. Arquette's siblings include Rosanna and David Arquette, while Fisher is the daughter of Eddie Fisher and Connie Stevens. Carrie Fisher is her half sister.

"It just seemed right. . . . There's something kind of ancient about the name. It's got such a weight and beauty to it as well, and, I don't know, it just rolled off the tongue."
—HEATH LEDGER, ABOUT THE NAME OF HIS DAUGHTER MATILDA

Oh, Henry!

Julia Roberts and Danny Moder welcomed a son, Henry Daniel, following in the footsteps of Rachel Weisz and Darren Aronofsky, Dennis Hopper, Julia Louis-Dreyfus, Viggo Mortensen, Patricia Richardson, Emily Robison, Daniel Stern, Meryl Streep, and Jack White who all have heirs named Henry.

Who's Working It

Felicity Huffman
Samuel L. Jackson
Chloë Sevigny
Horatio Sanz

AmericanBaby.com

Which of these presidential names do you like the best?

William (Clinton) 51%
John (Kennedy) 33%
George (Bush) 10%
Ronald (Reagan) 6%
(TOTAL VOTES: 5,947)

Which of these classic actresses' names do you like the best?

Isabella (Rossellini) 40%
Sophia (Loren) 24%
Audrey (Hepburn) 19%
Katharine (Hepburn) 16%
Ingrid (Bergman) 1%
(TOTAL VOTES: 6,292)

CASE HISTORY:
Stacie Fenster and Alec Merber, parents of Eliza Jane

"Alec and I thought we were having a boy. We were going to name him Max. When they told us it was a girl, we went back and forth trying to come up with a name. For the longest time it was Juliet, but he wanted to spell it Juliette, which I didn't like. Then I wanted Jane but Alec thought it was too plain. So, about 3 weeks before my due date we went through a book and came up with Eliza, but I really wanted to use Jane as the middle name.

"Fast forward to me in the hospital the night after I've given birth—I'm flipping through the channels and credits for *Little House on the Prairie* go by. And, I kid you not, the character Eliza Jane appears in the listings! I felt like such an idiot. It all came flooding back—I remembered Eliza Jane was Almanzo's spinster schoolteacher sister. Ugh—me and my popular culture fixations!"

The Charles River

Charlemagne was the original Charles the Great. Celebrities who count Charles among their children include Russell Crowe, Jodie Foster, Julia Louis-Dreyfus, Emily Robison, Chris O'Donnell, and Cynthia Nixon.

who's done it

Adelaide	Rachel Griffiths & Andrew Taylor
Ava	Reese Witherspoon & Ryan Phillippe
Charlotte	Sigourney Weaver & Jim Simpson
Chester	Tom Hanks & Rita Wilson
Cicely	Sandra Bernhard
Clyde	Catherine Keener & Dermot Mulroney
Colette	Dylan McDermott & Shiva Rose
Eleanor	Diane Lane & Christopher Lambert
Ella Rae	Mark Wahlberg & Rhea Durham
Esme	Katey Sagal & Kurt Sutter
Eulala	Marcia Gay Harden & Thaddaeus Scheel
Gable Ness	Kevin Nealon & Susan Yeagley
Hazel Patricia	Julia Roberts & Danny Moder
Isabella	Nicole Kidman & Tom Cruise
Julian Murray	Lisa Kudrow & Michel Stern
Julitta Dee	Marcia Gay Harden & Thaddaeus Scheel
Lila Grace	Kate Moss & Jefferson Hack
Lucy	Scott Weiland & Mary Forsberg
Mabel	Tracey Ullman & Allan McKeown
Matilda Rose	Heath Ledger & Michelle Williams
Orson	Lauren Ambrose & Sam Handel
Owen	Kevin Kline & Phoebe Cates
Pearl	Maya Rudolph & Paul Thomas Anderson
Phinnaeus Walter	Julia Roberts & Danny Moder
Ramona	Maggie Gyllenhaal & Peter Sarsgaard
Sadie	Adam Sandler & Jackie Titone
Samuel Jason	Jack Black & Tanya Haden
Sophie	Eric Clapton & Melia McEnery
Tallulah Belle	Demi Moore & Bruce Willis
Theodora	Keith Richards & Patti Hansen
Theodore "Theo"	Bryce Dallas Howard & Seth Gabel

all around the world

IMPORTING NAMES TO EMBRACE A FOREIGN CULTURE

Foreign names can add worldly allure to an otherwise average John, Matthew, or Sophie. Don't care for Ernest—then how about Ernesto? Anne finds new footing as Anya or Anoushka. International names show an intrigue or passion with faraway lands. They may be familiarly rooted in past history and heritage or reveal a cosmopolitan sophistication and fascination with the foreign and new.

Generations ago ethnic names were pushed aside in favor of more "All-American" monikers. Today that trend has reversed. With the increasing interconnectedness of world cultures and economies, the diplomatic skills and presence of these exotic globetrotters are a plus. On the downside these foreign names may be hard to pronounce, or may get lost in translation.

What This Style Says About You

You are worldly and wise. You see your child as a citizen of the world. You enjoy learning about foreign and indigenous cultures and are quick to embrace or adopt local languages and customs when traveling. In new situations you show great flexibility and strength.

Who's Working It

Ashanti, Leonardo DiCaprio, Emilio Estevez, Mariska Hargitay, Angelina Jolie, Viggo Mortensen, Joaquin Phoenix, Liev Schreiber, Ivanka Trump

Birthday Twins

Former basketball teammates and rivals Shaquille O'Neal and Kobe Bryant welcomed baby girls on the same day. Me'arah Sanaa O'Neal and Gianna Maria-Onore Bryant were both born on May 1, 2006, six minutes apart.

In another ironic twist, Brooke Shields' and Tom Cruise's daughters also arrived on the same day, April 18, 2006. Shields, whose 2005 memoir, *Down Came the Rain*, describes her struggles with postpartum depression, found herself publicly criticized by Cruise for her use of antidepressants. Despite their opposing stances, the two families found themselves on the same hospital floor for the births of Grier Hammond Henchy and Suri Cruise. Cruise later apologized to Shields privately and the two families are now friends.

TIP #1

Always speak the name out loud. Names that look stunning on paper can fall flat with a thud on the tongue. Thijs is nice, but it's easier in Dutch.

TRY THIS AT HOME

Travel light for greater mobility and accessibility. Go with Bella over Isabella or zip around with Finn instead of Finnegan.

who's done it

Aoki	Russell Simmons & Kimora Lee Simmons
Amai	Marlon Wayans & Angelica Zackary
Arpad Flynn	Elle Macpherson & Arpad Busson
Augustin James	Linda Evangelista
Aurelius Cy	Elle Macpherson & Arpad Busson
Bella	Mark Ruffalo & Sunrise Coigney
Coco Riley	Courtney Cox Arquette & David Arquette
Cosimo Henri	Beck & Marissa Ribisi
Cruz	Victoria & David Beckham
Eliana Sophia	Christian Slater & Ryan Haddon
Enzo	Patricia Arquette & Paul Rossi
Estela	Ali Landry & Alejandro Gomez Monteverde
Giacomo	Sting & Trudie Styler
Gianna	Kobe Bryant & Vanessa Laine Bryant
Isabella	Nicole Kidman & Tom Cruise
Italia	LL Cool J & Simone Smith
Joaquin	Kelly Ripa & Marc Consuelos
Johan	Heidi Klum & Seal
Katia	Denzel & Pauletta Washington
Magnus	Kristy Swanson & Lloyd Eisler
Maison	Rob Thomas & Marisol Maldonado
Mandla Kadjaly	Stevie Wonder & Kai Millard Morris
Mattea Angel	Mira Sorvino & Christopher Backus
Matteo	Colin Firth & Livia Giuggioli
Mattias	Will Ferrell & Viveca Paulin
Me'arah Sanaa	Shaquille O'Neal & Shaunie Nelson
Mercedes	Val Kilmer & Joanne Whalley
Mia Honey	Kate Winslet & Jim Threapleton
Milán Hayat	Scott Stapp & Jaclyn Nesheiwat
Milo	Ricki Lake & Rob Sussman
	Camryn Manheim
	Liv Tyler & Royston Langdon
	Sherry Stringfield & Lawrence Joseph
Paloma	Emilio Estevez & Carey Salley
Rocco	Madonna & Guy Ritchie
Stella Busina	Dave Matthews & Dr. Ashley Harper
Stellan	Jennifer Connelly & Paul Bettany
Suri	Tom Cruise & Katie Holmes
Thijs	Matt Lauer & Annette Roque
Zahara	Angelina Jolie & Brad Pitt
Zahra Savannah	Chris Rock & Malaak Compton Rock
Zolten	Penn Jillette & Emily Zolten

No Smelly Heads Here

In Malaysia, a country of 26 million, there is no shortage of names that are considered "undesirable." According to Malaysia's National Registration Department, parents are strongly discouraged from naming their babies after animals, colors, numbers, fruits, vegetables, or insects. Names with objectionable meanings in the languages used by the country's Malaysian, Chinese, and Indian populations are also considered no-no's. Blacklisted monikers include Chow Tow and Sum Seng, which in Chinese mean smelly head and gangster.

"My wife was born in Sweden, and we loved the idea of a Scandinavian name. I've gotten a lot of flak: 'What kind of ego do you have to have to name your child the great one?' That is not it at all."
—WILL FERRELL ON NAMING HIS SON MAGNUS

TIP #2
Check the meaning of a word before you use it as a name. For her daughter, Catherine Zeta-Jones chose Carys, the Welsh word for love.

"It's an awful name. It's probably the most oft-mispronounced name in showbiz." —LIEV SCHREIBER ON WHY HIS CHILD WITH NAOMI WATTS WON'T BE CALLED "LIEV."

TIP #3

Latin names conquer like no others. Remember, you don't have to be in Rome to do as Cate Blanchett, Debra Messing, and Harvey Keitel have done—just go ahead and name your son Roman.

BEYOND BORDERS

Often a name can find more than one meaning or translation across languages. For example, Zahara "shines" in Hebrew and "flowers" in Swahili.

CASE HISTORY: Kira Arné, writer-producer:

"I've only met one other Kira in my life besides Kyra Sedgwick. She was Irish-American and in my high school. She spelled her name differently from me, K-i-e-r-a, and she had a twin brother, Kieran. Kira is a name that travels across cultures. I've been told that it's an African name. I've had people tell me that it's Russian and ask if I have any Russian relatives. It's an Irish name, a Celtic name. I've also been told that it's Japanese. As a kid I really loved my name because it was so cross-cultural."

AmericanBaby.com

What is your favorite form of Catherine/Katherine?

Caitlyn	32%
Kate	32%
Kathleen	12%
Caterina	9%
Catalina	8%
Cathy	7%

(TOTAL VOTES: 5,935)

Which Irish surname would make a cool first name?

Kennedy	29%
Delaney	27%
Quinn	26%
Tierney	11%
Rafferty	4%
Murphy	3%

(TOTAL VOTES: 1,128

The Luck of the Irish

Celtic names have timeless and lyrical appeal. Recent imports from the Emerald Isle include Caitlin, Aiden, Liam, and Finn. Surnames such as Riley, Finley, Reagan, and Sullivan are wildly popular too. Of course, you could just name your child Ireland as Alec Baldwin and Kim Basinger did. And what could be better than one Irish name? Try two . . . and follow in the footsteps of Patrick Dempsey or Ben Stiller.

Name	Parents
Aidan	Faith Daniels
Bailey	Melissa Etheridge & Julie Cypher
Bronwyn Golden	Angela Bassett & Courtney B. Vance
Cashel	Daniel Day-Lewis & Rebecca Miller
Connor	Nicole Kidman & Tom Cruise
Darby Galen	Patrick Dempsey & Jillian Fink-Dempsey
Declyn Wallace	Cyndi Lauper & David Thornton
Delaney	Martina & John McBride
Finley	Chris O'Donnell & Caroline Fentress
Finn	Christy Turlington & Ed Burns
Finnigan	Eric McCormack & Janet Leigh Holden
Laird	Sharon Stone
Liam	Tori Spelling & Dean McDermott
Mackenzie	J.K. Rowling & Dr. Neil Murray
McCanna	Gary Sinise & Moira Harris
McKenna	Mary Lou Retton & Shannon Kelly
Quinlin Dempsey	Ben Stiller & Christine Taylor
Quinn	Sharon Stone
Rafferty	Jude Law & Sadie Frost
Reilly	Roma Downey & David Anspaugh
Riley	Lisa Marie Presley & Danny Keough
Roan	Sharon Stone & Phil Bronstein
Ronan	Daniel Day-Lewis & Rebecca Miller
Sullivan Patrick	Patrick Dempsey & Jillian Fink-Dempsey

to surname with love

WHEN LAST NAMES COME IN FIRST

Just as marriage traditionally consolidated the power and wealth of two families or clans, the merger of two last names generates twice as much credibility and prestige as one. The use of a surname as a first name commands respect. It's a heady combination for parents who want to make a strong impression for a child right out of the gate.

It was also a practice and privilege formerly reserved for heirs, namely sons. Modern parents have capitalized on this trend to herald the birth of sons and daughters. Surnames, such as Kennedy and Parker, are no longer the exclusive domain of descendants from the family tree but for parents who are equally tradition-minded and forward-thinking.

What This Style Says About You

Mergers & Acquisitions: Can you say dynasty, boys and girls? Your family is a tremendous source of pride and satisfaction to you. Protective and clear-eyed, you are aware of family traditions and power structures and may choose to uphold them or strike out on your own. Depending on the clan, power may be defined by wealth, political clout, intellectual freedom, creativity, sports achievement, or mobility.

THE LATEST TWIST

A mother's last name can make an ideal first name for a daughter, as Gabrielle Reece and Mary Matalin discovered.

"Here's the real story: Campbell is my mother's maiden name. My full name is Alma Dale Campbell Brown. My great-grandmother was named Alma, and she married John Dale. My grandmother was then named Alma Dale, and she married Richard Campbell. My mother was named Alma Dale Campbell, and then she married a Brown. I'm the fourth in a generation. It's so Southern. Everyone thinks I made it up for television. The story is too ridiculous to make up."
—CAMPBELL BROWN

TIP #1

You also can use a mother's last name for a boy's first name as Penn Jillette did for his son Zolten.

In the Crossfire

Political pundit and journalist Tucker Carlson has four—count 'em four!—surnames in his name: Tucker Swanson McNear Carlson.

Great Scott!

In Scotland the practice of using surnames as first, or given, names is an early and ancient tradition. Cameron, Campbell, and Scott are Scottish surnames that have found starring roles as first names. Douglas, Fraser, Graham, Keith, and Leslie are Scottish surnames that have evolved into proper English first names.

"And now we'd like to interview a man with two last names and a woman with two first names: Wentworth Miller and Evangeline Lilly."

—CONAN O'BRIEN, HOSTING THE 2006 EMMY AWARDS

Shirley Valentine

Before Charlotte Bronte's novel Shirley was published in 1849, Shirley was a surname frequently used for boys as a first name. During the 1930s and 1940s, the name became wildly popular with the meteoric rise of child star Shirley Temple.

CASE HISTORY:
Jane Armstrong, mother of Cameron, Kelly, Carson, and Campbell

"We have a Campbell and a Kelly, both girls, and Cameron and Carson are our boys. I never really thought about it, but I guess they all do have names that could be last names. Cameron was going to be Cameron no matter if he was a girl or a boy because that's my husband's middle name and I have always loved it. Growing up I knew no Camerons. He is the only Cameron in his grade, and there are over 325 kids. I only knew one Campbell during college and over the past few years have heard of a couple of Campbells in New Canaan, all babies.

"I wanted to pick names that were a little out there but not too much so because my husband was very concerned about our kids having 'freakish' names. There are so many common names these days that you hear constantly and I didn't want that for my kids. I wanted a Georgia, but my husband liked Kelly, so he got to pick that one. And she really does look like a Kelly, tall and blond. And although her name starts with a 'K,' it still has the hard 'C' sound so it fit in perfectly. For Carson, I wanted him to be Cooper initially but then my brother-in-law suggested Carson and we just went with it.

"It was while I was watching TV during my fourth pregnancy that I came up with the name Campbell after watching TV newscaster Campbell Brown. I remember remarking to my husband what a cool name I thought it was and when my husband didn't object to it, I held onto it until she was born. And so Campbell it was."

The Dynasty of Drew

Everyone knows that Drew Barrymore's last name belongs to her grandfather, legendary actor John Barrymore, but did you know her first and middle names are also family surnames? Drew is the maiden name of paternal grandmother, Georgiana Drew. Blyth is the original surname of great-grandfather Maurice Barrymore, patriarch of the Barrymore acting dynasty. Herbert Arthur Chamberlayne Blyth adopted the stage name of "Maurice Barrymore" when his father felt embarrassed by his son's theatrical choice of profession.

TIP #2

Too much of a good thing? Pile up too many surnames and you could have a name that's more suitable for a law firm than a baby.

AmericanBaby.com

Do you like the idea of passing on family names?

It depends on the name	58%
Yes, I love it	31%
I don't like it	11%

(TOTAL VOTES: 2,704)

Who's Working It

Campbell Brown, Tucker Carlson, Anderson Cooper, Schuyler Fisk, Lachlan Murdoch, Hayden Panettiere, Mackenzie Phillips

word up!

When it came to pioneering words as names, the Puritans were the first to rock the boat. Rejecting Old English names from the Church of England, they were fond of using names from the Bible, along with virtue names such as Prudence, Constance, Temperance, Fearnot, Mindwell, Safely-on-high, and Hate-Evil.

Word names state the obvious, whether you're calling your child Baby, Prince, or Journey. (Quincy Jones' middle name is Delightt.) Other desirable qualities that have turned up in the top 1,000 names recently are Sincere, Sterling, and Maverick for boys, and Precious and Unique for girls. Justice is in demand for both sexes, although it's slightly more popular for males.

What This Style Says About You
Words are sacred to you. Honest and literal, you often surprise people with your directness. You are idealistic and not afraid to take a stand for your beliefs. What you see is what you get.

CASE HISTORY: History in the Making
Krishna Stone, mother of Parade Diosa Stone

"If I had a boy child, I would have named him March. March Dios. I thought March would be a perfect boy's name. I was born in 1959 and I sat on my father's shoulders when he took me to hear Martin Luther King Jr.'s 'I Have a Dream' speech in D.C. I was really too young to remember the Civil Rights marches. I felt like I had missed all that.

"Parade and I have participated in a number of marches, protests, and parades. She has been to many demonstrations. She was 3 months old when she marched in the Lesbian, Gay, Bisexual, and Transgender Pride March with her godfathers.

"And she is a Parade. When you see her, there is just no way this child could not be Parade. She is a sensational person, even in her worst moments. It fits her. And that is very clear. Some children, they really are their name."

I Know This Much Is True

Forest Whitaker has a daughter named True. True is also the name of Joely Fisher's daughter. The word also works as a middle name for Kirstie Alley and Parker Stevenson's adopted son, William, and Meg Ryan's adopted daughter, Daisy.

TIP #1

Two words are sometimes better than one.

TRY THIS AT HOME

Make a list of the qualities you respect and admire.

WHAT GOES AROUND COMES AROUND Race car driver Kenny Brack and rapper Ludacris both have daughters named Karma.

"I always tell people my name was a birthday present from my parents. A gift in the truest sense—a great big name I had my whole life to grow into and one that, for me, conjures up dignity and beauty and femininity and watchfulness. My middle name, Unit, was given to me because I was the firstborn child, and then we became a family unit."

—MOON UNIT ZAPPA

"I think it's time for Kid Rock to drop the 'Kid.' He's getting older; he should change his name to Soft Rock. Or Smooth Jazz."

—CRAIG FERGUSON

CASH ON DELIVERY

Annabeth Gish delivered a son, Cash Alexander. Guns N' Roses guitarist Slash Hudson also has a son named Cash, and one of Finola Hughes' sons is named Cash Justice. Forget about showing the love—just show us the money!

Danger is my middle name!

At least it is for the son of Green Day lead singer Billie Joe Armstrong, named Jakob Danger. Australian rugby player Mat Rogers is no stranger to danger either. He welcomed a son, Maxwell Danger, to the world.

CASE HISTORY: Paisley Park
Lindsay Nohr Beck, founder and executive director of Fertile Hope

Lindsay Nohr Beck is the founder and executive director of Fertile Hope, an organization that educates and assists cancer patients with fertility issues. She and her husband, Jordan, wanted to find a name that honored her grandmother, Eve, from Scotland. "We looked at the Scottish names to see if there was anything we liked," she remembers, "and Paisley really stood out to us. We just loved it. It was one of those things. When we read it, we felt like, 'That's it!'"

The couple road-tested the name first, using it to make restaurant reservations and while shopping in the mall. "We wanted to see how people reacted or if they had a hard time saying it," Beck says. "Everyone would say, 'Wow, I love your name! I've never heard of that before.' That really helped us to decide. We wanted her name to be unique and we loved the Scottish heritage, but we didn't want it to be so off-the-wall that it would drive her crazy her whole life. Someone described Paisley as a little girl of many colors. The name suits her. Her personality is very colorful."

Another detail they love is their daughter's initials. "Her name is Paisley Jane Beck, so her monogram is PBJ, which is like peanut butter and jelly. My brother calls her Peanut Butter."

who's done it

Audio Science	Shannyn Sossamon & Dallas Clayton
Braison Chance	Billy Ray Cyrus & Leticia "Tish" Finley Cyrus
Cannon (b)	Larry King & Shawn Southwick
Chance (b)	Larry King & Shawn Southwick
Henry Chance	Rachel Weisz & Darren Aronofsky
Denim Cole (b)	Toni Braxton & Keri Lewis
Destiny "Miley"	Billy Ray Cyrus & Leticia "Tish" Finley Cyrus
Diezel Ky (b)	Toni Braxton & Keri Lewis
Dream Sarae (g)	Ginuwine & Solè
Felicity-Amore	Keisha Castle-Hughes & Bradley Hull
Freedom (b)	Ving Rhames & Deborah Reed
Honor (g)	Tilda Swinton & John Byrne
Justice	John Mellencamp & Vicky Granucci
Keen (b)	Mark Ruffalo & Sunrise Coigney
Liberty (g)	Casey Kasem & Jean Kasem
Lillie Price	Kirstie Alley & Parker Stevenson
Lyric (g)	Robby Benson & Karla DeVito
Mateo Bravery	Benjamin Bratt & Talisa Soto
Praise Mary Ella	DMX & Tashera Simmons
Prima	John Tesh & Connie Selleca
Seven Sirius (b)	Erykah Badu & André 3000
Sonnet (g)	Forest Whitaker & Keisha Nash
Story (g)	Ginuwine & Solè
Story Elias Elfman	Jenna Elfman & Bodhi Elfman
Sugar McQueen (g)	Nikka Costa & Justin Stanley
Sunny Bebop (g)	Flea & Frankie Rayder
Trinity (g)	Dennis Rodman & Michelle Moyer
Tu Morrow (g)	Rob Morrow & Debbon Ayer
Zephyr (b)	Robby Benson & Karla DeVito

TIP #2

A little wit goes a long way. Just say no to any puns ("Tu Morrow") that sound like put-downs.

Who's Working It

Ever Carradine, Jewel, Kid Rock, Prince, Diamond Blue Smith and Spectacular Blue Smith from the hip-hop group Pretty Ricky

plain janes and cool joes

KEEPING IT REAL

Traditional and functional names hold classic and timeless appeal for parents. From the proudly regal to the playfully modest, they allow a child to shine without any distractions. Whether you fancy Abby or Abigail, Billy or William, these normal names will blend effortlessly into any family, lifestyle, or career without offending or shocking anyone.

In an age of anything-goes baby names, ordinary names sit perfectly at ease in the world. Straightforward and approachable, they frame a person's identity, without overwhelming it.

Need more proof? Look at the long list of celebrities who have changed their given names—and the equally long list of celebrities who have kept them. Many of the biggest names in business, sports, and entertainment started out quite simply and humbly.

THE LATEST TWIST

Use a nickname properly. Bypass the longer and stuffier version for Maggie (Faith Hill and Tim McGraw's daughter) or Charlie (Soledad O'Brien's son).

What This Style Says About You

You are a realist. Grounded and level-headed, you possess sound judgment and common sense. You are a dependable and thoughtful parent who wants your child to fit in to society and feel accepted. You do not want your child to feel embarrassed by his or her name or to struggle with it unnecessarily. You are practical, choosing the tried and true over the trendy.

Take It Back!

Not every celebrity scion signs up for the free publicity that comes with an unusual name. Free Carradine, son of David Carradine and Barbara Hershey, changed his name to Tom. David Bowie's son, Zowie (aka Duncan Zowie Heywood Jones), was called Joe or Joey for years. Bob Geldof's daughter, whose full name is Peaches Honeyblossom Michelle Charlotte Angel Vanessa Geldof, recently asked celebrity parents to stop giving their children ridiculous names. She said, "I hate ridiculous names. My weird name has haunted me all my life."

TIP #1

Make every letter count. Use initials. Think L. A. Reid and KT Tunstall. LL Cool J stands for Ladies Love Cool James!

Hot or Not

It's hard to imagine Johnny Depp swashbuckling as John Christopher or Will Smith cracking wise as Willard. Ditto for Jude Law, whose first name is David, and Brad Pitt, who was born William Bradley Pitt.

MARY, MARY, QUITE CONTRARY

Meryl Streep's first name was Mary. Mary was also the first name of Debbie Reynolds, Sissy Spacek, Marg Helgenberger, Lily Tomlin, Bo Derek, Debra Winger, Lauren Hutton, and Sean Young.

who's done it

Billie	Carrie Fisher & Bryan Lourd
Billie Ray	Tim Burton & Helena Bonham Carter
Harry	David Letterman & Regina Lasko
Jack	Matt Lauer & Annette Roque
Jack Henry	Susan Sarandon & Tim Robbins
James Leroy	Jerry Hall & Mick Jagger
Joe Alfie	Kate Winslet & Sam Mendes
John David	Denzel Washington & Pauletta Washington
Peter	Stephanie Seymour & Peter Brant
Sam Alexis (g)	Tiger Woods & Elin Nordegren
Sam J.	Charlie Sheen & Denise Richards
Will	Christopher Reeve & Dana Reeve

TIP #2

Choose names that sound like nicknames and end with the long "ee" sound, spelled with a, y, i, ie, or ee.

"I wanted to give him a good, normal name. You can't move to Des Moines with a name like Pineapple."
—JOHN O'HURLEY, WHO NAMED HIS SON WILLIAM

CASE HISTORY:
Victoria and Brad Colyer are the parents of James, Andrew, Henry, and John. Victoria is from Spain and Brad is American. The family is bilingual.

"I like traditional names and I like short names, if possible. We liked James in both languages, English and Spanish. They all translate well and they sound normal in both languages. They go well with our last name, and you don't have to ask if they're a boy or a girl. You know right away that they are boys. There is a James, an Andrew, and a John. We have three disciples. I don't know what happened with Harry. Harry should have been Phillip or Peter, and he does have the personality of Peter. When Harry, our third son, was born, we named him John. I said, 'He just doesn't look like a John,' and Brad said, 'What does a John look like? What are you looking for?' So he became Harry and our next son was John."

Destiny's Child

There were no achy-breaky hearts when Billy Ray Cyrus and his wife, Tish, named their daughter Destiny Hope Cyrus. The youngster was so happy and smiley, it wasn't long before she was called Smiley, and then Miley. And the nickname stuck. By the time the teenaged actress-singer was starring in Disney's *Hannah Montana* series, it was clearly her destiny to perform.

"When I was little, I would stand up on couches and say, 'Watch me,'" remembered Miley. "We had these showers that are completely glass, and I would lock people in them and make them stay in there and watch me perform. I'd make them watch." Maybe that's why her grandmother is the only one who still calls her Destiny.

Who's Working It

Billie Joe Armstrong, Jack Black, Christie Brinkley, Tim Burton, Jim Carrey, George Clooney, Katie Couric, Billy Ray Cyrus, Matt Damon, Jennifer Garner, Bill Gates, Al Gore, Tom Hanks, Kate Hudson, Ricki Lake, Jason Lee, Edward Norton, Sandra Oh, Mary-Kate Olsen, Mary-Louise Parker, Matthew Perry, Jane Pratt, Denise Richards, Will Smith, Howard Stern, Billy Bob Thornton

MIX IT UP

Naomi Watts and Liev Schreiber mixed the formal with the informal for son, Alexander Pete, who was named in tribute of Liev's grandfather and Naomi's father.

occupied by a name

JOB HUNTING

Like the form says, state your name and occupation. The utilitarianism of occupational names has a stark and modern effect. They can possess the blunt, earthy appeal of men at work or sound shocking and sensational. There can be a real Barnum & Bailey brand of showmanship at work or a surreal Ripley's Believe It or Not effect.

Parents who name their kids after a trade are heading into uncharted territory. They may

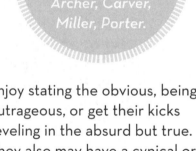

TIP #1
Tradesmen names often end in -er: Archer, Carver, Miller, Porter.

enjoy stating the obvious, being outrageous, or get their kicks reveling in the absurd but true. They also may have a cynical or ironic sense of humor and way of looking at the world.

What This Style Says About You
If you find yourself occupied by a name, you are a free thinker, original and unconventional. You like to defy labels and easy categorization. You tend to be suspicious of authority figures and the government. You enjoy debunking myths and may harbor more than a few conspiracy theories of your own.

TRY THIS AT HOME

To make a bigger splash, use your child's middle name for the full effect, as in Moxie CrimeFighter or Pilot Inspektor.

Sailing

For Christie Brinkley a family history of sailing and exploration led her and Peter Cook to name their daughter Sailor. "Peter's family dates back to Captain Cook, who discovered the Big Island of Hawaii," the supermodel recalls. "It's also where we found out we were pregnant, so we called her Captain Cook during the pregnancy. That evolved into Sailor."

Who's Working It

Taylor Hicks, Gypsy Rose Lee, Judge Reinhold, Fisher Stevens, Parker Stevenson, Hunter S. Thompson, Booker T. Washington

Ready or Not

Film director Robert Rodríguez has four sons—Rocket, Racer, Rebel, and Rogue—and a daughter, Rhiannon. He has joked that another child would be "Redundant."

RIDE Kate Hudson has remarked that her son, Ryder, often kicked in utero to his father's song "Ride."

Regis Philbin: "So today's dancer was Gypsy Light, Gypsy Light from Endicott, New York. Yeah, Gypsy!"
Kelly Ripa: "It's very nice when you're born with your stripper name. That's very important."
—LIVE WITH REGIS AND KELLY

who's done it

Barron	Donald & Melania Trump
Deacon	Reese Witherspoon & Ryan Phillippe
Duke	Diane Keaton
Gunner	Nikki Sixx & Brandi Brandt
Mason Olivia	Kelsey Grammer & Camille Donatacci
Moxie CrimeFighter	Penn Jillette & Emily Zolten
Pilot Inspektor	Jason Lee & Beth Riesgraf
Piper Maru	Gillian Anderson & Clyde Klotz
Pirate Howsmon	Korn's Jonathan Davis & Devon Davis
Poet Sienna Rose	Soleil Moon Frye & Jason Goldberg
Ryder Evan	Faith Evans & Todd Russaw
Shepherd Kellen	Jerry & Jessica Seinfeld

TIP #2

Many last names are also occupational names.

"Somehow the name Bob has become normal. Why Bob? That's something you do for apples on Halloween!"

–JASON LEE, FATHER OF PILOT INSPEKTOR

CASE HISTORY: Strummer
Gavin Edwards, music journalist

Gavin Edwards is a music journalist, a contributing editor for *Rolling Stone*, and the author of *Is Tiny Dancer Really Elton's Little John? Music's Most Enduring Mysteries, Myths, and Rumors Revealed*. He remembers the night his wife suggested a name for their son: "We had kicked around a lot of names, and we weren't agreeing on anything. A month before our son was born, we went to Joe's Pub and there was a cool band, the New Standards, doing covers. They did "London Calling" and Jen leaned over and said, 'What about Strummer?' I've always liked Joe Strummer. He was a hero, but he wasn't my all-time hero. You can do a lot worse than represent The Clash. When they hear my son's name, most people will respond with, 'That's the coolest thing ever.' They'll address it in some way and then it dies down pretty quickly after that. Sometimes they'll say, 'I guess he's going to be a rock star with a name like that,' but that's not the point. I mean, if he is, great, but it's just his name."

The Man from Utopia

Frank Zappa once said, "Consider for a moment any beauty in the name Ralph." The outspoken musician and composer was a mother of invention when he blessed his brood with names that were both iconoclastic and bizarre—Moon Unit, Dweezil, Ahmet Emuukha Rodan, and Diva Thin Muffin Pigeen. Diva received her name because she was screaming louder than all the other babies in the hospital nursery. Dweezil was a nickname that Frank had bestowed on the oddly curled pinky toe of his wife, Gail. When the hospital refused to register the baby as Dweezil, the name that appeared on the birth certificate was Ian Donald Calvin Euclid Zappa. This situation was remedied when Dweezil turned 5 and insisted that his name be changed legally.

AmericanBaby.com

Which of these occupational names works for you?

Tailor/Taylor	40%
Ryder	37%
Porter	12%
Miller	7%
Pilot	2%
Pirate	2%

(TOTAL VOTES: 4,711)

All in the Family

Cuba Gooding Jr. and his wife, Sarah, are the parents of sons Spencer (keeper of provisions) and Mason and daughter, Piper.

i need a hero

ROCKERS, REVOLUTIONARIES, AND GRANDMAS TO THE RESCUE

When it comes to paying tribute to icons, think outside the box. Take a risk with someone who took a stand or dreamed about a world filled with possibilities. Remember, "cool" isn't limited to celebrities. Teachers, athletes, coaches, and relatives can be role models and heroes too.

History is packed with the names of social revolutionaries, pioneers, rockers, and visionaries who dared to be different and made a difference. The category has expanded to include musicians, saints, composers, and sports greats.

TIP #1

Don't forget the peacemakers. History is full of do-gooders like Sojourner Truth, Andrew Carnegie, Abraham Lincoln, and Martin Luther King Jr.

What This Style Says About You

You're a rebel who doesn't mind shaking up the status quo. Your tradition is to break with tradition. You will, as the Fleetwood Mac song says, go your own way. You march to the beat of your own drum.

"We shoot guns in movies; we have motorbikes and planes and mummies covered in tattoos. All that's left for them to do is become Mormons."
—ANGELINA JOLIE ON IMAGINING HOW HER KIDS
MIGHT REBEL ONE DAY

All That Jazz

Woody Allen and Soon-Yi Previn named their adopted daughters, Bechet and Manzie, after jazz greats Sidney Bechet and Manzie Johnson. He also has a biological son, Satchel, with Mia Farrow, named after Satchel Paige, a legendary baseball pitcher who played in the Negro Leagues and Major League Baseball. (The younger Satchel later changed his name to Ronan.) Spike Lee named his daughter, Satchel, after the same pioneering hero.

TRY THIS AT HOME

When it comes to rock heroes, try the last name and not the first. Go with Presley over Elvis and swagger with Jagger instead of Mick.

WHEN DIDDY BECAME THE DADDY OF TWINS

Sean "Diddy" Combs and Kim Porter named their twin daughters, Jessie James and D'Lila Star, after the great-grandmothers. Jessie James honors Jessie Smalls, the music mogul's grandmother, while D'Lila Star pays tribute to Kim Porter's grandmother, Lila Star.

AmericanBaby.com

Which of these bad boy rocker names do you find the most appealing?

Dylan	52%
Presley	25%
Jagger	10%
Axl	7%
Ozzy	6%

(TOTAL VOTES: 1,091)

Which classic rocker girl's name do you like best?

Carly (Simon)	59%
Stevie (Nicks)	16%
Janis (Joplin)	14%
Joanie (Mitchell)	8%
Carole (King)	3%

(TOTAL VOTES: 4,911)

BAND TOGETHER

Korn's Jonathan Davis named his third son Zeppelin. Recently a Swedish couple received permission to name their infant daughter Metallica. Sounds like Angel Ray Keala, son of Metallica guitarist Kirk Hammett, has a new fan.

Who's Working It

Lance Armstrong, Orlando Bloom, Jesse G. James, Liv Tyler

CASE HISTORY: The Road to Oz

Thomas Rubinson, deputy district attorney, and Melissa Karz, career coach, parents of Oz Lennon Karz Rubinson

Thomas says: "We are Jewish and we wanted a name that was meaningful in Hebrew. In Hebrew Oz means 'strength.' The only change we made was in the pronunciation. In Hebrew it's Oz [with a long "O" sound]. We thought the name was unusual and unique. We liked names with a "Z" but we especially liked names ending with "Z." We didn't pick it because of *The Wizard of Oz*. It was easy to call him Ozzie, which we sometimes do.

"It's funny when people ask and we say Oz; sometimes we get this blank look or stare. They need it repeated or spelled. Most people say, 'That's a great name. How beautiful. How cool.' Others don't seem to know what to do with it and that's OK. It doesn't bother us at all.

"It's exciting now that he is starting to learn his name and respond to it. Once they start to grow a little bit, you can't imagine calling them anything else. Nothing else fits.

"Oz has two middle names. The first middle name is Lennon and the second middle name is Karz, my wife's last name. It was important to have her last name included as well. In the Jewish tradition you honor a recently passed-away relative with your child's name. The last person who passed away was my grandfather and I was very close to him. His name was Irving. We didn't find any "I" names that we liked. His middle name was Leonard and we played off Leonard and modernized it to get Lennon. We liked the interplay between Oz, meaning strength, and Lennon's embodiment of peace. We liked that combination: strength with peace. It honored my grandfather. I have a buddy who owns a music store and he was thrilled. He said, 'Between Ozzie and Lennon, what a rocker!'"

Man in the Mirror

In addition to eldest child, LaPrincia, Bobby Brown has a son, Bobby III, and a daughter, Bobbi Kristina. Michael Jackson gave his name to all three of his children: Michael Joseph Jackson Jr., otherwise known as "Prince," Paris Michael Katherine Jackson, and Prince Michael Joseph Jackson II, who is affectionately called Blanket.

It wasn't self-promotion but fatherly love that led boxing champion George Foreman to name each of his five sons George Edward Foreman. He wanted to give a sense of identity and belonging to his 10 children, which is why he named one daughter Freeda George and another Georgetta. (His remaining daughters are named Michi, Natalie, and Leola.)

who's done it

Bechet Dumaine (g)	Woody Allen & Soon-Yi Previn
D'Lila Star	Sean "Diddy" Combs & Kim Porter
Elvis	Anthony Perkins & Berry Berenson
Hendrix	Zakk & Barbaranne Wylde
Jesse James	Jon Bon Jovi & Dorothea Hurley
Jessie James	Sean "Diddy" Combs & Kim Porter
Lennon	Patsy Kensit & Liam Gallagher
Lincoln	Bill Murray & Jennifer Butler
Malcolm	Denzel Washington & Pauletta Washington
Manzie (g)	Woody Allen & Soon-Yi Previn
Marlon	Keith Richards & Anita Pallenberg
Dylan Jagger	Pamela Anderson & Tommy Lee
Jagger	Creed's Scott Stapp & Hillaree Burns
Presley (b)	Cindy Crawford & Randy Gerber
Satchel (b)	Woody Allen & Mia Farrow
Zeppelin	Jonathon Davis & Devon Davis

a boy named sue, a girl named owen

UNISEX NAMES AND GENDER BENDERS

Many celebrity parents, such as Brooke Shields and Michelle Branch, are choosing boys' names for their daughters. As trends go it's far more socially acceptable for a girl to have a boy's name than the other way around. Once a male name becomes widely adopted for girls, it often drops out of use for boys, making the number of truly masculine names scarce. With the proliferation of androgynous names and the migration of so many boys' names to the girls' camp, it's become increasingly difficult to tell the sex of an individual from his or her name alone.

This begs the question: Does giving a child a gender-neutral name render a girl more masculine, a boy more feminine, or does it just confuse everybody?

continued on page 60

Who's Working It

Drew Barrymore, Lindsey Buckingham, Dana Carvey, Alice Cooper, Lil' Corey, Jamie Lee Curtis, Fergie, Kelsey Grammer, Jerry Hall, Ashley Hamilton, Billie Holiday, Stacey Keach, Martie Maguire, Marilyn Manson, Mandy Patinkin, Stevie Nicks, Courtney B. Vance, Reese Witherspoon, Evan Rachel Wood

A Boy Named Brian

Marilyn Manson was born Brian Hugh Warner. To create a memorable stage name, he took his first name from screen siren Marilyn Monroe and his last name from serial killer Charles Manson. "I guess a lot of people will find it easier to classify me and understand me if they think that when I go home I'm somebody else," said the shock rocker. "But there are plenty of different levels to my personality and plenty of different vibes to the way I behave.... But for me there's not one that's Marilyn Manson and one that's not. It's all the same. And Marilyn Manson to me is just another way of describing myself. It's not another person. It's just a name."

TRY THIS AT HOME

Double your trouble. Diane Keaton dressed her adopted daughter in not one but two male names: Dexter Dean. How very Annie Hall!

TIP #1

A tomboyish nickname can be playful when used with a more formal and feminine first name. Try Sam for Samantha, Jack for Jacqueline, or Mad for Madeline.

IN THE NAME OF THE FATHER

Sidney Poitier named his daughter Sydney. Both Brooke Shields and Helen Hunt honored their fathers by using their dads' first names for their daughters' middle names: Rowan Francis and Makena'lei Gordon.

Perhaps that is the point—to move into a space where these considerations don't, or shouldn't, matter. In an ideal world a boy or girl could grow up to receive equal footing and opportunities no matter what his or her name. And you know what that means—To be truly radical and daring, you'd have to name your son Beatrice.

What This Style Says About You

You are ahead of the curve. A trailblazer, you are independent and confident, even cheeky. You believe in equality of the sexes and that people can transcend stereotype, gender, and bias. An idealist, you see limitations, prejudices, and labels as boundaries to blur and overcome.

CASE HISTORY:
Jonatha Brooke, singer-songwriter

Jonatha Brooke is a singer-songwriter, who kept her first and middle names and dropped her last name, Nelson, because it sounded too much like "Jonathan Nelson."

"People never get my name correctly. It's kind of mind-boggling because it's so similar to Jonathan that you think people would just say Jonatha. But no! I get Janotha or Johanna, Jo-mama, Joniqua, Jananda, Johnathana. It's just so crazy! I used to hate it because no one would ever get it. People would always think they were so funny, saying, 'Oh, did your parents want a boy? Hahahahaha.' I'd be like, 'No, I have two older brothers, thank you so much.' As a grown-up, I appreciate it much more because it's unusual. I do really like it now. It's pretty but it's not weird. It's just different.

"Most people correct it for me. I'll turn up at gigs and hotels and wherever and they'll have 'Jonathan Brooke' on the roster or the itinerary or the reservation at the airline, so I'm always correcting people, and they're always surprised that a chick is showing up instead of a guy.

"Friends of my parents had a daughter named Jonatha. They were the Kings. Jonatha King. And I did run into her once. We ended up on the same tiny commuter plane to Maine. The flight attendant said, 'There's more than one Jonatha. That's so weird.'

"I think names are probably more important than we know. We have these weird associations with them whether we realize it or not. My husband's name is Patrick, and I just think it's a perfect name for him and I'm not sure why. It just gives me this sense of strength and constancy and centeredness. Names have certain meanings that they take on in your mind and in your soul. It may not be from any association with certain people—but just the sound of them and how it feels to say it."

Branching Out

Michelle Branch and husband, Teddy Landau, were sure they were having a boy and picked out the name Owen. "Once we found out we were having a girl, we were still in love with the name Owen," Branch remembers. "We gave her a very feminine middle name—Isabelle—so if she hates it she can switch." Branch herself is named after The Beatles' song "Michelle."

AmericanBaby.com

Did you have names in mind for your baby before you even conceived?

1. Yes, I already had names for both genders. — 40%
2. I had a name for one gender, but not the other. — 26%
3. I had a lot of ideas, but nothing narrowed down. — 24%
4. No, I hadn't given it a thought. — 10%

(TOTAL VOTES: 2,704)

BILLIE JEAN OR BILLY GENE?

Pick a name that could work for a boy or a girl. Homophones are words or names that share a common pronunciation but vary in meaning and spelling. Examples of his-and-hers homophones include Tony and Toni, Lou and Lu, and Terry and Terri.

TIP #2

Designate the child's gender by using a masculine or feminine middle name, like Evan Rachel Wood.

TRUMP THIS

Donald Trump Jr. and his wife, Vanessa, named their daughter, Kai Madison, after her maternal grandfather. "It's Danish," Trump explains. "He's a Danish musician and we wanted to keep it as a family name."

who's done it

Aidan Rose (g)	Faith Daniels
August Anna (g)	Garth Brooks & Sandy Brooks
Bridget Michael (g)	Sting & Trudie Styler
Dexter Dean (g)	Diane Keaton
Dylan Frances (g)	Sean Penn & Robin Wright Penn
Eliot Pauline (g)	Sting & Trudie Styler
Elliott Anastasia (g)	George Stephanopoulos & Alexandra Wentworth
Emerson Rose (g)	Teri Hatcher & Jon Tenney
Finley Faith (g)	Angie Harmon & Jason Sehorn
Johnnie Rose (g)	Melissa Etheridge & Tammy Lynn Michaels
Kai Madison (g)	Donald Trump Jr. & Vanessa Haydon Trump
Noah Lindsey (g)	Billy Ray Cyrus & Leticia "Tish" Finley Cyrus
Oren Lily (g)	Eyal Podell
Owen Isabelle (g)	Michelle Branch & Teddy Landau
Rory John (b)	Bill Gates & Melinda Gates
Rowan Francis (g)	Brooke Shields & Chris Henchy
Ryan Elizabeth (g)	Rodney Peete & Holly Robinson Peete
Taylor Mayne (g)	Garth Brooks & Sandy Brooks
Toby Cole (g)	Emme & Phillip Aronson

SAM I AM

Tiger Woods picked a sentimental favorite, Sam, for his daughter. "My father had always called me Sam since the day I was born," recalled the champion golfer, whose real name is Eldrick. "He rarely ever called me Tiger. I would ask him, 'Why don't you ever call me Tiger?' He said, 'Well, you look more like a Sam.'"

Crossover Artists

During medieval times Jocelyn was considered a male name. Among the male names that have evolved into female names: Ashley, Courtney, Hilary, Lindsey, and Vivian. Notable exceptions to this trend: Cameron, Dakota, Dylan, and Jordan. Although these names are considered unisex, male Camerons, Dakotas, Dylans, and Jordans still outnumber female ones.

Special K

Kelsie B. Harder's life was changed forever by his name. His parents liked his sister's name, Elsie, so much that they put a "K" in front of it for their son. Although he frequently had to explain that he was not a girl, Harder grew up with a fascination with names that led him to become a leading onomastician, specializing in place names. He would later preside over the American Name Society and write or edit more than 1,000 books, articles, and reviews during his career. As he once observed, "We are at the mercy of our name givers. These things influence us for the rest of our lives, and we have nothing to do with it." Even so, he stuck with tradition to the end, naming one of his sons Kelsie.

"Oren is actually a boy's Hebrew name. I wanted something that started with an "O" because I wanted to honor my grandfather Odif. That wouldn't be a great name for a girl, but we liked Oren. She's absolutely beautiful."
—THE YOUNG AND THE RESTLESS' EYAL PODELL

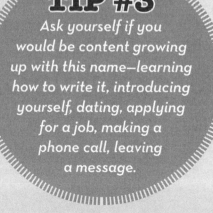

TIP #3

Ask yourself if you would be content growing up with this name—learning how to write it, introducing yourself, dating, applying for a job, making a phone call, leaving a message.

pageturners & masterpieces

THE ART OF NAMING

Masterpieces are great works of art. Little wonder then that many parents feel inspired by the classics in literature, art, film, theater, and pop culture when naming their progeny.

The literary landscape is well populated with authors, beloved characters, and comic book superheroes. From Irish poet and novelist Samuel Beckett to French diarist Anais Nin, writers and characters are finding themselves reborn on the cultural landscape as namesakes.

Recently celebrity parents have brought attention to the works of more obscure artists, such as novelist and writer Wilkie Collins, Australian poet Andrew Barton "Banjo" Patterson, and 16th century English dramatist Thomas Kyd.

The names of two of Demi Moore and Bruce Willis' daughters were inspired by literature: Rumer was named after British author Rumer Godden, and Scout was the narrator in the Harper Lee classic, *To Kill a Mockingbird*. Parents are not limiting themselves to literature. *My Name Is Earl* actress Jaime Pressly is a huge *I Love Lucy* fan. She named her son Dezi James after the show's bandleader husband, Desi Arnaz, and her father, James.

continued on page 66

TIP #1

Check out other "classic" pop culture forms: video games, soap operas, anime, sci-fi, and pulp fiction. After the horror movie The Ring was released in 2002, the name Samara jumped from #925 to #365 in two years.

Brandon vs. Dylan

Before MTV's reality programs *Laguna Beach* and *The Hills*, there was Aaron Spelling's fictional nighttime soap, *Beverly Hills, 90210*. Among the series' break-out stars were Jason Priestley, who played clean-cut, school newspaper editor Brandon Walsh and Luke Perry as the misunderstood, surfer bad boy, Dylan McKay. The male leads carried their heartthrob status into the popularity charts, with Brandon vaulting to the top 10 and Dylan rising from #83 in 1990 to #21 in 2001.

creative license

Dixie Chicks lead singer Natalie Maines and Heroes star Adrian Pasdar named their son Beckett Finn, after author Samuel Beckett and Neil Finn, the lead singer for the bands Crowded House and Split Enz.

ALICE, WARRIOR QUEEN

Tina Fey was born Elizabeth Stamatina Fey. Her daughter with Jeff Richmond is named Alice Zenobia. Zenobia is the name of a rebel Syrian queen who defied Rome. Zenobia is also the name of a character in an Edith Wharton novel.

Which of these famous male artists' names do you like best?

Jasper (Johns)	28%
Pablo (Picasso)	9%
Henri (Matisse)	18%
Jean (Basquiat)	5%
Keith (Haring)	40%
(TOTAL VOTES: 5,106)	

Which of these contemporary female writer names do you like best?

Zadie (Smith)	31%
Joan (Didion)	4%
Mary (Gaitskill)	10%
René (Steinke)	23%
Jeanne (Birdsall)	4%
Adele (Griffin)	22%
Deborah (Wiles)	6%
(TOTAL VOTES: 9,006)	

AmericanBaby.com

What This Style Says About You

Literary and artistic, you are open to new ideas, philosophies, and influences. You are fascinated by what you read and hear. You find letters, conversations, art, literature, and poetry illuminating and enlightening.

TIP #2

Avoid tragedy by being aware of a name's literary history and image. Hamlet, Ophelia, and Oedipus may require heavy lifting.

CASE HISTORY:
Steve Turre, Akua Dixon, Andromeda Turre, and Orion Turre

Trombonist and jazz musician Steve Turre and his wife, cellist Akua Dixon, made a deal when it came to naming their children. Steve would select two names for consideration, and Akua, whose Ghanian name means "girl child born on a Wednesday," would get to pick the final name.

For their first child, Steve suggested Andromeda, the princess from Greek mythology, and Ananda, which means "bliss" in Sanskrit.

Steve subscribes to many science magazines so he can read about astronomy and cosmology. "The Andromeda Galaxy is the closest to the Milky Way," he says. "In Greek lore Andromeda was an Ethiopian princess renowned for her beauty. So in the name Andromeda, you got a princess, a galaxy, and a constellation in the heavens."

"Having a name like Andromeda is a conversation starter," agrees Andromeda. "People will ask me questions, or they'll associate it with that Michael Crichton novel *The Andromeda Strain*. Everybody has heard of the name Andromeda, but they've never met an Andromeda. I've never met another Andromeda, not even when I was in Greece. I've been to 26 countries, and everybody knows that name and has heard of it."

When Andromeda was almost 10, Akua became pregnant with a son. Again Steve presented two names to her: Orion and Apollo. "In Greek mythology Orion is a great hunter. Orion is also the name of actual real physical astronomical entities. There's an Orion nebula and an Orion constellation."

From the beginning Andromeda was vocal that they pick the name Orion. "My brother loves his name," the actress and singer says proudly.

"I think as I've gotten older, my name has gotten better," says Orion, now a teenager. "When you're young people think it's odd. As you get older, you meet people who are more mature and more aware."

Besides, he doesn't think the name Apollo suits his temperament. "I'm pretty mellow," observes Orion. "I'm patient. I wait a long time for things to happen. Orion is the patient hunter in Greek mythology."

who's done it

TRY THIS
AT HOME

Go visual. Check out art and photography books and websites, comic books, graphic novels, galleries, and museums.

IT'S NOT A CRIME

Cate Blanchett's son Dashiell was named after novelist Dashiell Hammett, who is best known for penning *The Maltese Falcon* and *The Thin Man*.

Novelties

Both Heath Ledger's and Wentworth Miller's names were inspired by characters in British literature. Heath is short for Heathcliff, the brooding loner from Emily Bronte's *Wuthering Heights*, while Miller was named after Captain Wentworth in Jane Austen's novel *Persuasion*. You might think Orlando Bloom was named after Virginia Woolf's gender-bending hero of *Orlando*, but he was actually named after the 17th-century composer Orlando Gibbons.

name brands

A FEW OF MY FAVORITE THNGS

If you think of your baby's name as the garment of a lifetime, it's easy to see why some parents are searching for the best that money can buy. Endorsing your baby with a well-known label is the ultimate in product placement and brand loyalty. Imagine walking hand in hand with your son Timberland or cheering at sports games with your ballplayer, ESPN.

Popular brands that have made parents and consumers go Gucci Gucci Goo over the years include Armani, Canon, L'Oreal,

> ### Who's Working It
> *Chevy Chase, Mercedes Ruehl, Tiffani Thiessen, Timbaland*

Del Monte, and Courvoisier. Clearly advertising has left its mark on the American psyche. "Moxie is a name that was created by an American for the first national soft drink and then went on to mean 'chutzpah,' " says illusionist Penn Jillette, the father of Moxie CrimeFighter.

What This Style Says About You
When you like something, you really, really like it. Everyday objects can find themselves elevated to the status of sacred relics in your home. You have a practical nature that delights in innovation and design. Passionate and enthusiastic, you may act impulsively when you see something you want or gotta have.

TIP #1
Oh, the perils of playing I-Spy! When you're pregnant, it's easy to mistake hormone-induced delirium with passion. Test-drive any names first.

For Real

There have been a handful of baby boys named after the popular sports network ESPN. Pronounced "Espen," they turned up in Biloxi, Mississippi; Corpus Christi, Texas; Pampa, Texas; and Michigan. But only Leann and Rusty Real named their son, ESPN Montana, after the cable network and football great Joe Montana. Perhaps one day he will be known as "The Worldwide Leader in Sports."

who's done it

Camera (g)	Arthur Ashe & Jeanne Moutoussamy Ashe
Chanel	Nelly
Jett	George Lucas
	John Travolta & Kelly Preston
Frances Pen (g)	Amanda Peet & David Benioff
Tiffany	Donald Trump & Marla Maples

AmericanBaby.com

What brand name would make the best baby name?

Tiffany	32%
Lexus	23%
Chanel	22%
Dyson	13%
Canon	9%
ESPN	1%

(TOTAL VOTES: 1,144)

LET YOUR FINGERS DO THE WALKING

Pringles Potato Crisps was one brand name that came directly out of the phone book. Marketing experts at Procter & Gamble decided to look for a name that already existed instead of inventing one. Flipping through the phone book brought them to Pringle Avenue, a street in a Cincinnati suburb named Finneytown.

TWO FOR ONE

Many product names were the result of coining new words or combining words for a unique effect. Ore-Ida blends two states, Oregon and Idaho, while Microsoft is an abbreviation of "microcomputer software."

"I would like to thank my wonderful children, Paris, Prince, and Blanket, for their unconditional love and support."

—MICHAEL JACKSON, THANKING HIS CHILDREN IN AN ACCEPTANCE SPEECH AT THE WORLD MUSIC AWARDS

CASE HISTORY: Field of Dreams
Rachel Sapienza and Brian Hunt are the parents of Wrigley Ann Hunt.

Rachel remembers: "It's funny. There was an old lady in my building and she asked me my daughter's name. Then she said, 'What do you mean Wrigley? Like the gum? Oh, she's going to hate you forever.' Then she turned to her friend and explained, 'It's like the gum!'

"I actually came up with it. Everyone thinks that my husband picked it because Brian is from Chicago and he's a huge fan of the Chicago Cubs. It was just really hard to come up with a name. He'd be driving and I would have the book and I would be reading the names. Sammy Sosa was big at the time and he said, 'Oh, what about Sammy?' He really liked the name Addison, which is one of the four streets bordering Wrigley Field along with Clark, Sheffield, and Waveland. I thought Addison was OK but his sister's daughter's name is Madison—Madison, Addison—and I just thought the names were too similar. And then I said, 'What about Wrigley?' As soon as it came out of my mouth, we both knew. We sat with the name for a day. We didn't tell anyone until she was born. No, I didn't want to hear it! I always joke that we could never move to Chicago. It would be very confusing for her. We have pictures of her at Wrigley Field. We took her to Chicago for Memorial Day weekend, and she went to three games. She slept through two of them. Most people like it, at least that's what they tell me, even if they don't think immediately of Wrigley Field or Wrigley gum. You definitely think of the stadium but now Wrigley is so her name, I just think of her when I hear Wrigley. We call her Wrigley. Some people call her Wrigs, the Wrigster. When she was a baby, we called her 'my wiggly Wrigley.' I never had any regrets. I never thought about her not liking it. And we did give her a middle name, Ann—that's my mother's name and my sister's name—so we gave her an out. People want to know if Wrigley is a family name and we say, 'Yes, but it's not our family name.' It's very freeing to know that you can do your own thing."

70

Tiffany & Co.

In 1988 14-year-old Tiffani-Amber Thiessen tied with Tiffany Weber for *Teen* magazine's Great Model Search. Tiffany ranked #41 the year the future *90210* star was born, although she later chose to drop the Amber professionally. The name debuted on the popularity charts in 1962—one year after the movie *Breakfast at Tiffany's* was released in 1961. It peaked at #13 in 1982 and 1988 and remains in the top 200 names for girls today. Back then, the store was known as a purveyor of stationery and costume jewelry in lower Manhattan and accepted cash only. Years later the store would introduce the concept of the engagement ring and its coveted "Tiffany Setting" before moving to its current posh Fifth Avenue location.

TRY THIS AT HOME

Chasing cars! Take automotive names for a spin: Mercedes, Infiniti, Kia, Chevy, and Celica.

TIP #2

After reading the label consider any designer names as limited editions. Think classic, not dated.

Drive!

Lexus recently has vroomed into the top 1,000 names for girls.

branching out

Families grow with each new face. Each birth represents a branch of the family tree. To guide you in this process, this book features a pull-out family tree for your planning and convenience. Jot down names and keep it handy as a reference whenever you need to visualize your child's place in the family history. Often the name of the newest addition can become an intense matter of debate as members try to figure out which traditions to follow, whose opinion carries the most weight, and who deserves to be a namesake.

Ultimately the responsibility and decision for your child's name rests with you, although there have been cases when parents have let a grandparent or sibling decide what the name of a baby will be. The names of siblings also may share a similar style, common initials, or a unifying bond or theme.

TRY THIS AT HOME

Remember, tradition is in the eye of the beholder. The name of a child becomes a "family" name the moment it's given.

Silver and Gold

The oldest female twins were from Japan and were named Kin Narita and Gin Kanie, or gold and silver respectively in Japanese. Kin (Gold) was 107 when she died in 2000, and Gin (Silver) was 108 when she passed away a year later.

Stepdad

No one has heard of President Leslie Lynch King Jr. That's because when Lynch was a toddler, his mother legally changed his name from Leslie Lynch, the name of his biological father, to Gerald Rudolph Ford Jr. after his stepfather who adopted him.

SAY UNCLE!

Keanu Reeves' full name is Keanu Charles Reeves. He was named after his uncle, Henry Keanu Reeves. Keanu is a derivation of Keaweaheulu, the name of the actor's great-great uncle, and means "cool breeze over the mountains" in Hawaiian.

Given it Back

After years of estrangement with her father, Angelina Jolie legally dropped her last name, Voight, in the summer of 2002. Both Angelina and her brother, James Haven, use their middle names as their last names.

TIP #1

Many families reserve a child's middle name to honor a family member.

"We said . . . What do you want to call your brother? And his first option was Pumpkinhead. But then the next day he revised it and he changed it to Stinky."
—RUSSELL CROWE ON ASKING HIS FIRST SON, CHARLES, WHAT THEY SHOULD CALL HIS BROTHER, TENNYSON

Which family member would you like to name your baby after?

My grandparent	38%
My parent	35%
A close friend	12%
Spouse's parent	8%
Spouse's grandparent	7%

TOTAL VOTES: 1,908

LIKE A STAR

Stella McCartney was named after her two grandmothers. Both of her maternal grandmothers were named Stella. Coincidentally both Stella and her older sister, Mary, married men named Alasdhair, or Alastair.

TIP #2

Sibling names may share certain traits—starting or ending with the same letter, following a particular style, or possessing a common set of initials.

Me, Jane

Jane Pauley and Jane Seymour aren't twins, although they sound like they could be. In the pre-Friends year of 1983, Jane Pauley named her duo Ross and Rachel. (Her other son is named Thomas, which means "twin.") In 1995 Jane Seymour named her twins Johnny and Kris after friends Johnny Cash and Christopher Reeve.

CASE HISTORY: It's a Family Affair
Neal Casal, singer-songwriter, photographer, and musician

"My mom wanted to name me Phillip, but my grandmother had a brother who died in a fire when he was 12. The kid's name was Cornelius, and she tried to guilt my mom into naming me Cornelius. My mom was having none of that and made a deal with her. She said, 'Tell you what, Mom. If it's a boy, I'll name him Neal.' Grandma said, 'Neil.' My mom stood her ground and said, 'No, Neal,' and so it was. Weird story, huh? I'm kind of named after a kid who died in a fire."

Twin Sets

Twins and multiples are in a category all their own. They also present the opportunity to come up with more than one name and middle name. Do you want to mix or match them? Should they all begin or end with the same letter or sound?

Some parents like their twins' names to match—and some don't. Geena Davis stuck to the letter "K" for sons Kian and Kaiis, while Peri Gilpin placed a common "A" in back for daughters Stella and Ava. If matching monikers don't work for you, you can take a cue from Marcia Gay Harden, who picked the intrepid Hudson for one twin and the striking Julitta for the other.

After all, Mary-Kate and Ashley Olsen may be identical twins, but their names are anything but similar.

Then there are the parents who stick to a common trend or theme. Marcia Cross was inspired by Eden and Savannah for her daughters. Sean "Diddy" Combs took a villainous turn with Jessie James and D'Lila Star.

"My daddy was a Ray. I was a Ray Ray. I want a Ray Ray Ray!"
—MY NAME IS EARL

adoption

HOMEWARD BOUND

What do Angelina Jolie, Brad Pitt, Tom Cruise, Nicole Kidman, Steven Spielberg, Kate Capshaw, Sharon Stone, Kirstie Alley, Madonna, Hugh Jackman, Ewan McGregor, Michelle Pfeiffer, Meg Ryan, and B.D. Wong all have in common? They are the proud parents of adopted children.

When it comes to choosing a name for an adopted child, there are unique factors to consider. As with a birth child, the gift of a name symbolizes a powerful hope for the future. For an adopted child a new name can also represent a new beginning, encourage a sense of belonging, and signify a break from a painful or hurtful past.

Experts generally agree that a name change will not have great impact on a baby, but those concerns change as a child grows older. A child older than 2 can remember his or her given name and identify with it. For this reason older children may feel rejected or experience a loss of identity when their names are changed. The opposite also can be true. They may revel in their new names and the changed status it brings them.

Even so, the naming process can be complicated, as Meg Ryan discovered when she adopted her daughter, Daisy True, from China in 2006. "I already had to change her name," the actress explained to Oprah, "because there she is, just about a year old, and I thought she was Charlotte and she's just not. She's a Daisy. She's got the most open, beautiful, honest face you'll just ever see."

TRY THIS AT HOME

Many adoptive parents choose a new first name and continue to use the child's original name as a middle name. If the child is adopted from a foreign country, an ethnic name may represent a child's roots in his or her native homeland.

CASE HISTORY: From Kate to KT
KT Tunstall, singer-songwriter

Singer-songwriter KT Tunstall was born in Edinburgh, Scotland, the daughter of a Chinese mother and an Irish father. Adopted as an infant, she spent her childhood in St. Andrews, raised by a physicist dad and a schoolteacher mom. As she recounts on her website, her awareness of her adoption meant that "I grew up knowing I could have had a million different lives. It makes your life mysterious and your imagination go wild." Recently she spoke about adoption and changing her name from Kate to KT.

When did you decide to call yourself KT and why?
When I was about to release my album in late 2004, my label, management, and I all sat around a table and made a list of the female artists releasing albums at that time. We came up with around 10—all using their full names, one of which was Katie Melua. So I thought *time to grab some attention*. A friend at uni had always scribbled 'KT' as my moniker on my door, and it felt right. As a big PJ Harvey fan, it felt like a good way of sticking out of the crowd.

What's it like to grow up as Kate and perform as KT?
I always felt the name Kate was too folksy for the kind of music I was making, and I'm really glad I didn't use it as my stage name. I'm Kate to my family and friends, and it's lovely to leave the 'KT' in my unpacked bag full of gig clothes when I get home. Conversely, I now react to 'KT' by snapping into my stage headspace. It's very useful.

How has being adopted affected your identity and artistry?
I can't provide an objective answer to that. I know it adds mystery to my imagination, but I'm very close to my family and they have always encouraged me to be myself. I have rarely had to question who I am.

Do you have any advice for parents when it comes to naming their children?
As I am not a parent, I have no experience, but I would hope that if and when I have children myself, I will be flexible with names; I'm sure my partner and I will have ideas, but meeting them may change our minds completely! I do feel that giving a child an unusual name perhaps makes for a more unusual life experience, and that, in my book, is always good.

Sweet Child O' Mine
Sheryl Crow adopted an infant son in May 2007. The singer-songwriter named him Wyatt Steven, after her father, Wyatt, and brother, Steven.

and you are?

ADVICE FOR DILEMMAS AND DEAL-BREAKERS

Dealing with family conflicts, naming dilemmas, and potential deal breakers is never easy, but with pluck, perseverance, grace, and creativity, you will find a name for your baby that you can give—and call out—with confidence and love. Here are a few trying scenarios that parents commonly face with relatives, friends, strangers, and each other.

Who did you tell about baby's name before he or she was born?

Anyone who asked	45%
Some friends and family	23%
Not a soul!	21%
Our families only	11%

(TOTAL VOTES: 3,200)

A HOME RUN Kevin James named second daughter Shea Joelle after dad Joe, who took him to Mets games. "I can't believe this got by my wife," he exclaimed.

"We're going to wait and see. When you're writing you pick names for characters, but it's harder in real life."
—SOFIA COPPOLA ON THE DIFFICULT TASK OF NAMING HER FIRST CHILD

TIP #1
Remember, you're in the process of selecting a name, not lobbying for one! Landing everyone's approval is nice but not necessary.

Q **My husband and I have different naming styles. He is much more traditional and conservative, while I am drawn to more creative, unusual names. What can we do?** —*Tug of War*

Dear Tug,

You could flip a coin to decide who gets to pick the first name and who gets to select the middle name, but that wouldn't make either of you very happy. It also would result in the kind of divisiveness that leads to dueling names or a dull compromise that nobody likes.

If your and your husband's lists are far apart stylistically, they don't have to remain so. Keep an open mind and you may be surprised by what you discover. There are so many names to choose from and to combine that the possibilities are unlimited. Consider creating a new name from one of his favorites and one of yours. If his top pick of Emily is too conventional for you, you could suggest Emilie or Emme or Amelia or Emerson.

Don't shortchange the process or each other. Take turns suggesting potential names, listen to each other's choices respectfully, and agree from the start to choose a name that you both like and accept. This way you will be sure to defuse any power struggles and move that much closer to achieving a happy collaboration.

Here's one exercise that always gets people to cooperate: Start with a list of names you both hate and work your way up from there.

Q **My wife is dead set on naming our daughter after her favorite aunt, Sylvia. I used to be horribly bullied by a tyrant called Sylvia in the fourth grade. How can we honor her aunt and not rake up unpleasant memories for me?** —*Traumatized by Sylvia*

Dear Traumatized,

I am very sorry to hear about your unfortunate experience in fourth grade; however, keep in mind that it was fourth grade. I also understand your wife's wish to honor her aunt. There are many ways to celebrate a namesake. You could open up the field of choices by picking a name that begins with the same letter, S, to come up with Serena or Stella. You could choose a name that ends in "ia," such as Mia or Olivia. You also could use the letters in Sylvia to start other names, like Isla, Lia, and Ivy. International variations of Sylvia include the French Sylvie and the Italian Silvana. Since Sylvia means "forest," you could try planting a tree name, such as Laurel, in her honor. Did Aunt Sylvia have a favorite soap opera character named Greenleigh? Maybe the flower she most admired was the calla lily, in which case you could call your daughter Calla or Lily. There is no shortage of inspiring ideas once you put your heads together.

Q&A continued on page 80

Q I have always loved the name Theodore and have told anyone and everyone who would listen that if I had a son, his name would be Theodore. The problem? My college roommate just announced that she is going to name her son Theodore too. I am so upset my favorite name is taken that I can't even think about finding a replacement or attending our next reunion. —*How Dare She?*

Dear Dare,

It's not so surprising that if you had anything at all in common with your friend, you would like the same name or types of names. Before you accuse your former roomie of being a name robber, remember: You are not living with her anymore, and there is plenty of room for more than one Theodore in the world. The truth of the matter is no matter how many Theodores you encounter and meet in your lifetime, none will ever mean as much to you as your own. Your little Teddy will be special and unique to you because he's yours. And who knows? She might choose to call her son Theo, Eddie, or Teo.

Q Help! My in-laws reject and pooh-pooh every name my husband and I suggest before we've even finished speaking. Do I have to tell them what our son's name will be? —*Rolling My Eyes*

Dear Rolling,

You are going to have to tell them your son's name eventually, but if you know they won't like what you tell them, you can always be smart about when you tell them.

Many couples don't divulge their child's name until after the baby is born and the ink on the birth certificate has dried. Decide on a name together with your husband and present a united front to your relatives. What you and your partner decide to name the baby is up to the two of you. You are not obligated to explain your choice, only to love it.

Q We're in a Lamaze class where people are very direct and nosy. Lately, they have been demanding to know what we are going to name our child or what our top picks are. We don't want to hurt anyone's feelings, but we are very private people. What should we say? —*Mobbed*

Dear Mobbed,

You could always refer to the baby by a top-secret code name like Baby X or Cherry Garcia. One ingenious couple we know actually picked the most awful names they could find, like Muppim and Huppim. Do what feels right to you. If being private and reserved makes you feel more secure, then silence is golden. If you are one of those folks who treat every new acquaintance as a possible test-market subject or sounding board, then chatter away. It's perfectly fine to say, "We're not sure yet. We're still working on it." Or change the subject and redirect the focus on them by asking, "Have you heard of any names you like yet?"

games people play

CHANNELING CHILDHOOD CLASSICS

And for all you gamers out there, here's a primer to prepare you for being a player in the name game. By paying attention to the classic board games and nostalgic toys of your childhood, you too can tap into your inner child to name your newborn.

1 The Lesson of the Slinky: Be flexible and forward-moving.

2 Silly Putty: Don't be afraid to soak up new experiences, words, and names. Even newspaper pages and comic strips can serve as wondrous sources of inspiration.

3 Monopoly: No one can steal your favorite name "properties" if you keep them in the bank.

4 Battleship: Some names were meant to be torpedoed and sunk.

5 Scrabble: It's not the letters you have but what you do with them that counts.

6 Etch A Sketch: Empty your mind, wipe the slate clean, and start again.

7 My Little Red Wagon: There's a parade inside every person. Once you've picked out a name for your baby, don't forget to take a walk in your neighborhood and show it off.

the portrait of a name

The following listings are comprised of the most popular name spellings based on information released by the Social Security Administration in 2007. At first glance they may seem like humble and modest offerings, but in their own compact and powerful way they represent the culmination of many hours of exhaustive, detailed research and intelligence gathering. Use them as convenient and handy references for the naming road ahead. For many of you the listings will be a natural starting point from which you can venture forth to sort out your preferences and favorites. You can look up a name to find out more about its origin, meaning, and variations. Not sure if you're having a boy or a girl? You'll find suggestions for both genders so that Grandma Emily can be honored by your little Emma, Emmett, or Emery. To give you a true picture of the popularity of a name over the last decade, all the alternate spellings have been combined and graphed, because how else would you know how popular Caitlyn or Katelyn or Catelin really is? (If a rank or graph is not included, the name has dropped off the Social Security list, was rarely on it to begin with, or is a recent and new addition.)

Finding out the origins of a name can be a tricky business. Included are the most widely accepted derivations and meanings, but this is by no means the last or final word. That's because names change. They are fluid, organic, even fickle entities whose meanings and spellings (even gender associations) may change over time, across countries or decades or cultures. Their origins reflect their travels and their roots, but since no one has been able to interview the first Adam or Eve (or Apple), we must fill in the blanks and spaces on our own.

Names will resemble or share traits with others the way that siblings in a family will reflect a common upbringing or background. There should be enough wiggle room in a name to embrace a few nicknames or similar-sounding peers, and you'll find the most prominent examples listed here. (As you'll discover, even if you never use a nickname with your child, chances are fair to excellent that someone else will.)

For better or worse we've included the notable people who've shared a particular name for the impressions they've made in the public consciousness. While these namesakes should not be treated as standard-bearers, they may evoke strong reactions in you or others. An awareness of their history and context can help you determine if a name is appropriately fitting for your child.

RANK
The current rank as released by the Social Security Administration in 2007. If rank is not included, the name has dropped off the top 1,000.

GRAPH
A visual representation of each name's popularity during the last 100 years. All alternate spellings of the name have been combined for a more accurate ranking.

ORIGIN
A common source of the name.

MEANING
A feeling that goes hand in hand with the origin. Alternate meanings do exist.

ALTERNATE SPELLINGS
Common and unique spellings including international variants.

GENDER VARIATIONS
Adaptations of the name for the opposite sex.

NICKNAMES
Short forms that are also given independently.

SIMILAR NAMES
Names with a similar sound or feeling.

Emma   Rank: 2
Origin: Old German
Meaning: Whole, universal
Alternate Spelling: Ema
Gender Variations: Emery, Emmet
Nicknames: Em, Emmie
Similar Names: Emelia, Emerald, Emily, Emmaline, Emmalynn
Namesakes: Emma Samms (British actress), Emma Thompson (British actress), Emma Watson (British actress)
⇨ Originally a shortened form of the medieval names Irmgard and Ermintrude that was introduced to England by the Normans. Used by English writer Jane Austen for the title character of her 19th century novel that was adapted into a movie in 1996. Also the name of Rachel's baby on the TV show *Friends*. Listed among the top 100 since 1973 and is often combined with other names such as Emma Justine, Emma Marie, and Emma Rose.

NAMESAKES
Historical figures and current headliners who come to mind.

⇨
Facts including historical references, current trends, along with past and present influences.

Aaliyah
Rank: 91
Origin: Arabic
Meaning: Lofty, sublime
Alternate Spellings: Alea, Aleah, Alia, Aliya, Aliyah, Aliyya, Aliyyah, Alya
Gender Variation: Aali
Similar Names: Aamina, Alina, Jaliyah, Kaliyah, Maliyah, Taliyah
⇨ A feminine form of Ali that first landed on the popularity chart in 1994 and quickly rose among the top 100 names. Known for the Grammy- and Academy Award-nominated singer and actress Aaliyah Haughton, who died in a plane crash in 2001.

Abby
Rank: 205
Origin: Hebrew
Meaning: A father's joy
Alternate Spellings: Abbe, Abbee, Abbey, Abbi, Abbie, Abbye, Abe, Abee
Gender Variations: Abbey, Abiah, Addy
Nickname: Ab
Similar Names: Abella, Abena, Abery, Abia, Abigayle, Abriana, Abrielle, Addy, Aggy, Tabby
Namesakes: Abby Wambach (Olympic soccer medalist), Dr. Abby Lockhart (*ER* character)
⇨ Short form of Abigail from the Hebrew name Avigayil. Used for boys but more commonly given to girls as an independent name. Faded from the popularity chart in the late 19th century but returned in 1952. Bearing a variation of the name, Abbie Burgess was a famous lighthouse keeper known for her bravery in tending the Matinicus Rock Light in Maine during a 1856 winter storm. Inspired, starting in the 1950s, by advice columnist "Dear Abby," formerly written by Pauline Esther Friedman Phillips and currently written by her daughter, Jeanne Phillips. The name peaked in 2001 and 2003 at No. 163.

Abigail
Rank: 6
Origin: Hebrew
Meaning: A father's joy
Alternate Spellings: Abagail, Abegail, Abbigail, Abbygael, Abigael, Abigale, Abigayl, Abigayle
Gender Variations: Aaron, Abel
Nicknames: Abby, Gayle
Similar Names: Abida, Abril, Adelaide, Avigail, Gayla
Namesake: Abigail Breslin (actress)

⇨ The name of the third wife of King David in the Old Testament who referred to herself as David's "handmaid," which paved the way for its use in literature for a lady's servant. The name has steadily climbed in popularity since the 1940s, breaking into the top 100 in 1989. First lady and wife of former U.S. president John Adams is a namesake. Known today as the pen name for advice columnist Abigail Van Buren.

Abril
Rank: 845
Origin: Latin
Meaning: Open
Gender Variations: Abel, Abil
Similar Names: Abegail, Abila, Adela, April, Avril
⇨ Related to the Latin word *aprilis* that comes from the same root as the fourth calendar month of the year, marking the spring season when the flowers open. Spanish film actress Victoria Abril is a famous bearer of the surname.

Ada
Rank: 715
Origin: Hebrew/German
Meaning: Adornment or noble
Alternate Spellings: Adda, Aida, Aidah, Ayda
Gender Variations: Adair, Adam, Addison
Similar Names: Adalia, Adara, Adelaide, Adeline, Adella, Addi, Addiah, Adina
⇨ Possibly a variation of the Hebrew name Adah or the short form of the German Adelaide from the element *adal* associated with 19th-century renowned mathematician Ada King, the Countess of Lovelace and daughter of English poet Lord Byron. The name peaked during the late 19th century and fell off the chart 100 years later, reappearing again in 2004 as part of a biblical naming trend.

Adamaris
Rank: 920
Origin: American
Gender Variation: Adam
Nicknames: Ada, Maris
Similar Names: Adalia, Adelaide, Adeline, Adelle, Amaris, Damaris
⇨ An invented name that blends the elements "ada" and "maris" debuting as a girl's given name in 2006.

Addison   Rank: 27

Origin: Old English
Meaning: Adam's son
Alternate Spellings:
Addeson, Addisson,
Addisyn, Addyson, Adisen, Adison,
Adisson, Adisynne, Adysen, Adyson
Gender Variations: Addison, Aden, Adrian
Nickname: Addie
Similar Names: Ada, Addia, Addis, Adelaide,
Adeline, Adisa, Adrienne, Madyson
Namesakes: Dr. Addison Montgomery-
Shepherd in *Grey's Anatomy*
➡ Female use of a male name, even more
unique when spelled with a "y." A surname
that originated from a personal name.
Derived from Addie or Adie which was a
pet form of Adam during the Middle Ages.
Consistently rising in popularity as a girl's
name since entering the chart in 1994.

Adelaide   Rank: 921

Origin: Old German
Meaning: Noble, kind
Alternate Spelling: Adelade
Gender Variations: Adlai
Nicknames: Addie, Adel, Adela
Similar Names: Adelaida, Adelhaide, Adella,
Adelle, Adelina, Adeline
➡ A common royal name notable for the
wife of the Holy Roman Emperor Otto the
Great who was revered as a saint and for
the wife of King William IV who lent her
name to the capital of South Australia. It was
popularized by Nathan Detroit's girlfriend in
the 1950 hit musical *Guys and Dolls* that was
adapted into a film in 1955. The name is
derived from the elements "adal" and "heid."

Adeline   Rank: 467

Origin: German
Meaning: Noble
Alternate Spellings:
Adaline, Adalline, Adilene
Gender Variation: Addison
Nicknames: Addie, Aline
Similar Names: Adela, Adelaide, Adele,
Adelina, Adelita, Alina
➡ The French diminutive of Adele that was
popular during the 19th century, then faded
out during the mid-1950s, and made a comeback
in 1999. "Sweet Adeline," the ballad that was
first published in 1903 and is often performed
as a barbershop quartet, comes to mind.

Adriana   Rank: 106

Origin: Latin
Meaning: From Haydia
Alternate Spellings:
Adrianah, Adrianna,
Adrieanna
Gender Variations: Adriam, Adrian, Adric,
Adson
Nicknames: Adra, Adri, Aida
Similar Names: Abriana, Adreika, Adriel,
Adrienne, Andriana, Arianna, Audriana,
Auriana, Brianna, Marianna, Anna
Namesakes: Adriana Behar (Brazilian
Olympic volleyball player), Adriana Lima
(Brazilian Victoria's Secret model)
➡ Feminine form of Adrian, derived from Latin
word Hadrianus, meaning a town in northern
Italy. Two forms of the feminine name placed
within the top 200 and peaked in 2006.
Shows potential to increase in popularity
with its trendy spellings and variations.

Adrienne   Rank: 736

Origin: Latin
Meaning: From Adria
Alternate Spellings:
Adrean, Adriaan, Adrian,
Adriane, Adrianne, Adrien, Edrian
Gender Variations: Adrian, Adrianus, Adriel
Nickname: Adria
Similar Names: Adina, Adrianna
Namesake: Adrienne Goodson (WNBA all-star)
➡ The French feminine form of Adrian that
became a favorite after the release of the
Rocky film series with actress Talia Shire in
the role of Rocky's girlfriend. Listed among
the top 100 boy's names.

Aileen   Rank: 537

Origin: Scottish
Meaning: From the
green meadow
Alternate Spelling: Aileene,
Ailene, Eileen, Eileene, Ilean, Ileane, Ileen,
Ileene, Ilene, Illene
Gender Variations: Aidan, Alan, Alastair
Nickname: Ailie
Similar Names: Aindrea, Ainsley, Aline,
Avaline, Avelina, Evelyn, Leanne, Lena, Lianna
Namesake: Eileen Brennan (actress)
➡ The Scottish variation of Eileen that's
derived from Eibhlin. In use since the 19th
century and especially popular in Scotland.
Considered a variation of Evelyn and Helen.

Ainsley   Rank: 456

Origin: Old English
Meaning: Hermitage field
Alternate Spellings:
Ainslee, Ainsleigh, Ainslie,
Ansley, Aynslee, Aynsley, Aynslie
Gender Variations: Aidan, Alan
Similar Names: Aileen, Aislin, Alaina,
Alanis, Alanna
⇒ Derived from *ansetl* and *leah*, which is
a variation of the surname Ainslie originally
used as a place name for Annesley in
Nottinghamshire or Ansley in Warwickshire.
Steadily used for girls since 2001 and
occasionally used for boys.

Aisha   Rank: 683

Origin: Arabic
Meaning: Alive
Alternate Spellings: Aesha,
Aiesha, Ayeisha, Ayesha,
Ayishah, Ieasha, Ieashia, Iesha, Ieesha, Ieeshia
Gender Variation: Ali
Similar Names: Aida, Ailey, Aimee, Asia,
Keisha, Nieshia, Tyeisha
⇒ The third and favorite wife of the prophet
Muhammad. This form is the most popular
spelling of the name.

Akeelah   Rank: 711

Origin: Arabic
Meaning: One who
reasons, intelligent
Alternate Spellings: Akela,
Akiela, Akilah
Similar Names: Aisha, Akira, Alima,
Aliyah, Alya
⇒ Possibly a form of the Arabic name
Akilah that debuted on the popularity
chart in 2006 coinciding with the release
of the 2006, film *Akeelah and the Bee* about
an 11-year-old girl who participates in the
Scripps National Spelling Bee.

Akira   Rank: 965

Origin: Japanese
Meaning: Clear, bright, dawn
Gender Variation: Akira
Similar Names: Aika,
Akeelah, Aki, Akiko
Namesake: *Akira* (1988 animated film)
⇒ A Japanese unisex name that first
debuted for girls in 2002 and disappeared
until 2006.

Alaina   Rank: 248

Origin: Old German
Meaning: Precious
Alternate Spellings: Alainah,
Alainna, Alainnah, Allaina,
Allainah, Alayna, Alaynah, Alaynna, Alaynnah
Gender Variations: Alain, Alan
Nicknames: Alai, Alain
Similar Names: Alaia, Alaida, Alaine, Alaisa,
Alana, Alawna, Aleena, Aleia, Alena, Alina
⇒ Feminine form of Alain which is associated
with Alan, that debuted on the chart in 1978,
peaking in 2006 among the top 300 for its
trendy "a" ending and many variations
spelled with an "ai" or "y."

Alana   Rank: 166

Origin: Old German
Meaning: Precious
Alternate Spellings:
Alanah, Alanna, Alannah,
Alawna, Allana, Elana, Ilana
Gender Variations: Alan, Alden
Nicknames: Alie, Lana
Similar Names: Alani, Alanis, Alayne, Alayna,
Alleene, Allina, Allyn, Alona
Namesakes: Alana Davis (singer), Alana
Hamilton Stewart (former wife of both
George Hamilton and Rod Stewart)
⇒ A modern feminine form of Alan that
debuted on the popularity chart in 1944
during the peak of actress Lana Turner's
career during the 1940s and 1950s. Lana,
who bears a form of the name, starred in
26 films between 1937 and the year Alana hit
the chart. The name climbed into the top
300 in 1996, following the 1995 hit release
of *The Brady Bunch Movie*, starring Alanna
Ubach. It was influenced more recently by
the character Alana on Disney's *That's So
Raven* introduced in 2004 and portrayed
by Cheetah Girl Adrienne Bailon, which
led the name into the top 200.

Alani   Rank: 933

Origin: Hawaiian
Meaning: Orange-bearing
tree
Gender Variation: Alan
Similar Names: Aileen, Aimee, Alaina, Alaine,
Alamea, Alana
⇒ The Hawaiian name for several species
of shrubs and trees first used as a girl's name
in 2003.

Alejandra Rank: 232
Origin: Greek
Meaning: Defender of mankind
Alternate Spellings: Aleiandra, Allejandra
Gender Variations: Alejandrino, Alejandro
Nickname: Aleja
Similar Names: Alandra, Alejanda, Alejandria, Alejandrina, Alejandro, Alessandra, Alexandra, Alexandria
➡ Spanish feminine form of Alexander that debuted on the chart in 1972 and peaked in 1993 and 1994 around the same time its short form, Alonda, became popular.

Alena Rank: 665
Origin: Hebrew
Meaning: Watchtower
Alternate Spellings: Aleena, Alina, Alleena, Allena
Gender Variation: Allen
Nickname: Lena
Similar Names: Adeline, Alana, Alene, Malene, Marlena, Shelena
➡ The short form of Magdalena or a variation of Alina that uses the feminine "a" ending currently in fashion.

Alessandra Rank: 361
Origin: Greek
Meaning: Defender of man
Alternate Spelling: Alesandra, Alessandre, Allessandra, Alyssandra
Gender Variations: Alessandro, Alexander
Nicknames: Alessa, Sandra
Similar Names: Alejandra, Alexa, Alexandra, Alexandria, Alexandrina
➡ The Italian and Spanish form of Alexandra that became fashionable during the mid-1980s. Brazilian supermodel Alessandra Ambrosio, who first became known in the late 1990s, is a namesake.

Alexa Rank: 39
Origin: Greek
Meaning: Man's defender
Alternate Spelling: Allexa
Gender Variations: Alex, Alexis, Alexius
Nicknames: Alex, Lexa
Similar Names: Aleka, Alessa, Alessia, Alexia, Alexina, Alexis, Alyssa

Namesake: Alexa Vega (actress)
➡ The feminine form of Alexis or the short form of Alexandra that became fashionable during the early 1970s and currently in vogue with its "a" ending. The name of singer and songwriter Billy Joel and model Christie Brinkley's daughter.

Alexandra Rank: 40
Origin: Greek
Meaning: Man's defender
Gender Variations: Alex, Alexander
Nicknames: Alex, Andra, Lexa
Similar Names: Alessandra, Alexandria, Alexandrina, Alexandrine, Alexia, Alexie, Alexine, Sandra
Namesakes: Alexandra Holden (actress), Alexandra Paul (actress)
➡ The feminine form of Alexander. A royal name known for Alexandra Feodorovna, the last Czarina of Russia and mother of the famous Anastasia. Thought to be an artistocratic name in the United Kindom during the end of the 19th century because of its ties to Queen Alexandra, consort to Edward VII. Listed among the top 100 in the U.S. since 1984.

Alexandria Rank: 147
Origin: Greek
Meaning: Defender of mankind
Alternate Spelling: Alexanderia, Alexandrea, Alexzandrea, Alexzandria, Alixandria, Allexandria, Alyxandria
Gender Variations: Alex, Alexander, Alexjandro, Alexter, Xander
Nicknames: Alex, Alyx, Andria, Lexi
Similar Names: Alejandra, Alexa, Alexanda, Alexandra, Alexandrina, Alexsandra, Alexsi, Alexsia, Alexys, Xandra
➡ Feminine form of Alexander and the name of Egyptian city founded by Alexander the Great. Also a place name in Louisiana, Minnesota, and Virginia that debuted on the chart in 1969 and moved into the top 200 in 2002 as a popular choice for girls. A trendy form of the name because of its "ia" ending.

Alexia   Rank: 164

Origin: Greek
Meaning: Defender, protector
Alternate Spellings: Aleksaya, Aleksia, Aleksiah, Aleksyah, Alexiah, Alexsia, Alexsiya, Allexia, Alyxia
Gender Variations: Alex, Alexander
Nicknames: Alex, Lexi
Similar Names: Aleshia, Alexa, Alexandra, Alexandria, Alexcia, Allexus
⇒ Feminine form of Alexius that debuted on the popularity chart in 1981. Also a name for a princess in the Netherlands, Greece, and Denmark. Climbed up the chart to the top 200 and peaked in 2002 as one of the favorite choices for girls, especially because it ends with the popular "ia."

Alexis   Rank: 14

Origin: Greek
Meaning: Defender, protector
Alternate Spellings: Alexus, Alexys
Gender Variations: Alexius
Nicknames: Alex, Alexi, Lexi, Lexis
Similar Names: Alexa, Alexana, Alexanne, Alexia, Alexina, Alexine, Alexius, Alix, Lexia
Namesake: Alexis Bledel (actress)
⇒ Derived from the Greek Alexios that was originally considered a boy's name but is now more commonly used for girls. The name debuted on the popularity chart in 1943 and first broke into the top 100 in 1982, possibly influenced by Alexis Carrington Colby from the 1980s TV series *Dynasty*.

Alice   Rank: 383

Origin: German
Meaning: Of noble kind
Alternate Spellings: Alise, Allice, Allis, Allise, Allys, Alyce, Alyse
Gender Variations: Alec, Allan
Nickname: Ali
Similar Names: Adelaide, Alicia, Aline, Alivia, Aliyah, Allysa, Allyson, Lissa
Namesakes: Alice Sebold (author), Alice Walker (author)
⇒ The short form of Adelheidis, which led to Adelaide, both common names during the Middle Ages. Author Lewis Carroll used the name for the title character in his famed 1865 novel *Alice's Adventures in Wonderland*. Listed among the top 100 from the 1880s to the 1950s and has continued to stay among the top 500 names.

Alicia   Rank: 167

Origin: German
Meaning: Of noble kind
Alternate Spellings: Alisha, Allicia, Allycia, Allysha, Allyssha, Alycia, Alyicia, Alysha, Alyshah, Alyssha
Gender Variations: Alijah, Asa
Nicknames: Ali, Licia
Similar Names: Alecia, Aleecia, Aleesa, Aleeza, Aleisha, Alieshea, Alyssa, Elicia, Melisha, Talicia
⇒ Modern Latin form of Alice, which is a short form for the Old French name Adelais. Trendy choice for girls because of the "ia" combination and the long "ee" sound in its variations. Influenced by actress Alicia Silverstone and continues to hold on to its popularity in the 2000s with the help of award-winning R & B singer Alicia Keys.

Alina   Rank: 355

Origin: Latin/Arabic
Meaning: Noble, illustrious
Alternate Spellings: Aleena, Alena, Alenah, Allena, Allina, Allyna, Allynah
Gender Variations: Alan, Alistair
Nicknames: Ali, Lina
Similar Names: Adelina, Adelaide, Alaina, Alana, Alinda, Aline
⇒ Either the pet form of Adelina or a name that means "noble and illustrious" in Arabic. Also used in Scotland as the feminine form of Alistair. The name debuted on the popularity chart in 1975 and is currently at its peak.

Aliza   Rank: 856

Origin: Hebrew
Meaning: Joyful
Alternate Spellings: Aleeza, Aleezah, Alizah
Gender Variation: Elias
Nickname: Ali
Similar Names: Alice, Alicia, Alissa, Alizabeth, Alize, Eliza
⇒ A contemporary Hebrew name that's been used occasionally since 2000 and may have gotten its start from Alice.

Alize

Rank: 959

Origin: Hebrew
Meaning: Joyful
Gender Variation: Elijah
Nickname: Ali
Similar Names: Alice, Allison, Aliza, Elsa, Elsie, Elyse

➡ A new twist on Alice or a form of the Hebrew name Aliza in popular use since the mid-1990s.

Allie

Rank: 229

Origin: German
Meaning: Sweet
Alternate Spellings: Aley, Ali, Alie, Aly, Alle, Allee, Alley, Alli, Ally, Allye
Gender Variations: Albert, Albie, Atlie
Nickname: Al
Similar Names: Ailie, Allecia, Alleese, Allena, Allia, Allice, Ellie, Ollie

➡ The pet form of Alison, ultimately derived from the German name Adalheidis, and adopted as a nickname for Alfreda, Alice, Alison, Allegra, Allison, Alva, and Alvina. The name faded from the popularity chart in 1950 but returned in 1986 due to the instant success of the 1980s television comedy *Kate & Allie* that was followed by the 1997 to 2002 television series *Ally McBeal*. Occasionally used as a boy's name.

Allison

Rank: 46

Origin: Old German
Meaning: Noble, truth
Alternate Spellings: Alisanne, Alison, Alisoun, Allyson, Allysoun, Allysson, Alyson
Gender Variations: Alex, Allen
Nicknames: Al, Allie
Similar Names: Alessa, Alexis, Alice, Alicia, Alisa, Alicia, Alyssa
Namesake: Allison Janney (actress)

➡ A Norman French variation of Alice that was originally used as a surname. Actress June Allyson first brought attention to a form of the name during the 1940s and 1950s, now becoming trendy with a "y" in the middle.

Alma

Rank: 616

Origin: Latin/Spanish
Meaning: Nourishing or the soul
Alternate Spellings: Allma, Almah

Gender Variation: Allan
Similar Names: Almina, Almira, Alva, Amalie, Amelia

➡ The name came into fashion in 1854 after the Battle of Alma was fought near the Alma River in the Crimea. It's related to the term "alma mater" that means "fostering mother" in Latin and was used in ancient Rome for the mother goddess, in medieval Christianity for the Virgin Mary, and recently for the college or university that a person attended. The name was listed among the top 100 from the end of the 19th century until 1927 and has faded in usage.

Alondra

Rank: 170

Origin: Greek
Meaning: Defender of mankind
Alternate Spellings: Alandra, Allondra, Alondre
Gender Variations: Aleksandar, Aleksandro, Aleksanteri, Alessandro, Alex, Sandro, Zander
Nicknames: Alond, Alonn, Ola
Similar Names: Aleksandrina, Alessandra, Alexa, Alexandra, Alonnah, Alonzia, Alyx, Malandra, Saundra, Zandra

➡ Short for Alejandra, the Spanish form of Alexandra that first debuted on the popularity chart in 1993. Also derived from the *Spanish* word *alondra*, meaning "lark," and represents an increasingly common choice for girls because of its peak position in 2005. Popular for its "a" ending.

Alyssa

Rank: 19

Origin: Greek
Meaning: Noble, rational
Alternate Spellings: Alisa, Alissa, Allissa, Alysa, Elisa, Elissa, Ellisa, Elyssa, Illissa, Ilyssa
Gender Variation: Allan
Nicknames: Aly, Alys, Lissa, Lissie, Lyssa
Similar Names: Alecia, Alice, Alicia, Alyssia, Ilissa, Ilssa

➡ Derived from the yellow, white, pink, or purple alyssum flower. First used in popularity as a girl's name in 1963 and listed among the top 100 in 1986, just two years after actress Alyssa Milano began her career on the television sitcom *Who's the Boss?* The name has continued to climb among the top 20.

Amanda   Rank: 102

Origin: Latin
Meaning: Lovable
Alternate Spelling: Amandah
Gender Variations: Amery, Armand
Nicknames: Manda, Mandy
Similar Names: Amalia, Amarilla, Amber, Amelia, Amy
Namesakes: Amanda Bynes (actress), Amanda Coetzer (South African tennis player), Amanda Peet (actress), Mandy Moore (singer/actress)
⇨ The feminine form of Amandus that was first recorded as a given name in Warwickshire, England, in 1212. It became a literary name picked up by several playwrights and novelists during the 17th and 18th centuries. It was steadily used during the 19th century and slowly faded until the 1970s. The name was listed among the top 10 from 1976 to 1995 influenced by principal characters on the 1980s and 1990s television series *Dynasty*, *Scarecrow and Mrs. King*, and *Melrose Place*.

Amani   Rank: 687

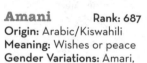

Origin: Arabic/Kiswahili
Meaning: Wishes or peace
Gender Variations: Amari, Amir
Nicknames: Aman
Similar Names: Amara, Amari, Amaris, Amaya, Armani
⇨ Originated as either an Arabic name that means "wishes" or from Kiswahili meaning "peace." The name debuted on the popularity chart in 1996 and recently fell out of the top 500.

Amara   Rank: 573

Origin: Greek/Latin
Meaning: Unfading, immortal or bitter, sour
Gender Variations: Ammar, Amir
Nickname: Amar, Mara
Similar Names: Amanitare, Amari, Amina
⇨ Possibly derived from a the Greek *amarantos* or the Latin *amarus* that's been listed among the top 1,000 names since 2000 and is currently at its peak. The name also refers to a genus of carabid beetles.

Amari   Rank: 519

Origin: African
Meaning: Having great strength
Alternate Spellings: Amare, Amary
Gender Variation: Amari
Similar Names: Amalie, Amara, Amaris, Amaya, Amayeta, Damaris, Kamaria
⇨ A form of Amar that first arrived on the chart in 1996 and is slightly more popular as a boy's name.

Amaris   Rank: 909

Origin: Hebrew
Meaning: The Lord promises
Gender Variations: Amare, Amariah
Nickname: Maris
Similar Names: Adamaris, Amariah, Amarise, Amarissa, Amarit, Amaya
⇨ A form of the Hebrew name Amariah used occasionally since 2003.

Amaya   Rank: 215

Origin: Basque
Meaning: The end
Alternate Spellings: Amaia, Amaiah, Amayah, Amiya, Amiyah, Amya, Amyah
Gender Variations: Ameya, Amrian, Aman
Nickname: Amay
Similar Names: Amada, Amalya, Amana, Amanda, Amara, Amari, Amarilla
⇨ Variant of Amaia that is also the name of a mountain and village in the Basque region of Spain. It first appeared on the chart as a popular choice for girls in 1999 and reached its peak at No. 181 in 2003. Still currently ranked among the top 300 for its trendy "a" ending and spelling with a "y" that most parents prefer.

Amber   Rank: 136

Origin: Arabic
Meaning: Amber
Alternate Spellings: Aamber, Ambar, Amberre, Ambor, Ambur, Ambyre
Gender Variations: Amber, Ambez, Ambrose, Lambert
Nickname: Amb

Similar Names: Ambereen, Amberetta, Amberkalay, Amberlee, Amberlynn, Amberzina, Ambilena, Ambree, Ambrielle, Ambrosia
Namesakes: Amber Valletta (actress), Ambrosia Kelley (model/actress)
➡ Traces back to Arabic *anbar* and defines itself with English vocabulary word "amber," a gemstone from fossilized tree resin or its golden color. First entered the popularity chart in 1945, following the publication of U.S. best-selling novel *Forever Amber* by Kathleen Winsor, and peaked in the top 20 between 1981 and 1993. Continues to hold value as a nature name for boys and girls, but more widely used for girls. Frequently combined with other elements to create trendy versions like Amberlynn and Amberkalay or hyphenated names such as Amber-Rose and Amber-Rae.

Amelia Rank: 82

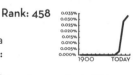

Origin: Latin
Meaning: Industrious
Alternate Spellings: Aemilia, Amilia, Emelia, Emilia, Emilija, Emiliya
Gender Variations: Emile, Emilian, Emilio
Nicknames: Amy, Melia, Milly
Similar Names: Amalia, Ameliana, Amelie, Emelina, Emeline, Emma
➡ Possibly the Latin feminine form of Aemilius or a combination of Emelia and Amalia. The name has been used for the title character in the novel *Amelia* by Henry Fielding and associated with Amelia Bloomer, a 19th-century women's rights and temperance advocate, and famed aviation pioneer Amelia Earhart.

America Rank: 458

Origin: Latin
Meaning: America
Gender Variation: Amerigo
Similar Names: Africa, Amera, Ami, Amica
➡ A form of the Latin geographical name Americus that refers to the continent discovered by Amerigo Vespucci in 1507. Used sporadically as a given name since the late 1800s until actress America Ferrera became known to audiences first in the 2002 and 2005 films *Real Women Have Curves*

and *The Sisterhood of the Traveling Pants* before landing the starring role in the popular television series *Ugly Betty* in 2006.

Amina Rank: 978

Origin: Arabic
Meaning: Truthful
Alternate Spellings: Ameena, Ameenah, Amena, Aminah, Amineh, Amynah
Gender Variations: Amias, Amin
Similar Names: Amia, Amica, Amie, Aminta
➡ The name of the Prophet Muhammad's mother who died when he was six. Also used as the short form of Williamina.

Amira Rank: 571

Origin: Arabic/Hebrew
Meaning: Princess, treetop
Alternate Spellings: Ameera, Ameerah, Amera, Amerah, Amirah, Amyra, Amyrah
Gender Variation: Amir
Nickname: Mira
Similar Names: Amara, Amina, Amiram, Amita, Amora
➡ The feminine form of Amir that caught on with parents in 1998.

Amy Rank: 128

Origin: Old French
Meaning: Beloved
Alternate Spellings: Aimee, Aimie, Aimy, Amee, Ami, Amie, Amiee, Amye, Aymee, Aymi
Gender Variations: Ameen, Ameer, Ames, Amicus, Amiel
Similar Names: Amada, Amata, Amecia, Amelia, Amiah, Amice, Amita, Amya, Esma
Namesakes: Amy Irving (actress), Amy Madigan (actress)
➡ Derived from Old French *aimee* and heavily influenced by the instant success of Amy Grant, contemporary Christian and pop singer, when she debuted in 1977, produced her first No. 1 hit in 1979, and released a platinum album in 1982. Name listed among the top 10 from 1969 to 1981 and is still popular today for its trendy long "ee" sound, yet traditional "y" spelling.

Anahi
Rank: 287

Origin: Persian
Meaning: The immaculate one
Alternate Spelling: Anahai
Gender Variations: Anais, Anayat
Nickname: Ana
Similar Names: Anahit, Anahita, Anai, Anaily, Anais, Anaya
⇨ Short form of Anahita, the name for a water goddess in Persian mythology. First appeared on the chart in 1997 and currently ranks among the top 300 most popular names for girls.

Anais
Rank: 869

Origin: French
Meaning: Grace
Alternate Spelling: Annais
Gender Variation: Ansel
Nickname: Ana
Similar Names: Agnes, Anna, Annalie, Annalisa, Anne, Annis, Annisa, Annise
⇨ The Provencal and Catalan form of Anna that's best-known for French-born writer Anais Nin, who became famous after the publication of her personal diaries starting in 1966. The name recently made a comeback on the popularity chart attributed to Latin pop singer Anais, who released her debut album in 2006.

Anastasia
Rank: 288

Origin: Greek
Meaning: Resurrection
Alternate Spellings: Anastacia, Anastasha, Anastashia, Anastasija, Anastasiya, Anastassia, Anastazia, Anasztaizia, Anasztasia, Annastasia
Gender Variations: Anastasio, Anastasios, Anastasis
Nicknames: Ana, Staz, Tasya
Similar Names: Anastaise, Anastay, Anstice, Asta, Anya, Asia, Nastasia, Stacia
⇨ Feminine form of Anastasius derived from the word *anastasis*. Best known for the daughter of Nicholas II, the last Russian czar, who supposedly survived the massacre of the royal family and whose story was adapted into a 1956 movie and a 1998 animated film. Nastassja Kinski, the prolific German actress who appeared in more than 60 films, bears a form of the name. Popular with parents because of its feminine "ia" ending and optional "z" and "y" spellings.

Andrea
Rank: 59

Origin: Greek
Meaning: Manly, courageous
Alternate Spellings: Anderea, Andreea, Andreia, Andria, Andrija,
Gender Variations: Anders, Andre, Andreas, Andrew
Nicknames: Andie, Drea, Rea
Similar Names: Andra, Andreana, Andree, Andrina, Joandra
Namesake: Andrea Jaeger (tennis player)
⇨ The feminine form of Andrew or Andreas used exclusively as a masculine name in some parts of the world. Associated with the S.S. *Andrea Doria*, an Italian luxury ocean liner, which collided with another ship in 1956 and due to advanced communications technology, most passengers and crew members survived.

Angel
Rank: 160

Origin: Greek
Meaning: Messenger of God
Alternate Spellings: Angele, Angell, Angil, Anjel
Gender Variations: Angel, Angelo, Dangelo
Nicknames: Ang
Similar Names: Angela, Angelea, Angeli, Angelica, Angelina, Angeline, Angie
⇨ Form of the Latin masculine name Angelus, derived from Angel, the name of a heavenly creature. Even though it is also a name for boys, it has listed within the top 200 since 1972 as a long-standing choice for girls. Its early popularity may be attributed to actress Angel Tompkins and her appearances in various television shows and films in the 1970s and 1980s.

Angela
Rank: 114

Origin: Greek
Meaning: Messenger of God
Alternate Spellings: Angala, Angella, Angila, Anjela, Anngela, Anngilla, Annjela
Gender Variations: Angelino, Angelo, Angelos
Nicknames: Ange, Angel
Similar Names: Angeleah, Angelee, Angelene, Angelica, Angelita, Angelynn
⇨ Feminine form of Angelus derived from Angel, the name of a heavenly creature. Landed a spot in the top 10 in 1965, following

the Oscar-nominated performance of actress Angela Lansbury in the 1962 movie *The Manchurian Candidate*. Name also inspired by actress Angela Cartwright in the 1965 film *The Sound of Music*, where her role as Brigitta von Trapp first made her famous. The fame of actresses Angela Bassett, Angie Harmon, and Angelina Jolie continued its success among parents.

Angelica   Rank: 208

Origin: Greek
Meaning: Messenger of God
Alternate Spellings: Angelika, Angalka, Anjelica, Anjelika, Anjellaca, Anjillica
Gender Variations: Angel, Angelito, Angelo
Nicknames: Angel, Angie
Similar Names: Angeliki, Angeline, Angelique, Angelita, Angelina, Angelia, Aniela, Anielica
Namesake: Angelica Boss (Russian model)
➡ Derived from the Latin word *angelicus*, meaning "angelic," but ultimately related to the Greek word *angelos*. An elaborated form of Angela that peaked on the popularity chart in 1993 and again in 1996. Recently influenced by actress Angelica Bridges, the lead singer of the sultry pop group Strawberry Blonde. Angelica Pickles, a character from the animated television show *Rugrats*, also comes to mind.

Angelina   Rank: 48

Origin: Latin
Meaning: Angel
Alternate Spellings: Angelona, Angellina
Gender Variations: Angel, Angelo
Nicknames: Angel, Angie
Similar Names: Angela, Angelia, Angelica, Angeline, Angelita
➡ A form of Angela that's been used in its own right since before the turn of the 20th century and shot up the popularity chart because of famed actress and U.N. Goodwill Ambassador Angelina Jolie.

Angeline   Rank: 863

Origin: Latin
Meaning: Angel
Alternate Spellings: Angelyne, Angyline
Gender Variations: Angel, Angelo, Angelos
Nicknames: Angel, Angie, Ann

Similar Names: Angela, Angelia, Angelica, Angelina, Angelique, Angelita, Angelle
➡ The French pet form of Angela that made a comeback in 2005 after a 17-year absence from the popularity chart.

Angelique   Rank: 693

Origin: Greek
Meaning: Messenger
Gender Variation: Angel
Nicknames: Angel, Angie
Similar Names: Angela, Angelica, Angelina, Angeline
➡ The French form of Angelica that spiked during the mid-1960s when the Gothic television soap opera *Dark Shadows* debuted with a character named Angelique. Today it's associated with Angelique Kidjo, the four-time Grammy-nominated singer-songwriter from Western Africa.

Angie   Rank: 389

Origin: Latin
Meaning: Angel
Alternate Spellings: Ange, Angee, Angey, Angi, Angy, Anjee, Anjey, Anjie
Gender Variations: Angelo, Angrej
Nickname: Ang
Similar Names: Agie, Andie, Angel, Angela, Angelica, Angelina, Annie
➡ A variation of Angela that became a top 300 name in the late 1800s and again in 1960. It peaked in the mid- to late 1970s, influenced by the 1973 song "Angie" by the Rolling Stones, and was followed by the No. 1 hit for Australian singer Helen Reddy called "Angie Baby" in 1974 and actress Angie Dickinson's role as Sgt. Leann "Pepper" Anderson in the popular 1970s crime drama *Police Woman*.

Aniyah   Rank: 220

Origin: Russian
Meaning: Grace
Alternate Spellings: Ania, Aniya, Anya
Gender Variations: Anil, Annan
Nickname: Ani
Similar Names: Aina, Aliya, Anisa, Anita, Anivah, Anna, Jaliyah, Janiya, Saniya, Taniyah
➡ Debuted in 1999 and climbed to No. 220 by 2006. Aniya is a variation of the name also currently ranked within the top 300.

Anna
Rank: 23

Origin: Hebrew
Meaning: Grace, charm
Alternate Spelling: Ana
Gender Variations:
Andreas, Andrew
Nicknames: Anne, Annie
Similar Names: Anelie, Anita, Anneka, Anneliese, Annetta, Annmarie, Leanna, Marianne, Rosanna
Namesakes: *Anna and the King* (1999 film), Anna Kournikova (Russian tennis player), Anna Paquin (actress), Anna Pavlova (Russian gymnast), Anna Sewell (author)
⇨ Derived from the Hebrew Channah, which is a form of Hannah and the name of a New Testament prophetess who recognized Jesus as the Messiah. Also known for Saint Anne, the mother of the Virgin Mary and the patron of Quebec and Brittany. A royal name for an 18th-century Russian empress who ruled from 1730 to 1740. In literature, the name of the title character in the novel *Anna Karenina* by Russian author Leo Tolstoy. The late model, actress, and sex symbol Anna Nicole Smith, born Vicki Lynn Marshall, also comes to mind. Used to form several name combinations such as Annabella, Annabeth, and Anna-Lisa.

Annabella
Rank: 556

Origin: Latin
Meaning: Lovable
Alternate Spellings:
Annabela, Anabella,
Gender Variations: Anando, Anatoli, Andrei
Nicknames: Anna, Bella
Similar Names: Annalie, Annalisa, Annamarie, Annaple, Anneliese, Annemarie
Namesake: Annabella (French actress)
⇨ The Latinate form of Annabel or a combination of "Anna" and the fashionable "Bella" that was first introduced on the popularity chart in 2001 and has climbed among the top 600 names.

Annabelle
Rank: 206

Origin: Latin
Meaning: Lovable
Alternate Spellings:
Anabel, Anabele, Anabelle, Annabell, Annahbell, Annahbelle, Annebell, Annebelle, Annibelle, Annybelle
Gender Variation: Anais
Nicknames: Ann, Anna

Similar Names: Amabelle, Andrell, Annabella, Annalisa, Annelle
⇨ Variation of Annabel ultimately derived from Amabel, derived from the Latin word *amabilis*. A combination name, blending Anna and Belle. Common in the 19th century because of "Annabel Lee," a famous 1849 poem by Edgar Allan Poe. After fading in 1951, it returned to popularity in 1995 and continued to rise partly because of character Annabelle Farrell played by actress Brooke Langton in the 2000 film *The Replacements*.

Annalise
Rank: 589

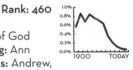

Origin: German/Scandinavian
Meaning: Graced with God's bounty
Alternate Spellings:
Annalies, Annaliese, Annelies, Anneliese, Annelise
Gender Variations: Anselm, Anshel
Nicknames: Anna, Lise
Similar Names: Anais, Anastasia, Annalisa, Annelie, Annella, Annise
⇨ A modern spelling of the German and Scandinavian compound name Anneliese that has risen in popularity since 1997. Anneliese van der Pol, who played the role of Chelsea on Disney's hit series *That's So Raven* from 2003 to 2007, is a namesake.

Anne
Rank: 460

Origin: Hebrew
Meaning: Grace of God
Alternate Spelling: Ann
Gender Variations: Andrew, Andy, Anthony
Nickname: Annie
Similar Names: Andrea, Angela, Anna, Annette, Hannah, Rexanne, Ysanne
Namesakes: Ann Bancroft (actress), Ann Landers (columnist), Anne Heche (actress), Anne Murray (Canadian singer)
⇨ The classic French form of Hannah that spent 65 years among the top 100 and is often combined or blended to create names such as Anise, Anita, Marianne, and Roseanne. It's accepted as the name of the mother of the Virgin Mary, although it's not mentioned in the Bible, and known for Anne Boleyn, the second wife of King Henry VIII and the mother of Queen Elizabeth I. Canadian author L. M. Montgomery used it for the title character in her 1908 novel *Anne of Green Gables*.

Annette   Rank: 881

Origin: Hebrew
Meaning: Grace of God
Alternate Spelling: Anette
Gender Variation: Arnett
Nicknames: Anne, Annie
Similar Names: Anissa, Annabelle, Annalisa, Annelie, Anneliese, Annetta, Annice, Anthea
Namesake: Annette O'Toole (actress)
➡ The French form of Anne that was popularized by singer and actress Annette Funicello who was discovered in the mid-1950s by Walt Disney and cast as one of the original Mouseketeers in the televised *Mickey Mouse Club*. Actress Annette Bening is a current bearer of the name.

Annie   Rank: 398

Origin: Hebrew
Meaning: Gracious
Alternate Spellings: Anie, Anne, Annee, Anney, Anni, Anny
Gender Variations: Aneel, Aneis
Nicknames: Ann
Similar Names: Agnie, Andie, Angie, Ann, Anna, Annise
Namesakes: Annie Borckink (Olympic speed skater), Annie Leibovitz (portrait photographer)
➡ A form of Ann and Hannah that peaked among the top 20 in the 1800s and early 1900s. American comic strip *Little Orphan Annie* by Harold Gray first appeared in 1924 during the name's top 50 ranking on the chart. Another notable bearer is *Annie Hall*, a 1977 film with Diane Keaton. An influence throughout the years is *Annie*, the 1977 stage musical.

Annika   Rank: 335

Origin: Hebrew
Meaning: Grace of God
Alternate Spellings: Aneeka, Aneka, Anica, Anika, Anikka, Anneka, Annica, Annicka, Annikka, Aunika
Gender Variations: Anik, Anil, Anis
Nicknames: Ani, Anick
Similar Names: Anela, Anelia, Anesha, Anna, Annaka, Annikke, Annina, Annisa, Annita
Namesake: Annika Sorenstam (Golf Hall of Famer)
➡ Associated with the name Anna, which ultimately derives from the Hebrew name

Channah and may be a contemporary blend of independent "Ann" names, like Angelika and Anita. It debuted on the popularity chart in 1995 and peaked in 2003.

Anya   Rank: 405

Origin: Hebrew
Meaning: Grace of God
Alternate Spelling: Anja
Gender Variation: Andrei
Similar Names: Aniyah, Anika, Anissa, Anita, Anna, Annie, Channah, Hania, Hannah
➡ The Russian form of Anna that's been on the rise since 1998 as part of a foreign trend.

Apple

Origin: Old English
Meaning: Sweet red fruit, temptation
Alternate Spellings: Apel, Appel
Gender Variations: Apollo, Apsel
Similar Names: Aphra, Apollonia, April, Opal
Namesake: apl.de.ap (Black Eyed Peas hip-hop group)
➡ A nature name for a tree that bears rounded red, yellow, or green fruit that has a strong biblical connotation as the temptation of Adam and Eve in the Garden of Eden. It's also associated with a brand of personal computers. Grammy Award-winning singer-songwriter Fiona Apple is a famous bearer of the surname. Celebrity couple Gwyneth Paltrow and Chris Martin named their daughter Apple Blythe Allison.

April   Rank: 319

Origin: Latin
Meaning: To open
Alternate Spellings: Aipril, Aprele, Aprelle, Apriel, Apriell, Aprielle, Aprill, Aprille, Apryl, Apryll
Gender Variations: Aneil, Aquil, Averill
Similar Names: Abril, Aniela, Anjil, Apree, Aprila, Aprilete, Avril
Namesakes: Eileen April Boylan (actress), April Gornik (painter), April Sinclair (author)
➡ The month of the year as a given name, often symbolizing spring. Originally derived from the Latin word *aperire*, referring to the opening of flowers during that month. Also the name of one of the most light-hearted days of the year, referred to as April Fool's Day. It appeared on the chart in 1939 and peaked in 1979 after the popularity had waned for similar seasonal names such as May and June.

Ar ⇨ girls' names

Arabella
Rank: 653
Origin: Latin
Meaning: Yielding to pray
Alternate Spelling: Arabela
Gender Variations: Ari, Ariel
Nicknames: Ara, Arabel, Bella
Similar Names: Aracely, Arbella, Arella, Arely, Ariel, Orabella, Orabelle
⇨ Possibly derived from the Latin *orabilis* or a variation of Annabelle. The name of a character in Charles Dickens' first novel *The Pickwick Papers,* and an opera by German composer Richard Strauss that was first performed in 1933. Considered an upper-class name, it was used sporadically during the late 19th century and made a sudden reappearance on the popularity chart in 2005 following a recent trend of names that end in "ella."

Araceli
Rank: 570
Origin: Latin
Meaning: Altar of heaven
Alternate Spelling: Aracely
Gender Variation: Arcadio
Similar Names: Arabella, Aracelia, Aracelis, Ariela
⇨ The name of a province located in the Philippines that's been used for girls since 1968 and recently fell out of the top 500.

Arely
Rank: 576
Alternate Spellings: Areli, Arelie
Gender Variation: Arland
Similar Names: Aracely, Arella, Aria, Ariel, Ariella, Arlene, Arlie
⇨ The exact origin and meaning of this name is unknown. Possibly a form of the surname Arley or a variation of Aurelia that's been used as a girl's given name since 2000.

Aria
Rank: 661
Origin: Italian
Meaning: Song, melody
Alternate Spelling: Arya
Gender Variations: Ariel, Aryan
Similar Names: Arabella, Aracely, Arianna, Ariel
⇨ The vocabulary word for an expressive melody sung by a single voice usually with an orchestral accompaniment as in an opera. Follows a recent trend to use a vocabulary word as a girl's given name.

Ariana
Rank: 78
Origin: Greek/Latin
Meaning: Melody and very holy one
Alternate Spellings: Arianna, Arieana, Arionna, Arriana, Aryana, Ayyanna, Aryonna
Gender Variations: Arden, Aric
Nicknames: Ari, Aria, Riana
Similar Names: Adriana, Ariadna, Ariadne, Arianne, Ariella, Arielle, Arin, Brianna, Marianna
⇨ The Italian form of Ariadne that debuted on the popularity chart in 1978 at No. 925 and finding sudden popularity among the top 100 names with its fashionable "a" ending.

Ariel
Rank: 202
Origin: Hebrew
Meaning: Lion of God
Alternate Spellings: Aeriel, Aeriell, Ariele, Arielle
Gender Variation: Ariel
Nickname: Arie
Similar Names: Aeriela, Ariellel, Ariellia, Auriel, Oriel
⇨ A unisex name that entered the chart in 1978 and peaked for girls among the top 100 from 1990 to 1992 due to the popular character in the 1989 Disney movie *The Little Mermaid.* Also a biblical place name in the Old Testament, used as another name for Jerusalem.

Armani
Rank: 936
Origin: Persian
Gender Variations: Armani, Armand, Armando
Nickname: Arman
Similar Names: Amani, Anya, Araceli, Arely, Ariana, Arnina
⇨ A surname used as a given name that was brought to parents' attention by famed Italian fashion designer Giorgio Armani when he introduced a menswear label in 1974 and a women's line in 1975. Ranks among the top 700 names for boys.

Ashanti
Rank: 882
Origin: African
Meaning: Thank you
Alternate Spellings: Ashante, Ashantee, Ashaunte, Ashauntee, Ashaunti
Gender Variations: Asher, Ashton

Nicknames: Shan, Shanti, Shany
Similar Names: Asante, Asha, Ashley, Shantay, Shantel, Shantrel
➯ This name's rise in popularity began with Grammy Award-winning singer Ashanti, who rose to fame in 2002 when she became the first female performer to hold the top two places on the Billboard Hot 100 singles chart. Also the name of a settlement of people located in southern Ghana. Often used by African Americans in celebration of their history.

Ashley
Rank: 12
Origin: Old English
Meaning: Ash meadow
Alternate Spellings: Ashlea, Ashleah, Ashlee, Ashlei, Ashleigh, Ashlie, Ashly, Ashlye
Gender Variations: Ashley, Ashton
Nicknames: Ash, Lee
Similar Names: Ashlan, Ashling, Ashlynn, Ashton
Namesake: Ashley Judd (actress)
➯ A common English surname until the 16th century that was first used as a given name for boys and is now more fashionable for girls. The name first landed on the popularity chart in 1964 and peaked at No. 1 in 1991 and 1992, influenced by Ashley Olson who started her career with twin sister, Mary-Kate at the age of 6 months on the 1987 to 1995 television show *Full House*.

Ashlyn
Rank: 140
Origin: American
Alternate Spellings: Ashlin, Ashlynn
Gender Variations: Austyn, Ayden
Similar Names: Annabelle, Annabeth, Annmarie, Ashton
➯ A fashionable update to Ashley by simply adding an "lyn" ending. The name has never looked back since it first hit the popularity chart in 1986.

Ashton
Origin: Old English
Meaning: Ash tree town
Alternate Spellings: Ashten, Ashtun
Gender Variations: Asher, Ashton
Nickname: Ash
Similar Names: Ashanti, Ashley, Ashling, Ashlyn, Asia

➯ A surname that was derived from a place name that's been used for girls since 1986, peaking the same year it debuted. It started out as a boy's name, but was surpassed by girls during the mid-1980s and taken over by boys again in 1997 when actor Ashton Kutcher became known for his role on the television series *That '70s Show*.

Asia
Rank: 332
Origin: Greek/Latin
Meaning: Rising sun
Alternate Spellings: Aisia, Aja, Asa, Ashia, Asiah, Assia, Asya, Asyah, Azha, Azia
Gender Variations: Aisan, Asa, Atsa
Similar Names: Anastasia, Asian, Asiray, Asrai, Assyria, Asta, Aziah, Azizia, Azra, Khadija

➯ From the name of the continent, which is possibly derived from the Assyrian word *asu*, meaning "east." According to the Koran, it is the name of Pharaoh's wife who raised Moses as her own son. Sometimes used as a short form of trendy names ending with "ia," such as Anastasia or Aspasia. It debuted on the chart in 1979. Also a variation of Aisha, the name of Muhammad's favorite wife, referred to as one of the four "perfect women."

Aspen
Rank: 572
Origin: Old English
Meaning: Aspen tree
Gender Variation: Austin
Similar Names: Ailsa, Aimee, Ainsley, Aisha, Ashley, Asta

➯ Taken from the word referring to the aspen tree that's part of the willow family. The popular ski resort city Aspen, Colorado, is named for the many aspen trees surrounding the area.

Athena
Rank: 504
Origin: Latin
Meaning: Wise
Alternate Spellings: Atheena, Athene, Athina
Gender Variations: Achilles, Apollo, Auster
Nickname: Athie
Similar Names: Aphrodite, Artemis, Aurora
➯ Known in Greek mythology as the goddess of war, handicraft, and practical reason and identified with the Roman goddess Minerva. She fought alongside the Greek heroes in Homer's *Iliad*.

Aubrey
Rank: 92
Origin: Old German
Meaning: Elf counsel
Alternate Spellings: Aubary, Aubery, Aubre, Aubree, Aubri, Aubrie, Aubry, Aubrye
Gender Variations: Auberon, Aubrey, Auburn
Nickname: Bri
Similar Names: Abrah, Abree, Albreda, Aubreigh, Aubrette, Aubriana, Aubrianne, Aubrielle, Auburn, Audrey

➡ Norman French form of the Old German name Alberich. Also a place name in three states that was originally meant for boys but has been given more frequently to girls since the 1970s. Appeared on the popularity chart in 1973 following the release of the fifth successful album from soft rock band Bread, featuring the hit song "Aubrey," that greatly influenced its classic comeback from the Middle Ages.

Audrey
Rank: 68
Origin: Old English
Meaning: Noble strength
Alternate Spellings: Audree, Audri, Audrie, Audry, Audrye
Gender Variations: Auberon, August, Austin
Nickname: Audie
Similar Names: Aubrey, Audra, Audrea, Audriana, Augusta, Aura

➡ Derived as the pet form of Ethelreda, who was known as a 6th-century saint. The name was picked up by Shakespeare at the beginning of the 17th century and used in his play As You Like It. Undoubtedly best known for Academy Award-winning actress Audrey Hepburn whose roles during the 1950s and 1960s led to five Academy Award nominations and one win for the 1953 film Roman Holiday. The name peaked in 1929 at No. 58 and appears to be making a comeback.

Aurora
Rank: 312
Origin: Latin
Meaning: Dawn
Alternate Spelling: Aurorah
Gender Variations: Aurele, Oron, Ory
Nicknames: Rora, Rory
Similar Names: Aurea, Aureal, Auroosa, Aurore, Ora, Orie, Zora

➡ In Roman mythology Aurora was the Roman goddess of sunrise and the equivalent of the Greek goddess Eos. It was influenced during the 1800s by "Aurora Leigh," an 1856 poem by Elizabeth Barrett Browning and character Aurora Raby in Lord Byron's chief masterpiece and comic epic, Don Juan, which he wrote from 1818 until nearly the end of his life. The name eventually reached a top 400 spot in 2003 and continued to climb to its current peak. It's also known by Disney fans as the name of Sleeping Beauty in most versions of the classic fairy tale. It follows the trend of the popular "a" ending.

Autumn
Rank: 95
Origin: Latin
Meaning: Season of harvest
Gender Variations: August, Austin
Similar Names: Aubrey, Aubrianne, Audra, Audrey, Audrina, Aurelia, Aurora

➡ Derived from autumnus for the vocabulary word that refers to the name of the fall season. Used for girls since 1969 and has already passed its peak but is still listed among the top 100. Surpassed the name Summer in popularity in 1982.

Ava
Rank: 5

Origin: Latin
Meaning: Like a bird
Alternate Spelling: Avah
Gender Variations: Avery, Avner
Similar Names: Avalee, Avelina, Avelyn, Avis, Chava, Eva, Eve, Evelyn, Evita

➡ Of uncertain origin, it's possibly a variation of the medieval names Avis and Aveline, a phonetic variation of Eva and Evelyn, or a form of the Hebrew Chava. Actress Ava Gardner, whose film career started in 1941, largely influenced the name.

Avery
Rank: 52

Origin: Old English
Meaning: Elf counsel
Alternate Spellings: Aeverie, Averie, Averi, Avrie
Gender Variations: Alfred, Averill
Similar Names: Ava, Avalon, Avelina, Aveline, Avis, Avril

➡ The Norman French feminine form of Alfred that debuted in 1989 and is currently at its peak. A place name for several cities across the U.S. Also used as a boy's name, but not as frequently.

Ayanna Rank: 527

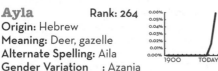

Origin: American
Alternate Spellings: Aiyana, Ayana, Iyana, Iyanna
Gender Variation: Ayesha
Similar Names: Anna, Anya, Aryana, Ayania, Aysha, Ayla
➡ A modern created name that possibly started as an elaboration of Anna or a pet form of Juliana. The name has been in popular use since 1971 and recently fell out of the top 500.

Ayla Rank: 264

Origin: Hebrew
Meaning: Deer, gazelle
Alternate Spelling: Aila
Gender Variation : Azania
Similar Names: Ayala, Ayesha, Aylin, Aysha, Azalea
➡ A literary name used by Jean Auel for the heroine in her 1984 novel *The Clan of the Cave Bear* and subsequent sequels. The name also means "circle of light around the sun or moon" in Turkish and has been used synonymously with "moonlight." Climbed among the top 300 names in 2006.

Aylin Rank: 776

Origin: Turkish
Meaning: Moon halo
Gender Variation: Aylwin
Nickname: Lin
Similar Names: Aya, Ayana, Ayesha, Ayla, Aysha, Jaylan, Kaylin
➡ Possibly inspired by Aylin Aslim, the Turkish pop-rock singer who released her first album in 2000.

Bailey Rank: 112

Origin: French/English
Meaning: Bailiff
Alternate Spellings: Baeli, Baileah, Bailee, Bailei, Baileigh, Baillie, Bailly, Baylee, Baylie, Bayly
Gender Variations: Bailey, Bailio, Blaine
Nicknames: Baye, Lee
Similar Names: Baiesha, Bali, Balita, Bayla, Baytee
➡ Feminine use of occupational surname for a bailiff or administrative official. Significantly more popular as a girl's name in the U.S., especially after the rise of the character Bailey Quarters on the hit 1978 to 1982

television series *WKRP in Cincinnati*. Continues to be a top choice for female television characters, such as Dr. Miranda Bailey on *Grey's Anatomy*.

Barbara Rank: 561

Origin: Greek
Meaning: Foreign
Alternate Spelling: Barbra
Gender Variations: Barnabas, Barnaby
Nicknames: Babs, Barb, Barbie
Similar Names: Babette, Barbette, Bobbie, Bonnie
Namesakes: Barbara Bush (former first lady), Barbara Eden (actress)
➡ The feminine form of Barbarus meaning "foreign," referring to the chatter made by non-Greek speaking people. A common Christian name known for St. Barbara, considered one of the most popular saints, she was martyred by her father who was in turn killed by lightning during the 3rd century. Irish writer George Bernard Shaw gave the name a literary distinction when he published the play *Major Barbara* in 1907. It was clearly influenced by actress Barbara Stanwyck, who started her career in films during the late 1920s and television in the 1960s. Singer, actress, and film director Barbra Steisand brought attention to a form of the name.

Beatrice Rank: 966

Origin: Latin
Meaning: Voyager, traveller
Alternate Spellings: Beatrise, Beatrycze
Gender Variation: Beau
Nicknames: Bea, Beattie, Trice
Similar Names: Beata, Beatricia, Beatrix, Beatriz
Namesakes: Beatrice Arthur (actress), Beatrix Potter (author)
➡ The Italian and French form of Beatrix used in literature as Dante Alighieri's guide in his long poem *The Divine Comedy* and the name of a character in Shakespeare's play *Much Ado About Nothing*. It was popular in England during the Middle Ages and became royally known for the daughter of Queen Victoria and the granddaughter of Queen Elizabeth II, Princess Beatrice of York. It dropped off the chart in 2002 and reappeared in 2006 with other vintage names.

Belinda   Rank: 809

Origin: Latin
Meaning: Beautiful
Alternate Spelling:
Bellinda, Bellynda, Belynda
Gender Variations: Belen, Beltran
Nicknames: Belle, Linda, Lindy
Similar Names: Beatrice, Bedelia, Belen, Belicia, Belita, Belva, Benita
⇨ A literary name first used in the 17th century by Sir John Vanbrugh for a character in *The Provok'd Wife* and then in the 18th century by Alexander Pope in "The Rape of the Lock." The origin and meaning is unknown but might possibly be a combination of *bella*, which means "beautiful," with the suffix "linda." The name was known during the 1980s for Belinda Carlisle, the lead singer of the all-female rock group The Go-Go's, but it subsequently dropped off the chart during the late 1990s only to return in 2005, influenced by Grammy-nominated Mexican singer and actress Belinda Peregrin Schull, who goes by the stage name "Belinda."

Bella   Rank: 181

Origin: Latin
Meaning: Beautiful
Alternate Spellings: Bela, Belah, Belau, Belia, Beliah, Bellah, Bellau
Gender Variations: Bela, Bellal, Belvin
Nicknames: Bell
Similar Names: Arabella, Belladonna, Bellamy, Bellissa, Belva, Belynda, Beyla, Claribel, Labella
⇨ The short form of Isabel or Isabella that also means "God's promise" in Hebrew. Notable bearers of the name are Bella Freud granddaughter of psychoanalysis inventor Sigmund Freud, and Bella Savitsky Abzug, a famous American political figure and a leader of the 20th-century women's movement. The name has recently been influenced by the popularity of Disney character Belle from the 1991 movie *Beauty and the Beast*.

Bethany   Rank: 244

Origin: Hebrew
Meaning: House of figs
Alternate Spellings:
Bethanee, Bethaney,
Bethani, Bethanie, Bethanney, Bethannie,
Bethanny, Betheney, Bethenie, Betheny
Gender Variations: Bevan, Beynan
Nicknames: Beth, Betha
Similar Names: Bethann, Bethia, Bethzaida, Bevalee, Bevany, Devany
Namesakes: Bethany Dillon (Christian singer)
⇨ A biblical place name in the New Testament that was the home of Lazarus and his two sisters, Mary and Martha, that's also considered a combination name using Beth and Ann. First debuted on the chart in 1949 and was listed among the top 200 from 1976 to 2002. The name is currently known for actress and singer Bethany Joy Galeotti, best known for her role as Haley James Scott in the television drama *One Tree Hill*.

Betsy   Rank: 743

Origin: Hebrew
Meaning: My God is an oath
Alternate Spellings: Betsey, Betsie, Bethzy
Nicknames: Bette
Similar Names: Annabeth, Babette, Bess, Bessie, Beth, Bethan, Betty, Buffy
Namesakes: Betsey Johnson (fashion designer), Betsy King (LPGA golfer)
⇨ The pet form of Elizabeth and a blend of the names Betty and Bessie that recently became fashionable following a trend of vintage names. Seamstress Betsy Ross, who is said to be the designer of the first U. S. flag, is a famous bearer of the name.

Bianca   Rank: 182

Origin: Italian
Meaning: White, pure
Alternate Spelling:
Beonca, Beyonca, Biancha, Bianka, Bionca, Byanca
Gender Variations: Bijan, Blane, Breon
Nicknames: Bi
Similar Names: Bellanca, Biana, Bianey, Biranda, Bitonnica, Blanca, Blanche, Vianna
Namesakes: Bianca Lawson (actress), Bianca Morales (jazz artist)
⇨ A variation of the French name Blanche that debuted on the popularity chart in 1973. The name of two Shakespeare characters, the meek younger daughter in *The Taming of the Shrew* and a courtesan in *Othello*. Also the subject of a song in *Kiss Me, Kate*, a Tony Award-winning 1948 musical spin-off of Shakespeare's earlier play. The name was

later inspired by activist Bianca Jagger, who became famous as the first wife of Rolling Stones singer Mick Jagger and is now known as a peace worker and diplomat.

Blanca
Rank: 800

Origin: Spanish
Meaning: White
Alternate Spelling: Blanka
Gender Variations: Blanco, Blane
Similar Names: Bianca, Blanche, Blythe, Branca
➡ Literally means "white" in Spanish and is also a form of the name Blanche. May have first been used by King Garcia VI of Navarre, who used the name during the 12th century for one of his daughters, which led to the use of both Blanca and Blanche among other royal families. It's predominantly considered a Hispanic name.

Braelyn
Rank: 855

Origin: American
Alternate Spelling: Braylyn
Gender Variations: Braeden, Braylon
Nickname: Lynn
Similar Names: Bradyn, Breana, Briallen, Briley, Brynn, Caralyn, Cherlyn
➡ An invented name that blends "Brae" with the popular suffix "lyn." New to the girl's popularity chart in 2006. Braylon is a similar variation for boys, listed among the top 500 names.

Brandy
Rank: 801

Origin: Dutch
Meaning: Distilled wine
Alternate Spellings: Brande, Brandey, Brandi, Brandie, Branndi
Gender Variations: Brandon, Brendan
Nickname: Bran
Similar Names: Breena, Brenda, Brenna, Briallen, Briana
➡ The vocabulary word for the alcoholic drink derived from the Dutch *brandewij*, but probably created as the feminine form of Brandon. The name spiked in 1973, a year after the pop music group Looking Glass hit No. 1 with "Brandy (You're a Fine Girl)" that has since been recorded by the rock band Red Hot Chili Peppers and country singer

Kenny Chesney. Actress and Grammy Award-winning R&B singer Brandy Rayana Norwood, who goes by the stage name "Brandy," is a famous bearer.

Bree
Rank: 955

Origin: Irish Gaelic
Meaning: Upbeat
Alternate Spellings: Brea, Brei, Bria, Brie
Gender Variations: Brede, Brent, Brett
Similar Names: Breanna, Breena, Briallen, Brielle, Brier, Brisa
➡ The anglicized form of the Irish Gaelic name Brighe and used as the short form of names like Breanna and Sabrina. The name was popularized during the 1970s by Jane Fonda's character in the 1971 film *Klute* and recently made a comeback influenced by Bree Hodge, the fictional *Desperate Housewives* character played by Marcia Cross.

Brenda
Rank: 239

Origin: Old Norse
Meaning: Sword
Alternate Spellings: Brendah, Brennda, Brenndah, Brinda, Brynda
Gender Variations: Brendan, Brendt, Brenon
Nicknames: Bren
Similar Names: Branda, Breanda, Brendalynn, Brendell, Brendette, Brendie, Brendolyn, Brendyl, Breonda, Labrenda
Namesakes: Brenda Blethyn (English actress), Brenda Vaccaro (actress)
➡ Derived from Old Norse word *brandr* and is also related to the English word "brand," meaning "to mark by burning." The name has become more popular in Gaelic-speaking countries because of its similarity to the male name Brendan and was mainly used in Scotland and Ireland until the 20th century. It debuted on the chart in 1925 and peaked at No. 11 in 1961 during the fame of singer Brenda Lee, who is credited for having the most successful hits of any woman during the 1960s and was one of the earliest pop stars to have a major contemporary international following. A current namesake is actress Brenda Lee Strong, who plays the role of Mary Alice Young in the television series *Desperate Housewives*.

101

Brenna
Rank: 381

Origin: Old Norse
Meaning: Sword
Alternate Spellings:
Brenah, Brennah, Brennaugh, Brinna, Brynna
Gender Variations: Brehn, Brennan, Brenly, Brentan
Nicknames: Bren, Brennie
Similar Names: Breana, Breena, Breina, Brenie, Brenin, Breonna, Brienna, Brynn
⇒ Either a variation of Brenda or a modern feminine form of Brennan. May also be taken from the Irish male name Bréanainn, meaning "prince." Peaked in 1995, following the release of the 1994 movie *Guarding Tess*, starring actress Brenna McDonough. Currently a top 400 name for its trendy "a" ending.

Bria
Rank: 870

Origin: Irish
Meaning: Strong, high noble
Alternate Spellings: Brea, Breah, Breea, Brya
Gender Variation: Brian
Nickname: Bree
Similar Names: Breda, Bren, Brenna, Bretta, Briallen, Briana, Brina, Briney, Brisa, Brita
⇒ The short form of Brianna used as an independent name since 1991.

Brianna
Rank: 20

Origin: Irish
Meaning: Strong, high noble
Alternate Spellings:
Breana, Breanna, Breayanna, Breeanna, Briahna, Briana, Briannah, Briaunna, Brieanna, Brienna, Bryanna
Gender Variation: Brian
Nicknames: Anna, Bree, Bria
Similar Names: Adrianna, Arianna, Breanne, Brenna, Briannon, Brieon, Brina, Briney, Brionna, Marianna
⇒ The female variation of the name Brian that's rapidly risen in popularity since 1976, entering the top 100 in 1988.

Bridget
Rank: 347

Origin: Irish Gaelic
Meaning: Exalted one
Alternate Spellings:
Bridgett, Bridgit, Bridgot, Briget, Briggette, Briggitte, Brigitt, Brydget, Brygette, Bryjit

Gender Variations: Bridger, Brigdon
Nicknames: Biddy, Bri, Bridie
Similar Names: Berett, Berget, Birgitt, Birgitta, Birkita, Breda, Bree, Brietta
Namesake: Bridget Hall (supermodel)
⇒ A form of the Irish name Brighid that's associated with the Greek goddess of fire, poetry, and wisdom. It became known during the 1950s and 1960s for French actress and sex symbol Brigitte Bardot. More recently influenced by actress Bridget Fonda, the daughter of Peter Fonda and granddaughter of Henry Fonda, and model and actress Bridget Moynahan. The 2001 movie *Bridget Jones's Diary* brought attention to the name in the 2000s.

Brielle
Rank: 459

Origin: Hebrew
Meaning: God is my strength
Alternate Spellings: Briele, Briell, Briyel, Bryel, Bryelle
Gender Variations: Gabe, Gabriel
Nicknames: Brie, Elle
Similar Names: Breena, Briallen, Briana, Gabby, Gabriela, Gabrielle
⇒ The short form of Gabrielle that uses the trendy "elle" ending. It has been used independently as a given name since 1991, steadily climbing to its current position today.

Brisa
Rank: 605

Origin: Spanish
Meaning: Breeze
Alternate Spellings: Briza, Bryssa
Gender Variations: Brice, Bryce
Similar Names: Bree, Breezy, Bria, Briana, Brielle, Brylee
⇒ The Spanish word for breeze referring to a light, gentle wind that's been used as a girl's given name since 2000.

Brittany
Rank: 318

Origin: Latin
Meaning: From Great Britain
Alternate Spellings:
Bretteny, Brettney, Bridney, Britani, Britanny, Britianee, Britney, Brittney, Bryttany, Bryttnee
Gender Variations: Brentan, Brett, Brittan
Nickname: Brit
Similar Names: Bethany, Brett, Bretta, Brittann, Brittanya, Brittell, Brittlynn

Namesake: Brittany Daniel (actress)

➡ From the name of the region in the northwest of France called French Bretagne, named for the Briton people who fled to that area after the Anglo-Saxon invasion of England. The entire region was later called Britain. The name was influenced starting in the 1990s by singer and actress Brittany Murphy and pop singer Britney Spears, who uses a form of the name.

Brooke   Rank: 44

Origin: Old English
Meaning: Brook, stream
Alternate Spellings: Bhrooke, Brook
Gender Variations: Brock, Brook
Nickname: Brookie
Similar Names: Brookanne, Brookelle, Brookia, Brookline, Brooklyna, Brooks
Namesakes: Brooke Bennett (Olympic swimmer), Brooke Burns (actress), Brooke Langton (actress)

➡ Enduring name significantly influenced by the accomplishments of model and actress Brooke Shields. An English surname also taken from the vocabulary word "brook," meaning "a small freshwater stream." First peaked in the top 100 in the late 1970s and has continued to hold a strong position since 1987. A suitable name for boys but more common for girls.

Brooklyn   Rank: 67

Origin: American
Alternate Spellings: Brookelynn, Brookelynne, Brooklen, Brooklin, Brooklyne, Brooklynn, Brooklynne
Gender Variations: Brook, Brooks
Nicknames: Brook, Lyn
Similar Names: Braelyn, Bryanne, Brynne, Brylee, Cailyn, Caitlyn

➡ The combination of "Brook" with the popular feminine suffix "lyn" that's associated with the New York City borough and a Broadway musical that debuted in 2004.

Brylee   Rank: 885

Origin: American
Alternate Spellings: Brilee, Briley, Brylea, Bryleigh
Gender Variations: Berle, Bralen, Bryan, Burley

Nicknames: Bry, Lee
Similar Names: Baylee, Beryl, Bree, Breila, Brenna, Brielle, Bryanna, Brynn

➡ A new twist on Rylee that uses the "ee" ending that's in vogue with parents today.

Brynn   Rank: 402

Origin: Welsh
Meaning: Hill, mount
Alternate Spellings: Brin, Bryn, Bryne, Brynne
Gender Variations: Bryn, Brynnen
Similar Names: Brynna, Brynnalyn, Brynnley

➡ A form of the place name Bryn that has gone in and out of popularity since 1980 and is currently among the top 500 names.

Cadence   Rank: 214

Origin: English
Meaning: Rhythm, flow
Alternate Spellings: Kadence, Kaydence
Gender Variations: Caden, Cadence
Nicknames: Cay, Cade, Cady
Similar Names: Caden, Cadyna, Jaden, Kadeidra, Kadelyn

➡ It's taken from the vocabulary word that can be applied to the rhythmic sequence in many areas, such as music, speech, dance, running, and the military. Also the name of a 1991 film directed by and starring Martin Sheen and actor Charlie Sheen as an inmate in a U.S. Army stockade. This film is based on a 1968 novel by Gordon Weaver, *Count a Lonely Cadence*. Possibly favored in the U.S. because of the patriotism and support of the military troops.

Caitlyn   Rank: 199

Origin: Irish
Meaning: Pure
Alternate Spellings: Caetlin, Caitlin, Kaitlin, Kaitlyn, Kaitlynn, Katlyn
Gender Variations: Carey, Carson
Nicknames: Cait, Lyn
Similar Names: Caelie, Cailyn, Caitrin, Caryn, Catalin, Catalina, Catarina, Catherina, Catherine, Cathleen
Namesake: Caitlin Wachs (actress)

➡ A trendy variation of Caitlin and a form of Katherine. Listed among the top 200 names since 1990.

103

Callie
Rank: 303

Origin: Greek
Meaning: Beautiful
Alternate Spellings:
Calee, Cali, Calie, Calley,
Calli, Kalee, Kali, Kallee, Kalli, Kallie
Gender Variations: Cal, Caley, Calin, Calray
Nickname: Cal
Similar Names: Cailie, Calan, Calandra,
Caleena, Caletta, Calina, Calissa, Callia, Callista
⇒ The short form of Callista that appeared
among the top 200 from the 1880s until
1900. Faded from the chart in 1963, returned
in 1973, and is currently making a comeback.
Influenced by fictional character Calliope
"Callie" Iphegenia Torres from the popular
television drama *Grey's Anatomy*. A popular
name favored for its long "ee" sound that
many parents prefer today.

Cameron
Rank: 289

Origin: Scottish Gaelic
Meaning: Crooked nose
Alternate Spellings:
Cameran, Cameren,
Camerin, Camerun, Cameryn, Camren,
Camron, Camryn, Kamrin, Kamryn
Gender Variations: Cambell, Cambridge,
Camden, Cameron
Nickname: Cami
Similar Names: Camara, Cambrya, Camden,
Camelina, Camelot, Cameo, Camerino,
Camylle, Caryn, Tamryn
Namesake: Cameron Diaz (actress)
⇒ A Scottish Highlands clan name and
surname possibly derived from *camsron* or
a place name that means "crooked stream."
A top 100 name for boys that debuted in
1980 for girls. Actress Camryn Manheim uses
a trendier form of the name with its "y."

Camila
Rank: 180

Origin: Latin
Meaning: Attendant at a
religious service
Alternate Spellingss:
Camilah, Camilla, Camillah, Cammila,
Cammilah, Cammilla, Cammylla, Camyla,
Chamila, Kamila
Gender Variations: Camiel, Camillo, Camren
Nickname: Cami
Similar Names: Caila, Camala, Camille,
Camri, Camryn, Carmela, Carmila, Jamila
Namesake: Camilla Belle (actress)

⇒ Spanish and Portuguese form of Camilla,
associated with the Old Roman family name
Camillus. Was also the name of a legendary
warrior maiden of the Volscians in Virgil's
Latin epic *Aeneid*. One of three variations, all
listed on the popularity chart, that first ranked
in 1997. Camilla, Prince Charles' wife and Her
Royal Highness, The Duchess of Cornwall, is
a notable bearer of a form of the name.

Camille
Rank: 308

Origin: Latin
Meaning: Attendant at a
religious service
Alternate Spellings: Camiel,
Camielle, Camile, Cammile, Cammille,
Cammyl, Cammylle, Camylle, Kamille, Kamylle
Gender Variations: Camille, Camilo, Camrin
Nickname: Cami
Similar Names: Camelina, Cameron, Camilla,
Cammilyn, Camino, Camri, Carille, Jamille
⇒ The French form of Camilla considered
a unisex name until it faded for boys in 1915.
It peaked for girls during the 1990s and
2000s among the top 300. It was influenced
in 2007 by the film *Camille*, starring Sienna
Miller and James Franco.

Campbell
Rank: 659

Origin: Scottish Gaelic
Meaning: Crooked mouth
Alternate Spelling:
Campbel
Gender Variations: Callum, Cameron,
Campbell
Nickname: Cami
Similar Names: Cameron, Camille, Carson
⇒ Originated as a surname derived from
the Gaelic *cam beul* that belonged to a
powerful Scottish Highland clan. Also used
as a boy's name, it currently ranks higher for
girls in the short time it's been listed on the
popularity chart.

Camryn
Rank: 216

Origin: Scottish Gaelic
Meaning: Crooked nose
Alternate Spellings:
Cameran, Cameren,
Cameryn, Camren, Camrin, Camron,
Kameron, Kamran, Kamren, Kamryn
Gender Variations: Cameron, Camon,
Camerson
Nicknames: Cam, Cami

Similar Names: Cambri, Camilyn, Camria, Camry, Camylle, Caryn, Tamryn
➪ The feminine form of Cameron that debuted on the chart in 1997, influenced by actress Camryn Manheim, who played attorney Ellenor Frutt on the legal drama *The Practice* that premiered the same year. The name is currently listed among the top 300 because of its trendy "y" spelling.

Carissa   Rank: 585

Origin: Greek
Meaning: Grace
Alternate Spellings: Caressa, Carisa, Carrisa, Carrissa, Charissa, Karisa, Karissa
Gender Variations: Casey, Cassidy
Nicknames: Cari, Caris, Rissa
Similar Names: Cara, Caresse, Carey, Clarissa, Karis, Larissa, Marisa
➪ A shortened form of Charissa or an elaboration of Carys that uses the feminine "issa" ending. The name is associated with ancient towns in Spain and Turkey and a genus of shrubs native to Africa and Asia. It debuted on the popularity chart in 1970 and peaked in 1992 at No. 239.

Carly   Rank: 251

Origin: Old German
Meaning: Free man
Alternate Spellings: Carlee, Carley, Carli, Carlie, Carlye, Karlee, Karley, Karli, Karlie, Karly
Gender Variations: Carl, Carlos, Carlson, Carlton, Karlton
Nickname: Carl
Similar Names: Cally, Carey, Carla, Carlyn, Caroly, Charly, Harly
➪ A variant of many names including Carla, Carlie, Carol, Caroline, and Charlotte. The feminine form of Carl and the German form of Charles that debuted on the chart in 1973 as a fashionable name for girls because of Carly Simon, the two-time Grammy Award-winning American musician and one of the top leaders of the early 1970s singer-songwriter movement. Carly was inducted into the Songwriters Hall of Fame in 1994, shortly before the name peaked on the charts in 1995. Continues to be a trendy choice because of the up-and-coming young actress Carly Schroeder. Favored because of its "y" spelling combined with the long "ee" sound.

Carmen   Rank: 258

Origin: Hebrew
Meaning: Fruitful orchard
Alternate Spellings: Carman, Carmyn, Karman, Karmen, Karmyn
Gender Variations: Carmelo, Carmen, Carmine
Similar Names: Carma, Carmania, Carmanya, Carmelia, Carmelina, Carmelita, Carmia, Carmie, Carmine, Carmyna
Namesake: Carmen Kass (Estonian supermodel)
➪ Spanish form of Carmel shaped by the Latin word *carmen*, meaning "song." Influenced by the name of the main character in George Bizet's French opera *Carmen* that premiered in 1875. Maria do Carmo Miranda da Cunha, a Portuguese-Brazilian samba singer and motion picture star known for her enormous fruit-laden hats in the 1940s, influenced the name when she was nicknamed "Carmen" because of her father's love for opera. Actress Carmen Electra later inspired the name in the 1990s and 2000s with her television and film roles.

Carol   Rank: 968

Origin: Old German
Meaning: Free man
Alternate Spellings: Carole, Carrol, Carroll, Caryl, Karel, Karol, Karole, Karyl, Karryl, Keryl
Gender Variations: Carl, Carroll, Charles
Nickname: Caro
Similar Names: Carla, Carlotta, Carly, Carola, Caroleen, Carolina, Caroline, Carrie, Charla, Charleen
Namesakes: Carol Blazejowski (Basketball Hall of Famer), Carol Channing (comedienne/actress), Carole King (singer)
➪ First used as a masculine name derived from Carolus and later became a short form of Caroline. It's also associated with the vocabulary word that refers to a song or hymn, especially at Christmastime. The name was listed among the top 100 from 1928 to 1971. It was known during the 1920s, 1930s, and early 1940s for comedic actress Carole Lombard, who used the French form of the name. Comedienne and actress Carol Burnett, the host of a successful television variety show from 1967 to 1978, is another famous bearer.

Carolina — Rank: 281

Origin: Old German
Meaning: Free man
Alternate Spellings: Caralina, Carilena, Carolena, Caroliana, Carollina, Carrolina, Karalina, Karolina, Karolyna
Gender Variations: Carrick, Carroll, Carron
Nickname: Lina
Similar Names: Calina, Carlina, Carmelina, Carola, Carolann, Carolinda, Caroline, Carolyn, Carrina, Catalina
⇨ Latin and feminine form of Carolus, ultimately derived from Charles. The name of two U.S. states, North and South Carolina, that were named for King Charles I of England. Currently not as popular as Caroline but has ranked among the top 300 since 1993 and keeps up with today's trends by ending with an "a."

Caroline — Rank: 89

Origin: Old German
Meaning: Free man
Alternate Spellings: Carolin, Carolyn, Carolyne, Carolynne, Karoline, Karolyn, Karolyne, Karolynn
Gender Variations: Carl, Charles
Nicknames: Carol, Carrie
Similar Names: Cara, Carlene, Carley, Carla, Carolann, Carolina, Charleen, Charlotte
Namesakes: Caroline in the City (TV series), Caroline Kennedy Schlossberg (author, philanthropist), Caroline Rhea (Canadian comedian/actress)
⇨ The Italian feminine form of Charles considered a classic by today's standards. Brought into England during the 18th century by the queen consort of George II and is still considered a royal name today used by Princess Caroline of Monaco. It was fashionable during the 19th century but started to lose its appeal during the 20th century. The name made a comeback during the 1980s and peaked at No. 62 in 2001.

Carolyn — Rank: 517

Origin: Old German
Meaning: Free man
Alternate Spellings: Carolin, Caroline, Carolyne, Carolynn, Carollyn, Carrolyn, Karolyn
Gender Variation: Charles

Carrie — Rank: 859

Nicknames: Carol, Lyn
Similar Names: Callie, Careen, Carly, Carolina, Carry, Charline
⇨ The modern form of Caroline with its "y" in the suffix spelling that's used mainly in the U.S. The name was listed among the top 100 from 1927 to 1970, peaking at No. 10 in 1942.

Origin: Old German
Meaning: Free man
Alternate Spellings: Carey, Cari, Carri, Carry, Kari, Kerrie, Kerry
Gender Variation: Carson
Similar Names: Careen, Carla, Carley, Carlisa, Carol, Caron, Carreen, Karen
Namesakes: Carrie (1976 and 2002 films), Carrie Fisher (actress)
⇨ The pet form of Caroline used independently as a given name since the 19th century. It's considered a literary name for Theodore Dreiser's novel Sister Carrie published in 1900 and Stephen King's 1974 novel Carrie that was adapted into a film in 1976. It became widely known for fictional character Carrie Bradshaw on the cable television series Sex and the City, which was shown from 1998 to 2004 and is currently aired in syndication. The name is also associated with singer Carrie Underwood, the fourth-season winner of American Idol.

Casey — Rank: 411

Origin: Celtic/Gaelic
Meaning: Brave or watchful
Alternate Spellings: Caisee, Caisey, Casee, Caisie, Casie, Kaci, Kacey, Kasey, Kaycee, KC
Gender Variations: Casey, Cassian
Similar Names: Cassie, Cassandra, Cassarah, Cassia, Cassidy
⇨ Derived from the Irish surname Cathasaigh and a form of Cassie. The name peaked for both boys and girls during the mid-1980s but is currently more common as a boy's name. Known for fictional Senior Assistant District Attorney Casey Novak from the top-rated television show Law & Order: Special Victims Unit. Some parents prefer an "ee" ending for a fashionable twist.

Cassandra Rank: 219

Origin: Greek
Meaning: Shining upon man
Alternate Spellings: Casandra, Casaundra, Cassaundra, Cassondra, Kasandra, Kasaundra, Kasondra, Kassandra, Kassondra
Gender Variations: Casdin, Cassandra, Cassell, Cassius
Nicknames: Casi, Cass, Cassy
Similar Names: Cassia, Cassidi, Casslyn, Cason, Kasander, Kasani, Kassey, Sandee, Saundra, Zandra
Namesake: Cassandra Wilson (jazz singer/ songwriter)
➡ A form of the name Kassandra, which is derived from *kekasmai*. In Greek mythology, Cassandra was a Trojan princess, also known as Alexandra, who was given the gift of prophecy. She was cursed by Apollo so no one would believe she didn't return his love. The name peaked in 1990, following the the rise in fame of actress and horror host Cassandra Peterson, who first became known in 1981 as Elvira, Mistress of the Dark. Singer, model, and actress Casandra Ventura, professionally known as Cassie, also comes to mind. The name was occasionally used between the Middle Ages and the 18th century but is still fashionable today.

Cassidy Rank: 198

Origin: Irish Gaelic
Meaning: Clever, curly haired
Alternate Spellings: Casadee, Casidy, Cassadie, Cassiddy, Cassidee, Cassidey, Cassidi, Kassidy, Kassidie
Gender Variations: Casdin, Cassell, Cassuis
Nicknames: Cass, Cassie
Similar Names: Casie, Cassidena, Castle, Cazlin, Cazi, Kasmira, Kastin
Namesakes: Joanna Cassidy (actress)
➡ From an Irish surname that was taken from Ó Caiside and ultimately from the Gaelic word *cas*. Debuted on the chart in 1981, possibly inspired by Shaun Cassidy, musician, actor, and television producer. who became a major teen idol with his late 1970s successful singles and role on the television series *The Hardy Boys*. Used for boys but more common for girls, which follows a trend to use surnames as given names.

Cassie Rank: 732

Origin: Greek
Meaning: Shining upon man
Alternate Spellings: Cassi, Cassy, Kassi, Kassie
Gender Variations: Caspar, Cassian, Cassius
Nickname: Cass
Similar Names: Casey, Cassandra, Cassia, Cassidy
➡ The pet form of Cassandra that's been used as an independent name since the 19th century. Namesake Cassandra Ventura, professionally known as Cassie, is a popular R&B singer, model, and actress.

Catalina Rank: 696

Origin: Greek
Meaning: Pure
Alternate Spelling: Katalina
Gender Variations: Carmelo, Catalin
Nicknames: Cat, Cate, Catie
Similar Names: Caitlin, Catarina, Catherine, Cathleen, Cathy, Catia, Catrina
Namesake: Catalina Castano (Colombian tennis player)
➡ The Spanish form of Catherine or Katherine that's also associated with an island off the shores of Los Angeles. Used sporadically as a given name starting in 1917. Associated with a fictional Hispanic maid on the television sitcom *My Name Is Earl.*

Catherine Rank: 122

Origin: Greek
Meaning: Pure
Alternate Spellings: Catharin, Catharine, Catharyne, Catheryn, Cathrine, Cathryn, Cathrynn, Katharine, Katharyne, Katherine
Gender Variations: Carl
Nicknames: Cath, Cathy, Caty
Similar Names: Camryn, Camilla, Carissa, Caroline, Catalina, Cathleen, Cathleena
➡ The French form of Katherine that's derived from the Greek Aikaterine. A royal name for the three wives of King Henry VIII of England including his first wife, Catherine of Aragon, and two empresses of Russia but best-known for Catherine II, also called Catherine the Great, who ruled during the 18th century. Actress Catherine Zeta-Jones has recently had an impact on the name. Katherine is currently the most popular form.

Cecilia   Rank: 265

Origin: Latin
Meaning: Blind
Alternate Spellings:
Cecelia, Cecilija, Cecillia,
Cecylia, Cycilia, Sacilia, Sesilia, Sesseelya,
Siselya, Sisiliya
Gender Variations: Cecil, Cecilio, Celica
Nicknames: Cecil, Ceil, Celia, Celie, Sissy
Similar Names: Cecelyn, Cecilee, Ceciliane,
Cecilio, Cecilyann, Celina, Cesya, Cicily,
Sheila, Zelia
Namesake: Cecilia Bartoli (opera singer)
⇒ Latin and feminine form of the Roman
family name Caecilius. A notable bearer of
the name is legendary Saint Cecilia, a 3rd-
century martyr who became the patron saint
of music and musicians. Recognized as the
feminine form of Cecil.

Celeste   Rank: 327

Origin: Latin
Meaning: Heavenly
Alternate Spellings:
Celleste, Saleste, Seleste
Gender Variations: Esteven, Lestel, Selley
Nickname: Cela
Similar Names: Celebrity, Celesse Celesta,
Celestena, Celestia, Celestiel, Celestin,
Celia, Celize, Silestyne
⇒ Associated with French name Caelestis
that was popular among early Christians.
The name may be associated with Queen
Celeste, the fictional wife in Jean and
Laurent de Brunhoff's 1930s children's book,
Babar, the Elephant. A notable bearer of the
name is actress Celeste Holm, famous for her
Academy Award-winning role in the 1947 film,
Gentleman's Agreement.

Celia   Rank: 707

Origin: Latin
Meaning: Heaven
Alternate Spelling: Cellia
Gender Variations: Cecil,
Cecilio
Nicknames: Cele, Celie
Similar Names: Cecile, Cecilia, Cecily,
Celeste, Celina, Celine, Cerise, Cerys
Namesake: Celia Cruz (Cuban-American
singer)
⇒ The feminine variation of the Roman
family name Caelius and the short form of
Cecilia derived from Caelia. Shakespeare

used the name for a character in his play
As You Like It. It peaked prior to the
beginning of the 20th century.

Chana   Rank: 990

Origin: Hebrew
Meaning: Grace of God
Alternate Spellings:
Chanah, Channa, Channah
Gender Variation: Chayim
Similar Names: Anna, Charna, Chava, Chaya,
Chloe, Hanela, Hannah, Hannalee
⇒ A variation of Channah that is the
Hebrew form of Hannah favored among
Jewish families.

Chanel   Rank: 917

Origin: French
Meaning: Pipe, channel
Alternate Spellings:
Chanelle, Channel,
Channelle, Shanel, Shanell, Shanelle,
Shannel, Shannelle
Gender Variation: Charles
Similar Names: Chanah, Chandi, Chantal,
Charlena, Charlene
⇒ Derived from a surname influenced by
20th-century French fashion designer
Gabrielle Bonheur "Coco" Chanel whose
most successful product, Chanel No. 5
perfume, was introduced in 1922. The name
became popular for girls in 1973 and peaked
in 1991 at No. 383. The "sh" spelling is a
reflection of the French pronunciation.

Charity   Rank: 673

Origin: Late Latin
Meaning: Christian love
Alternate Spellings:
Charitee, Chariti
Gender Variation: Charles
Similar Names: Charisma, Charissa, Charita,
Chasity, Chastity, Cherish, Cherry, Karita
⇒ Picked up directly from the vocabulary
word derived from the Late Latin *Caritas*
from *Carus* that referred to a Christian's love
for his fellow man. Mentioned by Paul in the
New Testament when he encouraged the
followers of Jesus to live in "faith, hope, and
charity" and emphasized "charity" as the
"greatest." Considered a virtue name by the
Puritans during the 17th century. It is often
Associated with the 1967 Broadway musical
Sweet Charity which was adapted into a

1969 film and helped lead to the name's comeback in the late 1960s. It peak during the mid-1970s.

Charlie
Rank: 761

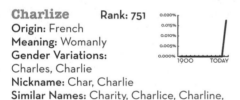

Origin: Old German
Meaning: Free man
Alternate Spellings: Char, Charlee, Charley, Charly
Gender Variations: Charles, Charlie
Similar Names: Carley, Charline, Charlize, Charlotte, Sherill
➡ The feminine form of Charles that made a comeback in 2005 as a girl's given name. Associated with Revlon's Charlie perfume introduced in 1973. Listed among the top 400 for boys.

Charlize
Rank: 751

Origin: French
Meaning: Womanly
Gender Variations: Charles, Charlie
Nickname: Char, Charlie
Similar Names: Charity, Charlice, Charline, Charlinna, Charlisa, Charlita, Charlotte
➡ A twist on the name Charlie that became fashionable when South African actress and former fashion model Charlize Theron won an Academy Award for Best Actress for her role in the 2003 film *Monster*.

Charlotte
Rank: 123

Origin: Old German
Meaning: Free man
Alternate Spellings: Charlet, Charlette, Charlot, Sharlet, Sharlette, Sharlot
Gender Variations: Carl, Charles, Charleson
Nicknames: Char, Charlie, Lotti
Similar Names: Carla, Carly, Chara, Charlesetta, Charlesina, Charlotta, Charlyne, Charmaine, Cheryl, Sharla
➡ French feminine form of Charles that listed among the top 100 in the 1880s until 1890. Used in England since the 17th century, and popularized by Queen Charlotte, George III's wife, in the 19th century. This top 200 name was also inspired by classic English novelist Charlotte Bronte, the eldest of the three literary Bronte sisters who was famous for *Jane Eyre* in 1847. E. B. White's 1952 book, *Charlotte's Web*, has continued to influence this classic name throughout the years.

Chasity
Rank: 744

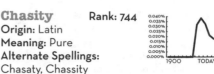

Origin: Latin
Meaning: Pure
Alternate Spellings: Chasaty, Chassity
Gender Variation: Chase
Nickname: Chas
Similar Names: Charity, Chasida, Chasta, Chastina, Chastine, Chastity
➡ The simplified form of the vocabulary word "chastity." Considered to be one of the virtue names derived from *castus*. Both Chasity and Chastity made their debut on the popularity chart in 1972 when Chastity Bono started appearing on *The Sonny & Cher Comedy Hour* with her famed parents.

Chaya
Rank: 785

Origin: Hebrew
Meaning: Life
Gender Variations: Chaim, Chayim, Hymie
Similar Names: Charity, Charo, Chava, Chavi, Chelsea, Cher, Chloe
➡ The feminine form of Chayim derived from the Hebrew word *chai* that carries a prophetic meaning for a newborn child.

Chelsea
Rank: 192

Origin: Old English
Meaning: Landing place for chalk or limestone
Alternate Spellings: Chelcea, Chelcee, Chelcie, Chelcy, Chellsie, Chelse, Chelsee, Chelsei, Chelsey, Chelsi
Gender Variations: Cheney, Chesley, Chesney, Chevi
Nicknames: Chel, Chels
Similar Names: Chelbi, Chelese, Chellie, Chenelle, Cheralee, Cherese, Cherylee, Cheslee, Shelsea
Namesake: Chelsea Clinton (former first daughter)
➡ A place name for a district in London and several locations in the U.S that debuted on the chart in 1969, possibly influenced by the song "Chelsea Morning," released by famed songwriter and folk singer Joni Mitchell that same year. Chelsea Noble, notable actress and wife of actor Kirk Cameron, is best known for her role on the television series *Growing Pains*.

Cheyenne   Rank: 171

Origin: Native American
Meaning: Native American plains tribe
Alternate Spellings: Cheyan, Cheyanne, Cheyene, Chian, Chianne, Chyann, Chyanne, Sheyanne, Shian, Shyan
Gender Variations: Cheyenne, Cheyney, Chez
Nickname: Chi
Similar Names: Chaya, Chelan, Cheyenna, Cheyla, Cheylynne, Cheyna
⇨ A name for both boys and girls that derived from the Dakota word *shahiyena* meaning "unintelligible speakers." A place name for the capital of Wyoming and also the name of a 2006 MTV television show, starring singer-songwriter Cheyenne Kimball. Favored by parents because of its unique spelling and pronunciation and the popular "y" in the middle.

Chloe   Rank: 18

Origin: Greek
Meaning: Young green shoot
Alternate Spellings: Chloee, Cloe, Cloey, Khloe, Khloey, Kloe
Gender Variations: Chris, Christian
Nickname: Chlo
Similar Names: Chloris, Christa, Cleo, Clorinda, Crystal
Namesakes: Chloe (*The Big Chill* character), Chloe Sevigny (actress), Chloe (*Smallville* character)
⇨ Mentioned in the New Testament by Paul and used as an alternate name for the goddess Demeter in Greek mythology. Fashion designer Karl Lagerfeld received international fame during the early 1970s for his creative involvement with fashion labels including the *Chloe* brand of clothing and perfume. Derived from *chloos*, the name has been in use since prior to the turn of the 20th century and is currently at its peak.

Christiana   Rank: 984

Origin: Greek
Meaning: Follower of Christ
Alternate Spellings: Christianna, Cristiana, Cristianna, Kristiana
Gender Variation: Christian
Nicknames: Chris, Christi
Similar Names: Christa, Christabel, Christel, Christiania, Christiann, Christin, Christina,
Christine, Christobel
⇨ The feminine form of Christian with the "a" ending that's in vogue for girls today.

Christina   Rank: 158

Origin: Latin
Meaning: Christian
Alternate Spellings: Christeena, Christyna, Chrystina, Cristina, Crystena, Khristena, Khristina, Khristyna, Khrystina, Kristina
Gender Variations: Christan, Christian, Christiano, Christo
Nicknames: Chris, Chrissy, Christie, Tina
Similar Names: Christa, Christabel, Christana, Christen, Christian, Christine, Christini, Chrystal, Kirsten, Kirstie
Namesake: Christina Ricci (actress)
⇨ Feminine form of Christian and a name of a 17th-century Swedish queen, who was interested in the arts and philosophy and gave up her crown to become a Roman Catholic. It peaked in the 1970s and 1980s in the top 20 also because of supermodel Christie Brinkley and tennis star Chris Evert, who both bear a variation of the name. It has become a more recent trend with its "y" spelling and the influence of pop singer Christina Aguilera when she first captured audiences in 1998.

Christine   Rank: 437

Origin: Latin
Meaning: Annointed Christian
Alternate Spellings: Christeen, Christene, Cristine, Crystine, Khristine, Kristine
Gender Variations: Christian, Christianus
Nicknames: Chris, Chrissie, Christy, Kirstie
Similar Names: Christa, Christelle, Christen, Christianne, Christiana, Christina
Namesakes: *Christine* (horror novel by Stephen King), Christine Ebersole (actress), Christine Lakin (actress), Christine McVie (singer/songwriter)
⇨ The French form of Christina that was a favorite during the Middle Ages and used interchangeably with Christian. The name grew in popularity during the 19th century in England and started the 20th century off in the U.S. among the top 200. The name peaked at No. 14 during the 1960s and has faded to its current position.

Ciara
Rank: 213

Origin: Gaelic
Meaning: Small and dark skinned
Alternate Spellings: Ceara, Ciaara, Ciaera, Ciaira, Ciarah, Ciarrah, Cyara, Cyarah, Cyarra, Kiara
Gender Variations: Ciaran, Kian, Kiernan
Nicknames: Ci, Ciar
Similar Names: Chara, Chiara, Ciaran, Ciaria, Cilena, Ciora, Claire, Syarra, Tiara
➡ Feminine form of Ciaran and the name of Saint Ciara, an Irish nun who established a monastery at Kilkeary in the 7th century. Name can also be traced back to Chiara that shares its "k" pronunciation or Sierra pronounced with the "s" sound. This popular choice for girls debuted on the chart in 1982 and took a drastic jump between 2004 and 2005 because of Ciara, the Grammy Award-winning singer-songwriter, record producer, and performer, who released her first album in 2004, making her name a trendy choice for girls today.

Cindy
Rank: 365

Origin: Greek
Meaning: From Mount Kynthos
Alternate Spellings: Cindee, Cindi, Cindie, Cyndee, Cyndi, Cyndie, Cyndy, Sindee, Sindi, Sindy
Gender Variations: Cindeo, Simeon, Sydney
Nickname: Cyn
Similar Names: Cinda, Cindel, Cinderella, Cindia, Cinnamon, Cintia, Sidonia, Sidra, Sydney
➡ Originally a pet form of Cynthia now commonly used as an independent name. It's best-known for supermodel Cindy Crawford and 1980s New Wave singer Cyndi Lauper. Cindy Brady, the youngest of the fictional *The Brady Bunch* kids, and Cindy Vortex from the 2002 first computer-animated Nicktoon *The Adventures of Jimmy Neutron: Boy Genius* also come to mind.

Citlali
Rank: 948

Origin: Nahuatl
Meaning: Star
Alternate Spellings: Citlalli, Citalaly
Gender Variation: Cillian
Nickname: Lali
Similar Names: Cicely, Cilla, Citrone
➡ Used occasionally as a name since 2001.

Claire
Rank: 86

Origin: Latin/French
Meaning: Famous
Alternate Spellings: Clair, Clare, Klare
Gender Variation: Sinclair
Similar Names: Clara, Claretta, Clarette, Claribel, Clarinda, Clarissa
Namesakes: Claire Danes (actress), Claire Forlani (English actress), Clare Boothe Luce (playwright/author)
➡ The French form of Clare that's derived from the Latin *clarus*. Associated with Saint Clare of Assisi who founded the "Poor Clares," an order of nuns descending from the Franciscan order founded in Assisi, Italy, during the 13th century. The piano composition "Claire de Lune" by 20th-century French composer Claude Debussy also comes to mind. The name became popular among television characters and has been used in the shows *The Cosby Show*, *Lost*, and *Six Feet Under*.

Clara
Rank: 233

Origin: Latin
Meaning: Clear, bright, famous
Alternate Spellings: Claara, Claarah, Claira, Clairah, Clarah, Klaara, Klaarah, Klara, Klarah, Klarra
Gender Variations: Klay, Klayton
Nickname: Clar
Similar Names: Clarabelle, Claran, Claresta, Claretha, Clarice, Clarie, Clarinda, Clarine, Clarita, Claritza
➡ Derived from Clare, a medieval name taken from the Latin word *clarus*. Peaked among the top 10 in the 1800s and top 20 at the turn of the 20th century, possibly influenced by Clara Schumann, composer and one of the leading pianists of the Romantic era as well as the wife of composer Robert Schumann. Also noted for the fictional character from *The Nutcracker* ballet. Most productions of the ballet center their plots on a German girl named Clara. The name was popularized in the 1920s because of Clara Bow, often referred to as the greatest silent film actress in history. It declined in popularity during the 1970s and 1980s but began climbing again in 1990, taking the name to its current position among the top 300.

Clarissa Rank: 468

Origin: Latin
Meaning: Clear, bright
Alternate Spellings:
Clairissa, Clarisa, Clayrissa,
Clerissa, Klarissa
Gender Variation: Clarence
Nicknames: Clari, Rissa
Similar Names: Chryssa, Crystal, Claire,
Clara, Clarette, Clarinda, Clarisse, Clarity
⇒ A form of the Latin Clarice that was
popularized during the 18th century by
Samuel Richardson's novel *Clarissa*. More
recently associated with the 1990s television
series *Clarissa Explains It All* with actress
Melissa Joan Hart in the title role. The name
has been moderately popular, especially with
its feminine "issa" ending.

Claudia Rank: 339

Origin: Latin
Meaning: Lame
Alternate Spellings:
Claudea, Claudiah, Clawdia,
Clawdiah, Clodia, Klaudia, Klodia
Gender Variations: Claude, Claudino,
Claudio, Claudius
Nicknames: Claude, Claudee
Similar Names: Clauda, Claudella, Claudelle,
Claudette, Claudex, Claudianne, Claudine,
Claudio, Claudyna, Claunese
Namesakes: Claudia Cardinale (Italian
actress), Claudia Muzio (Italian opera singer)
⇒ The feminine form of Claudius, derived
from the Latin word *claudus*. A biblical
name for a Christian woman of Rome who
was greeted by Paul in his second letter to
Timothy. Notable for Broadway and film
actress Claudette Colbert, who uses a
form of the name. Recently known for
German supermodel and actress Claudia
Schiffer, who reached her height of
popularity during the 1990s.

Colleen Rank: 902

Origin: Irish Gaelic
Meaning: Girl
Alternate Spellings:
Coleen, Colene, Coline,
Colline, Koleen, Kolleen, Kolline
Gender Variations: Cole, Colin
Nickname: Colly
Similar Names: Coletta, Colette, Colina, Corinne
Namesake: Colleen Dewhurst (actress)

⇒ Derived from *cailin* and sometimes
considered the feminine form of Colin or a
variation of Colette. Popular use of the name
started in the early 1900s and peaked at
No. 92 in 1966. Australian author Colleen
McCullough, best known for the 1977 novel
The Thorn Birds, is a famous bearer.

Cora Rank: 384

Origin: Greek
Meaning: Maiden
Alternate Spelling: Kora
Gender Variation: Corey
Similar Names: Corabel, Corabell, Coralee,
Coralynn, Coretta, Corie, Corina, Corinne,
Corissa
⇒ Possibly invented by writer James
Fenimore Cooper for a character in his 1826
historical novel *The Last of the Mohicans*,
adapted into a film in 1992. Could also be the
feminine form of Corey or the short form of
Corinna. A classic name that hit its peak prior
to the turn of the 20th century. Coretta Scott
King, civil rights activist and wife of Martin
Luther King Jr., used a form of the name.

Corinne Rank: 826

Origin: Greek
Meaning: Maiden
Alternate Spellings: Coreen,
Corin, Corine, Corinn,
Corrin, Corrine, Koreen, Korinne, Korrine
Gender Variations: Cornelius, Cornell
Nicknames: Cor, Cori
Similar Names: Cora, Corianne, Corinna,
Corinthia, Cornelia, Corona, Courtney
⇒ The French form of Cora that peaked
prior to the turn of the 20th century. The
name is known today for British singer-
songwriter Corinne Bailey Rae, whose first
album debuted at No. 1 in 2006.

Courtney Rank: 190

Origin: Old French
Meaning: Courteous
Alternate Spellings:
Corteney, Cortnee,
Cortneigh, Cortney, Cortnie, Cortny,
Courteney, Courtnee, Courtnie, Kourtney
Gender Variations: Cort, Cory
Nickname: Court
Similar Names: Coralee, Cordney, Cortenay,
Corynn, Courtland, Courtlyn
Namesake: Courtney Love (singer/entertainer)

➡ Taken from a French surname derived from either a place name meaning "domain of Curtis" or nickname meaning "short nose." Faded from the popularity chart in 1886 and returned in 1962 to quickly reach its peak in 1990 and again in 1995. It was greatly influenced by actress Courtney Thorne-Smith, who appeared on *Melrose Place* from 1992 to 1997. Also inspired by actress Courteney Cox Arquette, who found fame on the hit television series *Friends*.

Crystal   Rank: 201
Origin: Greek
Meaning: Crystal
Alternate Spellings: Cristal, Cristel, Cristelle, Crystall, Crystel, Crystyl, Kristall, Kristell, Krystal, Krystle
Gender Variations: Cris, Crispin, Cristo, Cristopher
Nickname: Cris
Similar Names: Crysta, Crystalyn, Crystelia, Crystina, Kristee, Krystalina, Krystene, Krystlea
➡ The vocabulary word derived from *krystallos* for colorless glass that is sometimes cut into the shape of a gemstone. Krystle Carrington, played by actress Linda Evans on the prime-time soap opera *Dynasty*, led the name to its peak at No. 9 in 1982. Linda Evans, with her tie to "Krystle," was also selected as the spokesperson for Crystal Light, the name of a powdered sugar-free drink introduced by Kraft Foods in 1984. Considered a trendy choice by itself with its "y" in the middle spelling or when it's combined and hyphenated with another name, such as Crystal-Ann and Crystal-Marie.

Cynthia   Rank: 240
Origin: Greek
Meaning: From Mount Kynthos
Alternate Spellings: Cinthia, Cinthiah, Cinthiya, Cinthiyah, Cynthea, Cynthya, Synthee, Synthia, Synthya
Gender Variations: Cian, Sina, Sindley
Nicknames: Cindy, Cinnie, Cyn
Similar Names: Cinnia, Cintia, Cinzia, Cynda, Cyndia, Cyndra, Cytia, Kynthia, Xanthia
Namesake: Cynthia Gregory (prima ballerina)
➡ In mythology Kynthia was one of the names of Artemis, the goddess of the moon, that referred to her birthplace on Mount Kynthos. The name peaked in the late 1950s and early 1960s and held a strong position among the top 50 because of the fictional character Cynthia "Cindy" Brady from *The Brady Bunch* fame. Another notable bearer of the name is actress Cynthia Nixon, known for her award-winning role as lawyer Miranda Hobbes in the popular series *Sex and the City*. Preferred by parents for its "ia" ending and variations spelled with a "y."

Daisy   Rank: 149
Origin: Old English
Meaning: Day's eye
Alternate Spellings: Daisee, Daisey, Daisi, Daisie, Dasie, Daysi
Gender Variations: Davis, Dayton
Nicknames: Dai, Dais
Similar Names: Dacey, Daizy, Dasya, Daya, Daysha, Dayva, Desiree, Deysi, Taisa
➡ Name derived from daegeseage, but simply means "daisy," a white flower. Has been used as a nickname for Margaret in France, where the flower is a marguerite. Existed as a popular name on the chart in the top 100 in the 1880s. This nature name later reentered the top 200 in 1990 for a long stay influenced by television show host and actress Daisy Fuentes. A place name in at least four states that also climbed the charts because of Daisy Duke, a character from *The Dukes of Hazzard*.

Dakota   Rank: 191
Origin: Native American
Meaning: Friend, ally
Alternate Spellings: Dackota, Dacoda, Dacodah, Dacota, Dacotah, Dakoda, Dakodah, Dakotah, Dekoda, Dekota
Gender Variations: Dackota, Dacota, Dakaota
Nicknames: Coda, Codi, Dak
Similar Names: Dakima, Dakisha, Dekedra, Dekendra, Dekenya
Namesake: Dakota Staton (jazz vocalist)
➡ The tribal name of a Native American people of the northern Mississippi valley. It debuted on the chart in 1990 as a popular name for girls and is currently at its peak in 2006 because of award-winning performances by young actress Dakota Fanning. Also a place name for North and South Dakota. The name is slightly more popular for boys.

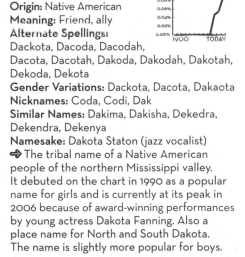

Dalia   Rank: 849

Origin: New Latin
Meaning: Flower name
Alternate Spellings: Dahlia, Daliah, Daliya, Daliyah, Dallia, Dalya, Dalyah
Gender Variations: Dale, Dallas
Similar Names: Daisy, Dale, Dalila, Delia, Delilah, Della
⇨ A form of Dahlia taken from the flower that was named after 18th-century Swedish botanist Anders Dahl. It's been used as a girl's given name since the mid-1990s.

Damaris   Rank: 609

Origin: Greek
Meaning: Calf
Alternate Spellings: Damaress, Damariss, Damariz, Dameris, Damerys, Dameryss, Demaras, Demaris, Demarys
Gender Variation: Damen
Nicknames: Mari, Maris
Similar Names: Damara, Damia, Damris, Tamaris
⇨ A biblical name for a woman converted to Christianity by Saint Paul after hearing him preach in Athens. It's part of a resurgence in biblical names and is currently at its peak.

Dana   Rank: 395

Origin: Old English
Meaning: From Denmark
Alternate Spellings: Daena, Daina, Danah, Dayna
Gender Variations: Dan, Dana, Dane, Daniel
Similar Names: Dani, Danica, Daniella, Danielle, Danita, Deana, Diana
Namesake: Dana Delany (actress)
⇨ Originated as a surname for a person who was Danish and considered a variation of the boy's name Daniel. Listed among the top 100 from 1963 to 1988, peaked in 1971 at No. 44. The name is currently in vogue with its "a" ending.

Dania   Rank: 985

Origin: Hebrew
Meaning: God is my judge
Alternate Spellings: Danea, Dannia, Danya
Gender Variations: Dan, Daniel
Nickname: Dani
Similar Names: Dalia, Dana, Danelle, Danica, Danice, Daniella, Danielle, Danna, Daria
⇨ The Spanish pet form of Daniela used occasionally as a girl's given name since 1996. Also the name of a beach community in Florida.

Danica   Rank: 352

Origin: Slavic
Meaning: Morning star
Alternate Spellings: Danika, Dannica, Dannika
Nickname: Dani
Similar Names: Dana, Danae, Dania, Daniela, Danielle, Danna
Namesake: Danica Patrick (race car driver)
⇨ A contemporary name that's rise in popularity began with actress Danica McKellar, who's best known for her role as Winnie Cooper on the television show *The Wonder Years* that aired from 1988 to 1993.

Daniela   Rank: 132

Origin: Hebrew
Meaning: Judged by God
Alternate Spellings: Daniella, Daniellah, Danniella, Danyela, Danyella
Gender Variations: Dane, Daniel, Danny
Nicknames: Dani, Nelly, Ella
Similar Names: Daniala, Danielan, Danielle, Danille, Danneley, Dannibella
⇨ Feminine form of Daniel that has escalated into the top 200 since it first appeared on the chart in 1973. Similar to Danielle but coincides with the popular trend of ending with an "a." Well-known Daniela Pestova, a three-time *Sports Illustrated* cover model from Czechoslovakia, also had baby in 2002 named Ella, which is a shortened form of the name.

Danielle   Rank: 116

Origin: Hebrew
Meaning: Judged by God
Alternate Spellings: Dannielle, Danyell, Danyelle, Dhanielle
Gender Variations: Daniel, Danilo, Danny, Dantrell
Nicknames: Danna, Danee, Dani, Elle
Similar Names: Danelle, Danelley, Danette, Dania, Danica, Daniella, Danita, Dannyce, Danya
Namesakes: Dani Evans (*America's Next Top Model* winner), Danielle Panabaker (actress)

➡ Feminine form of biblical name Daniel with a 27-year stay in the top 50. Initially influenced by Danielle Steel's first novel, *Going Home,* published in 1973 and the first of 69 best sellers. Most trendy form currently includes spellings with a "y."

Danna   Rank: 518

Origin: Hebrew
Meaning: God is my judge
Alternate Spellings: Dannah, Dhanna
Gender Variations: Dane, Daniel, Danny
Nicknames: Dan, Dani
Similar Names: Dana, Danelle, Danette, Dania, Danice, Danielle, Danita, Dannalee, Dannelle, Danya
➡ The feminine variation of the Hebrew name Daniel. Dannah is also a place name in the Bible for a city in Judea. It made a comeback in 2002 and has since climbed to its highest ranking as part of a biblical naming trend. Also known as the Japanese word for "master."

Daphne   Rank: 606

Origin: Greek
Meaning: Laurel tree
Alternate Spellings: Dafne, Dafnee, Dafni, Dafnie, Daphney, Daphnie, Daphny
Gender Variations: Danny
Similar Names: Daffodil, Dahlia, Daisy, Daphna
Namesake: Daphne du Maurier (British novelist)
➡ Originated in Greek mythology for a nymph who was changed into a laurel tree by the river god to escape the affections of Apollo. Also the name of a shrub that is recognized by its handsome foliage and fragrant flowers in use during the 19th century when plant names came into fashion. More recently known for cartoon character Daphne Blake from *Scooby-Doo* and fictional character Daphne Moon from the television show *Frasier.*

Dayanara   Rank: 435

Origin: Latin
Meaning: Heavenly, divine
Alternate Spellings: Dayanarah, Dayanaira, Dayanairah, Deyanaira, Deyanairah

Gender Variations: Daylan, Daymon, Dayyon
Nicknames: Day, Nara
Similar Names: Dayana, Dayani, Dayanne, Daylan, Dyandra, Dyia
➡ A variation of Dayana and form of Diana. Debuted on the chart in 2003, peaking in 2005 as a top 400 name. Dayanara Torres Delgado is a Puerto Rican actress, singer, model, and former 1993 Miss Universe.

Deanna   Rank: 532

Origin: Old English
Meaning: From the valley
Alternate Spelling: Deana
Gender Variation: Dean
Nicknames: Anna, Dee
Similar Names: Danna, Deanne, Deena, Deondra, Diana, Diane, Diantha
Namesake: Deanna Troi (*Star Trek: The Next Generation* character)
➡ Variation of Diana or the feminine form of Dean. Influenced by Deanna Durbin, born Edna Mae Durbin, who gained fame during the 1930s and 1940s as a singer and actress. The name landed on the popularity chart in 1936 and peaked in 1969 at No. 88.

Deborah   Rank: 676

Origin: Hebrew
Meaning: Bee
Alternate Spellings: Debora, Debra, Debrah
Gender Variation: Dean
Nicknames: Deb, Debbie
Similar Names: Debralee, Debriana, Devora, Devorit
Namesakes: Debbie Armstrong (Olympic alpine skier), Debbie Reynolds (actress), Deborah Gibson (singer/songwriter), Deborah Harry (musician), Deborah Norville (TV host), Debra Winger (actress)
➡ The name of a biblical prophetess and judge of the Israelites who wrote the Song of Deborah in celebration of the Israelites' victory over the Canaanites. It became popular with 17th-century Puritans because the bee was a symbol of industriousness. It was influenced by British film actress Deborah Kerr during the late 1940s, 1950s, and 1960s, which led to the name's top 25 ranking during that time. It's frequently used by Jewish families. The alternate spelling Debra came along during the 1930s.

Deja
Rank: 753

Origin: French
Meaning: Already
Alternate Spellings: Deija, Deijah, Dejah
Gender Variation: Deion
Similar Names: Deandra, Deanne, Deirdre, Deka, Delia, Delice, Delicia
Namesakes: *Deja Vu* (2006 film)
⇨ Taken from the French phrase *deja vu* meaning "already seen" that debuted as a girl's given name in 1988 and climbed among the top 200 in 1996, then faded to its current position.

Delaney
Rank: 193

Origin: French
Meaning: From the elder-tree grove
Alternate Spellings: Dalanee, Dalaney, Delainey, Delainie, Delanee, Delani, Delayne, Delaynie, Dellanee, Dellani
Gender Variations: Delan, Delandon, Delaney, Delawrence
Nicknames: Del, Della
Similar Names: Delacey, Delaina, Deleena, Delia, Delilah, Delonda, Delonna, Delsey
Namesake: Shelagh Delaney (British playwright)
⇨ From the Norman surname "De l'aunaie" that also holds the Irish meaning "descendant of the challenger." This boy's and girl's name first appeared on the chart in 1991 and moved into the top 200 by 2002. Possibly inspired by actress Kim Delaney and her career from the 1980s to the 2000s with her most notable roles in *NYPD Blue* and *Tour of Duty*. A fashionable name that follows a trend to use surnames as given names.

Delilah
Rank: 548

Origin: Hebrew
Meaning: Delicate
Alternate Spellings: Dalila, Delila
Gender Variation: Lyle
Nicknames: Dee, Lilah
Similar Names: Delia, Delice, Delicia, Della, Tallulah
Namesake: Delilah Rene (national radio personality)
⇨ A biblical name for the famed seductress who enticed Samson into revealing the source of his great strength only to betray him with the knowledge. Their story has been the subject of several films and a painting by Flemish master Peter Paul Rubens. It's been used sporadically since the 19th century and is slowly climbing the chart as part of a biblical name revival.

Denise
Rank: 379

Origin: Greek/English
Meaning: Follower of Dionysius
Alternate Spellings: Denese, Denice, Deniece, Denis, Denisse, Dennise, Denyce, Denys, Denyse, Denize
Gender Variations: Deniz, Dennis, Denzil
Similar Names: Danise, Deneigh, Deni, Denisa, Dennette
Namesakes: Denise Austin (fitness/exercise expert), Denise Crosby (actress/entertainer), Denise Huxtable (*Cosby Show* character)
⇨ The feminine form of Dennis. Singer Deniece Williams inspired a variation of the name in the 1970s and 1980s with popular songs such as "Let's Hear It for The Boy" and "Silly." Actress and former wife of actor Charlie Sheen, Denise Richards brought attention to the name in the late 1990s, especially for her role as Dr. Christmas Jones in the 19th film in the James Bond series.

Desiree
Rank: 300

Origin: French
Meaning: Desired, wished
Alternate Spellings: Desairee, Desaree, Desaraye, Deseree, Deserie, Desirae, Desirea, Desirey, Dezaray, Deziree
Gender Variations: Desi, Desiderio, Destin, Destrey
Nicknames: Desi, Dez
Similar Names: Desara, Desedria, Desendra, Desert, Desiah, Desiana, Desirah, Desire, Destiny
⇨ Traced back to the Puritans who used Desire as a given name. It debuted on the popularity chart in 1954 influenced by the release of the film *Desiree*, starring Jean Simmons and Marlon Brando and based on the best-selling novel by Annemarie Selinko. Also associated with the 1977 song by Neil Diamond. More recently used as the name of a fictional villain from Nickelodeon's animated television series *Danny Phantom*

that first aired in 2004. The most famous bearer of the name was Lucille Desiree Ball, a four-time Emmy Award-winning actress and charter member of the Television Hall of Fame.

Destiny   Rank: 37
Origin: Old French/ Late Latin
Meaning: One's certain fortune, fate
Alternate Spellings: Destanee, Destine, Destinee, Destiney, Destini, Destinie, Destyni
Gender Variations: Derrick, Devin
Similar Names: Deirdre, Desiree, Dominique
Namesake: Destiny Davis (reality TV star)
➡ Derived from the Old French *destinee* and the Late Latin *destinata*. A vocabulary word that has gained popularity as a given name since 1975. Actress and musician Destiny Hope "Miley" Cyrus, who plays the title character on the Disney television series *Hannah Montana*, is a namesake.

Diamond   Rank: 316
Origin: Latin
Meaning: Diamond
Alternate Spellings: Diamonde, Dimond, Dimonde
Gender Variations: Diamante, Diamond, Diamonte
Nicknames: Di, Dia, Diamon
Similar Names: Demanda, Diamanda, Diamanta, Diamante, Diamantra, Diamonda, Diamonia, Diamonique, Diamontina
Namesake: *Diamonds* (1999 film)
➡ The brilliant birthstone of April that was first used as a girl's given name in the 1890s during the popular gemstone trend. It debuted on the chart in 1986, one year before famed brass musician Herb Alpert released his second single, "Diamonds," to mark his musical comeback. Also associated with one of four suits used in playing cards, the name of a baseball field, and a type of highway interchange.

Diana   Rank: 120
Origin: Roman
Meaning: Heavenly, divine
Alternate Spellings: Dayana, Dianha, Dianna, Dijana, Dyana

Nicknames: Di, Anna
Similar Names: Deana, Deanne, Deena, Diane, Diantha, Kiana
Namesakes: Diana DeGarmo (American Idol finalist), Diana Krall (jazz singer/pianist), Diana Nyad (swimmer), Diana Ross (singer), Diana Taurasi (WNBA basketball player)
➡ The name was picked up from the Roman goddess of nature, fertility, and childbirth who is often shown as a huntress and the equivalent of the Greek goddess Artemis. The late Princess of Wales proved to be an inspiration for the name when nearly one billion people across the globe watched her marry Prince Charles in a 1981 televised ceremony.

Dominique   Rank: 648
Origin: Latin
Meaning: Of God
Alternate Spellings: Domanique, Domenique, Domineek, Domineke
Gender Variations: Domingo, Dominic
Nickname: Dom
Similar Names: Domini, Dominica, Domitia
Namesakes: Dominique Dawes (Olympic gymnast), Dominique Moceanu (Olympic gymnast), Dominique Swain (actress)
➡ The French feminine form of Dominic that's been used for both girls and boys and given in the past for a child born on Sunday, regarded by some as the Lord's day. Also the title of a song performed by the Singing Nun during the 1960s. The name is already past its peak and has declined in recent years.

Donna   Rank: 832
Origin: Gaelic
Meaning: World mighty
Gender Variation: Donald
Similar Names: Donalda, Donaldina, Donella, Donelle, Ladonna, Madonna
Namesakes: Donna Karan (fashion designer), Donna Summer (singer)
➡ The Italian feminine form of Donald used as a title similar to Don for men. It was influenced in 1958 when singer Ritchie Valens used the name as a title for a song that he performed on Dick Clark's *American Bandstand* and actress Donna Reed debuted as housewife Donna Stone on the television series *The Donna Reed Show.*

117

Dulce
Rank: 274

Origin: Spanish
Meaning: Sweet
Alternate Spellings: Dulcea, Dulci, Dulcie, Dulcy, Dulsea
Gender Variations: Durel, Dushane
Similar Names: Dalise, Delice, Dulcia, Dulciana, Dulcibella, Dulcibelle, Dulcina, Dulcinea, Dulsine, Dilys
Namesakes: Dulce María Loynaz (author/poet), Dulce María (actress/singer)
➡ Spanish name derived from the Latin word, *dulcis* that was revived in the 20th century. Also makes reference to *dulce nombre de Maria*, meaning "the sweet name of Mary." Gaining in popularity since its debut on the chart in 1990, it continues to be favored as a top choice in the U.S. for its pleasant meaning and unique pronunciation and spelling. Irmã Dulce was a Brazilian Catholic nun who founded the Obras Sociais Irmã Dulce in 1959, the Charitable Works Foundation of Sister Dulce, and who was also named Servant of God by Pope John Paul II in 2003.

Dylan
Rank: 733

Origin: Welsh
Meaning: Son of the sea
Alternate Spellings: Dylanne, Dylon
Gender Variations: Dillon, Dylan
Similar Names: Dayana, Delaney, Devyn, Dilys, Dyan
➡ A surname used as a given name that's also associated with the god of the sea in Welsh mythology. Listed among the top 50 for boys, which spilled over as a girl's given name. Parents looking for a more feminine form should try the "Dylanne" spelling.

Eden
Rank: 320

Origin: Hebrew
Meaning: Delightful
Alternate Spellings: Eadan, Eaden, Eadin, Eadon, Edan, Edin, Edon, Edyn, Edyne
Gender Variations: Edsen, Egen, Ethen
Nickname: Ede
Similar Names: Edena, Edene, Edenia, Edesia, Edian, Edlyn, Edna, Edonia, Edrea, Jaden
➡ Associated with the Old Testament Garden of Eden where Adam and Eve lived before they were expelled. Occasionally used as a boy's name, it first debuted on the girls popularity chart in 1986. It's associated with the surname of film and television actress and singer Barbara Eden, who is most famous for her role in *I Dream of Jeannie* from 1965 to 1970. Also considered a literary name for the novel *East of Eden*, by Nobel Prize winner John Steinbeck in 1952 that was adapted into a 1955 film starring James Dean in his first major film role, and the 1986 novel *The Garden of Eden* by Ernest Hemingway that was published after his 1961 death.

Edith
Rank: 638

Origin: Old English
Meaning: Rich, war
Alternate Spellings: Edyth, Edythe
Gender Variations: Eddie, Edgar, Edmond
Nicknames: Eda, Edie
Similar Names: Edit, Edita, Edlyn, Edna, Edria, Edytha
Namesakes: Edith Head (costume designer), Edith Wharton (novelist)
➡ Derived from the elements *ead* and *gyo* that became known among royalty and saints. It was given to the daughter of Edgar the Peaceful during the 10th century when it was commonplace to repeat name elements within a family. The name survived the Norman Conquest and became a favorite in England. In the U.S., it rose into the top 100 during the 19th century and stayed there until 1937 when it started to fade. Best-known for television character Edith Bunker on the acclaimed 1970s comedy *All in the Family*. Today's parents may prefer the fashionable "y" in the middle spelling.

Elaine
Rank: 719

Origin: Greek
Meaning: Torch
Alternate Spellings: Ellaine, Elayn, Elayne
Gender Variations: Elan, Elden
Nickname: Lainey
Similar Names: Alana, Elaina, Elanna, Eleanor, Eleanora, Eleni, Helene, Lena
Namesake: Elayne Boosler (comedienne)
➡ The Old French form of Helen associated with the figure in Arthurian legend who was the lover of Sir Lancelot and mother of Galahad. The legend was picked up by English poet Alfred, Lord Tennyson, who gave the tale a tragic ending. Today the *Seinfeld* television

character played by Julia Louis-Dreyfus during the 1990s and the literary restaurant located in New York City come to mind.

Eleanor
Rank: 277

Origin: French/Greek
Meaning: Torch
Alternate Spellings: Aleanor, Aleonore, Elenore, Eleonore, Elinor
Gender Variations: Elendor, Elmore
Nickname: Ella
Similar Names: Eleana, Eleanora, Eleni, Elnora, Lenore, Leonora, Leora, Nelly
➡ Of uncertain origin possibly from the French form of Alienor or taken from the Greek name Helen. It was borne by 12th-century Eleanor of Aquitaine, the wife of both Louis VII, the king of France, and Henry II, the king of England. The name was known during the 1930s and 1940s for both film actress and tap dancer Eleanor Powell and Eleanor Roosevelt, the activist, diplomat, and wife and first lady of U.S. president Franklin D. Roosevelt. The Beatles helped popularize the name during the mid-1960s with the song "Eleanor Rigby." The name acquired literary fame from Elinor Dashwood, a fictional character and the main protagonist in Jane Austen's 1811 novel *Sense and Sensibility*.

Elena
Rank: 187

Origin: Greek
Meaning: Torch
Alternate Spellings: Elaina, Elainah, Elainea, Elainna, Elana, Elayna, Elaynah, Elenah, Elenna, Ellena
Nickname: Lena
Similar Names: Eladia, Elayni, Eleena, Eleni, Eleanora, Eleora, Eliana, Elina, Helen
Namesakes: Elena Baranova (Russian WNBA player), Elena Zamolodchikova (Russian Olympic gymnast)
➡ Variation of Helen that has been listed among the top 500 names since 1953, and recently climbed in popularity because of its fashionable "a" ending.

Eliana
Rank: 282

Origin: Hebrew/Greek
Meaning: My God has answered, sun
Alternate Spellings: Eleana, Eleanah, Elianna, Elleana, Elliana, Ellianna,
Elyana, Ileana, Iliana, Ilianah
Gender Variations: Elia, Eliazar, Eloitt
Nicknames: Eli, Elia
Similar Names: Elaina, Elana, Elania, Eliane, Elina, Eliotta, Liana, Oliana
➡ The Italian and Spanish form of Eliane associated with the Roman family name Aelianus that was derived from the Greek word *helios*, meaning "sun." The name peaked in 2002 following the recent popularity of Venezuelan jazz artist Eliana Cuevas. Currently more popular than variations Elaina and Elliana, also listed on the chart.

Elise
Rank: 218

Origin: Hebrew
Meaning: My God is an oath
Alternate Spellings: Alise, Alisse, Alyse, Eilis, Elese, Elisse, Ellyce, Elyse, Elysse, Elyce
Gender Variations: Elisay, Eliseo, Ellis
Nicknames: Eli, Lese, Lis
Similar Names: Elisa, Elisia, Elita, Eliz, Eliza, Else, Felise, Melise
➡ Short form of Elizabeth that has recently held a strong position on the chart because of its long "ee" sound that is popular with parents today. "Für Elise," which means "For Elise" in German, is the popular name of a piano solo written by Ludwig van Beethoven during the 19th century.

Eliza
Rank: 325

Origin: Hebrew
Meaning: My God is an oath
Alternate Spellings: Aliza, Alyza, Elizah, Elizea, Elizeah, Elizza, Elizzah, Elliza, Ellyzah, Elyza
Gender Variations: Elijiah, Eliya
Nicknames: Eli, Eliz, Liz, Liza
Similar Names: Elia, Elisa, Elisabeth, Elise, Elita, Eliya, Elizabee, Elizabeth, Elizaida, Elza
Namesake: Eliza Dushku (actress)
➡ Short form of Elizabeth widely used by the 16th-century poets of Queen Elizabeth I. The name was popularized by George Bernard Shaw in his 1913 play *Pygmalion*, based on the fictional character Eliza Doolittle, that became a 1956 Broadway hit, setting a record for the longest run of any major theater production in history. It was later adapted into the 1964 film *My Fair Lady* starring Audrey Hepburn in the role of Eliza.

Elizabeth   Rank: 11

Origin: Hebrew
Meaning: My God is
an oath
Alternate Spelling:
Elisabeth
Gender Variation: Elian
Nicknames: Beth, Betsy, Betty, Eliza, Elle,
Libby, Liz, Liza, Lizbeth
Similar Names: Bess, Eliana, Elisheba,
Elisheva, Elsa, Elsie, Elspeth, Isabel, Lisa,
Lisette
Namesakes: Queen Elizabeth II, Elizabeth
Barrett Browning (poet), Elizabeth Hurley
(actress), Elizabeth Taylor (actress)
➡ Derived from the Greek form of the
Hebrew name Elisheva. The name of Aaron's
wife in the Old Testament and the mother of
John the Baptist in the New Testament.
Influenced by the long and successful rein of
Queen Elizabeth I, which resulted in numerous
variations. Also a literary name for one of the
principal characters in Jane Austen's novel
Pride and Prejudice. Consistently ranked
among the top 25 for more than 100 years.

Ella   Rank: 21

Origin: Greek
Meaning: Torch
Alternate Spelling: Ela
Gender Variations: Elliott,
Ellis
Nicknames: Elle, Ellie
Similar Names: Alice, Allie, Elaine, Eleanor,
Eleanora, Elena, Eleni, Elnora, Elsie, Nellie
Namesake: Ella Wheeler Wilcox (poetess)
➡ Introduced to England by the Normans.
Derived from a part of the compound name
ali and used as the short form of Ellen.
Famed jazz singer Ella Fitzgerald brought
attention to the name during a career that
spanned six decades. The name of the title
character in the 2004 film *Ella Enchanted*.
The classic fairy tale about the cinder girl
who meets prince charming with the help
of her fairy godmother also comes to mind.
A top 20 name in several countries other
than the U.S.

Elle   Rank: 480

Origin: Greek
Meaning: Torch
Gender Variations: Elkan,
Elliot, Ellis

Similar Names: Elaine, Elena, Ella, Ellen, Ellie,
Elma, Eloise, Elsa, Elsie
Namesake: Elle Fanning (actress)
➡ The French short form of Ellen. Inspired
by Australian supermodel and actress Elle
Macpherson who became internationally
known when she appeared in *Elle* magazine
for six consecutive years. The name first
appeared on the popularity chart in 2002
and is listed among the top 500.

Ellen   Rank: 544

Origin: Greek
Meaning: Torch
Alternate Spellings: Elan,
Elen, Elin, Ellan, Ellin, Ellyn,
Elyn
Gender Variations: Elliot, Ellis
Nickname: Elle
Similar Names: Elena, Elene, Eleni, Elina,
Elinor, Ella, Ellenor, Ellie
Namesakes: Ellen Barkin (actress), Ellen
Burstyn (actress), Ellen Goodman (columnist)
➡ A variation of Helen and sometimes used
as the short form of Eleanor. The name
hovered around the top 100 starting in the
late 19th century until the early 1960s when
interest began to wane. Actress and talk
show host Ellen DeGeneres has kept the
name in front of the public since 1986 when
she was the first comedienne invited to visit
with Johnny Carson on *The Tonight Show*.

Ellie   Rank: 175

Origin: Greek
Meaning: Torch
Alternate Spellings: Elah,
Ele, Ellee, Elle, Elli, Elly
Gender Variations: Eland, Eli, Ellex
Nicknames: Ell
Similar Names: Allie, Elanna, Elanor, Ella,
Ellia, Ellice, Elsie, Ellin, Eliz
➡ The short form of Eleanor and other
names beginning with "el" and may also be
taken from the French form of the Provençal
name Alienor. Faded from chart in 1931 and
returned in 1992, quickly rising to the top 200
in 2003. Recently attention has been brought
to the name by the 2005 movie *Ellie Parker*,
starring actress Naomi Watts in the title role
and fictional wooly mammoth character Ellie,
voiced by actress Queen Latifah in the 2006
film *Ice Age: The Meltdown*.

Elsa   Rank: 792

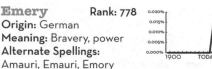

Origin: Hebrew
Meaning: My God is
an oath
Gender Variation: Elroy
Nickname: Else
Similar Names: Elisa, Elise, Ella, Elsbeth,
Elsie, Eliza, Elizabeth, Ellie, Ilsa
➡ Princess Elsa of Brabant was a fictional
character in early German Arthurian
literature popularized by composer Richard
Wagner in his 1848 opera *Lohengrin*.
The German short form of Elizabeth, the
name has been used steadily since the 19th
century, peaking in 1895 at No. 215. Mexican
supermodel Elsa Benitez is a famous bearer.

Elsie   Rank: 879

Origin: Hebrew
Meaning: My God is
an oath
Alternate Spelling: Elsey
Gender Variations: Ellery, Elroy, Elsdon
Similar Names: Elissa, Eloise, Elsa, Elsbeth,
Elspet, Elspeth, Elyse, Liesl, Lisbet, Lise
➡ A variation of Elspie which is a pet form
of Elspeth and ultimately the Scottish short
form of Elizabeth. Used independently since
the 19th century, peaking at No. 31 during the
1890s. Considered a literary name used by
poet Henry Wadsworth Longfellow in *Golden
Legend* and author Oliver Wendell Holmes
in the novel *Elsie Venner*. After a 29-year
absence from the popularity chart, it made
a comeback in 2005 as part of a vintage
naming trend.

Emerson   Rank: 305

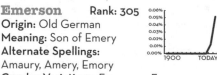

Origin: Old German
Meaning: Son of Emery
Alternate Spellings:
Amaury, Amery, Emory
Gender Variations: Emerson, Emery
Nicknames: Em, Emmie
Similar Names: America, Emelia, Emerald,
Emery, Emily
➡ A surname derived from a medieval
personal name that has been in use longer
for boys but more widely used for girls since
2005. Parents have favored surnames as
given names for both boys and girls for quite
some time.

Emery   Rank: 778

Origin: German
Meaning: Bravery, power
Alternate Spellings:
Amauri, Emauri, Emory
Gender Variations: Emerson, Emery
Nickname: Em
Similar Names: Ember, Emelia, Emeline,
Emelyn, Emily, Emma
➡ A surname derived from a medieval
personal name composed of the elements
amal and *ric* that was introduced by the
Normans into England. It was first used as
a boy's name that eventually faded out in
1982 and caught on as a given name for
girls in 2005.

Emilia   Rank: 420

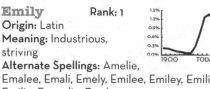

Origin: Latin
Meaning: Industrious,
striving
Alternate Spellings: Amelia,
Amilia, Amillia, Emelia, Emilija, Emilya
Gender Variations: Emil, Emiliano, Emilio
Nicknames: Em, Emmie, Milia
Similar Names: Aemilia, Aemilie, Emila,
Emiliana, Emilina, Emily, Lila, Milana
➡ The feminine form of Aemilius that's
sometimes confused with the similar
sounding Amelia. The name has been in
popular use for over a century and is
currently among the top 500.

Emily   Rank: 1

Origin: Latin
Meaning: Industrious,
striving
Alternate Spellings: Amelie,
Emalee, Emali, Emely, Emilee, Emiley, Emili,
Emilie, Emmelie, Emylee
Gender Variations: Emil, Emilio
Nicknames: Em, Emmie, Milly
Similar Names: Amelia, Emaline, Emila, Emilia
Namesakes: Emily Post (etiquette expert),
Emily Robison (musician), Emily Watson
(British actress)
➡ The top-ranked name in the U.S. and
Canada for more than 10 years and recently
fell to No. 5 in England during 2006. Listed
among the top 50 names since 1975. Derived
from the medieval feminine form of Aemilius
that became a literary name associated with
British writer Emily Bronte and U.S. poet
Emily Dickinson.

Emma   Rank: 2

Origin: Old German
Meaning: Whole, universal
Alternate Spelling: Ema
Gender Variations: Emery, Emmet
Nicknames: Em, Emmie
Similar Names: Emelia, Emerald, Emily, Emmaline, Emmalynn
Namesakes: Emma Samms (British actress), Emma Thompson (British actress), Emma Watson (British actress)
⇨ Originally a shortened form of the medieval names Irmgard and Ermintrude that was introduced to England by the Normans. Used by English writer Jane Austen for the title character of her 19th-century novel that was adapted into a movie in 1996. Also the name of Rachel's baby on the TV show *Friends*. Listed among the top 100 since 1973 and is often combined with other names such as Emma Justine, Emma Marie, and Emma Rose.

Emmalee   Rank: 685

Origin: American
Gender Variations: Emery, Emmet
Nicknames: Emma, Lee
Similar Names: Emmaline, Emmylou, Evelynne
⇨ A modern twist of the highly ranked name "Emma" combined with "lee." Debuted on the popularity chart in 1999.

Erica   Rank: 222

Origin: Old Norse
Meaning: Ever ruler
Alternate Spellings: Arica, Ericca, Ericha, Ericka, Erika, Erikah, Erikka, Eryca, Erycah, Eryka
Gender Variations: Eric, Erron, Jarric
Nickname: Ricki
Similar Names: Alricka, Erical, Erin, Erlina, Erykia, Jerica, Rica
⇨ The feminine form of Eric that also means "heather" in Latin. A classification name of more than 700 species of flowers in the family *Ericaceae* often referred to as "heath" or "heather." The name debuted on the popularity chart in 1945 and peaked at No. 31 from 1986 to 1988. *Erica Kane* is the title of songs by singer Aaliyah in 2002 and alternative rock band Urge Overkill in 1993, both written about Susan Lucci's famous character on the soap opera *All My Children*. Since the drama first aired in 1970, Erica Kane is considered the most popular character in daytime television history. Another well-known fictional character who who comes to mind is Dr. Erica Noughton from the television medical drama *Nip/Tuck*.

Erin   Rank: 130

Origin: Irish Gaelic
Meaning: Ireland
Alternate Spellings: Earin, Erienne, Erinn, Erinna, Erinne, Errin, Erynn
Gender Variations: Aaron, Eric, Erino, Errant, Erry
Similar Names: Arin, Arrine, Arwyn, Eiren, Erenia, Eri, Erinetta, Iren, Irina, Taryn
⇨ Derived from Eireann and is a poetic name for Ireland. Name's extended position in top 100 from 1971 to 2004 was notably fashioned by the popularity of actress Erin Moran of *Happy Days* and the character Erin Walton from the *The Waltons*. Also recently influenced by the 2000 movie *Erin Brockovich*, starring actress Julia Roberts. Name used for both boys and girls, but a more trendy choice for girls, especially when spelled with a "y" or with variations ending in "a" or "ia."

Esmeralda   Rank: 224

Origin: Spanish
Meaning: Prized green gemstone
Alternate Spellings: Esmaralda, Esmerelda, Esmerilda, Esmiralda, Ezmaralda, Ezmerelda, Ezmirilda
Gender Variations: Esmel, Esmond
Nicknames: Esme
Similar Names: Emerald, Esmerald, Esmerazda, Espedaniza, Esperanza
⇨ A variation of the vocabulary word "emerald" and gem name that was first associated with the famed fictional character in the 1905 film *The Hunchback of Notre Dame*, based on the 1831 novel by Victor Hugo. The name peaked toward the end of the 20th century following the 1996 release of the Disney film version of *The Hunchback of Notre Dame*, starring an updated Esmeralda character. The name was also inspired by the fictional maid played by actress Alice Ghostley on the 1964 to 1972 television show *Bewitched*.

Esperanza Rank: 675

Origin: Spanish
Meaning: Hope
Alternate Spelling: Espranza
Gender Variation: Estaban
Similar Names: Ernesta, Esmeralda, Esperaza, Estebana

➡ Spanish for "hope" that follows a current vocabulary word naming trend. It was used by writer Sandra Cisneros as the heroine's name in her 1984 novella *The House on Mango Street*. Favored among Hispanic families.

Essence Rank: 839

Origin: Latin
Meaning: To be
Gender Variation: Esmond
Similar Names: Electra, Ernesta, Ernestine, Eslanda, Essie, Estella, Estelle

➡ A vocabulary word used as a given name derived from "esse." Parents may also recognize it as the name of a fashion, lifestyle, and entertainment magazine targeted at African-American females.

Estefani Rank: 905

Origin: Greek
Meaning: Crown
Alternate Spellings: Estefanie, Estefany, Estephanie, Estephany
Gender Variations: Esteban, Estevan, Stefano
Similar Names: Estebana, Estefania, Stefana, Stefania, Stephani

➡ A variation of Estefania, which is the Spanish form of Stephanie, used as a girl's given name since 2002.

Esther Rank: 298

Origin: Persian
Meaning: Star
Alternate Spellings: Ester, Esthur
Gender Variations: Estel, Estes, Estevan
Nicknames: Es, Essa, Essie
Similar Names: Asta, Easter, Esta, Estee, Esterel, Hesther, Istar
Namesake: Esther Jones (Olympic runner)

➡ In the Bible, Esther, originally named Hadassah, was the Jewish wife of the Persian king, who helped save the Jews from persecution. A book in the Bible bears her name. Considered a vintage name that peaked prior to the turn of the 20th century, it's best known for swimming actress Esther Williams, who became a popular star during the 1940s and 1950s. Also the name of the protagonist in Sylvia Plath's semi-autobiographical novel *The Bell Jar* published in 1963.

Estrella Rank: 311

Origin: Latin
Meaning: Star
Alternate Spellings: Estrela, Estrelah, Estrellya, Estrelya
Gender Variations: Esteban, Estevan, Estraton
Nicknames: Esta, Trella
Similar Names: Asta, Astrea, Estefani, Estelinda, Estelle, Esteva, Estevana, Esther, Estrellita, Stella
Namesakes: Estrella Alfon (storywriter/playwright), Linda Estrella (Filipina actress), Estrella Morente (Spanish flamenco singer)

➡ Spanish form of Stella and the name of the Sierra Estrella mountain range southwest of Phoenix, Arizona. Debuted on the chart in 1997. Possibly influenced by *Estrella de Mar*, the breakthrough album from Spanish pop/rock group Amaral, released in Spain in 2002.

Eva Rank: 124

Origin: Hebrew
Meaning: Giver of life
Alternate Spelling: Evah
Gender Variations: Evan, Everett
Nickname: Ev
Similar Names: Ava, Evalea, Evana, Evanesa, Eve, Eveleena, Evella, Evelyn, Evette, Evia

➡ Latinate form of Eve derived from the Hebrew word *chavah*. Has many pronunciations from other countries, but most often pronounced with the long "ee" sound in the U.S. Listed on the popularity chart in 1880 at No. 41 and stayed within the top 50 choices for girls until 1913. Trendy when used as a combination name, such as Evamarie, or with a hyphen. With creative variations to choose from, this name is becoming increasingly popular once again in families, especially for its similarity to current No. 5 name, Ava.

Evangeline   Rank: 597
Origin: Greek
Meaning: Good news
Gender Variations: Evan
Nicknames: Angeline
Similar Names: Evangela, Evangelia, Evangelina, Evangelyn, Evelina, Evelyn
⇨ A form of Evangelina that disappeared in the late 1960s and surfaced among the top 600 names in 2006 inspired by Canadian actress Evangeline Lilly, who's best-known for her role in the hit drama *Lost*.

Eve   Rank: 590
Origin: Hebrew
Meaning: Life giver
Gender Variations: Evan, Everett
Nickname: Evie
Similar Names: Eva, Evaleen, Evalina, Evelia, Evelyn, Evetta, Evette, Eviana, Evita, Hava
Namesake: Eve Arden (actress)
⇨ The biblical name for the first woman who was Adam's wife and the mother of Cain and Abel and derived from the Latin "chavvah." The name is known for actress Eve Plumb who played middle sister Jan on the 1970s television sitcom *The Brady Bunch,* and for rapper, singer, and actress Eve Jihan Jeffers, who goes by the stage name "Eve."

Evelyn   Rank: 65
Origin: Norman
Meaning: Lively, pleasant
Alternate Spelling: Evalin, Evaline, Evalyn, Eveline, Evelyne, Evelynn, Evelynne
Gender Variations: Evan, Evander
Nicknames: Eve, Evie, Lyn
Similar Names: Avaline, Avelina, Eileen, Eva, Evelina
Namesake: Evelyn Ashford (Olympic sprinter)
⇨ Derived from the surname Aveline and considered an elaborated form of Ava. Generally used as a male name, associated with British writer Evelyn Waugh, before it caught on for females prior to the turn of the 20th century. The name peaked in 1915 and appears to be making a comeback possibly due to the fashionable "y" in the suffix.

Faith   Rank: 64
Origin: Latin
Meaning: To trust
Alternate Spellings: Faithe, Fayth, Faythe
Gender Variations: Faegan, Fairfax
Similar Names: Charity, Faye, Fayette, Fidelia, Fidelity, Hope, Patience
Namesakes: Faith Evans (singer), Faith Ford (actress), Faith Ringgold (artist), *Hope & Faith* (TV sitcom)
⇨ Parents have been drawn to this vocabulary word derived from *fidere* for more than a century. Considered a virtue name, it was introduced by the Puritans during the 16th century along with Hope and Charity. Country singer Faith Hill, born Audrey Faith Perry, brought the name to the forefront with her successful debut album in 1993.

Fatima   Rank: 228
Origin: Arabic
Meaning: To abstain
Alternate Spellings: Fatema, Fateema, Fateemah, Fatimah, Fatyma, Fatymah
Gender Variation: Faton
Nickname: Tee
Similar Names: Asia, Fathema, Fatime, Fatina, Fatmah, Khadija
⇨ A Muslim name often associated with the Prophet Muhammad's daughter, Fatima Zahra, or given in honor of "Our Lady Fatima," the title bestowed on the Blessed Virgin Mary by the Roman Catholics. The name first appeared on the chart in 1973 and peaked in 2001. A town in Portugal and essential Christian pilgrimage center also bears the name, along with *Fatima The Gracious,* a book by Shi'a scholar Abu Muhammad Ordoni about Fatima Zahra. More recently, Fatima Blush is a fictional character from the unofficial 1983 James Bond film *Never Say Never Again.*

Felicity   Rank: 617
Origin: Latin
Meaning: Happy
Gender Variations: Feliciano, Felix
Nickname: Felice
Similar Names: Felicia, Feliciana, Felicidad, Felicita, Felicitas, Felixa
Namesake: *Felicity* (TV series)

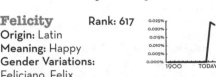

➡ A vocabulary word derived from *felicitas* meaning "good luck" that was considered a virtue name by 17th-century Puritans. Felicitas was the name of several saints and the Roman goddess of good luck and success. Actress Felicity Huffman, best-known for her role on the television series *Desperate Housewives*, is a famous bearer.

Fernanda   Rank: 431

Origin: Old German
Meaning: Adventurous
Gender Variations: Ferdinand, Ferdinando
Nicknames: Fern, Nan, Nanda
Similar Names: Fenicia, Ferdinanda, Fernande
Namesake: Fernanda Torres (Brazilian actress)
➡ The Spanish and Portuguese feminine form of Ferdinand and Fernando. The name landed on the popularity chart in 1995 and is currently in vogue with other foreign names.

Finley   Rank: 910

Origin: Gaelic
Meaning: Fair hero
Alternate Spellings: Findlay, Finlay, Finnlay, Finnley
Gender Variations: Finley, Finn
Nickname: Finn
Similar Names: Fenella, Finola, Fiona, Fionnnula
➡ A Scottish surname that became fashionable as a girl's given name in 2005 and caught on for boys in 2006.

Fiona   Rank: 333

Origin: Irish Gaelic
Meaning: Fair, pale
Alternate Spellings: Ffiona, Ffyona, Fionna, Fyona
Gender Variation: Fiore
Nickname: Fee
Similar Names: Fione, Fiorella, Fiorenza, Fiorina
➡ Name debuted on the chart in 1990 after U.S. rock singer Fiona released three albums. Grammy-winning singer and songwriter Fiona Apple also drew attention to the name with her 1996 debut album *Tidal* as well as Princess Fiona, the popular character in the 2001 film *Shrek*. The name also peaked in 2004 at No. 327, the same year fictional character Fiona was introduced in *The Grim Grotto*, one of *Lemony Snicket's A Series of Unfortunate Events* books.

Flor   Rank: 1000

Origin: Spanish/Portuguese
Meaning: Flower
Gender Variation: Florencio
Nickname: Flo
Similar Names: Fleur, Flora, Florence, Florencia, Floria, Floris, Florrie, Floria
➡ The Spanish and Portuguese word for "flower" and the short form of names like Flora, Florence, and Florencia. Flor, born Florencia Caserta, is an Argentine pop singer who released her first album in 2006.

Frances   Rank: 779

Origin: Latin
Meaning: Free
Gender Variations: Francis, Frank
Nicknames: Fran, Franny
Similar Names: Fannie, Franca, Francesca, Francetta, Francette, Francie, Francine, Francisca
Namesake: Frances McDormand (actress)
➡ The feminine form of Francis associated with Saint Frances Xavier Cabrini who was the first American to be canonized by the Roman Catholic Church. It was the title of a 1982 film that depicted the life of actress Frances Farmer, starring Jessica Lange in the title role. Frances Hodgson Burnett, author of several children's stories including the 1909 novel *The Secret Garden*, is another famous bearer of the name.

Francesca   Rank: 428

Origin: Latin
Meaning: Free
Alternate Spellings: Franceska, Franchesca
Gender Variations: Francesco, Francis
Nicknames: Fran, Franci, Frannie
Similar Names: Franca, Frances, Francetta, Francine, Francisca
➡ The Italian feminine variation of Franciscus and the name of the first U.S. saint. It was more recently used for the fictional Italian Iowa housewife in the 1992 best-selling novel *The Bridges of Madison County* by Robert James Waller.

Frida
Rank: 836
Origin: German
Meaning: Peace
Alternate Spellings: Freada, Freda, Freeda, Freida, Frieda, Fryda
Gender Variations: Frederick, Freeman
Similar Names: Frederica, Freya, Friede
⇒ The Swedish and Hungarian form of Friede that's derived from *frid* or *fried* and influenced by 20th-century Mexican painter Frida Kahlo, whose life was depicted in a 2002 Academy Award-winning film. The name made its debut on the popularity chart in 2001.

Gabriella
Rank: 50
Origin: Hebrew
Meaning: God is my strength
Alternate Spellings: Gabrieala, Gabriela, Gabryella
Gender Variations: Gabe, Gabriel, Gabriels, Gavril
Nicknames: Gabi, Briella
Similar Names: Gabrielle, Gabriellen, Gabrila, Gaela
Namesakes: Gabriela Sabatini (tennis player), Gabriela Szabo (Romanian Olympic track and field medalist)
⇒ The Italian female variation of the Christian name Gabriel that's been listed among the top 100 since 2000. The name of one of the lead characters on the 2006 Disney Channel original movie *High School Musical*.

Gabrielle
Rank: 62
Origin: Hebrew
Meaning: God is my strength
Alternate Spellings: Gabriele, Gabriell, Gabriyel, Gabryel, Gabryelle
Gender Variations: Gabe, Gabriel, Gabriels, Gavril
Nicknames: Gabby, Brielle
Similar Names: Gabriella, Gail, Gaila
Namesakes: Gabrielle (*Xena: Warrior Princess* character), Gabrielle Reece (model/volleyball player), Gabrielle Union (actress), Gabrielle "Coco" Chanel (french fashion designer
⇒ The French feminine form of the biblical name Gabriel that's quickly climbed up the popularity chart since 1957.

Genesis
Rank: 169
Origin: Hebrew
Meaning: Beginning
Alternate Spellings: Genesiss, Genicis, Genises, Genisus, Genysis
Gender Variations: Genard, Generoso, Geno
Nicknames: Gen, Genee, Genes
Similar Names: Genesse, Genesha, Genesia, Genesio, Genessa, Genessie, Genita, Jessie
⇒ Biblical name of the first book of the Old Testament. Has been considered a popular name for girls since 1998 when it debuted on the chart and climbed into the top 200 in 2004. Parents are welcoming this trendy name and possibly choosing it for its biblical reference.

Genevieve
Rank: 368
Origin: Celtic or German
Meaning: Of the race of women
Gender Variations: Gene, Geoffrey
Nicknames: Gen, Genny
Similar Names: Gena, Genette, Geneva, Genevra, Guinevere
⇒ The exact origin of the name is unclear but possibly derived from the Celtic words meaning "people," "tribe," and "woman." Saint Genevieve, known as the patron of Paris, is credited with saving the city from the Huns during the 5th century. Introduced to Britain from France during the 19th century, the name has been used steadily in both the United Kingdom and the U.S. Canadian actress Genevieve Bujold, who's best known for her television and film roles during the 1960s and 1970s, is a namesake.

Georgia
Rank: 273
Origin: Greek
Meaning: Farmer
Alternate Spellings: Giorga, Giorgia, Gorgia, Jeorga, Jeorgia, Jorga, Jorgia, Jorja,
Gender Variations: George, Georgio, Geordie
Similar Names: Georgeann, Georgeanna, Georgene, Georgette, Georgiana, Georgie, Georgina
Namesake: Georgia Cobb (actress/model)
⇒ A state name and feminine form of George. A famous bearer was painter

Georgia O'Keeffe, a major figure in U.S. art since the 1920s who is mostly known for her expression of nature. Inspiring the name during its stay among the top 200 was actress Georgia Ellis who was featured as Kitty in the popular 1950s Western radio drama *Gunsmoke*, considered one of the finest radio dramas of all time. The 1925 song "Sweet Georgia Brown" is a jazz and pop tune and the theme song of the Harlem Globetrotters basketball team. It follows the popular trend of spellings with an "ia."

Gia
Rank: 643

Origin: Greek
Meaning: The planet Earth
Gender Variation: Gino
Similar Names: Gaia, Gaiana, Gala, Gianna, Gigi, Gina, Ginessa
➡ A variation of Gianna that's known for Gia Carangi, a fashion model during the late 1970s and early 1980s before her untimely death in 1986. Acknowledged as the first supermodel, she was depicted in a 1998 television film called *Gia* starring Angelina Jolie in the title role. Possibly a variation of Gaia, the mother goddess in Greek mythology.

Gianna
Rank: 98

Origin: Hebrew
Meaning: God is gracious
Alternate Spellings: Geonna, Giana, Gionna, Jiana
Gender Variations: Gianni, John, Johnny
Nicknames: Anna, Gia, Gina
Similar Names: Ginara, Gianella, Giannina, Giannetta, Giacinta, Ginevra, Giovanna
➡ Feminine Italian form of John and short form of Giovanna that first appeared on the popularity chart in 1989. Continues to climb in the U.S. and become more common for girls as parents prefer trendy names ending with "a."

Gillian
Rank: 758

Origin: Latin
Meaning: Downy
Alternate Spelling: Jillian
Gender Variation: Giles
Nicknames: Gill, Gilly
Similar Names: Gilana, Gilda, Gillaine, Giulia, Giuliana, Jillianne

➡ The English feminine form of Julian that first hit the chart in 1968 but has never been as frequently used as "Jillian," which is currently listed among the top 200. Actress Gillian Anderson of the television show *X-Files* fame, brought attention to the name during the show's run from 1993 to 2002.

Gina
Rank: 712

Alternate Spellings: Geena, Geina, Gena, Jeana, Jeena
Gender Variations: Gene, Gino
Nickname: Gin
Similar Names: Gia, Gianina, Gianna, Ginamarie, Ginessa, Ginette, Ginevra, Ginger, Ginny
Namesakes: Geena Davis (actress), Gena Rowlands (actress), Gina Gershon (actress)
➡ The short form of names that end in "gina" such as Georgina, Luigina, and Regina that's been used as a given name since the 19th century, sporadically at first then steadily starting in the mid-1940s. Italian actress Gina Lollobrigida brought attention to the name when she first began appearing in Italian language films in 1947 and U.S. films in 1953. It's a popular name for combinations and blends.

Giovanna
Rank: 723

Origin: Hebrew
Meaning: God is gracious
Alternate Spellings: Geovana, Geovanna, Giovana
Gender Variations: Gianni, Giovanni
Nickname: Gio, Vanna
Similar Names: Gianetta, Gianmaria, Gianna, Gina, Ginette, Ginevra
Namesake: Giovanna Mezzogiorno (Italian actress)
➡ The Italian feminine form of Giovanni that's been used steadily in the U.S. since 1991 and has risen in popularity following foreign naming trend. Princess Giovanna of Italy, the last Tsaritsa of Bulgaria before it was invaded by the Soviet Union, is a namesake.

Giselle
Rank: 168

Origin: German
Meaning: Hostage, pledge
Alternate Spellings:
Ghisele, Gisel, Gisele, Gisell,
Gisselle, Gizelle, Gysel
Gender Variations: Gill, Gillis, Gjon, Guss
Nickname: Giz
Similar Names: Gazelle, Gisela, Giselda,
Gisena, Giza, Gynell, Jiselle, Joselle
⇨ Derived from the German element *gisel*,
that's most often pronounced "je-ZELL,"
and the title of a well-known 19th-century
ballet from the Romantic period by French
composer Adolphe Adam that adds
character and poise to the name. It debuted
on the popularity chart in 1983 and recently
moved into the top 200 names in 2003,
following the breakout of Brazilian supermodel
Gisele Bundchen, who was said to be "the
most beautiful girl in the world" in 2000.

Gloria
Rank: 453

Origin: Latin
Meaning: Glory
Alternate Spellings:
Glaurea, Glorea, Gloreya,
Glorya
Similar Names: Glorianna, Glorianne,
Gloribel, Gloris, Glory
Namesakes: Gloria Estefan (singer), Gloria
Naylor (novelist), Gloria Steinem (feminist/
journalist), Gloria Vanderbilt (clothing
designer)
⇨ A form of the name Gloriana that was
used by poets during the 17th century in
reference to Queen Elizabeth I. Playwright
George Bernard Shaw was possibly the first
to shorten the name to Gloria for a character
in his 19th-century play *You Can Never Tell*.
It was listed among the top 100 from the
1920s to the 1960s, which coincided with
the film career of actress Gloria Swanson.

Grace
Rank: 17

Origin: Latin
Meaning: Grace
Alternate Spelling: Grayce
Gender Variations:
Graham, Grant
Nickname: Gracie
Similar Names: Graceland, Gracelyn, Gracia,
Graciana, Graciela, Gracielle, Gracious,
Grata, Gratiana, Gratiella

Namesakes: Grace Jones (singer), Grace Park
(LPGA golfer)
⇨ A derivative of the Latin word *gratia* that
was introduced to England by the Puritans in
the late 16th century and who then brought
the name to America. Currently ranks
among the top 10 in England and Australia.
Associated with the Three Graces, who were
the goddesses of nature in Greek mythology.
Actress Grace Kelly, who later held the title
of Princess of Monaco, also comes to mind.

Gracelyn
Rank: 759

Origin: American
Alternate Spellings:
Gracelin, Gracelynn,
Gracelynne
Gender Variations: Grayson, Gregory
Nicknames: Grace, Gracie, Lyn
Similar Names: Graceland, Gracella,
Graciana, Graciela
⇨ A combination of the names "Grace" and
"Lyn" that first landed on the popularity chart
in 2004.

Gracie
Rank: 103

Origin: Latin
Meaning: Grace
Alternate Spellings:
Gracee, Gracey
Gender Variations: Grady, Gray, Grayson
Nickname: Grace
Similar Names: Casey, Lacy, Macy, Tracy
⇨ A form of Grace, which is a derivative of
the Latin word *gratia*. The name was
popularized by comedian Gracie Allen
who teamed up with husband George
Burns in 1922 to work in vaudeville, films,
radio, and television.

Greta
Rank: 680

Origin: Greek
Meaning: Pearl
Alternate Spellings: Gretta,
Grette
Gender Variation: Grey
Similar Names: Greer, Gressa, Gretel,
Gretchen, Grete, Gretna
Namesake: Greta Van Susteren (journalist/
TV personality)
⇨ The short form of Margaret inspired by
Swedish-born actress Greta Garbo, who was
considered one of the most glamorous stars
during the 1920s and 1930s. The name

peaked in popularity in 1932, then dropped out of sight during the 1980s and 1990s and is slowly starting to make a comeback.

Gretchen   Rank: 771
Origin: Greek
Meaning: Pearl
Gender Variation: Greville
Similar Names: Greta, Grete, Gretel, Grethel, Gretna, Gretta, Megan
Namesakes: Gretchen Mol (actress), Gretchen Wilson (country singer)
➡ The German diminutive of Margaret used by Johann Wolfgang von Goethe for a character in his 18th-century play *Faust*. Popular use of the name began in the late 19th century, peaking in 1973 at No. 192.

Guadalupe   Rank: 255

Origin: Spanish
Meaning: Valley of the Wolves
Gender Variations: Gualterio, Guillermo
Nicknames: Guada, Lupe
Similar Names: Guadalupa, Guadalupi, Lupita
➡ The Spanish name for the biblical Virgin Mary, often referred to as "Our Lady of Guadalupe," who is known for protecting the Mexican people against floods, earthquakes, and epidemics. The name peaked in 1997 at No. 209.

Gwendolyn   Rank: 631
Origin: Welsh
Meaning: White ring
Alternate Spellings: Guendolen, Guendolin, Guendolynn, Gwendaline, Gwendalyn, Gwendolen, Gwendoline, Gwendolynne
Gender Variations: Wendell, Wynn
Nickname: Gwen
Similar Names: Guenna, Gwenda, Gwenette, Gwenyth, Winnie
➡ A variation of Gwendoline, which led to the more popular name Wendy. In Arthurian legend sometimes referred to as the name of the wife of Merlin the magician. Singer and songwriter Gwen Stefani and actress Gwyneth Paltrow use forms of the name.

Hadley   Rank: 494
Origin: Old English
Meaning: Heather field
Alternate Spellings: Hadlea, Hadleigh, Hadly
Gender Variations: Haden, Harley
Similar Names: Haidee, Hailey, Haldana, Halle, Halia
➡ A surname derived from a medieval place name for any one of several locations. It was picked up and used by parents as a girl's name in 1998 and has risen in popularity since that time. Writer Ernest Hemingway's first wife was named Elizabeth Hadley Richardson.

Hailey   Rank: 25
Origin: Old English
Meaning: Hay clearing
Alternate Spellings: Haile, Hailee, Hailie, Haleigh, Haley, Halie, Haylee, Hayleigh, Hayley, Haylie
Gender Variations: Hal, Hale
Similar Names: Bailey, Hadley, Halle, Harley, Kailey
➡ A place name derived from *heg* and *leah*. Also used as a form of Haley and Hayley that was influenced by British actress Hayley Mills, who was discovered at 12 and propelled to stardom in the title role of the 1960 Walt Disney film *Pollyanna*. The name came into popular use during the 1970s and 1980s and ranks highly in Canada.

Halle   Rank: 493

Origin: Old English
Meaning: From the hall
Alternate Spellings: Halli, Hallie, Hally
Gender Variations: Hal, Hale
Similar Names: Hadley, Hadyn, Hailey, Holly
➡ A variation of Hallie, which is the pet form of Harriet. The name was made famous by actress Halle Berry, whose parents named her after Halle's Department Store in Cleveland, Ohio, credited as the first African-American woman to win an Academy Award for Best Actress. Considered fashionable today for its long "ee" sound.

Hannah   Rank: 8
Origin: Hebrew
Meaning: Grace of God
Alternate Spellings: Hana, Hanah, Hanna
Gender Variations: Hammond, Hanan, Hananiah
Nicknames: Hann, Hannie
Similar Names: Alannah, Anna, Chana, Hanne, Ioanna, Johanna
Namesakes: Daryl Hannah (actress), Hannah Mandlikova (tennis player), *Hannah Montana* (Disney TV series), Hannah Storm (news anchor)
⇒ A biblical name for the mother of the prophet Samuel who was barren until she asked God to bless her with a child. Derived from the Hebrew name Channah, the name precisely means "God has graced me with a son." Anna is the Latin variation. *Hannah and Her Sisters* was a popular Woody Allen film released in 1986.

Harley   Rank: 388
Origin: Old English
Meaning: Hare meadow
Alternate Spellings: Harlea, Harleah, Harlee, Harleeh, Harleey, Harlei, Harlie, Harly
Gender Variations: Charlie, Harlen, Harley, Hartley
Similar Names: Carley, Charlee, Hailey, Harlene, Harleyann, Harleyanna, Harper, Hartley
⇒ A surname and place name from Old English *hara* and *leah*. A name for both boys and girls but more popular as a female name, unlike Charlie, which is still more common for boys. Trendy because of its long "ee" sound that most parents prefer in a name. It reached its height of popularity in 2003 at No. 312. Fictional character Harley Cooper, played by actress Beth Ehlers, is featured on daytime soap opera *Guiding Light* and was named after "her father's" favorite motorcycle. Actress and author Harley Jane Kozak is another popular bearer.

Harmony   Rank: 342
Origin: Greek
Meaning: Unity, concord
Alternate Spellings: Harmonee, Harmoney, Harmonie
Gender Variations: Hammond, Harmon
Similar Names: Essence, Journey, Justice
⇒ The vocabulary word derived from the Greek "harmonia" that means a tuneful sound. In Greek mythology, Harmonia was the daughter of Aphrodite and known as the goddess of order. Debuted on the popularity chart in 1975 and has climbed steadily with other vocabulary word names. Occasionally used as a boy's name.

Harper   Rank: 510
Origin: Old English
Meaning: Harp player
Gender Variations: Harper, Harry
Similar Names: Harley, Harmony, Haven
⇒ An occupational surname that was originally given to someone who played the harp. Associated with 20th-century Southern novelist Harper Lee, best known for her 1960 Pulitzer Prize-winning novel, *To Kill a Mockingbird*. It's climbed the popularity chart as a given name for girls since 2004 and made a reappearance for boys in 2006.

Haven   Rank: 610
Origin: Old English
Meaning: A place of safety
Alternate Spelling: Haeven
Gender Variation: Harvey
Similar Names: Harleen, Harley, Harmony, Hava, Hayley, Heaven
⇒ Adopted from the vocabulary word derived from the Old English *haefen*. It was the title of a 2004 film starring Orlando Bloom and a 2001 television miniseries starring Natasha Richardson. Used as a girl's given name since 1996.

Hayden   Rank: 416
Origin: Old English
Meaning: Hay valley
Alternate Spellings: Haden, Hadon, Haiden, Haydn
Gender Variations: Hardy, Haydn, Hayward
Similar Names: Hadley, Hannah, Harper, Haven, Hayley
⇒ A surname and place name derived from *heg* and *denu*. First used as a boy's name then gained popularity as a girl's name in 1998 and is especially stylish with the "y" in the middle. Actress and singer Hayden Panettierre has kept the name in front of the public in recent years.

Hazel Rank: 465

Origin: Old English
Meaning: The hazel tree
Alternate Spellings: Hazal, Hazell, Hazelle, Hazle
Gender Variations: Haven, Hayden
Similar Names: Hattie, Haya, Hayley
Namesake: Sister Hazel (musical group)
➡ A name used in nature that refers to the nut-bearing shrub or small tree related to the birch family or a color that ranges from light brown to yellowish brown. It got its start as a girl's given name during the 19th century when botanical names became popular. It was the title of a comic strip about a fictional live-in maid who works for a middle class family that was first published in 1943 and adapted into a television series in 1961. Actress Julia Roberts and Danny Moder have a daughter named Hazel.

Heather Rank: 341

Origin: Middle English
Meaning: A flowering plant
Alternate Spellings: Heathar, Hethar, Hether
Gender Variations: Heath, Heaton
Similar Names: Heath, Heatha, Heatherly, Heathshia, Heaven, Heavenly, Hester
Namesake: Heather Graham (actress)
➡ A flower and nature name associated with the variety of small shrubs with pink or white flowers that usually grow in rocky areas. Derived from the Middle English word *hather*, it debuted on the chart in 1935 when British actress Heather Angel became known as an U.S. film star. The name's most famous bearer is actress Heather Locklear, who has inspired the name since the 1980s.

Heaven Rank: 253

Origin: English
Meaning: Paradise
Alternate Spellings: Heavan, Heavin, Heavon, Heavyn, Heavynne, Hevean, Heven, Hevin
Gender Variations: Haven, Hervin
Similar Names: Deven, Heather, Heavenley, Helen, Helena, Nevaeh, Raven
➡ A place name from the vocabulary word often described by Christians as the holiest possible place where sin is absent. It debuted on the chart in 1990 as a given name for girls and climbed to its current peak among the top 300 names during the era of two popular television series: *Highway to Heaven*, airing from 1984 to 1989, and *7th Heaven* from 1996 to 2007. The name has also been the subject of songs, films, and novels.

Heidi Rank: 295

Origin: German
Meaning: Sweet, noble
Alternate Spellings: Haidee, Heide, Heidey, Heidie, Heidy, Hidee, Hidey, Hidie, Hiedi, Hydee
Gender Variations: Heikki, Hien, Hiran, Hiten
Similar Names: Hedda, Hedi, Heida, Heidiann, Heidilin, Heike, Heili
➡ The short form of Adelaide or Adelheid that became a famous literary name for the Swiss Alps girl in Johanna Spyri's 1880 well-loved children's novel, *Heidi*. The book was adapted into a 1937 film starring child-actress Shirley Temple in the title role, which led to its debut on the chart in 1939. Heidi Klum, the German supermodel and actress, is a famous bearer.

Helen Rank: 343

Origin: Greek
Meaning: Torch
Alternate Spellings: Helan, Helean, Helenh, Helin, Hellan, Hellen, Hellon, Hellyn, Helon, Helyn
Gender Variations: Elvan, Elin, Elwin, Helden
Nickname: Heli
Similar Names: Ailene, Alanna, Elayne, Eleanor, Eleni, Ella, Ellen, Helena, Hellenor, Leonora
Namesakes: Helena Bonham-Carter (British actress), Helen Gurley Brown (author/publisher), Helen Mirren (British actress)
➡ From the Greek word, *helene* that's known in Greek mythology for Zeus' mortal daughter, Helen of Troy, whose abduction led to the Trojan War. Saint Helena was the mother of Constantine the Great, whose purity allowed her to discover the True Cross. Prominently known for Helen Keller, the author and educator who became blind and deaf at the age of 19 months, and actress Helen Hayes, often referred to as the First Lady of the American Theatre. More recently associated with Helen Hunt, best-known for her role on the television sitcom *Mad About You*, and Australian pop singer Helen Reddy, one of the most successful female recording artists of the 1970s.

131

Helena
Rank: 508

Origin: Greek
Meaning: Torch
Alternate Spellings:
Hellena, Helenna, Helana
Gender Variation: Henry
Nickname: Helen
Similar Names: Helene, Helga, Heloise,
Henrietta, Henriette
➡ The Latin form of Helen that first became
popular in northern Europe. The name
peaked prior to the turn of the 20th century.
Danish supermodel Helena Christensen and
British actress Helena Bonham Carter are
famous bearers of the name.

Hillary
Rank: 982

Origin: Greek/Latin
Meaning: Filled with
pleasure
Alternate Spellings: Hilary,
Hillery
Gender Variations: Hilarius, Hilary
Nicknames: Hilly
Similar Names: Hila, Hilaria, Hilda, Hildegard
Namesakes: Hilary Duff (actress/singer),
Hilary Swank (actress)
➡ A variation of Hilary that is the medieval
form of Hilarius or Hilaria. A common boy's
name until 1931, it debuted for girls in 1963
and peaked in 1992 at No. 131. Former first
lady and junior senator from New York,
Hillary Rodham Clinton, is a famous bearer
of the name.

Holly
Rank: 346

Origin: Old English
Meaning: Holly tree
Alternate Spellings: Holea,
Holee, Holey, Holleah,
Hollee, Holleigh, Holley, Holli, Hollie, Hollye
Gender Variations: Holland, Hollis
Nickname: Hol
Similar Names: Hally, Holeen, Holissa,
Holland, Hollis, Hollyann, Hollyanna, Hollyn
Namesake: Holly Marie Combs (actress)
➡ Associated with the name of a tree,
ultimately derived from the Old English word
holen first used in the early 20th century.
Often given to daughters born on or near
Christmas. Influenced early on by Holly
Golightly, the heroine in the 1961 film
Breakfast at Tiffany's, played by famed
actress Audrey Hepburn. Holly Hobbie,
a writer and illustrator born in 1944, became
famous for her children's books but even
more so for her 1974 Holly Hobbie licensed
character and rag dolls that carried the name
to its peak position in 1979, then redesigned
by Mattel as *Holly Hobbie and Friends* in
2006. The name was also given to well-known
actress Holly Hunter, who popularized the
name from the 1980s through the 2000s.

Hope
Rank: 200

Origin: Old English
Meaning: Expectation,
belief
Gender Variations: Holton,
Hoyle
Similar Names: Happy, Holle, Honesty,
Honey, Honor, Verity
➡ Taken from the vocabulary word derived
from "hopian" that means to desire with
anticipation and represents one of three
biblical qualities, along with faith and charity,
found in the New Testament. The name was
first commonly used by the Puritans and
favored for triplets who are given all three
names. Actress Hope Lange was a notable
bearer of the name who came to fame during
the 1950s in her first two film roles in *Bus
Stop* and *Peyton Place*.

Iliana
Rank: 727

Origin: Greek
Meaning: Trojan
Alternate Spellings: Ileana,
Ileanna, Illiana
Gender Variation: Ilan
Nicknames: Ilia, Ana
Similar Names: Ilana, Ilayne, Ileanne, Ilene,
Iloana, Ilone, Iolana, Iolyn
➡ A variation of Ilion, which is another name
for the ancient city of Troy. This is one of the
many names ending in "ana" and "ian" that
has become fashionable with parents.

Imani
Rank: 409

Origin: African
Meaning: Faith
Gender Variation: Immanuel
Similar Names: Iliana, Iman,
Iolani, Ivana, Iyana
➡ A variation of Iman that means "faith" in
Swahili. Already peaked during its 15-year-
plus placement on the popularity chart but
still listed among the top 500.

India　　Rank: 568

Origin: English
Meaning: From India
Alternate Spelling: Indya
Gender Variation: Indiana
Similar Names: America, Brooklyn, Ireland, London

➡ A geographical name for the country located in southern Asia that's derived from the Indus River. The name has been used since the 19th century and peaked in 2001 at No. 298. Sometimes used because of a family link with the country. Also a literary name used by Margaret Mitchell for *Gone with the Wind* character India Wilkes.

Ingrid　　Rank: 619

Origin: Scandinavian
Meaning: Fair, beautiful
Gender Variation: Ingemar
Nickname: Inge
Similar Names: Inga, Inger, Ingmar, Inigo

➡ An Old Norse personal name combining the name of the fertility god "Ing" combined with the suffix for "beautiful." A royal name for Princess Ingrid of Sweden, the queen consort of King Frederik IX of Denmark. It's best-known for three-time Academy Award-winning Swedish actress Ingrid Bergman, who is remembered for her role in the 1942 classic film *Casablanca*. Actress Isabella Rossellini named her daughter Elettra Ingrid after her famous mother.

Irene　　Rank: 593

Origin: Greek
Meaning: Peace
Alternate Spellings: Eireen, Eirene, Ireen, Irine
Gender Variations: Ira, Iram
Nicknames: Rena, Rene, Renie
Similar Names: Arina, Careen, Irayna, Irena, Renee, Salena
Namesakes: Irene Cara (singer/songwriter/actress), Irene Dunne (actress)

➡ The name of the Greek goddess of peace, a 4th-century saint who was martyred with her two sisters in Macedonia, and an 8th- century Byzantine empress who became the first woman to rule an empire. Formerly spelled "Irenee" or "Irenie" by the Greeks who pronounced the name with three syllables. It became popular during the 19th century and peaked in 1918 and 1919 before falling to its current ranking.

Iris　　Rank: 369

Origin: Greek
Meaning: Rainbow
Alternate Spellings: Iriss, Irisse, Irys, Iryse, Irysse
Gender Variations: Iric, Iren, Irish
Similar Names: Ariza, Iria, Iridiana, Iridianny, Irina, Irisa, Irisha, Irita, Orchid, Rainbow

➡ Associated with the messenger-goddess in Greek mythology who made deliveries for Olympus by riding rainbows between heaven and earth. Also known as a flower name and a vocabulary word for the colored part of the eye. It moved into the top 400 on the chart influenced by the 1998 song "Iris", by alternative rock band the Goo Goo Dolls.

Isabel　　Rank: 87

Origin: Hebrew
Meaning: God is my oath
Alternate Spellings: Isabele, Isabell, Isabelle, Isobel, Isobelle, Izabele, Izabelle
Gender Variation: Isandro
Nicknames: Izzy, Sabel
Similar Names: Eliza, Ellie, Ilsa, Isabella, Libby, Liesa, Liesel, Lisette
Namesake: Isabelle Adjani (French actress)

➡ The Portuguese and Spanish form of Elizabeth. A literary name for the heroine in the Henry James novel *Portrait of a Lady*, published in 1881. The name has been in popular use since before the turn of the 20th century and hit its peak in 2003 at No. 83.

Isabella　　Rank: 4

Origin: Hebrew
Meaning: Devoted to God
Alternate Spelling: Isabela, Isebella, Izabela, Izabella
Gender Variations: Elian, Isidoro
Nicknames: Bella, Belle, Isa, Izzie, Sabella
Similar Names: Elizabeth, Elise, Eliza, Elsa, Isabel, Isbel, Isidora
Namesake: Queen Isabella of Spain

➡ The Italian form of Elizabeth that was brought into France in the early Middle Ages and then carried into England. The name became popular among royalty and was best-known for Isabella of France who married King Edward II of England and became the queen consort during the 14th century. Italian actress and model Isabella Rossellini is a recent namesake.

Isis

Rank: 566

Origin: Egyptian
Meaning: Throne
Gender Variation: Isidoro
Nickname: Issy
Similar Names: Isidora, Isidore, Isla, Ismaela, Isolde

⇨ One of the most powerful goddesses in Egyptian mythology, she was the wife of the god Osiris and the mother of Horus. The Egyptians worshipped her as the perfect wife and mother. The name is derived from the Greek form of the Egyptian Aset. It's been listed among the top names since 1994.

Itzel

Rank: 378

Origin: Mayan
Meaning: Rainbow lady
Alternate Spellings: Itcel, Itchel, Itesel, Itsel, Itssel, Itzell, Ixchel
Gender Variations: Itzak, Itzjac, Itztli
Nickname: Itz
Similar Names: Itza, Itzallana, Itzayana

⇨ Possibly a variant of Ixchel, the Mayan goddess of the earth, the moon, and medicine. The name debuted on the chart in 1993, moving up to its current ranking among the top 400 because of its trendy "z" spelling.

Ivy

Rank: 334

Origin: Old English
Meaning: Ivy
Alternate Spellings: Ivee, Ivey, Ivie, Ivye, Ivyie
Gender Variations: Iv, Iva, Ivan
Nickname: Iv
Similar Names: Ava, Ave, Eva, Eve, Iva, Ivalyn, Ivia, Ivianna, Ivree, Ivyanne

⇨ A nature name for the evergreen climbing plant with small yellow flowers ultimately derived from the Old English *ifig*. Used as a girl's given name since the 1800s and peaked prior to the turn of the 20th century.

Jacey

Rank: 747

Origin: American
Alternate Spellings: Jaci, Jacie, Jaycee, J. C.
Gender Variations: Jack, Jaden, Jalen
Similar Names: Jacelyn, Jacinda, Jacine, Jackie, Jade, Jael, Jaina, Jala, Jalena, Jalila

⇨ An invented name phonetically based on the initials J. C. or possibly the short form of Jacinda.

Jacqueline

Rank: 118

Origin: Hebrew
Meaning: Holder of the heel
Alternate Spellings: Jacalynn, Jackelyn, Jacklynne, Jaclyn, Jacqualine, Jacqualyn, Jacquelyn, Jaculine, Jaklyn, Jaqueline
Gender Variations: Jack, Jackson
Nicknames: Jacquel, Jacqui
Similar Names: Jacketta, Jacquella, Jacquelle, Jacquenetta, Jacquette, Jacquine, Jaeyln, Jakayla

⇨ Feminine form of Jacques, the French version of James and Jacob. Existed on the popularity chart since the turn of the 19th century but peaked at No. 37 in 1961 and 1964 due to first lady Jacqueline "Jackie" Bouvier Kennedy. Actress and clothing designer Jaclyn Smith and actress Jacqueline Bisset helped keep the momentum going for the name's top 100 ranking during the 1960s until 2003.

Jada

Rank: 93

Origin: Hebrew
Meaning: Wise
Alternate Spellings: Jaeda, Jaida, Jayda
Gender Variation: Jaden
Similar Names: Jade, Jadeana, Jaden, Jaelyn, Jakayla, Jaelyn

⇨ A trendy variation of Jade that uses the popular "a" ending. The name peaked in 2002 at No. 86 but has stayed among the top 100 names. Influenced by actress and singer Jada Pinkett Smith, the wife of actor Will Smith, whose career started with a role on the television sitcom *A Different World*. Originated as a Hebrew name for a minor male character in the Bible.

Jade

Rank: 111

Origin: Spanish
Meaning: Jade
Alternate Spellings: Jaide, Jayde
Gender Variations: Jad, Jadaryl, Jaden, Jader, Jadot
Nickname: Jaye
Similar Names: Jada, Jadeana, Jadee, Jaden, Jadira, Jadra, Jadrienne, Jaydra, Zhade

➡ Associated with a precious stone that is often used in carvings and probably derived from *ijada* meaning "stone of the colic." A jewel name that debuted on the popularity chart for girls in 1975, shortly after the birth of singer Mick Jagger's daughter Jade in 1971. Peaked in 2002 as one of the most unique names for girls, even though sometimes given to boys.

Jaelyn
Rank: 442

Origin: American
Meaning: Bird of light
Alternate Spellings: Jaelynn, Jailyn, Jalyn, Jalynn, Jaylin, Jaylinn, Jaylynn
Gender Variation: Jalen
Nicknames: Jae, Lyn
Similar Names: Jacelyn, Jadyn, Jaida, Jakayla, Jaliyah, Jaylee, Jaylene, Jazlyn, Joellyn, Joslin
➡ A contemporary blend of the late 1990s that uses "Jae" and "lyn" and currently ranks as the most popular form with its trendy "lyn" ending. A good choice for parents looking for a variety of spelling options.

Jakayla
Rank: 730

Origin: American
Gender Variation: Jake
Nickname: Kayla
Similar Names: Jadyn, Jailyn, Jaliyah, Makayla
➡ A created name inspired by the popular Makayla that parents are drawn to because of it's "y" spelling. The name came into regular use in 1999.

Jaliyah
Rank: 762

Origin: American
Alternate Spellings: Jalia, Jaliah, Jaliya
Gender Variations: Jaelen, Jamaal
Similar Names: Aaliyah, Jael, Jalani, Jalila, Jaliyah, Kaliyah, Maliyah, Taliyah
➡ A creative blend that adds the prefix "Ja" to the top 100 name "Aliyah"; used by parents since 2002.

Jamie
Rank: 242

Origin: Hebrew/Latin
Meaning: Supplanter
Alternate Spellings: Jaime, Jaimee, Jaimey, Jaimi, Jaimie, Jaimy, Jamee, Jamey, Jami, Jaymee
Gender Variations: James, Jamie, Jamiel
Nickname: Jae
Similar Names: Amie, Emmie, Jamya, Jamyla, Jamyra, Janee, Jemmie
Namesake: Jamie Salé (Olympic figure skater)
➡ Feminine form of James that dramatically peaked on the chart in the late 1970s due to award-winning television and film actress Jamie Lee Curtis Also given to actress and singer Jamie Lynn Marie Spears, the younger sister of pop singer Britney Spears and star of the current Disney series *Zoey 101*. Trendy as a combination name such as Jamielee or Jamielynn, for variations spelled with a hyphen like Jamie-Marie or Jamie-Rae, or simply because of its preferred long "ee" sound.

Jamya
Rank: 737

Origin: American
Alternate Spelling: Jamia
Gender Variations: James, Jamie
Similar Names: Jaina, Jaliyah, Jamie, Jana, Janae, Janiah
➡ A modern created name using a blend of "jam" with the "ya" ending that was first introduced in 2001 and has climbed to its current standing. A popular choice among African-American families.

Janae
Rank: 679

Origin: Hebrew
Meaning: God is gracious
Alternate Spellings: Janay, Janaye, Jeanay, Jenae, Jenay, Jenee, Jennae, Jennay
Nickname: Jan
Similar Names: Jana, Jane, Janel, Janene, Janet, Jayna, Jaynie
➡ Great for parents looking for a new twist on a classic name. A contemporary form of Jane with the feminine "ae" ending that's been listed among the top names since 1976.

Jane   Rank: 478

Origin: Hebrew
Meaning: God is gracious
Alternate Spellings: Jaine, Jayne
Gender Variations: John
Nickname: Janey
Similar Names: Jan, Jana, Janeen, Janelle, Janet, Janetta, Janice, Janis, Jean, Jenna
Namesakes: Jane Austen (English novelist), Jane Pauley (television host)
⇨ The Old French feminine form of Johannes. An enduring name that has been in and out of the top 100 since the 19th century, fading in recent years and currently among the top 500. Historically associated with Lady Jane Grey, the granddaughter of King Henry VII, who was proclaimed queen of England for nine days. Also considered a literary name for the main character in Charlotte Bronte's 19th-century novel *Jane Eyre*. Popular among actresses including Jane Russell, Jane Fonda, and Jane Seymour. Often combined or blended with other elements such as Sarah-Jane and Janeane.

Janelle   Rank: 390

Origin: Hebrew
Meaning: God is gracious
Alternate Spellings: Janel, Janell, Jannelle, Jenell, Jenelle
Gender Variations: Jared, Jarrett
Nicknames: Jan, Nell
Similar Names: Janae, Jane, Janeeta, Janessa, Janice, Janine, Jeanelle
⇨ A pet form of Jane that became the forerunner of similar names that use the popular "elle" ending such as Danielle and Jonelle. First landed on the chart in 1931 and peaked during the late 1970s.

Janessa   Rank: 594

Origin: Hebrew
Meaning: God is gracious
Alternate Spellings: Janesa, Jannessa
Gender Variations: Jan, Janos
Nickname: Jan
Similar Names: Janae, Janella, Janene, Janesse, Janetta, Janice, Janissa
⇨ An elaborate form of Jane with the feminine "ssa" ending that's also found in names such as Alissa, Marissa, and Vanessa.

Janet   Rank: 562

Origin: Hebrew
Meaning: God is gracious
Alternate Spelling: Janette
Gender Variation: Jan
Nickname: Jan
Similar Names: Jana, Jane, Janelle, Janessa, Janetta, Janine
Namesakes: Janet Evanovich (writer), Janet Evans (Olympic swimmer), Janet Leigh (actress), Janet Reno (former attorney general)
⇨ A pet form of Jane that originated as Janeta. Influenced by actress Janet Gaynor in 1928, who became the first recipient of the Academy Award for Best Actress, which led to the name's first appearance among the top 100. Pop singer Janet Jackson is a current bearer of the name.

Janice   Rank: 994

Origin: Hebrew
Meaning: God is gracious
Alternate Spellings: Janis, Janiss, Jannice, Janyce
Gender Variation: Jan
Similar Names: Jana, Jancis, Jane, Janessa, Janette, Janina, Janine, Janita
Namesake: Janice Dickinson (model/reality TV star)
⇨ A blend of the name "Jane" with the suffix "ice" that was possibly created by Paul Leicester Ford for a character in his 19th-century novel *Janice Meredith*. Singer Janis Joplin popularized a form of the name during the 1960s and 1970s. Also used for a fictional character on the TV series *The Sopranos* and a recurring character on the sitcom *Friends*.

Janiya   Rank: 386

Origin: Hebrew
Meaning: Grace of God
Alternate Spellings: Jania, Janiah, Janiyah, Jinia, Jinya
Gender Variations: Jan, Janile, Janina
Nickname: Jan
Similar Names: Aniyah, Dania, Hania, Jaliyah, Jamia, Janina, Rania, Saniya, Shaniya, Taniya
⇨ A creative variation of the name Aniya, which derives from Anya and may also be a form of Jane with a similar meaning, "God is gracious." It peaked in 2004, the same year Aniyah moved up into the top 300, and is considered trendy for its "y" spelling and feminine "a" ending.

Jasmine　Rank: 29
Origin: Persian
Meaning: Flower in the olive family
Alternate Spellings: Jasmin, Jasmyn, Jasmyne, Jassmine, Jazmin, Jazmine, Jazmyn, Jazzmyn
Gender Variations: Jareth, Jason
Similar Names: Jessamine, Yasmin, Yasmina
Namesakes: Jasmine Guy (actress/singer), Jasmine Trias (*American Idol* finalist)
➡ Derived from Yasmin, which is the vocabulary word for a climbing shrub with sweet-scented white or yellow flowers. Princess Jasmin, the fictional character from the three Disney animated films based on *Aladdin and the Magic Lamp*, comes to mind.

Jayden　Rank: 203
Origin: Hebrew
Meaning: God has heard
Alternate Spellings: Jaden, Jadon, Jadyn, Jaeden, Jaedon, Jaiden, Jaidon, Jaidyn, Jaydn, Jaydon
Gender Variations: Jaden, Jadon, Jadyn, Jayden
Nicknames: Jae, Jayde
Similar Names: Jadeann, Jayanna, Jayda, Jaydee, Jayla, Jaylen, Jayran, Jazlyn
➡ Possibly a form of Jadon, a biblical figure in the Old Testament, or derived from jade, the name of a precious stone. A more common name for boys but increasing in popularity for girls with its debut on the chart in 1998. The name features three different spelling forms charted among the top 300, with this variation rising above them all using the trendy "y" in the middle of the name.

Jayla　Rank: 99
Origin: Latin
Meaning: Happy
Alternate Spellings: Jaylaa, Jaylah, Jayleah
Gender Variations: Jay, Jaylon, Jaymie, Jayryl
Nicknames: Jay
Similar Names: Gayla, Jaya, Jayda, Jaylan, Jaylia, Jaylie, Jaymee, Jayna, Kayla
➡ A created name combining "Jay" with the popular suffix "la" that debuted on the chart in 1995 and peaked in popularity in 2006. It's favored by parents for its "y" spelling and "a" ending.

Jaylee　Rank: 818
Origin: American
Alternate Spelling: Jayleigh
Gender Variation: Jaylen
Nicknames: Jay, Lee
Similar Names: Jada, Jade, Jadyn, Jayla, Jayleen, Jaelyn, Jaliyah
➡ A modern combination of the names "Jay" and "Lee" that's risen in popularity for girls since 2004, incorporating the trendy "y" in the middle spelling.

Jaylene　Rank: 912
Origin: American
Alternate Spelling: Jayleen, Jaline
Gender Variations: Jaydon, Jaylen, Jayson
Nickname: Jay
Similar Names: Jailyn, Jayla, Jaylee, Jelena, Jillian, Jolene, Juliana, Juliane
➡ A modern blended name using the popular prefix "Jay" with "lene" that's been in popular use since 1999.

Jazlyn　Rank: 533
Origin: American
Alternate Spellings: Jaslyn, Jaslynn, Jazlynn, Jazzlyn
Gender Variation: Jasper
Similar Names: Jaklyn, Jazmyn, Jozlyn
➡ A modern invented name with a blend of "jaz" and the feminine "lyn" ending that came along in 1996, possibly influenced by Jasmine or Joslyn.

Jenna　Rank: 88
Origin: Latin
Meaning: Gracious, fair spirit
Alternate Spellings: Genna, Jena, Jennah
Gender Variation: Gene
Nicknames: Jen, Jeni
Similar Names: Jeana, Jenae, Jenelle, Jenessa, Jennie
Namesake: Jenna Elfman (actress)
➡ The Latinate form of Jenny that debuted on the popularity chart in 1971 and climbed into the top 100 in 1984. Influenced by Priscilla Presley from 1983 to 1988 when she played the role of Jenna Wade on the prime-time television drama *Dallas*. The name is occasionally used for blends such as Jennalyn, Jennabel, and Jennalee.

Jennifer Rank: 51

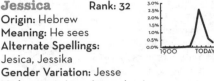

Origin: Welsh
Meaning: Fair one
Alternate Spellings:
Genifer, Geniffer, Jenefer, Jenifer
Gender Variations: Jenkin, Jenson
Nicknames: Jen, Jenny
Similar Names: Gaynor, Genevieve, Guinevere, Jenelle, Jenessa, Jennica, Jenna
Namesakes: Jennifer Connelly (actress), Jennifer Garner (actress), Jennifer Lopez (singer/actress), Jennifer Love Hewitt (actress)
➡ A former No. 1 name during the 1970s and 1980s and listed among the top 100 since 1956. Originated from Guinevere who was the wife of Arthur, the legendary king of Britain. Gained popularity as a literary name in George Bernard Shaw's 1906 play, *The Doctor's Dilemma*. Several actresses have kept the name in front of the public throughout the years, including Jennifer Jones who won several coveted roles during the 1940s and 1950s, Jennifer O'Neill who starred in the 1971 blockbuster film *Summer of '42*, and more recently Jennifer Aniston who played Rachel Green on the hit television series *Friends*.

Jenny Rank: 475

Origin: Welsh
Meaning: White wave
Alternate Spellings: Genny, Jenney, Jenni, Jennie
Gender Variation: Jenkin
Nickname: Jen
Similar Names: Jena, Jenae, Jenelle, Jenilee, Jenine, Jenise, Jennetta, Jennica, Jennifer, Jennis
Namesakes: *Jennie Gerhardt* (novel by Theodore Dreiser), Jenny Fields (*The World According to Garp* character), Jenny Thompson (Olympic swimmer)
➡ The Scottish pet form of Jane or Janet, and more recently the short form of Jennifer. Used independently since the 19th century when Swedish-born opera singer Jenny Lind became internationally known to audiences. The name received a boost in 1970 when Ali MacGraw appeared in the film that was based on the best-selling novel *Love Story* in the role of Jenny Cavalleri. Associated today with model and actress Jenny McCarthy.

Jessica Rank: 32

Origin: Hebrew
Meaning: He sees
Alternate Spellings: Jesica, Jessika
Gender Variation: Jesse
Nicknames: Jess, Jessa, Jessie
Similar Names: Jennica, Jessalyn, Jessamine
Namesakes: Jessica Alba (actress), Jessica Andrews (singer), Jessica Biel (actress), Jessica Capshaw (actress), Jessica Dube (Canadian figure skater), Jessica Fletcher (*Murder She Wrote* character), Jessica Mitford (British writer), Jessica Sierra (*American Idol* finalist), Jessica Simpson (singer/actress)
➡ A form of the Old Testament name Iscah or Jesca found in early translations of the Bible. Shakespeare changed the name to Jessica and used it for a young Jewish girl in his play *The Merchant of Venice*. The name became a favorite among Jewish families. It held the No. 1 position nine times during the 1980s and 1990s, influenced by award-winning actresses Jessica Tandy and Jessica Lange. A top 20 name in several countries besides the U.S.

Jessie Rank: 558

Origin: Hebrew
Meaning: He sees
Alternate Spellings: Jessi, Jessy, Jessye
Gender Variations: Jesse, Jessie
Nickname: Jess
Similar Names: Jessa, Jessalyn, Jessamae, Jessana, Jessandra, Jessica, Jesslyn
Namesake: Jessye Norman (opera singer)
➡ The short form of Jessica that's also used in Scotland as a pet form of Jean and diminutive of Janet. The name recently dropped out of the top 500 for girls. Jesse is the most common spelling for boys.

Jewel Rank: 861

Origin: Old French
Meaning: Gemstone
Alternate Spellings: Jewell, Jewelle
Gender Variation: Joel
Similar Names: Jill, Jillian, Jiselle, Jolie, Juliana, Julianne, Julie
➡ A vocabulary word name derived from *jouel* referring to a precious stone. It became

fashionable during the 19th century along with other gemstone names, fading during the early 1970s, and reappearing in 1997. It was popularized by singer and songwriter Jewel Kilcher, known simply by her first name, whose 1995 debut album stayed on the Billboard 200 for an impressive two years.

Jillian
Rank: 174

Origin: Latin
Meaning: Youthful
Alternate Spellings: Gilian, Gillian, Gillyan, Jilian, Jiliann, Jilianne, Jilliann, Jillion, Jilliyn
Gender Variations: Giuliano, Julian, Julius
Nicknames: Gili, Jill
Similar Names: Elliana, Iliana, Leilani, Lilianna, Lillian, Jilianna, Jilisa, Jillana, Jillayne, Jillissa
➡ Variation of Gillian and the feminine form of Julian, it first appeared on the chart in 1976 and moved up almost 400 spots that same year. Peaked in 1982 during its long stay in the top 200 from 1978 to 2006, partially due to actress Ann Jillian, who is best known for the early 1980s television sitcom *It's a Living*. Also influenced by actress Jillian Armenante, famous for her role on the 1995 to 2005 television show *Judging Amy*. Popular actress Jill "Jillian" Hennessy from *Law & Order* and *Crossing Jordan* also comes to mind.

Jimena
Rank: 472

Origin: Hebrew/American
Meaning: Listening
Alternate Spellings: Jemena, Jemenah, Jimenah, Jimina, Jiminah
Gender Variations: Jimenez, Simon
Nickname: Jimi
Similar Names: Amena, Jimae, Jimella, Jimisha, Jimiyah, Kimana, Siena, Simmona, Ximena
➡ A variation of Ximena and also the U.S. form of Jimi derived from James. Appeared on the chart in 2001, peaking in 2005, as did its variation Ximena. However not as popular as the spelling with an "x." Contributing to the awareness of the name is Mexican pop singer Jimena who released her first album in 2003 entitled *Jimena*, followed by two more successful albums in 2005 and 2006.

Joanna
Rank: 256

Origin: Hebrew
Meaning: God is gracious
Alternate Spellings: Joahnna, Joana, Joannah, Joeanna, Johannah
Gender Variations: Joanel, Jonah, John
Nicknames: Jo, Joan
Similar Names: Joananna, Joandra, Joanelle, Joann, Joannanette, Joannie, Jolanda, Josann, Jovannah
➡ The latinized form of Ioanna and the feminine form of Ioannes that is ultimately derived from John. The name peaked on the chart in 1984 and 1985 during the fame of film and television actress Joanna Cassidy. A popular name for girls because of its trendy "a" ending and its classic blend of two independent names, "Jo" and "Anna."

Jocelyn
Rank: 73

Origin: Old German
Meaning: Happy, joyful
Alternate Spellings: Jocelin, Joceline, Jocelyne, Josceline, Joscelyn, Joselin, Joselyn, Joslyn, Josselyn, Jossline
Gender Variations: Joshua, Josiah
Nickname: Joss
Similar Names: Jolene, Josephine, Joyce, Joye
Namesake: Jocelyn Brown (singer)
➡ Originated from the Germanic tribe the Gauts, which led to its use as a boy's given name and an English surname. It was possibly linked with Joyce when parents first began using it for girls during the early 20th century. The name's current popularity may be attributed to its fashionable "y" in the suffix.

Johanna
Rank: 376

Origin: Hebrew
Meaning: God is gracious
Alternate Spellings: Johana, Johannah
Gender Variations: Johan, Johannes, John, Johnnie
Nicknames: Hanna, Jo
Similar Names: Joan, Joanna, Joanne, Johanne, Johnna, Johnnie, Jonelle
➡ The Latin feminine form of Johannes or the Icelandic feminine form of John. The name peaked prior to the turn of the 20th century but is still listed among the top 400.

Jolie   Rank: 614

Origin: French
Meaning: Pretty
Alternate Spellings: Jolee, Joleigh, Joley, Joli, Joly
Gender Variation: Joel
Similar Names: Joelle, Joely, Jolan, Joliet, Jolietta, Joline, Julie

⇨ The feminine form of the adjective *joli* that possibly derives from the Old Norse *jul* meaning "yule." Listed on the popularity chart from 1968 to 1975, the name suddenly faded and reappeared in 2000, influenced by actress and U.N. Goodwill Ambassador Angelina Jolie, who was born Angelina Jolie Voight.

Jordan   Rank: 97

Origin: Hebrew
Meaning: To flow down
Alternate Spellings: Jordann, Jordanne, Jorden, Jordin, Jordon, Jordyn
Gender Variations: Jonah, Joseph
Nickname: Jori
Similar Names: Georgia, Jordana, Jordane, Joselyn

⇨ A biblical name for the river in Palestine where Christ was baptized by John the Baptist. The name was traditionally given to either a male or female child who had been baptized in holy water brought from this famed river. It's still used today as a unisex name and ranks among the top 100 for both boys and girls.

Josephine   Rank: 221

Origin: Hebrew
Meaning: God will increase
Alternate Spellings: Josaffine, Josaphine, Josefine, Josephene, Josephin, Josephyn, Josephyne, Jozafine, Jozefine, Jozephine
Gender Variations: Joseph, Josey
Nicknames: Josee, Sefa
Similar Names: Josafata, Josepha, Josephina, Josette, Jozetta

⇨ The French feminine form of Joseph that was among the top 100 girls' names for more than 60 consecutive years. One notable bearer of this name was the first wife of Napoleon Bonaparte in 1796. It is also the literary name for Josephine March in Louisa May Alcott's famous 1868 novel, *Little Women*, that influenced its high ranking at the time. Peaked in 1916 and 1917 during the era of Academy Award- and Golden Globe-winning actress Josephine Hull, most remembered for her long-standing fame on stage before the release of her popular films, such as *Arsenic and Old Lace* in 1944 and *Harvey* in 1950.

Josie   Rank: 291

Origin: Hebrew
Meaning: God will add
Alternate Spellings: Josee, Josey, Josi, Josy, Jozee, Jozey, Jozi, Jozie, Jozy
Gender Variations: Jose, Josemar, Joseph
Nickname: Jos
Similar Names: Jacie, Jessie, Joselyn, Josephine, Josette, Josianne, Josina, Joyse, Jozette

⇨ The pet form of Josephine that peaked prior to the turn of the century and seems to be making a comeback because of its long "ee" sound and optional spelling with a "z." Known during the 1990s for actress Josie Bissett, who played the role of Jane Andrews Mancini on the television series *Melrose Place*. The name was also influenced when supermodel Josie Maran appeared in three consecutive issues of the *Sports Illustrated Swimsuit Issue* between 2000 and 2002. A popular combination and blended name such as Joselyn or Josette, or Josieann.

Journey   Rank: 822

Origin: Latin
Meaning: Day's journey
Gender Variations: Jeremy, Joran
Similar Names: Jorene, Jorey, Justice

⇨ A vocabulary word that means "to travel from one place to another"; used as a girl's given name since 1999.

Joy   Rank: 507

Origin: Latin
Meaning: To rejoice
Alternate Spellings: Joi, Joie, Joye
Gender Variation: Joss
Similar Names: Joya, Joyann, Joyce, Joyelle, Joyita
Namesakes: Joy Adamson (author), Joy Behar (comedian/television co-host)

⇨ The vocabulary word that means "a state of happiness" derived from the Anglo-French *joie* and the Latin *gaudia*. Widely used by the Puritans during the 17th century who felt it was their duty to be "joyful in the Lord." The name is given by parents today as a reflection of happiness in their child's birth or to wish her a happy life, peaking during the mid-1970s.

Joyce   Rank: 831

Origin: Latin
Meaning: Joy
Alternate Spellings: Joice, Joyse
Gender Variation: Joss
Nickname: Joy
Similar Names: Josie, Joyceanne, Joycelyn, Joselyn, Joyita, Joyous
Namesakes: Joyce Carol Oates (author), Joyce DeWitt (actress)
➡ Derived from the male personal name *Josce* that was ultimately taken from *Iodoc* that was used by a 7th-century Breton saint. The surname may have originated from *Judocus* and the feminine form may have gotten its start from *Jocosa*. It was considered a literary name during the 19th century and hit its stride with parents from the mid-1920s to the mid-1960s when it ranked among the top 100. Family psychologist and advice columnist Dr. Joyce Brothers is a famous bearer of the name.

Judith   Rank: 577

Origin: Hebrew
Meaning: Woman from Judea
Alternate Spellings: Judithe, Judyth, Judythe
Gender Variations: Judge, Jules
Nickname: Judi
Similar Names: Jodelle, Jodene, Jody, Judit, Judita, Juditha
Namesakes: Dame Judith Anderson (Australian actress), Judit Polgar (chess champion), Judith Crist (film critic), Judith Krantz (novelist), Judith Viorst (writer), Judy Blume (author), Judy Garland (actress/singer)
➡ A biblical name for one of the wives of Esau. Also the name of a Jewish widow who saved her people from an invading Assyrian army as related in the book of Judith in the Apocrypha. The name is derived from "Yehudit" that refers to the ancient region in Israel called Judea. Popular among Jewish families, it peaked during the 1940s and is starting to make a comeback with other biblical names.

Julia   Rank: 31

Origin: Latin
Meaning: Youthful
Alternate Spellings: Giulia, Julija, Jullia
Gender Variations: Jules, Julian
Similar Names: Jewel, Jilian, Jill, Jilly, Julian, Juliana, Julie
Namesakes: *Being Julia* (2004 film), *Julia* (Beatles song), *Julia* (Eurythmics song), Julia Alvarez (poet/novelist), Julia Child (chef), Julia Duffy (actress), Julia Louis-Dreyfus (actress), Julia Ormond (British actress), Julia Stiles (actress)
➡ The feminine form of the Roman family name Julius. A Christian woman mentioned in the Bible. A literary name for a character in Shakespeare's play *The Two Gentlemen of Verona*. Peaked prior to the turn of the 20th century possibly influenced by abolitionist and poet Julia Ward Howe, the author of the "Battle Hymn of the Republic," first published in 1862. Surged in popularity during the 1990s, inspired by film actress Julia Roberts, born Julie Fiona Roberts.

Juliana   Rank: 162

Origin: Latin
Meaning: Youthful
Alternate Spellings: Juleana, Julianna, Julieanna, Jullianna
Gender Variations: Juliano, Julius, Julyan
Nickname: Juel
Similar Names: Judyanna, Julee, Julia, Julian, Julianne, Yuliana
➡ Feminine form of Julianus, ultimately derived from Roman name Julius. This name was given to many saints, princesses, and essential women, such as 14th-century mystic and author Juliana of Norwich and 1948 to 1980 Queen Juliana of the Netherlands. Ranked in the top 100 on the chart between 1994 and 2001, peaking in 1997, most likely because of singer Juliana Hatfield who gained favor from parents by being a positive role model for preteen and teenage girls and for addressing serious issues faced by young women in her songs. Sometimes spelled separately such as Julie Anna or hyphenated such as Juli-Anna.

Julianne   Rank: 884

Origin: Latin
Meaning: Youthful
Alternate Spellings:
Julian, Juliane, Julienne
Gender Variations: Julian, Julio, Julius
Nicknames: Anne, Julie
Similar Names: Jillian, Julia, Juliana, Juliette, Julissa
⇨ The feminine form of Julianus that was derived from Julius. The name of several early saints, Julian was used in medieval England for both boys and girls. The more feminine spelling using the "anne" ending came along in 1930. Actress Julianne Moore is a famous bearer.

Julie   Rank: 296

Origin: Latin
Meaning: Youthful
Alternate Spellings: Jule, Julee, Juli, Jullie, July
Gender Variations: Jule, Juliano
Nickname: Jewel
Similar Names: Julayne, Juleanna, Juleen, Julet, Julian, Julica, Julise, Julixa
⇨ The French form of Julia ultimately derived from the masculine name Julius. A top 100 name on the chart from 1951 to 1992 because of award-winning British actress, singer, and author Julie Andrews. Trendy when combined with other independent names, such as Julieanne and Julieanna, or used in popular blends like Julissa.

Juliet   Rank: 581

Origin: Latin
Meaning: Youthful
Alternate Spelling: Juliette
Gender Variations: Jules, Julian, Julius
Nicknames: Jules, Julie
Similar Names: Jillian, Julia, Juliana, Julianne, Julitta
Namesakes: Juliet Mills (British actress), Juliet Stevenson (British actress)
⇨ A pet form of Julie that's best known for Shakespeare's star-crossed heroine in the 16th-century tragedy *Romeo and Juliet* and adapted into several films, most recently in 1996 with Claire Danes and Leonardo DiCaprio in the titles roles. Associated today with French actress Juliette Binoche and actress and musician Juliette Lewis, who use the French form of the name.

Julissa   Rank: 225

Origin: American
Alternate Spellings: Julisa, Julyssa
Gender Variations: Jules, Juliano, Jullian
Nicknames: Jewel, Jules
Similar Names: Alissa, Jalissa, Jelissa, Jolissa, Julia, Julie, Julise, Julisha, Julius, Julixa
⇨ A contemporary blend of Julie and Alissa that debuted on the popularity chart in 1969, faded from the chart in 1976, and returned in 1988, the same year its variations were also highly ranked. Popular with parents for its feminine blend using "lissa" and trendy "a" ending.

Justice   Rank: 547

Origin: Latin
Meaning: Judge, office of justice
Alternate Spellings: Justiss, Justyce
Gender Variation: Justin
Similar Names: Faith, Harmony, Justina, Justine, Liberty
⇨ Either taken from the vocabulary word that's derived from the Latin *justitia* or the Old French occupational surname for someone who maintains justice. Parents started using the name on a regular basis in the early 1990s.

Justine   Rank: 950

Origin: Latin
Meaning: Just
Alternate Spelling: Justene, Justyne
Gender Variations: Justin, Justinas, Justus
Nickname: Justy
Similar Names: Janine, June, Junita, Justina
Namesake: Justine Henin (Belgian tennis player)
⇨ The French feminine form of Justinus that was used as the title of a novel published in 1957 by British writer Lawrence Durrell. The name reached its peak when Justine Bateman played the role of Mallory Keaton during the run of the popular 1980s television sitcom *Family Ties*.

Kaitlyn
Rank: 41

Origin: Irish
Meaning: Pure
Alternate Spellings: Caetlin, Caitlyn, Kaitlin, Kaitlynn, Katelin, Katelyn, Katelynn, Katlyn, Katlyne
Gender Variations: Kale, Karlin
Nickname: Kait
Similar Names: Kailey, Kailyn, Kalena, Kara, Karyn, Katalin, Katarin, Katarina, Kathlyn, Kathryn
Namesakes: Kaitlin Cooper (*The O.C.* character), Kaitlin Olson (actress), Kaitlin Sandeno (Olympic swimmer)
➡ A spelling variation of Kaitlin and the Irish form of Katherine. Currently the most widely used spelling of the name, possibly due to the trendy "y" in the middle spelling. Debuted on the popularity chart in 1983 and quickly climbed to its current ranking. A good choice for parents who are looking for a name with several spelling choices. See Caitlin.

Kaliyah
Rank: 755

Origin: American
Gender Variation: Kalen
Nicknames: Kali, Liya
Similar Names: Aaliyah, Jaliyah, Kaila, Kailynn, Kaleah, Maliyah, Taliyah
➡ A modern blend of the prefix "Ka" added to the top 100 name "Aliyah" that became popular with parents in 2001.

Kara
Rank: 279

Origin: Greek
Meaning: Pure
Alternate Spellings: Cara, Kaira, Karah, Karrah
Gender Variations: Karas, Kareb, Karon
Nickname: Kar
Similar Names: Karalee, Karalyn, Karee, Kariana, Kariann, Karielle
Namesake: Kara Lawson (WNBA player)
➡ Either a pet form of Katherine, a variant of Cara, or a diminutive of Karina. A place name in India and Africa and the name of a sea in the Arctic Ocean. Fictional character, Kara Milovy, played by Maryam d'Abo, in the 1987 James Bond film *The Living Daylights*, brought considerable attention to the name and took it to its peak position on the chart in 1988. Popular for its "a" ending and association with other existing favorites such as Karen and Carrie.

Karen
Rank: 173

Origin: Greek
Meaning: Pure
Alternate Spellings: Caren, Carin, Caryn, Karan, Karin, Karon, Karren, Karrun, Karyn, Keren
Gender Variations: Kaden, Kaelen, Kagen, Karam
Nickname: Ren
Similar Names: Carina, Kara, Karalynn, Kareen, Karel, Karenah, Karenza, Karessa, Karey, Taryn
➡ Danish form of Katherine and ultimately derived from the name Aikaterina. Has placed among the top 200 on the chart since 1935 and peaked in 1965 at No. 3, the same year singer Karen Carpenter joined her brother Richard's band, The Richard Carpenter Trio. In 1969 Karen and her brother formed the famous duo The Carpenters just before their first two breakthrough 1970 hits, "Close to You" and "We've Only Just Begun." Since 1999, one-eyed villain character "Plankton," from Nickelodeon's hit television show *SpongeBob SquarePants*, has a computer wife that also bears this name.

Karina
Rank: 227

Origin: Greek
Meaning: Pure
Alternate Spelling: Carena, Carenah, Carina, Carinna, Kareena, Karena, Karenah, Karinna, Karrina, Karrinah
Gender Variations: Karlen, Karon, Karrol,
Nicknames: Kar, Kari
Similar Names: Karen, Karenza, Karessa, Karima, Karinya, Karisma, Karlena, Karolina, Katrina, Korina
➡ Polish and Russian form of Karin and is ultimately associated with Katherine. Achieved its peak in popularity in 1996 and currently ranks among the top 300 names because of its international flair. Possibly inspired recently by Karina Smirnoff, a world champion professional dancer from Kharkiv, Ukraine, who was featured on the television series *Dancing with the Stars* in 2006 with actor Mario Lopez and in 2007 with singer and actor Billy Ray Cyrus.

143

Karis
Rank: 942

Origin: Greek
Meaning: Grace, kindness
Alternate Spellings: Caris, Carys
Gender Variations: Kasen, Paris
Nickname: Karie
Similar Names: Charissa, Cherish, Chris, Chrissie, Chryssa, Kari, Karin, Karima, Karisma, Karissa
⇒ A spelling variation of Charis and a place name for a province located in southern Finland.

Karla
Rank: 209

Origin: Old German
Meaning: Free man
Alternate Spellings: Carla, Carlah, Carlla, Carllah, Karlah, Karlla, Karllah
Gender Variations: Carl, Charles, Karlen, Karlos, Karlton
Nickname: Karl
Similar Names: Carlyle, Carol, Darla, Karlee, Karleen, Karleta, Karlissa
⇒ The short form of Caroline and feminine form of Charles that debuted on the chart in 1936, about 10 years after "Carla" became popular. The named reached its peak in 2002.

Karma
Rank: 852

Origin: Hindi/Sanskrit
Meaning: Fate, destiny
Alternate Spellings: Carma, Karmah
Gender Variation: Karmel
Similar Names: Kara, Karasi, Karen, Karima, Karis, Karisma, Karissa, Karmina
⇒ Defined in Indian philosophy as the influence of a person's past actions on the person's future lives. First used as a girl's given name in 2005.

Kate
Rank: 142

Origin: Greek
Meaning: Pure
Alternate Spellings: Kait, Kaite, Kayt, Kayte
Gender Variations: Katarius, Katray, Katrel
Nickname: Kay
Similar Names: Katasha, Kately, Katelyn, Katerina, Katessa, Katherine, Katie
Namesakes: Kate Jackson (actress), Kate Winslet (actress), Kate Beckinsale (actress)
⇒ The short French form of Katherine taken from the Greek Aikaterine. It was a top 100 name in the 1880s that is making a comeback in popularity partly because of the well-known actress and daughter of Goldie Hawn, Kate Hudson, whose breakthrough role was in the 2000 film *Almost Famous*. It has also been shaped by Kate Austen, the leading female and fictional character in the television series *Lost* since its pilot aired in 2004, and by Kate Bosworth and her performance as Lois Lane in the 2006 movie *Superman Returns*. Trendy when combined with other names such as Katelee and Katelynn.

Katherine
Rank: 36

Origin: Greek
Meaning: Pure
Alternate Spellings: Catherine, Katharine, Kathryn
Gender Variations: Kallum, Kameron
Nicknames: Kate, Katie, Kathy
Similar Names: Kaitlin, Kaleigh, Kalena, Katerina, Katharina
Namesakes: Katharine McPhee (*American Idol* runner-up), Katharine Graham (publisher), Katherine Heigl (actress)
⇒ Derived from Aikaterina and is currently the most popular spelling of the name. Associated with short story writer Katherine Anne Porter, awarded the Pulitzer Prize and National Book Award in 1966. Best known for screen legend Katharine Hepburn, whose film career started in the 1930s and spanned seven decades. Katharine is the occasionally used German form.

Kathleen
Rank: 371

Origin: Greek
Meaning: Pure
Alternate Spelling: Cathleen
Gender Variation: Karl
Nicknames: Kate, Kathy, Katie
Similar Names: Katalin, Katarin, Katarina, Katelyn, Katharina, Katherine, Kathlyn, Kayleigh
⇒ The Irish form of Caitlin that was listed among the top 100 from 1920 to 1990, peaking at No. 9 in 1949. The name received a hike in popularity when actress Kathleen Turner launched a successful career in 1978 when she starred in the film *Body Heat*.

Kathy Rank: 907

Origin: Greek
Meaning: Pure
Alternate Spellings:
Cathey, Cathi, Cathie,
Cathy, Kathi, Kathie, Kathey
Gender Variation: Kato
Nickname: Kath
Similar Names: Kaelea, Kailyn, Kaisa, Kaitlin, Kate, Katey, Katia, Katina, Katlyn, Katrin
Namesakes: Kathie Lee Gifford (TV host/actress/singer), Kathy Bates (actress)
➡ The short form of Katherine that's been used as an independent name along with its counterpart Cathy since the 1930s, both peaking in 1958. The "C" spelling faded in 1991, while namesakes like supermodel, actress, and entrepreneur Kathy Ireland and country musician Kathy Mattea have kept the "K" variation in front of the public.

Katie Rank: 107

Origin: Greek
Meaning: Pure
Alternate Spellings: Catie, Caty, Kady, Katee, Katey, Kati, Katy, Kaydee, Kaydi
Gender Variation: Karl
Similar Names: Kassidy, Kassie, Kat, Katelyn, Kathy, Katia, Katianne, Katrina, Kaycee, Kaylee
Namesakes: Katie Couric (news anchor), Katie Douglas (WNBA basketball player), Katie Smith (WNBA basketball player)
➡ The short form of Katherine that's been used as an independent name since before the turn of the 20th century. Actress Katie Holmes kept the name in front of the public when she became known for her role as Joey Potter on the drama *Dawson's Creek* that aired from 1998 to 2003. She has since received international fame as the wife of superstar Tom Cruise.

Katrina Rank: 382

Origin: Greek
Meaning: Pure
Alternate Spellings:
Catreena, Catreina, Catrina,
Katreena, Katreina, Katryna, Ketreina,
Ketrina, Ketryna
Gender Variations: Kato, Katriel, Katriot
Nicknames: Kat, Trina
Similar Names: Kaitrona, Karina, Katerina, Katherine, Kathrina, Katrin, Katriona, Kotryna

Namesake: Katrina Kaif (actress/model)
➡ Variation of Catriona and short form of Katherine that gained popularity during the 1980s because of Katrina and the Waves, a pop rock band, best known for their 1985 hit "Walking on Sunshine." Still a common name girl's name because of the character Katrina in Christopher Paolini's *Eragon*. Hurricane Katrina, the catastrophic 2005 hurricane that devastated New Orleans and the Mississippi Gulf Coast, also bears this name.

Kaya Rank: 640
Origin: Native American Hopi
Meaning: My elder sister
Alternate Spellings: Kaia,
Kaiya, Kya
Gender Variation: Kai
Similar Names: Kai, Kaisa, Kaitha, Kaiysha, Kaja, Kayla, Kaylee, Kazia
➡ One of the trendy girl's names that end with "a" with three additional spelling variations, all listed among the most popular names.

Kayden Rank: 624
Origin: English
Meaning: Spirited
Alternate Spellings: Caden,
Caeden, Caiden, Cayden,
Kaden, Kadin, Kadyn, Kaeden, Kaiden
Gender Variations: Caden, Jaden, Paden
Nickname: Kade
Similar Names: Cadence, Hayden, Jayden, Kadena, Kaya, Kaydee, Kayla, Kaylee, Kaylin
➡ This is the only form of the top 100 boy's name that made it onto the chart as a girl's given name. A great choice for parents who like the trendy "y" in the middle or a large selection of spelling options.

Kayla Rank: 26
Origin: American
Alternate Spellings: Caela,
Caila, Cayla, Kaelah, Kaila,
Kala, Kaylah, Keyla
Gender Variations: Kale, Kaleb
Nickname: Kay
Similar Names: Kara, Kate, Katelyn, Kathleen, Kayley, Kelly
➡ A trendy combination of "Kay" with the suffix "la" also used as the short form of Michaela that's jumped in popularity since 1959. The name of a character on the long-running soap opera *Days of Our Lives*.

145

Kaylee
Rank: 42

Origin: American
Alternate Spellings: Kailee, Kailey, Kaleigh, Kaley, Kali, Kayleigh, Kayley, Kayli, Kaylie
Gender Variations: Kaleb, Kevyn
Nicknames: Kay, Lee, Kailey
Similar Names: Kallie, Kayla, Kaylene, Kaylin, Keeley, Kylie
⇨ A combination name that uses the elements "Kay" and "lee" that's possibly a form of Keeley or Kayla. Favored by parents because of its many spelling options, the name has quickly climbed the popularity chart since 1984.

Kaylin
Rank: 399

Origin: American
Alternate Spellings: Cailyn, Kaelyn, Kailyn, Kaylen, Kaylyn, Kaylynn
Nicknames: Kay, Lin
Similar Names: Kallie, Kara, Karyn, Katelyn, Kathy, Katie, Kaylie, Keila
⇨ A combination of "Kay" and the suffix "lin" considered fashionable for its "y" in the middle spelling. The name has increased in usage since debuting on the chart in 1987 at No. 984.

Keely
Rank: 698

Origin: Gaelic
Meaning: Slender
Alternate Spellings: Kealey, Kealie, Kealy, Keeley, Keelie Keighley, Keiley, Keilly, Keily
Gender Variation: Keelin
Similar Names: Keelia, Keelyn, Keilah, Kella, Kellen, Kelly
Namesake: Keely Shaye Smith (actress)
⇨ An Irish surname that became a given name derived from the Gaelic word *caol*. Used occasionally since 1959.

Keira
Rank: 109

Origin: Irish Gaelic
Meaning: Black haired
Alternate Spellings: Keirra, Keirrah, Kiera, Kierra, Kira, Kyra
Gender Variations: Keiran, Kyran
Similar Names: Ciara, Cierra, Keara, Keera
⇨ A variation of Kiera that first hit the chart in 2000, most likely due to British actress Keira Knightly.

Kelly
Rank: 212

Origin: Irish Gaelic
Meaning: Descendant of Ceallach
Alternate Spellings: Kelle, Kellee, Kelleigh, Kelley, Kelli, Kellie, Kellye
Gender Variations: Kellen, Keller, Kelley, Kelson
Nickname: Kel
Similar Names: Callie, Keely, Kellar, Kellene, Kellianne, Kellina, Kellyn, Kelsey, Kelty
Namesakes: Kelly McGillis (actress), Kelly Ripa (TV host/actress), Kelly Preston (actress)
⇨ Transferred use of surname that started out as a boy's name but is currently more common for girls. Originally an English form of the ancient Irish Gaelic name Ceallach, which debuted on the chart in 1944 and rose to a strong position among the top 100 in 1959. Peaked at No. 10 in 1977 because of fictional character Kelly Garrett, played by actress Jaclyn Smith on the 1976 to 1981 television series *Charlie's Angels*. Singer Kelly Clarkson, the 2002 first-season winner of *American Idol,* also comes to mind. Trendy name with a "y" spelling and long "ee" sound and either by itself or combined with other names like Kellyjo or Kelly-Ann.

Kelsey
Rank: 184

Origin: Old English
Meaning: Victorious ship
Alternate Spellings: Kelcey, Kelcie, Kelcy, Kellsey, Kellsie, Kelsee, Kelseigh, Kelsi, Kelsie, Kelsy
Gender Variations: Kelley, Kelson, Kelton, Kelsy
Nicknames: Kel, Kelse
Similar Names: Casey, Chelsea, Kalyssa, Kelli, Nelsey
⇨ A name for boys and girls that debuted on the chart in 1977 with the premiere of hit television series *Lou Grant* starring Linda Kelsey as reporter Billie Newman. Grew in popularity and peaked from 1992 to 1993 during the fame of actor Kelsey Grammer as Frasier on the two television sitcoms *Cheers* and *Frasier*. Name is more favored as a girl's name and is popular for its spelling with a "y."

Kendall   Rank: 148
Origin: Old English
Meaning: Kent river valley
Alternate Spellings:
Kendahl, Kendal, Kendyl,
Kendyle
Gender Variations: Kendall, Kenden,
Kendric, Kenneth
Nicknames: Kena, Keni
Similar Names: Kendalla, Kendell, Kendralla,
Kendri, Kendria, Kennah, Kenndra, Kimball,
Kyndal
➩ Surname used as a given name since the
19th century that also derived from the name
of a city in northwest England. Reentered
the top 200 in 2002 and has more trendy
spellings today, such as variations with "ia,"
ending with "a," or including a "y" in the
suffix. Mostly given to boys in the past but
becoming more popular for girls after
debuting on the chart in 1964.

Kendra   Rank: 243
Origin: Welsh/Old English
Meaning: Chief hero or
royal ruler
Alternate Spellings:
Keandra, Keandre, Kendrah, Kendre,
Kenndra, Kindra, Kyndra
Gender Variations: Ken, Kendal, Kenya
Nickname: Ken
Similar Names: Candra, Keaundra, Kenda,
Kendell, Kendellyn, Kendria, Kenna, Kentra
➩ Feminine form of Kendrick that may be
taken from the Old Welsh personal name
Cynwrig or the Old English personal name
Cynric. May also be a combination name or
modern blend of Ken with Sandra or Andrea.
Listed among the top 200 names from
1974 to 1986, peaking a year later at No. 77.
Possibly influenced in recent years by
Kendra Todd, the first female and youngest
candidate to be hired by Donald Trump
on the 2005 Season 3 conclusion of the
television reality series The Apprentice.

Kenna   Rank: 924
Origin: Scottish Gaelic
Meaning: Fair one,
fire-sprung
Gender Variations:
Kenneth, Kenny
Nickname: Ken

Similar Names: Kendall, Kendra, Kenia,
Kenina, Kennedi, Kenya, Kenzie, Kiana,
McKenna
➩ The feminine form of Kenneth that
may also be a modern twist on the top 100
name Jenna.

Kennedy   Rank: 115
Origin: Irish Gaelic
Meaning: Armoured head
Alternate Spellings:
Kenadee, Kennedi, Kennedie
Gender Variations: Kennedy, Kenneth
Nicknames: Ken, Kenz
Similar Names: Kandy, Kennette, Kendyl,
Kenna, Kennesha, Kennia, Kennina, Kennya,
Kenzy, Kinsey
➩ Surname used as a given name from
the Gaelic term Cinnéidigh that means
"misshapen head." Originally given to boys
in honor of assassinated U.S. president
John F. Kennedy. After landing on the
popularity chart in 1994, it has been an
increasingly more common name for girls,
particularly when spelled with "y," "ia,"
or long "ee".

Kenya   Rank: 523
Origin: African
Meaning: Kenya
Alternate Spellings:
Kenia, Kennya
Gender Variations: Kanye, Ken, Kenny
Similar Names: Kenda, Kendall, Kendra,
Kenia, Kenna
Namesake: Kenya Moore (actress)
➩ Adopted as a girl's given name in 1968
for the eastern African country. A popular
choice among African-American families and
also used occasionally as a boy's name.

Kenzie   Rank: 557
Origin: Scottish Gaelic
Meaning: Son of Coinneach
Alternate Spelling: Kenzy
Gender Variation: Ken
Similar Names: Kelsie, Kenda, Kendra,
Kenisha, Kennis, Kenza, Keziah, Kinzie
➩ A contemporary short form of Mackenzie
that's been used independently since 1994
and notable for its feminine "ie" ending.

Kiana   Rank: 401

Origin: American
Alternate Spellings:
Keanna, Keiana, Keona,
Keonna, Kiahna, Kianna,
Kiauna, Kiona, Kionah, Kionna
Gender Variations: Keanu, Keona
Nickname: Kia
Similar Names: Ciana, Giana, Keena, Kiani,
Kinna, Qiana
⇒ May be the Hawaiian form of Diana or a
variation of Kian, an Irish Gaelic name meaning
"ancient." Could also be associated with the
name Anna. A modern name especially
favored in Hawaii, perhaps because of the
popular boy's name Keanu. Possibly used
frequently for girls because of the fame of
actor Keanu Reeves from the 1990s through
the 2000s. Actress Kiana Tom may have
inspired the name with her 1999 role in the
hit movie *Universal Soldier: The Return*.

Kimberly   Rank: 58

Origin: Old English
Meaning: Land belonging
to Cyneburg
Alternate Spellings:
Kimberlea, Kimberlee, Kimberleigh,
Kimberley, Kimberli, Kimberlie, Kymberlee,
Kymberleigh, Kymberley, Kymberly
Gender Variations: Kim, Kimball
Nicknames: Kim, Kimber, Kimmy
Similar Names: Kimba, Kimberlyn, Kim Marie
Namesake: Kimberly Williams (actress)
⇒ A surname and place name for a city in
South Africa named for English statesman
John Wodehouse, 1st Earl of Kimberley. Used
as both a boy's and girl's name around the
middle of the 20th century. The boy's name
faded in 1980 while the girl's continued to
thrive, peaking in 1966 and 1967 at No. 2.

Kimora   Rank: 422

Gender Variations: Kanye,
Kim
Nickname: Kim
Similar Names: Kamara,
Kamari, Kiara, Kierra, Kimana, Kyra
⇒ A recent addition to the popularity chart
with an unknown meaning and origin. The
name was inspired by former Chanel model
and actress Kimora Lee Simmons, who is
currently the head of design for Baby Phat,
a clothing line for women and girls.

Kinley   Rank: 904

Origin: American
Gender Variation: Finley
Similar Names: Finley, Kiley,
Kinsey, Kinsley, Lynley
⇒ The short form of the girl's name McKinley.

Kinsey   Rank: 898

Origin: Old English
Meaning: Victorious prince
Alternate Spellings:
Kinnsee, Kinnsey, Kinnsie,
Kinsee, Kinsie, Kinzee, Kinzie
Gender Variations: Kingsley, Kinsey
Similar Names: Kenzie, Kimberly, Kinley, Kinsley
⇒ A surname used as a girl's given name
since 1992 with the "ey" ending currently in
vogue. Sue Grafton, author of the award-
winning Kinsey Milhone mystery series, also
known as the alphabet novels, has kept the
name in front of the public.

Kinsley   Rank: 876

Origin: American
Gender Variation: Kingsley
Similar Names: Ainsley,
Ansley, Kiley, Kimberly,
Kinley, Kinsey, Paisley
⇒ An invented name possibly used as a form
of Kinsey that became fashionable in 2005
with its feminine "ey" ending.

Kirsten   Rank: 407

Origin: Latin
Meaning: Christian
Alternate Spellings:
Keerstin, Keirstin, Kersten,
Kerstin, Kiersten, Kierstin, Kierstynn, Kirstin,
Kirstyn, Kyrstin
Gender Variations: Christian, Kresten, Kritee
Similar Names: Kirstie, Kirstine, Kristyn
⇒ Scandinavian form of Christina, which
traces back to the Latin name Christian and
has been widely used in Scotland for many
years and first appeared on the popularity
chart in 1957. The name peaked from 1989
to 1997 among the top 200 during the initial
fame of actress Kirsten Dunst, best known
for the role as Mary Jane Watson in the
Spider-Man film series. Actress Kirstie Alley
bears a form of the name.

Krista Rank: 701

Origin: Latin
Meaning: Christian
Alternate Spellings:
Christa, Crista
Gender Variations: Kristian, Kristopher
Nickname: Kris
Similar Names: Krissa, Krissie, Kristia, Kristie, Kristen, Krysia, Krystal
Namesake: Krista Allen (actress)
➡ The short form of Kristina that's been used independently since 1950 and is notable with its feminine "a" ending. The name spent one year among the top 100 during the mid-1980s and has since declined.

Kristen Rank: 374
Origin: Latin
Meaning: Christian
Alternate Spellings:
Christen, Khristin, Kristan, Kristin, Kristyn, Krysten, Krystin, Krystyn, Krystynn
Gender Variations: Christian, Kresten, Krishen
Nickname: Kris
Similar Names: Kiersten, Kirsten, Krissie, Krista, Kristabell, Kristeen, Kristel, Kristi, Kristina, Krysia
Namesakes: Kristin Scott Thomas (British actress)
➡ The Danish form of Christian and a variation of Kristin that was originally a male name but is now more widely given to girls. It debuted on the popularity chart in 1946 and currently ranks the highest among its variations. The name peaked during the 1980s when former astronaut Sally Kristen Ride became famous as the first U.S. woman to reach outer space. Actress Kristin Davis influenced the name's top position in the 1990s and 2000s with television roles in *Melrose Place* and *Sex and the City*. Kristen Johnston, best known for her Emmy Award-winning role in the television series *3rd Rock From the Sun*, also comes to mind.

Kyla Rank: 204
Origin: Scottish
Meaning: Narrow piece of land
Alternate Spellings: Kiela, Kieyla, Kila, Kilah, Kylah
Gender Variations: Kylan, Kyle

Nickname: Ky
Similar Names: Keyla, Kylara, Kylee, Kylia, Kylle, Kyna, Kyrah
➡ Feminine form of Kyle that debuted on the popularity chart in 1974, climbed among the top 200 in 2002, and peaked in 2004. Popular due to rising television and film actress Kyla Pratt and Filipino singer Melanie Hernandez Calumpad, who goes by the stage name of "Kyla." A contemporary name that stands out because of its "a" ending and similarity to the ever popular Kylie.

Kylie Rank: 66
Origin: Australian
Meaning: Boomerang
Alternate Spellings: Kiley, Kilie, Kylee, Kyleigh, Kyli
Gender Variations: Kyle, Kyler, Kyran
Similar Names: Kellie, Kyla, Kyra, Krysten
➡ Possibly adopted from the aboriginal word for "boomerang" or may have been influenced by Kelly and Kyle. Associated with Australian singer and songwriter Kylie Minogue, who started her career as a dance-pop artist in the late 1980s. Currently the most popular form of the name with its trendy "y" in the middle spelling.

Kyra Rank: 195
Origin: Greek
Meaning: Lady
Alternate Spellings:
Cyra, Cyrah, Kira, Kyrah
Gender Variations: Ciro, Kyros
Similar Names: Kylie, Kyria, Krystle, Kyrsten
Namesake: Kyra Phillips (news anchor)
➡ The feminine form of Cyrus, considered a good choice for parents who like the fashionable "y" in the middle spelling. Actress Kyra Sedgwick, best known for her role in the television police drama *The Closer,* has been a recent influence. The name was used sporadically during the 1970s, then hit its stride during the 1980s. Kyra Panagia is an island located along the east coast of Greece.

La ⇨ girls' names

Lacey
Rank: 446

Origin: Old French
Meaning: Cheerful
Alternate Spellings: Lacee, Laci, Lacie, Lacy, Laicee, Laicey, Laisey, Laycie, Laysie
Gender Variations: Laird, Lambert
Similar Names: Lacene, Laciann, Laila, Lainey,
⇨ A surname derived from Lassy taken from the name of a town in Normandy and brought into England and Ireland after the Norman conquest. Also associated with the delicate fabric made of thread or yarn. A top name since 1975, it peaked during the 1980s when Lacy J. Dalton became known as a country singer.

Lana
Rank: 412

Origin: Old German
Meaning: Precious
Alternate Spelling: Lanna
Gender Variations: Alan, Lance, Lane
Similar Names: Alaina, Alanis, Alanna, Alayna, Lane, Lani
⇨ The short form of Alana or the feminine form of Alan. Influenced by actress Lana Turner, born Julia Jean Mildred Frances Turner, who was discovered at the age of 16 in a cafe by the publisher of the *Hollywood Reporter*. She eventually became a well-known star and pinup girl during the 1940s and 1950s. The name peaked on the popularity chart in 1948 and appears to be making a comeback.

Laney
Rank: 483

Origin: Greek
Meaning: Torch
Alternate Spellings: Lainey, Lanie
Gender Variations: Lance, Lane, Lanford
Nickname: Lane
Similar Names: Lacey, Laila, Laina, Lana, Lara, Linn, Linnea
⇨ A variation of Lainey and ultimately the pet form of Elaine that's been used steadily as a given name since 2000.

Lara
Rank: 834

Origin: Latin
Meaning: Protection
Alternate Spelling: Larra
Gender Variations: Larry, Lawrence

Similar Names: Laraine, Lareina, Larissa, Laura, Laurel, Lauren, Lauretta
Namesake: Lara Flynn Boyle (actress)
⇨ The short form of Larisa that was popularized by one of the main characters in Boris Pasternak's 1956 novel *Dr. Zhivago*, adapted into a film in 1965. The name debuted on the chart in 1966 and saw a moderate rise in popularity with the release of the 2001 film *Lara Croft: Tomb Raider*, starring actress Angelina Jolie in the title role.

Larissa
Rank: 633

Origin: Latin
Meaning: Cheerful, lighthearted
Alternate Spellings: Larisa, Larysa, Laryssa, Lerissa, Lorissa
Gender Variations: Larry, Lars
Nicknames: Lari, Rissa
Similar Names: Lara, Laraine, Lareyna, Laurie, Lissa, Latasha, Laura
Namesake: Larissa Lazutina (Russian Olympic skier)
⇨ Derived from *hilaris* which is also the root of Hilary. Possibly adapted from the Russian Larisa or used as the feminine form of Larry. The name caught on during the 1960s and recently dropped out of the top 500. Also known as a city in north central Greece and the name of one of Neptune's moons.

Laura
Rank: 172

Origin: Latin
Meaning: Crowned with laurel
Alternate Spellings: Laurah, Laure, Lawra, Lawrah, Lawrea, Loura
Gender Variations: Lauren, Lauro, Lawrence
Similar Names: Lauralee, Lauralyn, Laurkin, Laureanne, Laurella, Laurence, Lauretta, Laurin, Laurka, Lavra
Namesake: Laura Bush (first lady of the U.S.)
⇨ Feminine form of the late Latin name Laurus, meaning "laurel." A name that has ranked within the top 100 for the majority of the 19th and 20th centuries, many of those years peaking in the top 20. It's also known for famed author Laura Ingalls Wilder, who wrote the series of historical fiction books for children based on her pioneer childhood, which led to the long-running television show *Little House on the Prairie*, starring Melissa Gilbert as Laura Ingalls. The name was

inspired during the 1980s for fictional duo Luke and Laura, the signature supercouple of the soap opera *General Hospital*. Their marriage on the show in 1981 attracted 30 million viewers, making it the highest-rated hour in soap opera history.

Laurel   Rank: 846

Origin: Latin
Meaning: Laurel garland
Alternate Spellings: Laurell, Laurelle, Loralle, Lorel, Lorelle
Gender Variations: Laurie, Loren
Similar Names: Lara, Laura, Lauren, Laurene, Laurie, Laurissa, Lorelei, Lorelle
➡ A nature name that refers to an evergreen shrub or tree and possibly used as a pet form of Laura. The name hit its height in popularity during the mid-1950s.

Lauren   Rank: 24

Origin: Latin
Meaning: Crowned with laurel
Alternate Spellings: Lauran, Laurin, Laurren, Lauryn, Loren, Loryn
Gender Variations: Laurence, Lawson
Nickname: Laurie
Similar Names: Lara, Laryn, Laurel, Laurena, Laurencia, Laurentino, Lena, Lorenza
Namesakes: Lauren Graham (actress), Lauren Holly (actress), Lauren Sevian (jazz musician)
➡ The feminine form of Laurence and a variation of Laura. Influenced by stage and screen actress Lauren Bacall, born Betty Joan Perske, who became an instant star after she appeared in the film *To Have or Have Not* in 1944. Today the name is as fashionable as the clothing designed by namesake Ralph Lauren. Popular in several European countries.

Layla   Rank: 100

Origin: Arabic
Meaning: Night
Alternate Spelling: Laela, Laella, Laila, Lala, Lalah, Lalla, Laylah, Leila, Leyla
Gender Variations: Layne, Layton
Nicknames: Lae
Similar Names: Bayla, Dayla, Gayla, Jayla, Kayla, Lelah, Lyla

➡ This is the name of the central character in poems by the 7th-century Arab poet known as Qays. The poem *Leyli and Majnun*, later inspired British rock guitarist Eric Clapton to write one of rock music's famous love songs "Layla" in 1970. The name debuted on the popularity chart in 1972, the same year the song first landed a spot on the music charts. Boxing champion Laila Ali uses a form of the name.

Leah   Rank: 69

Origin: Hebrew
Meaning: Delicate
Alternate Spellings: Lea, Leia, Leya, Lia
Gender Variations: Lee, Levi
Nickname: Lee
Similar Names: Leann, Lecia, Leda, Leesa, Leila
Namesake: Leah Remini (actress)
➡ A biblical name for the first wife of Jacob and the mother of six leaders of Israel's 12 tribes. The name was influenced during the 1980s and 1990s by actress Lea Thompson, best known for her role in the *Back to the Future* film trilogy and as the star of the television sitcom *Caroline in the City*. Occasionally used as a combination or blended name such as Leanna, Leanora, and Leatrice.

Leilani   Rank: 313

Origin: Hawaiin
Meaning: Heavenly lei
Alternate Spelling: Lalani
Gender Variations: Lei, Leighton, Lelio
Nicknames: Lani, Lei
Similar Names: Elliana, Iliana, Jillian, Leia, Leilah, Leilena, Leilia, Leina, Lilian, Lilyana
➡ A combination of the elements *lei*, which is a Hawaiian necklace symbolizing regard and love for the person to whom it is given, with "lani." It's faded on and off the chart since its debut in 1937 but began a steady growth period in 1996, taking the name to its current peak among the top 400. The fictional Princess Leia of *Star Wars* fame in the 1970s and 1980s made it a popular choice.

Lena
Rank: 489

Alternate Spellings: Leana, Leena, Leina, Lenah, Lina
Gender Variations: Lennie, Leon
Similar Names: Alena, Ileana, Lainey, Lana, Leanna, Leigh, Lenora, Maddalena, Marlena
⇨ The short form of several names including Helena, Magdalena, Shelena, and Yelena. It was popularized by singer and actress Lena Horne whose claim to fame during the 1940s was her role in the film *Stormy Weather* and rendition of the title song. The name has been used independently since the 19th century.

Leslie
Rank: 108

Origin: Scottish Gaelic
Meaning: Garden of hollies
Alternate Spellings: Leslee, Lesleigh, Lesley, Lesli, Lesly, Lesye
Gender Variations: Lesley, Lessie, Lestel
Nicknames: Lee, Lesa, Les, Lessie, Lizzy
Similar Names: Lesia, Leslea, Lezlee
Namesakes: Lesley-Anne Down (British actress), Leslie Ann Warren (actress)
⇨ Surname and Scottish place name first used in the 18th century. Variation with a "z" preserves the original Scottish pronunciation and even more fashionable today when spelled with "ee." First long-lasting placement in the top 100 in the 1900s began with Leslie Caron's performance in nine-time Oscar winner *Gigi* in 1958. Well-known as a boy's name in England and Scotland but typically given to girls in the U.S.

Leticia
Rank: 797

Origin: Latin
Meaning: Great joy
Alternate Spellings: Laetitia, Laticia, Latisha, Letisha, Letitia, Letycia
Gender Variation: Latrell
Nicknames: Letty, Tisha
Similar Names: Latasha, Latrice, Lecrecia, Letizia, Lettice
⇨ The Spanish and Portuguese form of Letitia popular among African-American families since the 1950s.

Lexi
Rank: 345

Origin: Greek
Meaning: Defender of mankind
Alternate Spellings: Leksi, Lexie, Lexey, Lexy
Gender Variations: Lex, Lexander, Lexin
Nickname: Lex
Similar Names: Alexi, Laci, Lesy, Lexa, Lexia, Lexina, Lexine, Lexus, Roxi
Namesake: Lexi Kercher (jazz artist)
⇨ Pet form of Alexandra and variation of Alexis that is currently striving for another peak since its first one in 2005. Debuting in 1993, it's currently ranked considerably higher than its variation spelled with an "ie" and is widely used because of its association with the even more popular names, such as Alexa, Alexandra, Alexandria and Alexia. Actresses Lexie Bigham and Lexi Randall brought attention to the name during the 1990s.

Liana
Rank: 721

Origin: French
Meaning: To twine
Alternate Spellings: Leana, Leanna, Leiana, Liahna, Lianna
Gender Variation: Liam
Similar Names: Iliana, Lia, Lianne, Lilian, Liliana, Lina
Namesake: Liana Liberato (actress)
⇨ The short form of Eliana, Juliana, and Liliana and also the name of a vine that grows in tropical moist forests and rain forests. Notable for parents who like names with the trendy "a" on the end.

Libby
Rank: 798

Origin: Hebrew
Meaning: My God is an oath
Alternate Spellings: Libbee, Libbey, Libbie
Gender Variations: Liam, Linley
Nickname: Lib
Similar Names: Liberty, Libra, Lilibeth, Lisa, Lisette, Liz, Liza, Lizbeth
⇨ The pet form of the Hebrew name Elizabeth that's been used independently since the 19th century and made a comeback in 2002.

Liberty

Rank: 539

Origin: Latin
Meaning: Liberty
Gender Variation: Liam
Nickname: Libby
Similar Names: America, Freedom, Harmony, Journey, Patience
Namesake: Liberty X (British pop group)
➡ Taken directly from the vocabulary word that means the state of being free, it's often associated with the Statue of Liberty in New York. The name has been used sporadically in the past, listed among the top names in 1918 and during the bicentennial in 1976 before climbing the chart since 2001.

Lila

Rank: 329

Origin: Arabic
Meaning: Night
Alternate Spellings: Lilah, Lyla
Gender Variation: Lyle
Similar Names: Leila, Lilac, Lilia, Lillian, Lillith, Lily, Lola
➡ The short form of Leila that was steadily used during the first half of the 20th century, peaking at No. 170 in 1930. The name faded during the 1970s and made a comeback in 1998 inspired by country singer Lila McCann, who was named "Most Successful New Artist" by *Time* magazine.

Lilia

Rank: 930

Origin: Latin
Meaning: Lily
Alternate Spellings: Lillia, Lilya
Gender Variation: Lindall
Nickname: Lil
Similar Names: Lila, Lilac, Lilana, Lilian, Lillith, Lily
➡ An elongated form of Lily that's been used sporadically since the 19th century.

Liliana

Rank: 150

Origin: Latin
Meaning: Lily
Alternate Spellings: Lilianna, Lilliana, Lillieana, Lillieanna, Lilijana, Lilyana, Lilyanna, Lilyannah
Gender Variations: Liel, Liltony, Linell
Nicknames: Lil, Lily
Similar Names: Elliana, Gillian, Iliana, Jillian, Leilani, Lileas, Liliah, Lilibeth, Lillian, Lilyanne

➡ Derived from the Latin word *lilium*, and is a variant of Lillian and Lily. A popular latecomer to the chart that arrived in 1972.

Lillian

Rank: 38

Origin: Latin
Meaning: Lily
Alternate Spellings: Lilian, Liliane, Lilianne
Nicknames: Lil, Lilli
Similar Names: Liana, Lianne, Lila, Liliana, Lilias, Lilibeth, Lilith, Lillia
Namesake: Lillian Hellman (playwright)
➡ Possibly derived from the flower, it's been in popular use since the 19th century and peaked around 1900 when nature names were in vogue. Actress and singer Lillian Russell and silent film star Lillian Gish brought attention to the name during the late 19th century and early 20th century.

Lily

Rank: 33

Origin: Latin
Meaning: Lily
Alternate Spellings: Lile, Lili, Lillie, Lilly
Gender Variations: Lindall, Linden
Nickname: Lil
Similar Names: Laila, Lillia, Lillian, Lilyanne, Lilibeth, Lola
Namesake: Lily Tomlin (comedian/actress)
➡ Derived from *lilium* which is a direct pickup from the name of the perennial flower. A form of Lillie associated with the 20th-century British actress Lillie Langtry, born Emilie Charlotte Le Breton. Listed among the top 100 since 2002, it's also used as a popular combination name such as Lily-Anne and Lily-Rose.

Lina

Rank: 981

Origin: Arabic
Meaning: Palm tree or tender
Alternate Spellings: Leena, Leina, Lena, Linah, Lyna
Gender Variations: Liam, Linley
Similar Names: Alina, Lana, Liana, Linda, Linn, Linnea, Liona, Livana
➡ The short form of names such as Angelina or Carolina and also considered an Arabic name. It's been used as an independent name since the 1850s and peaked prior to the turn of the 20th century.

Linda   Rank: 462

Origin: Spanish
Meaning: Beautiful
Alternate Spellings:
Lynda, Lynnda
Gender Variations: Linden, Lyndon
Nickname: Lin
Similar Names: Lina, Lindsay, Lissa, Lyndie, Lynette
Namesakes: Linda Evangelista (Canadian model), Linda Evans (actress), Linda Gray (actress), Linda Ronstadt (singer)
⇒ Possibly derived from several sources, such as the shortened form of Belinda or Melinda, from the Spanish *linda* meaning "beautiful," or the short form of Germanic names ending in "lind" meaning "tender, soft." The name was listed among the top 10 from 1940 to 1965 due to the success of actresses Linda Darnell and Linda Christian. The name has faded since that time but is still listed among the top 500.

Lindsey   Rank: 186

Origin: Scottish
Meaning: Lincoln's wetland
Alternate Spellings:
Lindsay, Lindsea, Lindsee, Lindsie, Lindsy, Lindzie, Lyndsey
Gender Variations: Linden, Lindsey, Linster, Linwood
Nicknames: Lin, Linds
Similar Names: Linda, Lindey, Lindita, Linelle, Linese, Linsey
⇒ Derived from a Scottish surname that was originally taken from a place name. Has proven to be a more common name for girls than boys since its 1974 debut on the chart and positions in the top 100 and 200 since 1977. Lindsay, a variation of the name also preferred among parents, is listed among the top 300. Both spellings are popular with the "y" ending, but are even more trendy when spelled with a "z" or combined with other names such as Lindseylee or Lindsey-Anne.

Lisa   Rank: 503

Origin: Hebrew
Meaning: My God is an oath
Alternate Spellings: Leesa, Liesa
Gender Variations: Linus, Lionel
Nickname: Lis
Similar Names: Leeza, Lisabet, Lise, Lisette, Liza, Lizanne, Lizbeth
Namesakes: Lisa Bonet (actress), Lisa Fernandez (Olympic softball player), Lisa Leslie (basketball player), Lisa Marie Presley (singer)
⇒ The pet form of Elizabeth that's been steadily used as a name in its own right since 1937, spending eight years at No. 1 during the 1960s. Associated with Leonardo da Vinci's famed 16th-century painting the *Mona Lisa*, and more recently known for actress Lisa Kudrow from *Friends* fame. A popular blend or combination name such as Annalisa, Lisa-Marie, Melissa, and Talisa.

Litzy   Rank: 829

Origin: Hebrew
Meaning: My God is an oath
Alternate Spellings: Litsea, Litsee, Litsey, Litsy, Litzea, Litzee, Litzey
Gender Variation: Liton
Nickname: Litz
Similar Names: Lizzie, Mitzi, Nitsa, Ritsa
Namesakes: Litzy Vannya Rodríguez Balderas (pop singer)
⇒ A form of Elizabeth that debuted on the chart in 2000. Similar to Litsea, a form of Liza that sounds like the name. Passed its peak in 2005 but still popular for its "z" spelling and trendy long "ee" sound.

Lizbeth   Rank: 323

Origin: Hebrew
Meaning: My God is an oath
Alternate Spellings:
Lisbeth, Lysbeth, Lyzbeth
Gender Variations: Lison, Liznadro
Nicknames: Liz, Lizzy, Beth
Similar Names: Elizabeth, Lisabet, Lisset, Lizabeth, Lizandra, Lizbet, Lizeth, Lizmarie, Lizzieann, Lyzette
⇒ Short form of Elizabeth and also a contemporary combination of Liz and Beth. It debuted on the chart in 1988 when Elizabeth ranked among the top 10. It peaked in 2002 as a preferred choice for girls because of its blend of two already-popular independent names.

Lizeth   Rank: 691

Origin: Hebrew
Meaning: My God is an oath
Gender Variation: Litton
Nicknames: Liz, Lizzie
Similar Names: Lilith, Lisbet, Lisbeth, Lizabeth, Lizbeth, Lizette, Lysanne

➡ Possibly a shortened form of Elizabeth or a variation of its pet form Lizette used occasionally as a given name since 1989.

Logan
Rank: 432

Origin: Scottish Gaelic
Meaning: Little hollow
Alternate Spelling: Logann
Gender Variations: Linden, Logan, Lonnie
Similar Names: Lillias, Lindsey, London, Lora, Lorna
➡ A surname that was derived from a Scottish place name. Consistently more common as a boy's name, it was first brought to parents' attention by fictional character Brooke Logan from the soap opera *The Bold and the Beautiful,* who was referred to by her last name.

Lola
Rank: 280

Origin: Spanish
Meaning: Sorrows
Alternate Spellings: Lolah, Lolla, Lollah
Gender Variations: Lonell, Lora
Nickname: Lo
Similar Names: Lala, Lela, Lila, Loela, Loila, Loletta, Lolita, Lula, Lyla
Namesake: *Run Lola Run* (1998 film)
➡ Short form of Dolores, which is taken from the Spanish title of the Virgin Mary, María de los Dolores, meaning "Mary of Sorrows." Associated with "La Bella Lola" or "Beautiful Lola," also known as the "Hymn of the Sailor." Also known for fictional character Lilly Truscott on the hit 2006 Disney show *Hannah Montana,* who attends Hannah's concerts under the alias Lola. The name recently made a comeback in 2002 after fading.

London
Rank: 353

Origin: English
Meaning: Fierce ruler of the world
Gender Variations: Linden, London
Similar Names: Dakota, Ireland, Paris
Namesakes: LaToya London (*American Idol* finalist), London Tipton (*The Suite Life of Zack and Cody* character)
➡ The city that is the capital of the United Kingdom. It's been in use as a girl's given name since 1994 and for boys starting in 2000.

Lorelei
Rank: 740

Origin: German
Meaning: Luring rock
Alternate Spellings: Loralei, Loralai, Lorelai, Loreley
Gender Variation: Loren
Nickname: Lora
Similar Names: Loralee, Loralynn, Lorelle, Lorena, Lorene, Lorinda, Lorna
➡ A place name for a rock located on the eastern bank of the Rhine River derived from "lureln" and "ley." Also the name of a legendary maiden who lured navigators to the river and ultimately their death with her singing. It was popularized by Marilyn Monroe when she played the role of Lorelei Lee in the 1953 film *Gentlemen Prefer Blondes* that was based on the 1925 novel by Anita Loos. The name recently made a comeback influenced by Lorelai Gilmore, the fictional character from the popular television series *Gilmore Girls.*

Lorena
Rank: 705

Origin: Latin
Meaning: Crowned with laurel
Alternate Spellings: Laurena, Lorrina
Gender Variations: Laurence, Loren, Lorne
Nickname: Lori
Similar Names: Laryn, Lorene, Lorenza, Lorinda, Lorna, Lorraine
Namesakes: Lorena Ochoa (Mexican LPGA golfer)
➡ The latinized form of Lauren that peaked just prior to the turn of the 20th century but still in steady use among the top 800 names. It's also the title of a song considered a favorite of Confederate soldiers during the U.S. Civil War.

Lucero
Rank: 973

Origin: Spanish
Meaning: Light
Gender Variations: Lucas, Luke
Nickname: Luce
Similar Names: Lucerna, Lucia, Luciana, Lucille, Lucina, Lucinda, Lucrecia, Luisa, Luna
➡ A surname derived from "luz," which also means "morning or evening star." Used as a girl's given name since 1990.

Lucia
Rank: 340

Origin: Latin
Meaning: Light
Gender Variation: Lucian
Nickname: Lucy
Similar Names: Lucecita, Luciana, Lucila, Lucilda, Lucinda, Lucrecia, Luisa
Namesake: Lucia Rijker (Dutch boxer/kickboxer)
➡ Derived from the Latin *lux* and the feminine form of the Old Roman name Lucius. Saint Lucia of Syracuse was a 4th-century Christian martyr, known as the patron of blindness. Also the name of an island in the British West Indies. A good choice for parents looking for a trendy foreign name.

Luciana
Rank: 927

Origin: Latin
Meaning: Illumination
Alternate Spelling: Lucianna
Gender Variation: Lucian
Nicknames: Ana, Luci, Lucia
Similar Names: Luana, Lucerne, Lucette, Luciane, Lucille, Lucina, Lucinda, Lucine, Lumina, Luziana
Namesakes: Luciana Serra (Italian soprano)
➡ The feminine form of Lucian and the name of a character in Joseph Heller's 1961 classic novel, *Catch-22*. Brazilian jazz singer and composer Luciana Souza, who has been nominated for three Grammy awards, also comes to mind.

Lucille
Rank: 728

Origin: Latin
Meaning: Light
Alternate Spelling: Lucile
Gender Variations: Lucian, Luciano
Nickname: Lucy
Similar Names: Lucetta, Lucette, Lucia, Luciana, Lucienne, Lucilla, Lucinda, Lucinde, Lucita
➡ The French form of Lucilla known for comedienne and actress Lucille Ball who started her career in films during the 1930s and 1940s before moving to television to star in several successful shows starting with *I Love Lucy* that aired during the 1950s. Also the name blues singer-songwriter B. B. King gives to each of his guitars.

Lucy
Rank: 152

Origin: Latin
Meaning: Illumination
Alternate Spelling: Lucey, Luci, Lucie
Gender Variations: Lucas, Lucian, Lucio
Nicknames: Lu, Luce
Similar Names: Lucelle, Lucetta, Luciann, Lucienne, Lucilla, Lucille, Ludy, Lusinda, Lulu, Lucza
Namesakes: Lucy Lawless (*Xena* actress)
➡ English feminine form of Lucius. Peak positions on the chart in the 1880s inspired by one of the most popular first ladies of the 19th century, Lucy Hayes, wife of President Rutherford B. Hayes. Probably most remembered bearer of the name is actress Lucille Ball, especially known for her 1950s sitcom, *I Love Lucy*. Lucille's daughter and actress, Lucie Arnaz, bears a variation of the name. Another 1950s influence is Lucy van Pelt, character in the syndicated comic strip *Peanuts*, by Charles Schulz. More recently actress Lucy Liu has kept the name strong because of her successful film performances.

Luna
Rank: 516

Origin: Latin
Meaning: Moon
Gender Variation: Lundy
Similar Names: Livana, Lumina, Lunetta, Lunette, Selina
➡ In Roman mythology Diana, also referred to as Luna, was the goddess of the moon, whose counterpart in Greek mythology was Selene. Also considered an astrological name for people born under the sign of Cancer, which is ruled by the moon. It's been in use since the 19th century, then faded out in 1922, and saw a modest revival in 2003.

Luz
Rank: 591

Origin: Latin
Meaning: Light
Gender Variation: Luis
Similar Names: Lucinda, Lucita, Lucy, Luisa, Lumina, Luminosa, Luzette, Luziana
➡ The Spanish word for "light" that's used in reference to the Virgin Mary, often called "Our Lady of Light." The name has been in use since the 19th century.

Lydia Rank: 131

Origin: Greek
Meaning: From Lydia
Alternate Spellings: Lidea, Lidia, Lidiah, Lidiya, Lyydia
Gender Variations: Ledon, Lindan
Nickname: Lydie
Similar Names: Lada, Leyda, Lidka, Lidochka, Lidona, Linda, Lydah, Lydiana, Lyllian, Lyyti
➡ Surname and female first name derived from the Greek term *ludia* that is most preferred when spelled with a "y" in the middle. Also a biblical name for a New Testament woman converted to Christianity by Saint Paul. Lydia, played by actress Winona Ryder in the movie *Beetlejuice* in 1988, may have contributed to the name's comeback in popularity.

Lyric Rank: 644

Origin: Greek
Meaning: Lyric
Gender Variation: Lyndon
Similar Names: Lark, Lyra, Lyris, Lysette, Lyssa, Melody
➡ The musical vocabulary word for a verse that's sung to a melody that's derived from the Greek *lyrikos*. It's been used as a given name for girls since 1995 and peaked in 1996.

Mackenzie Rank: 53

Origin: Scottish Gaelic
Meaning: Son of Coinneach
Alternate Spellings: Mackenzey, Makensie, Makenzie, Mckenzie
Gender Variations: Mack, Mckenzie
Nickname: Kenzie
Similar Names: Macy, Maura, Maurine
Namesake: Mackenzie Rosman (actress)
➡ Originated from the Gaelic surname Mac Coinnich that was eventually used as a given name for boys. Actress Mackenzie Phillips, who played Julie on the 1970s sitcom *One Day at a Time*, paved the way for its use as a girl's name, leading to its debut on the popularity chart in 1976.

Macy Rank: 267

Origin: French
Meaning: Weapon
Alternate Spellings: Mace, Macee, Macey, Maci, Macie, Macye, Maicey, Maicy, Maisy, Massey
Gender Variations: Macedonio, Macer, Macy, Mason
Nicknames: Mae, Mace
Similar Names: Lacy, Macelia, Macia, Maciena, Masina, Mason, Massiel, Mazey
➡ Boy's and girl's name possibly derived from a surname taken from the short form of Thomas. Touched the chart in the late 1880s and early 1900s, but it wasn't until 1990 when the name came back for a consistent climb up the ranks inspired by the Grammy Award-winning R&B and soul singer and songwriter Macy Gray. Macy's, a chain of U.S. department stores founded in 1858, also comes to mind.

Madeline Rank: 71

Origin: Hebrew
Meaning: Woman from Magdala
Alternate Spellings: Madalyn, Madalynn, Madeleine, Madelyn, Madelynn, Madilyn
Gender Variations: Marc, Marcel
Nickname: Maddie
Similar Names: Madelia, Madge, Magdalene, Marcelle, Marcelline, Marlena
Namesakes: Madeleine L'Engle (children's author), Madeleine Stowe (actress)
➡ Derived from the French Madeleine that was taken from Magdala, a biblical place name for a village located on the Sea of Galilee and the home of Mary Magdalene, a follower of Jesus. Also a literary name for the heroine in a series of children's books created by author Ludwig Bemelmans. Listed among the top 100 since 1994.

Madison Rank: 3

Origin: English
Meaning: Son of Maud
Alternate Spellings: Maddison, Madisen, Madissyn, Madisyn, Madyson
Gender Variations: Mackenzie, Maddox
Nickname: Maddie
Similar Names: Addison, Madelina, Madelyn, Maegan
➡ The name was derived from an English surname associated with former U.S. President James Madison and his wife, Dolley. It was influenced by actress Daryl Hannah in the 1984 film *Splash* whose character adopted the name after seeing a street sign for Madison Avenue in New York.

Maeve
Rank: 645
Origin: Irish Gaelic
Meaning: Intoxicating
Alternate Spellings:
Mave, Meave
Gender Variation: Maitland
Nickname: Mae
Similar Names: Maeva, Maude, Maura, Mavis
⇨ The name of a legendary queen of Ireland who was known for her strong will and determination. The anglicized form of *Meadhbh*, it's been listed among the top girl's names since the late 1990s. Irish novelist Maeve Binchy, author of *Circle of Friends* that was adapted into a 1995 film starring Chris O'Donnell and Minnie Driver, is a famous bearer.

Magdalena
Rank: 908
Origin: Greek
Meaning: Watchtower
Alternate Spellings:
Magdalina, Magdelena, Magdelina
Gender Variations: Magnus
Similar Names: Madeline, Madonna, Magdalene, Maggie, Margaret, Marlena, Marlene
Namesake: Magdalena Maleeva (Bulgarian tennis player)
⇨ A form of the biblical name Magdalene associated with the village of Magdala located on the Sea of Galilee. The name is known for Mary Magdalene, also referred to as Mary of Magdala, a follower of Jesus. It was introduced into the United Kingdom from France during the Middle Ages, which led to the names Madeline and Madeleine.

Maggie
Rank: 189
Origin: Greek
Meaning: Pearl
Alternate Spellings:
Maggey, Maggi, Maggey, Maggy
Gender Variations: Magee, Magnus
Nicknames: Magg, Mags
Similar Names: Madge, Magda, Magena, Marga, Margie, Megan
Namesakes: Maggie Grace (actress), Maggie Gyllenhaal (actress)
⇨ The short form of Margaret that peaked prior to the turn of the 20th century and slowly decreased in popularity until 1971

when Scottish/English singer Rod Stewart released the song "Maggie May" that topped the charts in the United Kingdom and the U.S. Longtime British actress Maggie Smith, who plays Professor McGonagall in the *Harry Potter* films, is a famous bearer of the name.

Maia
Rank: 506
Origin: Latin
Meaning: Great
Alternate Spellings:
Maiya, Maja, Maya, Miah, Miya, Mya, Myah
Gender Variations: Mike, Miles, Milo
Similar Names: Maisie, Mamie, Mary, May, Mia, Mira
⇨ Associated with the Roman goddess of spring who gave her name to the fifth calendar month of the year. In Greek mythology she was the mother of the god Hermes. Popular use of the name began in 1996.

Makayla
Rank: 45
Origin: Hebrew
Meaning: Who resembles God
Alternate Spellings:
Macaela, Makaila, McKayla, Micaela, Michaela, Michela, Mikaela, Mikalah, Mikayla
Gender Variations: Michael, Mickey
Nicknames: Kayla, Mike
Similar Names: Michaelina, Michaeline, Michal, Michelle
⇨ A form of Michaela that was originally derived as the feminine variant of Michael. Also a possible combination of the Scottish Gaelic surname McKay with Kayla. Popularized by actress Jane Seymour during the 1990s when she played Dr. Michaela "Mike" Quinn on television's *Dr. Quinn, Medicine Woman*. Parents are drawn to the trendy "y" in the suffix.

Malaya
Rank: 939
Origin: American
Gender Variation: Malachi
Similar Names: Mahalia, Makayla, Malana, Malery, Malhala, Malia, Malie,

⇨ A geographical name for the southern part of the Malay Peninsula or a twist on the popular Makayla. The name made its debut in 2006 and uses the trendy "ya" ending.

Malia Rank: 410

Origin: Hebrew
Meaning: Sea of sorrow
Alternate Spellings:
Malaea, Maleah, Maliyah
Gender Variation: Maleko
Similar Names: Emalia, Maraea, Mele, Mere
➡ The Hawaiian form of Mary and Maria first listed among the most popular names in 1977.

Mallory Rank: 234

Origin: Old French
Meaning: Unlucky
Alternate Spellings:
Mallary, Mallerey, Mallery,
Mallorey, Mallori, Mallorie, Malorey,
Malori, Malorie, Malory
Gender Variations: Mallory, Miller, Muller
Nickname: Malo
Similar Names: Malley, Mallica, Mallisa,
Malorey, Meliora, Mellony, Melorie
➡ Originally a common surname that became a popular first-name choice for girls during the 1980s due to the fictional character played by Justine Bateman on the 1982 to 1989 television series *Family Ties*. The 1995 to 1999 sci-fi television series *Sliders* possibly influenced the name when it featured three characters with the names Quinn Mallory, Colin Mallory, and Mallory.

Mara Rank: 681

Origin: Hebrew
Meaning: Bitter
Alternate Spelling: Marah
Gender Variation: Malachi
Similar Names: Amara, Maralina, Maraline,
Maralyn, Maria, Mary, May, Tamara
Namesake: Mara Wilson (actress)
➡ An Old Testament name adopted by Naomi who was grief-stricken after the deaths of her husband and sons. Possibly a variation of Mary or the short form of Tamar. It's been listed among the top names since 1950.

Margaret Rank: 161

Origin: Greek
Meaning: Pearl
Alternate Spellings:
Margeret, Margret,
Gender Variation: Marius
Nicknames: Greta, Gretchen, Madge, Marga,
Maggie, Margie, Meg, Megan, Peggy, Rita
Similar Names: Madge, Mamie, Maret,

Margaux, Margery, Margharita, Marguerite,
Marketa, Marta
Namesakes: Marg Helgenberger (actress),
Margaret Mead (anthropologist), Margaret
Mitchell (author), Margaret Sullavan (actress)
➡ A popular name from the Middle Ages that's been associated with 19 royal figures, including Margaret of Anjou, the wife of King Henry VI of England; Margaret Tudor, the sister of Henry VIII; and Princess Margaret, the younger sister of British monarch Elizabeth II. It's also the name of nine saints and was used by Shakespeare in four plays. Margaret Thatcher, the only woman to have held the office of prime minister of the United Kingdom, is a recent bearer. Actress Meg Ryan, born Margaret Mary Emily Hyra, uses a pet form. It was listed among the top 10 until 1939 and the top 100 until 1975.

Margarita Rank: 944

Origin: Greek
Meaning: Pearl
Alternate Spellings:
Margareta, Margarida,
Margrieta, Marguerita
Nicknames: Marga, Marge, Margie, Rita
Similar Names: Margaret, Margery, Margo,
Marguerite, Marketa
➡ A form of Margaret often found in several languages including Spanish. Also a popular alcoholic beverage.

Maria Rank: 47

Origin: Hebrew
Meaning: Sea of sorrow
Alternate Spellings:
Marea, Mariae
Gender Variations: Mario, Mark
Similar Names: Mara, Mare, Maresol, Mariah,
Marian, Mariel, Mariette, Marissa, Mary, May
Namesakes: Maria Bello (actress), Maria
Sharapova (tennis player), Maria Shriver (TV journalist)
➡ The Latin variation of Mary widely used among Spanish- and non-Spanish-speaking countries. The name was highly ranked during the 1950s and 1960s, influenced by the musical *West Side Story* that featured the song "Maria." Also used as a combination and blended name such as Marianna and Mariangela. Listed among the top 100 since 1944.

Mariah   Rank: 81

Origin: Hebrew
Meaning: Sea of sorrow
Alternate Spellings:
Maraia, Marayah, Mariahe,
Mariyah, Marryah, Meriah, Mireya,
Moraiah, Moriah, Myriah
Gender Variations: Mariano, Mario
Nicknames: Riah
Similar Names: Maiah, Marah, Maria,
Mariam, Marian, Marianna, Marietta,
Mariette, Marika, Mayra
Namesake: Mariah Stewart (author)
⇒ Most commonly identified with the song
"They Call the Wind Mariah" from the 1951
musical *Paint Your Wagon*, but attributes its
appeal to the prominent success of singer
Mariah Carey. Variant of Mary that began
a 10-year placement within the top 100 in
1991 and is still widely used today.

Mariam   Rank: 692

Origin: Hebrew
Meaning: Sea of sorrow
Alternate Spellings:
Maryam, Meriam
Gender Variation: Marius
Similar Names: Maria, Mariah, Marian,
Mariana, Mariel, Marion, Mary, Miriam
⇒ A variation of the Hebrew name Miriam
that's been used sporadically since the 19th
century, listed among the top 700 names.

Mariana   Rank: 176

Origin: Ancient Rome
Meaning: Manly
Alternate Spellings:
Marianna, Marriana,
Maryana, Miriana
Gender Variations: Mariano, Marinus, Mario
Nicknames: Ana, Mary
Similar Names: Brianna, Kariana, Maria,
Mariam, Marianda, Marianella, Marianne,
Maribella, Marizela, Mary
⇒ The feminine and Italian form of the
Roman family name Marianus. Since its first
appearance on the chart in 1980, this name
has steadily climbed. *Mariana* is the name
of a poem written by Alfred, Lord Tennyson
in 1830. Also a place name for the Mariana
Trench, the deepest location in the earth's
crust, located in the floor of the Pacific
Ocean.

Maribel   Rank: 803

Origin: Spanish/French
Meaning: Beautiful Maria
Alternate Spellings:
Maribell, Maribelle,
Marybelle, Meribel, Meribelle
Gender Variations: Mariano, Mario
Nicknames: Mari, Belle
Similar Names: Mariana, Maribella, Marieta,
Marina, Marisol
⇒ A modern blend of the Spanish "Maria"
with the French "belle" that became popular
in the early 1960s and peaked in 1980.

Marie   Rank: 578

Origin: Hebrew
Meaning: Sea of sorrow
Alternate Spelling: Maree
Gender Variation: Mark
Nickname: Mari
Similar Names: Maria, Mariah, Marianne,
Maribel, Mariel, Mariela, Marielle, Marietta,
Marina
Namesake: Marie Osmond (singer/actress)
⇒ The French, Czech, and German form
of Maria. Historically known for Marie
Antoinette, the 18th-century queen consort
of King Louis XVI. Also associated with Marie
Curie, the 20th-century Polish-born French
physicist famous for her work on radioactivity
and a two-time winner of the Nobel Prize.
The name is often combined and blended
with other elements such as Anamarie,
Marie-Charlotte, and Marie-Lou.

Mariela   Rank: 808

Origin: Hebrew
Meaning: Sea of sorrow
Alternate Spelling: Mariella
Nickname: Marie
Similar Names: Marcela, Maricela, Mariele,
Marlee, Marvela, Maryla, Marylou
⇒ The Italian diminutive of Maria with the
fashionable "ela" ending that's been used as
a given name since 1990 and peaked just two
years later.

Marilyn   Rank: 514

Origin: Hebrew
Meaning: Sea of sorrow
Alternate Spellings:
Maralyn, Marelyn, Marilin,
Marilyne, Marilynn, Marilynne, Marylin
Gender Variations: Marley, Marlon

Nicknames: Mary, Lynn
Similar Names: Madilyn, Madisyn, Marianne, Maribel, Marielle, Marieke, Marilena, Marilene, Marinda, Marlie
➡ The combination of "Mary" and "lyn" that possibly originated during the 18th century as a blend of Mary and Ellen. Widely used since 1906 and listed among the top 100 from 1925 to 1958. The name is best known for sex symbol Marilyn Monroe, born Norma Jean Mortenson, who became one of the most popular film actresses during the 1950s and early 1960s before her untimely death.

Marin   Rank: 953

Origin: Latin
Meaning: Of the sea
Alternate Spellings: Maren, Marinn, Marrin, Maryn
Gender Variations: Marinus, Marlin
Similar Names: Marian, Mariana, Marina, Maris, Marna, Marnie
➡ The French, Romanian, and Croatian form of Marinus that first landed on the popularity chart as a girl's given name in 2004.

Marina   Rank: 406

Origin: Latin
Meaning: From the sea
Alternate Spellings: Mareena, Mareina, Marena, Marinna
Gender Variations: Marino, Marinus
Nicknames: Mari, Rina
Similar Names: Marian, Mariana, Marna, Marnetta, Marin, Marnie
➡ The feminine form of Marinus that's also known as a vocabulary word for a port where boats and yachts are kept. Shakespeare used the name in his play *Pericles, Prince of Tyre* for the daughter of the title character. The name has faded in popularity during the past 10 years but is still listed among the top 500.

Marisol   Rank: 321

Origin: Spanish
Meaning: Our lady of solitude
Alternate Spellings: Maresol, Marysol
Gender Variations: Marino, Mario
Nicknames: Mari, Sol
Similar Names: Maria, Marie, Marissa, Marisse, Mariske

➡ A combination name using Maria and Soledad. Spanish singer and actress Josefa Flores Gonzalez, better known as Marisol, had an impact on the name starting in the 1960s, which led to its debut on the popularity chart in 1962.

Marissa   Rank: 104

Origin: Latin
Meaning: Of the sea
Alternate Spellings: Marisa, Marrissa, Marysa, Maryssa, Merissa, Meryssa, Morissa
Gender Variations: Marinus, Mario
Nicknames: Issa, Mari, Maris
Similar Names: Carissa, Clarisssa, Larissa, Marianna, Marice, Mariella, Marietta, Marisol
Namesake: Marissa Jaret Winokur (actress)
➡ An elongated form of Maria that was listed among the top 100 from 1989 to 2005. The name is fashionable with its "issa" ending.

Maritza   Rank: 496

Origin: Latin
Meaning: Star of the sea
Alternate Spelling: Maritsa
Gender Variations: Marino, Martin
Similar Names: Maria, Marianela, Maribel, Maricela, Maricruz, Marisela, Marisol, Marissa, Maristela
➡ The Spanish form of Maria that landed on the popularity chart in 1956 and peaked in 2005. A good choice for parents who are looking for a trendy foreign name.

Marlene   Rank: 515

Origin: Hebrew
Meaning: Woman from Magdala
Alternate Spellings: Marleen, Marline
Gender Variations: Marley, Marlon
Nickname: Marla
Similar Names: Madeleine, Marilena, Marilene, Marilyn, Marinda, Marion, Marlena, Marley, Marlyne
➡ A blend of the names Maria and Magdalene that was influenced by German-born actress and singer Marlene Dietrich. It's been listed on the popularity chart since 1920, peaked during the mid-1930s, and has slowly faded to its current position.

Marley Rank: 415

Graph: 0.00%–0.06%, 1900 to TODAY

Origin: Old English
Meaning: Pleasant wood
Alternate Spellings: Marlea, Marlee, Marlie, Marly
Gender Variations: Marlin, Marlon
Similar Names: Mariel, Marilee, Marilyn, Marla, Marlaine, Marlene, Marlow, Marlyn
⇨ Originated from a surname and place name, and considered a pet form of Marlene that's been used consistently for girls since 1994. Parents may have picked up the name from the surname of Jamaican reggae musician Bob Marley or fictional character Jacob Marley from Charles Dickens' *A Christmas Carol*, who are both bearers of the surname. Academy Award-winning actress Marlee Matlin uses the trendy "ee" spelling.

Martha Rank: 526

Graph: 0.0%–0.8%, 1900 to TODAY

Origin: Aramaic
Meaning: Mistress of the house
Alternate Spelling: Marthe
Gender Variations: Martin, Marty
Nicknames: Marth, Martie
Similar Names: Marta, Martella, Martina, Martita, Mattie
Namesakes: Martha Graham (dancer choreographer), Martha Plimpton (model/actress)
⇨ A biblical name for the sister of Mary and Lazarus who pleaded with Jesus for her brother's resurrection. The name is historically known for Martha Washington, the wife of George Washington, the first U.S. president. It's best known today for lifestyle expert Martha Stewart, who turned a catering business into an international publishing, television, radio, and merchandising success story. The name peaked prior to the turn of the 20th century and has slowly declined in use.

Mary Rank: 84

Graph: 0%–6%, 1900 to TODAY

Origin: Hebrew
Meaning: Sea of sorrow
Alternate Spellings: Mari, Merry
Gender Variations: Marcus, Marty, Marvin
Nickname: Mare
Similar Names: Maria, Mariah, Mariam, Marica, Marie, Mariel, Marissa, Marla, Maura, Myriam

Namesakes: Mary J. Blige (singer/songwriter), Mary Chapin Carpenter (singer/songwriter), Mary Martin (actress), Mary Matalin (political strategist), Mary Pickford (actress), Mary Pierce (tennis player), Mary Shelley (author)
⇨ Perhaps the most widely used female name in history, ranking No. 1 prior to the turn of the 20th century until the beginning of the 1960s. A Christian name best known for the virgin mother of Jesus, his faithful follower Mary Magdalene, and several saints. Also considered a royal name used by two queens of England and one queen of Scotland. Occasionally combined with other names and popularized by actress Mary-Kate Olsen.

Maryam Rank: 954

Origin: Hebrew
Meaning: Sea of sorrow
Alternate Spelling: Mariam
Gender Variation: Marian
Nickname: Mary
Similar Names: Mariana, Marika, Mariya, Mary, Maryama, Maryamie, Maryanne, Marylin, Miriam
Namesakes: *Maryam* (2002 film), Maryam d'Abo (actress)
⇨ The Arabic form of Miryam that's predominantly used for Arab and Muslim girls.

Mattie Rank: 827

Graph: 0.0%–0.5%, 1900 to TODAY

Origin: German
Meaning: Strength in battle
Alternate Spellings: Maddie, Matti, Matty
Gender Variations: Mathis, Matias, Mattie
Nickname: Mat
Similar Names: Madison, Marta, Matilda, Maude
⇨ The pet form of Matilda that enjoyed early popularity as a given name, peaking in 1882, and was listed among the top 100 until 1920. It's also used as the short form of the boy's name Matthew.

Maura Rank: 922

Graph: 0.000%–0.020%, 1900 to TODAY

Origin: Gaelic
Meaning: Great
Alternate Spelling: Mora
Gender Variations: Maurice, Maurus
Similar Names: Mara, Maria, Marie, Marla, Marlis, Mary, Maureen, Mauve, Moira
Namesake: Maura Tierney (actress)

➡ Possibly from the Gaelic *mor* meaning "great" or the feminine form of Maurus prominently used in Ireland. The name of a saint who was martyred during the 4th century. It's been in popular use since 1948 and peaked during the 1960s.

Maya   Rank: 57

Origin: Sanskrit
Meaning: Illusion
Alternate Spellings: Maia, Maiya, Miah, Miya, Mya, Myah
Gender Variations: Myles, Myron
Similar Names: Macie, May, Mayme, Mayra
Namesake: Maya Rudolph (actress)
➡ Associated with the birth mother of Gautama Buddha as well as an alternate name of the Hindu goddess Durga from Indian mythology. Also used in reference to the Indian tribe located in southern Mexico and northern Central America. Best known for African-American author and poet Maya Angelou, born Marguerite Johnson, who assumed her professional name as a dancer during the 1940s. Its increase in popularity might be due to the trendy "a" on the end.

Mayra   Rank: 656

Origin: Latin
Meaning: Myrrh
Alternate Spelling: Mira
Gender Variations: Maynard, Myron
Nickname: May
Similar Names: Maria, Maya, Myria, Myrna, Myrtle
➡ First joined the popularity chart during the late 1960s as a variation of Myra, created by 17th-century poet Fulke Greville, which he possibly adopted from the aromatic gum tree resin.

Mckenna   Rank: 217

Origin: Scottish Gaelic
Meaning: Son of Coinneach
Alternate Spellings: Mackena, Mackenah, Makena, Makenah, Makenna, Mckennah, Mckinna, Mykena, Mykenah, Mykenna
Gender Variations: Mckade, Mckean, Mckell, Mckinley
Nicknames: Ken, Kenna

Similar Names: Macarena, Mckayla, Mckaylee, Mckell, Mckella, Mckendra, Mckenzie, Mckinley
➡ From the Gaelic surname Mac Cionnaith and also a form of Mackenna. Is possibly most remembered as the surname of main character Elise McKenna in the famed 1980 movie *Somewhere in Time*, played by actress Jane Seymour. Since its debut in 1991, this contemporary choice peaked in 2002 and is one of three variations of the name ranked among the most popular on the chart.

Mckinley   Rank: 964

Origin: Scottish
Gender Variations: Kingsley
Nickname: Kinley
Similar Names: Kenya, Kenzie, Keshia, Kimberly, Kinsey
➡ A Scottish surname derived from the early personal name Fionnlaoch. Also associated with Mount McKinley, located in Alaska and known as the highest peak in North America.

Meadow   Rank: 804

Origin: Old English
Meaning: To mow
Gender Variations: Leaf, Linden
Similar Names: Magnolia, Mahogany, Marigold, Meagan, Meena, Melanie, Shadow
➡ Taken from the vocabulary word for a low-lying grassland and derived from *mawan*. Debuted as a girl's given name in 2001.

Megan   Rank: 60

Origin: Greek
Meaning: Pearl
Alternate Spellings: Maegan, Maeghan, Magan, Magen, Maygan, Meagan, Megann, Megen, Meghan, Megyn
Gender Variations: Mead, Morgan
Nicknames: Meg, Meggie
Similar Names: Madge, Maggie, Maisie, Margo, Marje, Mayme, Merit, Midge
Namesake: Megan Quann (Olympic swimmer)
➡ Derived from *marged* and considered the Welsh pet form of Margaret. Debuted on the chart in 1952 and peaked three times during the 1980s and 1990s at No. 10.

Melanie   Rank: 83
Origin: Greek
Meaning: Black, dark
Alternate Spellings: Melainy, Melanee, Melany, Melony
Gender Variations: Melville, Melvin
Nickname: Mel
Similar Names: Melania, Melinda, Melissa, Melody, Millicent, Millie, Mindy
Namesake: Melanie Griffith (actress)
⇨ Derived from the Greek *melas* and associated with two Roman saints during the 5th century, a grandmother and granddaughter. Saint Melania the Younger sold all of her property after inheriting her father's wealth and gave the money to the poor. The "ie" ending was introduced to England by France during the Middle Ages. Influenced by Melanie Wilkes, the fictional character from *Gone with the Wind*.

Melina   Rank: 546
Origin: Greek
Meaning: Honey
Alternate Spellings: Malina, Mallina, Meleana, Meleena, Mellina
Gender Variation: Melek
Nickname: Mel
Similar Names: Malinda, Melanie, Melinda, Meline, Melissa, Melita, Mindy
Namesakes: Melina Mercouri (actress), Melina Perez (professional wrestler)
⇨ The name has been in use since the 19th century and recently climbed among the top 600. Influenced by actress Melina Kanakaredes, who had a starring role of Stella Bonasera on the series *CSI: NY*.

Melissa   Rank: 117
Origin: Ancient Greek
Meaning: Bee
Alternate Spellings: Malissa, Melessa, Melisa, Meliza, Melizah, Mellisa, Melyssa
Gender Variations: Mel, Melesio, Messiah
Nicknames: Lissa, Mel, Missy
Similar Names: Elissa, Lisa, Meleasa, Melicia, Melisanda, Melise, Melitta, Mellicent, Melosa
Namesake: Melissa Etheridge (musician/singer)
⇨ Greek mythological name given to forest nymph who was turned into a bee when caught saving young Zeus from his father,

Cronus. Stood out in the top 10 due to the premiere and success of the 1974 to 1983 *Little House on the Prairie* television series, starring Melissa Gilbert and Melissa Sue Anderson. Also influenced by singer and songwriter Melissa Manchester when her debut album was released in 1973. The name has many variations, but most trendy when spelled with "z," "ah," "y" or pronounced with the long "ee" sound.

Melody   Rank: 299
Origin: Greek
Meaning: Music, song
Alternate Spellings: Mellodey, Mellodi, Mellodie, Mellody, Melodea, Melodee, Melodey, Melodi, Melodie, Melodye
Gender Variations: Meldon, Meliton
Nickname: Mel
Similar Names: Harmony, Melendy, Melida, Melodia, Melony, Melory, Melyta, Memorie, Milada
⇨ From the vocabulary word that derives from the Greek word *melos* and *aeido*, referring to the rhythmic succession of single tones. It debuted on the popularity chart as a girl's given name in 1942 and peaked in 1960. Notable for Melody Thomas Scott, best-known for her current role as Nikki Newman on the daytime serial *The Young and the Restless*, and singer and songwriter Melody Thornton, from the Pussycat Dolls.

Mercedes   Rank: 440
Origin: Spanish
Meaning: Mercy
Alternate Spellings: Mercedeas, Mercedees, Mercedies, Mercedeez, Mercedez, Mersades, Mersadies
Gender Variation: Mercer
Nickname: Mercy
Similar Names: Mercede, Mercedis, Mercia, Mercilla, Mersera, Mery
⇨ Associated with the Virgin Mary, also called Santa Maria de las Mercedes, meaning Our Lady of Mercies. Related to the names Mercy and Mersera. Possibly inspired by Alexandre Dumas' 1846 novel *The Count of Monte Cristo*, featuring Mercedes as the lost love of character Edmond Dantes. Mercedes Ruehl, an Academy Award-winning theater and film actress, influenced the name

beginning in the 1970s. It peaked among the top 200 between 1990 and 1995. Also the name of the German luxury car.

Meredith
Rank: 310

Origin: Welsh
Meaning: Noted ruler
Alternate Spellings: Meredeth, Meredithe, Meredyth, Meredythe, Meridith, Meridyth, Merridithe, Merridyth, Merrydith, Merrydyth
Gender Variations: Meredith, Merek, Meril
Nicknames: Mere, Meri
Similar Names: Merediff, Meredy, Meregon, Merescil, Merielle, Merilyn, Meritt
➡ Derived from the Welsh names Maredudd and Meredydd, it's been more popular for girls in English-speaking countries since the mid-1920s. It debuted in 1910 with its most popular period ranked among the top 200 from 1971 to 1992, influenced by actress Meredith Baxter, best known for her role on the television sitcom *Family Ties*. Recently inspired by Meredith Grey, a fictional character from the popular television series *Grey's Anatomy,* and Meredith Vieira, who co-hosts NBC's *Today*.

Mia
Rank: 13

Origin: Italian
Meaning: Sea of sorrow
Alternate Spellings: Mea, Meya, Miah, Miya, Mya, Myah
Gender Variations: Micah, Mike
Similar Names: Maria, Mariah, Marie, Marilyn, Marisa, Marisol, Mary, Maya, Michelle, Nia
Namesakes: Mia Hamm (soccer player), Mia Tyler (model)
➡ The Danish and Swedish pet form of Maria. Actress Mia Farrow, whose birth name is Maria, first brought attention to the name during the 1960s, which led to its debut on the popularity chart in 1964. More recently associated with the name of the leading character in Disney's *Princess Diaries* movies.

Micah
Rank: 714

Origin: Hebrew
Meaning: Humble
Alternate Spellings: Mica, Micaiah, Micha, Michah, Mika, Mikah, Mikka, Myca, Mycah, Myka
Gender Variations: Micah, Michael

Similar Names: Mia, Micaela, Michal, Michalina, Michele
➡ A biblical name for a minor prophet and author of the book that bears his name. Generally considered a boy's name, it made its debut on the girl's chart in 1978, recently climbing as part of a resurgence in biblical names.

Michelle
Rank: 80

Origin: Hebrew
Meaning: Who resembles God
Alternate Spellings: Machelle, Mashelle, M'chelle, Mechelle, Meshell, Michele, Mishelle, Mychele, Mychelle, Myshell
Gender Variations: Michael, Mick, Mitchell
Nicknames: Chelle, Shelly
Similar Names: Mia, Michaela, Michalina, Michelyne, Micki, Miguela, Misha
Namesakes: Michelle Branch (singer/songwriter), Michelle Kwan (Olympic figure skater), Michelle Pfeiffer (actress), Michelle Wie (LPGA golfer)
➡ The French feminine form of Michael that debuted on the popularity chart in 1938 and has been listed among the top 100 since 1954. The name spent nine years at No. 5 after the 1965 release of The Beatles' song "Michelle" known for its bilingual lyrics.

Mila
Rank: 749

Origin: American
Alternate Spelling: Myla
Gender Variations: Miles, Milo
Similar Names: Melia, Milada, Milan, Milena, Milessa, Mileta, Miley, Mina, Mira, Miya
➡ The short form of several names such as Camila, Ludmila, Milena, and Emilia. Mila Kunis, who played the role of Jackie Burkhart on *That '70s Show,* is a namesake.

Mina
Rank: 995

Origin: Arabic/Hindi/Persian
Meaning: Seaport, love, precious stone, daisy flower
Alternate Spellings: Minah, Myna, Mynah
Gender Variation: Micah
Similar Names: Mia, Micah, Mila, Mira
➡ The short form of names ending in "mina" used independently since the 19th century.

Mira Rank: 935
Origin: Latin/Slavic/Hindi
Meaning: Wonderful, peace, prosperous
Alternate Spellings: Mirra, Myra
Gender Variation: Myron
Similar Names: Maria, Marie, May, Mia, Mirana, Mirella, Myria, Myrna
⇒ A variation of Myra and Miranda that's been sporadically used since it first joined the popularity chart during the 19th century. The name is known for actress Mira Sorvino, who won an Academy Award for Best Supporting Actress for her role in Woody Allen's 1995 film *Mighty Aphrodite*.

Miracle Rank: 482
Origin: Latin
Meaning: To wonder at
Gender Variation: Michael
Similar Names: Harmony, Journey, Liberty, Patience
⇒ Derived from *mirari* and taken from the vocabulary word that means "an extraordinary event." Part of a recent trend to use word names such as Harmony and Journey, which are also currently listed among the top 1,000.

Miranda Rank: 139
Origin: Latin
Meaning: Admirable
Alternate Spellings: Meranda, Merinda, Mirannda, Mirandah, Mirranda, Mirrandah, Muranda
Gender Variations: Miron, Morell, Murray
Nicknames: Mia, Mira, Miran, Miri
Similar Names: Maranda, Marenda, Mariana, Marindi, Merina, Mirella, Mirian, Mirinda, Mironda, Randa
Namesake: Miranda Cosgrove (actress)
⇒ Derived from the Latin word, "mirandus," it was the name created by Shakespeare for the heroine in the play, *The Tempest*. This is also the name of one of the 27 known moons of Uranus discovered in 1948. It peaked as a top 100 choice for girls from 1991 to 1999 and continues to be popular partly due to actress Miranda Otto who appeared in *The Lord of the Rings* movies in 2002 and 2003. Actress Miranda Richardson also comes to mind. A trendy name with its "a" ending.

Miriam Rank: 292
Origin: Hebrew
Meaning: Sea of sorrow
Alternate Spellings: Mariam, Maryam, Meriam, Miriame, Miriem, Mirriam, Miryam, Miryem, Myriam, Myryam
Gender Variations: Mira, Miro, Miron
Nickname: Mimi
Similar Names: Mairwen, Miracle, Miram, Miriama, Mirian, Mirinda, Mirit, Miyana
⇒ Original Hebrew form of Mary that was given to the elder sister of Moses and Aaron in the Old Testament. The name was revived in the 18th century and peaked on the popularity chart in 1917. A well-known bearer of the name was painter and sculptor Miriam Davenport, who helped European Jews escape the Holocaust during World War II.

Molly Rank: 105
Origin: Hebrew
Meaning: Sea of sorrow
Alternate Spelling: Mollie
Gender Variations: Moe, Monroe, Monty
Nickname: Mol
Similar Names: Maleah, Mally, Manon, Mara, Mare, Mariah, Marie, Mary, Moira, Mona
Namesakes: Molly Ringwald (actress), Molly Shannon (actress/writer)
⇒ The Irish pet form of Mary that was first coined during the 18th century. Throughout the years the name has been associated with the popular Irish song "Sweet Molly Malone," the old-time radio show *Fibber McGee and Molly*, the movie *The Unsinkable Molly Brown*, and the television show *The Days and Nights of Molly Dodd*.

Monica Rank: 250
Origin: Latin
Meaning: Advisor
Alternate Spellings: Moneka, Monicah, Monicka, Monika, Monnica, Monnicah, Monnicka, Monnyca, Monyca, Monycka
Gender Variations: Monico, Monnie
Nickname: Moni
Similar Names: Mona, Monicia, Monikue, Moniqua, Monisha, Monita
Namesake: Monica Seles (tennis player)
⇒ Possibly derived from the Latin word, *moneo*, but it's most likely of unknown North

African or Phoenician origin. Inspired by Monica, a Grammy Award-winning R&B singer-songwriter who debuted in 1995 and became the youngest recording act with two consecutive chart-topping hits on the U.S. Billboard Top R & B Singles chart. Another well-known bearer is actress Monica Bellucci, whose film career began in the early 1990s. Also known for fictional character Monica Geller on the famed television sitcom *Friends*, originally airing from 1994 to 2004.

Monique
Rank: 655

Origin: Latin
Meaning: Advisor
Alternate Spellings: Monika, Mo'Nique
Gender Variation: Montague
Nicknames: Mique
Similar Names: Mona, Monica, Monice, Monifa
Namesake: Monique Hennagan (Olympic track and field medalist)
➡ The French form of Monica that's been used in the U.S. and the United Kingdom since the 1950s. The name peaked in the U.S. in 1980 at No. 93 and is listed among the top 700.

Monserrat
Rank: 702

Origin: Latin
Meaning: Jagged mountain
Alternate Spelling: Montserrat
Gender Variation: Montague
Similar Names: Mona, Monique, Montana
➡ A variation of Montserrat, which is the name of a mountain near Barcelona and the site of a Benedictine abbey. The island of Montserrat, located in the Caribbean Sea, was named after the mountain climbed by Christopher Columbus on his second voyage to the New World in 1493. It's been used as a girl's given name since 2000.

Morgan
Rank: 35

Origin: Welsh
Meaning: Born from the sea
Alternate Spellings: Morgaine, Morgann, Morganne, Morgen, Morgin, Mourgan
Gender Variations: Morgen, Mortimer
Similar Names: Meghan, Moreen, Morgana, Morganetta, Moriah
Namesakes: Lorrie Morgan (musician), Morgan York (actress)

➡ Derived from Morcant, which is a popular Welsh family name. In literature Morgan le Fay was the sister of King Arthur in Sir Thomas Malory's 15th-century book *The History of the Renowned Prince Arthur, King of Britain*. Influenced by actress Morgan Fairchild, born Patsy Anne McClenny, during the 1980s when she appeared in the prime-time soap opera *Flamingo Road*. Also used for boys but considerably more popular for girls.

Myla
Rank: 918

Origin: English
Meaning: Merciful
Alternate Spelling: Mila
Gender Variation: Myles
Similar Names: Myisha, Mylea, Myleen, Mylie, Mylinda, Myra
➡ The contemporary feminine form of Myles, known for novelist Myla Goldberg, author of the critically acclaimed *Bee Season* that was adapted into a 2005 film.

Nadia
Rank: 188

Origin: Russian
Meaning: Hope
Alternate Spellings: Nadea, Nadiah, Nadija, Nadiya, Nadiyah, Nadya
Gender Variations: Nader, Nahemiah, Nandan, Naul
Nickname: Nadi
Similar Names: Nada, Nadejda, Nadezhda, Nadie, Nadija, Nadine, Nadzia, Natka, Nydia
➡ A popular name in Russia and in the Middle East that originated as the French and English form of Nadya and short form of Nadezhda. It was inspired by 14-year-old Russian gymnast Nadia Comaneci who became one of the stars of the 1976 Olympic Games in Montreal as the first recipient of a perfect 10 for her performance on the uneven bars.

Naima
Rank: 888

Origin: Arabic
Meaning: To be contented
Alternate Spellings: Naema, Naimah, Na'imah, Neima
Gender Variation: Na'im
Similar Names: Nabiha, Nabila, Nahla, Naomi, Nayeli
➡ The feminine form of Na'im that's been used in popularity since 2005.

Nancy

Rank: 326

Origin: Hebrew
Meaning: Gracious
Alternate Spellings: Nancea, Nancee, Nancey, Nanci, Nancie, Nancsi, Nancye, Nanncy, Nansee, Nansi
Gender Variations: Nandan, Nasir
Nickname: Nanc
Similar Names: Nanami, Nancia, Nancine, Nandani, Nandi, Nandria, Nanice, Nannah, Nattie
Namesakes: Nancy Allen (actress), Nancy Wilson (singer)
⇒ The pet form of Anna and associated with a city in the northeast of France. A literary name for fictional detective Nancy Drew heroine of a popular mystery series created in 1930 by Edward Stratemeyer. The name is notable for the first lady and wife of 40th U.S. President Ronald Reagan and singer Nancy Sinatra, best known for her 1966 hit, "These Boots Are Made for Walkin'." Influenced during the 1990s by Olympic and World Championship ice skater Nancy Kerrigan.

Naomi

Rank: 129

Origin: Hebrew
Meaning: Pleasantness
Alternate Spellings: Nayomee, Naomee, Naomey, Naomie, Naomy
Gender Variations: Nathan, Noah, Nolan
Nicknames: Naome, Naya, Nayo
Similar Names: Naoma, Naomia, Naonna, Naovanni, Natoya, Naylia, Nayrobi, Naytalia, Neomee
Namesake: Naomi Watts (actress)
⇒ Biblical name most well-known because of Naomi, Ruth's mother-in-law in the Old Testament book of Ruth. Also recognized because of country music singer Naomi Judd, along with her daughter Wynona who formed the 1980s duo, The Judds. Name reentered the top 200 on the chart in 1997 and is even more popular today because of its long "ee" sound and its classic flair.

Natalia

Rank: 94

Origin: Latin
Meaning: Born on Christmas Day
Alternate Spellings: Natalya, Nathalia, Nathalya

Nickname: Nattie
Similar Names: Natala, Natalie, Natasha, Nathalie, Nettie, Talia
Namesake: Natalia Vodianova (Russian model)
⇒ The Italian, Polish, and Spanish form of the name Natalie. Used by the early Christians in honor of a 4th-century saint. The name has risen in popularity since the 1970s, recently landing among the top 100.

Natalie

Rank: 16

Origin: Latin
Meaning: Born on Christmas day
Alternate Spellings: Natalee, Nataly, Natelie, Nathalee, Nathalie, Nathaly, Natilie, Natily
Gender Variations: Nathan, Nathaniel
Nicknames: Nata, Nattie
Similar Names: Catalina, Natalia, Natalina, Natalya, Natasha, Natisha
Namesakes: Natalie Cole (singer) Natalie Maines (musician), Natalie Portman (actress)
⇒ From the Latin name Natalia, which refers to Christmas or the birthday of Christ. Actress Natalie Wood, born Natalya Nikolaevna Zakharenko, first brought attention to the name when she appeared in the 1947 film *Miracle on 34th Street* at the age of nine.

Natasha

Rank: 357

Origin: Latin
Meaning: Born on Christmas day
Alternate Spellings: Natacha, Natascha, Natashah, Natashia, Natashja, Natasshah, Natasshia, Natosha, Natossha
Gender Variations: Nash, Natal, Natanael
Nickname: Nat
Similar Names: Latasha, Natalia, Natalie, Nastalya, Natashenka, Natasia, Natisha, Natucha
Namesake: Natasha Henstridge (Canadian fashion model/actress)
⇒ Variation of Natalie, which is ultimately derived from the Latin name Natalia or Latin words *natale domini*. Also possibly a contemporary blend of Natalie and Tasha. Considered a literary name for Natasha Rostova, the main female character in Leo Tolstoy's novel *War and Peace*, published

during the 19th century. British film and stage actress Natasha Richardson was named after this fictional character.

Nayeli
Rank: 394

Origin: Latin
Meaning: Horn
Alternate Spellings: Naeyli, Nayelee, Nayelie, Nayelli, Nayellie, Nayolly, Nayelley, Nayely, Nayeley
Gender Variations: Nayan, Nayati
Nicknames: Nate, Nay, Eli
Similar Names: Natalia, Nayel, Nayila, Naylibbi, Nela, Nelia, Nekeisha
➪ A form of Nelia derived from the name Cornelia. May also have the Native American meaning "I love you" in the Zapotec language. First appeared on the chart in 1993 and climbed all the way to No. 175 by 2001. Popular for its "y" spelling.

Nevaeh
Rank: 43

Origin: American
Alternate Spelling: Neveah
Gender Variation: Neville
Similar Names: Nevah, Nevara, Neve
➪ A created name for heaven spelled backward that quickly became fashionable after debuting at No. 266 in 2001, possibly following a recent biblical naming trend.

Nia
Rank: 380

Origin: Gaelic/African
Meaning: Lustrous, purpose
Alternate Spellings: Nea, Niah, Nya, Nyah
Gender Variations: Niall, Nick
Similar Names: Neve, Niamh, Nichelle, Nicola
Namesakes: Nia (Blackalicious hip-hop album), Nia Long (actress), Nia Peeples (singer/actress)
➪ The Welsh form of Niamh and also means "purpose" in Swahili. The name peaked in 2001, influenced by actress Nia Vardalos who wrote and starred in the 2002 film *My Big Fat Greek Wedding*.

Nicole
Rank: 74

Origin: Greek
Meaning: Victorious people
Alternate Spellings: Nichole, Nicholl, Nicholle, Nicol, Nikole

Gender Variations: Nicholl, Nicholas, Nick
Nicknames: Nicki, Nico
Similar Names: Colette, Nichelle, Nichola, Nicolette
Namesakes: Nicole Eggert (actress), Nicole Hollander (cartoonist)
➪ The French feminine form of Nicholas used as a given name since the 1940s. It was influenced by Australian actress Nicole Kidman, whose successful career started in the U.S. in 1989.

Nicolette
Rank: 997

Origin: Greek
Meaning: Victorious people
Alternate Spellings: Nicolet, Nicollette, Nikolett
Gender Variations: Colin, Nichol, Nicholas
Nicknames: Colette, Nic, Nicky
Similar Names: Nichola, Nicoletta, Nicolina, Nicoline
➪ A variation of Nicole ultimately used as the French feminine form of Nicholas. Actress Nicollette Sheridan from *Desperate Housewives* fame uses an alternate spelling of the name.

Nina
Rank: 272

Origin: Spanish
Meaning: Little girl
Alternate Spellings: Neena, Neenah, Neina, Nena, Neneh, Nenna, Nyna
Gender Variations: Ninious, Nino
Nickname: Nin
Similar Names: Ninete, Ninetta, Ninon, Ninoska, Ninya, Nona
➪ The short form of names that end in "nina," such as Antonina, and related to the Spanish word *niña* and the Hebrew name Ann. Listed among the top 200 from the 1880s until 1941 due to the fame of Ballerina Dame Ninette de Valois, the founder of London's renowned Royal Ballet in 1931. The name maintained its popularity with the inspiration of singer, songwriter, and civil rights activist Nina Simone, who released more than 40 albums between the 1950s and 1990s. Also influenced by rock singer Nina Rachel Shapiro Gordon, the co-founder of the band Veruca Salt, who moved on to a successful solo career after leaving the band in 1998. Also the name of one of Christopher Columbus's three ships.

Noelia
Rank: 795

Origin: French
Meaning: Christmas
Alternate Spellings: Noellia, Noe
Gender Variation: Noel
Nickname: Elia
Similar Names: Natalia, Natasha, Natividad, Noela, Noelene, Noelle, Nola
⇨ The Spanish and Italian feminine form of Noel, often given to girls born during the Christmas season.

Noelle
Rank: 451

Origin: Old French
Meaning: Christmas
Alternate Spellings: Noele, Noell, Nowel, Nowell
Gender Variation: Noel
Similar Names: Noelene, Noelia, Noeline, Noella, Noelynn
⇨ The feminine form of Noel, which is a festive name related to the Christmas holiday. Parents started using the name on a regular basis during the mid-1960s.

Noemi
Rank: 634

Origin: Hebrew
Meaning: Pleasantness
Alternate Spelling: Noeme
Gender Variations: Noah, Noam
Nickname: Mimi
Similar Names: Naomi, Naomia, Neomi, Nona, Nonie
⇨ The Spanish and Portuguese form of Naomi that became popular in the mid-1950s and peaked among the top 600 names before falling to its current position. A popular choice among Hispanic parents.

Nora
Rank: 245

Origin: Greek
Meaning: Torch
Alternate Spellings: Noora, Norah, Norra, Norrah
Gender Variations: Norlan, Norrel, Norton
Nickname: Noor
Similar Names: Lanora, Noralee, Norangelice, Nordia, Noreena, Norella, Norelle, Norissa, Norry, Norwanna
Namesake: Nora Huntington (*Desperate Housewives* TV character)
⇨ Either the short form of Greek names Eleanora and Eleanor or the Latin name Honora, meaning "honor." Used as an independent name in Scotland and often the feminine form of Norman. The name made a more recent jump back among the top 300 on the chart with the fame of singer-songwriter Norah Jones, who has become one of the most successful recording artists of the 2000s.

Nyasia
Rank: 807

Origin: Greek
Meaning: Goal
Gender Variation: Nye
Nickname: Nya
Similar Names: Nisha, Nissa, Nydia, Nyree, Nysa, Nysse
⇨ A form of Nyssa that debuted on the popularity chart in 1999.

Nyla
Rank: 385

Origin: Gaelic
Meaning: Champion
Alternate Spellings: Nylah, Nylla, Nyllah
Gender Variations: Nylan, Nyle, Nyron
Similar Names: Nela, Nile, Nola, Nula, Nya, Nyasia, Nyda, Nyia, Nyleen, Nyna
⇨ Feminine form of Nyles, which is ultimately derived from Neil. It peaked on the chart in 2005, the same year IQ, the U.S. teenage pop and hip-hop girl group, began performing with rapper and vocalist Nyla Williams, an up-and-coming bearer of the name. Trendy for its "y" in the middle spelling.

Olivia
Rank: 7

Origin: English
Meaning: Olive tree
Alternate Spellings: Alivia, Olivea, Olivya
Gender Variation: Oliver
Nicknames: Liv, Liva, Livia, Livie, Olia, Ollie, Olva
Similar Names: Olia, Oliva, Olive, Olivetta, Olivette, Olivie, Olivine
Namesake: Olivia de Havilland (actress)
⇨ Shakespeare is credited with inventing the name for the rich heiress wooed by a duke in his play *Twelfth Night*. Possibly taken from the Latin word *oliva* which means "olive." The name was influenced during the 1970s by Australian singer and actress Olivia Newton-John and first entered the top 100 in 1990.

Paige Rank: 76
Origin: Old French
Meaning: Young servant
Alternate Spellings:
Page, Payge
Gender Variations: Paden, Patton
Similar Names: Pagett, Paisley, Pamela,
Paula, Peggy
Namesake: Geraldine Page (actress)
➡ Derived from the occupational surname
generally given to a young boy who was
a page to a lord during the Middle Ages.
Debuted on the popularity chart during the
early 1950s, which coincided with the rise to
fame of country and pop singer Patti Page.
Also the name of a character on the
television sitcoms *Ellen* and *Charmed*.

Paisley Rank: 835
Origin: Scottish
Meaning: Tear-drop print
Gender Variation: Parry
Similar Names: Ainsley,
Kinsley, Pacey, Paige, Pansy, Payton
➡ A Scottish surname and place name for a
royal burgh in Scotland that became famous
for manufacturing the Paisley patterned
fabric during the 19th century.

Paloma Rank: 853
Origin: Spanish
Meaning: Dove
Alternate Spellings:
Palloma, Peloma
Gender Variation: Pablo
Nickname: Aloma
Similar Name: Paola
Namesake: Paloma Picasso (French/Spanish
fashion designer)
➡ The Spanish word for dove often referred
to as the bird of peace. French and Spanish
fashion designer Paloma Picasso, daughter of
Spanish painter and sculptor Pablo Picasso,
is a famous bearer of the name.

Pamela Rank: 530
Origin: Greek
Meaning: All honey
Alternate Spellings: Pamala,
Pamalla, Pamella, Pamila,
Pamilla, Pammela
Gender Variation: Palmer
Nicknames: Pam, Pammy
Similar Names: Palma, Paloma, Pamelia, Tamela

Namesake: Pam Shriver (tennis player)
➡ Invented during the 16th century by poet
Sir Philip Sidney for his poem *Arcadia*. The
name was also used by 18th-century writer
Samuel Richardson for the title character in
his best-selling novel *Pamela*. The name was
influenced from 1978 to 1991 by character
Pam Ewing on the popular prime-time
television soap opera *Dallas*. Canadian
actress, model, and television personality
Pamela Anderson is a current namesake.

Paola Rank: 302
Origin: Latin
Meaning: Little
Gender Variations: Paul,
Paulo
Similar Names: Paloma, Pascuala, Patricia,
Paula
➡ The Italian and Spanish feminine form
of Paul that was derived from the Roman
family surname Paulus. Also used as a
variation of Paula, it debuted on the
popularity chart in 1983.

Paris Rank: 260
Origin: French
Alternate Spellings:
Parice, Parise, Pariss,
Parisse, Parris, Parys, Paryse,
Paryss, Parysse
Gender Variations: Paris, Parish, Parry
Similar Names: Paradise, Parasly, Paria,
Parisa, Pascale
➡ The meaning is unknown. Derived from
from the ancient Celtic tribe known as the
Parisii. A place name for the fashionable
capital city of France that is used for both
boys and girls. Becoming more popular for
girls, especially because of hotel heiress
and socialite Paris Hilton.

Parker Rank: 637
Origin: Old French
Meaning: Keeper of the
park
Gender Variations:
Parker, Parry, Porter
Similar Names: Paris, Patience, Patrice
Namesake: Parker Posey (actress)
➡ An occupational surname for someone
who works as a gamekeeper, especially
popular for boys that more than likely spilled
over when it debuted as a girl's name in 1999.

Pa ⇒ girls' names

Patience
Rank: 580

Origin: Latin
Meaning: Patience
Gender Variations:
Parker, Patrick
Similar Names: Charity, Faith, Hope, Patricia, Patsy, Pattie

⇒ Taken directly from the vocabulary word that's derived from the Latin *patientia*. It's considered one of the virtue names used by the Puritans during the 16th century. Popular 20th-century British poet Patience Strong, born Winifred Emma May, is a namesake.

Patricia
Rank: 413

Origin: Latin
Meaning: Nobleman
Alternate Spellings:
Patriceia, Patricja, Patrisha, Patrishia, Patrizia, Patrizzia
Gender Variations: Patrice, Patrick
Nicknames: Pat, Patti, Tricia, Trish
Similar Names: Beatrice, Patrell, Patrese, Patrica, Patrina, Patryce, Patsy
Namesakes: Pat Nixon (former first lady), Patsy Cline (country/pop singer)

⇒ Feminine form of Patricius, taken from the male name Patrick and derived from the Latin word *patrician*, one of two Roman social and political classes. The name climbed in popularity when Queen Victoria's granddaughter, Princess Patricia, was born in 1886 and eventually became known as Patsy to family and friends. It was influenced by the fame of Academy Award-winning actress Patricia Neal and actress Patty Duke, who uses a shortened form of the name. Several notable musicians who bear a form of this name are Grammy Award-winning R & B soul singer Patti LaBelle and four-time Grammy Award-winning rocker Pat Benatar. Also a popular hyphenated name, such as Patricia-Anne or Patricia-Lynn.

Paula
Rank: 671

Origin: Latin
Meaning: Small
Gender Variations:
Paolo, Paul
Similar Names: Paola, Pauleen, Paulette, Paulina, Pauline, Polly
Namesakes: Paula Deen (TV cook), Paula Poundstone (comedienne), Paula Prentiss (actress), Paula Zahn (TV host)

⇒ The feminine form of Paul derived from *paulus* and used among early Christians in honor of the biblical figure. The name was inspired during the 1960s after the release of the No. 1 song "Hey, Paula." It's currently known for 1980s and 1990s pop singer and *American Idol* judge Paula Abdul.

Paulina
Rank: 499

Origin: Latin
Meaning: Small
Alternate Spelling: Polina
Gender Variations: Paul, Paulino
Nickname: Paula
Similar Names: Paolina, Pasha, Pauletta, Paulette, Pauline
Namesake: Paulina Rubio (Mexican singer/actress)

⇒ A form of Pauline and the feminine form of the Late Latin name Paulinus that was used by several early martyrs. The name is known today for Cezch-born supermodel and actress Paulina Porizkova, who became a top model in Paris during the early 1980s and rose to fame in the U.S. when she first appeared in the *Sports Illustrated* Swimsuit Issue in 1983.

Penelope
Rank: 481

Origin: Greek
Meaning: Weaver
Alternate Spelling:
Pennelope
Gender Variation: Pelham
Nicknames: Pen, Penny
Similar Names: Penlcia, Penina, Penna, Penninnah
Namesakes: Dr. Penelope Leach (British parenting expert), *Penelope* (2006 film), Penelope Ann Miller (actress), Penelope Cruz (Spanish actress)

⇒ Adopted from Greek mythology for the wife of Odysseus, who spent time weaving while she waited 20 years for her husband's return from the Trojan War. The name has since been associated with faithfulness. It's been used sporadically since the 19th century but influenced since 2001 by Penelope Cruz, the first Spanish actress to be nominated for an Academy Award in the best actress category. The name is also linked with *penelops*, which means "duck."

Perla   Rank: 387
Origin: Latin
Meaning: Pearl
Alternate Spellings:
Pearla, Pearlah, Pearlea,
Pearleah, Perlah
Gender Variations: Peralt, Perez, Pernell
Nickname: Perl
Similar Names: Diamond, Opal, Pearl,
Pearlina, Pearlita, Pearly, Pella, Pera, Verla
Namesake: Perla Adea (actress)
➥ Italian and Spanish form of Pearl, which is
the vocabulary word for concretions formed
inside certain mollusk shells and a jewel
name for the birthstone of June that is
supposed to bring health and wealth. The
name debuted on the popularity chart in 1979
and saw a surge in popularity in 2003. Young
U.S. actress Perla Haney-Jardine, who starred
in *Kill Bill Vol. 2* in 2004 and *Spider-Man 3* in
2007, has kept the name among the top 400.
Considered a trendy name because of its
jewel association.

Peyton   Rank: 138
Origin: Old English
Meaning: Village of the
warrior
Alternate Spellings: Paten,
Patin, Paton, Payton
Gender Variations: Patrick, Patton, Paden
Nicknames: Pet, Pey, Tae
Similar Names: Padon, Petra, Petrina, Tayton
➥ Variation of Payton, which can also be found
in the top 200 on the popularity chart. From
a surname which was derived from an English
place name meaning "Poega's town." Popular
spelling with a "y" also contributes to its success
as a name of choice. Also used as a boy's
name, but slightly more fashionable for girls.

Phoebe   Rank: 366
Origin: Greek
Meaning: Bright, radiant
Alternate Spellings:
Pheabe, Phebe, Pheby,
Pheobe, Phoebey, Phoibe
Gender Variations: Philip, Phineas
Similar Names: Phemie, Philomena, Philippa,
Phoena, Phylicia, Phyllis
Namesake: Phoebe Cates (actress)
➥ A biblical name mentioned in the New
Testament for a deacon of the church
at Cenchreae. In Greek mythology, Phoebe's

daughter Leto was the mother of Apollo and
Artemis. The name became known to millions
of fans of the television series *Friends* for
fictional character Phoebe Buffay.

Phoenix   Rank: 816

Origin: Greek
Meaning: Dark red
Alternate Spellings:
Fenix, Phenix, Phoenyx
Gender Variation: Phoenix
Similar Names: London, Montana, Paris,
Raven, Sydney
Namesakes: *Phoenix* (1998 film)
➥ A mythical bird that dies in flames and is
reborn from the ashes every 500 years and
the capital city of Arizona, so named because
it was born from the ruins of a former
civilization. Derived from the Greek *phoinix*
and used as a girl's given name starting in
2003. Listed among the top 500 for boys.

Piper   Rank: 246
Origin: Old English
Meaning: Pipe player
Alternate Spellings: Pipere,
Pipper, Pyper, Pypper
Gender Variations: Piper, Pippin
Nickname: Pip
Similar Names: Pipiena, Pipina, Pippa,
Pippen, Pippi
➥ This boy's and girl's name derived from
an occupational surname that was originally
given to someone who played a pipe. The
name graced the chart in 1990, best known
for film and television actress Piper Laurie
whose career has spanned more than six
decades. Actress Piper Perabo and one of
the leading characters in the TV series
Charmed also come to mind.

Precious   Rank: 555
Origin: Latin
Meaning: Precious
Gender Variations:
Prentice, Prescott, Price
Similar Names: Preita, Prima, Princess,
Prudence, Purity
➥ Taken from the vocabulary word that's
derived from the Latin *pretiosus* that means
"of great value." It's been listed among the
top names since 1978. Historically the
Catholics have used the name in reference
to the "precious blood of Christ."

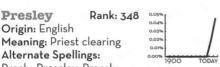

Presley
Rank: 348
Origin: English
Meaning: Priest clearing
Alternate Spellings:
Presly, Pressley, Pressly
Gender Variations: Preston
Similar Names: Paisley, Precious, Priscilla
Namesakes: Jaime Pressly (actress), Lisa Marie Presley (singer), Priscilla Presley (actress)
⇒ A surname derived from a place name that's often used in honor of legendary singer Elvis Presley, who's widely known as the King of Rock and Roll. First listed among the top names almost 10 years ago and has climbed to its current standing today.

Princess
Rank: 709
Origin: English
Meaning: Princess
Gender Variation: Prince
Similar Names: Precious, Prima, Princella, Princessa, Priscilla, Prisma
⇒ The vocabulary word for a female member of a royal family used as a given name since 1979.

Priscilla
Rank: 372
Origin: Latin
Meaning: Ancient, venerable
Alternate Spellings:
Pracilla, Precilla, Prescilla, Pricila, Pricilla, Priscella, Prisila, Priscylla, Prisilla, Prysilla
Gender Variations: Presley, Prescott, Price
Nicknames: Cilla, Pris, Prisca
Similar Names: Percilla, Precia, Prescill, Prisciliana
⇒ The pet form of Prisca and a biblical name mentioned in the New Testament for a Christian woman who became a companion to Paul. It appeared in Edmund Spenser's book *The Faerie Queene* and was used by Longfellow as the heroine of his poem "The Courtship of Miles Standish," which led to the name's use among the Puritans during the 17th century. A surge in popularity began in 1980 when Priscilla Presley, wife of famous rock and roll singer Elvis Presley, played the role of Jenna Wade on the series *Dallas*. Her autobiography and best seller *Elvis and Me* was released in 1985. The name is still commonly used today because of its trendy "a" ending.

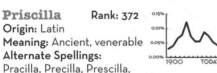

Quinn
Rank: 540
Origin: Irish Gaelic
Meaning: Descendant of Conn
Alternate Spelling: Quin
Gender Variations: Quincy, Quinn, Quintin
Similar Names: Queen, Queenie, Quenna, Quianna, Quintessa
⇒ A surname used as a given name and possibly the short form of the boy's names Quincy and Quintin. It was inspired as a given name for girls by the Emmy Award-winning television series *Dr. Quinn, Medicine Woman* that aired during the 1990s with Jane Seymour in the title role.

Rachel
Rank: 49
Origin: Hebrew
Meaning: Ewe
Alternate Spellings:
Rachael, Racheal, Rachell, Rachele, Rachelle, Raechel, Raechell, Raychel, Raychelle, Rachyl
Gender Variations: Ray, Ralph
Nicknames: Ray, Shell
Similar Names: Raelyn, Raquel, Rochelle, Shelley
Namesakes: Rachel Hetherington (LPGA golfer), Rachel Hunter (model), Rachel Ward (actress)
⇒ An Old Testament name for the wife of Jacob and mother of Joseph and Benjamin. Perceived as a Jewish name during the Middle Ages but now widely used among all ethnic groups. It's recently come into vogue along with other biblical names. Associated with Jennifer Aniston's character Rachel Green on the popular television sitcom *Friends*.

Raina
Rank: 925
Origin: Latin
Meaning: Queen
Alternate Spellings:
Rayna, Reina, Reyna
Similar Names: Raya, Rayann, Raylina, Regana, Regena, Regine, Reyney
⇒ A variation of Rayna that's either the Bulgarian form of Regina or the feminine form of Rayno. Also used as the short form of Lorraina or Lorraine. The name has been in sporadic use since 1970.

Raquel
Rank: 500

Origin: Hebrew
Meaning: Ewe
Alternate Spellings: Racquel, Racquell, Raquelle
Gender Variation: Raphael
Similar Names: Rachalle, Rachana, Rachel, Rachela, Raquella

➡ The Spanish and Portuguese form of Rachel influenced by actress Raquel Welch, born Jo Raquel Tejada, who became one of the biggest sex symbols of the 1960s and 1970s. The name peaked in 1970 at No. 215.

Raven
Rank: 441

Origin: Old English
Meaning: Raven
Alternate Spellings: Ravenne, Ravyn, Rayvinn
Gender Variations: Ray, Rayner
Nickname: Ray
Similar Names: Raschelle, Ravenna, Ravina, Raylene

➡ Derived from the vocabulary word for the large black bird that's part of the crow family and the subject of an 1845 poem by writer and poet Edgar Allan Poe. The name has recently been influenced by actress and musician Raven-Symone, who launched her career in 1989 at the age of three on *The Cosby Show*.

Rayne
Rank: 992

Origin: French/Yiddish
Meaning: Queen, mighty, pure
Alternate Spellings: Rain, Raine, Reine
Gender Variation: Rain
Similar Names: Rayna, Raynee, Reanna, Reena, Reenie

➡ A variation of Rayna popularized because of its trendy "y" in the middle spelling.

Reagan
Rank: 155

Origin: Irish Gaelic
Meaning: Descendant of the little king
Alternate Spellings: Ragan, Raegan, Regan, Reghan
Gender Variations: Beagan, Reagan, Keegan
Nickname: Rae
Similar Names: Regeanah, Reggie, Rejean, Meagan, Teagan

➡ A form of Regan, derived from the surname O'Riagain. Highly recognized because of U.S. president Ronald Reagan and has joined other presidential names as popular choices for both boys and girls. After fading from the chart, this name reappeared in 1993 and moved quickly up the ranks to within the top 200 in 2004. More favored as a trendy name for girls because of actress Reagan Dale Neis and her performance in the 2006 movie *Material Girls*.

Rebecca
Rank: 96

Origin: Hebrew
Meaning: Bound, tied
Alternate Spellings: Rebakah, Rebeca, Rebeccah, Rebecka, Rebeckah, Rebeka, Rebekah, Rebekka
Gender Variations: Reagan, Reed
Nicknames: Becca, Beck, Becky
Similar Names: Reanna, Reba, Reece, Reena, Riva
Namesakes: Rebecca DeMornay (actress), Rebecca West (British-Irish writer)

➡ The Latin form of the biblical Rebekah, known as the wife of Isaac and the mother of Esau and Jacob in the Old Testament. Also the title of a 1938 novel by British author Daphne du Maurier that was adapted into a 1940 film directed by Alfred Hitchcock. An enduring name widely used during the 19th century that has since faded in and out of the top 100, peaking at No. 10 during the mid-1970s.

Reese
Rank: 159

Origin: Welsh
Meaning: Enthusiastic
Alternate Spellings: Reece, Rees
Gender Variations: Reese, Reeve, Reez
Nickname: Ree
Similar Names: Reed, Reesa, Reesey, Reeve, Reez, Resi, Rise, Rose

➡ British form of Rhys that debuted on the chart in 2000 and is currently at its peak influenced by Academy Award-winning actress Reese Witherspoon, whose career began when she answered an open casting call and won the lead role in the 1991 film *The Man in the Moon*. It's considered a trendy name for girls because of its Hollywood spotlight and its favored long "ee" sound. It's currently listed among the top 500 for boys.

Regina
Rank: 603
Origin: Latin
Meaning: Queen
Alternate Spellings:
Regeena, Regena, Reginna
Gender Variations: Reggie, Reginald
Nickname: Gina
Similar Names: Raina, Raya, Regana, Regine, Reginia, Rina
Namesakes: Regina Belle (singer), Regine Velasquez (Filipino singer/actress)
⇨ Adopted from the Latin vocabulary word that means "queen." Roman Catholics used the name starting in the 8th century in reference to the Virgin Mary, Regina Coeli, "Queen of the Heavens." The name reappeared during the 19th century influenced by Queen Victoria's full official name, Victoria Regina. The name is past its peak and recently dropped out of the top 600.

Renee
Rank: 582
Origin: Late Latin
Meaning: Reborn
Alternate Spellings: Ranae, Ranee, Renae, Renay, Rene
Gender Variations: Renato, Rene
Nickname: Renny
Similar Names: Reena, Reenie, Rena, Renata, Renate, Renelle, Renita
Namesakes: Renee O'Connor (actress), Renee Richards (tennis player), Renee Russo (actress), Renee Zellweger (actress)
⇨ The feminine form of Renatus and the French form of Renata that was used by the early Christians as a baptismal name to honor rebirth in Christ. It entered the top 1,000 just after the turn of the 20th century and peaked during the late 1960s, fading to its current standing today.

Reyna
Rank: 595
Origin: Spanish
Meaning: Queen
Alternate Spellings:
Raina, Rayna, Reina
Gender Variations: Reynard, Reynold
Similar Names: Raven, Rea, Reanna, Ren, Rena, Renee, Rhiannon
⇨ A variation of the name Reina that means "queen" in Spanish. The name has been listed among the top 1,000 for the past 25 years.

Rhiannon
Rank: 738
Origin: Welsh
Meaning: Great queen
Alternate Spellings:
Reannon, Riannon, Rianon
Gender Variation: Ryan
Similar Names: Rhiann, Rhianna, Rhyan, Rihana, Riona
⇨ The name of the goddess of fertility and the moon in Welsh mythology derived from the Old Celtic Rigantona. It was influenced by the 1975 Fleetwood Mac song "Rhiannon (Will You Ever Win)" and made its debut on the popularity chart the following year.

Rihanna
Rank: 528
Origin: Welsh
Meaning: Maiden
Alternate Spellings:
Reanna, Reannah, Rheanna, Rhiana, Rhianna, Rianna, Riannah
Gender Variations: Reyham, Reynard, Ryan
Similar Names: Rhian, Rhiannon, Rianne, Riona
⇨ A created name that's possibly a variation of Rhiannon or a longer form of Rhian, popularized by the Barbadian singer Rihanna, who became internationally known after the release of her first album in 2005.

Riley
Rank: 55
Origin: Irish Gaelic
Meaning: Rye clearing
Alternate Spellings: Rilee, Rileigh, Rylee, Ryleigh, Ryley, Rylie
Gender Variations: Reilley, Ryan
Similar Names: Rya, Ryann
⇨ A surname used as a first name for boys since the 19th century. Popular usage for girls started in 1990 and surpassed the boys in 2002. Country singer Jeannie C. Riley brought attention to the surname in 1968 with her No. 1 country and pop hit, "Harper Valley PTA."

Riya
Rank: 958
Origin: Hindu
Meaning: Singer
Alternate Spelling: Riyah
Gender Variations: Rishi, Ryan
Similar Names: Liya, Miya, Raya, Ria, Ryan, Rylie

➔ A contemporary variation of Ria used occasionally as a girl's name since 2002. Indian film actress and model Riya Sen is a famous bearer.

Rocio
Rank: 940

Origin: Spanish
Meaning: Dew
Gender Variations: Rico, Roberto, Rosario
Similar Names: Roberta, Romina, Rosa, Rosario, Rosita
➔ A biblical name given in honor of the Virgin Mary referred to as Maria del Rocio that means "Mary of the Dew." Spanish singer and actress Rocio Durcal, known to millions in Mexico and Latin America, was a famous bearer of the name.

Rosa
Rank: 400

Origin: Latin
Meaning: Rose
Gender Variation: Ross
Nickname: Rose
Similar Names: Rhoda, Rocio, Rosalba, Rosalind, Rosamond, Rosario, Roseanne, Rosita
➔ The Latin and botanic name for the flowering shrub that's often used as a blend or combination such as Rosalie, Rosabel, and Rosemary. Rosa Parks, the famed civil rights activist who refused to give up her seat on a Montgomery, Alabama, bus in 1955, is a namesake.

Rose
Rank: 350

Origin: Latin
Meaning: Rose
Alternate Spellings: Rosse, Roze
Gender Variations: Roshe, Rossi, Rosze
Similar Names: Rosa, Rosalia, Rosalie, Rosalin, Roseanne, Rosemary, Roses, Rosetta, Rosie, Rozina
Namesakes: Rosario Dawson (actress), Rose McGowan (actress)
➔ Possibly associated with the vocabulary word for the fragrant flower derived from rosa or a short form of names beginning with the Germanic element hros meaning "horse." A top 50 name from the 1880s until 1943. Influenced early on by the famous nursery rhyme "Ring a Ring O'Roses" or "Ring Around the Rosie" when it was first printed in 1881. A prominent bearer of the name is Rose Fitzgerald Kennedy, who was the mother of nine children including former U.S. president John F. Kennedy. Also inspiring the name is Rose Marie, an actress who began her career as a child star under the name Baby Rose Marie and is most famous for her role as Sally Rogers on the 1960s *Dick Van Dyke Show*.Rosie O'Donnell, an 11-time Emmy Award-winning talk show host, television personality, comedian, and actress is another famous bearer. "The Rose" is the title of song sung by Bette Midler and featured in the 1979 movie of the same name. A strong independent name for years, but may also be popular as a combination name like Rosemarie or Roseanne.

Roselyn
Rank: 706

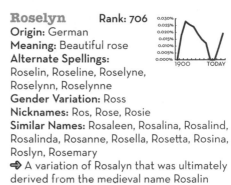

Origin: German
Meaning: Beautiful rose
Alternate Spellings: Roselin, Roseline, Roselyne, Roselynn, Roselynne
Gender Variation: Ross
Nicknames: Ros, Rose, Rosie
Similar Names: Rosaleen, Rosalina, Rosalind, Rosalinda, Rosanne, Rosella, Rosetta, Rosina, Roslyn, Rosemary
➔ A variation of Rosalyn that was ultimately derived from the medieval name Rosalin that's been in use since the early 1900s.

Rosemary
Rank: 703

Origin: Latin
Meaning: Dew of the sea
Alternate Spellings: Rosemaree, Rosemaroy, Rozmary
Gender Variations: Roosevelt, Rosario, Ross
Nicknames: Mary, Rose
Similar Names: Rosalie, Rosaline, Rosanna, Roseanne, Roselani, Rosemarie, Rosemaria
Namesake: *Rosemary's Baby* (1968 film)
➔ Either a combination of the names Rose and Mary or taken from the herb with fragrant needlelike leaves used as a seasoning in cooking derived from *rosmarinus*. The name was popular during the 1940s and 1950s for jazz singer Rosemary Clooney, aunt of actor George Clooney.

Rowan
Rank: 642

Origin: Gaelic
Meaning: Little redhead
Alternate Spellings:
Roanne, Rohan, Rowanne, Rowen
Gender Variations: Rowan, Rowland
Similar Names: Roanna, Romy, Rona, Roni, Rosanne, Rowena
⇒ Originated as a surname derived from *Ruadhan* that became a given name for both boys and girls. The girl's name is most likely associated with the tree known for its clusters of red berries. Actress Kelly Rowan, best known for her role as Kirsten Cohen on the television series *The O.C.*, is a famous bearer of the surname.

Ruby
Rank: 137

Origin: Latin
Meaning: Ruby
Alternate Spellings:
Rubee, Rubey, Rubi, Rubie, Rubye
Gender Variations: Ruben, Rudy, Rugby, Ruy
Nicknames: Rube, Rue
Similar Names: Ruberta, Rubina, Rubra, Rubyn, Ruchelle, Rudee, Rudina, Ruth
⇒ Associated with the precious stone that ultimately derived from Latin *ruber* "red," the birthstone of July. Also considered the short form of the biblical name Reuben, meaning "behold, a son" in Hebrew. It first became known for actress and famous tap performer Ruby Keeler whose breakthrough performance in the 1933 musical *42nd Street* led to its top 50 ranking. Also inspired by Emmy Award-winning actress and activist Ruby Dee, whose extensive career has lasted more than seven decades. Along with being a trendy choice for parents because of its "y" spelling, it may be preferred more recently because of the popular children's television show *Max and Ruby*, based on the books by Rosemary Wells.

Ruth
Rank: 373

Origin: Hebrew
Meaning: Companion
Alternate Spellings:
Rhouth, Ruthe
Gender Variations: Ru, Rubin, Rudy, Ruwan
Similar Names: Rutha, Ruthann, Ruthelle, Ruthellen, Ruthi, Ruthina, Ruza

⇒ In the Old Testament book by the same name, Ruth was a young Moabite widow who was devoted to her mother-in-law, Naomi. Victorian poets valued her sentiments, and the name has been popular since the 17th century and joined the top 10 on the chart in 1892 and stayed there until 1930, peaking at No. 3 in 1893. Bringing attention to the name in the late 1960s and early 1970s was actress Ruth Buzzi, especially known for her performances on the comedy show *Rowan & Martin's Laugh-In*. Also influenced by award-winning British mystery writer Ruth Rendell who is often referred to as the Queen of Crime. Popular as a combination name, such as Ruthanne or Ruthellen.

Ryan
Rank: 455

Origin: Irish Gaelic
Meaning: Little king
Alternate Spellings: Rian, Riane, Rianne, Riayn, Ryane, Ryann, Ryanne, Ryen, Ryenne
Gender Variations: Bryan, Ryan
Similar Names: Rina, Riya, Ruby, Ryba, Ryley
⇒ Originally a surname that may have been influenced by Rhiannon. Often considered a boy's name, it's never hit the same heights in popularity for girls since it debuted on the chart in 1974. Sometimes blended with "ann" or "anne" to add a feminine touch. Actress Meg Ryan is a bearer of the surname.

Sabrina
Rank: 197

Origin: Gaelic
Meaning: Welsh river name
Alternate Spellings: Sabreena, Sabrena, Sabrinah, Sabrinna, Sabryna, Sabrynna, Sabrynah, Sebreena, Sebrina, Subrina
Gender Variations: Sabastian, Saber, Sabino, Sabron
Nicknames: Bri, Breena
Similar Names: Breena, Sabana, Sabelia, Sabina, Sable, Sabreen, Sabria, Sebyne, Zabrina
Namesake: Sabrina Lloyd (actress)
⇒ Taken from the River Severn located in Wales that was originally called Habren. In Celtic legend Sabrina was a princess who drowned in the Severn. The name first appeared on the chart in 1954 influenced by the film of the same name starring Audrey Hepburn in the title role. The name peaked

in 1997 because of the popular 1996 to 2003 television series *Sabrina the Teenage Witch*, starring actress Melissa Joan Hart. A fashionable girls name favored by parents because of its popular long "ee" sound, "y" and "z" spelling variations, and its "a" ending.

Sadie   Rank: 157

Origin: Hebrew
Meaning: Princess
Alternate Spellings: Sadee, Sadi, Sadye, Saidee, Saidey, Saidie, Sayde, Saydie, Saydi, Saydee
Gender Variations: Sade, Sage, Sanders
Nicknames: Sae, Sayd
Similar Names: Sada, Sadelle, Sadia, Sadra, Saechelle, Sage, Sydella, Zadie
➡ The pet form of Sarah that was used as an independent name at the start of the 20th century. It was a top 100 name during the 1880s and early 1900s, later influenced by 1928 film *Sadie Thompson* starring Gloria Swanson and the updated 1953 version *Miss Sadie Thompson* starring actress Rita Hayworth. The name continues to be a favorite because of the Disney 2005 show *Naturally, Sadie*.

Sage   Rank: 417

Origin: Latin
Meaning: Have good taste, be wise
Alternate Spellings: Saeg, Saege, Saig, Saige, Sayg, Sayge
Gender Variations: Saif, Sage
Nickname: Sai
Similar Names: Basil, Cinnamon, Curry, Sagal, Sagara, Sagen, Sagia, Sajedah, Skye
➡ From the English vocabulary word, which denotes either a type of spice or else a wise person. A name for both boys and girls that is associated with sagebrush, cowboys, and the Wild West. A spice name that debuted on the chart in 1993 and peaked in 2004, but still ranks high among the top 500, much higher than its variation with an "ai," and the boy's name with the same spelling.

Salma   Rank: 752

Origin: Arabic
Meaning: Safe, unharmed
Alternate Spellings: Salmah, Sahlma
Gender Variations: Salah, Salama, Salim

Similar Names: Saml, Sahar, Salwa, Sana
➡ The feminine form of Salim derived from *salima* that's most identified with Academy Award-nominated Mexican-American actress Salma Hayek who has appeared in more than 30 films.

Samantha   Rank: 10

Origin: Hebrew
Meaning: Name of God
Alternate Spellings: Samanntha, Samentha, Sammantha, Semantha, Simantha, Symantha
Gender Variations: Samson, Samuel
Nicknames: Sam, Sammi
Similar Names: Samanta, Samara, Samuela
Namesake: Samantha Mathis (actress)
➡ Possibly the female form of the Hebrew name Samuel. Popularized by Cole Porter in the song "I Love You, Samantha" that was featured in the 1956 film *High Society*. The name was influenced during the 1960's by the principal character of the television show *Bewitched*.

Samara   Rank: 351

Origin: Hebrew/Arabic
Meaning: Watchtower, Elm tree seed, night talk
Alternate Spellings: Saimara, Samarra, Samarrah, Samera, Samira, Samirah, Sammara, Semara, Semarah
Gender Variations: Samar, Samier
Nickname: Sam
Similar Names: Samar, Samaria, Samarie, Samarol, Samaya, Sameria
➡ Possibly derived from the biblical place name Samaria. First appeared on the chart in 1997 at No. 991 and jumped all the way to No. 351 by 2006, its current peak position. Also a river name in France, Ukraine, and Russia. A preferred choice for its "a" ending and similarity to the Top 10 name Samantha.

Sanaa   Rank: 607

Origin: African
Meaning: Work of art
Alternate Spelling: Sana
Gender Variation: Salim
Similar Names: Samya, Sanai, Saniyya, Sanura, Sara, Sarahi, Sarai
➡ An African name in popular use since 2003; notable for film and television actress Sanaa Lathan.

Sanai   Rank: 974

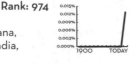

Origin: Unknown
Similar Names: Sana, Sancia, Sandi, Sandia, Sanne, Sanya
⇒ The origin and meaning is unknown, possibly receiving its inspiration from the biblical Mount Sinai where Moses received the 10 Commandments from God. It made its debut as a girl's given name in 2006.

Sandra   Rank: 364

Origin: Greek
Meaning: Defender of mankind
Alternate Spellings: Sahndra, Sandera, Sandira, Sanndra
Gender Variations: Sandan, Sanders, Sandro
Similar Names: Sandee, Sandralynn, Sandreea, Sandrella, Sandrelle, Sandrette, Sandrina, Sandya, Saundra, Zandra
⇒ The shortened form of Alexandra and the feminine version of Alexander. Known for 1950s teen icon and actress Sandra Dee, most famous for her role as *Gidget* in the 1959 television film with the same name. Famous bearers include Sandra Day O'Connor, who served as the first female Justice of the Supreme Court, and film actress Sandra Bullock.

Saniya   Rank: 522

Origin: Arabic
Meaning: Radiant, brilliant
Alternate Spellings: Saniyah, Saniyya, Saniyyah
Gender Variation: Samir
Similar Names: Aniyah, Janiyah, Samira, Shaniya, Taniyah
⇒ Possibly derived from the Arabic *sana* blended with the "iya" ending. Listed among the top names since 2003.

Sarah   Rank: 15

Origin: Hebrew
Meaning: Princess
Alternate Spellings: Saira, Sairah, Sara, Sarra, Sarrah, Sera, Serah
Gender Variation: Sal
Nickname: Sari
Similar Names: Sadie, Sahara, Sally, Sarai, Saranna, Sarena, Sariah, Sarina, Zara, Zarita

Namesakes: Sarah Evans (country singer), Sarah Ferguson (Duchess of York), Sarah Hughes (Olympic ice skater), Sarah McLachlan (singer/songwriter), Sarah Michelle Gellar (actress), Sarah Jessica Parker (actress)
⇒ In the Old Testament Sarah was the wife of Abraham and the mother of Isaac. God changed her name from Sarai to Sarah when she was 90. An enduring name that has been generally listed among the top 100 names since prior to the turn of the 20th century. Famed jazz singer Sarah Vaughan kept the name in front of the public during a career that spanned six decades. Sarah-Jane has been a popular combination since the late 1960s.

Sarahi   Rank: 842

Origin: Hebrew
Meaning: Princess
Gender Variation: Seriah
Similar Names: Sarah, Sarene, Sari, Sariah, Zarah
⇒ A form of the name Sarah that's been used occasionally as a girl's name since 1996.

Sarai   Rank: 443

Origin: Hebrew
Meaning: Princess
Alternate Spelling: Sariah
Gender Variation: Seraiah
Nickname: Sara
Similar Names: Sadie, Sally, Sarah, Sarahi
⇒ A variation of the name Sarah known in the Old Testament as Abraham's wife before God changed her name to Sarah. Currently fashionable along with other biblical names.

Sasha   Rank: 336

Origin: Greek
Meaning: Defender of mankind
Alternate Spellings: Sahsha, Sascha, Saschae, Sashae, Sashah, Sashia, Sashiah, Sashsha, Sashya, Sausha
Gender Variations: Sascha, Saschel
Nickname: Sash
Similar Names: Jasha, Sachie, Sachio, Sashai, Sashana, Sashay, Sashel, Sashenka, Zasha
Namesake: Sasha Alexander (actress)
⇒ Russian pet form of Aleksandr or Aleksandra and also a variation of the Greek name Alexander and French name Sacha.

Predominantly given to male children in Eastern Europe but almost exclusively for girls in the U.S. It rose among the top 200 in 1987 when Mexican singer Sasha Sokol launched her solo career, following a successful singing career with award-winning group Timbiriche since 1981. One of the most famous recent bearers of the name is figure skater Sasha Cohen, the 2006 Olympic silver medalist and 2006 U.S. National Champion. Trendy for its popular "a" ending and association with highly-ranked names, such as Alexandra and Alexandria.

Savannah   Rank: 30

Origin: Spanish
Meaning: Treeless plain
Alternate Spellings: Savana, Savanna, Savanah, Savanha, Savannha, Sevanna
Nickname: Vanna
Similar Names: Anna, Hannah, Sarah, Saranna, Zavanna
Namesakes: *Savannah* (TV series)
➡ Possibly derived from *zavana*, taken directly from the vocabulary word for a large grassland with few trees. The S.S. *Savannah* was the first steamship to cross the Atlantic Ocean. Also a place name for a city in Georgia, located along the Savannah River. Comedian and actor Chris Rock has a daughter named Zahra Savannah.

Scarlett   Rank: 297

Origin: Late Latin
Meaning: Red
Alternate Spellings: Scarlet, Scarlette
Gender Variation: Scott
Similar Names: Salina, Sariah, Satin, Savannah
➡ Derived from "scarlata," which was an occupational surname given to a person who dyed or sold brightly colored fabrics. The name landed on the popularity chart after the debut of the 1939 award-winning film *Gone with the Wind* based on the novel by Margaret Mitchell featuring heroine Katie Scarlett O'Hara, better known simply as Scarlett. It's currently associated with film actress Scarlett Johansson, who first made a name for herself in the 1998 film *The Horse Whisperer*.

Selah   Rank: 838

Origin: Hebrew
Meaning: Rock
Alternate Spellings: Seela, Seelah, Sela
Gender Variation: Selby
Similar Names: Cecilia, Celeste, Celine, Salah, Selena, Seleta, Selia, Selima, Selinda, Selma
Namesake: Selah (Christian band)
➡ A biblical name for the ancient capital of Edom and a musical term that possibly means "pause" or "reflection," frequently mentioned in the book of Psalms. Actress Sela Ward uses an alternate spelling of the name.

Selena   Rank: 285

Origin: Greek
Meaning: Moon
Alternate Spellings: Celina, Salena, Sallyna, Salyna, Selina, Selyna, Sillenna, Sylena
Gender Variations: Salene, Selden, Selwyn
Nicknames: Sela, Sely, Selen
Similar Names: Salinda, Salynn, Sela, Selene, Selenia, Selona
Namesake: Selena Gomez (actress)
➡ Latin form of Selene that is most noted for the famous Mexican-American singer who was called "the queen of Tejano music" during the late 1980s and 1990s and whose fame continued long after her untimely death in 1995. Her Grammy Award-winning album, *Selena Live!* was released in 1993, just shortly before the name hit top rankings on the popularity chart. Also inspired by the 1997 movie *Selena*, starring actress and singer Jennifer Lopez in the title role. Trendy name among parents because of its popular "a" ending and use of the long "ee" sound.

Selene   Rank: 987

Origin: Greek
Meaning: Moon
Alternate Spellings: Celene, Celine
Gender Variations: Salome, Sereno
Similar Names: Salma, Selah, Selena, Selima, Selma, Serene, Serenity
➡ The name of the goddess of the moon in Greek mythology whose Roman counterpart is Artemis. Appropriate for girls who are born under the sun sign of Cancer ruled by the moon in astrology. Canadian award-winning singer Celine Dion uses a form of the name.

Serena
Rank: 396

Origin: Latin
Meaning: Serene, calm
Alternate Spellings:
Cerena, Sarena, Saryna, Sereena, Serenah, Serenna, Serienna, Serinah, Seryna, Syrena
Gender Variations: Sereno, Severan
Nickname: Seree
Similar Names: Reena, Serene, Seretha, Seretta, Serenity, Serissa, Sirena
⇒ From a Late Latin name that was derived from the word *serenus*, it was featured in Edmund Spenser's 1590 poem, *The Faerie Queene*. A popular choice today for its "a" ending and its similarity to top choice Selena. The name peaked on the chart during the fame of tennis player and Olympic gold medalist Serena Williams, who became a professional in 1995 at age 14 and in 2002 ranked No. 1 in the world.

Serenity
Rank: 135

Origin: Latin
Meaning: Calm
Alternate Spellings:
Serenitee, Serenitsey, Serenitie
Gender Variations: Sereno, Sergio
Nicknames: Sera, Seren
Similar Names: Serena, Serendipity, Serene, Seretha, Serienna, Serissa
⇒ A vocabulary word expressing a feeling of inner peace of the mind and body considered a virtue name similar to Purity and Verity. Associated with "The Serenity Prayer," an originally untitled prayer written by theologian Reinhold Niebuhr in the 1930s or early 1940s. First entered the popularity chart in 1997 and rose nearly 700 spots into the top 300 in 2002, influenced by the name of a spaceship originally featured in the 2002 science fiction television series *Firefly*.

Shakira
Rank: 791

Origin: Arabic
Meaning: Thankful
Alternate Spellings:
Shakeera
Gender Variation: Shakir
Similar Names: Shahira, Shakila, Sharifa, Shazi, Shula
⇒ The feminine form of Shakir known for the two-time Grammy Award-winning and eight-time Latin Grammy Award-winning Colombian singer and songwriter who goes simply by Shakira.

Shania
Rank: 487

Origin: Native American
Meaning: On my way
Alternate Spelling: Shaniya
Gender Variation: Shane
Nickname: Shan
Similar Names: Shana, Shandy, Shanee, Shanelle, Shanice, Shanna, Shannon, Shantelle
⇒ Singer Shania Twain, born Eileen Regina Edwards, changed her name in the early stages of her career to the Ojibwa or Chippewa words created by her adopted father. The name landed on the popularity chart in 1995, the same year she released her second album that topped country charts and crossed over to mainstream charts peaking at No. 5. Also considered a variation of Shayna or an elaborate form of Shan.

Shannon
Rank: 359

Origin: Gaelic
Meaning: Wise river
Alternate Spellings:
Shanan, Shanen, Shanon, Shannan, Shannen, Shannin, Shannun, Shannyn, Shanyn
Gender Variations: Shanley, Shannon
Nickname: Shay
Similar Names: Shana, Shanadoah, Shanae, Shandra, Shane, Shanene, Shannah, Shannel, Shantell, Sheannon
⇒ From the name of the Shannon River, the longest river in Ireland, created using the Gaelic elements *sean* and *abhann* and is also considered the feminine form of the Irish masculine name Seanan. It ranked among the top 100 from 1968 to 1997. The name has also been associated with actress Shannon Doherty, fictional character Shannon Rutherford from the hit television series *Lost*, and the singer known simply as Shannon, who started her career in the 1980s.

Sharon
Rank: 623

Origin: Hebrew
Meaning: Fertile plain
Alternate Spellings:
Sharan, Sheren, Sharenne, Sharin, Sharren, Sharrin, Sharron, Sharyn

Gender Variations: Shane, Shannon
Similar Names: Shara, Shareen, Sharelle, Sharena, Sharla, Sharney, Sharona, Sharonda, Sharonna, Sherri
Namesakes: Sharon Gless (actress), Sharon Lawrence (actress), Sharon Osbourne (television personality)
➡ Mentioned in the Bible as the name of the coastal plain near Israel and for the rose of Sharon, which is a type of flowering shrub. Actress, producer, and former fashion model Sharon Stone is a famous bearer of the name. Used sporadically for boys until 1967.

Shayla   Rank: 330

Origin: Gaelic
Meaning: From the fairy palace
Alternate Spellings: Shaela, Shaila, Shaylah
Gender Variations: Shayne, Shea
Nickname: Shay
Similar Names: Shailyn, Shaylee, Shayleen, Shayna, Shea, Sheila
Namesake: Shae-Lynn Bourne (Canadian ice dancer)
➡ A variation of Sheila or the rhyming form of the top 25 name Kayla. Influenced by the song of the same name from Blondie's No. 1 *Eat to the Beat* album released in 1979. Suddenly in fashion with its trendy "a" ending.

Shaylee   Rank: 788

Origin: American
Alternate Spellings: Shaelee, Shalee, Shealee
Gender Variation: Shea
Nicknames: Shay, Lee
Similar Names: Sharla, Sharlee, Sharlene, Shayla, Shayleen, Sheila, Shelley
➡ An invented name that combines "Shay" and "lee" in popular use since 1997.

Shayna   Rank: 810

Origin: Yiddish
Meaning: Beautiful
Alternate Spellings: Shaena, Shaina, Shaynah, Sheina
Gender Variation: Shane
Nickname: Shanie
Similar Names: Shayla, Shania, Shanna, Shawna, Shayndel, Sheena, Sheila

➡ A contemporary name used by parents since 1976 that either originated as a form of Sheena or as a Yiddish name.

Shea   Rank: 893

Origin: Gaelic
Meaning: Admirable
Alternate Spellings: Shae, Shay
Gender Variations: Shane, Shaun
Similar Names: Lashay, Shaelyn, Shauna, Shayla, Shaylee, Shayna, Shayndel
➡ An Irish surname derived from Seaghdha, also the name of a tropical African tree that bears a fruit, referred to as a nut, used to make shea butter. It's been used as a girl's given name since 1971 and for boys since 1970.

Sheila   Rank: 946

Origin: Latin
Meaning: Blind
Alternate Spellings: Sheela, Sheelah, Sheelagh, Sheilah, Shela, Shelagh, Shelah, Shelia, Sheyla, Shiela
Gender Variations: Cecil, Shea
Similar Names: Cicily, Sela, Selia, Shayla, Shilea, Shyla, Sissy
Namesakes: Sheila E. (musician), Sheila Taormina (Olympic triathlete)
➡ The Irish Gaelic form of Cecily and the anglicized form of "sile" commonly used in Australia and New Zealand as a slang term for a woman. The name has been used in the title of several songs including a 1962 No. 1 single by Tommy Roe and a 1998 song by The Smashing Pumpkins.

Shelby   Rank: 133

Origin: Old English
Meaning: Willow farm
Alternate Spellings: Schelby, Shelbe, Shelbey, Shelbi, Shelbie, Shellby, Shellbee, Shellbey, Shellbi, Shellbie
Gender Variations: Shelby, Sheldon, Shelton
Nicknames: Shel, Shelb
Similar Names: Selbey, Shelba, Shelbiana, Shea, Shreya
➡ Originated as a surname and variant of Selby that debuted on the popularity chart in 1935 and rose into the top 100 in 1990. Suitable for both boys and girls yet more frequently chosen for girls. Trendy for its long "ee" sound and its popular "y" spelling.

Sherlyn   Rank: 362

Origin: American
Alternate Spellings:
Cherlyn, Cherlynn,
Cherlynne, Sherlyn,
Sherlyne, Sherlynne, Shirlyn, Shirlynn,
Shirlynne
Gender Variations: Sheldon, Sheridan
Similar Names: Sharlyn, Sherilyn, Sherry,
Sheryl, Sherylann, Sheryn, Shirley
⇒ A modern variation of Sherilyn or a
combination of the popular "Sher" with "lyn"
that appeals to parents with the "y" spelling.

Shiloh

Origin: Hebrew
Meaning: He who is to be sent
Alternate Spellings: Shilo, Shiloe, Shylo,
Shyloh
Gender Variation: Shiloh
Nicknames: Shi, Lo
Similar Names: Shilah, Shilea, Shelah, Sherah
⇒ A name rooted in history as a biblical
sanctuary where the Israelites kept the
famed Ark of the Covenant, but also as the
site of a battle during the U.S. Civil War.
Celebrity couple Brad Pitt and Angelina Jolie
named their daughter Shiloh Nouvel Jolie-
Pitt. The name is used for both boys and girls.

Shyla   Rank: 919

Origin: Latin
Meaning: Blind
Alternate Spelling: Shylah
Gender Variation: Shiloh
Similar Names: Sharla, Shayla, Shaylee,
Sheila, Shelby, Shelley, Sheryl, Shula
⇒ One of several contemporary forms of
Sheila that was introduced on the popularity
chart in 1999 and made a comeback in 2006.

Sienna   Rank: 177

Origin: English
Meaning: Reddish brown
color
Alternate Spellings:
Ciana, Siena
Gender Variations: Seina, Seneca, Siera
Nicknames: Si, Enna
Similar Names: Seina, Seini, Selina, Senia,
Sianna, Sianni, Sierra, Sina, Sirena, Syon
⇒ Derived from the name of a city in Italy
noted for its mines that produced a
reddish-brown colored soil. It debuted

as a girl's given name in 1995 and quickly
rose to its current peak influenced by British
actress Sienna Miller and British actress
and model Sienna Guillory. Widely used
because of its "a" ending and popular long
"ee" sound.

Sierra   Rank: 141

Origin: Spanish
Meaning: Mountain range
Alternate Spellings: Ciera,
Cierra, Searah, Searra, Siera,
Sierrah, Syerra, Syerrah
Gender Variations: Sirage, Sirius
Similar Names: Sarra, Seeria, Sera, Siara,
Siedah, Sienna, Sierea, Syarra
⇒ Place name for many geographic sites,
including the Sierra Mountains, that became
a fashionable choice in 1993 when it entered
the top 100. High position on chart in 2000
partially due to PepsiCo's release of new
lemon-lime soft drink Sierra Mist. A nature
name more frequently given to girls and one
that is trendy when it expresses the long "ee"
sound or when variations are spelled with
"ia," "ra," or "y."

Simone   Rank: 564

Origin: Hebrew/Greek
Meaning: God is listening
Alternate Spellings:
Cymone, Symone
Gender Variations: Simon, Simeon
Similar Names: Simeona, Simona, Simonetta,
Simonette
Namesakes: Simone Foster (*Head of the
Class* character)
⇒ The French feminine form of Simon.
The name entered the U.S. in 1937 then
faded until 1960, around the time actress
Simone Signoret became the first French
woman to win the Academy Award for Best
Actress after appearing in a foreign film.
Singer and actress Raven-Symone uses a
form of the name.

Skye   Rank: 433

Origin: Old Norse
Meaning: Cloud
Alternate Spellings:
Skie, Sky
Gender Variations: Skyler
Similar Names: Echo, Iris, Lily, Spring,
Summer

➡️ A form of the nature word sky that gained popularity in 1987. Also possibly used as the short form of Skylar and Skyler. Recognized by music fans for Canadian singer Skye Sweetnam, whose parents named her after the Isle of Skye located off the west coast of Scotland.

Skyla
Rank: 598

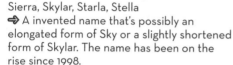

Origin: American
Gender Variation: Sky
Nickname: Skye
Similar Names: Sela, Sharla, Sierra, Skylar, Starla, Stella
➡️ A invented name that's possibly an elongated form of Sky or a slightly shortened form of Skylar. The name has been on the rise since 1998.

Skylar
Rank: 145

Origin: Dutch
Meaning: Scholar
Alternate Spellings: Schiler, Schylar, Schyler, Skyelar, Skyeler, Skyelur, Skyler, Skylor, Skylyr
Gender Variations: Scully, Skye, Skylar
Nicknames: Sky, Skye
Similar Names: Skyla, Skylia, Skylee, Skylena, Skylynne, Skyra
➡️ A contemporary spelling of the Dutch surname Schuyler that was brought to New York by 17th-century settlers. Since first listing on the popularity chart in 1990, the name quickly moved into the top 200 in 1998. The most recent influence on the name comes from Skylar Stevens, a character played by actress Candace Bailey on the postapocalyptic drama *Jericho* that premiered in 2006. Name is given to both boys and girls and coincides with current trends of spellings with a "y."

Sonia
Rank: 599

Origin: Greek
Meaning: Wisdom
Alternate Spellings: Sonja, Sonje, Sonya
Gender Variation: Sonny
Similar Names: Sofia, Sondra, Sophie
Namesake: Sonia Braga (Brazilian actress)
➡️ The Russian pet form of Sophia that's been used independently since the early 1900s. Norwegian figure skater Sonja Henie, who was a three-time Olympic champion

during the 1920s and 1930s before moving on to a successful film career, used the German form. Russian author Fyodor Dostoevsky used Sonya for one of the main characters in his 19th-century novel *Crime and Punishment*. Currently a royal name for Queen Sonja of Norway, the consort of King Harald V.

Sophia
Rank: 9

Origin: Greek
Meaning: Wisdom
Alternate Spellings: Sofia, Sofija, Sofiya, Sofya
Gender Variation: Sonny
Nickname: Sophie
Similar Names: Saffi, Sonya, Sophie, Zofia, Zofie, Zosia
Namesakes: Sophia Bush (actress), Sophia Myles (English actress)
➡️ Derived from the Greek word that grew in popularity during the 17th and 18th centuries in England, most likely influenced by the heroine in Henry Fielding's 1749 novel, *Tom Jones*. Italian actress and Academy Award-winner Sophia Loren brought attention to the name during the 1960s. Sophie is the French form of the name.

Sophie
Rank: 125

Origin: Greek
Meaning: Wisdom
Alternate Spellings: Sophy, Sofie, Sophey
Gender Variations: Solomon, Sophen, Soren
Nickname: Soph
Similar Names: Sobia, Sofenya, Sonni, Sophal, Sophia, Sophronia
➡️ French form of Sophia that was most often given to women of royalty in previous years. Ranked high among the top 200 from the 1880s until the mid-1920s possibly because of famous author Sophie Kerr, who wrote 23 novels and several poems and short stories beginning in 1916. A classic name that faded and reentered chart in 1984, rising to the top 200 in 1999. Continues to be a popular choice as a girl's name partially due to character Sophie Neveu in Dan Brown's 2003 novel *The Da Vinci Code*, followed by the movie released in 2006, and for its association with its more commonly used variations Sophia and Sofia.

Stacy
Rank: 672

Origin: Greek
Meaning: Fruitful
Alternate Spellings:
Stacee, Stacey, Staci, Stacie,
Stasey, Stasie, Staycee, Staycey, Slaysie,
Gender Variations: Stacey, Stacy
Nickname: Stace
Similar Names: Stacia, Star, Starla, Stella,
Steph, Tacy, Tasya
Namesakes: Stacey Q (singer), Stacy Dragila
(Olympic pole vaulter)
⇒ A variation of Stacey that originated
during the Middle Ages as a short form of
Eustace. It became fashionable for girls in
1949 and peaked during the 1970s at No. 32.
It dropped off the chart as a given name
for boys in 1993.

Stella
Rank: 241

Origin: Latin
Meaning: Star
Alternate Spellings:
Stela, Stelah, Stellah
Gender Variation: Stellan
Nicknames: Ell, Ella, Stell
Similar Names: Estelle, Estrella, Steile,
Stellina
⇒ A place name and a given name used after
the 16th century that's often associated with
the Virgin Mary by Roman Catholics because
of her title "Stella Maris" which means "star
of the sea." The name is best remembered
in Tennessee Williams' 1947 *A Streetcar
Named Desire* for character Stella Kowalski.
Another notable bearer is English fashion
designer Stella McCartney, the daughter of
Paul McCartney.

Stephanie
Rank: 70

Origin: Greek
Meaning: Crown
Alternate Spellings:
Stefani, Stefanie, Steffaney,
Steffanie, Steffenie, Stephani, Stephannie,
Stephany, Stepheney
Gender Variations: Stephen, Steven, Steve
Nicknames: Steph, Stephie
Similar Names: Stephana, Stephania, Stevie
Namesake: Steffi Graf (German tennis player)
⇒ The French feminine form of the early
Christian name Stephen. Listed among the
top 100 since 1961, the name peaked during
the 1980s, influenced by actresses Stephanie

Powers, who starred on the television series
Hart to Hart, and Stephanie Zimbalist from
television's *Remington Steele*.

Summer
Rank: 154

Origin: Old English
Meaning: Summer
Alternate Spellings:
Somer, Sommer, Sumer,
Summar
Gender Variations: Sumir, Summet, Sumner
Nickname: Sum
Similar Names: Sumiya, Sammara,
Summerlee, Summers, Sumnar, Sumreen,
Sumura, Sunnie, Sunshyne
Namesake: Summer Sanders (Olympic
swimmer)
⇒ A nature name derived from the Old
English word *sumor*. This trendy seasonal
name, similar to Spring and Autumn, peaked
on the chart in 1977, due to Suzanne Somers
and her performance as Chrissy Snow on the
sitcom *Three's Company* and the outbreak of
exceptional musician and performing artist
Donna Summer in the 1970s. Listed among
the top 200 since 1993.

Suri

Origin: Persian/Hebrew/Sanskrit
Meaning: Red rose, princess, the sun
Similar Names: Sarah, Sarai, Sari, Sura,
Surata, Surya
⇒ Suri carries multiple origins and is known
as the Yiddish form of Sarah, a surname in
India, and the name of a tribe in Ethiopia and
Afghanistan. It became fashionable around
the world when celebrity couple Tom Cruise
and Katie Holmes named their daughter Suri.

Susan
Rank: 611

Origin: Hebrew/Greek
Meaning: Lily
Alternate Spellings:
Susann, Susanne, Suzan
Gender Variation: Sutcliff
Nicknames: Sue, Susie
Similar Names: Sueanne, Sukie, Susanka,
Susannah, Susette, Suzanne, Suzetta
Namesakes: Sue Bird (WNBA basketball
player), Susan Cheever (writer), Susan Dey
(actress)
⇒ The short form of the Hebrew name
Susanna. Historically known for Susan B.
Anthony, the 19th-century women's rights

leader who was honored with her image on a dollar coin minted in 1979, 1980, 1981, and 1999. The name is currently inspired by Academy Award-winning actress Susan Sarandon, whose successful film career started in 1970. It peaked during the 1950s at No. 2 for four consecutive years and is sometimes used as a blended name such as Susanetta or Susannah.

Susana
Rank: 875

Origin: Hebrew/Greek
Meaning: Lily
Alternate Spellings: Susanna, Susannah, Suzanna, Suzannah
Nicknames: Ana, Sue, Susan, Susie
Similar Names: Shana, Shoshana, Sueann, Suellen, Susanita, Susette, Suzanne
➡ A biblical name using its original form of Susanna derived from the Hebrew Shoshana and ultimately *shoshan*. Often associated with the song "Oh! Susanna" written by Stephen Foster in 1847.

Sydney
Rank: 34

Origin: Old French/English
Meaning: Of Saint Denis or wide island
Alternate Spellings: Sidnee, Sidney, Sydne, Sydnee, Sydnie
Gender Variation: Sidney
Nickname: Syd
Similar Names: Denisa, Denise, Skylar, Sylvana
Namesake: Sydney Penny (actress)
➡ Variation of Sidney that's associated with the name of a city in Australia. Popular use has been almost completely taken over by girls, possibly influenced by Sydney Biddle Barrows, who ran an escort service in New York City and is the author of *Mayflower Madam: The Secret Life of Sydney Biddle Barrows*.

Sylvia
Rank: 524

Origin: Latin
Meaning: Woods
Alternate Spellings: Silvia, Silvija, Silviya, Silvya
Gender Variations: Silvio, Silvius
Nickname: Sylvi
Similar Names: Silva, Silvana, Silvianne, Sylvette, Sylvie

Namesakes: Sylvia (country/pop singer), Sylvia Plath (poet)
➡ A variation of Silvia, which is the feminine form of Silvius. Rhea Silvia was the mother of Romulus and Remus in Roman mythology, and Saint Silvia was the mother of Pope Gregory I. Shakespeare used the name for a character in his comedy *The Two Gentlemen of Verona*. Today it's known for Queen Silvia of Sweden, who is the consort of King Carl XVI Gustaf and mother of the heir apparent to the throne.

Tabitha
Rank: 534

Origin: Aramaic
Meaning: Gazelle
Alternate Spellings: Tabatha, Tabbitha, Tabetha, Tabotha, Tabytha
Gender Variations: Tad
Nickname: Tabbi
Similar Names: Tacita, Talia, Talitha, Tamara, Tamsin, Tamia, Tansy
➡ A biblical name for a woman who was restored to life after Saint Peter prayed beside her body. She was also referred to as Dorcas, which is the Greek form of the name. It debuted on the popularity chart in 1966 the same year Samantha Stephens gave birth to Tabitha on the successful television series *Bewitched*. *Tabitha* became a spin-off of the show and aired from 1977 to 1978.

Talia
Rank: 363

Origin: Hebrew
Meaning: Dew from heaven
Alternate Spellings: Talea, Tahlia, Taliah, Taliya, Taliyah, Tallia, Talya, Talyah, Thalia
Gender Variations: Talain, Talha, Tallis
Nickname: Tali
Similar Names: Dalia, Natalie, Taliatha, Talenia, Talieya, Talinda, Talyn, Talisa, Tulia
➡ Variation of Talya and Taliah and a short form of Natalia. Probably the most famous bearer of the name is actress Talia Shire, popular for her roles in the 1972 movie *The Godfather*; its sequels; and her more recent role as Adrian, the girlfriend and later wife of boxer Rocky Balboa in the *Rocky* movies beginning in 1976. It has been a top 400 name for the past 10 years for its contemporary spelling with an "ia."

Tamara   Rank: 678

Origin: Hebrew
Meaning: Palm tree
Alternate Spellings:
Tamarra, Tamera, Tamira,
Tammara, Tammera, Tamora, Tamyra
Gender Variation: Tanner
Nicknames: Tam, Tammy
Similar Names: Tam, Tamaka, Tamar, Tambre,
Tamela, Tamesis, Tamra, Tamsin, Tara
Namesakes: Tamara McKinney (Olympic
skier), Tamera Mowry (actress)
⇨ The Russian form of Tamar who was
the daughter of King David in the Bible. It
became a royal name during the 12th century
for a queen of Georgia and was frequently
used in Russian literature. The pronunciation
varies outside the U.S.. Also means "spice"
in Sanskrit.

Tamia   Rank: 575

Origin: Hebrew
Meaning: Palm tree
Alternate Spelling: Tamya
Gender Variation: Tanner
Nicknames: Tam, Tami
Similar Names: Tam, Tama, Tamar, Tamara,
Tamika, Tamela, Tamra
⇨ A twist on the name Tamara that is
derived from the Hebrew Tamar. It is notable
with its "ia" ending.

Tania   Rank: 447

Origin: Russian
Meaning: Fairy princess
Alternate Spellings:
Tahnya, Taniyah, Tanja,
Tannia, Tanya, Tonnya, Tonya, Tonyah
Gender Variation: Tanner
Similar Names: Talia, Tana, Taneka, Tanesha,
Tara, Tarana, Tariana, Tatianna, Tatienne
⇨ The short version of Tatiana and the
feminine form of the Roman family name
Tatius. Tanya has been the most widely used
spelling, influenced by country singer Tanya
Tucker. The "ia" spelling surfaced in 1960 and
became the favorite form of the name in 1996.

Tara   Rank: 463

Origin: Irish Gaelic
Meaning: Hill
Alternate Spellings: Tarah,
Tarra, Tarrah, Terra
Gender Variation: Tory

Similar Names: Tamara, Tansy, Taryn, Tasha
Namesakes: Tara Lipinski (Olympic skater),
Tara Reid (actress)
⇨ An Irish place name derived from the
Gaelic *teamhair* for the sacred hill in Meath
where the high kings resided. Best known for
the fictional O'Hara plantation in Margaret
Mitchell's 1936 novel *Gone with the Wind*,
debuting on the popularity chart in the late
1940s after the release of the 1939 film. Also
the name of the Hindu astral goddess and
means "star" in Sanskrit.

Taryn   Rank: 444

Origin: American
Alternate Spellings: Taran,
Tarin, Tarren, Tarryn, Teryn
Gender Variation: Taylor
Similar Names: Tamra, Tamsyn, Tansy, Tanzi,
Tara, Tarina, Tarnia
⇨ A contemporary, longer version of Tara
that's been in popular use since 1955 and
currently back in style because of its "y"
spelling. Taryn Manning, who began acting
during the 1990s and formed the band
Boomkat with her brother in 2003, is a
namesake.

Tatiana   Rank: 283

Origin: Russian
Meaning: Fairy princess
Alternate Spellings:
Taitianna, Tatayana,
Tateanna, Tateonna, Tatianah, Tatianna,
Tatihana, Tatiyana, Tatyana, Tatyanah
Gender Variations: Tatiano, Tatius, Tatum
Nicknames: Ana, Tati
Similar Names: Tamia, Taniya, Tasanna,
Tassiana, Tatania, Tatia, Tatrian, Tatrina,
Tatum, Titania
Namesakes: Tatiana Golovin (French tennis
player), Tatiana Celia Kennedy Schlossberg
(daughter of Caroline Kennedy Schlossberg),
Tatiana Troyanos (opera singer)
⇨ Associated with Saint Tatiana, who was
martyred during the 2nd century in Rome
and is now considered the patron saint of
students. The name debuted on the chart
in 1980 and peaked in 1999, shortly following
the performance of actress Tatyana Ali on
the television show *The Fresh Prince of
Bel-Air* from 1990 to 1996. Popular, trendy
name because of its "ia" combination and
"a" ending.

Tatum Rank: 349
Origin: Old English
Meaning: Tate's homestead
Alternate Spellings:
Tadum, Tatumn
Gender Variations: Tate, Tation
Nickname: Tate
Similar Name: Tatie
➡ From a surname that was originally derived from a place name used for girls since 1994. Actress Tatum O'Neil, best known for her role in the 1973 movie *Paper Moon*, became the youngest actor to win an Oscar at the age of 10. It's currently listed among the top 400.

Tayla Rank: 923
Origin: American
Gender Variations:
Talen, Taylor
Nickname: Tay
Similar Names: Kayla, Shayla, Tanya, Taylor, Twyla
➡ A created name with the feminine "la" ending used sporadically since 1995. It's most likely been influenced by the top 25 name Taylor or as a rhyming variation of Kayla.

Taylor Rank: 22
Origin: English
Meaning: To cut
Alternate Spellings: Taelir, Taelor, Talor, Tayler, Taylir, Tayllor, Taylyr, Teighlor
Gender Variations: Taylor, Tyler
Similar Names: Taya, Tayla, Talora, Tyla, Tyller
Namesakes: Ann Taylor (retail store), Lord & Taylor (department store), Taylor Caldwell (author), Taylor McKessie (Disney *High School Musical* character)
➡ Originated as an occupational surname for someone who tailors clothing that became popular as a given name for boys until 1989 when it moved into the top 100 for girls spurred on by characters from *The Bold and the Beautiful, All My Children, Melrose Place,* and *The O.C.* Singer and actress Taylor Dayne is a famous bearer of the given name. Actress Elizabeth Taylor and model Nikki Taylor are bearers of the surname.

Teagan Rank: 425
Origin: Irish
Meaning: Attractive
Alternate Spellings: Teegan, Tegan, Teigan, Tiegan
Gender Variations: Teagan, Tiernan
Similar Names: Reagan, Teal, Teige, Tierney
➡ A unisex name that debuted in 1999 for girls and is currently almost twice as popular as the boy's name. Derived from the Irish *tadhg* and was originally used as a surname.

Teresa Rank: 535

Origin: Greek
Meaning: The harvester
Alternate Spellings: Terese, Theresa, Therese
Gender Variation: Terry
Nickname: Teri
Similar Names: Teresita, Teressa, Terrise, Tess, Tessa, Theresia, Tracey, Tressa
Namesake: Theresa Russell (actress)
➡ The Italian and Spanish form of Theresa that's widely used by Roman Catholics in honor of Saint Teresa of Avila, a 16th-century Spanish nun. Nobel Peace Prize recipient Mother Teresa chose the name in honor of Saint Teresa when she took her vows as a nun in 1931. Theresa was the most widely used form until 1960.

Tess Rank: 734
Origin: Greek
Meaning: The harvester
Gender Variations: Terence, Terry
Nickname: Tessie
Similar Names: Teresa, Teresia, Teresita, Teressa, Teri, Tessa, Thera, Trace, Traci
Namesake: Tess Harper (actress)
➡ The short form of Theresa and the name of the unfortunate heroine in Thomas Hardy's 19th-century novel *Tess of the d'Urbervilles*. The name was also used for Dick Tracy's girlfriend, Tess Trueheart, in the popular comic strip that debuted in 1931 and was adapted into a film in 1990. It's been used as a girl's given name since 1983.

Tessa
Rank: 252
Origin: Greek
Meaning: The harvester
Alternate Spellings: Tesa, Tesah, Tessah
Gender Variations: Terrace, Tex
Nicknames: Tess
Similar Names: Dessa, Tassa, Terri, Tessan, Tessia, Tessie, Teza, Theresa
Namesake: Tessa Sanderson (Olympic javelinist)
⇨ The short form of Theresa but now commonly used as an independent name that may also mean "fourth child" in Greek. Associated with *Tessa Noël*, a fictional character on the 1992 to 1998 show *Highlander: The Series*, portrayed by Belgian actress Alexandra Vandernoot.

Thalia
Rank: 774
Origin: Greek
Meaning: To blossom
Alternate Spellings: Thaleia, Thalya
Gender Variations: Thelonius, Theo
Similar Names: Talia, Thalie, Thana, Thea, Theda
⇨ Picked up from Greek mythology for one of the nine Muses as well as the name of one of the Three Graces. Derived from *thallo*, it debuted in 1932, then suddenly fell off the chart for 60 years, resurfacing in 1992 and used steadily since that time.

Tia
Rank: 608
Origin: Spanish
Meaning: Aunt
Alternate Spelling: Tea
Gender Variations: Theo, Tito
Similar Names: Thea, Thera, Tiana, Tiara, Tiernan, Tierney
Namesake: Tia Mowry (actress)
⇨ The short form of names that begin or end in *tia*, such as Tiana and Lucretia, and also used independently as a given name since 1957. Hawaiian-born actress and singer Tia Carrere has brought attention to the name. A popular choice for Hispanic parents.

Tiana
Rank: 477
Origin: Latin
Meaning: Anointed Christian
Alternate Spelling: Tianna
Gender Variations: Christian, Cristiano
Nickname: Tia
Similar Names: Christiana, Christiane, Taryn, Tatiana, Tiara, Tierney, Tina
⇨ An elaborated form of Tia or the short form of Christiana and Tatiana. The name was moderately popular when it debuted in 1975 and has climbed among the top 500 with its catchy "a" ending.

Tiara
Rank: 551
Origin: Latin
Meaning: Headdress
Alternate Spellings: Teara, Tiarah, Tiare, Tiarra
Similar Names: Ciara, Sierra, Tia
⇨ Taken directly from the vocabulary word that refers to a jeweled or flowered head piece often designed in a semicircle also called a crown. It's been steadily used as a girl's given name for more than 25 years.

Tiffany
Rank: 210
Origin: Greek
Meaning: Manifestation of God
Alternate Spellings: Tifanee, Tifaney, Tifani, Tiffaney, Tiffannie, Tiffanny, Tiffeney, Tiffini, Tiphanie, Tiphany
Gender Variations: Theophanes, Tiesen, Tiffan, Tillman
Nicknames: Tiff, Tiffy
Similar Names: Symphony, Tifara, Tiffan
Namesakes: Tiffany Trump (daughter of Donald Trump)
⇨ Medieval form of Theophania and feminine form of Theophanes. A name traditionally given to girls born on the January 6 festival Epiphany, commemorating the visit of the Magi to the infant Jesus. First appeared on the chart in 1962 following the release of the famed 1961 Academy Award-winning film *Breakfast at Tiffany's*, starring Audrey Hepburn. A surge in popularity in 1988 was influenced by teen pop singer Tiffany Renee Darwish, known simply as Tiffany, who had multiple hits during the late 1980s including the song "Could've Been," which shot to the No. 1 spot of the Billboard charts in February 1988.

Tina
Rank: 932

Origin: Greek
Meaning: Follower of Christ
Alternate Spellings:
Teena, Teina, Tena
Gender Variations: Titus
Similar Names: Tayla, Tiana, Tiara, Tillie, Tine, Toni, Tori, Trina, Trine
Namesakes: Tina Louise (actress), Tina Thompson (WNBA basketball player)
➡ The short form of Christina and other names ending with "tina" that spent 28 years among the top 100 names from 1956 to 1982. The name was inspired by seven-time Grammy Award-winning singer-songwriter Tina Turner, who rose to superstardom during the 1960s and 1970s with Ike Turner and then launched a successful solo career starting in the mid-1980s.

Toni
Rank: 819

Origin: Latin
Meaning: Priceless, praiseworthy
Alternate Spellings:
Toney, Tonie, Tony
Gender Variations: Tonio, Tony
Similar Names: Toinette, Tonelle, Tonette, Tonia, Tonisha, Tori
Namesake: Toni Collette (Australian actress/musician)
➡ The short form of Antonia that's been used independently since 1923 and achieved its highest ranking in 1963 at No. 146. The name is known for Nobel Prize-winning author Toni Morrison and six-time Grammy Award-winning singer and songwriter Toni Braxton.

Tori
Rank: 452

Origin: Japanese
Meaning: Bird
Alternate Spellings:
Torey, Torree, Torrey, Torri, Torrie, Torry, Torrye, Tory
Gender Variations: Tory, Victor
Similar Names: Terri, Toni, Tonya, Tora, Tracy
Namesake: Tori Amos (singer)
➡ Either of Japanese origin or the pet form of the Latin name Victoria. The name has been used independently since 1959 and peaked in 1994 at No. 142, influenced by actress Tori Spelling, who's best known for her role as Donna Martin in *Beverly Hills, 90210*. Occasionally used as a boy's name.

Trina

Origin: Greek
Meaning: Pure
Alternate Spellings:
Treana, Treanah, Treena, Treenah, Treina, Trena, Trinah, Tryna, Trynah, Trynya
Gender Variations: Darin, Tarin, Torin
Similar Names: Tina, Triana, Trice, Tricia, Trine, Trini, Trinity, Trish, Trista
Namesakes: Trina (rap artist), Trina Echolls (*Veronica Mars* TV character)
➡ The short form of Katrina used independently since the 1940s. The name peaked at No. 172 in 1970 and 1971 and faded 20 years later.

Trinity
Rank: 63

Origin: Latin
Meaning: Threefold
Alternate Spellings:
Trinitee, Trinitey
Gender Variations: Tristan, Tristram
Nickname: Trini
Similar Names: Trina, Trinidad
➡ Derived from the vocabulary word *trinus*. Used in Christianity to describe the unity of the Father, Son, and Holy Spirit. The name debuted on the popularity chart in 1974 and rose into the top 100 in 2000, influenced by the character in *The Matrix* movies.

Trisha

Origin: Latin
Meaning: Nobleman
Alternate Spellings:
Trecia, Tresha, Tricia, Trisia, Trissha, Trysha, Tryshah
Gender Variations: Parish, Tris, Tristan
Nickname: Trish
Similar Names: Teisha, Tisha, Tresha, Trishelle, Trissa, Trista
➡ The short form of Patricia used independently since 1961. Tricia Nixon, daughter of the late U.S. President Richard M. Nixon, popularized both forms of the name when her father was inaugurated in 1969. The name has been recently influenced by three-time Grammy Award-winning country music singer Patricia "Trisha" Yearwood. Also used as the short form of Beatrice.

Trista
Rank: 812

Origin: Celtic/Gaelic
Meaning: Sad
Alternate Spelling: Trysta
Gender Variations: Tristan, Tristram
Similar Names: Christa, Christine, Crystal, Kirsten, Kristen, Trisha, Tristana
⇨ Invented as the feminine form of Tristan that's gone in and out of popularity since 1970.

Tyler
Rank: 741

Origin: Old English
Meaning: Tiler, roofer
Alternate Spellings: Tilar, Tylar, Tylor
Gender Variations: Tyler, Tyrone
Nickname: Ty
Similar Name: Taylor, Twyla, Tylena, Tyna, Tyra
Namesakes: Mary Tyler Moore (actress)
⇨ An occupational surname for someone who makes tiles that's been predominantly given to boys and crossed over as a girl's name in 1984. Actress Liv Tyler is a famous bearer of the surname.

Tyra
Rank: 662

Origin: Old English
Meaning: Thor's battle
Gender Variations: Tyrell, Tyrone
Nickname: Ty
Similar Names: Tara, Thora, Tiana, Tierney, Tierra, Tirzah, Tory, Tyree, Tyreeka
⇨ The feminine form of Tyrone and a place name for a town in Ireland. Supermodel Tyra Banks brought attention to the name when she was the first African American to be featured on the cover of the *Sports Illustrated* Swimsuit Issue in 1996.

Unique

Origin: Latin
Meaning: Only one
Alternate Spelling: Unike
Gender Variations: Enrique, Rique
Nickname: Uni
Similar Names: Anique, Jonique, Monique, Uniqua, Uniquia, Unity, Urania
⇨ Derived from the Latin vocabulary word *unicus* that means to be without a like or equal. It first gained attention as a girl's given name in 1993 and has slowly faded in recent years. Possibly influenced by the Latin Monique.

Valentina
Rank: 438

Origin: Latin
Meaning: Strong, healthy
Gender Variation: Valentino
Nicknames: Tina, Val, Valen
Similar Names: Valencia, Valene, Valetta, Valonia, Valtina, Vanda
Namesake: Valentina (Danish model)
⇨ The feminine form of Valentine associated with two Roman martyred saints whose feast day is celebrated on February 14. The day has traditionally been recognized as a romantic holiday in which Valentine's cards are exchanged. Popular use of the girl's name started in 1994 and was recently used in 2007 by Salma Hayek for her daughter, Valentina Paloma, with Francois-Henri Pinault.

Valeria
Rank: 90

Origin: Latin
Meaning: Strong
Alternate Spellings: Valaria, Valiria, Vallaria, Valleria, Valliria
Gender Variations: Valerio, Vallen, Valtez
Nickname: Val
Similar Names: Falecia, Valena, Valera, Valeriana, Valerie, Valetta, Valkyria, Vallia, Valoria
⇨ Feminine form of Valerius and the name of a 3rd-century saint. It fell from the popularity chart in 1977 but returned in 1985 following the release of the 1982 movie *Conan the Barbarian*, featuring the character Valeria, a strong female warrior, alongside Conan. It was also inspired by actress Valeria Golino and her performance as Susanna in the 1988 release of *Rain Man*. Jumped to its current peak in 2006 because of its popular "ia" ending and association to Valerie, a top 200 name.

Valerie
Rank: 127

Origin: Latin
Meaning: Strong
Alternate Spellings: Valaree, Valarey, Valarie, Valeree, Valery, Valerye, Vallarie, Valleree, Vallerie, Valorie
Gender Variations: Valdez, Valencio, Valerius, Vallen
Nickname: Val
Similar Names: Valentina, Valera, Valeria, Valeriana, Vallen, Valese, Valley, Vallrie

→ Feminine form of Valerius and a Roman family name derived from the Latin *valere*. It is the French form of an early Christian name Valeria that peaked in popularity in 1959 and reached another high position again in 1985 because of actress Valerie Bertinelli who played Barbara Cooper on the 1970s and 1980s television show *One Day at a Time* and actress Valerie Perrine, whose most famous role was in the 1978 film *Superman*. The name also kept a top 100 position on the chart between 1951 and 1987 because of the influence of Emmy Award-winning actress Valerie Harper, best known for her role as Rhoda Morgenstern on the 1970s television show *The Mary Tyler Moore Show*.

Vanessa Rank: 79

Origin: Greek
Meaning: Butterfly
Alternate Spellings: Vanesa, Vanesse, Vannessa, Venesa, Venessa
Gender Variations: Vance, Vaughan
Nickname: Nessa
Similar Names: Vanda, Vanecia, Vanetia, Vanetta, Vania, Vanna
Namesakes: Vanna White (TV personality), Vanessa Williams (singer/actress)
→ Invented by Irish author Jonathan Swift for a poem he published in 1726 titled "Cadenus and Vanessa." He created the name using "Van" from his friend Esther Vanhomrigh's surname and adding "Esse," which is the pet form of Esther. The name was influenced by British actress Vanessa Redgrave, whose five-decade career in film, stage, and television started in the late 1950s. It's recently known for singer and actress Vanessa Hudgens of Disney's *High School Musical* fame. Also the name of a genus of butterflies.

Veronica Rank: 211

Origin: Latin
Meaning: True image
Alternate Spellings: Varonica, Varonicca, Varonika, Verhonica, Veronika, Veronnica, Vironica, Vironika, Vyronica, Vyronicah
Gender Variations: Verlondan, Vermont, Von
Nicknames: Roni, Veronic
Similar Names: Verinica, Vernica, Vernice, Vernisha, Vernita, Verntoria, Verona

→ Latin form of Berenice, influenced by the ecclesiastical Latin phrase *vera icon*. Also the name of a legendary saint who wiped Jesus's face with a towel and then found his image imprinted in the fabric. The name was influenced by British child actress Veronica Cartwright starting in the late 1950s. Also associated with Veronica "Ronnie" Lodge, the fictional character from the *Archie* comic book series created in 1942, who has kept an ageless influence on the name as a high school teenager for more than 65 years.

Victoria Rank: 28

Origin: Latin
Meaning: Victory, victorious
Alternate Spellings: Vicktoria, Vicktorya, Vyctoria, Vyctorya, Viktorija
Gender Variations: Victor, Victorio
Nicknames: Tor, Tori, Toria, Vicka, Vicke, Vicki, Vics
Similar Names: Ria, Toya, Victorina, Vikiana, Victoriana, Victorine, Victory, Vittoria, Vita
Namesakes: Victoria's Secret (retail chain)
→ The feminine form of Victorius and the name of the Roman goddess of victory. It became fashionable during the 19th century for Queen Victoria, whose reign is currently the longest of any British monarch. Famous bearers include actress Victoria Principal from the 1980s prime-time drama *Dallas* and former Spice Girl Victoria Beckham, wife of soccer star David Beckham. The name has been listed among the top 100 since 1981.

Viola

Origin: Latin
Meaning: Violet
Alternate Spellings: Violah, Vyola, Vyolah
Gender Variations: Cole, Virgil
Nickname: Vi
Similar Names: Finola, Iola, Lilla, Nola, Verla, Viole, Violetta, Viona, Virgilia, Willa
→ Derived from the Latin *violet* known for the white, yellow, or purple flower and the color that is similar to purple. Considered a literary name for Shakespeare's heroine from the play *Twelfth Night*, who disguises herself as a young man named Cesario. Also refers to the bowed stringed instrument in the violin family.

Violet
Rank: 261

Origin: Latin
Meaning: Purple
Alternate Spellings:
Villette, Violete, Violett,
Violette, Viollet, Viollette, Vyolet,
Vyolete, Vyolett, Vyolette
Gender Variations: Vi, Vernet, Viresh
Nickname: Vi
Similar Names: Valeta, Viola, Violaine,
Violanta, Viole, Violetta, Volett, Yolanda,
Yolane, Yolanthe

⇒ The vocabulary word for the color and
also one of the earliest flower names, first
used during the 1830s. Shakespeare used
a form of the name, Viola, for the heroine
in *Twelfth Night*. Popular in early 20th
century, it faded from the chart in the early
1980s and returned in 1998 for a strong
climb to its current position at No. 261.
French ballerina Violette Verdy inspired
the name before its drop in popularity
starting in 1945.

Virginia
Rank: 511

Origin: Latin
Meaning: Maiden
Gender Variations: Virgil
Nicknames: Ginia, Ginnie,
Virge, Virgie, Virginie
Similar Names: Gigi, Gina, Ginger, Vivian,
Viviette
Namesakes: Virginia Madsen (actress),
Virginia Wade (tennis player), Virginia Woolf
(author)

⇒ The feminine form of the Roman family
name *Virginius* and associated with a
legendary woman killed by her father to
ward off the attempts of suitors. The state
of Virginia and the first American child born
of English parents were named in honor of
Queen Elizabeth I, who was referred to as
the "Virgin Queen." The name was widely
used during the first half of the 20th century
and peaked at No. 6 in 1921.

Vivian
Rank: 223

Origin: Latin
Meaning: Alive
Alternate Spellings:
Vivianne, Vivien, Vivienne,
Vivyan, Vyvyan, Vyvyanne
Gender Variations: Vinson, Vivek, Volan
Nicknames: Vi, Viv, Vivee

Similar Names: Bibiana, Bibiane, Vibiana,
Vivia, Viviana
Namesakes: C. Vivian Stringer (Women's
Basketball Hall of Famer)

⇒ The name has been commonly used since
the 19th century and given most often to girls.
The name peaked in 1920 during a long stay
among the top 100 on the chart. Strongly
favored as a fashionable name because of
actress Vivian Blaine, known for her role as
Adelaide in the 1950 musical theater
production *Guys and Dolls*; Emmy Award-
winning actress and singer Vivian Vance, best
known as Ethel in the 1950s classic sitcom,
I Love Lucy; and two-time Academy Award-
winning British Actress Vivien Leigh, most
famous for her role in the film *Gone with the
Wind* in 1939. Currently ranked among the
top 300 choices for its distinguished flair
and trendy creative spellings.

Viviana
Rank: 449

Origin: Latin
Meaning: Alive
Alternate Spellings:
Vivianna, Vivyana
Gender Variations: Victor, Vincent
Nicknames: Viv, Vivi, Vivia
Similar Names: Vianne, Vivianne, Viviette

⇒ The feminine form of Vivianus associated
with the Roman saint who was martyred
during the 4th century. First listed among
the top names in 1979 at No. 487.

Wendy
Rank: 354

Origin: English
Meaning: Friend
Alternate Spellings:
Wendey, Wendi, Wendie
Gender Variation: Wendell
Similar Names: Gwen, Gwendolyn,
Wenda, Windy
Namesakes: Wendy Wasserstein (playwright)

⇒ Possibly first coined as "friendy-Wendy"
by a young friend of Scottish novelist and
playwright J. M. Barrie for a character in his
1904 play *Peter Pan* or a form of the Welsh
name Gwendolen. It became a favorite in the
United Kingdom during the 1960s, influenced
by three actresses including Dame Wendy
Hiller who won an Academy Award in 1959.
The name peaked in popularity just 10 years
later when Dave Thomas opened his first
Wendy's fast-food restaurant.

Whitney   Rank: 531

Origin: Old English
Meaning: White island
Alternate Spellings:
Whitnea, Whitnee,
Whitneigh, Whitni, Whitnie, Whitny,
Whittney, Whittnie
Gender Variations: Whitaker, Whitney
Nickname: Whit
Similar Names: Whitley, Willa, Willow,
Winnifred, Winona
➡ A surname that was derived from a place
name for any number of local areas in
England. Considered a boy's name until 1962
when it first appeared on the girl's popularity
chart at No. 757. Singer and actress Whitney
Houston had an impact in 1985 when her
debut album became a best seller and led
the name into the top 100.

Willow   Rank: 529

Origin: Old English
Meaning: Slender, graceful
Gender Variations: Will,
William, Willoughby
Nickname: Will
Similar Names: Wilhelmenia, Willa,
Wilma, Wilona
➡ A nature name picked up from the tree
and shrub that's derived from the Old English
welig. The name has been in popular
use since 1998 possibly influenced by
television anchor and host Willow Bay,
who started out as the face model for
Estee Lauder cosmetics during the 1980s,
and character Willow Rosenberg who
appeared on the 1997 to 2003 series *Buffy
the Vampire Slayer*.

Winona

Origin: Native American
Meaning: First-born
daughter
Alternate Spellings:
Wanona, Wenona, Wenonah, Winnona,
Winonah, Wynnona, Wynona
Gender Variations: Winn, Winston, Winthrop,
Winton
Nicknames: Win, Winnie
Similar Names: Willa, Willow, Wilma,
Winema, Winfred, Winifred, Wyanet, Wynne
➡ A Sioux girl's nickname usually given to
the first-born daughter. Popularized by film
actress Winona Ryder, who was named after

the city of Winona, Minnesota. Country
music singer Wynnona Judd, born Christina
Claire Ciminella, uses a form of the name.

Ximena   Rank: 393

Origin: Hebrew/Greek
Meaning: Listening
Alternate Spellings:
Ximenah, Xymena, Xymenah
Gender Variations: Simon, Ximen, Ximenes
Similar Names: Amena, Jimena, Kimana,
Siena, Simona, Sirena, Xena, Ximona,
Xiomara, Xirena
➡ A Spanish or Basque feminine form of
Simone, taken from the Greek form of the
Hebrew name Shimon. It debuted on the
chart in 2001 and peaked in 2005 and has
been a top 400 name for the past few years,
partly due to Ximena Abarca, a Chilean pop
singer and actress who made her debut in
2003 as a solo artist. The name stands out
because of its "X" spelling but silent
pronunciation.

Xiomara   Rank: 806

Origin: German
Meaning: Famous in battle
Gender Variation: Xavier
Nickname: Mara
Similar Names: Ximena, Xylina, Xylona
Namesake: Xiomara Reyes (Cuban ballerina)
➡ Possibly the Spanish feminine form of
Guiomar that uses the element "Mara" from
the Hebrew word that means "bitter" and is
mentioned twice in the Bible. It caught on
as a popular given name for girls in 2004.

Yadira   Rank: 541

Origin: Hebrew
Meaning: Friend
Alternate Spellings:
Yadeera, Yadeerah, Yadirah,
Yadirha, Yadirya, Yadyra
Gender Variation: Yancy
Nickname: Dira
Similar Names: Yaira, Yakira, Yashmine,
Yasmine, Yasmina, Yemena, Yolanda, Ysbel
➡ New to the popularity chart in 1975, the
name has climbed to its current peak as part
of a trend of names that end in "a."

Yahaira

Origin: American
Meaning: First-born daughter
Alternate Spellings: Jahaira, Jahara, Yahara, Yahayra, Yajaira
Gender Variations: Johar, Tahir, Zahir
Nickname: Win, Winnie
Similar Names: Akyra, Jadira, Jakira, Nahara, Sahara, Tahira, Yahira, Zahara, Zahira
⇒ Possibly a form of of the Hebrew name Yakira that first landed on the popularity chart in 2003 and faded just a couple of years later.

Yareli — Rank: 627

Origin: American
Gender Variations: Yahir, Yair
Similar Names: Yadira, Yahaira, Yaloni, Yareli, Yaritza
⇒ A modern invented name that first hit the popularity chart in 2002 and may have been influenced by Mexican/Cuban/American actress Yareli Arizmendi, known for her role in the 1992 foreign film *Like Water for Chocolate*.

Yaretzi — Rank: 837

Origin: American
Similar Names: Maritza, Yaritza, Yarmilla, Yazmin
⇒ A variation of the invented name Yaritza that joined the popularity chart in 2006.

Yaritza — Rank: 897

Origin: American
Alternate Spellings: Yaritsa, Yaritsah, Yaritzah
Gender Variation: Yale
Similar Names: Maritza, Yana, Yanamaria, Yara, Yarrow, Yasmin
⇒ A combination of "Yara" and "itza" that debuted on the popularity chart in 1993.

Yasmin — Rank: 324

Origin: Persian
Meaning: Flower in the olive family
Alternate Spellings: Yasamin, Yasimine, Yasmeen, Yasmen, Yasmenne, Yasmine, Yassmyn, Yazemen, Yazmin, Yazzmine
Gender Variations: Yasin, Yasmanny, Yasser
Nickname: Yaz

Similar Names: Jasmina, Jasmine, Yashmine, Yasmaine, Yasmina, Yasminda, Yasset
⇒ A variation of Jasmine and the vocabulary word for a climbing shrub with sweet-scented white or yellow flowers derived from *yasamin*. Notable bearers of the name are Princess Yasmin Aga Khan, a U.S. philanthropist and daughter of movie actress Rita Hayworth and Prince Ali Khan, and Yasmin Le Bon, well-known model and wife of pop rock group Duran Duran's Simon Le Bon. Actress Yasmine Bleeth influenced the name with her role on television series *Baywatch*. Also popular because of its contemporary "z" spellings.

Yesenia — Rank: 418

Origin: Spanish/Arabic
Meaning: Flower
Gender Variations: Yosef, Yusuf
Similar Names: Yasmin, Yemena, Yoselin, Yuliana
⇒ Derived from Jessenia, which is a type of palm tree found in South America. Also the title of a limited-run television serial released in Mexico in 1971, the same year the name debuted on the popularity chart in the U.S. Currently past its peak but still listed among the top 500 and considered part of a foreign naming trend.

Yoselin — Rank: 600

Origin: Old German
Meaning: Happy, joyful
Nicknames: Lin
Similar Names: Jaslyn, Jessalyn, Joselina, Joselyn, Joslin, Roselin, Roselina, Yolanda, Yvonne
⇒ A form of the top 100 name Jocelyn that's rapidly climbed the popularity chart since 2001.

Yuliana — Rank: 947

Origin: Latin
Meaning: Youthful
Alternate Spelling: Yulyana
Gender Variations: Yul
Nicknames: Yulia, Ana
Similar Names: Eliana, Iliana, Julia, Juliana, Juliane, Lucia, Luciana
⇒ The Russian and Bulgarian form of Juliana that's declined in popularity since it debuted in 2001.

Yuridia
Rank: 894

Origin: American
Gender Variation: Yuri
Similar Names: Yasmin, Yolanda, Yordana, Ysanne, Yuridiana
➡ An invented name that's rise in popularity began with Mexican singer Yuridia Gaxiola, who became internationally known after appearing on the reality show *La Academia*. Her 2004 debut album became one of the fastest selling in Mexican history.

Yvette
Rank: 913

Origin: French
Meaning: Archer
Alternate Spellings: Evette, Ivett, Ivette, Yvet
Gender Variation: Yves
Similar Names: Yasmin, Yelena, Yolanda, Yvetta, Yvonna, Yvonne
➡ The French feminine form of Yves and also the name of a small river in southern France. It debuted on the chart in 1912 and rose to No. 125 during the mid-1960s, popularized by actress Yvette Mimieux.

Zahara

Origin: Swahili/Hebrew
Meaning: Flower, to shine
Gender Variations: Zahari, Zahir
Nicknames: Za, Zar
Similar Names: Sahara, Zahira, Zahra, Zara, Zaray, Zaria, Zohara
➡ A multiethnic name that's associated with beauty and radiance. Possibly a form of the top 100 name Sara. It's become internationally known for Zahara Marley Jolie-Pitt, the adopted daughter of celebrity couple Angelina Jolie and Brad Pitt.

Zara
Rank: 858

Origin: Arabic
Meaning: Flower
Alternate Spellings: Zahrah, Zaira, Zarah
Gender Variations: Zane, Zarek
Similar Names: Zaina, Zanna, Zaray, Zaria, Zarifa, Zaylie
➡ Possibly derived from the Arabic *zahr* or a spelling variation of Sara. World champion equestrienne Zara Phillips, the only daughter of Princess Anne and Captain Mark Phillips, and the eldest granddaughter of Queen Elizabeth II, is a famous bearer of the name. It's gained popularity as a girls' given name since 2005.

Zaria
Rank: 718

Origin: Latin/Arabic
Meaning: Princess and blooming flower
Alternate Spellings: Zariah, Zarriah, Zarya, Zoria, Zoriah
Gender Variations: Zach, Zane, Zavier
Nickname: Zari
Similar Names: Zahrah, Zakia, Zanna, Zara, Zarita, Zaylie
➡ A city in northern Nigeria whose people are predominantly Muslim and also the name of the goddess of beauty in Slavic mythology. Picked up in 1996 as a girls' given name, it peaked in 2000 at No. 479.

Zion
Rank: 817

Origin: Hebrew
Meaning: Highest point
Gender Variations: Zimran, Zion
Similar Names: Zillah, Ziona, Zipporah, Zorah
➡ A symbolic name for the city of Jerusalem in the Bible. Mount Zion was the site of the temple that housed the famed ark of the covenant. More commonly used as a boy's name, it debuted for girls in 2006 as part of a biblical naming trend favored by Jewish families. Also a place name for Zion National Park located in Utah.

Zoe
Rank: 54

Origin: Greek
Meaning: Life
Alternate Spellings: Zoee, Zoie, Zoey, Zowie
Gender Variations: Zach, Zeb
Similar Names: Zena, Zita, Zola, Zorah
Namesake: Zooey Deschanel (actress)
➡ Popular among early Christians who used it in anticipation of eternal life. The name of two martyrs and a ruling Byzantine empress. Fashionable in the U.S. during the 19th century, however usage declined after the turn of the 20th century. The name suddenly hit a popularity streak and slid into the top 100 in 2000. Recently associated with the television show *Zoey 101* and a muppet on the long-running children's television series *Sesame Street*.

Aaron
Rank: 57

Origin: Hebrew
Meaning: Exalted, strong
Alternate Spellings: Aaran, Aaren, Aarron, Aeron, Ahron, Aren, Aron, Aryan, Ayran, Ayron
Gender Variation: Erin
Similar Names: Abel, Adam, Amos, Andrew, Asa, Asaiah
Namesakes: Aaron Carter (musician/actor), Aaron Eckhart (actor)
⇒ The brother of Moses in the Old Testament who was selected by God as the first high priest of Israel. A literary name for the villain in Shakespeare's *Titus Andronicus*. Influenced by baseball home run hitter Hank Aaron, whose career spanned from 1952 to 1976. Peaked at No. 28 in 1994.

Abdullah
Rank: 888

Origin: Arabic
Meaning: Servant of God
Alternate Spellings: Abd-Allah, Abdulah, Abdulla, Abdu'llah
Gender Variations: Aaliyah, Abla
Nickname: Abdul
Similar Names: Abbas, Abdalla, Abdul-Aziz, Abdul-Hamid, Adil
⇒ A commonly used name in the Islamic world that belonged to the father of Muhammad, the founder of the religion of Islam. Associated with Abdullah II of Jordan, reigning king since the death of his father in 1999. The name premiered on the popularity chart in 1996, but is seldom used.

Abel
Rank: 338

Origin: Hebrew
Meaning: Breath, child
Alternate Spellings: Abele, Abell, Able, Abyl
Gender Variations: Abbey, Abigail
Nickname: Abe
Similar Names: Abelard, Abelson, Abiel, Abiram, Abner, Abraham, Avel
Namesake: Abel Xavier (Mozambiquan soccer player)
⇒ Originated from the Hebrew name Hevel. A biblical name for the second son of Adam and Eve who was murdered by his envious brother Cain, and is often considered the first martyr. Preferred by parents in Spain.

Abraham
Rank: 183

Origin: Hebrew
Meaning: Father of a multitude
Alternate Spellings: Abrahem, Abrahim, Abrahym, Abreham, Abrehem, Abrehym, Abryham, Ebrahim
Gender Variations: Abigail, Abilene, Abital
Nickname: Abe
Similar Names: Aaron, Adam, Addison, Avraham, Efraim
⇒ A form of Avraham who is known as the biblical husband of Sarahi and the father of Isaac and Ishmael, originally called Abram. He is considered to be one of the first prophets of Islam and the first patriarch of the Jews. The name's popularity during the 1880s suggests it was greatly influenced by Abraham Lincoln, the 16th president.

Ace
Rank: 838

Origin: Latin
Meaning: Unit, copper coin
Gender Variations: Acacia, Lacey
Similar Names: Acer, Asa, Casey, Jace
⇒ Originally used as a nickname taken from the vocabulary word that means "highest rank." Associated with the playing card, a combat pilot who has brought down five or more enemy airplanes, a hole in one in golf, or a point scored in tennis. Jim Carrey popularized the name in his 1990 comedy *Ace Ventura: Pet Detective*. The name recently returned to the chart after an absence of more than 100 years, possibly inspired by *American Idol* finalist Ace Young.

Adam
Rank: 64

Origin: Hebrew
Meaning: Red earth
Alternate Spellings: Addam, Addem, Adem, Adham, Adim
Gender Variations: Adah, Adalia, Adamina
Nicknames: Ad, Addy
Similar Names: Adan, Addis, Addison
Namesakes: Adam Ant (musician), Adam Brody (actor), Adam Clayton (musician)
⇒ Derived from a Hebrew word referring to the color of the earth. In the Old Testament, Adam was the first man created by God to live in the Garden of Eden with his partner, Eve. Popularized in Great Britain during the 1960s by British pop star Adam Faith. Actor Adam Sandler is an influence today.

Addison   Rank: 562

Origin: Old English
Meaning: Adam's son
Alternate Spellings:
Addisen, Adison, Adyson
Gender Variations: Adamina, Addison, Addy
Nickname: Addie
Similar Names: Abraham, Adam, Absolm, Adrian
➡ A surname that originated from a personal name derived from Addie or Adie which was a pet form of Adam during the Middle Ages. Sporadically used during the late 19th century, it faded from use until 1986. More popular as a girl's name, especially when connected to Dr. Addison Montgomery Shepherd, the *Grey's Anatomy* character.

Aditya   Rank: 810

Origin: Sanskrit
Meaning: Belonging to Aditi
Alternate Spelling: Aaditya
Gender Variations: Adhita, Aditi
Similar Names: Adheesha, Agastya, Agni, Ananta, Aruna
➡ The name of several Hindu gods who are the children of Aditi and Kashyapa. Also a male Indian name that means "sun."

Adolfo   Rank: 581

Origin: German
Meaning: Noble wolf
Alternate Spelling: Adaulfo, Adolpho, Adulfo
Gender Variations: Adela, Adelinda
Nicknames: Adolf, Dolfo
Similar Names: Adolfus, Adulfo, Rodolfo
Namesakes: Adolfo Perez Esquivel (Nobel Peace Prize winner)
➡ The Italian and Spanish form of Adolf combining *adal* and *wulf*. The name of a 13th-century German bishop and a place name for a city located in Brazil. The name has been used sporadically since prior to the turn of the 20th century and has gained popularity since 1922.

Adonis   Rank: 822

Origin: Greek
Meaning: Handsome
Alternate Spelling: Adonys
Gender Variation: Adonia
Nickname: Adon
Similar Names: Adone, Alexandros, Athenios

➡ Derived from *adon* which means "lord." In Greek mythology, he's the attractive youth who was loved by Aphrodite. The name has become synonymous for a handsome young man and is used occasionally in the U.S.

Adrian   Rank: 63

Origin: Latin
Meaning: Man from Hadria
Alternate Spellings: Adrean, Adriaan, Adrien, Edrian
Gender Variations: Adria, Adrianna, Adrianne, Adrienne
Similar Names: Adriano, Adrianus, Aiden, Ainsley, Arie
Namesakes: Adrian Dantley (basketball player), Adrian Paul (actor)
➡ The English form of the Latin name Hadrianus. Hadria was a town in northern Italy that gave its name to the Adriatic Sea. Adrian Cronauer, the inspiration for the 1987 movie, *Good Morning, Vietnam*, bears the name. Actor Adrien Brody uses a form of the name. Also used by several early popes. It first entered the top 100 in 1985 and is currently at its peak.

Adriel   Rank: 707

Origin: Hebrew
Meaning: God's flock
Alternate Spelling: Adrial, Adriell, Adriyel
Gender Variations: Adrielle
Nicknames: Adrie
Similar Names: Adar, Adiel, Amiel, Aviel, Aviram, Avner
➡ A biblical name for King Saul's son-in-law who was married to Merab. In Native American it's a word for "beaver," which is a symbol of skill. The name has climbed the popularity chart since 2002 and is fashionable among Jewish families.

Agustin   Rank: 657

Origin: Latin
Meaning: Ingenious
Alternate Spellings: Agustyn, Augustin, Augustyn
Gender Variations: Agostina, Augusta, Augustina
Nicknames: August, Gus
Similar Names: Agostino, Agosto, August, Augustavo, Augustine, Augustini, Augustino
➡ The Spanish form of Augustine ultimately derived from the Roman name Augustus that's popular among Hispanic families.

Ahmad   Rank: 524

Origin: Arabic
Meaning: Highly praised
Alternate Spellings:
Amad, Ahmaad, Ahmod
Gender Variations: Amada
Similar Names: Adnan, Ahlam, Ahmed, Ahmet, Amjad, Anwar
Namesakes: Ahmad Rashad (sportscaster)
⇒ One of the names used by the Islamic prophet Muhammad. In fiction the name refers to the prince in the *Arabian Nights*. Former football star and Emmy-award-winning sportscaster Ahmad Rashad drew attention to the name during his career that started in 1972. Born Bobby Moore, he converted to Islam that same year and changed his name. Preferred by Muslims.

Aiden   Rank: 30

Origin: Celtic/Gaelic
Meaning: Little fire
Alternate Spellings: Adan, Aden, Adin, Aedan, Aeden, Aiden, Aidyn, Aydan, Ayden, Aydin
Gender Variations: Addison, Adrienne
Similar Names: Aiken, Angus, Braden, Brian, Kian, Kieran
Namesake: Aidan Quinn (actor)
⇒ A variation of Aidan, which is the anglicized form of Aodhan. It was influenced by fictional character Aidan Shaw, played by actor John Corbett in the hit series *Sex and the City*, and the fictional little boy in the 2002 horror film *The Ring*.

Alan   Rank: 122

Origin: Celtic
Meaning: Rock
Alternate Spelling: Alain, Allan, Alen, Allen, Alin, Allin, Alun, Allyn, Alyn
Gender Variations: Alana, Alayna, Alina, Lana
Similar Names: Albert, Alden, Alec, Alex, Alfred
Namesakes: Alan Arkin (actor), Alan Jackson (singer-songwriter), Alan Shepard (astronaut)
⇒ Brought into England by the Breton followers of William the Conqueror during the 11th century, most notably for Alan, the Earl of Brittany, which led to a large number of surnames during the Middle Ages. It was influenced by actor Alan Ladd when he appeared in *This Gun for Hire* in 1942 and

the classic western *Shane* in 1953. Today the name is best known for Alan Alda who played the irreverent Hawkeye Pierce in the popular television series *MASH*. Alain is the French form.

Albert   Rank: 354

Origin: Old German
Meaning: Noble, bright, famous
Alternate Spelling: Allbert
Gender Variations: Alberta, Albertina, Albertine
Nicknames: Al, Albie, Bert, Bertie
Similar Names: Adelbert, Alberto, Albertus, Albrecht, Aubert, Elbert
Namesakes: Albert Finney (actor), Albert Grimaldi (Prince of Monaco), Albert Schweitzer (Alsatian-German theologian/philosopher)
⇒ Brought into England by the Normans and quickly grew in popularity among European royalty, most notable for Prince Albert, Queen Victoria's consort of Great Britain and Ireland during the 19th century. Also known for the German-American physicist Albert Einstein, who developed the theory of relativity and received the 1921 Nobel Prize for physics.

Alberto   Rank: 315

Origin: Old German
Meaning: Glorious nobility
Alternate Spelling: Allberto
Gender Variations: Alberta
Nicknames: Al, Bert, Berto
Similar Names: Albert, Elbert, Enrique, Ernesto, Filiberto, Ulberto
⇒ Italian, Portuguese, and Spanish form of Albert and the name of 28 saints. Slightly more popular than Albert, most likely due to increased usage by Hispanic families.

Alden   Rank: 811

Origin: Old English
Meaning: Old friend
Alternate Spellings: Aldan, Aldin, Aldon
Gender Variations: Alda, Aleen
Similar Names: Aldous, Aldwin, Alwine, Elden, Eldwyn
⇒ A surname used as a given name derived from Aldwyn. In occasional use since before the turn of the 20th century. Pilgrim John

Alden who emigrated to America in 1620 on the *Mayflower* is a famous bearer of the surname. Also notable for Astronaut Neil Alden Armstrong, the first person to set foot on the moon.

Aldo Rank: 587

Origin: Old German
Meaning: Noble
Gender Variations: Alda, Aldona
Similar Names: Alden, Aldis, Aldwin, Arnell, Arness, Arnold
Namesake: Aldous Huxley (author)
➡ The short form of the German name Aldous that first appeared on the popularity chart in 1911. It was possibly inspired by fictional character Aldo Burrows from the popular television series *Prison Break*.

Alec Rank: 328

Origin: Greek
Alternate Spellings: Aleck, Alek, Alic, Alick
Gender Variation: Alecia
Nickname: Al
Similar Names: Alex, Alexei, Alexander, Alejandro, Xander
Namesake: Alec Baldwin (actor)
➡ A nickname for Alexander used independently since the 19th century. English actor Sir Alec Guinness is a famous bearer of the name. He received an Academy Award for his role in the 1957 film *The Bridge on the River Kwai*, but is perhaps best known for his role as Ben Obi-Wan Kenobi in the *Star Wars* film trilogy.

Alejandro Rank: 96

Origin: Greek
Meaning: Defender of mankind
Gender Variations: Alejandra, Alexa, Alexandria
Nicknames: Al, Jandro
Similar Names: Alejandrino, Alejo, Alendro, Alessandro, Alexander, Alexandro, Alexandros, Alistair
Namesakes: Alejandro Fernandez (Mexican singer), Alejandro Sanz (Spanish musician)
➡ The Spanish form of the name Alexander derived from a blend of *alexein* with *andros* listed among the top 100 since 1997.

Alessandro Rank: 608

Origin: Greek
Meaning: Defender of mankind
Gender Variations: Alessa, Alessandra
Nicknames: Al, Sandro
Similar Names: Alastair, Alejandro, Alesander, Alexander, Alexandros, Alister
➡ The Italian form of Alexander historically known for Italian physicist Alessandro Volta, the inventor of the battery.

Alex Rank: 67

Origin: Greek
Meaning: Defender of mankind
Alternate Spellings: Alecks, Aleks, Alix, Allex, Alyx
Gender Variations: Alexa, Lexa, Lexie
Similar Names: Alasdair, Alastair, Alec, Alexander
Namesakes: Alex Haley (novelist), Alex Karras (football player), Alex Rodriguez (baseball player), Alex Trebek (game show host)
➡ The shortened form of Alexander that's also used as an independent name. It jumped in popularity during the 1980s run of *Family Ties*, starring Michael J. Fox in the role of Alex P. Keaton.

Alexander Rank: 12

Origin: Greek
Meaning: Defender of mankind
Alternate Spellings: Aleksandar, Aleksander, Aleksandr, Alexandre, Alexzander, Alixandre
Gender Variations: Alexandra, Alexandria, Alexis
Nicknames: Alex, Xander
Similar Names: Alasdair, Alastair, Alejandro, Alessandro, Alexandro, Alexius, Alistair, Alister
Namesakes: Alexander Ovechkin (Russian hockey player), Jason Alexander (actor), Shaun Alexander (football player)
➡ Alexander the Great brought worldwide attention to the name during the 4th century BC. Since that time, three emperors, numerous kings and saints, and eight popes have taken the name. Alexander Graham Bell, the inventor of the telephone, comes to mind. Naomi Watts and Liev Schreiber chose Alexander Pete for their son.

Alexis
Rank: 130

Origin: Greek
Meaning: Defender, protector
Alternate Spelling: Alexus
Gender Variations: Alexa, Alexis, Lexa
Nicknames: Al, Alex
Similar Names: Alejo, Aleksei, Alexandre, Alexei, Alexios, Alexius
Namesakes: Alexis Cruz (actor), Alexei Kovalev (Russian hockey player)
⇒ A form of Alexius associated with the 19th century French political thinker and historian, Alexis de Tocqueville. The name was originally used for boys but is now more common for girls.

Alfred
Rank: 755

Origin: Old English
Meaning: Elf counsel
Alternate Spellings: Alfrid, Elfred
Gender Variations: Alfreda
Nicknames: Al, Alf, Alfie, Fred, Freddie, Fredo
Similar Names: Adelfried, Alfredo, Alvere, Avery
Namesakes: Alfred E. Neuman (*MAD* magazine fictional mascot), Alfred, Lord Tennyson (poet), Alfred Hitchcock (director)
⇒ A combination of *aelf* and *raed* used in honor of the 9th-century King of Wessex, Alfred the Great, who defended England against the Danes. Because of his popularity the name stayed in use after the Norman Conquest and was picked up by Queen Victoria as the name of her second son. It was listed among the top 50 around the turn of the 20th century, but has steadily decreased since that time. Comic book buffs may think of Batman's butler Alfred Pennyworth.

Alfredo
Rank: 334

Origin: Old English
Meaning: Elf counsel
Gender Variations: Alfreda
Nicknames: Al, Alf, Fred, Freddie, Fredo
Similar Names: Adelfo, Adonaldo, Agustino, Alfonso, Alfred
⇒ The Italian, Portuguese, and Spanish form of Alfred used by a 4th-century saint. A favorite name among Hispanic families.

Ali
Rank: 360

Origin: Arabic
Meaning: High, exalted
Gender Variation: Aliyah
Similar Names: Abid, Adil, Ala, Amal, Asim, Attiah, Aziz
⇒ The son-in-law of the prophet Mohammed who came to be known as the first male convert to Islam and the last caliph. Best known for boxing champion, Cassius Clay, who changed his name to Muhammad Ali in 1975. The story *Ali Baba and the Forty Thieves*, also comes to mind.

Alonzo
Rank: 558

Origin: Old German
Meaning: Noble and ready
Alternate Spelling: Alonso
Gender Variations: Alanna, Alonza
Nicknames: Al, Alon, Lon, Lonnie
Similar Names: Adelfo, Ademar, Adolfo, Alberto, Alfredo, Alphone, Alphonse, Alvaro
Namesakes: Alonzo Babers (Olympic track and field medalist), Alonzo Mourning (basketball player)
⇒ The Spanish form of Alphonso, and Alonso is the name of a fictional character from Spanish author Miguel de Cervantes' 17th-century novel, *Don Quixote de la Mancha*. A popular choice among African-American families.

Alvin
Rank: 513

Origin: Old English
Meaning: Elf friend
Alternate Spelling: Alvan, Alven, Alvyn
Gender Variations: Alvina, Alvine, Elvina, Elwina
Nicknames: Al, Alvie
Similar Names: Alwyn, Calvin, Elvin, Elvis, Elwin, Malvin, Melvin
Namesake: Alvin Robertson (basketball player)
⇒ An Old English personal name derived from a blend of "aelf" and "wine." The name was popularized by Alvin York, the World War I hero and Medal of Honor recipient, whose life story was depicted in the 1941 film *Sergeant York*, starring Gary Cooper in the title role. Also known for the fictional singing group *Alvin and the Chipmunks* created in 1958 that led to the popular 1980s and 1990s television show. Listed among the top 100

from 1901 to 1938. A top 50 name in Sweden and a favorite among African-American parents.

Amari
Rank: 421
Origin: African
Meaning: Having great strength
Alternate Spelling: Amare, Amary
Gender Variation: Amara
Similar Names: Ali, Amil, Anadi, Ananya, Anil
➡ A form of Amar that debuted on the popularity chart in 1997 and is currently listed among the top 500 names.

Amir
Rank: 324
Origin: Arabic/Hebrew
Meaning: Prince, treetop
Alternate Spelling: Ameer, Ameir, Emeer, Emir
Gender Variations: Almira, Amira
Similar Names: Ali, Amin, Amiri, Ammar, Aziz
➡ Originally used as a title for a ruler or military leader in several Muslim countries. The name has swiftly moved up the chart since its debut in 1976.

Anders
Rank: 987
Origin: Greek
Meaning: Manly
Gender Variations: Andra, Andrea
Nicknames: Ander, Andy
Similar Names: Anderson, Andor, Andras, Andre, Andreas, Andro, Andros
➡ The Scandinavian form of Andrew which led to the surname Anderson. The name is historically associated with Swedish astronomer Anders Celsius, the inventor of the Celsius temperature scale.

Anderson
Rank: 399
Origin: Greek
Meaning: Son of Andrew
Alternate Spelling: Andersen, Andersson
Gender Variations: Andrea, Andriana, Andrine
Nicknames: Ander, Anders, Andy
Similar Names: Andre, Andreas, Andres, Andrew, Andro, Andros
➡ A common surname derived from the personal name Anders. Actor Richard Dean Anderson from the 1985 to 1992 television series *MacGyver* is a famous bearer of the surname. It's also known for Emmy Award-winning television personality Anderson Cooper. It peaked as a given name during the 1880s.

Andre
Rank: 207
Origin: Greek
Meaning: Man
Alternate Spellings: Andrei, Andreiy, Andrey
Gender Variations: Andrea, Andrina
Nicknames: Andy
Similar Names: Andreas, Andres, Andrew
Namesakes: Andre Agassi (tennis player), Andre Braugher (actor), Andre the Giant (wrestler), Andre Previn (pianist)
➡ The French and Portuguese form of Andrew that peaked in popularity in 1984 at No. 119. The 1982 film *My Dinner with Andre* may come to mind.

Andreas
Rank: 880
Origin: Greek
Meaning: Manly
Alternate Spellings: Aindreas, Andreus
Gender Variations: Andra, Andrea
Nickname: Andy
Similar Names: Ander, Andras, Andre, Andres, Andrew, Deandre
➡ The original New Testament form of Andrew that debuted on the popularity chart in 1963. Preferred in in Austria, Denmark, Norway, and Sweden.

Andres
Rank: 161
Origin: Greek
Meaning: Manly
Gender Variations: Andra, Andrea, Andriana
Nickname: Andy
Similar Names: Andre, Andreas, Andris, Andrius, Andrus
Namesakes: Andres Escobar (Colombian Soccer Hall of Famer), Andres Nocioni (Argentine basketball player)
➡ The Spanish form of the name Andrew. Andres Segovia, considered to be the father of the modern classical guitar, is a namesake. Popular in Catalonia, Chile, and Spain.

Andrew   Rank: 8

Origin: Greek
Meaning: Manly
Alternate Spelling: Andrue
Gender Variation: Andrea
Nicknames: Andy, Drew
Similar Names: Ander, Anders, Anderson, Andras, Andre, Andreas, Andres, Evander
Namesake: Andrew Wyeth (artist)
⇨ A biblical name for the first apostle chosen by Christ derived from the Greek Andreas. The name has seen much popularity in Scotland and renewed interest in Great Britain since the birth of Prince Andrew in 1960. Historical namesakes include two presidents and industrialist Andrew Carnegie.

Andy   Rank: 204

Origin: Greek
Meaning: Manly
Alternate Spelling: Andie
Gender Variations: Andie
Similar Names: Anders, Andre, Andreas, Andres, Andrew
Namesakes: Andy Roddick (tennis player)
⇨ A popular nickname for Andrew that's also used as an independent name. Associated with *Amos 'n' Andy*, a radio comedy that became popular in the 1920s, and the doll that started as a character in the 1920 book *Raggedy Andy Stories*. Pop artist Andy Warhol and actor Andy Garcia are famous bearers of the name.

Angel   Rank: 31

Origin: Greek
Meaning: Messenger of God
Alternate Spellings: Angell, Anjel
Gender Variations: Angela, Angelina, Angie
Nickname: Ange
Similar Names: Angelino, Angelo, Angelos, Dangelo, Deangelo
Namesake: Angel Cordero Jr. (Puerto Rican jockey)
⇨ The biblical name for a spiritual being who acts as God's messenger. Popular in Spanish-speaking countries, the name has steadily increased in popularity since the 1940s and is the title of numerous movies, television series, and songs, including the 1999 to 2004 supernatural drama that originated as a spin-off of the series *Buffy the Vampire Slayer*. Antonio Banderas played the role of Angel Gimenez in the 1986 film *Matador*.

Angelo   Rank: 262

Origin: Greek
Meaning: Messenger of God
Gender Variations: Angela, Angelia, Angelica, Angeline
Nicknames: Ange
Similar Names: Angel, Angelino, Angelo, Dangelo, Deangelo, Michelangelo
⇨ The Spanish and Italian form of Angel that peaked in popularity in 1914 and 1916. A literary name used by Shakespeare in his play *Measure for Measure*.

Anthony   Rank: 9

Origin: Latin
Meaning: Priceless, praiseworthy
Gender Variations: Antonia, Antoinette, Toni, Tonya
Nicknames: Tone, Tony
Similar Names: Antoine, Anton, Antone, Antonio, Antonius, Antony
Namesakes: Anthony Edwards (actor), Carmelo Anthony (basketball player)
⇨ Derived from the old Roman family name Antonius. Associated with early saints and an Egyptian hermit who founded monasticism. Listed among the top 100 names since 1881 and the top 50 since 1936. Influenced by the long career of Welsh actor Anthony Hopkins. Puerto Rican-American singer Marc Anthony is a famous bearer of the surname.

Antoine   Rank: 631

Origin: Latin
Meaning: Priceless, praiseworthy
Alternate Spelling: Antwan
Gender Variations: Antoinetta, Antoinette
Nicknames: Anton, Tone, Tony
Similar Names: Anthoney, Antonius, Antonio, Antony
Namesake: Antoine Carr (basketball player)
⇨ The French variation of Anthony that has faded during the past 10 years. A top 50 name in Belgium and France.

Anton   Rank: 725

Origin: Latin
Meaning: Priceless, praiseworthy
Gender Variations: Antonella, Antonellina, Tonya
Nickname: Tony

Similar Names: Antone, Antonio, Antonius, Antony, Antwan

➥ The German form of Anthony that peaked in popularity toward the end of the 19th century. Russian short story writer and playwright Anton Chekhov is a famous bearer. The name is preferred in several English-speaking countries.

Antonio   Rank: 93

Origin: Latin
Meaning: Priceless, praiseworthy
Gender Variations:
Antonella, Antonia, Antonietta
Nicknames: Tonio, Tony
Similar Names: Anthony, Anton, Antonino, Antonius, Antony
Namesakes: Antonio Freeman (football player), Antonio Sabato Jr. (actor), Antonio Tarver (Olympic medalist/boxer/actor)

➥ The Italian and Spanish form of Anthony. A top 100 name since 1972. Influenced by Spanish film actor Antonio Banderas, who first came to fame when he began appearing in American films in 1992. The name is preferred in Catalonia, Chile, and Spain.

Antony   Rank: 815

Origin: Latin
Meaning: Priceless, praiseworthy
Alternate Spelling: Antoney
Gender Variations: Antoni, Antonia
Nickname: Tony
Similar Names: Anthony, Antoine, Anton, Antono, Antonio, Antonius

➥ Variation of Anthony that is ultimately derived from Antonius. Roman politician and general Mark Antony, who committed suicide with his lover, Egyptian queen Cleopatra, is a famous bearer of the surname. It first listed on the popularity chart in 1953.

Ari   Rank: 634

Origin: Hebrew/Old Norse
Meaning: Lion, eagle
Alternate Spellings:
Aree, Arie, Arri, Ary
Gender Variations: Aria, Ariel
Similar Names: Aric, Arion, Aristide, Aristo, Aristos

➥ The short form of several names including the biblical Ariel and the Greek Aristotle. It also refers to the Greek name for the planet

Mars and the English translation for Ares, the Greek god of war. Aristotle Onassis, the Greek shipping magnate, and Greek philosopher Aristotle are two famous bearers commonly referred to as "Ari."

Ariel   Rank: 471

Origin: Hebrew
Meaning: Lion of God
Alternate Spelling: Ariell
Gender Variations:
Ariella, Arielle
Nickname: Ari
Similar Names: Aaron, Abel, Abiel, Abijah, Abiram, Abisai

➥ Mentioned in the Old Testament as a symbolic name for the city of Jerusalem. Shakespeare used the name for a spirit in his 17th-century play The Tempest. Famous bearer Ariel Sharon is the former Israeli prime minister and military leader. The name has faded in popularity for boys and increased for girls.

Arjun   Rank: 720

Origin: Sanskrit
Meaning: White, clear
Gender Variations:
Arjane, Marjan
Similar Names: Aditya, Agni, Ananta, Anil, Arjuna, Aruna
Namesakes: Arjun Rampal (Indian actor/model), Arun Sarja (Indian actor/director)

➥ A variation of Arjuna, the name of a hero in the Hindu epic Mahabharata that was adapted into a 1985 theatrical play. Influenced by professional golfer Arjun Atwal, the first Indian to become a member of the U.S.-based PGA Tour. The name debuted on the popularity chart in 2001 and is also preferred in Canada.

Armando   Rank: 264

Origin: German
Meaning: Soldier, warrior
Alternate Spelling:
Armondo
Gender Variations: Armina, Hermine
Nicknames: Arman, Armand
Similar Names: Alberto, Anatolio, Apollo, Ariano, Armin, Arnoldo, Ermanno, Harmon, Herman
Namesake: Armando Benitez (Dominican Republic baseball player)

➥ The Spanish, Italian, and Portuguese form of Herman that usually indicates a hero in the army. The name has gained in popularity since 1985.

Armani   Rank: 698

Origin: Persian
Meaning: Desire, goal
Alternate Spellings:
Armanie, Armoni
Gender Variations: Armina
Nickname: Arman
Similar Names: Armand, Armando, Armin, Armon, Arnaud
➡ A surname derived from the medieval personal name Armanno. Influenced by Italian fashion designer Giorgio Armani, which led to its debut on the popularity chart in 1994.

Arthur   Rank: 377

Origin: Celtic/Irish
Meaning: Bear, stone
Alternate Spellings:
Arther, Arthor
Gender Variations: Arthuretta, Arthurina, Arthurine
Nicknames: Art, Artie
Similar Names: Artair, Arthus, Artor, Artur, Arturas, Arturo
Namesakes: Arthur Conan Doyle (British author), Arthur Garfunkel (musician), Arthur Miller (playwright)
➡ Possibly derived from the Celtic *Artos* or the Irish *Art* and associated with the legendary King Arthur who was popularized in literature. The name was influenced during the 19th century by the British military successes of Arthur Wellesley, Duke of Wellington, who defeated Napoleon at Waterloo. It peaked prior to the turn of the 20th century and was listed among the top 100 until 1969.

Arturo   Rank: 323

Origin: Celtic/Irish
Meaning: Bear, stone
Alternate Spelling: Artero
Gender Variations: Arthuretta
Nickname: Art
Similar Names: Alberto, Alfonso, Alfredo, Alturo, Arthuro, Auturo
Namesakes: Arturo Gatti (Canadian boxer)
➡ The Italian and Spanish form of Arthur.

Asa   Rank: 623

Origin: Hebrew
Meaning: Healer
Gender Variations: Asia

Nicknames: Ase
Similar Names: Asaiah, Asaph, Asher, Azel, Esau, Ethan, Ezra, Ezri, Isiah
➡ A biblical name for the third king of Judah who reigned for 41 years and became popular among the Puritans during the 17th century. More common in the U.S. prior to the turn of the 20th century. A favorite Jewish name.

Asher   Rank: 252

Origin: Hebrew
Meaning: Happy, blessed
Alternate Spellings:
Ashor, Ashur
Gender Variation: Ashley
Nickname: Ash
Similar Names: Abe, Alon, Anschel, Arik, Asa
➡ In the Old Testament, the name of the second son of Jacob and Leah's handmaid, Zilpah, who became the leader of one of the 12 tribes of Israel. The name has drifted in and out of popularity and is currently at its peak following a biblical naming trend. Commonly used among Jewish families.

Ashton   Rank: 121

Origin: Old English
Meaning: Ash tree town
Alternate Spellings:
Ashten, Ashtun
Gender Variations: Ashley, Ashlynn
Nickname: Ash
Similar Names: Asa, Ashby, Asher, Astin, Aston
➡ A surname derived from a place name taken from several possible locations in England. It took a jump in popularity during the late 1990s when actor Ashton Kutcher first became known in the television series *That '70s Show*. Occasionally used as a girl's name.

Atticus   Rank: 767

Origin: Latin
Meaning: From Attica
Gender Variations: Astrid
Similar Names: Amadeus, Antonius, Arcadia, Aston, Atholl, Augustus, Aurelius
➡ A Roman name for someone who lived in the Attica region that surrounds Athens in Greece. A literary name for attorney Atticus Finch from *To Kill a Mockingbird*. In popular use in 1881, then completely faded away until reappearing again in 2004. Actor Billy Crudup and actress Mary-Louise Parker named their son William Atticus.

August
Rank: 618

Origin: Latin
Meaning: Great, magnificent
Alternate Spelling: Auguste
Gender Variations:
Augusta, Augustina
Nicknames: Augie, Gus
Similar Names: Agustin, Augustine, Augusto,
Augustus, Austin
Namesakes: Auguste Renoir (painter),
Auguste Rodin (sculptor)
➡ The eighth calendar month of the year
and the short form of Augustus associated
with the Roman emperor. It peaked prior
to the turn of the 20th century. Emmy
award-winning actress Mariska Hargitay
has a son named August.

Augustus
Rank: 831

Origin: Latin
Meaning: Exalted
Gender Variations:
Augusta, Augustia, Augustina
Nicknames: Augie, August, Gus
Similar Names: Agostino, August, Augustin,
Augustine
➡ A title used by all of the Roman emperors
starting with Gaius Julius Caesar Octavianus,
the adopted son of Julius Caesar. who was
referred to as Augustus Caesar after 27 BC.
The name became popular in England during
the 18th century and peaked in the U.S. in
1916. Dixie Chick Emily Robison named her
son Charles Augustus.

Austin
Rank: 41

Origin: Latin
Meaning: Ingenious
Alternate Spelling: Austen,
Austyn, Osten, Ostin, Ostyn
Gender Variations: Austina, Austine
Similar Names: Agustin, Auberon, Aubrey,
August, Augustus
Namesakes: Austin Carr (basketball player),
Steve Austin (The Six Million Dollar Man
character)
➡ A surname derived from Augustinus that's
historically known for American colonizer
Stephen Austin, one of the founders of the
Republic of Texas and the namesake for the
state capital. Today it's associated with the
lead character in the Austin Powers films that
premiered in 1997. The name peaked in 1996
and 1997 at No. 9.

Avery
Rank: 212

Origin: Old English
Meaning: Elf counsel
Alternate Spellings:
Averey, Averi, Averie, Avry
Gender Variations: Avery
Similar Names: Alfred, Aubrey, Austin
Namesakes: Avery Brooks (actor/singer),
Steve Avery (baseball pitcher)
➡ A surname that originated during the
Middle Ages from Alfred. Animator and
cartoon director, Tex Avery, who created the
characters Daffy Duck, Droopy, Chilly Willy,
and coined the phrase "What's up Doc?"
for Bugs Bunny, is a bearer of the surname.
Predominantly used as a girl's name.

Axel
Rank: 295

Origin: German/Scandinavian
Meaning: Father of peace
Alternate Spellings: Axell,
Axil, Axill, Axl
Gender Variations: Avril
Nicknames: Acke, Ax
Similar Names: Azel, Azarel, Azariah
Namesake: Axel Foley (Beverly Hills Cop
character)
➡ The Scandinavian form of Absalom.
Its rise in popularity began with Axel
Munthe, a 20th-century Swedish physician
and psychiatrist, who wrote an autobiography
called The Story of San Michele. Axl Rose,
the lead singer of the rock group Guns N'
Roses, uses a variation of the name.

Bailey
Rank: 635

Origin: French/English
Meaning: Bailiff
Alternate Spellings:
Bailee, Bailie, Baily, Baylee,
Bayley, Baylie
Gender Variation: Bailee
Nickname: Bail
Similar Names: Baylor, Beckett, Chandler,
Gardner, Hunter, Parker
Namesake: Will Bailey (West Wing actor)
➡ An occupational surname for a bailiff or
administrative official. The name was in use
at the turn of the 20th century and then
sporadically until 1992. A top 100 name in
Australia, England, New Zealand, and Wales.
Significantly more popular as a girl's name.

Barrett Rank: 762

Origin: Middle English/German
Meaning: Dispute, argument, bear-strength
Alternate Spellings: Barat, Baret, Barratt, Barret, Barrette
Gender Variation: Barrett
Nickname: Barry
Similar Names: Barnett, Barrington, Barry, Barrymore, Bennett, Bradley, Garrett, Jarrett
Namesake: Roger Keith "Syd" Barrett (English musician)
⇨ Derived from *baret* and predominantly used as a surname until the 19th century when it was influenced as a given name for both boys and girls by English poet Elizabeth Barrett Browning. It peaked in 1981 and is slowly coming back into fashion.

Beau Rank: 438

Origin: French
Meaning: Handsome, beautiful
Alternate Spelling: Bo
Gender Variation: Bo
Similar Names: Beaufort, Beaumont, Beauregard, Boyce, Brett, Brock, Bryce
Namesakes: Bo Diddley (musician), Bo Jackson (baseball/football player)
⇨ A nickname meaning handsome that originated with Englishman George Bryan Brummell, better known as Beau Brummell, a fashion leader during the 19th century. A literary name for the central character in P.C. Wren's 1924 novel *Beau Geste* or character Beau Wilkes in *Gone with the Wind*. Used in the U.S. since 1967, which led to the less popular form, Bo. Influenced during the 1970s and 1980s by actor Beau Bridges. Among the top 100 names in Australia.

Beckett Rank: 758

Origin: Old English
Meaning: Beehive, bee cottage
Alternate Spelling: Becket
Gender Variation: Becca
Nickname: Beck
Similar Names: Beck, Benedict, Bennett, Burkett
⇨ Possibly an occupational surname that may also be related to Beck. Irish dramatist, novelist, and poet Samuel Beckett is a famous bearer of the surname. New to the popularity chart in 2006 as part of a surname trend.

Ben Rank: 555

Origin: Hebrew
Meaning: Son of the right hand
Alternate Spelling: Benn
Gender Variations: Bea, Becca
Nickname: Benny
Similar Names: Benjy, Benny, Bent, Bentley, Benton, Bill, Bob
Namesakes: Ben Affleck (actor), Ben Hogan (Hall of Fame golfer), Ben Johnson (Canadian Olympic medalist), Ben Stiller (actor)
⇨ The short form of Benjamin or Bennett used as an independent name since before the turn of the 20th century.

Benjamin Rank: 24

Origin: Hebrew
Meaning: Son of the right hand, son of the south
Alternate Spellings: Benjaman, Benjamen, Benjamon, Benjiman, Benjimin, Benjimon
Gender Variation: Benjamina
Nicknames: Ben, Benjy, Benny
Similar Names: Barnabus, Bartholomew, Benedict, Bennett, Benson, Bentley, Benton
Namesakes: Benjamin Bratt (actor), Benjamin Harrison (23rd U.S. president), Benjamin McKenzie (actor), Benny Goodman (band leader)
⇨ In the Old Testament the youngest son of Jacob and his wife, Rachel, who died giving birth. During the Middle Ages, the name was given to sons whose mothers had died during childbirth. Known for 18th-century statesman and inventor Benjamin Franklin, who signed the Declaration of Independence. Listed among the top 50 names since 1974 and tops the chart in Chile.

Bennett Rank: 369

Origin: Latin
Meaning: Little blessed one
Alternate Spellings: Benet, Benett, Bennet
Gender Variations: Annette
Nicknames: Ben, Benny
Similar Names: Benedict, Benoit, Benson, Bentley, Benton
⇨ A form of Benedict used by both men and women during the Middle Ages. Usage today is related to the surname. Singer Tony Bennett, whose career has remarkably

spanned six decades, is a famous bearer. The name has declined in recent years but seems to be making a comeback.

Benny
Rank: 962

Origin: Hebrew
Meaning: Son of the right hand
Gender Variation: Bente
Nickname: Ben
Similar Names: Benedict, Benicio, Benjamin, Benjy, Benoit, Benroy, Bent, Bentley, Bernie
➡ The pet form of Benjamin, Benedict, or Ebenezer also used as a surname. Known for comedian and entertainer Jack Benny and jazz musician and band leader Benny Goodman.

Bernard
Rank: 945

Origin: German
Meaning: Bold as a bear
Alternate Spelling: Bernhard
Gender Variations: Bernadette, Bernadina, Bernadine, Bernette
Nicknames: Bern, Bernie
Similar Names: Barnard, Barney, Bernardo, Bernhardt
Namesakes: George Bernard Shaw (playwright), Bernard Malamud (novelist)
➡ A combination of the elements bear and hard that was brought by the Normans into England. The name of several saints, including Saint Bernard of Menthon who built hospices in the Swiss Alps during the 10th century. The monks in this order were often accompanied by herding dogs who later became known as Saint Bernards.

Bernardo
Rank: 975

Origin: German
Meaning: Bold as a bear
Alternate Spellings: Barnardo, Bernhardo
Gender Variations: Bernadine, Bernardine, Bernardita
Nicknames: Bernie, Nardo
Similar Names: Barney, Bernardino, Bernat, Bernhard
➡ The Italian, Portuguese, and Spanish form of Bernard.

Billy
Rank: 473

Origin: Old German
Meaning: Determined
Alternate Spelling: Billie
Gender Variations: Billie, Willa
Nickname: Bill
Similar Names: Blake, Blane, Will, Willie, Wilmer
Namesakes: Billy Crystal (actor), Billy Crudup (actor), Billy Joel (singer/musician), Billy Squier (rock musician)
➡ The pet form of William infamously known for 19th-century American outlaw Billy the Kid, who went by the name of Henry McCarty as a child. Both actors and musicians have combined Billy with a one-syllable name, such as actor Billy Bob Thornton and country singer and actor Billy Ray Cyrus. It peaked in popularity during the 1920s and is occasionally used as a girl's name.

Blaine
Rank: 572

Origin: Cetic
Meaning: Slender, thin
Alternate Spellings: Blain, Blane, Blayne
Gender Variation: Blanche
Nickname: Blaney
Similar Names: Baird, Birk, Blair, Blaise, Blake, Boyd, Brice
➡ Originated as a surname given in honor of the 6th-century Scottish Saint Blaan. An enduring name that peaked during the 1880s and is now listed among the top 600. Also a place name with several locations in the U.S.

Blaise
Rank: 985

Origin: Latin
Meaning: One who stammers
Alternate Spellings: Blais, Blaize, Blase, Blayze, Blaze
Gender Variation: Blanca
Similar Names: Biaggio, Biagino, Blaine, Blair, Blake, Brais
➡ A variation of Blasius and the name of a 4th-century saint who was gifted with miraculous healing powers and known as the patron saint of sore-throat sufferers. French mathematician and physicist Blaise Pascal was a 17th-century child prodigy who invented a calculating machine before he died at age 39.

209

Blake Rank: 97

Origin: Old English
Meaning: Black, pale
Gender Variation: Blake
Similar Names: Blachard, Blaine, Blair, Blakely
Namesakes: Blake Edwards (filmmaker), Blake Shelton (country singer), James Blake (tennis player), Robert Blake (actor)
⇒ Originally a nickname given to someone who had light or dark skin or hair. English poet and artist William Blake first brought attention to the surname during the 19th century. It was popularized during the 1980s by fictional character Blake Carrington from the the prime-time television soap opera *Dynasty*. Occasionally used as a girl's name.

Bode Rank: 848

Origin: Old English
Meaning: To wait
Alternate Spellings: Bodie, Body
Gender Variations: Codie, Dodie
Similar Names: Bede, Boden, Boyd, Cade, Cody, Dade
⇒ New to the popularity chart in 2006, the name was influenced by alpine skier Bode Miller who became the first American in 22 years to win the overall alpine skiing World Cup title. Also the name of a river in Germany.

Boston Rank: 626

Origin: American
Alternate Spelling: Bostin
Gender Variation: Aubrey
Similar Names: Austin, Bastien, Bolton, Dallas, Denver, Easton, Houston
Namesake: Boston (rock band)
⇒ A geographical name for the capital of Massachusetts occasionally used as a given name since prior to the turn of the 20th century. It's taken a giant leap in popularity since 2005, possibly influenced by the song released in 2005 by the California rock band Augustana that propelled them into the spotlight.

Brad Rank: 897

Origin: Old English
Meaning: Broad clearing
Alternate Spelling: Bradd
Gender Variations: Brandy
Similar Names: Bradford, Bradley, Brady, Brant, Brent, Brett
Namesake: Brad Renfro (actor)

⇒ The short form of Bradley or Bradford that peaked as a given name in 1975 at No. 98. Best known for actor and film producer Brad Pitt, born William Bradley Pitt, who became famous in film roles during the mid 1990s but is even better known for his highly scrutinized personal life.

Bradley Rank: 188

Origin: Old English
Meaning: Broad clearing
Alternate Spellings: Bradlea, Bradlee, Bradleigh, Bradlie, Bradly
Gender Variation: Bradlee
Nicknames: Brad, Lee
Similar Names: Bartlett, Bradford, Brady, Brandon, Brayden, Braylen
⇒ A surname and place name that may have been influenced by World War II General Omar Bradley. A top 200 name since 1948 that's also popular in England and Wales.

Brady Rank: 105

Origin: Irish Gaelic
Meaning: Descendant of Bradach
Alternate Spellings: Bradey, Bradie, Braedy, Braidie, Braidy, Braydie
Gender Variation: Brandy
Similar Names: Brad, Braden, Bradford, Bradley, Brody
⇒ An old Irish nickname that's also used as a surname. Greg, Peter, Bobby, Marcia, Jan, and Cindy, otherwise known as The Brady Bunch from the classic television show that aired from 1969 to 1974, left an indelible mark on the name.

Brandon Rank: 27

Origin: Old English
Meaning: Hill covered with broom
Alternate Spellings: Brandan, Branden, Brandin, Brandyn
Gender Variations: Brandy, Brenda, Brenna
Nicknames: Bran, Brand
Similar Names: Braden, Brannon, Braylon, Brendan, Brennan, Brenton, Bronson
Namesakes: Brandon Lee (actor), Brandon Routh (actor), Brandon Tartikoff (NBC executive)
⇒ Originated as a surname and place name that debuted on the charts in 1950 possibly influenced by actor Marlon Brando. The name peaked during the run of the 1990s

television series *Beverly Hills, 90210*, starring character Brandon Walsh. Occasionally used as a female name.

Branson
Rank: 862

Origin: English
Meaning: Son of Brand
Alternate Spelling: Bransen
Gender Variations: Briannon
Nickname: Bran
Similar Names: Brandon, Branston, Branton, Bronson
Namesakes: Sir Richard Branson (British entrepreneur)
➜ A variation of the name Brandon that first charted in 1995. A place name for the popular vacation spot located in Branson, Missouri.

Braxton
Rank: 224

Origin: Old English
Meaning: Brock's town
Alternate Spellings: Brackston, Braxten, Braxtin, Braxtyn, Braxxton
Gender Variation: Braelyn
Nickname: Brax
Similar Names: Brack, Braden, Brandon, Brant, Branton, Caxton, Paxton
➜ Originated as a surname and place name that's huge jump in popularity is most likely associated with Grammy Award-winning singer and songwriter, Toni Braxton.

Brayden
Rank: 79

Origin: Irish
Meaning: Descendant of Bradan
Alternate Spelling: Braden, Bradin, Bradyn, Braeden, Braedon, Braiden, Braydon
Gender Variation: Brady
Similar Names: Brad, Bradley, Brady, Brandon, Braylen, Brendan, Brennan, Brycen, Bryden, Bryen
➜ A variation of Braden that originated from the surname O Bradain. In vogue since 1991, it's a good choice for parents who are looking for a name with several spelling options.

Braylon
Rank: 401

Origin: American
Alternate Spellings: Braelon, Braylen
Gender Variations: Braelyn,

Breelyn, Briallen
Nicknames: Bray, Lon
Similar Names: Bradley, Braedon, Brandon, Brendon, Brennen
Namesake: Braylon Edwards (football player)
➜ A trendy combination of the names Braydon and Lynn that first listed on the popularity chart in 2004 at No. 703.

Brendan
Rank: 185

Origin: Irish
Meaning: Prince
Alternate Spellings: Brenden, Brendon
Gender Variations: Brenda, Brenna
Nicknames: Bren, Brend
Similar Names: Braydon, Brandon, Branson, Brennan, Brenton
Namesakes: Brendan Fehr (Canadian actor), Brendan Gaughan (NASCAR truck champion)
➜ The anglicized form of the Irish Breandan ultimately derived from "Breanainn." Saint Brendan was an Irish abbot during the 6th century who was reported to be the first European to travel to North America. The name peaked in 1999 at No. 96 influenced by by Canadian-American actor Brendan Fraser, star of the 1999 hit film *The Mummy*.

Brennan
Rank: 299

Origin: Irish Gaelic
Meaning: Moisture, drop
Alternate Spellings: Brenan, Brennen, Brennin, Brennon, Brenyn
Gender Variations: Brenda, Brenna
Nickname: Brenn
Similar Names: Braedon, Branden, Brannen, Brendan
➜ Originally a form of the more popular name Brendan or an Irish surname derived from "O Braonain."

Brent
Rank: 481

Origin: Old English/Celtic
Meaning: Hill
Alternate Spellings: Brennt, Brentt
Gender Variations: Bretta
Similar Names: Brandon, Brant, Brenton, Bronson
Namesakes: Brent Musburger (sportscaster)
➜ A surname derived from an English place name and used as the short form of Brenton.

Brenton Rank: 942

Origin: Old English
Meaning: Bryni's town
Gender Variation: Brenna
Nickname: Brent
Similar Names: Braedon, Brandon, Branton, Brendon, Trent, Trenton
⇨ A surname derived from a local place name located near Exminster, England, and sometimes used as a variation of Branton. First listed on the popularity chart in 1966, it peaked in 1984 at No. 259.

Brett Rank: 304

Origin: Latin
Meaning: One from Brittany
Alternate Spellings: Bret, Brette
Gender Variations: Bretta, Britt, Brittany
Similar Names: Brad, Brent, Bretton, Brice
Namesakes: Bret Saberhagen (baseball player), Brett Favre (football player)
⇨ A surname that originated as an ethic name during the Middle Ages for a native of Brittany. It received a boost from 1957 to 1962 when James Garner played gambler Bret Maverick on the television western *Maverick*. It climbed among the top 100 names during the baseball career of Kansas City Royals third baseman George Brett.

Bridger

Origin: Old English
Meaning: One who builds bridges
Gender Variation: Bridget
Nickname: Bridge
Similar Names: Brigham, Briscoe, Bristol, Brock, Brody, Brook, Brooks
⇨ An occupational surname for someone who constructs bridges. The name is associated with James "Jim" Bridger, the 19th-century American fur trader and frontiersman who established a way station for travelers on the Oregon Trail and the namesake of several landmarks located in Montana and Wyoming. Rarely used.

Brock Rank: 261

Origin: Old English
Meaning: Badgerlike
Alternate Spellings: Broc, Broch, Brocke, Brok
Gender Variation: Brooke
Similar Names: Broderick, Brook, Bruce, Bruno, Bryce, Byron

Namesake: Lou Brock (Baseball Hall of Famer)
⇨ A surname derived from *broc* and originally used as a nickname for someone who resembles a badger. The name is just past its 2003 peak.

Broderick Rank: 884

Origin: Norse
Meaning: Brother
Alternate Spellings: Broderic, Brodric, Brodrick, Brodryck
Gender Variation: Brooke
Nicknames: Brod, Brody
Similar Names: Bertram, Bertrand, Brody, Richard, Roderick
⇨ A surname derived from the Norse Brodhir that was once commonly given to a second son. Popular usage started during the 1950s with Academy Award-winning film actor Broderick Crawford, born William Broderick Crawford, who used his mother's maiden name for a middle name. Film actor Matthew Broderick is a bearer of the surname.

Brody Rank: 147

Origin: Gaelic
Meaning: Ditch
Alternate Spellings: Brodee, Brodey, Brodie
Gender Variations: Brady, Trudy
Similar Names: Braden, Bradley, Brady, Brendan, Brennan, Brian, Brogan
⇨ A surname taken from Brodie Castle in Scotland possibly derived from the Gaelic *brothhach*. It debuted on the popularity chart in 1976 and is currently at its peak possibly influenced by notable television and film actor Adam Brody who played Seth Cohen on the television show *The O.C.*

Brogan Rank: 999

Origin: Irish Gaelic
Meaning: Sturdy shoe
Alternate Spelling: Groggan
Gender Variation: Brady
Similar Names: Bergen, Braeden, Brendan, Brody, Bronagh
⇨ A surname in Ireland derived from the word *brogue*. The name of several saints including Saint Patrick's scribe and nephew. Also a term in clothing for a heavy ankle-high shoe or boot. The name first debuted on the popularity chart in 2006.

Bronson

Origin: Old English
Meaning: Son of a brown man
Alternate Spellings:
Bronnson, Bronsen, Bronsin,
Bronsonn, Bronsson
Nickname: Bron
Similar Names: Brander, Brandon, Branson,
Branston, Brennan, Bronius, Bronson,
Bronwen, Browen
➡ A variation of the names Brandon and
Branson that originated as a surname. It made
its debut on the popularity chart in 1970 and
peaked in 1987. Film and television actor
Charles Bronson is a bearer of the surname
and was best known for his tough-guy roles.

Brooklyn

Origin: American
Alternate Spellings: Brookelynn,
Brookelynne, Brooklen, Brooklin, Brooklyne,
Brooklynn, Brooklynne
Gender Variation: Brooklyn
Nicknames: Brook, Lyn
Similar Names: Brock, Broderick, Brodie,
Brogan, Brooks
➡ The combination of "Brook" with the popular
suffix "lyn" that's associated with the New York
City borough. Celebrity couple Victoria and
David Beckham have a son named Brooklyn.

Brooks   Rank: 592

Origin: Old English
Meaning: Water, small stream
Alternate Spelling: Brookes
Gender Variation: Brooke
Nickname: Brook
Similar Names: Brandon, Brennan, Brent,
Brenton, Brian, Briscoe, Bristol, Brody, Bryce
➡ Derived from a surname for someone who
lived near a brook.

Bruce   Rank: 482

Origin: Norman/French
Meaning: Thicket,
woodlands
Gender Variation: Brucine
Nickname: Brucie
Similar Names: Blake, Brett, Brice, Brock, Brook
Namesakes: Bruce Springsteen (musician),
Bruce Willis (actor)
➡ Originally a place name brought into Scotland
by the Normans. It became a popular Scottish
surname during medieval times. Historically

known for Robert the Bruce who freed
Scotland from English rule in the 14th century.

Bruno   Rank: 793

Origin: Old German
Meaning: Brown
Gender Variations:
Bruna, Brunella, Brunetta
Nickname: Broun
Similar Names: Bjorn, Boris, Braun, Bruin,
Bryn, Burkhard
Namesake: Bruno Kirby (actor)
➡ Typically used by families of German
descent. Associated with Saint Bruno, an
11th-century German monk who founded the
Carthusian Order. Also considered a royal
name in Germany during the Middle Ages.
It was possibly inspired by Lewis Carroll's
19th-century novel *Sylvie and Bruno*.

Bryan   Rank: 66

Origin: Celtic/Gaelic
Meaning: High, noble
Alternate Spellings: Brian,
Brien, Brion, Bryen, Bryon
Gender Variations: Briana, Brianda, Briane
Similar Names: Brogan, Bryant, Brynley,
Bryson, Byran
Namesakes: Brian De Palma (director), Brian
Piccolo (football player), Brian Setzer (musician),
Bryan Adams (singer/songwriter)
➡ A variation of Brian that got its start
largely due to the popularity of Brian Boru,
the last high king of Ireland, who ruled during
the 10th and 11th centuries. It's been listed
among the top 100 since 1959 and follows
the current trend with "y" in the middle.

Bryant   Rank: 389

Origin: Celtic/Gaelic
Meaning: High, noble
Alternate Spellings:
Briant, Bryent
Gender Variations: Brianne, Bryanna
Nicknames: Bryan
Similar Names: Brant, Bryce, Brynley, Brynn,
Bryon, Bryson, Byron
Namesakes: Bryant Gumbel (television
personality), Paul "Bear" Bryant (football
coach), William Cullen Bryant (poet)
➡ A surname derived from the given name
Brian. Best known as the surname of
basketball player Kobe Bryant, the first guard
in NBA history to be drafted out of high school.

Bryce
Rank: 109

Origin: Scottish
Meaning: Speckled
Alternate Spellings:
Brice, Brise, Bryse
Gender Variation: Brylee
Similar Names: Bruce, Bryden, Brynley, Bryson
Namesake: Bryce Wilson (actor/musician)
⇨ Scottish surname derived from the medieval given name Brice. Follows the popular trend with its "y" in the middle and has been the preferred spelling of the name since it debuted on the popularity chart in 1918. A place name for Bryce Canyon National Park located in Utah.

Bryson
Rank: 176

Origin: Welsh
Meaning: Son of Brice
Alternate Spellings: Brycen, Brysen, Brysin
Gender Variation: Brynn
Nickname: Bryce
Similar Names: Bryant, Bryce, Bryden, Bryon
⇨ A common surname and variation of Bryce. Part of a fashionable "y" in the middle trend, the name has steadily gained in popularity since it debuted on the chart in 1979.

Byron
Rank: 523

Origin: Old English
Meaning: At the byres or cattlesheds
Alternate Spellings: Biron, Byram, Byran
Gender Variations: Brynn
Similar Names: Bradley, Bryan, Bryson, Burgess, Burton, Buxton,
Namesake: Byron Raymond White (U.S. Supreme Court Justice)
⇨ A surname and place name first used as a given name in honor of Lord Byron, the English poet, best known for the poem *Don Juan*. Although it peaked early, it's still considered fashionable with "y" in the middle.

Cade
Rank: 288

Origin: Old English
Meaning: Round
Alternate Spellings: Caide, Cayde, Kade, Kayde
Gender Variation: Cadence
Similar Names: Cadell, Caden, Cain, Cal, Caleb
⇨ A surname that started as a nickname listed among the top 300 since 1999.

Caden
Rank: 91

Origin: Gaelic
Meaning: Son of Cadan
Alternate Spellings:
Cadan, Caeden, Caiden, Cayden, Kaden, Kadin, Kadyn, Kaeden, Kaiden, Kayden
Gender Variation: Cadence
Nickname: Cade
Similar Names: Cade, Cadell, Caedmon, Cael, Camden, Cane, Cayen, Hayden, Jaden, Paden
⇨ Possibly a variation of McCadden, which is an anglicized form of Mac Cadain. It debuted on the popularity chart in 1992 and quickly climbed among the top 100, favored by parents with its "en" ending.

Cale
Rank: 733

Origin: American
Alternate Spellings: Cael, Cail, Cayle, Kael, Kail, Kale
Gender Variations:
Calista, Callie
Similar Names: Cal, Calbert, Caleb, Callum, Calvin, Kai
Namesakes: Cael Sanderson (Olympic medalist), J. J. Cale (songwriter/musician)
⇨ A common surname and possibly used as the short form of Caleb. Racing fans will think of William Caleb "Cale" Yarborough, the only NASCAR Winston Cup driver to win three consecutive championships during a career that spanned four decades.

Caleb
Rank: 34

Origin: Hebrew
Meaning: Faithful
Alternate Spellings:
Calib, Cayleb, Kaleb, Kayleb, Kaylob
Gender Variations: Calah, Caleigh
Nickname: Cale
Similar Names: Cael, Cain, Cal, Callum, Christian, Clement
Namesakes: Caleb Carr (novelist), William Caleb "Cale" Yarborough (NASCAR driver)
⇨ In the Old Testament, Caleb was one of 12 spies sent into Israel by Moses and lived long enough to enter the promised land of Canaan. Also the name of several fictional television characters on the shows, *American Gothic, Buffy the Vampire Slayer*, and *The O.C.* Listed among the top 100 since 1989, favored by parents because of its biblical roots.

Calvin
Rank: 220

Origin: French
Meaning: Little bald one
Alternate Spellings:
Kalvin, Kalvyn
Gender Variation: Callie
Nickname: Cal
Similar Names: Cale, Callum, Calvino, Camden, Galvin, Kellen, Kelvin
Namesakes: *Calvin and Hobbes* (comic strip), Calvin Coolidge (30th U.S. president)
➡ Derived from the surname Chauvin that was ultimately taken from *chauve* influenced during the 16th century by John Calvin, the French theologian and reformer whose interpretation of Christianity was later called Calvinism. Later known for fashion designer Calvin Klein, who launched his own company in 1968.

Camden
Rank: 221

Origin: Scottish
Meaning: From the winding valley
Alternate Spellings:
Camdin, Camdon, Kamden, Kamdon
Gender Variation: Camilla
Nickname: Cam
Similar Names: Braden, Branden, Caden, Callum, Calvin, Cameron, Campbell
➡ A place name and surname known for English historian William Camden who wrote the first historical account of the reign of Queen Elizabeth I. The name has steadily gained in popularity since 1990 and received a boost from the hit show *7th Heaven* that follows fictional characters Reverend Eric Camden and family.

Cameron
Rank: 52

Origin: Scottish Gaelic
Meaning: Crooked nose
Alternate Spellings:
Camaeron, Camren, Camron, Camryn, Kameron, Kamran, Kamren, Kamron
Gender Variation: Cameron
Nickname: Cam
Similar Names: Caden, Callum, Campbell, Carson, Cary
Namesakes: Cameron Crowe (director), James Cameron (director), Kirk Cameron (actor)
➡ A Scottish clan name that didn't catch on as a given name until the 1950s. It was later inspired by actor and teen idol Kirk Cameron, who played Mike Seaver on the 1985 to 1992 sitcom *Growing Pains*. Preferred in England, Scotland, and Wales, and also gaining in popularity as a girl's name.

Campbell

Origin: Scottish Gaelic
Meaning: Crooked mouth
Alternate Spelling: Campbel
Gender Variation: Campbell
Similar Names: Callum, Cameron, Carson, Colin, Conall, Craig
Namesakes: Campbell Scott (actor), Earl Campbell (Football Hall of Famer)
➡ The name of a powerful Scottish Highland clan derived from the Gaelic *cam beul*. Declining in use as a boy's name and increasing in popularity for girls. Also associated with a soup company founded in 1869.

Cannon
Rank: 796

Origin: French
Meaning: Official of the church
Alternate Spelling: Canan, Canon, Kannon, Kanon
Gender Variation: Camryn
Similar Names: Camden, Cameron, Conan, Kamen, Kenyon
➡ An occupational surname that debuted on the chart as a given name in 2003, climbing to its current position. Parents may have been inspired by award-winning broadcaster and television host Larry King, who named his son Cannon Edward in 2000.

Carl
Rank: 429

Origin: Old German
Meaning: Free man
Alternate Spellings: Carel, Carle, Karel, Karl, Karle
Gender Variations: Carla, Carlene, Carly
Similar Names: Carlo, Carlos, Carlton, Charles, Chuck
Namesakes: Carl Bernstein (journalist), Carl Jung (Swiss psychologist), Carl Lewis (Olympic medalist), Carl Reiner (actor/comedian), Karl Marx (German philosopher),
➡ A variation of Karl and the German form of Charles. A royal name in Sweden, Austria, and Norway. Associated with poet, historian, and novelist Carl Sandburg and astronomer and astrobiologist Carl Sagan. The name has gradually declined in use over the past 150 years.

Ca ⇒ boys' names

Carlo   Rank: 937

Origin: Latin
Meaning: Free man
Alternate Spellings:
Carlow, Carrlo, Kaarlo, Karlo
Gender Variations: Carley, Carlisa, Carlotta
Nickname: Carl
Similar Names: Cale, Carlin, Carlito, Carlos, Carroll, Charles, Cyril
Namesake: Carlo Ponti (film director)
⇒ Variation of the Latin name Carolus and the Italian form of Charles. The name is past its peak but is still in regular use.

Carlos   Rank: 70

Origin: Old German
Meaning: Free man
Alternate Spellings:
Carrlos, Kaarlos, Karlos
Gender Variations: Carla, Carlota
Similar Names: Carl, Carlito, Carlo, Charles
Namesakes: Carlos Alberto Torres (Brazilian Soccer Hall of Famer), Carlos Arroyo (Puerto Rican basketball player), Carlos Moya (Spanish tennis player)
⇒ The Spanish and Portuguese form of Charles that's steadily climbed the popularity charts since the 1920s, peaking at No. 59 in 1999 and 2001. A royal name for Juan Carlos I, King of Spain, but perhaps best known for Grammy Award-winning Mexican-born musician Carlos Santana.

Carlton

Origin: Old English
Meaning: Free peasant settlement
Alternate Spellings:
Carleton, Karlton
Gender Variation: Charlene
Nickname: Carl
Similar Names: Carlson, Carsten, Carson, Carver
Namesakes: Carlton Banks (*The Fresh Prince of Bel-Aire* character), Carlton Fisk (Baseball Hall of Famer), Steve Carlton (Baseball Hall of Famer)
⇒ A place name associated with any number of locations in England. A form of Charlton, which denotes the Anglo-Saxon pronunciation, as opposed to Carlton, which represents the Anglo-Scandinavian. The name peaked during the 1930s.

Carmelo   Rank: 870

Origin: Hebrew
Meaning: Fruitful orchard
Alternate Spellings:
Carmello, Karmelo, Karmello
Gender Variations: Carmela, Carmelita, Carmella, Carmen, Carmina
Nickname: Carmel
Similar Names: Carmillo, Carmine, Carlo, Carlos, Cecilio, Marcelo
Namesake: Carmelo Anthony (basketball player)
⇒ The Spanish form of Carmel, derived from the Hebrew word that means vineyard. Mount Carmel is a mountain range located in northern Israel referred to in the Old Testament. It debuted on the chart as a boy's given name in 1911 and is occasionally used today.

Carmine   Rank: 785

Origin: Latin
Meaning: Song
Alternate Spelling: Karmine
Gender Variations:
Carmen, Carmina
Nickname: Carm
Similar Names: Calvino, Carlo, Carmelo, Celino, Celio, Cesare
⇒ The Italian form of Carmel that faded from the chart in 1973 and reappeared in 2005, climbing to its present position today. Fans of the television sitcom *Laverne and Shirley*, that aired from 1976 to 1983, will think of fictional character Carmine Ragusa. Popular among Italian families.

Carson   Rank: 87

Origin: Scottish
Meaning: Son of Carr
Alternate Spellings:
Carsen, Karsen, Karson
Gender Variation: Carson
Similar Names: Carlton, Carter, Case, Casey, Cason, Cassidy
Namesakes: Carson Palmer (football player), Johnny Carson (TV host)
⇒ A Scottish surname influenced during the 19th century by legendary Missouri frontiersman and scout Kit Carson, who helped expand the U.S. boundaries westward. Carson City, the capital of Nevada, was named in his honor. Known today for television personality Carson Daly. Also preferred in Canada and occasionally used as a girl's name.

Carter

Rank: 75
Origin: Old English
Meaning: Driver of a cart
Alternate Spelling: Karter
Gender Variations: Cara, Careen
Similar Names: Carson, Cartier, Cartrell, Carver, Cary
Namesakes: *Coach Carter* (2005 film), Gary Carter (Baseball Hall of Famer), Jimmy Carter (39th U.S. president)
⇨ An occupational surname for a person who transports goods in a cart. Nick Carter was a member of the Emmy-nominated pop group the Backstreet Boys, and is a famous bearer of the surname. It's steadily gained popularity as a given name since 1981.

Case

Rank: 951
Origin: Gaelic
Meaning: Vigilant
Gender Variation: Casey
Similar Names: Cade, Cale, Casey, Cash, Chase, Jase
⇨ Possibly a short form of Casey or picked up from the vocabulary word that has multiple meanings. The name first hit the popularity chart in 2006 and is best-known as the surname for Steve Case, the cofounder and former CEO of America Online.

Casey

Rank: 308
Origin: Gaelic
Meaning: Vigilant
Alternate Spellings: Cacey, Cacy, Casy, Cayce, Kace, Kacey, Kasey, KC
Gender Variations: Cass, Cassie, Cassandra, Kacey
Similar Names: Cade, Caleb, Cary, Casen, Cody, Kale
Namesakes: Casey Affleck (actor), Casey Kasem (radio personality/voice actor)
⇨ From the Irish surname derived from O Cathasaigh. Known for John Luther "Casey" Jones, the locomotive engineer who died in 1900 saving the lives of passengers on the Cannonball Express. He was born in Cayce, Kentucky, where he received his nickname. Baseball Hall of Famer Charles Dillon "Casey" Stengel who was given the nickname Casey from the initials for his hometown of Kansas City, Missouri, is another famous bearer. Also among the top 500 for girls.

Cash

Rank: 378
Origin: Norman French
Meaning: Case
Gender Variation: Cassia
Similar Names: Cade, Caden, Cale, Camden, Cason, Chad, Chance
⇨ An occupational surname for a box maker derived from the Norman French *casse* and a vocabulary word that refers to money. Sporadically used as a given name since 1881. Singer and songwriter Johnny Cash, also known as the "man in black," was a notable bearer of the surname.

Cedric

Rank: 595
Origin: Old English
Meaning: Chief
Alternate Spellings: Cedrick, Cedrik, Cedrych, Sedric, Sedrick, Sedrik
Gender Variation: Cedrica
Nicknames: Ced, Ric
Similar Names: Cecil, Chad, Chadwick, Chance, Cian
⇨ Originated as a literary name created by Sir Walter Scott for a character in his 1819 novel *Ivanhoe*. The name was picked up by Frances Hodgson Burnett for the title character in her 1886 novel *Little Lord Fauntleroy*. More recently associated with actor and comedian Cedric Antonio Kyles, better known as Cedric the Entertainer.

Cesar

Rank: 168
Origin: Latin
Meaning: Hair
Alternate Spellings: Caesar, Caezar, Cesare, Cezar, Seasar
Gender Variation: Cesarina
Similar Names: Celestino, Cesaire, Cesarino, Cesario, Kaiser
Namesakes: Cesar Chavez (Mexican-American civil rights leader), Cesar Romero (actor)
⇨ The Spanish and Portuguese form of Caesar derived from *caesaries* best-known for Julius Caesar, the Roman political leader who brought worldwide attention to the imperial family name. Caesar dropped off the chart in 1953, while Cesar has been steadily climbing since 1948, popular among Hispanic families.

Chad
Rank: 375

Origin: Old English
Meaning: Warlike, warrior
Alternate Spellings: Chadd
Gender Variation: Charity
Nickname: Chaddie
Similar Names: Chadburn, Chadrick, Chadwick, Chaim, Chance, Chris
Namesake: Chad Lowe (actor)
⇨ Derived from Ceadda, the name of a 7th-century English saint who was Archbishop of York. Singing duo Chad and Jeremy, part of the British music invasion into the U.S., influenced the name during the mid 1960s. Actor Chad Everett, from the popular 1970s television series *Medical Center*, pushed the name into the top 50 during the show's run. A place name for a country in Africa.

Chaim
Rank: 946

Origin: Hebrew
Meaning: Life
Alternate Spelling: Chayyim
Gender Variations: Chaya, Eve
Similar Names: Chayim, Chesed, Chayim, Haim, Henry, Hyman, Hymie
⇨ A variation of Hyam commonly used by Jewish families particularly during the Middle Ages. It debuted on the popularity chart in 1959.

Chance
Rank: 273

Origin: Anglo Norman
Meaning: Good fortune
Gender Variations: Chana
Similar Names: Chancellor, Charles, Chas, Chase, Chauncey
Namesake: *Chance* (1913 novel by Joseph Conrad)
⇨ Derived from "cheaunce" originally used as a nickname for a gambler or for someone who survived an accident because of luck. The name of Paul Newman's character in the 1962 Tennessee William's film *Sweet Bird of Youth* and Peter Seller's character in the 1979 film *Being There*. English actress Rachel Weisz named her son Henry Chance.

Chandler
Rank: 402

Origin: Old French
Meaning: Candle maker
Gender Variation: Chandler
Nickname: Chan
Similar Names: Chadwick, Chance, Chapman, Charlton, Chase, Chauncey

Namesakes: Jeff Chandler (WBA boxing champion), Kyle Chandler (actor), Tyson Chandler (basketball player)
⇨ Originated as an occupational surname for someone who made and sold candles. Actor Matthew Perry kept the name in front of the public from 1994 to 2004 when he played Chandler Bing on the hit television series, *Friends*. Occasionally used as a girl's name.

Charles
Rank: 60

Origin: Old German
Meaning: Free man
Gender Variations: Charlesina, Charletta, Charlotte
Nicknames: Charlie, Chas, Chaz, Chuck
Similar Names: Carl, Carlo, Carlos, Charleson, Charlton
Namesakes: Charles Barkley (basketball player), Charles de Gaulle (French military leader), Charles Osgood (TV commentator), Charles Schulz (cartoonist)
⇨ A variation of Karl popularized by Charles the Great, also referred to as Charlemagne, who ruled over much of Western Europe during the late 8th and early 9th centuries. The name and its variations have been used by royalty in several countries including the heir to the British throne, Prince Charles. Naturalist Charles Darwin and novelist Charles Dickens are other famous bearers of the name.

Charlie
Rank: 337

Origin: Old German
Meaning: Free man
Alternate Spellings: Charley, Charly

Gender Variations: Charline, Charlotte
Nickname: Chuckie
Similar Names: Carl, Carlo, Carlos, Charles, Charlton
Namesakes: Charlie "Bird" Parker (jazz musician), Charlie Chan (fictional detective), Charlie Chaplin (British actor)
⇨ The pet form and feminine form of Charles. Perhaps best known for fictional character Charlie Brown from the comic strip *Peanuts* that debuted in 1950. The name peaked prior to the turn of the 20th century and was listed among the top 100 names until 1934. Actor Charlie Sheen is another famous bearer of the name.

Chase
Rank: 83

Origin: English
Meaning: Hunter
Alternate Spellings: Chace, Chayce, Chayse
Gender Variation: Chaya
Similar Names: Casey, Charles, Chasen, Chaz, Chuck
➡️ A surname that started as a nickname for a person who hunts. The name took a huge jump in popularity in 1982, most likely influenced by the career of actor and comedian Chevy Chase.

Chris
Rank: 358

Origin: Greek
Meaning: Christ-bearer
Alternate Spellings: Cris, Kris, Krys
Gender Variations: Chris, Chrissy, Christy
Similar Names: Chad, Craig, Curt, Cy, Kip, Kit
Namesakes: Chris Elliott (actor/comedian), Chris Farley (actor/comedian), Chris O'Donnell (actor), Chris Tucker (actor)
➡️ A variation of Christopher and Christian that's also used as an independent name, peaking in 1961 at No. 57. Actor and comedian Chris Rock is a famous bearer of the name.

Christian
Rank: 21

Origin: Greek
Meaning: Follower of Christ
Alternate Spellings: Christiaan, Cristian, Kristian, Krystian
Gender Variations: Christiana, Christianne, Christy, Kristy
Nickname: Chris
Similar Names: Christan, Christiano, Christo, Christophe, Christopher, Christos
Namesakes: Hans Christian Andersen (children's author), Christian Dior (French fashion designer), Christian Slater (actor)
➡️ Started as a girl's name during the Middle Ages but became more common for boys during the 18th century, possibly due to the main character in John Bunyan's book *Pilgrim's Progress*. Popular in Austria and Denmark.

Christopher
Rank: 7

Origin: Greek
Meaning: Christ-bearer
Alternate Spellings: Christofer, Christoffer, Cristofer, Kristofer, Kristoffer, Kristopher

Gender Variations: Christa, Christina, Christine, Christy
Nicknames: Chris, Christoph, Kip, Kit, Topher
Similar Names: Christian, Christos, Cristobol, Cristo, Cristoforo, Christophe
Namesake: Christopher Reeve (actor)
➡️ The patron saint of travelers who is said to have carried the Christ child across a river. The name increased in popularity during the 1940s because of fictional character Christopher Robin in A. A. Milne's classic, *Winnie the Pooh*. Italian explorer Christopher Columbus is a historical namesake.

Clarence
Rank: 818

Origin: Latin
Meaning: One who lives near the River Clare
Alternate Spellings: Clarance, Clarrence, Klarance
Gender Variations: Clara, Clare, Clarette
Nickname: Clare
Similar Names: Claiborne, Clancy, Clarendon, Clark, Claron, Clement
Namesakes: Clarence Day (author), Clarence Thomas (U.S. Supreme Court justice)
➡️ A title that was created in 1362 for the third son of Kind Edward III when he married the heiress of Clare. The title Duke of Clarence is now given to junior members of the English and British royal families. Influenced by renowned 20th-century criminal defense attorney Clarence Darrow. Clarence Oddbody, the angel from the 1946 film *It's a Wonderful Life*, also comes to mind.

Clark
Rank: 696

Origin: Latin
Meaning: Cleric, scholar
Alternate Spelling: Clarke
Gender Variations: Clarinda, Clarissa, Lark
Similar Names: Claud, Clay, Clayton, Clement, Cliff, Clint, Clive
Namesakes: Dick Clark (television host), William Clark (Scottish-American explorer)
➡️ An occupational surname for someone who was a clerk or scholar. Known for Superman alter ego Clark Kent, who made his first appearance as a comic book hero in 1932. Motion picture actor Clark Gable, referred to as the "King of Hollywood," made the biggest impact on the name. Born William Clark Gable, Clark was his maternal grandmother.

Clay
Rank: 708

Origin: Old English
Meaning: Moist earth
Alternate Spelling: Klay
Gender Variations:
Chloe, Cleo
Similar Names: Cal, Claude, Clayborne, Clayland, Clayton, Cleo, Cliff, Clint
Namesake: Andrew Dice Clay (comedian/actor)
⇨ A local name for someone who either lived on clay soil or worked with clay. Widely known for boxing champion Cassius Clay, who changed his name to Muhammad Ali in 1975. *American Idol* runner-up Clay Aiken recently brought attention back to the name. The short form of Clayton.

Clayton
Rank: 226

Origin: Old English
Meaning: Clay settlement
Alternate Spelling: Klayton
Gender Variations:
Claudine, Peyton
Nickname: Clay
Similar Names: Carlton, Clifton, Clinton, Colton, Layton, Preston, Trenton
Namesake: Clayton Farlow (*Dallas* character)
⇨ A surname and place name derived from *clag* and *tun*. Actor Clayton Moore, best known for his role on the television show *The Lone Ranger*, kept the name in front of parents during the 1950s. The name has seen little change in use during the past 125 years and is similar in popularity to other names ending in "ton" like Preston, Trenton, and Colton.

Clifford

Origin: Old English
Meaning: Ford by a cliff
Alternate Spellings:
Cliford, Clyfford, Clyford
Nickname: Cliff
Similar Names: Clayton, Clifton, Clinton, Gifford, Linford
⇨ A surname used as a given name starting in the 17th century. Film and television actor Cliff Robertson has kept the short form of the name in front of the public for more than 50 years. Also associated with Clifford the Big Red Dog, the children's book and television hero created in 1962. The name peaked during the early 1900s and has steadily faded since that time.

Clinton
Rank: 844

Origin: Old English
Meaning: Fenced settlement
Gender Variation: Clio
Nickname: Clint
Similar Names: Carlton, Claxton, Clayton, Clement, Clifton, Clive
⇨ Derived from a surname that denotes a common place. Associated with DeWitt Clinton, the former governor of New York, who was instrumental in the creation of the Erie Canal. Influenced by actor and director, Clint Eastwood, born Clinton Eastwood Jr., whose long-standing career started during the 1960s when he appeared in three Spanish-Italian westerns. Former president Bill Clinton is a bearer of the surname.

Cody
Rank: 106

Origin: Irish Gaelic
Meaning: Son of Oda
Alternate Spellings:
Codee, Codi, Codie, Kodey, Kodi, Kodie, Kody
Gender Variation: Cody
Similar Names: Coby, Colby, Cole, Colm, Cory
Namesakes: Cody Martin (*Suite Life of Zack and Cody* character)
⇨ Originated as an Irish surname popularized by American frontiersman and showman, William F. "Buffalo Bill" Cody, who toured with his "Wild West" show at the turn of the 20th century. He is credited as the founder and developer of Cody, Wyoming. Also associated with the fictional character from the *Agent Cody Banks* films released in 2003 and 2004. Occasionally used as a girl's name.

Cohen
Rank: 415

Origin: Hebrew
Meaning: Priest
Alternate Spellings:
Coen, Koen, Kohen
Gender Variation: Courtney
Similar Names: Amos, Asher, Daniel, Falk, Ira, Joel, Saul
Namesakes: David X. Cohen (television writer/producer), Sacha Baron Cohen (English actor)
⇨ A form of the Hebrew name Kohen considered a favorite among Jewish families. Comedian Rodney Dangerfield was born Jacob Cohen.

Colby
Rank: 271

Origin: Old English
Meaning: Coal town
Alternate Spellings: Colbee, Colbey, Colbie, Kolby
Gender Variation: Colleen,
Nickname: Cole
Similar Names: Carter, Coby, Cody, Colbert, Colton, Colvin, Colwyn
Namesakes: Colby Donaldson (*Survivor: The Australian Outback* runner-up), William E. Colby (former CIA director)
➡ A surname taken from a place name. The prime-time television soap opera *The Colbys*, a spin-off of the popular series *Dynasty*, kept the name current during the 1980s.

Cole
Rank: 84

Origin: Old English/French
Meaning: Black
Alternate Spellings: Col, Coll, Kole
Gender Variations: Colette, Colleen, Nicole
Similar Names: Colbert, Coleman, Colin, Colson, Nicol, Nicholas
Namesakes: Cole Sprouse (actor), Nat King Cole (singer)
➡ A surname derived from a medieval given name also used as the short form of Nicholas and other names beginning with Cole. The name has been listed among the top 100 since 1997 and is associated with composer and lyricist Cole Porter and outlaw Cole Younger.

Coleman
Rank: 661

Origin: Late Latin
Meaning: Dove
Alternate Spellings: Colemann, Colman, Kolman
Gender Variation: Colleen
Nickname: Cole
Similar Names: Callum, Colin, Colm, Columba, Malcolm
Namesakes: Coleman Hawkins (jazz musician), Dabney Coleman (actor), Gary Coleman (actor)
➡ A more popular variation of the name Colman that's ultimately derived from Columba. It's the name of several Irish saints including Saint Colman of Leinster who founded several monasteries in Europe during the 7th century. The name faded during the 1970s and appears to be making a comeback.

Colin
Rank: 111

Origin: Greek/Gaelic
Meaning: Victorious people
Alternate Spellings: Colan, Collan, Colen, Collen, Collin, Colyn, Collyn
Gender Variations: Colena, Coletta, Colette
Nickname: Col
Similar Names: Callum, Cole, Coleman, Cullin, Kalin
Namesakes: Colin Firth (English actor), Colin Powell (former U.S. secretary of state), Jesse Colin Young (musician)
➡ The short form of Nicholas that's been used independently since the Middle Ages. The name was reintroduced to England from Scotland during the 19th century where it was an anglicized form of the Gaelic *Cailean*. The name rose into the top 100 in 2003 influenced by Irish actor Colin Farrell.

Colt
Rank: 906

Origin: Old English
Meaning: Coal town
Alternate Spelling: Kolt
Gender Variation: Collette
Similar Names: Colbert, Colby, Cole, Collin, Colston, Colter, Colton, Coltrane, Colum
➡ The shortened version of the North American surname Colton that first gained popularity in 1982. Inventor Samuel Colt, credited with popularizing the revolver gun, is a famous bearer of the surname.

Colton
Rank: 133

Origin: Old English
Meaning: Coal town
Alternate Spellings: Coleton, Collton, Colten, Kolton
Gender Variation: Coleen
Nickname: Colt
Similar Names: Colbert, Colby, Cole, Coleman, Collin, Colston, Colville
Namesake: Graham Colton (musician)
➡ A surname originating from a place name for any number of locations in England and possibly derived from the personal name Cola. It's been used as a given name since 1982 and peaked in the mid-1990s.

Connor   Rank: 53

Origin: Irish Gaelic
Meaning: Lover of hounds
Alternate Spellings:
Conner, Conor, Konner,
Konnor, Konor
Gender Variation: Connie
Nickname: Conn
Similar Names: Cameron, Campbell,
Carson, Cary, Colin, Conan
⇒ Derived from Conchobhar, the legendary
Irish king of Ulster. The name has quickly
climbed the popularity chart since 1981
influenced by the surname of fictional
character John Connor in the three films
based on *The Terminator*. Also associated
with fictional character Connor MacLeod
played by Christopher Lambert in the 1985
Highlander film and sequels. Conor is the
preferred spelling in Ireland.

Conrad   Rank: 788

Origin: Old German
Meaning: Brave counsel
Alternate Spelling: Konrad
Gender Variation:
Constance
Nicknames: Con, Connie
Similar Names: Conrado, Conroy, Corrado,
Cort, Curt, Koen
Namesakes: Conrad Aiken (poet), Joseph
Conrad (Polish-born novelist)
⇒ Derived from the Germanic elements
kuon and *rad*, that's been popular as a given
name starting in the 19th century. The name
of a well-known 10th-century bishop from
Switzerland and several kings from Germany.
Hotelier Conrad Hilton is a famous bearer
of the name.

Cooper   Rank: 113

Origin: Old English
Meaning: Barrel maker
Alternate Spelling:
Couper
Gender Variations: Capri, Piper
Nickname: Coop
Similar Names: Carter, Connor, Conrad,
Conway, Corbin, Cordell, Corey
Namesakes: Alice Cooper (musician),
Anderson Cooper (television personality),
James Fenimore Cooper (novelist)
⇒ An occupational surname first used as
a given name during the 19th century.

Associated with the surname of two-time
Academy Award-winning actor Gary Cooper,
known by the nickname "Coop," whose
career started during the 1920s. The name
is currently at its peak.

Corbin   Rank: 289

Origin: Latin
Meaning: Raven-haired
Alternate Spellings:
Corban, Corben, Corbyn,
Korban, Korbin, Korbyn
Gender Variation: Cordelia
Nickname: Corby
Similar Names: Colby, Colman, Colton,
Corbett, Corbinian, Cordell, Corwin, Cory
⇒ Possibly derived as a short form of the
name Corbinian. Influenced by actor Corbin
Bernsen, best known for his role as Arnie
Becker on the prime-time television show
L.A. Law from 1986 to 1994. The name had
faded from view until that time and made
a comeback in 1987.

Corey   Rank: 234

Origin: Old Norse/Gaelic
Meaning: Hill hollow
Alternate Spellings: Corie,
Correy, Corrie, Corry, Cory,
Courey, Kori, Korey, Kory
Gender Variations: Cora, Coretta, Corrie
Similar Names: Carey, Cody, Conan, Conner,
Conrad, Cordell, Corwin
Namesakes: Corey Feldman (actor), Corey
Haim (Canadian actor), Corey Jerome Hodges
(singer "Lil' Corey"), Corey Pavin (PGA golfer)
⇒ A surname possibly derived from the Old
Norse name Kori. Among its many alternate
spellings, this form with its "ey" ending is the
most popular.

Cornelius   Rank: 939

Origin: Latin
Meaning: Horn
Alternate Spellings:
Cornelious, Cornilius,
Kornelious, Kornelius
Gender Variations: Cornelia, Cornelie
Nicknames: Neal
Similar Names: Cornelio, Cornell, Cornelis,
Cornelus
⇒ A common Roman family name used in the
New Testament for a Roman centurion who
was baptized by Peter and considered to be

the first Gentile to adopt the Christian faith. Also associated with 19th-century railroad entrepreneur Cornelius Vanderbilt. Cornelius Fudge is a fictional character in the *Harry Potter* series of novels. The name peaked in popularity prior to the turn of the 20th century.

Cortez
Rank: 938

Origin: Spanish
Meaning: Courteous, court dweller
Alternate Spellings: Cortes, Kortes, Kortez
Gender Variations: Corazon, Corina
Similar Names: Carlos, Carmen, Cesar, Claudio, Cristo, Cruz, Curtis
➡ A variation of Curtis. Historically known for Hernando Cortez, the 16th-century Spanish explorer who conquered the Aztec civilization of Mexico. Popular among Hispanic families. The name hit its height in popularity in 1990.

Craig
Rank: 548

Origin: Gaelic
Meaning: Crag or rocks
Alternate Spellings: Kraig, Kreig
Gender Variation: Christina
Similar Names: Callum, Carson, Cian, Colin, Crawford, Creighton, Crispin, Ewan, Greg, Gregor
Namesakes: Craig Newmark (Craigslist founder), Jim Craig (Olympic hockey player), Roger Craig (football player)
➡ A Scottish surname derived from *creag* for someone who lived near rocks. Listed among the top 100 names from 1947 to 1988 and possibly influenced by film and television actor Craig Stevens. Daniel Craig, the latest actor to portray fictional character James Bond, is a bearer of the surname. A place name for several cities, counties, and an air force base located in the U.S.

Cristobal
Rank: 991

Origin: Greek
Meaning: Christ-bearer
Gender Variation: Cristina
Nicknames: Cris, Cristo
Similar Names: Crisanto, Crisoforo, Cristian, Christoffer, Christophe, Cristovao
Namesake: Cristobal Huet (French hockey player)
➡ The Spanish form of Christopher that debuted in the U.S. in 1975. Also popular in Chile.

Cruz
Rank: 500

Origin: Latin
Meaning: Cross
Gender Variation: Cruza
Similar Names: Camilo, Cayetano, Cecilio, Cesar, Claudio, Clemente, Crisoforo, Cristian, Cristo, Cristobal
Namesakes: Alexis Cruz (actor), Brandon Cruz (actor/musician), *Cruz* (1998 film), Joaquim Cruz (Olympic medalist), Jose Cruz (baseball player/coach)
➡ Derived from the Spanish name *cruz* with a biblical meaning that refers to the cross upon which Jesus died. A common surname and popular choice among Hispanic families. English soccer star David Beckham and former Spice Girl Victoria Adams Beckham named their third son Cruz.

Cullen
Rank: 790

Origin: Irish Gaelic
Meaning: Good-looking lad, handsome
Alternate Spellings: Cullan, Cullin, Kullen
Gender Variation: Cynthia
Similar Names: Carlin, Coleman, Colin, Conan, Curt, Curtis, Keelan
Namesake: Cullen Bryant (football player)
➡ Nineteenth-century romantic poet William Cullen Bryant may have put this one on the map. The name has been used sporadically in the U.S. since 1880 but rose during the 1970s.

Curtis
Rank: 339

Origin: Old French
Meaning: Courteous, polite
Alternate Spellings: Curtice, Curtiss, Kurtis
Gender Variation: Cortney
Nickname: Curt
Similar Names: Cade, Chandler, Cortez, Cyril, Harcourt, Kort
Namesakes: Curtis Mayfield (musician), Curtis Strange (PGA golfer)
➡ A surname from the Middle Ages given to a courteous person. Listed among the top 100 names during the 1950s and 1960s, possibly influenced by the success of actor Tony Curtis. The name has faded from popularity in recent years.

Cyrus   Rank: 515

Origin: Persian
Meaning: The sun
Gender Variations:
Cyra, Kira
Nickname: Cy
Similar Names: Cirino, Ciro, Cyprian, Cyril, Kuros, Kyros
Namesakes: Cyrus McCormick (inventor), Cyrus Vance (former secretary of state)
⇒ The Greek form of Kurush that means "far sighted" or possibly related to the Persian word *khur* for the sun. The name of several kings of Persia, including Cyrus the Great, mentioned in the Old Testament as the conqueror of the Babylonians who freed the exiled Jews and founded the Persian empire. More recently known as the surname of "Achy Breaky Heart" singer and actor Billy Ray Cyrus and his daughter, Miley.

Dakota   Rank: 172

Origin: Native American
Meaning: Friend, ally
Alternate Spellings:
Daccota, Dackota, Dacoda, Dacodah, Dacota, Dacotah, Dakoda, Dakodah, Dakotah, Dekota
Gender Variation: Dakota
Nicknames: Cody, Cota
Similar Names: Cheyenne, Dack, Dakarai, Dallas, Montana
Namesake: *Dakota* (1988 film)
⇒ The name of a Native American people from the northern Mississippi valley, it peaked at No. 56 in 1995 and is a fashionable name for both boys and girls.

Dale   Rank: 745

Origin: Old English
Meaning: Valley
Alternate Spellings:
Dael, Daile, Dalle
Gender Variation: Dahlia
Similar Names: Daley, Dallas, Dallen, Dalton, Dell, Devon, Hale
Namesakes: *Chip 'n' Dale* (cartoon), Dale Carnegie (lecturer/author), Dale Hawerchuk (Hockey Hall of Famer), Dale Jarrett (NASCAR driver)
⇒ A surname and place name for someone who lived in a valley. Listed among the top 100 from 1921 to 1969 and is best-known for racing legends Dale Earnhardt and his son.

Dallas   Rank: 352

Origin: Scottish
Meaning: Resting place
Gender Variation: Dallas
Similar Names: Dale, Daley, Dalton, Dane, Dayton, Dean, Delaney, Denver
Namesakes: *Dallas* (album by Randy Meisner), Dallas Clark (football player)
⇒ A Scottish place name and surname used as a given name since the 19th century, peaking in 1938 at No. 217. Known for the city in Texas that lent its name to popular television soap opera *Dallas*, which aired from 1978 to 1991. Occasionally used as a girl's name.

Dallin

Origin: Old English
Meaning: From the valley
Alternate Spellings:
Dallan, Dallen, Dallon, Daylin
Gender Variation: Fallon
Similar Names: Daley, Dalton, Delaney, Dillon, Dilwyn
⇒ A place name related to Dale and discovered by parents in 1993.

Dalton   Rank: 199

Origin: Old English
Meaning: Settlement in the valley
Alternate Spellings:
Dallton, Dalten, Daulton
Gender Variation: Dalia
Similar Names: Daley, Dallas, Damian, Daniel
Namesake: Timothy Dalton (actor)
⇒ Taken from a surname and place name for any one of various places in England. The 19th-century English meteorologist and chemist John Dalton is a historical namesake. His early research on color blindness is sometimes referred to as Daltonism. Also associated with the infamous outlaw gang during the 19th century. Peaked during the 1990s.

Damarion   Rank: 646

Origin: American
Alternate Spelling:
Demarion
Gender Variation: Damaris
Similar Names: Amarion, Damian, Damon, Jamarion, Omarion
⇒ An invented name using the prefix "da" with "marion." It debuted on the popularity chart in 2003 and has steadily risen since

that time. The name Demarion followed soon after, making its first appearance in 2004.

Damian
Rank: 136

Origin: Greek
Meaning: To tame
Alternate Spellings: Dameon, Damien, Damion, Damyan
Gender Variation: Damiana
Similar Names: Damario, Damaso, Damiano, Damon
Namesake: Damian Marley (musician)
➡ Taken from *Damianos* and derived from *damao*. Saint Damian and his twin brother, Cosmo, were 4th-century Christian martyrs who became the patron saints of physicians.

Damon
Rank: 386

Origin: Greek
Meaning: To tame
Alternate Spellings: Daimon, Daemon, Daimen, Daman, Damen, Damone, Daymon
Gender Variations: Damaris, Damask
Similar Names: Damian, Damianos, Dana, Dimitrios
Namesake: Damon Wayans (actor/comedian)
➡ A variation of Damian derived from *damao*. Known in Greek mythology for the legend of Damon and Pythias, whose lives were spared after a demonstration of true friendship. Actor and screenwriter Matt Damon has kept the surname in front of the public in recent years.

Dandre
Rank: 992

Origin: American
Alternate Spelling: Dondre
Gender Variations: Danette, DeAndra
Nicknames: Dee, Andre
Similar Names: Dante, Deandre, Deangelo, Deion, Desmond, Keandre, Leandre
➡ A contemporary name that blends the letter "D" with the name "Andre." It debuted on the popularity chart in 1985 and is a favorite among African-American parents.

Dane
Rank: 393

Origin: Old English
Meaning: From Denmark
Alternate Spellings: Dain, Daine, Dane, Dayne
Gender Variations: Danae, Dania, Danice

Similar Names: Dan, Dana, Daniel, Dean, Duane
➡ The name for a citizen of Denmark commonly used for boys since 1945. Parents may think of fictional character Dane O'Neill from the best-selling novel *The Thorn Birds*.

Dangelo
Rank: 863

Origin: American
Gender Variations: Angela, DeAndra, Dee
Nicknames: Dan, Angelo
Similar Names: Angel, Angelino, Angelo, Daniel, Danilo, Dante, Deangelo
➡ A popular African-American combination of "D" with the name "Angelo."

Daniel
Rank: 6

Origin: Hebrew
Meaning: God is my judge
Alternate Spellings: Danial, Daniele, Danyal, Danyel, Danyele
Gender Variations: Dani, Danette, Daniella, Danielle, Danita
Nicknames: Dan, Danny
Similar Names: Danail, Danel, Dangelo, Danielo, Dante, David, Dennis, Donald
Namesake: Daniel Baldwin (actor)
➡ Derived from the Hebrew *Daniyyel* and known for the prophet whose story is told in the book of Daniel. His enemies sent him into the lion's den where God set him free. Famous bearers include English author Daniel Defoe and frontiersman and scout Daniel Boone. Recently influenced by British actor Daniel Radcliffe of *Harry Potter* fame.

Danny
Rank: 307

Origin: Hebrew
Meaning: God is my judge
Alternate Spelling: Dannie
Gender Variations: Dani, Dania, Danita
Nickname: Dan
Similar Names: Dana, Daniel, Dante, Denny, Donny, Jimmy, Johnny
Namesakes: Danny DeVito (actor), Danny Glover (actor), Danny Kaye (actor/entertainer)
➡ A nickname for Daniel that was seldom used until the love song "Danny Boy" was recorded for the first time in 1915. The name climbed to its all-time high in the 1950s and 1960s during the run of the television series *Make Room for Daddy*, starring Danny Thomas.

Dante
Rank: 291

Origin: Latin
Meaning: Lasting
Alternate Spellings: Dantae, Daunte, Dontae, Dontay, Donte
Gender Variation: Danita
Similar Names: Dandre, Dangelo, Danton, Durand, Durante
Namesake: *Dante's Peak* (1997 film)
⇨ The medieval short form of Durante historically known for 14th-century Italian poet Dante Alighieri who wrote *The Divine Comedy*, and 19th-century English poet and painter, Dante Gabriel Rossetti. Currently past its peak, but still in steady use. Football player Daunte Culpepper uses a form of the name.

Daquan

Origin: American
Alternate Spelling: Dequan
Gender Variation: Reagan
Similar Names: Deon, Deonte, Deshaun, Devyn, Dewayne, Jaquan
⇨ A trendy invented name that combines "Da" and "Quan" and is popular among African-American families. It debuted on the popularity chart in the late 1980s.

Darby

Origin: Irish Gaelic/Old Norse
Meaning: Free man, deer town
Alternate Spellings: Darbee, Darbey, Darbi, Darbie
Gender Variation: Darby
Nicknames: Arby, Dar, Darb
Similar Names: Darcy, Dari, Daria, Darian, Dario, Darius, Derby
Namesake: Kim Darby (actress)
⇨ A surname derived from the city of Derby or the district of West Derby near Liverpool in England. It's associated with the 1959 film *Darby O'Gill and the Little People*. The name was recently influenced by actor Patrick Dempsey and his wife, Jillian, who named one of their twin sons Darby.

Darian
Rank: 590

Alternate Spellings: Darien, Darion, Darrion, Derrien
Gender Variations: Darian, Darla

Similar Names: Dario, Darius, Darnell, Darragh, Darrin, Dorian
⇨ Of uncertain origin, possibly a form of Adrian or a combination of Darius and Darren. It first ranked among the top names in 1965, debuting at No. 899. Occasionally used as a girl's name.

Dario
Rank: 875

Origin: Greek
Meaning: He who upholds the good, wealthy
Gender Variations: Daria, Darian, Darinka
Nickname: Dar
Similar Names: Darien, Dario, Darion, Darnell, Darren, Darrow, Darry, Mario
Namesake: Dario Fo (Nobel Prize winner, Literature)
⇨ The Italian form of Darius preferred by parents in Spain.

Darius
Rank: 280

Origin: Greek
Meaning: He who upholds the good, wealthy
Alternate Spellings: Darias, Dariess, Darious, Darrius, Derrius
Gender Variations: Daria, Darian, Darice
Nickname: Darry
Similar Names: Darien, Darin, Dario, Dorian, Dory
Namesakes: Darius Danesh (Scottish musician/actor), Darius Kasparaitis (Lithuanian-Russian hockey player), Darius Miles (basketball player)
⇨ A form of Dareios and ultimately derived from Daryavahush. The name of several ancient Persian kings, including Darius the Great who reigned for 36 years. He is mentioned in the Bible, along with Darius the Mede, the ruler of Babylon. The name reached its height in popularity between 1990 and 1991.

Darnell
Rank: 711

Origin: Old English
Meaning: Hidden nook
Alternate Spellings: Darnal, Darnall, Darnel
Gender Variations: Daniella, Danielle, Darlene
Similar Names: Darnley, Darrell, Darren, Darwin, Derrick, Devin

⇒ A surname possibly derived from the Old English *derne* and *half* or from the Old French *darnel* for a type of grass. It may have been inspired by the surname of actress Linda Darnell who first appeared in films in 1939—the same year it debuted on the popularity chart as a boy's given name. It peaked during the 1980s.

Darrell   Rank: 597

Origin: Old English
Meaning: Beloved
Alternate Spellings: Darell, Darrel, Darrill, Darryl, Daryl, Derrell, Derryl
Gender Variation: Daryl
Similar Names: Darence, Darien, Darnell, Darren, Derek, Devin
Namesakes: Darrell Green (football player), Darrell Hammond (*Saturday Night Live* cast member), Darryl Strawberry (baseball player)
⇒ A surname that originated from a Norman baronial family name indicating someone from Airelle in France. Use as a given name started sporadically during the late 19th century and climbed to its highest level in the 1950s and 1960s.

Darren   Rank: 361

Origin: Irish Gaelic
Meaning: Great
Alternate Spellings: Daren, Darin, Darron, Deron, Derren, Derron, Darryn
Gender Variations: Darrene, Daryn
Nicknames: Dare
Similar Names: Darnell, Darrell, Darrion, Darwin, Derrick, Devin, Dorian
Namesake: Darren Hayes (Australian musician)
⇒ Possibly originated as an Irish surname or a form of Darryl. The name's debut on the chart during the 1950s was likely due to the popularity of actor, singer, and teen idol James Darren and rock and roll idol Bobby Darin. Its sudden rise during the 1960s is attributed to fictional character Darrin Stephens from the hit television show *Bewitched*, played by Dick York from 1964 to 1969 and Dick Sargent from 1969 to 1972.

Darwin   Rank: 772

Origin: Old English
Meaning: Dear friend
Alternate Spelling: Darwyn
Gender Variation: Darian
Similar Names: Darden, Darien, Darin, Darnell, Daryl, David, Davis
⇒ A surname derived from the English personal name Deorwine. English naturalist Charles Darwin, who founded the theory of evolution, is a famous bearer of the surname. A city in Australia was named in his honor.

David   Rank: 13

Origin: Hebrew
Meaning: Beloved
Alternate Spellings: Davidde, Davide, Davyd, Davydd
Gender Variations: Davina, Davinia
Nicknames: Dave, Davey
Similar Names: Daniel, Darrell, Darren, Davin, Davion, Davis, Dawson, Dennis, Donald
Namesakes: David Arquette (actor), David Bowie (musician), David Letterman (TV host), David Schwimmer (actor), Dave Winfield (Baseball Hall of Famer)
⇒ David slew Goliath with his slingshot and later became the second king of Israel in the Bible. Also a literary name for the title character in Charles Dickens' novel *David Copperfield*. Other famous bearers include a 5th-century saint from Wales, two kings of Scotland, and 19th-century explorer Dr. David Livingstone. The name has been listed among the top 35 since 1880 and held the No. 1 position in 1960. A popular name for future soccer stars thanks to English soccer player David Beckham.

Davin   Rank: 601

Origin: Hebrew/Scandinavian
Meaning: Beloved, Finnish person
Alternate Spellings: Davon, Davyn
Gender Variations: Davina, Davinia
Similar Names: Daley, Dalton, Damon, Darian, David, Davion, Davis
⇒ Possibly a variation of the Hebrew name David or Scandinavian in origin. Parents discovered the name in 1965 and have used it steadily since 1969.

Davion   Rank: 478

Origin: American
Alternate Spellings:
Daveon, Davian
Gender Variations: Davina,
Devin
Similar Names: Davey, Davin, Deangelo,
Deanthony, Demarco, Demason, Demichael
Devon
➽ A modern choice for parents who like
the blend of David and Darrion. The name
first hit the popularity chart in 1991.

Davis   Rank: 405

Origin: Hebrew
Meaning: Beloved
Alternate Spellings:
Davies, Daviss
Gender Variation: Davina
Nicknames: Dave, Davy
Similar Names: David, Davidson, Davison,
Dawson, Dayton, Devlin, Dewey
Namesakes: Jim Davis (*Garfield* cartoonist),
Miles Davis (jazz musician), Sammy Davis Jr.
(entertainer), Terrell Davis (football player)
➽ A surname taken from David used as
a given name in honor of Jefferson Davis,
president of the Confederate States.
PGA golfer Davis Love III is another
famous bearer.

Dawson   Rank: 233

Origin: Old English
Meaning: Son of David
Alternate Spelling: Dawsen
Gender Variation: Dawn
Similar Names: Dallas, Dalton, Darrin,
Darwin, David, Davis, Dewey
➽ Originated from a medieval surname and
pet form of David. Fictional character Jack
Dawson, played by Leonardo DiCaprio in
the 1997 megahit film *Titanic*, boosted the
name to popularity. Fictional lead character
Dawson Leery from the prime-time television
drama *Dawson's Creek* kept it in front of
the public from 1998 to 2003.

Dayton   Rank: 540

Origin: Old English
Meaning: Bright town
Alternate Spellings:
Daytan, Dayten
Gender Variation: Dayana
Nickname: Day

Similar Names: Dallin, Dalton, Dane, Dawson,
Payton, Tayton
➽ A surname that originated from a place
name that's known for several cities in the
U.S. including Dayton, Ohio. A good choice
for parents who are looking for a fresh
option for Darrell or Dustin.

Deacon   Rank: 687

Origin: Greek
Meaning: One who serves
Gender Variations:
Deanna, Deanne
Nicknames: Dee, Deke
Similar Names: Dean, Declan, Deforest,
Denny, Deon, Derrick, Devon
Namesakes: "Deacon Blues" (Steely Dan song)
➽ Derived from a surname that belonged
to a deacon or cleric in the Christian church.
Associated with Football Hall of Famer
Deacon Jones, one of the greatest defensive
ends of all time. He is credited with coining
the term "quarterback sack" which was
considered his specialty. Actress Reese
Witherspoon and actor Ryan Phillippe
named their son Deacon Reese.

Dean   Rank: 385

Origin: Old English
Meaning: From the valley,
dean
Alternate Spellings: Deane,
Dene
Gender Variations: Deana, Deanne, Deena,
Denise
Nickname: Dino
Similar Names: Dennis, Denton, Deon, Devin,
Dino, Dobbs, Dyer
Namesakes: Dean Cain (actor), Dean
McDermott (actor), Dean Smith (basketball
coach)
➽ A place name for someone who lives near
a valley that's also used as an occupational
name indicating the person is a church official
or head of a school. Actor James Dean is a
famous bearer of the surname. Actor and
entertainer Dean Martin also comes to mind.

Deandre   Rank: 452

Origin: American
Alternate Spellings:
D'Andre, DeAndre
Gender Variations: Deandra,
Deandria

Nicknames: Dee, Andre
Similar Names: Dandre, Deangelo, Demarcus, Deshawn, Desmond, Destin, Devin
➡ A combination of the popular prefix "De" with the name "Andre" that became popular in 1971. A favorite among African-American parents.

Deangelo   Rank: 794

Origin: Greek
Alternate Spellings: D'Angelo, Diangelo
Gender Variations: Angela, DeAndra, Deanna
Nicknames: Angelo, Dee
Similar Names: Angel, Angelo, Angelos, Dandre, Demarcus, Denzel, Deshawn
➡ A created name that blends the name Angelo with the prefix "De" and is widely used by African-American parents. It first appeared on the popularity chart in 1975.

Declan   Rank: 364

Origin: Gaelic
Meaning: Full of goodness
Gender Variation: Decla
Nickname: Dec
Similar Names: Darragh, Dean, Dermot, Devnet, Dylan
Namesakes: Declan Galbraith (English singer)
➡ A form of Deaglan that was first associated with the 5th-century Irish saint. English musician Declan Patrick MacManus, better known by his stage name, Elvis Costello, is a famous bearer. The name has shot up the chart since 1998.

Demarcus   Rank: 735

Origin: American
Alternate Spellings: Damarcus, Demarkes, Demarkis, Demarkus, D'Marcus
Gender Variations: Demetria, Demetris
Nicknames: Dee, Marc, Marcus
Similar Names: Demarko, Demarquez, Demetrius, Desmond, Lamarcus
Namesake: Demarcus Ware (football player)
➡ A contemporary blend of the prefix "De" with the name Marcus. Popular usage started in 1974 favored by African-American families.

Demetrius   Rank: 457

Origin: Greek
Meaning: Lover of the earth
Alternate Spellings: Demitrius, Dimetrius, Dimitrious, Dimitrius
Gender Variations: Demetria, Demi
Nickname: Dimitri
Similar Names: Demeter, Demetrio, Demetrios, Demetris, Demond, Desmond
➡ Latinized form of Demetrios, derived from the name of the Greek goddess Demeter. The name of royalty and several early saints, including Saint Demetrius, who was martyred during the 4th century. Shakespeare used the name in several of his plays, such as *A Midsummer's Night's Dream*, *Antony and Cleopatra*, and *Titus Andronicus*. It debuted on the popularity chart in 1954—the same year the film *Demetrius and the Gladiators* was released.

Dennis   Rank: 313

Origin: Greek/English
Meaning: Follower of Dionysius
Alternate Spellings: Denis, Dennys, Denys
Gender Variations: Denisa, Denise, Dionysia
Nicknames: Den, Denny
Similar Names: Dion, Dennison, Denton, Denzel, Dionysus
Namesakes: Dennis Franz (actor), Dennis Haysbert (actor), Dennis Hopper (actor), Dennis Miller (comedian/television personality), Dennis Rodman (basketball player)
➡ A variation of Dionysius, known in the Bible as a judge of Athens who converted to Christianity because of the apostle Paul. Perhaps best known for Dennis the Menace, the mischievous, blond, comic-strip character, who made his debut in 1951 in 16 newspapers. He was also the title character of a 1959 to 1963 television sitcom and a 1993 live-action film. Actor Dennis Quaid is another famous bearer. Listed among the top 100 names from 1934 to 1984.

Denzel   Rank: 940

Origin: English
Meaning: Fort or fertile upland
Alternate Spellings: Denzal, Denzell, Denzil, Denzill, Denzyl
Gender Variation: Denize
Nickname: Denny
Similar Names: Denis, Dennison, Denniston, Denziel, Deshawn, Desmond
Namesake: Denzil (English rock band)
⇨ Adopted from the Cornish surname Denzell, a personal name from a place in Cornwall. The name became popular by association to two-time Academy Award-winning actor Denzel Washington whose career started in television during the 1970s and 1980s before he moved to films. Parents discovered the name in 1990.

Deon   Rank: 849

Origin: Greek
Meaning: Man from Dionysus
Alternate Spellings: Deion, Dejon, Deonn, Deonne, Deyon, Dion, Dione
Gender Variation: Dionne
Nickname: Dee
Similar Names: Dean, Dennis, Dennison, Denzel, Deonte, Devon, Dionisio, Dyson
⇨ A variation of Dion and the short form of Dionysios, in Greek mythology, the name of the god of wine. It first charted in 1961 and is preferred by African-American families. Famed football player Deion Sanders uses a form of the name.

Derek   Rank: 159

Origin: German
Meaning: Ruler of the people
Alternate Spellings: Dereck, Derick, Derik, Derrek, Derrick, Derrik, Derryk
Gender Variation: Dereka
Similar Names: Dedrick, Dick, Dierk, Dietrich, Dirk, Jerrick
Namesakes: Derek and the Dominos (rock group), Derek Jeter (baseball player), John Derek (director/actor)
⇨ A form of Theodoric derived from the elements *peud* and *ric* that was brought into England during the Middle Ages by Flemish weavers. The name was listed among the top 100 from 1970 to 1995.

Deshawn   Rank: 518

Origin: American
Alternate Spellings: Dashaun, Dashawn, Deshan, Deshaun
Gender Variation: Lashawn
Nicknames: Dee, Shawn
Similar Names: Deambrose, Deandre, Deangelo, Dejuan, Keyshawn
Namesake: DeShawn Stevenson (basketball player)
⇨ The popular African-American combination of the prefix "De " with the name "Shawn." Considered a favorite since 1971.

Desmond   Rank: 464

Origin: Irish/Gaelic
Meaning: Man from South Munster
Alternate Spellings: Desmund, Dezmond
Gender Variations: Desdemona, Desiree
Nickname: Des
Similar Names: Demond, Desi, Devereux, Devin, Donovan, Redmond
⇨ A surname used as a given name derived from the Gaelic *Deasmhumhnach*, which refers to a province in Ireland called Munster that was once an ancient Irish kingdom. It was rarely used in the U.S. until the 1950s and was widely recognized during the 1980s for Desmond Tutu, the South African bishop and advocate against apartheid in South Africa, who was awarded the Nobel Peace Prize in 1984.

Destin   Rank: 960

Origin: American
Alternate Spellings: Deston, Destyn
Gender Variation: Destiny
Similar Names: Davin, Denton, Devin, Dustin, Justin
⇨ Possibly a shortened form of the female name Destiny. Also considered a place name after a beach community in Florida. It first appeared on the popularity chart in 1994. Parents may see this name as a fresh option for the well-used Dustin.

Devin
Rank: 100

Origin: Irish Gaelic
Meaning: Descendant of Damhan
Alternate Spellings: Devan, Deven, Devinn, Devon, Devyn, Devynn
Gender Variations: Devona, Devonne
Nickname: Dev
Similar Names: Davin, Davion, Derrick, Derrin, Desmond, Evan, Jevon, Kevin
➡ An Irish surname derived from O Damhain and also a place name for a town in southern Bulgaria. Listed among the top 100 since 1987 and used occasionally as a girl's name.

Dexter
Rank: 913

Origin: Old English/Latin
Meaning: One who dyes, right-handed
Gender Variation: Dextra
Nicknames: Dex, Dexy
Similar Names: Delbert, Delroy, Denholm, Dennis, Denton, Derrick
Namesake: *Dexter* (TV series), *Dexter's Laboratory* (animated series)
➡ Originally a surname for a woman who dyes fabric. Regularly used in United Kingdom during the 1940s and peaked in the U.S. during the late 1960s. A popular choice for African-American parents.

Diego
Rank: 56

Origin: Hebrew/Greek/Latin
Meaning: Supplanter
Nickname: Dee
Similar Names: Delmar, Dion, Domingo, James, Santiago
Namesakes: Diego Maradona (Argentine Soccer Hall of Famer), Don Diego de Vargas (Spanish explorer)
➡ The Spanish form of James and possibly used as the short form of Santiago. Diego Rivera, the Mexican painter and muralist, is a namesake. Also a place name for both the island of Diego Garcia and San Diego, California. Became more widely recognized as the title character in the children's animated series that grew as a spin-off of *Dora the Explorer*. Widely used among Hispanic parents.

Dimitri

Origin: Greek
Meaning: Devoted to
Alternate Spellings: Demetri, Dimitry, Dmitri, Dmitrij, Dmitriy, Dmitry
Gender Variations: Demetria, Demi, Dimity
Similar Names: Demeter, Demetrio, Demetrios, Dimitar
➡ The French and Russian variation of Demetrius that debuted in the U.S. in 1989 and is still widely used in France and Russia today.

Dominic
Rank: 85

Origin: Latin
Meaning: Of God
Alternate Spellings: Domenic, Dominick, Dominik, Dominique
Gender Variations: Dominica, Dominique
Nicknames: Dom, Nic, Nicky
Similar Names: Domenico, Domingo, Domini, Dominicus
Namesakes: Dominic Monaghan (English actor), Dominic Purcell (British-born actor), *Dominick and Eugene* (1988 film), Dominik Hasek (hockey player)
➡ Derived from the Latin name Dominus influenced in the 13th-century by Saint Dominic, founder of the Dominican order of friars. It was traditionally used for a child born on Sunday, regarded by some as the Lord's day. Television character Dominic Santini, from the 1980s series *Airwolf* comes to mind.

Dominique
Rank: 763

Origin: Latin
Meaning: Of God
Alternate Spellings: Domenic, Dominick, Dominik
Gender Variations: Dominica, Dominique
Nicknames: Dom, Nic, Nicky
Similar Names: Domenico, Domingo, Domini, Dominicus
➡ The French feminine and masculine form of Dominic that's slightly more popular as a girl's name. Associated with the French song that became known worldwide in 1963 by Soeur Sourire, also known as the Singing Nun. The name debuted on the popularity chart in 1973 and peaked in 1991 at No. 170.

Donald   Rank: 303

Origin: Gaelic
Meaning: World mighty
Alternate Spellings:
Donal, Donghal
Gender Variations: Dona, Donella, Donette
Nicknames: Don, Donny
Similar Names: Desmond, Donaldson, Donnell, Donnelly, Donovan, Duncan
Namesakes: Donald O'Connor (actor), Donald Sutherland (actor), Donald Trump (entrepreneur/TV personality)
⇨ A form of the Gaelic name Domhnall that's been used for centuries in Scotland and associated with the MacDonald clan. It became fashionable outside of Scotland during the 20th-century. English actor Donald Crisp is credited with the name's entry into the U.S. The name reached its peak from 1928 to 1938, around the time Donald Duck made his Disney debut.

Donovan   Rank: 198

Origin: Irish Gaelic
Meaning: Brown-haired man, chieftain
Alternate Spellings:
Donavan, Donavon, Donevon, Donoven, Donovon
Gender Variation: Donya
Nicknames: Don, Donnie, Van
Similar Names: Dominick, Donald, Donnelly, Doran, Dorian
Namesakes: Donovan McNabb (football player), Tate Donovan (actor)
⇨ A surname used as a given name popularized in the United Kingdom by the Scottish singer and songwriter Donovan Philips Leitch, who produced a series of hit albums and singles from 1965 to 1970. Brought into the U.S. at the beginning of the 20th century and currently at its peak.

Dorian   Rank: 469

Origin: Latin/Greek
Meaning: Man from Doris
Alternate Spellings: Dorien, Dorion, Dorrian, Dorrien
Gender Variations: Dora, Doria, Doriana, Dorie, Dorianne
Nickname: Dory
Similar Names: Damien, Darien, Darius, Demetrius, Dimitri, Dione, Doran
Namesakes: Dorian Lord (*One Life to Live* soap opera character)

⇨ Possibly derived from the Latin name Dorius. The name wasn't widely known until Irish playwright and poet Oscar Wilde used it for the central character in his first and only novel, *The Picture of Dorian Gray*, originally published in 1890, then revised and expanded in 1891.

Douglas   Rank: 365

Origin: Scottish Gaelic
Meaning: From the dark water
Alternate Spellings:
Douglass
Gender Variation: Douglasina
Nicknames: Doug, Dougie, Duggie
Similar Names: Dougal, Dugald, Dugan, Drummond, Dudley, Duncan, Dustin
Namesakes: General Douglas MacArthur (military leader), Dr. Douglas Ross (*ER* TV character),
⇨ Common Celtic river name that led to the surname of a powerful Scottish family. A popular girl's name during the 17th and 18th centuries, which has since faded. Noted for silent film actor Douglas Fairbanks and his son, actor Douglas Fairbanks Jr., and followed by Kirk Douglas and Michael Douglas, who continue to keep the name in front of the public. Ranked among the top 100 names from 1929 to 1989.

Drake   Rank: 239

Origin: Old English
Meaning: Dragon
Gender Variations:
Erika, Trace
Similar Names: Donald, Dorian, Douglas, Drew, Driscoll, Duane
Namesake: *Drake and Josh* (TV show)
⇨ Originated as a surname for the keeper of the inn with the dragon trademark. Interest in the name started with the surname of 16th-century English explorer Sir Francis Drake. It's been listed among the top 300 names since 1997.

Draven   Rank: 685

Gender Variations:
Dreda, Raven
Similar Names: Dobre, Drake, Dre, Drogo
⇨ Origin and meaning is unknown. Popular by association to Eric Draven, the lead

character in the 1994 film *The Crow*. Actor Brandon Lee played the role of Draven and was accidentally killed while filming one of the scenes. The name debuted on the popularity chart in 1995.

Drew
Rank: 205

Origin: Greek
Meaning: Manly
Alternate Spellings: Dru, Drue
Gender Variation: Drusilla
Similar Names: Doug, Drury, Duane, Dudley
Namesakes: Drew Bledsoe (football player), Drew Lachey (actor/singer)
➡ The short form of Andrew used sporadically as a given name starting in the 1880s, which increased to a steady usage in 1940. Actor and comedian Drew Carey comes to mind.

Duncan
Rank: 654

Origin: Scottish
Meaning: Dark-skinned warrior
Gender Variations: Dulce
Nicknames: Dun, Dunc
Similar Names: Douglas, Dudley, Duffy, Dunstan, Durand, Dustin
Namesakes: Duncan MacLeod (*Highlander* TV character), Duncan Sheik (singer/composer), Tim Duncan (basketball player)
➡ A form of the Gaelic name Donnchadh. The name of two Scottish Kings and several ships in the Royal navy. Duncan Phyfe, the renowned 19th-century furniture maker, is a namesake. A place name for several communities in the U.S. and British Columbia.

Dustin
Rank: 259

Origin: Old German
Meaning: Valiant fighter
Alternate Spellings: Dustan, Dusten, Duston, Dustyn
Gender Variation: Dustine
Nickname: Dusty
Similar Names: Destin, Duane, Dudley, Dunstan, Justin, Thurston
Namesake: Dustin Diamond (actor)
➡ Surname derived from an Old Norse given name popularized by two-time Oscar-winning actor Dustin Hoffman, whose mother named him after the silent-screen leading man Dustin Farnum.

Dwayne
Rank: 610

Origin: Gaelic
Meaning: Little and dark
Alternate Spellings: Dawayne, Dewayne, Duane, Duwayne, Dwain, Dwaine, Dwane
Gender Variation: Duana
Nickname: Wayne
Similar Names: Dougal, Dudley, Dwight, Dwyer, Dylan, Wayne
Namesake: Duane Eddy (musician)
➡ A variation of Duane, derived from the Irish name Dubhan. It peaked during the 1960s because of actor Dwayne Hickman, who played the title character in the television series *The Many Loves of Dobie Gillis*.

Dylan
Rank: 26

Origin: Welsh
Meaning: Son of the sea
Alternate Spellings: Dillan, Dillon, Dyllan, Dyllon, Dylon
Gender Variation: Dylan
Similar Names: Dalton, Desmond, Devon, Dion, Duane
Namesakes: Bob Dylan (musician), Dylan McDermott (actor), Dylan Sprouse (actor), Matt Dillon (actor)
➡ In Welsh mythology Dylan was a god of the sea. Welsh poet Dylan Thomas brought attention to the name in England and Wales during the 1940s until his untimely death in 1953. The name entered the top 100 and was influenced by *Beverly Hills, 90210* television character Dylan McKay.

Earl
Rank: 993

Origin: Old English
Meaning: Nobleman, warrior
Alternate Spellings: Earle, Erle
Gender Variations: Earla, Earleen
Similar Names: Edgar, Edison, Erie, Ernie, Errol
Namesakes: James "Jimmy" Earl Carter (former U.S. president), James Earl Jones (actor)
➡ An aristocratic title ranking below a marquess and above a viscount that peaked prior to the turn of the 20th century. Namesakes include country musician Earl Scruggs and Basketball Hall of Famer Earl "the Pearl" Monroe. Also associated with the Emmy Award-winning sitcom *My Name is Earl*.

Easton   Rank: 359

Origin: Old English
Meaning: From east town
Gender Variation: Eden
Similar Names: Ashton, Aston, Austin, Earnest, Eaton, Eldon, Elston, Esmond, Gaston
⇨ A place name that identified a section of town where the bearer lived. Used as a given name since 1995.

Eddie   Rank: 395

Origin: English
Meaning: Wealth, protector
Alternate Spelling: Eddy
Gender Variations: Eden, Edie
Nickname: Ed
Similar Names: Edgar, Edison, Edmund, Edward, Freddie, Neddie, Teddie
Namesakes: *Eddie and the Cruisers* (1983 film), Eddie Cahill (actor), Eddie Cibrian (actor), Eddie Van Halen (musician), Eddie Vedder (musician)
⇨ Nickname for Edward, Edgar, and other names beginning with "Ed" and used independently since the late 1800s. In recent years associated with comedian and actor Eddie Murphy.

Edgar   Rank: 171

Origin: Old English
Meaning: Wealthy spear
Gender Variation: Edie
Nicknames: Ed, Eddie
Similar Names: Edgard, Edgardo, Edmond, Edward, Edwin
Namesakes: Edgar Bergen (ventriloquist), Edgar Degas (French artist), Edgar Laprade (Hockey Hall of Famer), Edgar Rice Burroughs (author), J. Edgar Hoover (FBI director)
⇨ A royal name for a 10th-century Anglo-Saxon king given the nickname "the Peaceable," who was later revered as a saint. It was frequently used in England after the Norman Conquest. A literary name known for Edgar Allan Poe, the 19th-century author and poet of mystery and suspense, and a Shakespearean character from the play, *King Lear*.

Edison   Rank: 947

Origin: Old English
Meaning: Son of Edward
Alternate Spellings: Eddison, Edyson
Gender Variation: Edith
Nicknames: Ed, Eddie
Similar Names: Addison, Edgar, Edmund, Edson, Edward, Edwin
⇨ A surname best known for Thomas Edison, the inventor and businessman who patented an electric distribution system in 1880 that led to the invention of the electric lamp. The name is rarely used today.

Eduardo   Rank: 126

Origin: Old English
Meaning: Wealth protector
Alternate Spelling: Edwardo
Gender Variations: Eduarda
Nicknames: Duardo, Ed, Eddy
Similar Names: Edison, Eduard, Eduarelo, Edvard, Enrique
⇨ The Spanish and Portuguese form of Edward preferred by Hispanic parents.

Edward   Rank: 143

Origin: Old English
Meaning: Wealth protector
Alternate Spellings: Edouard, Eduard
Gender Variation: Edwardine
Nicknames: Ed, Eddie, Ned, Ted
Similar Names: Edison, Edvard, Edwardo, Edwin
Namesakes: Edward Kennedy (senator), Edward R. Murrow (newscaster)
⇨ Derived from the elements *ead* and *weard*. Greatly influenced during the 11th century by Edward the Confessor, who became king of England before the Norman Conquest. It remained a popular royal name in England. Also a literary name used by Shakespeare in several plays.

Edwin   Rank: 158

Origin: Old English
Meaning: Rich friend
Alternate Spelling: Edwyn
Gender Variation: Edwina
Nicknames: Ed, Eddie
Similar Names: Edgar, Edmond, Edsel, Edward, Egbert
⇨ The name of a 7th-century king of Northumbria, venerated as a Christian saint.

It saw a revival in popularity during the 19th century and has remained in regular use for the past 125 years. Astronaut Edwin "Buzz" Aldrin, the second man to walk on the moon, is a famous bearer.

Efrain
Rank: 663

Origin: Hebrew
Meaning: Fruitful
Alternate Spellings: Efren, Efrin, Ephrain
Gender Variations: Effemy, Effie
Similar Names: Eferino, Efraim, Ephron, Eran, Evron
➡ The Spanish form of Ephraim and the Old Testament name of Joseph's second son, who founded the tribe of Ephraim.

Eli
Rank: 139

Origin: Hebrew
Meaning: High
Alternate Spelling: Ely
Gender Variations: Eliada, Elise, Elita
Similar Names: Elias, Eliezer, Elijah, Eliot, Elisha
Namesakes: Eli Manning (football player), Eli Wallach (actor)
➡ The high priest of Israel and Samuel's teacher in the Old Testament. The name drifts in and out of popularity. Historically Eli Whitney, the inventor of the cotton gin, comes to mind.

Elian

Origin: Spanish
Meaning: He who is assured
Alternate Spelling: Elyan
Gender Variation: Eliana
Nicknames: Eli
Similar Names: Elan, Elia, Eliam, Elias, Elijah
➡ The combination of Elizabeth and Juan. A seldom-used name that received a surge of popularity during the Miami custody battle of Elian Gonzalez in 2000. Elian was returned to his father in Cuba, and the name has recently faded into the background.

Elias
Rank: 186

Origin: Hebrew
Meaning: The Lord is my God
Alternate Spelling: Elyas
Gender Variations: Eliza, Elizabeth
Nickname: Eli

Similar Names: Elia, Elijah, Elisha, Elliot, Ellis, Eliyahu
Namesakes: Elias Howe (sewing machine inventor), Elias Koteas (Canadian actor)
➡ Used in some versions of the New Testament when referring to the important prophet Elijah. Experiencing a resurgence in popularity in the U.S. Elias Canetti, who won the 1981 Nobel Prize for literature, and Elias James Corey, the 1990 Nobel Prize winner in chemistry, are among the namesakes.

Elijah
Rank: 29

Origin: Hebrew
Meaning: The Lord is my God
Alternate Spellings: Alijah, Elija, Elisha
Gender Variations: Elisha, Elisheba
Nickname: Eli
Similar Names: Elia, Eliab, Eliam, Elias, Elliot
Namesakes: Elijah Blue Allman (musician), Elijah Wood (actor)
➡ A great prophet in the Old Testament who ascends into heaven on a chariot of fire. A top 100 name since 1995.

Eliseo

Origin: Hebrew
Meaning: The Lord is my salvation
Gender Variation: Elisha
Nickname: Eli
Similar Names: Elian, Elias, Eloiso, Elysiuio, Emilio, Erasto, Erico
➡ The Italian and Spanish form of Elisha and the name of nine saints. Used sporadically in the past 125 years. Favored by Hispanic families.

Elliot
Rank: 372

Origin: Hebrew
Meaning: The Lord is my God
Alternate Spellings: Eliott, Elliot, Elliott, Elyot
Gender Variations: Ellie, Elita
Nickname: Eli
Similar Names: Elia, Elias, Elisha, Ellis, Elton
Namesakes: Chris Elliott (comedian/actor), Elliott Sadler (NASCAR driver)
➡ A surname that originated as a form of the given name Elias. Actor Elliott Gould has kept the name in front of the public since the 1960s. Parents may prefer the trendier "y" in the middle spelling. Occasionally used as a girl's name.

Ellis
Rank: 783

Origin: Hebrew
Meaning: The Lord is my God
Alternate Spelling: Ellys
Gender Variations: Elisha, Elsa
Similar Names: Eliakim, Elias, Eljas, Elliott, Ellis, Ellison, Ellsworth, Ely
Namesake: Ellis Burks (baseball player)
⇨ Derived from the Hebrew name Elijah. British writer and poet Emily Bronte chose the masculine sounding Ellis Bell as her pen name when she wrote her only novel, *Wuthering Heights*, published in 1847. The name reached its height in popularity prior to the turn of the 20th century.

Elmer
Rank: 907

Origin: Old English
Meaning: Famous nobleman
Alternate Spellings: Aylmar, Aylmer, Ellmer, Elmar, Elmir
Gender Variations: Alma, Edelmira
Similar Names: Adelmar, Aymer, Delmer, Delmore, Elman, Elmo, Elmore
Namesake: Elmer Rice (British playwright)
⇨ Used as a given name prior to the Norman Conquest then made a comeback during the 19th century. It was listed among the top 100 names from 1880 to 1932. It may have been adversely influenced by the 1927 Sinclair Lewis novel, *Elmer Gantry*, that portrays the title character as a rogue. The novel was adapted into a film in 1960. Also associated with fictional cartoon character Elmer J. Fudd, who made his first appearance in 1940.

Elvin
Origin: Old English
Meaning: Elf friend
Alternate Spellings: Elven, Elvyn
Gender Variations: Elva, Elvina, Elvira
Similar Names: Elton, Elvern, Elvis, Elwin, Kelvin, Melvin
⇨ This form of Alvin peaked during the 1920s.

Elvis
Rank: 761
Alternate Spelling: Elviss, Elvys
Gender Variation: Elvia
Similar Names: Alvin, Alvis, Elric, Elton, Elvin, Elwood, Elwyn

Namesakes: Elvis Costello (British musician), Elvis Stojko (Canadian Olympic medalist)
⇨ Origin and meaning is unknown. Popularized by singer and actor Elvis Presley, often referred to as the King of Rock and Roll, who was named after his father, Vernon Elvis Presley. He's regarded as one of the most influential entertainers of the past 50 years. Parents who use this name are generally fans of the pop icon.

Emerson
Rank: 539
Origin: Old German
Meaning: Son of Emerry
Alternate Spellings: Emersen, Emmerson, Emmyrson, Emyrson
Gender Variations: Emerson, Emery, Emily
Nickname: Emery
Similar Names: Amaury, Edison, Edward, Emanuel, Emery, Emile, Emmerich
Namesakes: Emerson Fittipaldi (Brazilian race car driver), Keith Emerson (musician)
⇨ A surname derived from a medieval personal name that was possibly given during the 19th century in honor of poet and essayist Ralph Waldo Emerson, leader of the transcendentalist movement. George Emerson, the principal male character in E. M. Forster's 1908 novel, *A Room with a View*, is another literary namesake. Ranks highly as a girl's name.

Emiliano
Rank: 332
Origin: Latin
Meaning: Rival
Gender Variations: Emelia, Emeliana, Emily
Nicknames: Emil, Milan
Similar Names: Emil, Emilian, Emilio, Emilianus, Emlyn
⇨ The Spanish and Italian form of the Roman family name Aemilianus, ultimately derived from *aemulus*. A notable bearer is 20th-century Mexican revolutionary Emiliano Zapata, who's considered a national hero of Mexico.

Emilio
Rank: 298

Origin: Latin
Meaning: Rival
Alternate Spellings: Amelio, Amilio

Gender Variations: Emelia, Emiliana, Emily, Emmie
Nickname: Emil
Similar Names: Emilian, Emiliano, Enrique, Erico, Ernesto, Esteban
Namesake: Emilio Estefan Jr. (music producer)
➡ The Italian, Portuguese, and Spanish form of Aemilius. The name is associated with actor and director Emilio Estevez, a member of the 1980s group of young movie actors referred to as the Brat Pack. It's a popular choice among Hispanic families.

Emmanuel Rank: 166

Origin: Hebrew
Meaning: God is with us
Alternate Spellings: Emanual, Emanuel, Emanuele, Emmanouil, Imanuel, Immanuel, Immanuele
Gender Variations: Emmanuelle, Manola, Manuelita
Nicknames: Eman, Manny, Manuel
Similar Names: Manolo, Manuel, Manuelo
Namesake: Emanuel Ungaro (fashion designer)
➡ The New Testament name for Jesus and a variation of the Hebrew name Immanuel, whose coming is prophesied in the Old Testament. Actor Emmanuel Lewis who starred in the title role of *Webster* brought attention to the name during the 1980s. It's considered a royal name in Italy.

Emmett Rank: 569

Origin: English
Meaning: Hard worker, truth
Alternate Spellings: Emmet, Emmit, Emmitt, Emmot, Emmott
Gender Variations: Emma, Emmie
Similar Names: Earnest, Edmund, Elmer, Emery, Emile, Emmanuel
➡ A surname derived from the female name Emma that became fashionable during the Middle Ages. It peaked prior to the turn of the 20th century but has endured as a boy's given name throughout the years. Possibly influenced by circus clown Emmett Kelly, who created the character Weary Willie. Another notable bearer is football player Emmitt Smith, the third-season winner of *Dancing with the Stars*.

Enrique Rank: 281

Origin: German
Meaning: Home ruler
Gender Variations: Enrica, Harriet, Henrietta, Henriette
Nicknames: Erik, Rico
Similar Names: Enrico, Enriques, Erico, Harry, Henrik, Henry, Ricardo, Richard, Rico
➡ The Spanish form of Heinrich and the name of 16 saints. It peaked in the at No. 221 in 2000 influenced by Grammy Award-winner Enrique Iglesias, the Spanish-born singer and songwriter.

Eric Rank: 77

Origin: Old Norse
Meaning: Ever ruler
Alternate Spellings: Aerick, Aric, Arrick, Eirik, Erek, Erich, Erick, Erik, Erric, Eryk
Gender Variation: Erica
Nickname: Ric
Similar Names: Erickson, Erico, Erie, Frederick, Rick
Namesakes: Eric Bana (actor), Eric Benet (singer/actor), Eric Clapton (musician), Eric McCormack (actor)
➡ A form of Erik derived from the Old Norse name *Eirikr*. Notable for 10th-century Viking explorer Eric the Red who founded the first Nordic settlement in Greenland. The name gained popularity during the 19th century when British writers Frederic Farrar and H. Rider Haggard used the name in literature. It's considered a royal name in Denmark, Sweden, and Norway. Actor Eriq La Salle uses a variant.

Ernest Rank: 723

Origin: Old German
Meaning: Serious
Alternate Spelling: Earnest
Gender Variations: Ernesta, Ernestina, Ernestine
Nicknames: Ern, Ernie
Similar Names: Ernesto, Ernst, Erwin, Eugene, Evert, Ewald
Namesake: Ernest Borgnine (actor)
➡ Variation of the German word *eornost* influenced by short-story writer and novelist Ernest Hemingway, who received the Pulitzer Prize in 1953 for *The Old Man and the Sea*. He also received the Nobel Prize in Literature in 1954. Oscar Wilde's play *The Importance of Being Earnest* also comes to mind.

Ernesto   Rank: 379

Origin: Old German
Meaning: Serious
Gender Variations: Erna, Ernesta, Ernestina, Ernestine
Nicknames: Ern, Ernie, Ernio, Nesto
Similar Names: Enrique, Erico, Ernest, Ernestor, Ernilo, Ernst
⇨ The Italian, Spanish, and Portuguese form of Ernest. The name has gone in and out of favor since the 19th century and is preferred by Hispanic families.

Esteban   Rank: 333

Origin: Greek
Meaning: Crown, garland
Alternate Spellings: Estaban, Estavan, Estaven, Estevan
Gender Variations: Estefania, Stefania, Stephanie
Similar Names: Esteve, Estevo, Stefan, Stefano, Stefanus, Stephen
Namesake: Esteban Ramirez (*The Suite Life of Zack and Cody* character)
⇨ The Spanish form of Stephen and a literary name for the main character in the 1982 novel *The House of Spirits* by Isabel Allende, adapted into a film in 1993. It's gained popularity since the mid-1950s and is also preferred in Chile.

Ethan   Rank: 4

Origin: Hebrew
Meaning: Firm, steadfast
Alternate Spellings: Eathan, Eathen, Eithan, Eithen, Ethen, Ethyn
Gender Variation: Ethana
Similar Names: Eldon, Emil, Enoch, Ephraim, Ernest, Esau, Eugene
Namesakes: Ethan Coen (film director/screenwriter), Ethan Embry (actor), Ethan Hawke (actor)
⇨ The name of a wise man in the Old Testament and the author of *Psalm 89*. The name Ethan Allen is notable for the Revolutionary War leader and general, a 19th-century firearm manufacturer from Massachusetts, and a furniture chain founded in 1932. American novelist Edith Wharton wrote *Ethan Frome* in 1911, which was adapted into a film in 1993.

Eugene   Rank: 647

Origin: Greek
Meaning: Well born
Gender Variations: Eugenia, Eugenie
Nickname: Gene
Similar Names: Euan, Eugen, Eugenio, Gene
Namesakes: Eugene Delacroix (French painter), Eugene Field (children's poet), Eugene Ionesco (French-Romanian playwright), Eugene Levy (actor)
⇨ Derived from Eugenios and the name of several early saints and four popes. Influenced by 20th-century playwright Eugene O'Neill, a four-time Pulitzer Prize winner who also won the Nobel Prize for Literature in 1936. It was popular throughout the late 19th century until the middle of the 20th century.

Evan   Rank: 42

Origin: Hebrew
Meaning: God is gracious
Alternate Spellings: Evann, Even, Evin, Evyn
Gender Variations: Evangeline, Evania, Evie
Similar Names: Evander, Evangelos, Everard, Everett, Evian, Ian, Ivan
Namesake: Evan Taubenfeld (musician)
⇨ The Welsh form of John and a shortened form of the Greek name Evangelos. Its popularity in Wales led to the surname Evans. It's been on the rise since 1990 and is occasionally used as a girl's name.

Everett   Rank: 451

Origin: Old English
Meaning: Strong boar
Alternate Spellings: Everet, Everette
Gender Variation: Evette
Nickname: Rett
Similar Names: Edgar, Edward, Egbert, Emmett, Ernest, Everton, Evert
Namesakes: Chad Everett (actor), C. Everett Koop (former surgeon general), Tom Everett Scott (actor)
⇨ A surname derived from Everard used as a given name starting in the 19th century. Best-selling novelist John Irving has a son named Everett. Actor Rupert Everett is a famous bearer of the surname.

Ezekiel
Rank: 269

Origin: Hebrew
Meaning: Strength of God
Alternate Spellings:
Ezechiel, Ezekial, Ezekyel,
Ezequiel, Ezikiel, Ezikyel, Ezykiel
Gender Variation: Eve
Nickname: Zeke
Similar Names: Elisha, Eliyahu, Emmanuel,
Ephraim, Ezra
➡ In the Old Testament, the name of a great
prophet exiled to Babylon who prophesies
that a field of dry bones will live again.
A book in the Bible bears his name. The
name's rise in popularity can be attributed
to a recent surge in biblical names.

Ezra
Rank: 340

Origin: Hebrew
Meaning: Help
Alternate Spellings: Esra,
Ezrah
Gender Variation: Azura
Similar Names: Ephraim, Ephron, Erez, Esau,
Ezekiel, Ezri
➡ A priest and scribe in the Old Testament
who is believed to be the author of the
Books of Ezra and 1 Chronicles in the Bible.
Children's writer and illustrator Ezra Jack
Keats and poet Ezra Pound also come to
mind. The name peaked prior to the turn of
the 20th century, but appears to be making
a comeback with other biblical names.

Fabian
Rank: 272

Origin: Late Latin
Meaning: Bean grower
Alternate Spellings: Fabien,
Fabion, Fabyan, Fabyen,
Fabyon, Faebian, Faybian, Faybien
Gender Variations: Fabia, Fabienne,
Fabiola
Nickname: Fabe
Similar Names: Fabiano, Fabio, Fabius, Fabo
➡ Originated from the Roman clan name
Fabianus which was derived from Fabius
and used by several emperors and 16 saints.
Influenced during the 1950s and 1960s by
teen idol Fabiano Anthony Forte, better
known as Fabian, who started his career
as a singer and later became an actor.

Felipe
Rank: 457

Origin: Greek
Meaning: Lover of horses
Alternate Spellings:
Felippe, Filep, Filip,
Fillip, Fyllip
Gender Variations: Filipa, Filipina, Pippa
Similar Names: Felipo, Ferdinand, Fernando,
Filemon, Philip
Namesakes: Felipe Alou (Dominican baseball
player), Felipe Calderon (President of Mexico),
➡ The Spanish form of Philip that became
a royal name in Portugal and Spain.

Felix
Rank: 397

Origin: Latin
Meaning: Happy
Alternate Spellings:
Feliks, Felyx
Gender Variations: Felice, Felicia,
Feliciana, Felicienne
Nickname: Fee
Similar Names: Feliciano, Felicien, Felicio,
Fenn, Fenton
Namesakes: Felix Leiter (*James Bond*
character), Felix Unger (*Odd Couple* character)
➡ A common name among early Christians
used by several saints and four popes.
Felix Mendelssohn, the 19th-century German
composer and conductor, is a namesake.
Felix the Cat was a popular cartoon
character who debuted during the 1920s.
It became an enduring name with parents
because of its favorable meaning.

Fernando
Rank: 151

Origin: German
Meaning: Daring,
adventurous
Alternate Spelling:
Ferdynand
Gender Variations: Ferdinanda, Fernanda
Nicknames: Ferdie, Nando
Similar Names: Ferdinand, Ferdinando,
Fernand, Fernedo, Ferran, Ferrer, Hernan,
Hernando
Namesakes: Fernando Botero (Colombian
artist), Fernando Lamas (Argentine actor),
Fernando Valenzuela (baseball player)
➡ The Spanish and Portuguese form of
Ferdinand that's currently past its peak
but still in regular use.

Fidel

0.010%
0.008%
0.006%
0.004%
0.002%
0.000%
1900   TODAY

Origin: Latin
Meaning: Faithful
Alternate Spellings:
Fidal, Fedele, Fidele
Gender Variations: Fidela, Fidelia
Similar Names: Fadelio, Fedele, Fidalio, Fidelix
⇨ Derived from the name Fidelis and is best-known for Cuban revolutionary leader Fidel Castro who became premier in 1959 and president in 1976. It's seldom used in the U.S.

Finley   Rank: 886

Origin: Irish Gaelic
Meaning: Golden ray of sun, fair-haired warrior
Alternate Spellings: Findley, Finlea, Finlee, Finnley
Gender Variations: Fina, Finella, Fiona
Nickname: Finn
Similar Names: Farley, Finn, Fionan, Linley
Namesake: Michael Finley (basketball player)
⇨ A variation of Finlay, which is the anglicized form of Fionnlagh. The name suddenly reappeared on the popularity chart after an absence of more than 85 years.

Finn   Rank: 456

0.030%
0.025%
0.020%
0.015%
0.010%
0.005%
0.000%
1900   TODAY

Origin: Irish Gaelic
Meaning: White, fair
Alternate Spellings:
Fin, Fyn, Fynn
Gender Variation: Fiona
Nickname: Finnie
Similar Names: Finlay, Finnegan, Finnian, Fionn, Phineas
⇨ A form of Fionn and often used as the short form of Finnegan that's known in Irish folklore for Finn MacCumaill, a legendary hero who was popular because of his fairness. Huckleberry Finn, the title character in Mark Twain's novel *The Adventures of Huckleberry Finn*, is a literary namesake. Widely used since 2000, the name also describes a native or inhabitant of Finland.

Finnegan   Rank: 779

0.015%
0.012%
0.009%
0.006%
0.003%
0.000%
1900   TODAY

Origin: Irish Gaelic
Meaning: Descendent of Fionnagan
Alternate Spelling: Finegan
Gender Variation: Fiona
Nickname: Finn
Similar Names: Finbar, Finley, Finnen, Finnian, Fionn
⇨ A surname derived from O Fionnagain associated with *Finnegan's Wake*, the last novel published by Irish writer James Joyce. New to the popularity chart in 2005. Finn, the short form of the name, has become more widely used.

Fisher

Origin: Old English
Meaning: Fisherman
Alternate Spellings: Fischer, Fisscher
Gender Variation: Sher
Nickname: Fish
Similar Names: Farrell, Finlay, Fitz, Fletcher, Flynn, Forrest
Namesakes: Fisher Stevens (actor)
⇨ An occupational name derived from *fiscare*. Eddie Fisher, a popular singer and entertainer during the 1950s and 1960s, is a bearer of the surname. Associated today with author and screenwriter Antwone Fisher whose 2001 autobiography, *Finding Fish*, was adapted into a film in 2002. Rarely used as a boy's name today.

Forrest

0.12%
0.10%
0.08%
0.06%
0.04%
0.02%
0.00%
1900   TODAY

Origin: Old French
Meaning: Woodland, forest
Alternate Spelling: Forest
Gender Variations: Fawn, Fern, Flora, Florence
Similar Names: Deforest, Forbes, Forrester, Forster, Foster
⇨ A surname used as a first name that was initially given to someone who lived or worked near a woodland. It was known during the 19th century for Confederate general Nathan Bedford Forrest. Film and television actor Forrest Tucker popularized the name from the 1940s until the 1980s. The name peaked in 1913 and climbed again in 1994 with the release of the film *Forrest Gump*. Oscar winner Forest Whitaker is another famous bearer. Also considered a nature name.

Francis
Rank: 561

Origin: Latin
Meaning: From France
Gender Variations: Fran, Frances
Nicknames: Fran, France, Frank, Frankie
Similar Names: Ferenc, Francois, Franco, Frank, Franklin, Franz, Franzen
Namesakes: Fran Tarkenton (Football Hall of Famer), Francis Ford Coppola (film director), Francis Scott Key (composer)
➡ Derived from Franciscus denoting a person from France. Saint Francis of Assisi, the 13th-century Italian friar and preacher who founded the Franciscan order, is a famous bearer. He was named Francisco in honor of his mother's heritage. Also known for English philosopher Sir Francis Bacon and English navigator Sir Francis Drake. Singer and actor Francis Sinatra, better known as Frank, kept the name in the public eye beginning in the 1940s.

Francisco
Rank: 157

Origin: Latin
Meaning: From France
Gender Variations: Fran, Francesca, Franci, Francisca
Nicknames: Cisco, Franc
Similar Names: Francesco, Francis, Franco
Namesake: Francisco Tarrega (Spanish composer/guitarist)
➡ The Spanish and Portuguese form of Franciscus historically known for Spanish painter Francisco de Goya and Spanish dictator Francisco Franco.

Franco
Rank: 918

Origin: Latin
Meaning: From France
Alternate Spelling: Franko
Gender Variation: Franca
Nicknames: Fran, Franc
Similar Names: Ferenc, Francois, Frankie, Franz
Namesake: James Franco (actor)
➡ The pet form of Francesco or Francisco. Generalisimo Francisco Franco, leader of Spain after the civil war, is a famous bearer of the surname. Occasionally used for boys since its 1967 debut on the popularity chart.

Frank
Rank: 245

Origin: Latin
Meaning: From France
Alternate Spellings: Franc, Franche, Franck, Francke, Franke
Gender Variation: Frances
Similar Names: Ferenc, France, Francis, Francisco, Franco, Francois, Franek, Franio, Frankin, Frantz
Namesakes: Frank Gifford (actor/football announcer), Frankie Muniz (actor)
➡ The short form of several names, including Franklin and Francis. The name was affected significantly by the fame and accomplishments of singer and actor Frank Sinatra and master architect Frank Lloyd Wright. It's been used as an independent name since the 17th century.

Frankie
Rank: 648

Origin: Latin
Meaning: From France
Alternate Spellings: Frankey, Franky
Gender Variations: Frances, Francesca, Frannie
Similar Names: Frances, Franco, Frank, Franklin, Franz
➡ The pet form of Frank or Frances. Singer Frankie Laine, whose career spanned most of the 20th century, greatly influenced the name. Also known for teen idol Frankie Avalon who released three No. 1 hits during the 1950s and starred in a string of beach movies during the 1960s.

Franklin
Rank: 439

Origin: Middle English
Meaning: Freeholder
Alternate Spellings: Francklyn, Franklyn
Gender Variations: Francie, Francine
Nicknames: Frank, Frankie
Similar Names: Francis, Francisco, Frank, Frankie, Fraser
➡ A surname given to someone who was a landowner. Mainly used in the U.S., its rise in popularity began with 18th-century statesman and inventor Benjamin Franklin, who signed the Declaration of Independence. The name peaked during the presidency of Franklin Delano Roosevelt.

Frederick   Rank: 483

Origin: Old German
Meaning: Peaceful ruler
Alternate Spellings:
Frederic, Frederich,
Frederik, Fredric, Fredrick, Fredrik
Gender Variations: Freda, Fredericka,
Frederique
Nicknames: Fred, Freddy, Fritz
Similar Names: Federico, Fred, Frederico,
Friedrich
Namesakes: Fred Flintstone (animated film/
TV character), Fred Savage (actor/director),
Reverend Frederick Rogers (*Mister Rogers*,
TV host)
⇒ A combination of *frid* and *ric* adopted by
the Normans and brought into England but
faded until the 17th and 18th centuries.
Known for 19th-century Polish-French
composer and pianist Frederic Chopin.
Dancer and actor Fred Astaire, born
Frederick Austerlitz, brought attention to
the shortened form. It was listed among the
top 100 names until 1957. The name of several
rulers of Prussia and Germany, including
Frederick II of Prussia, better known as
Frederick the Great.

Gabriel   Rank: 28

Origin: Hebrew
Meaning: God is my
strength
Alternate Spelling:
Gabriele
Gender Variations: Gabriela, Gabrielle
Nicknames: Gab, Gabe, Gaby
Similar Names: Gabriello, Gavriel, Gavril,
Gideon, Gilbert
Namesakes: Gabriel Byrne (actor), Peter
Gabriel (musician), Gabriel Garcia Marquez
(author/Nobel Prize winner), Roman Gabriel
(football player)
⇒ The name of one of seven archangels
in the Bible, who appeared to Daniel twice
and once to Zacharias to announce the
impending birth of Christ. Gabrielle is listed
among the top 100 girl's names.

Gael   Rank: 314

Origin: English
Meaning: Speaker of
Gaelic
Alternate Spellings: Gaell,
Gaelle, Gale

Gender Variations: Abigail, Gail
Similar Names: Cael, Collin, Gavin, Gill,
Glen, Kyle
Namesake: Gael Turnbull (Scottish poet)
⇒ A popular term that describes a person
of Irish or Scottish descent. Possibly picked
up by parents within the last few years to
honor their heritage. A form of the female
name Abigail.

Gage   Rank: 156

Origin: Middle English
Meaning: Measure
Alternate Spellings:
Gaige, Gauge
Gender Variations: Gaia, Gail
Similar Names: Gaiger, Gale, Galen, Garth,
Geoff, Gibb, Gill
Namesake: Thomas Gage (British general)
⇒ The English and French occupational
surname for an assayer, sometimes used as
a nickname for a money lender. The name
has ranked among the top 150 as a boy's
given name since 2001.

Gannon   Rank: 889

Origin: Irish Gaelic
Meaning: Fair-skinned
Alternate Spelling: Ganon
Gender Variation: Gana
Similar Names: Gallagher, Garvan,
Gilroy, Grady
⇒ A surname used as a given name
associated with fictional detective Bill
Gannon from the popular mid-1960s
television series *Dragnet* and made into
a 1987 film. The name was new to the
popularity chart in 2002.

Garrett   Rank: 138

Origin: Old German
Meaning: Rule of the spear
Alternate Spellings:
Garet, Garret, Garett
Gender Variation: Greta
Nickname: Gary
Similar Names: Garretson, Garson, Gerald,
Geraldo, Gerard, Jared, Jarrett, Jerry
Namesakes: Brad Garrett (actor)
⇒ A surname originating from Gerald and
Gerard best-known for lawman Pat Garrett,
who reportedly shot Billy the Kid in 1881. The
most popular among boy's names ending in
"ett" when compared to Barrett and Jarrett.

Garrison   Rank: 895

Origin: Middle English
Meaning: Spear-fortified town
Alternate Spelling:
Garrisson
Gender Variation: Carson
Nickname: Gary
Similar Names: Carson, Garrett, Garson, Gresham, Greyson
➡ A variation of Garret or taken from the local surname and place name meaning from Garriston in North Yorkshire, England. Notable bearer William Lloyd Garrison was a prominent abolitionist during the 19th century. It's best-known for radio personality Garrison Keillor, the host of *A Prairie Home Companion.*

Gary   Rank: 350

Origin: Old English
Meaning: Carries a spear
Alternate Spellings:
Garey, Gari, Garrey, Garrie, Garry, Gery
Gender Variation: Garnet
Nickname: Gar
Similar Names: Gareth, Garrett, Garrick, Garth, Garvey, Garvin, Gerald, Gervais, Gervis, Jareth
Namesakes: Gary Oldman (actor), Gary Sinise (actor), Gary Trudeau (cartoonist)
➡ Surname that became a given name. Actor Gary Cooper is credited with the name's enormous popularity during the 1940s and 1950s. Born Frank James Cooper, he picked up the stage name Gary from the city in Indiana. Azerbaijanian chess champion Garry Kasparov, who held the title of World Chess Champion from 1985 to 2000, also comes to mind.

Gavin   Rank: 38

Origin: Celtic
Meaning: Little hawk
Alternate Spellings: Gavan, Gaven, Gavyn, Gavynn
Gender Variation: Gavina
Nickname: Gav
Similar Names: Gallagher, Gareth, Garth, Gawain, Gilroy
Namesakes: Gavin MacLeod (actor)
➡ A variation of the medieval name Gawain, which was used in Arthurian legend by one of the knights of the famed Round Table. The name has quickly climbed the popularity chart since 1960 and is widely used in Ireland.

George   Rank: 153

Origin: Greek
Meaning: Farmer
Alternate Spelling: Georg
Gender Variations:
Georgene, Georgette, Georgia, Georgiana
Nickname: Georgie
Similar Names: Geordie, Georgios, Giorgio, Jorge, Joren, Jorgen, Jori
Namesakes: George Bush (U.S. president), George Carlin (actor/comedian), George Clooney (actor), George Foreman (boxer/entrepeneur), George Harrison (musician), George Lucas (producer/director)
➡ Taken from Georgos. The name of several saints, including a martyred Roman soldier known as a legendary dragon slayer. A favorite among royalty in England and Greece. Other famous bearers include authors George Eliot and George Orwell and George Washington, the 1st U.S. president, who made a huge impact on the name.

Gerald   Rank: 544

Origin: Old German
Meaning: Strong with a spear
Alternate Spellings:
Gerhold, Gerold, Jerald, Jerold
Gender Variation: Geraldine
Nicknames: Ged, Gerry
Similar Names: Garold, Geraldo, Gerard, Gerardo, Geraud, Jarrett, Jarod
➡ The name was brought into England by the Normans where it was often confused with Gerard. It faded in popularity until the 19th century and reached its peak in both Great Britain and the U.S. during the mid 1930s. It was kept in front of the public by Gerald Ford, the 38th president. Geraldo is the Spanish form.

Gerardo   Rank: 268

Origin: German
Meaning: Strong with a spear
Alternate Spellings:
Gherardo, Jerardo
Gender Variation: Gerardine
Nickname: Gerry
Similar Names: Garrett, Gerald, Geraldo, Gerard, Gerrold, Jarrett
Namesakes: Gerardo Diego (Spanish poet)
➡ The Italian and Spanish form of Gerard and the name of 16 saints.

German   Rank: 839

Origin: French/Latin
Meaning: From Germany
Alternate Spellings:
Jerman, Jermyn
Gender Variation: Germaine
Similar Names: Geoffrey, Gerard,
Germano, Jermaine, Kerman
⇨ The English form of the French Germain
and the Latin Germanus. The name of several
early saints that was revived in the U.S. in
1973, possibly used by parents in honor of
their heritage.

Giancarlo   Rank: 716

Origin: Italian
Alternate Spelling:
Gian-Carlo
Gender Variation: Giana
Nicknames: Carlo, Gian
Similar Names: Gianni, Giampaolo,
Giacomo, Gianmaria
⇨ A combination of the popular names
"Gian" and "Carlo" that's gained in popularity
since its debut in 1986 at No. 937.

Gideon   Rank: 591

Origin: Hebrew
Meaning: Feller of trees
Alternate Spellings:
Gedeon, Gideone
Gender Variation: Jaden
Nicknames: Gid, Giddy
Similar Names: Gabriel, Gaius, Gera,
Gershon, Gilead
Namesake: *Gideon's Trumpet* (1964
novel/1980 movie)
⇨ A biblical hero who was called on by
God to deliver Israel from the Midians.
Also known for The Gideons International,
a missionary team of men and women who
distribute Bibles and New Testaments
throughout the world. The name declined
at the beginning of the 20th century, then
reappeared in 1980.

Gilbert   Rank: 658

Origin: Old German
Meaning: Bright pledge
Alternate Spellings:
Gilburt, Guilbert
Gender Variation: Gilberta
Nicknames: Bert, Gibb, Gil

Similar Names: Colbert, Culbert, Giles,
Gilroy, Gilson
Namesake: Gilbert Gottfried (comedian)
⇨ Introduced to Britain by the Normans
which led to the creation of several surnames,
such as Gibbs and Gibson. Listed among the
top 200 names since its debut on the
popularity chart. Especially fashionable
during the 1920s and 1930s. Associated with
the name of the title character in the 1993
film, *What's Eating Gilbert Grape*, played by
Johnny Depp. Gilberto is the Spanish form.

Giovanni   Rank: 146

Origin: Hebrew
Meaning: God is gracious
Alternate Spellings:
Geovanni, Geovanny,
Giovani, Giovanny, Giovonni
Gender Variations: Gianna, Giovanna,
Giovannetta
Nicknames: Gio, Vanni
Similar Names: Gianni, Giannino, Giorgio,
John, Yanni
Namesakes: *Don Giovanni* (opera by Mozart),
Giovanni Hidalgo (Puerto Rican
percussionist), Giovanni Ribisi (actor)
⇨ The Italian form of John that has
increased in popularity since the 1960s.
Historical namesakes include Giovanni
Bellini, the Italian Renaissance painter, and
Giovanni Lorenzo Bernini, the 17th-century
Italian sculptor and architect.

Glenn   Rank: 850

Origin: Irish Gaelic
Meaning: Narrow valley
Alternate Spelling: Glen
Gender Variations:
Glenna, Glenys, Glynis
Similar Names: Craig, Glenton, Glenville,
Grant, Kyle
Namesakes: John Glenn (astronaut/senator),
Scott Glenn (actor)
⇨ A variation of the vocabulary word *glen*
from the Scottish surname derived from
gleann. Popular use in the U.S. may have
started with the famed composer and big-
band leader Glenn Miller, whose life is
chronicled in the 1953 film *The Glenn Miller
Story*. Canadian actor Glenn Ford, born
Gwyllyn Ford, whose career spanned from
the early 1950s until the 1990s, also
influenced the name.

Gonzalo　Rank: 925

Origin: German
Meaning: Fight, combat
Gender Variation: Consuelo
Nickname: Gonzi
Similar Names: Galeno, Genaro, Geraldo, Gerardo, Gilberto, Gonzales, Gregorio, Guillermo, Gumersindo
Namesake: Julie Gonzalo (actor)
➡ A personal name using a combination of *gund* and *salve* or *salvo*. Shakespeare used the name for a courtier in his 17th-century play *The Tempest*. Also the name of five saints. Occasionally used by parents in the U.S.

Gordon　Rank: 900

Origin: Old English/Gaelic
Meaning: Great hill
Alternate Spellings: Gordan, Gorden
Gender Variation: Jordan
Nicknames: Gord, Gordie
Similar Names: Gaylord, Geoffrey, George, Goddard, Godwin
Namesakes: Flash Gordon (comic book hero), Jeff Gordon (NASCAR driver), Gordon Smith (U.S. senator)
➡ A well-known Scottish clan name and place name. Popular in Scotland and with parents of Scottish descent during the 20th century and listed among the top 100 names from 1911 to 1943. The name has faded considerably in recent years.

Grady　Rank: 475

Origin: Irish Gaelic
Meaning: Noble
Alternate Spellings: Gradea, Gradee, Gradey, Graidey, Graidy
Gender Variations: Grace, Gracie
Similar Names: Galvin, Gannon, Gilroy, Glen, Gordy, Granville, Gray, Grayson
➡ An Irish surname derived from O Gradaigh that has seen a surge in popularity during the past five years.

Graham　Rank: 430

Origin: Old English
Meaning: Gravelly place
Alternate Spellings: Graeme, Grahame, Grahem, Gram
Gender Variations: Grania
Similar Names: Gibson, Glen, Gordon, Graham, Grant, Gray, Grierson, Guthrie
Namesakes: Alexander Graham Bell (inventor), Graham Kerr (Scottish cooking personality), Graham Nash (English musician)
➡ Originated as an English place name taken by Sir William de Graham during the 12th century into Scotland, where it became a well-known clan name. It peaked in 1986 at No. 339, but has never achieved the popularity in the U.S. that it has in Europe.

Grant　Rank: 155

Origin: Scottish
Meaning: Large
Gender Variations: Garnet, Granata
Similar Names: Graham, Grantley, Granville, Gray
Namesakes: Cary Grant (actor), Grant Wood (painter), Hugh Grant (English actor)
➡ A common surname used as a given name taken from a Highland Scottish clan from the 14th century. Ulysses S. Grant, American general and 18th president of the U.S., brought much attention to the surname. It peaked at No. 114 in 1997.

Grayson　Rank: 218

Origin: Middle English
Meaning: Son of the steward
Alternate Spellings: Graysen, Greyson
Gender Variations: Grace, Gracie
Nickname: Gray
Similar Names: Gardner, Garner, Garrison, Garritt, Geoffry, Graydon, Grayham
➡ Originated as a surname that was occasionally used in 1881, then disappeared for more than 100 years, before resurfacing again in 1984. Dick Grayson, the fictional hero in "DC Comics Universe," better known as Bruce Wayne's ward, Robin, is a bearer of the surname. Also the title of a 2004 film based on the same fictional character.

Gr ⇒ boys' names

Gregory   Rank: 208
Origin: Greek
Meaning: Watchful, vigilant
Alternate Spellings:
Greggory, Gregori
Gender Variation: Gregoria
Nicknames: Greg, Gregor
Similar Names: Greg, Gregor, Gregorio, Grenville, Greville, Grey, Grigor, Grigorios
Namesakes: Gregg Allman (musician), Greg Kinnear (actor), Greg LeMond (championship cyclist)
⇒ Derived from the Greek name Gregorios that was ultimately derived from *gregoros*. A common name among popes and saints that was only moderately used until actor Gregory Peck, born Eldred Gregory Peck, appeared in his first Academy Award-nominated film in 1944. Fictional character Greg Brady, from the television classic *The Brady Bunch*, brought much attention to the name's short form. Gregor is popular in Scotland.

Griffin   Rank: 254
Origin: MIddle English
Meaning: Griffin
Alternate Spellings:
Griffen, Griffon, Gryffen
Gender Variation: Griselda
Nickname: Griff
Similar Names: Garrett, Goddard, Godfrey, Greyson, Griffith, Grover
Namesakes: Alfredo Griffin (Dominican baseball player), Eddie Griffin (actor), Griffin Dunne (actor)
⇒ A form of *griffon* or *gryphon*, which is a mythical animal with the head and wings of an eagle and the body of a lion. A common surname used sporadically as a given name until the 1980s.

Guadalupe   Rank: 921
Origin: Spanish
Meaning: Our Lady of Guadalupe
Gender Variations:
Guadalupe, Lupita
Nickname: Lupe
Similar Names: Gaspar, Geraldo, Gerardo, Gervasio, Gregorio, Guillermo, Gustavo
⇒ Our Lady of Guadalupe is a popular religious and cultural image that originated from a Spanish title for the Virgin Mary.

The patron saint of Mexico, her feast day in December celebrates the account of her appearances to a native Mexican during the 16th century. Also a place name for a town located near Phoenix, Arizona. Popularity has recently faded for boys more than likely due to increased usage for girls. Ranks among the top 300 girls' names.

Guillermo   Rank: 440
Origin: German
Meaning: Protector with a strong will
Gender Variation: Guillema
Similar Names: Geraldo, Gerardo, German, Gilberto, Giermo, Gonzalo, Guillelmo
Namesake: Guillermo Canas (Argentine tennis player)
⇒ A variation of Guillaume and William and the name of several saints. Used steadily since the 1920s and is popular among Spanish-speaking countries.

Gunnar   Rank: 502
Origin: German
Meaning: Bold warrior
Alternate Spelling: Gunner
Gender Variations: Gaynor, Guinevere
Nickname: Gunne
Similar Names: Gundahar, Gunder, Gunter, Gunthar, Guntharius
Namesake: Ole Gunnar Solskjaer (Norwegian soccer player)
⇒ The Scandinavian form of Gunther, known as the legendary king of the Burgundians and the husband of the Icelandic queen Brynhild. The name has climbed steadily since 1991 and is among the top five names in Iceland.

Gustavo   Rank: 305
Origin: German
Meaning: Staff of the Goths
Alternate Spelling: Gustovo
Gender Variations: Gusta, Gustava
Nickname: Gus
Similar Names: Guido, Gustabo, Gustaf, Gustav, Gustavus
Namesake: Gustavo Kuerten (Brazilian tennis player), Gustavo Santaolalla (Argentine musician)
⇒ The Italian, Spanish, and Portuguese form of Gustav that debuted on the popularity

chart in 1935, faded until 1946, and climbed to its current position today.

Guy
Rank: 989
Origin: Old German
Meaning: Wood, wide
Gender Variation: Gytha
Similar Names: Guido, Gunnar, Gunther, Gustav, Gyles
Namesakes: Guy Pearce (Australian actor)
➡️ An Old French name that was originally a short form of Germanic names beginning with the *widu* or *wid*. The name was brought into England by the Normans and became known as Gy or Guido. British film director Guy Ritchie, married to pop singer and actress Madonna, is a famous bearer. Also a vocabulary word that refers to a man or the members of a group regardless of sex.

Harley
Rank: 522
Origin: Old English
Meaning: Hare meadow
Alternate Spellings: Harlea, Harlee, Harleigh, Harly
Gender Variation: Harley
Similar Names: Hale, Harding, Hardy, Harlan, Hartley
➡️ A place name and surname linked with Harley-Davidson, the motorcycle manufacturer. Listed among the top 400 names for girls.

Harold
Rank: 652
Origin: Scandinavian
Meaning: Army-power
Alternate Spellings: Harald, Herald
Gender Variations: Harley, Harper
Nicknames: Hal, Harry
Similar Names: Garold, Haraldo, Harlan, Harper, Harrell, Herrick
Namesakes: Harold Pinter (playwright), Harold Ramis (actor/director/writer), Harold Robbins (novelist)
➡️ The name of several kings in Denmark, England, and Norway, including Harold II, the last Anglo-Saxon king of England, who was killed at the Battle of Hastings, which led to the Norman Conquest. A form of the Old Norse name Haraldr. Listed among the top 100 names from 1884 to 1966, but has faded from use in recent years.

Harrison
Rank: 232
Origin: Old English
Meaning: Son of Harry
Alternate Spelling: Harrisson
Gender Variations: Harriet, Harrietta, Hattie
Nicknames: Harris, Harry
Similar Names: Garrison, Hank, Harry, Heinrich, Henderson, Henry
Namesake: George Harrison (musician)
➡️ A surname used as a given name influenced during the 1800s by William Henry Harrison, the 9th U.S. president, and then by his grandson, Benjamin Harrison, the 23rd U.S. president. More recently influenced by *Star Wars* and *Indiana Jones* actor Harrison Ford.

Harry
Rank: 593
Origin: Old German
Meaning: Home ruler
Alternate Spellings: Harri, Harrie
Gender Variations: Harriett, Harrietta
Similar Names: Enrico, Enzo, Hal, Hank, Harris, Harrison, Henrik
Namesakes: Harry Hamlin (actor), Harry Truman (33rd U.S. president), Harry Houdini (magician), *When Harry Met Sally* (1989 film)
➡️ The medieval English variation of Henry and the shortened form of Harrison. The name peaked before the turn of the 20th century but has lasted due to its many namesakes. Known for Dirty Harry Callahan, the fictional police detective played by Clint Eastwood in the 1970s and 1980s. Another namesake, Prince Henry of Wales, commonly known as Prince Harry, is third in line to the British throne. J.K. Rowling's fictional wizard, Harry Potter, has also greatly influenced the name.

Hassan
Rank: 765
Origin: Arabic
Meaning: Beautifier, handsome
Alternate Spelling: Hasan
Gender Variation: Hana
Similar Names: Harun, Hashim, Hasim, Hatim, Hayfa, Haytham
Namesake: Hassan Jones (football player)
➡️ A royal name in Morocco and the name of the first grandson of the Islamic prophet Muhammad. It made its debut in 1971 and is preferred by Arabic parents. Mount Hasan is an inactive volcano located in Turkey.

Hayden   Rank: 73

Origin: Old English
Meaning: Hay valley
Alternate Spellings:
Haden, Hadon, Haydan,
Haydn, Haydon, Heiden
Gender Variations: Hayden, Hayley
Similar Names: Hardy, Harlan, Harry, Haven
Namesakes: Hayden Desser (Canadian
singer/songwriter), Hayden Fox (*Coach* TV
character)
⇨ A surname first given in honor of Austrian
classical music composer Joseph Haydn
during the 18th century. Possibly influenced
by Canadian actor Hayden Christensen
who gained international attention playing
the young Anakin Skywalker in *Star Wars
Episode II: Attack of the Clones* and *Star
Wars Episode III: Revenge of the Sith*.
Also used as a girl's name.

Heath   Rank: 786

Origin: Old English
Meaning: Heath
Gender Variation: Heather
Similar Names: Hank, Henry,
Herb, Hollis, Hoyt, Hyatt
⇨ A place name for someone who lived on
a section of uncultivated land. The name
has been popular since 1966, influenced by
fictional character Heath Barkley, played by
actor Lee Majors, on the television Western
The Big Valley. It's best-known today for
Australian actor Heath Ledger, born
Heathcliff Andrew Ledger.

Hector   Rank: 175

Origin: Greek
Meaning: Holding fast
Alternate Spelling: Hecktor
Gender Variation: Victoria
Nicknames: Ector, Heck
Similar Names: Ettore, Heitor, Helio, Heraclio,
Herbert, Homer, Hubert, Hugo
Namesakes: Hector Berlioz (French
composer), Hector Elizondo (actor)
⇨ Derived from Hecktor, the name of a
legendary Trojan War hero killed by Achilles .
in Greek mythology. Also a literary name
for a fictional character in the Shakespearean
tragedy, *Troilus and Cressida*. It peaked at
No. 156 during the 1990s and is a favorite
in Spain.

Henry   Rank: 95

Origin: Old German
Meaning: Home ruler
Alternate Spellings:
Henri, Henrie
Gender Variations: Harriet, Henrietta,
Henriette
Similar Names: Enrico, Enrique, Enzo, Hal,
Hank, Heinrich, Hendrick, Henrik
Namesakes: Henri Matisse (artist), Henry
David Thoreau (author), Henry Fonda (actor),
Henry Ford (automaker), Henry James
(author), Henry Wadsworth Longfellow (poet)
⇨ A popular royal name used by six kings of
France and eight kings of England, including
the infamous King Henry VIII. Prince Henry,
third in line to the British throne and often
referred to as Harry, is a current namesake.
Also considered a literary name used by
Shakespeare in a series of historical plays. It
peaked prior to the turn of the 20th century but
remains in steady use. Enzo is the Italian form.

Hezekiah   Rank: 885

Origin: Hebrew
Meaning: God gives strength
Gender Variations: Hazel,
Hester
Similar Names: Hershel, Heskel, Hezeki,
Hezron, Hizkiah
⇨ Derived from the Hebrew name
Chizqiyahu associated with a king of Judah
and an ancestor of the prophet Zephaniah.
The name was in use during the turn of
the 20th century, then faded in 1924 and
reappeared again in 2006 as part of a biblical
naming trend.

Holden   Rank: 384

Origin: English
Meaning: From the hollow
in the valley
Alternate Spellings:
Holdan, Holdin, Holdyn
Gender Variations: Holly, Hope
Similar Names: Hampton, Harding, Harlen,
Harley, Hartford, Holman, Houston, Howard
⇨ Originally a place name and surname
widely known for actor William Holden, born
William Franklin Beedle Jr., whose career
spanned more than four decades. Literary
teenage character Holden Caulfield from the
1951 critically acclaimed J.D. Salinger novel,
The Catcher in the Rye, also comes to mind.

Houston
Rank: 837

Origin: Irish Gaelic
Meaning: Hill town
Gender Variations: Hope
Similar Names: Hubert, Hugh, Hugo, Hume

➡ A place name for the largest city in the state of Texas, named for Sam Houston, a 19th-century lawyer and politician, who served as president of the Republic of Texas, senator after it joined the Union, and governor. Used steadily as a given name from 1880 to 1958, and sporadically after 1959.

Howard
Rank: 836

Origin: Old English
Meaning: Noble watchman
Gender Variation: Hope
Nicknames: Howe, Howie
Similar Names: Holden, Hollis, Homer, Horace, Howell, Hoyt
Namesakes: Howard Cunningham (*Happy Days* TV character), Howard Keel (actor), *Howard the Duck* (1986 film), Ron Howard (actor/director)

➡ Originated as an surname for an English noble family. Notable for Oliver Otis Howard, a civil war officer and founder of Howard University. Also influenced by millionaire Howard Hughes, who became a manufacturer, aviator, and film producer during his lifetime. Listed among the top 100 names during the first half of the 20th century, the name has recently lost favor with parents.

Hudson
Rank: 249

Origin: Old English
Meaning: Son of Hudd
Gender Variation: Adison
Nickname: Hud
Similar Names: Hadley, Hanson, Hubert, Hugh, Hugo, Hunter, Hutton

➡ Surname derived from the medieval personal name Hudde, that's also considered a pet form of Hugh and Richard. Henry Hudson, the English navigator and explorer, is a namesake. A North American bay, river, and strait are named in his honor. Widely known for film and television actor Rock Hudson.

Hugh
Rank: 994

Origin: Old German
Meaning: Heart, mind, or spirit
Alternate Spellings: New, Newe
Gender Variations: Hughette, Hughina
Nickname: Hughie
Similar Names: Hewett, Howe, Hubert, Hudson, Hughes, Hugo
Namesakes: Hugh Hefner (magazine publisher), Hugh Laurie (actor)

➡ Introduced by the Normans into England during the Middle Ages, which led to surnames such as Howe, Howse, and Hughes. It peaked prior to the turn of the 20th century, but British actor Hugh Grant and Australian actor and film producer Hugh Jackman continue to keep the name in front of the public.

Hugo
Rank: 371

Origin: Latin
Meaning: Bright mind
Gender Variation: Huguette
Similar Names: Hudson, Huey, Hugh, Hughie, Keegan, Owen, Tyrone
Namesake: Hugo Weaving (English-Australian actor)

➡ A variation of Hugh that peaked prior to 1900, but still remains in use today. French novelist Victor Hugo, the author of *The Hunchback of Notre Dame* and *Les Miserables*, is a famous bearer of the surname.

Hunter
Rank: 54

Origin: Old English
Meaning: Hunter
Gender Variation: Hunter
Similar Names: Huntley, Mason, Palmer, Parker, Tanner
Namesakes: Charlie Hunter (musician), *Hunter* (TV series)

➡ An occupational surname given to someone who hunts that was known during the 1950s for actor and singer Tab Hunter. Journalist and author Hunter S. Thompson, known for creating "gonzo journalism," is another famous bearer. Occasionally used as a girl's name.

Ian
Rank: 81

Origin: Hebrew
Meaning: God is gracious
Alternate Spellings: Ean, Eion, Eon, Iain, Iann, Ion
Gender Variation: Ianna
Similar Names: Evan, Ewan, Ivan, John, Sian
Namesakes: Ian Anderson (musician), Ian Astbury (musician)
⇒ The Celtic form of John that first appeared in the U.S. in 1935 and rose to the top 100 in 1982. British novelist Ian Fleming, who created the fictional character James Bond, is a namesake. It was influenced during the 1990s by actor Ian Ziering of *Beverly Hills, 90210* fame.

Ibrahim
Rank: 594

Origin: Hebrew
Meaning: Father of a multitude
Alternate Spellings: Ebrahim, Ibraheem
Gender Variation: Abrahana
Similar Names: Abijah, Abram, Abraham, Avraham, Avram, Ithamar, Ithiel
⇒ The Arabic and Turkish form of Abraham that has climbed in popularity since 1990 following a biblical naming trend.

Ignacio
Rank: 703

Origin: Latin
Meaning: Fire
Gender Variations: Ignacia
Nickname: Nacio
Similar Names: Igacio, Ignaas, Ignace, Ignacy, Ignatius, Ignazio, Inacio
⇒ The Spanish form of the Roman family name Ignatius. Up and down in popularity, the name peaked in 1930 at No. 499. The name ranks highly with parents in Chile and Spain.

Imanol
Rank: 969

Origin: Hebrew
Meaning: God is with us
Gender Variations: Emanuelle, Manoela, Manola
Similar Names: Emanuel, Manel, Manny, Manoel, Manolo, Manuel
Namesake: Imanol Landeta (Mexican singer/actor)
⇒ The Basque form of Emmanuel referring to Jesus, whose coming is prophesied in the Old Testament. The name first appeared on the popularity chart in 2001 and disappeared until 2006 as part of a biblical naming trend.

Irvin
Rank: 670

Origin: Old English
Meaning: Sea friend
Alternate Spellings: Earvin, Ervin, Irvine, Irvyn
Gender Variations: Iris, Irma
Nickname: Irv
Similar Names: Erskine, Ira, Irving, Irwin, Isaac, Isaiah
Namesake: Michael Irvin (Football Hall of Famer)
⇒ A popular variation of Irving and Irwin derived from a Scottish place name. Basketball Hall of Famer Earvin "Magic" Johnson Jr. uses a form of the name. The name peaked prior to the turn of the 20th century.

Irving
Rank: (not listed)

Origin: Celtic
Meaning: Handsome, fair
Alternate Spelling: Erving
Gender Variation: Irma
Nickname: Irv
Similar Names: Erwin, Irvine, Isaac, Isaiah, Iser, Israel
Namesakes: John Irving (author), Irving Wallace (author), Washington Irving (author)
⇒ A Scottish place name used as a given name starting in the mid-19th century. Best known for famed composer Irving Berlin, born Israel Isidore Baline, whose name was misprinted as "I. Berlin" on the sheet music of his first song, which prompted the change in his name. He composed more than 3,000 songs including "Alexander's Ragtime Band," "God Bless America," and "White Christmas," one of the most-recorded songs in history. The name peaked in 1911 and has faded in popularity.

Isaac
Rank: 48

Origin: Hebrew
Meaning: He laughs
Alternate Spellings: Isaak, Isac, Isak, Issac, Izaac, Izaak, Izak
Gender Variation: Isabel
Nicknames: Ike, Zak
Similar Names: Ira, Irvin, Irving, Isaiah, Ishmael, Israel

Namesakes: Isaac Asimov (science fiction writer), Isaac Hayes (composer)
⇒ The son of Abraham and father of Esau and Jacob in the Old Testament. Popular during the 18th and 19th centuries known for Isaac Burns Murphy, who became the first jockey to win three Kentucky Derbies during the late 19th century. Other notable bearers include famed violinist Isaac Stern and English mathematician Sir Isaac Newton. Preferred by Jewish parents.

Isai
Rank: 706

Origin: Hebrew
Meaning: Salvation of God
Alternate Spelling: Isay
Gender Variation: Isadora
Similar Names: Esa, Isai, Isaiah, Isaias, Israel, Issur
⇒ The shortened form of Isaiah that first came into vogue in 1995 following a biblical naming trend.

Isaiah
Rank: 40
Origin: Hebrew
Meaning: Salvation of God
Alternate Spellings: Isaia, Isiah, Izaiah, Izayah
Gender Variation: Isadora
Nickname: Isai
Similar Names: Elisha, Esa, Ike, Isaias, Jeremiah, Josiah
⇒ A prophet in the Old Testament and the author of the book of Isaiah. The name has steadily increased in popularity since 1968 and is best known for former *Grey's Anatomy* star Isaiah Washington. Basketball star Isiah Thomas uses an alternate spelling of the name.

Isaias
Rank: 531
Origin: Hebrew
Meaning: Salvation of God
Gender Variation: Isabella
Nickname: Isai
Similar Names: Esa, Isaac, Isai, Isaiah, Iser, Israel
⇒ A variation of Isaiah that has slowly climbed the chart since 1980 along with other biblical names.

Ismael
Rank: 327

Origin: Hebrew/Arabic
Meaning: God hears
Alternate Spellings: Esmail, Ishmael, Ishmeil, Ismail
Gender Variations: Isobel, Isolde
Similar Names: Ichabod, Isaac, Isaiah, Ishmael, Israel
⇒ The Spanish form of Ishmael, the biblical name for the eldest son of Abraham and his wife's handmaiden, Hagar. He's later referred to as the patriarch of the Arabs. Also used in literature for the narrator of the 1851 novel, *Moby-Dick*, by Herman Melville, who refers to himself as "Ishmael" in the first line of the book.

Israel
Rank: 203

Origin: Hebrew
Meaning: God perseveres
Alternate Spellings: Isreal, Izrael, Izreal
Gender Variations: Isidora, Isla
Nickname: Izzy
Similar Names: Ira, Irvin, Irving, Isaac, Isaiah, Ishmael, Jacob
Namesakes: Israel Horovitz (playwright/screenwriter), Israel Houghton (musician)
⇒ Derived from the Hebrew *Yisrael* for the country in southwest Asia that borders on the Mediterranean Sea. In the Old Testament, God changed Jacob's name to Israel as a blessing. His ancestors became God's chosen people and were called Israelites. The name has risen in popularity due to a biblical naming trend.

Ivan
Rank: 127

Origin: Hebrew
Meaning: God is gracious
Gender Variations: Jeannie, Joana, Iva, Ivanna, Ivica, Vanna
Similar Names: Evan, Ian, Ira, Jack, John, Jovan, Shawn
Namesakes: Ivan Lendl (Czech tennis player), Ivan Turgenev (Russian novelist)
⇒ A variation of John in several countries, including Russia, Bulgaria, and Slovenia. The name of several Bulgarian and Russian tsars. Two Russian rulers, Ivan III, known as Ivan the Great, and Ivan IV, known as Ivan the Terrible, are famous bearers of the name.

Jace   Rank: 187

Origin: American
Alternate Spellings: Jaice, Jase, Jayce, Jayse
Gender Variations: Jaci, Jackie
Nickname: Jacey
Similar Names: Jack, Jake, Jason, Jay
⇒ A modern created name that can also be used as the short form of Jason.

Jack   Rank: 35

Origin: Hebrew
Meaning: God is gracious
Alternate Spellings: Jac, Jak
Gender Variations: Jackie, Jacqueline
Nicknames: Jackie, John
Similar Names: Jace, Jackson, Jacob, Jacobus, Jake, Jock
Namesakes: Jack Kerouac (author), Jack Lambert (Hall of Fame Hockey player), Jack Nicklaus (golfer)
⇒ A variation of the Hebrew name John. U.S. president John F. Kennedy was one of the more notable people who used Jack as a nickname. Other famous bearers include actor Jack Nicholson and novelist Jack London. The name climbed into the top 100 in 1996 and into the top 50 in 2000.

Jackson   Rank: 36

Origin: Old English
Meaning: Son of Jack
Alternate Spellings: Jacson, Jacksyn, Jakson, Jaxon, Jaxson
Gender Variations: Jacklyn, Jacquetta
Nicknames: Jack, Jackie, Jax
Similar Names: Jake, Jarrod, Jason, Johnson
Namesakes: Alan Jackson (musician), Bo Jackson (baseball/football player), Jackson Browne (musician), Michael Jackson (musician), Randy Jackson (*American Idol* judge), Samuel L. Jackson (actor)
⇒ Originated as a surname often given in honor of U.S. president Andrew Jackson or Confederate general Thomas "Stonewall" Jackson. It's been listed among the 100 most popular names since 1998 and the top 50 since 2004. American painter Jackson Pollock, considered one of the leaders in Abstract Expressionism, is a namesake. The story of his life was captured in the 2000 film *Pollock*. Also a place name for the state capital of Mississippi.

Jacob   Rank: 1

Origin: Hebrew
Meaning: Holder of the heel
Alternate Spellings: Jacobe, Jakob
Gender Variations: Jacoba, Jacobina
Nicknames: Jake, Jay
Similar Names: Jack, Jacobus, Jacoby, Jacomus, James
Namesake: Jacob Marley (*A Christmas Carol* character)
⇒ Jacob has come in and out of vogue for more than 100 years. It landed at No. 1 for the first time in 1999, knocking Michael off the top after 38 years. In the Old Testament, Jacob was born holding his twin brother Esau's heel. Namesake Jacob Grimm, the German linguist and writer, was the author of *Grimm's Fairy Tales* with his brother, Wilhelm. Jacobus is the Latin form of the name.

Jaden   Rank: 88

Origin: American
Alternate Spellings: Jadon, Jadyn, Jaeden, Jaedon, Jaiden, Jaidon, Jaidyn, Jayden, Jaydin, Jaydon
Gender Variations: Jada, Jade, Jadyn
Nickname: Jay
Similar Names: Aiden, Braiden, Jace, Jake, Jalen, Kaiden
⇒ A combination of the names Jay and Aiden that's seen a sudden burst of popularity during the past 10 years. A notable bearer is the son of Will Smith and Jada Pinkett Smith, who appeared with his dad in the 2006 film, *The Pursuit of Happyness*. A unisex name.

Jaime   Rank: 279

Origin: Hebrew
Alternate Spellings: Haime, Jaimee, Jaimey, Jaimie
Gender Variation: Jaime
Similar Names: Jacob, James, Jamie, Jermaine, Jerome, Jimmy
⇒ The Spanish and Portuguese form of James used in the U.S. since the 1940s. The name peaked in 1976 at No. 169. It's occasionally used as a girl's name, which may increase with the popularity of actresses Jaime King and Jaime Pressly.

Jair
Rank: 726

Origin: Hebrew
Meaning: He shines
Gender Variation: Jaira
Similar Names: Jabez, Jabin, Jael, Jahleel, Jairo, Jairus, Jamin, Jared
➡ A common biblical name for a judge of Israel and a descendant of Manasseh, both mentioned in the Old Testament. Possibly influenced by Jair Lynch, who became the first African-American male gymnast to medal at an Olympics. He earned the silver medal on the parallel bars in 1996, the same year the name debuted on the popularity chart.

Jake
Rank: 107

Origin: Hebrew
Gender Variation: Jackie
Similar Names: Jace, Jacey, Jack, Jacob, Jacobus, Jay
➡ The short form of Jacob influenced in Great Britain by singer-songwriter John Philip "Jake" Thackray, who produced seven albums between 1967 and 1991. In the U.S., the name has flirted around the top 100 since 1997 associated with actor Jake Gyllenhaal, who landed his first major film role in the 2001 cult hit *Donnie Darko*.

Jamal
Rank: 504

Origin: Arabic
Meaning: Beauty
Alternate Spellings: Jahmal, Jamaal, Jamael, Jamahl, Jamall, Jammal
Gender Variation: Jamila
Similar Names: Gamal, Gamali, Jamar, James, Jameson, Jamie
Namesake: Jamal Lewis (football player)
➡ Derived from Jamula, which means "to be handsome or good-looking." The name of the first Egyptian president, Jamal Abd al-Nasir, who created the United Arab Republic (UAR) between the republics of Egypt and Syria. Today more closely linked with actor Malcolm-Jamal Warner of *The Cosby Show* fame. The name has been in use in the U.S. since 1968.

Jamarcus
Rank: 914

Origin: American
Gender Variations: Marcia, Marcy
Nicknames: Jamar, Marcus
Similar Names: Jamar, Jamari, Jamarion, Marcus, Mark, Markell
➡ An invented name that blends "ja" with the name "Marcus" The name has been used sporadically since 1988 and reappeared on the chart in 2006, possibly influenced by football quarterback JaMarcus Russell, the No. 1 NFL draft pick for 2007.

James
Rank: 16

Origin: Hebrew/Latin
Meaning: Supplanter
Alternate Spelling: Jaymes
Gender Variations: Jamelia, Jamell, Jamesina, Jametta, Jamila, Jamille
Nicknames: Jamie, Jim, Jimmy
Similar Names: Jacobus, Jaime, Jameson, Jaques, Jay, Seamus
Namesakes: James Dean (actor), James Gandolfini (actor), James Spader (actor), James Taylor (musician), Jimmy Stewart (actor), LeBron James (basketball player)
➡ The English form of the Late Latin Jacomus derived from *Iakobos*. A biblical name for two apostles of Jesus. It grew rapidly in popularity when James Stuart ascended the throne of England in 1602. Listed among the top five names for 100 years, it faded in 1981, yet stayed within the top 20. Six presidents are also among the namesakes.

Jameson
Rank: 424

Origin: Old English
Meaning: Son of James
Alternate Spellings: Jaimison, Jamieson, Jamison
Gender Variation: Jamesina
Nicknames: James, Jamie
Similar Names: Jackson, Jacobus, Jamar, Jamarcus
➡ A surname that originated from a personal name. It peaked at No. 415 in 1985.

Jaquan
Rank: 656

Origin: American
Gender Variation: Jaqueline
Nickname: Jay
Similar Names: Daquan, Jaiden, Jaques, Jaylen, Jayson, Jaxon, Joaquin
➡ A created name that blends the elements "ja" and "quan" that first became popular in 1988.

Jared   Rank: 137

Origin: Hebrew
Meaning: Descending
Alternate Spellings:
Jarod, Jarred, Jarrid,
Jarrod, Jerad, Jered, Jerred, Jerrid, Jerrod
Gender Variation: Jayda
Similar Names: Jareth, Jarrett, Jerald,
Jerome, Jordan
Namesakes: Jared Harris (British actor),
Jared Martin (actor), Jared Padalecki (actor)
⇒ The biblical name for the father of Enoch
and the grandfather of Methuselah. It
jumped in popularity during the 1960s
because of fictional character Jarrod Barkley
on the TV western *Big Valley*. The name
peaked at No. 51 in 1998 and is associated
today with actor and musician Jared Leto.

Jaron   Rank: 819

Origin: American
Alternate Spellings:
Jaran, Jaren, Jarran,
Jarren, Jarrin, Jeran, Jeren,
Jerren, Jerrin, Jerron
Gender Variation: Janna
Similar Names: Aidan, Jaden, Javon, Yaron
⇒ A modern blend of Jared and Darren
popular since the mid-1970s. A good choice
for parents who are looking for a creative
name with numerous spelling options.

Jarrett   Rank: 659

Origin: German
Meaning: Rule of the
spear
Alternate Spellings: Jaratt,
Jarett, Jarratt, Jarret, Jerett,
Jerrett, Jerrot
Gender Variations: Geraldine, Jeri
Similar Names: Garrett, Gearalt, Geraldo,
Jared, Jerald, Jerard, Jerry
Namesakes: Dale Jarrett (NASCAR driver),
Keith Jarrett (pianist), Ned Jarrett (NASCAR
driver)
⇒ A surname and variation of Garrett used
sporadically during the late 19th century.
The name dropped out of sight in 1900 and
reappeared again in 1966.

Jarvis   Rank: 1,000

Origin: Old English
Meaning: Driver, a
conqueror
Gender Variation: Gervaise
Nicknames: Jarvey, Jary
Similar Names: Gervase, Gervasio, Gervasius,
Jarvell, Jervey, Jervis
Namesake: Jarvis Cocker (English musician)
⇒ A surname that originated from the given
name Gervaise. Used sporadically until the
1950s when parents started picking it up on
a regular basis. Rarely used today.

Jasiah   Rank: 933

Origin: American
Alternate Spelling: Jesiah
Gender Variation: Asiah
Similar Names: Isiah, Jediah, Jeriah,
Josiah, Josias
⇒ An invented name similar to Isiah, Josiah,
Jeriah, and Jediah that made its debut on
the popularity chart in 2006.

Jason   Rank: 55

Origin: Greek
Meaning: Healer
Alternate Spellings:
Jacen, Jaisen, Jaison, Jasen,
Jasin, Jasun, Jaysen, Jayson
Gender Variation: Jaslyn
Nicknames: Jase, Jay
Similar Names: Jared, Jeremiah, Jeremy,
Jerome, Jerry, Joshua
Namesakes: Jason Alexander (actor),
Jason Lee (actor), Jason Patric (actor),
Jason Priestley (actor)
⇒ In the New Testament, Jason was
converted to Christianity by Paul and Silas.
In Greek mythology he was the leader of
the Argonauts. Infamously known for Jason
Vorhees, the main character in the *Friday the
13th* horror films. A top 100 name since 1966.

Jasper   Rank: 568

Origin: Persian
Meaning: Treasurer
Alternate Spellings:
Jaspar, Jespar
Gender Variation: Jasmine
Similar Names: Gaspar, Jaser, Jason,
Jesper, Kaspar

Namesakes: Jasper Carrott (British comedian), Jasper Conran (English fashion designer), Jasper Johns (artist)
➡ In Christianity the name of one of the three kings, also known as the three Magi, who brought gifts to the newborn Christ child. Also the name of a gemstone that comes in a variety of colors. The name peaked prior to the turn of the century when gemstone names were popular, and it appears to be on the rise again.

Javier
Rank: 162

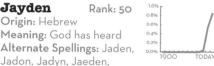

Origin: Portuguese/Spanish
Meaning: New house
Alternate Spellings: Xaviar, Xavier, Xavior, Xzavier, Zavier
Gender Variations: Xavia, Xaviera, Zavier
Similar Names: Jarvis, Javan, Jay, Jayden, Xaverius
➡ The Spanish form of Xavier predominantly used since 1940. The name peaked in 1991 and again in 2001 at No. 149.

Javon
Rank: 410

Origin: American
Alternate Spellings: Javan, Javen, Javonne, Jevan, Jevon
Gender Variation: Javonna
Similar Names: Jabez, Janale, Jared, Jason, Jazz
➡ A modern combination of "ja" and "von" that's become a favorite with African-American families since 1976.

Jay
Rank: 351

Origin: Latin
Meaning: Happy
Alternate Spellings: Jae, Jai, Jaye
Gender Variations: Jaya, Jayne
Similar Names: Jake, Jason, Jayce, Jayden, Jaylen
Namesakes: Jay McInerney (author), Jay-Z (hip-hop artist)
➡ The short form of Jason, Jacob, Jayden, and other names beginning with the letter "J." Possibly derived from the Latin name Gaius. Also an Indian name meaning "victory" in Sanskrit. Used as an independent name for more than 125 years. Talk show host and comedian Jay Leno is a recent bearer.

Jayden
Rank: 50

Origin: Hebrew
Meaning: God has heard
Alternate Spellings: Jaden, Jadon, Jadyn, Jaeden, Jaedon, Jaiden, Jaidon, Jaydin, Jaydon
Gender Variations: Jada, Jade, Jayden
Nickname: Jay
Similar Names: Aden, Cade, Jacob, Jason, Jaylen, Kaden, Payton
Namesake: Jadon Lavik (musician)
➡ A form of Jadon, a biblical figure from the Old Testament. It entered the top 100 in 2003. The name of the second son of Britney Spears and Kevin Federline. Also popular as a girl's name.

Jaylen
Rank: 191

Origin: American
Alternate Spellings: Jalen, Jalon, Jaylan, Jaylin, Jaylon
Gender Variations: Jalene, Jaylyn
Nickname: Jay
Similar Names: Jadon, Jamie, Jaquan, Jared, Jaron, Jason, Javen, Waylon
Namesakes: Jalen Rose (basketball player)
➡ A variation of Jalen and a modern blend of two short names, Jay and Len. It's climbed quickly up the popularity chart since 1993 preferred by parents with its "y" in the middle spelling. Also used as a girl's name.

Jean
Rank: 721

Origin: Hebrew
Meaning: God is gracious
Gender Variations: Hana, Jeane, Jeanelle, Jeannine, Johanna
Similar Names: Evan, Gianni, Giovanni, Johann, John, Sean
Namesakes: Jean-Luc Picard (*Star Trek* character), Jean Reno (French actor), Jean-Claude Van Damme (actor)
➡ A form of the Old French name Johannes, which is a variation of the Hebrew name John. Often seen hyphenated in true French flavor such as the philosopher Jean-Paul Sartre. The name received much of its popularity in Scotland during the Middle Ages. It peaked in 1928 at No. 307 and appears to be making a comeback.

Jefferson   Rank: 642

Origin: Old English
Meaning: Son of Jeffrey
Alternate Spelling: Jepherson
Gender Variation: Jennifer
Nicknames: Jeff, Jeffrey
Similar Names: Godfrey, Gottfried, Jeffery, Jeffers, Jepson
Namesakes: Jefferson Airplane (rock band), *The Jeffersons* (television series), William Jefferson Clinton (42nd U.S. president)
⇨ A surname primarily known for Thomas Jefferson, the 3rd U.S. president and principal author of the Declaration of Independence, and Jefferson Davis, who served as president of the Confederate States during the Civil War. The name peaked prior to the turn of the 20th century and is still listed among the top 700 names.

Jeffrey   Rank: 180

Origin: Old German
Meaning: Peace
Alternate Spellings: Geffrey, Geoffery, Geoffrey, Geoffry, Geofrey, Jeffery, Jeffree, Jeffrie, Jeffry
Gender Variation: Jenny
Nicknames: Jeff, Jeffy
Similar Names: Godfrey, Gottfried, Jeff, Jefferson, Jepson
Namesakes: Jeff Bezos (amazon.com founder), Jeff Bridges (actor), Jeff Foxworthy (comedian/actor), Jeff Gordon (NASCAR driver)
⇨ A variation of the name Geoffrey that was introduced by the Normans into England during the 11th century, which led to several popular surnames such as Jeffries and Jefferson. It first appeared as "Jeffrey" during the Middle Ages, now the most common form in the U.S. It spent four years among the top 10 during the 1960s.

Jeremiah   Rank: 71

Origin: Hebrew
Meaning: God will uplift
Alternate Spellings: Jeramiah, Jeremia, Jeremieh, Jerimiah
Gender Variations: Jemima, Jemma, Jerri
Nickname: Jerry
Similar Names: Jem, Jeremias, Jeremy, Jermaine, Jerome, Jerry, Jorma

⇨ A major prophet in the Old Testament and the author of the books of *Jeremiah* and *Lamentations*. Also a 1972 film starring Robert Redford in the lead role as *Jeremiah Johnson*. The name has gone in and out of popularity during the last 125 years and is currently at its peak.

Jeremy   Rank: 123

Origin: Hebrew
Meaning: Exalted by God
Alternate Spellings: Jeramee, Jeramey, Jeramy, Jeremey, Jeremie, Jeromy
Gender Variation: Jeri
Nickname: Jerry
Similar Names: Jermaine, Jeremiah, Jeremias, Jerome
Namesakes: *Jeremy* (1992 Pearl Jam song), Jeremy Irons (English actor)
⇨ The English form of Jeremiah, which can be found in some versions of the New Testament. The name took a huge jump in popularity in 1970, influenced by the character Jeremy Bolt in the television series, *Here Come the Brides*. It peaked at No. 14 in 1976, but still remains a favorite among parents today.

Jermaine   Rank: 474

Origin: Latin
Meaning: Brother
Alternate Spellings: Germain, Germaine, Germayne, Jermain, Jermane, Jermayne
Gender Variation: Jessamine
Nickname: Jerry
Similar Names: German, Jerome, Jerrard, Jerrauld, Jerrelle
Namesakes: Jermain Taylor (boxing champion), Jermaine Dupri (record producer/rapper)
⇨ A form of Germaine, best-known for singer Jermaine Jackson, former member of the Jackson Five, who embarked on a successful solo career during the 1970s and converted to Islam and changed his name to Muhammad Abdul Aziz in the 1980s.

Jerome   Rank: 577

Origin: Latin
Meaning: Sacred name
Alternate Spelling: Gerome
Gender Variation: Jerrie
Nicknames: Jerry

Similar Names: Jered, Jeremiah, Jeremy, Jermaine, Jeronimo, Jerrone
Namesakes: Jerome Bettis (football player), Jerome Robbins (choreographer)
➡ Historically known for Saint Jerome, a 4th-century Christian apologist, who translated the Bible from Greek and Hebrew into Latin. English novelist Jerome K. Jerome brought attention to the name in 1889 with the publication of *Three Men in a Boat*. It was further influenced by Jerome Kern, a prolific songwriter of both Broadway musicals and films during the 1920s, 1930s, and 1940s. The name peaked during this time.

Jerry
Rank: 318

Origin: Hebrew
Meaning: Exalted by God, strong with a spear
Alternate Spellings: Geri, Gerry, Jere, Jeri, Jerie, Jerri
Gender Variation: Gerri
Similar Names: Gerald, Geraldo, Gerard, Gerhart, Jarett, Jeremiah, Jeremy, Jerome
Namesakes: Jerry Garcia (singer/guitarist), Jerry Lee Lewis (musician), *Tom and Jerry* (animated series)
➡ Short form of Jeremy, Gerald, and other names beginning with "Jer" or "Ger." Used as an independent name since before the turn of the 20th century. Influenced by comedian and actor Jerry Lewis, who began his career as Dean Martin's partner during the 1940s. Actor and comedian Jerry Seinfeld has kept the name in front of parents more recently.

Jesse
Rank: 102

Origin: Hebrew
Meaning: God's gift
Alternate Spellings: Jessie, Jessey, Jessy
Gender Variations: Jessalyn, Jessamine, Jesse, Jessica
Nickname: Jess
Similar Names: Jessiah, Jethro, Joshua, Joss
Namesakes: Jesse Colin Young (musician), Jesse Jackson (politician), Jesse James (*Monster Garage* TV series), Jesse McCartney (musician)
➡ The father of King David in the Old Testament and infamously known for outlaw Jesse James, who was killed in 1882. American track-and-field athlete Jesse Owens, the winner of four Olympic gold medals, is another famous bearer. Also used as a girl's name.

Jesus
Rank: 74

Origin: Hebrew
Meaning: The Saviour, God is salvation
Alternate Spelling: Jesous
Gender Variation: Jesse
Similar Names: Isa, Jesusa, Josh, Joshua, Josue, Josias
Namesake: Jesus Shuttlesworth (*He Got Game* television and film character)
➡ A variation of the name Joshua and the central figure of Christianity. The four Gospels of the New Testament recount his life and teachings. Character Jesus Martinez, from the 1980s television show, *Hill Street Blues*, comes to mind. A common name in Hispanic cultures although the pronunciation varies. Listed among the top 100 names since 1990 following a biblical naming trend.

Jett
Rank: 535

Origin: American
Alternate Spellings: Jet, Jette
Gender Variation: Jetta
Similar Names: Jann, Jase, Jaye, Jedd, Jiles, Jody, Judd, Jude
➡ A modern invented name taken from a velvety black mineral or an aircraft. Famed actor James Dean played fictional character Jett Rink in his last film, *Giant*. Actor John Travolta, known as an avid aviator, chose the name for his son.

Jimmy
Rank: 325

Origin: Hebrew/Latin
Meaning: Supplanter
Alternate Spelling: Jimmee, Jimmey, Jimmie
Gender Variations: Jamila, Jinny
Nickname: Jim
Similar Names: James, Jameson, Jamie, Jim, Joaquin, Johnny
Namesakes: Jimmy Connors (tennis player), Jimmy Fallon (comedian/actor), Jimmy Kimmel (comedian/talk show host),
➡ A pet form of James and Jim, also used as a name on its own. Former U.S. president Jimmy Carter is a famous bearer of the name. He was awarded the Nobel Peace Prize in 2002. Other notable bearers include actor Jimmy Stewart and musician Jimmy Buffett.

Joan   Rank: 978

Origin: Hebrew
Meaning: God is gracious
Gender Variations: Joan, Joana
Similar Names: Euan, Gian, Jan, Jean, Joe, John, Juan
⇒ The English form of Johanne and a variation of John used sporadically as a given name for boys since 1929, peaking in 2002 at No. 777. Typically considered a girl's name in the English language, it may have been influenced by parents in Catalonia and Spain where it ranks highly for boys.

Joaquin   Rank: 286

Origin: Hebrew
Meaning: God will establish
Alternate Spellings: Joacheim, Joachim, Joakim, Joaquim
Gender Variation: Joaquima
Similar Names: Jaime, Jeremias, Jesus, Jonas, Jose, Juan, Judas
⇒ A biblical name, possibly derived from Johoiachin, that's popular due to early Christians who believe Joaquim to be the father of the Virgin Mary. The name has recently taken a jump in popularity influenced by actor Joaquin Phoenix, who went by Leaf as a child. The name ranks highly in Chile and Spain. Joachim is the Spanish form.

Joe   Rank: 370

Origin: Hebrew
Meaning: The Lord is God
Gender Variations: Jo, Jobeth, Joetta, Johanna, Josephine, Josette
Similar Names: Joel, Joey, Jose, Joseph
Namesakes: Joe Frazier (boxer), Joe Montana (football player), Joe Namath (football player)
⇒ The short form of Joseph and Joel that paved the way for several female variations. The name is popular among athletes, including famed baseball player Joe DiMaggio and boxer Joe Louis. Parents have used the name independently for more than 125 years.

Joel   Rank: 124

Origin: Hebrew
Meaning: The Lord is God
Gender Variations: Jo, Joella, Joelle
Nicknames: Joe, Joey

Similar Names: Joachim, Job, John, Jonah
Namesakes: Joel Coen (director), Joel Siegel (film critic), Joel Silver (producer)
⇒ A minor prophet in the Old Testament and the author of the book of *Joel*. Actor Joel McCrea brought much attention to the name when he was cast in his first major role in 1929. More recently known as the surname of six-time Grammy Award-winner Billy Joel. The name is popular among Jewish families.

Joey   Rank: 537

Origin: Hebrew
Meaning: The Lord is God
Gender Variations: Joan, Joanna, Joanne, Joellen, JoJo, Josiane
Nickname: Joe
Similar Names: Barry, Jaden, Jay, Jody, Joel, Jory, Joseph
⇒ The pet form of Joseph and Joel but often used as an independent name. Matt LeBlanc brought attention to the name when he played Joey Tribbiani on the TV series *Friends* and the spin-off *Joey*. Also the title of seven films released between 1964 and 2004. Occasionally used as a girl's given name.

Johan   Rank: 528

Origin: Hebrew
Meaning: God is gracious
Alternate Spellings: Johann, Johanne
Gender Variations: Joan, Johanna
Similar Names: Iohann, Ion, Ivan, John, Jonas, Jovan
⇒ The Czech, Low German, and Scandinavian form of Johannes. The name has climbed the popularity chart since its debut in 1998. Parents may see it as a new twist on John. A unisex name. German supermodel and actress Heidi Klum and British singer and songwriter Seal have a son by this name.

John   Rank: 20

Origin: Hebrew
Meaning: God is gracious
Alternate Spelling: Jon
Gender Variations: Jane, Janet, Jean, Joan, Joanna, Juana, Vanna
Nicknames: Jack, Johnny
Similar Names: Ian, Jean, Johannes, Johnson, Jonas, Jovan, Juan, Sean, Van, Yanni

Namesakes: Elton John (musician), John Coltrane (jazz saxophonist/composer), John Lennon (musician), John Travolta (actor), John Wayne (actor)

➡ Quite possibly the most popular name in history. It's been given to kings, popes, saints, presidents, and heroes. Listed as the No. 1 name from 1880 to 1923, it stayed among the top 10 until 1986. It also carries great Christian significance and is known for both John the Baptist and one of Jesus' apostles. An impressive array of celebrities have assisted in keeping the name listed among the top 20.

Johnny
Rank: 237

Origin: Hebrew
Meaning: God is gracious
Alternate Spellings: Johnie, Johnnie, Johny, Jonney, Jonnie, Jonny
Gender Variations: Gianna, Hannie, Joni, Jonina
Nickname: John
Similar Names: Gianni, Hanne, John, Jonah, Jonathan
Namesakes: Johnny Carson (television host), Johnny Cash (musician), Johnny Sauter (NASCAR driver)

➡ A pet name for John used for both boys and girls. It reached the height of popularity during the 1940s. Actor Johnny Depp has brought worldwide attention to the name. Gianni is the Italian form.

Johnpaul
Rank: 979

Origin: American
Gender Variation: Jonina
Nicknames: John, Paul
Similar Names: Gianpaolo, Giovannipaolo

➡ A combination of the names John and Paul, possibly given in honor of Pope John Paul II, leader of the Roman Catholic church from 1978 to 2005.

Jonah
Rank: 170

Origin: Hebrew
Meaning: Dove
Alternate Spelling: Jona
Gender Variation: Jonie
Similar Names: Jacob, Jon, Jonas, Joshua, Jude

➡ In the Old Testament, the prophet who sailed out to sea to avoid following God's command. He was swallowed by a fish and finally spewed out on dry land after three days. Sailors have long since associated the name with someone who brings bad luck. A top 200 name since 1999.

Jonas
Rank: 357

Origin: Hebrew
Meaning: Dove
Gender Variation: Joni
Similar Names: John, Jonah, Jonathan, Jones, Josias, Judas
Namesake: Jonas Brothers (rock/pop band)

➡ The Greek form of Jonah. Jonas Salk, the American physician and researcher, who developed the first polio vaccine is a famous bearer of the name. Also a popular trivia question for the given name of Skipper Jonas Grumby on the 1960s TV classic *Gilligan's Island*.

Jonathan
Rank: 22

Origin: Hebrew
Meaning: God has given
Alternate Spellings: Johnathan, Johnathon, Jonathen, Jonathon, Jonathyn
Gender Variations: Jolene, Jolie
Nicknames: Jon, Jonny, Nathan
Similar Names: Joel, John, Jonah, Jonas, Nate, Nathan
Namesake: Jonathan Taylor Thomas (actor)

➡ A combination of Jon and Nathan and a biblical name for the oldest son of Saul who became friends with David. Listed among the top 50 since 1969 and the top 25 since 1980. Irish author Jonathan Swift is a famous bearer.

Jordan
Rank: 46

Origin: Hebrew
Meaning: To flow down
Alternate Spellings: Jorden, Jordin, Jordon, Jordyn, Jourdan
Gender Variation: Jordan
Nicknames: Jordi, Jory
Similar Names: John, Jonah, Jonathan, Joseph, Joshua
Namesakes: Jordan Bridges (actor), Jordan Knight (musician)

➡ The name of the river that flows between the countries of Jordan and Israel. Jesus was baptized in the River Jordan at the beginning of his ministry. Basketball superstar Michael Jordan is a bearer of the surname. Listed among the top 100 for girls.

Jorge   Rank: 120

Origin: Greek
Meaning: Farmer
Gender Variations:
Georgia, Georgiana
Similar Names: George, Jarek, Joran, Jorgen, Jori, Jorje, Jurgen, Jurek
Namesakes: Jorge Garcia (actor), Jorge Posada (baseball player)
⇒ The Spanish and Portuguese form of George. Saint Jorge was a 4th-century soldier known for chivalry. The name peaked during the early 1990s and is commonly used by Hispanic families.

Jose   Rank: 32

Origin: Hebrew
Meaning: God will increase
Gender Variations: Josefina, Josefine, Josette, Josiane
Similar Names: Joe, Joey, Jonas, Jorge, Joseph, Joses, Yosef
⇒ The Spanish and Portuguese form of the name Joseph. Influenced by famed Puerto Rican singer Jose Feliciano and baseball star Jose Canseco, who published a tell-all book in 2005 that set off controversy about steroid use in major league baseball.

Joseph   Rank: 11

Origin: Hebrew
Meaning: God will increase
Alternate Spellings: Josef, Josephe, Joszef, Jozef
Gender Variations: Josepha, Josephine
Nicknames: Joe, Joey
Similar Names: Joachim, Joash, Joel, John, Jordan, Jose, Joshua, Josiah
Namesakes: Joseph Fiennes (actor), Joseph Hughes "Jacques" Laperriere (Hockey Hall of Famer), Joseph Pulitzer (publisher), Joseph Wambaugh (writer)
⇒ A biblical name mentioned in the Old Testament as the 12th son of Jacob, who was sold by his brothers into slavery, and in the New Testament the name of Jesus' earthly father. Also associated with the rich Jew Joseph of Armathea, who took Jesus down from the cross, wrapped him in a shroud, and buried him in a rock tomb. The name has dropped out of the top 15 only twice during the past 125 years. Joseph Alois Ratzinger, elected Pope Benedict XVI in 2005, is another famous bearer.

Josh   Rank: 714

Origin: Hebrew
Meaning: God is salvation
Gender Variation: Josette
Similar Names: Jesus, Jon, Joseph, Josiah, Joss, Josue
Namesakes: Josh Brolin (actor), Josh Groban (musician), Josh Hartnett (actor), Josh Holloway (actor)
⇒ The shortened form of Joshua that is also used as an independent name. It peaked prior to the turn of the 20th century but it is still steadily used.

Joshua   Rank: 3

Origin: Hebrew
Meaning: God is salvation
Alternate Spelling: Joshuah
Gender Variation: Jesusa
Nickname: Josh
Similar Names: Jacob, Jesus, Joachim, Jonathan, Joseph, Josiah, Joss
Namesakes: Joshua Gracin (*American Idol* finalist)
⇒ In the Old Testament, Joshua led the Israelites into the Promised Land and later succeeded Moses as leader of the Israelites. The name jumped in popularity during the late 1960s possibly due to fictional character Joshua Bolton on the television show *Here Come the Brides*. The name also ranks highly in England. Josh is a shortened form that's also used independently.

Josiah   Rank: 117

Origin: Hebrew
Meaning: Jehovah supports
Alternate Spellings: Joesiah, Josia, Joziah
Gender Variations: Josiane, Josie
Similar Names: Isiah, Josh, Joshua, Josias, Joss
Namesakes: Josiah "Jed" Bartlet (*The West Wing* television character), Josiah Wedgwood (English potter)
⇒ In the Old Testament, the son of King Amon and Jedidah who ascended the throne of Judah when he was 8 and became known as a religious reformer during his reign. Historically known for Josiah Bartlett, the physician and statesman who signed the Declaration of Independence. The name was in use at the turn of the 20th century, then faded until 1975, and is currently at its peak.

Josue   Rank: 193
Origin: Hebrew
Meaning: God is salvation
Alternate Spelling: Josu
Gender Variation: Josie
Similar Names: Jesus, Joseph, Josh, Joshua, Josiah
➡ The Spanish and French form of Joshua that first ranked in popularity in 1971. The name has steadily increased in usage along with other biblical names.

Jovan   Rank: 840
Origin: Hebrew
Meaning: Father of the sky
Gender Variations:
Jovana, Jovanka
Nicknames: Jov, Van
Similar Names: Giovanni, Ivan, Johann, Jon, Jonas, Jowan, Juan, Yann, Yanni
➡ A Serbian name for John or Ivan modestly used since 1976.

Jovani   Rank: 694
Origin: Hebrew
Meaning: Father of the sky
Alternate Spellings:
Jovanie, Jovanni, Jovannie, Jovanny, Jovany
Gender Variation: Jovana
Nickname: Jovan
Similar Names: Giovani, Jevon, Joran, Jorge
➡ A variation of Jovan occasionally used as a given name since the 1990s.

Juan   Rank: 61

Origin: Hebrew
Alternate Spelling: Juwan
Gender Variations: Juana, Juanita
Similar Names: Johannes, John, Jorge, Jose, Juanito, Julio
Namesake: Juan Carlos Ferrero (Spanish tennis player)
➡ The Spanish form of John popularized by the legendary Spanish lover Don Juan. A royal name for Juan Carlos I, the king of Spain. Basketball player Juwan Howard uses a variation of the name. Preferred among Hispanic families.

Judah   Rank: 493
Origin: Hebrew
Meaning: Praised one
Alternate Spelling: Juda
Gender Variations: Jude, Judy
Nicknames: Jud, Jude
Similar Names: Jedidiah, Jehiel, Jeriah, Jesher, Jesus, Joash, Jotham, Judas
➡ An Old Testament name for the fourth son of Jacob and Leah, and founder of one of the 12 tribes of Israel. The name has recently seen a resurgence in popularity along with other biblical names. New Zealand actress and singer Lucy Lawless has a son named Judah.

Jude   Rank: 330

Origin: Hebrew/Latin
Meaning: Praise of the Lord
Alternate Spelling: Jud
Gender Variations: Judith, Judy
Similar Names: Judah, Judas, Judd, Jules, Thaddeus
Namesake: *Jude* (1996 film)
➡ A variation of Judas with several possible namesakes mentioned in the Bible including the brother of Jesus and one of the 12 apostles, who is also referred to as Thaddeus. Known for the 1968 song "Hey Jude," which spent nine weeks at No. 1 in the U.S., the longest of any single by the Beatles. Actor Jude Law has brought much attention to the name in recent years.

Julian   Rank: 65

Origin: Latin
Meaning: Youth
Alternate Spellings:
Julien, Julion, Julyan
Gender Variations: Juliana, Juliane, Julien
Nicknames: Jule, Jules
Similar Names: Giuliano, Jude, Julianus, Julio, Julius
➡ A variation of Julianus that's common among early Christians. The name of several saints including Saint Julian, the patron of travelers and hospitality. It's best known for English musician Julian Lennon, the first son of Beatle John Lennon.

Julio
Rank: 240

Origin: Latin
Meaning: Youth
Alternate Spelling: Giulio
Gender Variations:
Julianna, Julianne, Julie
Similar Names: Jules, Julian, Juliano, Julius
Namesake: Julio Cesar Chavez (boxer)
⇒ The Spanish and Portuguese variation of Julian and Julius. Influenced by Julio Iglesias, the best-selling Spanish singer of all time.

Julius
Rank: 319

Origin: Latin
Meaning: Youthful
Gender Variations:
Julianne, Julie
Nicknames: Jul, Jule, Jules
Similar Names: Julian, Julianus, Julen, Julio, Justino
Namesake: Julius Erving (basketball player)
⇒ A popular Roman clan name most noted for military and political leader Gaius Julius Caesar, whose birth month *Quintilis* was renamed *July* in his honor. His life was immortalized by Shakespeare in the play *Julius Caesar*. Also the name of three popes. Jules is popular in France. Julio is preferred in Spain. In the U.S. the name peaked prior to the turn of the 20th century.

Junior
Rank: 627

Origin: Latin
Meaning: The young child
Gender Variation: June
Similar Names: Junius, Juno, Justin, Justus
⇒ A nickname generally given to a son who has the same given name as his father. It was used independently during the 19th century and peaked in 1925 at No. 116. The title of a 1994 film starring Arnold Schwarzenegger and Danny DeVito.

Justice
Rank: 411

Origin: Old French
Meaning: Judge, officer of justice
Alternate Spellings: Justis, Justus, Justyce
Gender Variations: Justina, Justine
Nickname: Just
Similar Names: Jaiden, Jordan, Justin, Justo
⇒ A variation of the occupational surname

Justus and a vocabulary word that means "the quality of being just, impartial, or fair." It was used in 1882, then disappeared until 1992, possibly influenced by baseball player, David Justice, who's listed among the top 500 home-run hitters of all time. A virtue name that parents should consider on its merit.

Justin
Rank: 45

Origin: Latin
Meaning: Just
Alternate Spellings:
Justan, Justen, Justyn
Gender Variations: Justina, Justine
Nickname: Juste
Similar Names: Dustin, Justain, Justinas, Justus, Justy
Namesake: Justin Guarini (*American Idol* finalist)
⇒ Taken from the Roman name Justinus, which was derived from Justus. It was the name of several early saints including Justin Martyr, a 2nd-century Christian apologist who was beheaded in Rome. Singer Justin Timberlake is credited with the name's jump into popularity today.

Kai
Rank: 238

Origin: German
Meaning: Keeper of the keys
Alternate Spellings: Cai, Kei, Ky, Kye
Gender Variations: Kaia, Kaila, Kailey
Similar Names: Kade, Kaden, Kale, Keanu, Kim, Kiran
Namesake: Kai Ryssdal (public radio host)
⇒ Originates from several possible sources, including the pet form of several Germanic names beginning with a K or G, a variation of the Latin name Gaius, or the short form of Kylie. It also means "sea water" in Hawaiian. The name has been rapidly catching on with parents since 1979 and is also popular in England, South Australia, and Wales.

Kane
Rank: 701

Origin: Irish Gaelic
Meaning: Warlike
Alternate Spellings:
Cain, Caine, Kain, Kaine, Kayne, Keyne
Gender Variations: Kara, Karen
Similar Names: Kaden, Kainen, Kathel, Kavan
Namesake: Christian Kane (actor/singer)

⇨ The anglicized form of the name Cathan, in common use since 1986. Charles Foster Kane, the main character in the 1941 classic *Citizen Kane*, is a bearer of the surname. Also a Japanese given name that means "doubly accomplished."

Kanye
Origin: American
Gender Variation: Kanya
Similar Names: Kane, Keane, Keanu, Ken, Kian, Kim
⇨ An invented name that was brought to parents' attention by Kanye West, the six-time Grammy Award-winning record producer and rapper. It debuted on the popularity chart in 2004 at No. 488 and has faded since that time.

Kareem   Rank: 713
Origin: Arabic
Meaning: Generous
Alternate Spelling: Karim
Gender Variations: Karima, Karma
Similar Names: Kadir, Kamil, Karam, Khalid, Khalil
⇨ A form of Karim influenced by basketball great Kareem Abdul-Jabbar, the recipient of six NBA Most Valuable Player Awards. Born Lew Alcindor, he changed his name in college when he converted to Islam. Popular among African-American families.

Kason   Rank: 752
Origin: American
Alternate Spellings: Casen, Cason, Kasen
Gender Variation: Cassidy, Kasey
Similar Names: Carson, Cassian, Jason, Karney, Mason
⇨ Parents started using this contemporary name on a regular basis in 2004 and it's moved steadily up the chart since that time. Cason ranks just one point behind at No. 753.

Keanu
Origin: Hawaiian
Meaning: Cool breeze
Gender Variations: Keana
Similar Names: Kane, Keane, Kearn, Keaton, Keenan, Kieran
⇨ Popular by association to famed Canadian film actor Keanu Reeves, who started appearing in high-budget action films during

the 1990s when the name coincidentally first hit the popularity chart. Of Hawaiian descent, he was named after his uncle Henry Keanu Reeves, ultimately derived from his great-great-uncle Keaweaheulu, which means "cool breeze over the mountains."

Keaton   Rank: 382
Origin: English
Meaning: Where hawks fly
Alternate Spelling: Keelon
Gender Variations: Katana, Peyton
Similar Names: Kaden, Kelly, Kendall, Kenton, Kerr, Kerry, Kieran
Namesake: Michael Keaton (actor)
⇨ A surname and place name that debuted on the popularity chart in 1985. The name may have received a boost from fictional character Alex P. Keaton, played by actor Michael J. Fox, on the 1980s television sitcom *Family Ties*.

Keegan   Rank: 225
Origin: Irish Gaelic
Meaning: Small flame
Alternate Spellings: Keagan, Keagen, Keegen, Keeghan, Kegan
Gender Variation: Keeley
Similar Names: Keaton, Keelan, Keenan, Keene, Kieran, Kiernan
Namesake: Andrew Keegan (actor)
⇨ Originated as a surname and anglicized form of the Gaelic Mac Aodhagain. It's moved steadily up the chart since 1979 because of its fashionable long "ee" sound.

Keenan   Rank: 607
Origin: Irish Gaelic
Meaning: Ancient
Alternate Spellings: Keanan, Keenon, Kenan, Kienan
Gender Variations: Keana, Keena
Nickname: Keen
Similar Names: Keegan, Keelan, Keen, Keiran, Keirnan, Kennan
⇨ Derived from the Irish surname O' Cianain, it debuted on the popularity chart in 1958, influenced by character actor Keenan Wynn. A recent bearer is Keenen Ivory Wayans, the comedian, director, and writer best known as the creator of the 1990s comedy series *In Living Color*.

Keith — Rank: 277

Origin: Scottish
Meaning: Wood
Alternate Spellings: Keath, Kieth
Gender Variations: Keita, Keitha
Similar Names: Keenan, Keiller, Keir, Kellen, Kelvin, Kenneth
Namesakes: Keith Sweat (singer/songwriter/producer), Toby Keith (country singer/songwriter)

➡ Originated as a surname and place name used by a line of Scottish earls from 1455 to 1715. The name caught on with parents outside of Scotland during the latter part of the 19th century. It peaked in the U.S. during the 1960s at No. 32, influenced by Keith Richards who founded the British rock group The Rolling Stones in 1962.

Kelton

Origin: Old English
Meaning: Town of the keels
Alternate Spellings: Kellton, Keltan, Kelten, Keltin, Keltonn
Gender Variation: Kelly
Similar Names: Kelvin, Kendall, Kendrick, Kenneth, Kenrick, Kenton, Kolton
➡ A place name that may refer to the town where ships were built. It's been used occasionally as a given name since 1993.

Kelvin — Rank: 434

Origin: Celtic/Gaelic
Meaning: From the narrow river
Alternate Spellings: Kellvan, Kellven, Kellvon, Kelvan, Kelven, Kelvon, Kelvyn
Gender Variations: Kelly, Kelsey
Nickname: Kel
Similar Names: Kalvin, Kellen, Kelly, Kelwin, Kevin
Namesakes: Kelvin Bryant (football player), Kelvin Cato (basketball player)
➡ Famed British physicist William Thomson was named Lord Kelvin after the river that runs through Glasgow into the Clyde. The name made its debut in 1950 and is currently listed among the top 500, possibly as a new twist on the name Kevin.

Kendall — Rank: 573

Origin: Old English
Meaning: Ruler of the valley
Alternate Spellings: Kendal, Kendel, Kendell, Kendill, Kendle, Kendyl
Gender Variations: Kenda, Kendalia, Kendaline
Nicknames: Ken, Kenny
Similar Names: Kendrick, Kenneth, Kenrick, Kenyon

➡ A surname and place name for a city in northwest England that stands in the valley of the river Kent. Used as a given name since the 19th century and also ranks highly for girls.

Kendrick — Rank: 527

Origin: Welsh/Old English
Meaning: Chief hero or royal ruler
Alternate Spellings: Kendric, Kendrik
Gender Variation: Kendra
Nicknames: Ken, Kenny
Similar Names: Hendrick, Kendall, Kennard, Kennedy, Kenneth, Kenrick, Kerrick

➡ A surname used as a given name during the 19th century possibly derived from the Old Welsh personal name Cynwrig, or the Old English personal name Cynric. It first gained popularity in 1964, peaked in 1991, and still remains in regular use.

Kennedy

Origin: Irish Gaelic
Meaning: Helmeted, chief
Alternate Spellings: Kennady, Kennedey, Kennedie
Gender Variation: Kennedy
Nicknames: Ken, Kenny
Similar Names: Keane, Keenan, Kelly, Kendall, Kendrick, Kenneth, Kian
Namesake: Edward Kennedy (senator)

➡ A Scottish and Irish clan name derived from Cinneidigh and the highly recognized surname of assassinated U.S. president John F. Kennedy, who held office from 1961 to 1963. His brother, Robert F. Kennedy, former Attorney General and state senator, was assassinated in 1968 during his own campaign for president. Rarely used as a boy's name, it ranks among the top 125 names for girls.

Kenneth   Rank: 128

Origin: Scottish Gaelic
Meaning: Fair one, fire-sprung
Alternate Spellings:
Keneth, Kenith, Kennith
Gender Variations: Kendra, Kenna, McKenna
Nicknames: Ken, Kenny
Similar Names: Kendrick, Kenelm, Kennard, Kennedy, Kenrick, Kent
Namesake: Kenneth Branagh (English actor)
➡ The anglicized form of Coinneach and Cinaed. Scottish bearers include several kings as well as novelist Kenneth Grahame, author of the children's classic *The Wind in the Willows*. It was listed among the top 100 names from 1898 to 2001 and reached its peak in 1939 at No. 13.

Kenny   Rank: 498

Origin: Scottish Gaelic
Meaning: Fair one, fire-sprung
Alternate Spellings:
Kenney, Kenni
Gender Variations: Kendra, Kenna
Nickname: Ken
Similar Names: Kelly, Kelvin, Kent, Kerry, Kevin, Kinney
Namesakes: Kenny (*The Cosby Show* television character), Kenny Loggins (musician)
➡ Pet form of Kendall, Kendrick, and Kenneth that's been used as an independent name since 1929. Notable bearers include country singers Kenny Rogers and Kenny Chesney, and saxophonist Kenny G.

Kenyon   Rank: 699

Origin: English
Meaning: Blond-haired
Alternate Spellings:
Kenyan, Kenyen, Kenyin
Gender Variation: Kenya
Similar Names: Kendall, Kendrick, Kennard, Kennedy, Kenneth, Kenrick, Kenton
Namesakes: Kenyon Martin (basketball player)
➡ A surname used as a given name since 1970. It peaked in 2005 at No. 663.

Keshawn   Rank: 823

Origin: American
Alternate Spellings:
Keshaun, Keyshaun,
Keyshawn
Gender Variations: Kesha, Keshia
Nickname: Shawn

Similar Names: Deshawn, Leshawn, Rayshawn, Tashawn
➡ A contemporary combination using the prefix "Ke" with the name Shawn that first charted in 1996 and is favored among African-American families.

Kevin   Rank: 37

Origin: Irish Gaelic
Meaning: Handsome, beautiful
Alternate Spellings: Cevin, Kavan, Kevan, Keven, Kevinn, Kevyn
Gender Variations: Keva
Similar Names: Calvin, Gavin, Keenan, Kellen, Kelvin, Kenneth
Namesakes: Kevin Bacon (actor), Kevin Costner (actor), Kevin Federline (entertainer), Kevin Henkes (children's author), Kevin McHale (basketball player)
➡ A form of the Old Irish name Caoimhin. Influenced by Saint Kevin who founded a monastery in Ireland during the 7th century and became the patron saint of Dublin. Also the name of the forgotten boy in the *Home Alone* films who made a star out of actor Macaulay Culkin. Listed among the top 50 names since 1952.

Khalil   Rank: 454

Origin: Arabic
Meaning: Good, best friend
Alternate Spellings:
Kahleil, Kahlil, Kaleel, Kalil, Khaleel
Gender Variation: Khalilah
Similar Names: Kamil, Karim, Khalid, Khalifa
➡ Occasionally used since 1989 mainly by parents of Middle Eastern descent. Khalil Gibran, the 20th-century Lebanese artist, poet, and writer, is a namesake.

Kian   Rank: 705

Origin: American
Alternate Spellings: Keon, Keyan, Keyon, Kion, Kiyan, Kyan
Gender Variation: Kiana
Similar Names: Ian, Kean, Keenan, Kyle, Kylen, Kyler, Kyran, Kyrell
➡ An invented name that blends the letter "K" to the name Ian that has been climbing up the popularity chart since 2000. Parents may prefer the trendier "y" in the middle spelling.

Kieran
Rank: 566

Origin: Gaelic
Meaning: Small and dark-skinned
Alternate Spellings: Ciaran, Keiran, Keiren, Keiron, Kiaran, Kieren, Kieron, Kyran
Gender Variations: Kiera, Kiersten
Similar Names: Kerr, Kern, Kerry, Kerwin, Kian, Kiernan
⇒ A form of Ciaran that debuted in 1992. Macaulay Culkins' little brother, Kieran, an actor in his own right, is a namesake. A runaway favorite in England, Ireland, Scotland, and Wales. A good choice for parents who are looking for a name with several spelling options.

King
Rank: 896

Origin: Old English
Meaning: King
Gender Variation: Kinsey
Similar Names: Kingsley, Kingston, Kingwell, Kinnard, Kinsey
⇒ A nickname from the vocabulary word for a male monarch or someone who holds a preeminent position, similar to names like Duke and Earl. A notable bearer of the surname was Martin Luther King, Jr., the U.S. civil rights leader. The name reappeared on the popularity chart in 2006 after an absence of 40 years.

Kingston
Rank: 941

Origin: Old English
Meaning: King's settlement
Gender Variations: Kiana, Kinsey
Nickname: King
Similar Names: King, Kingsley, Kingswell, Kinnard, Kinsey, Kinston
⇒ A place name for several locations in England, Australia, and Scotland and the capital of Jamaica. It first hit the chart as a boy's given name in 2006 influenced by singer and songwriter Gwen Stefani and British singer and guitarist Gavin Rossdale, who named their son Kingston.

Kobe
Rank: 543

Origin: American
Alternate Spellings: Cobe, Cobey, Cobi, Coby, Kobey, Kobi, Kobie, Koby
Gender Variations: Gabi, Kloe, Toby
Similar Names: Kelby, Kirby, Kody, Kolby, Kole
⇒ A variation of Coby or Colby and one of today's trendier choices. Also a place name for a prominent port city in Japan. Basketball star Kobe Bryant, drafted out of high school in 1996, put this name on the map. He was named after Kobe beef which his parents saw mentioned on a restaurant menu. The name debuted at No. 600 in 1997.

Krish
Rank: 625

Origin: American
Gender Variations: Kris, Trish, Trisha
Nickname: Kris
Similar Names: Koresh, Kris, Krishna, Kristos, Parish
⇒ An invented name that made its debut on the popularity chart at No. 625 in 2006.

Kurt
Rank: 699

Origin: Old German
Meaning: Courageous advice
Alternate Spelling: Curt
Similar Names: Koen, Konrad, Kord, Kort, Kurtis, Kyle
Namesakes: Kurt Cobain (singer), Kurt Warner (football player)
⇒ A form of Conrad used consistently as a given name starting in the 1920s. Novelist Kurt Vonnegut Jr. and actor Kurt Russell are famous bearers of the name.

Kyan
Rank: 899

Origin: American
Alternate Spelling: Keyan, Kian, Kion, Kiyan
Gender Variations: Keena, Kiana
Similar Names: Ian, Kean, Keenan, Kyle, Kylen, Kyran, Kyrell, Ryan
⇒ An invented name and alternative to Ryan that debuted on the popularity chart in 2004 at No. 588 and has faded since that time.

Kylan
Rank: 740

Origin: American
Alternate Spellings: Caelan, Kylen
Gender Variation: Cailyn
Similar Names: Callum, Collyn, Dylan, Kieran, Killian, Rylan, Wylan
⇒ An elaboration of the name Kyle that debuted on the popularity chart in 1998.

Favored by parents who prefer the trendy "y" in the middle.

Kyle
Rank: 80

Origin: Scottish
Meaning: Narrow piece of land
Alternate Spellings: Cyle, Kiel, Kile
Gender Variations: Kyla, Kylie, Kylin
Similar Names: Kyan, Kylan, Kyler, Kyrell, Kyros
Namesakes: Kyle Chandler (actor), Kyle MacLachlan (actor), Kyle Petty (NASCAR driver)
➡ A Scottish surname derived from the Gaelic word *caol* that refers to a narrow strait or channel. A trendy name that uses the "y" in the middle spelling.

Kyler
Rank: 265

Origin: Dutch
Meaning: Archer
Alternate Spellings: Cuyler, Kylar, Kylor
Gender Variations: Kyla, Kylie
Nickname: Kyle
Similar Names: Kurtis, Kyle, Kylen, Kyrell
➡ Possibly a Dutch surname and variation of Kyle that first hit the popularity chart in 1986.

Lamar
Rank: 672

Origin: Old German
Meaning: Well-known land
Alternate Spellings: Lamarr, Lamarre, Lemar, Lemarr
Gender Variation: Lana
Similar Names: Lambert, Lamont, Lance, Lander, Lanier
➡ A variation of Lamont that originated as a surname and peaked during the 1930s.

Lamont
Rank: 982

Origin: Spanish/Irish/Old Norse
Meaning: Mountain, man of the land, law man
Alternate Spellings: LaMont, Lamonte
Gender Variation: Lonette
Nickname: Lam
Similar Names: Lamar, Lambert, Landon, Langston
➡ A Scottish surname that debuted during the late 1930s and faded from use during 2005 only to return again in 2006. It may have been inspired by actor Lamont Bentley,

best known for his role as Hakeem Campbell on the television series *Moesha*, who met an untimely death in 2005. Popular among African-American families.

Lance
Rank: 321

Origin: Old German
Meaning: Land
Alternate Spelling: Launce
Gender Variations: Lana, Lanie
Similar Names: Lamar, Lambert, Lancelot, Lane, Lanz, Lanzo
Namesake: Lance Bass (singer/actor)
➡ The Germanic variation of Lanzo and often used as the short form of Lancelot. Actor Lorenzo Lamas kept the name in front of parents when he played fictional character Lance Cumson in the prime-time television soap opera *Falcon Crest* during the 1980s. Cyclist Lance Armstrong, the seven-time Tour de France winner, has been a recent influence.

Landon
Rank: 49

Origin: Old English
Meaning: Long hill
Alternate Spellings: Landan, Landen, Landin, Landyn
Gender Variation: Landra
Nickname: Lanny
Similar Names: Lando, Langdon, Langston, Lindall, Linden, Lindsey, Lyman
➡ A common surname and place name that reached the top 100 in 2003. Actor, producer, and director Michael Landon, whose television career spanned three decades, was a bearer of the surname.

Lane
Rank: 322

Origin: Old English
Meaning: Narrow road
Alternate Spellings: Laine, Layne
Gender Variation: Lainie
Similar Names: Lance, Lander, Landon, Landry, Langley
Namesake: Frankie Laine (singer)
➡ A surname for someone who lived near a lane. Nathan Lane, the Tony Award-winning stage and screen actor, is a famous bearer.

Larry   Rank: 381
Origin: Latin
Meaning: Crowned with laurel
Gender Variations:
Larch, Larissa
Similar Names: Lawler, Lawley, Lawrence, Lawson, Lawton, Lonnie, Loren, Lorenz, Loring, Lorne
Namesakes: Larry Bird (basketball player), Larry Hagman (actor), Larry Holmes (boxer), Larry King (radio/television host)
⇒ The short form of Lawrence that's also used independently. The name's popularity started in the 1930s, and was probably the influence of actor and comedian, Larry Fine of the *Three Stooges* fame.

Lawrence   Rank: 407
Origin: Latin
Meaning: Crowned with laurel
Alternate Spellings:
Laurence, Laurens, Lawrance
Gender Variations: Laurentia, Lauricia, Laurina
Nicknames: Larry, Lars, Laurie
Similar Names: Larkin, Larson, Lawford, Lawler, Lawson, Lawton, Loren, Lorenz, Lorenzo, Lowery
Namesakes: D. H. Lawrence (English author/poet), Martin Lawrence (actor/comedian), Tracy Lawrence (country musician)
⇒ The contemporary form of Laurence that's dominated the popularity chart since the late 1800s. Listed among the top 100 from 1880 to 1972, the name peaked at No. 30 during 1945. T. E. Lawrence, the 20th-century British archaeologist, soldier, and writer, internationally known by his nickname Lawrence of Arabia, is a famous bearer of the name. Actors Laurence Olivier and Laurence Fishburne use a form of the name.

Lawson   Rank: 673
Origin: Old English
Meaning: Son of Laurence
Gender Variations: Lara, Lavonne
Similar Names: Dawson, Larson, Lawford, Lawler, Lawry, Lawton
⇒ A surname derived from a personal name notable for 20th-century author and illustrator Robert Lawson, the first person

awarded both the Newbery Medal and Caldecott Medal. The name peaked prior to the turn of the 20th century, disappeared after 1950, and recently made a comeback.

Layton   Rank: 717

Origin: Old English
Meaning: Leek garden
Alternate Spellings:
Leighton, Leyton
Gender Variation: Layna
Similar Names: Landen, Langston, Lawler, Lawton
⇒ A variation of the surname Leighton. The "Leigh" spelling was used as a boy's name until 1946 and is now generally used for girls. The name has caught on with parents since 2001.

Leandro   Rank: 864
Origin: Greek
Meaning: Lion man
Alternate Spelling: Liandro
Gender Variations: Leanda, Leandra
Nickname: Lean
Similar Names: Leander, Leandre, Leodro, Leon, Leonardo, Leoncio, Leonardo
⇒ A variant of Leander that's been given to four saints, including a 6th-century bishop of Seville. Also a place name for San Leandro, California. Popular among Hispanic families.

Lee   Rank: 613
Origin: Old English
Meaning: Meadow
Gender Variations: Leah, Leanne, Leigh
Similar Names: Leaf, Leander, Leighton, Leland, Leo, Leonardo
Namesakes: Lee Majors (actor), Lee Marvin (actor), Tommy Lee (musician), Tommy Lee Jones (actor)
⇒ A surname derived from *leah* used during the 19th century in honor of Robert E. Lee, Confederate general during the Civil War. Listed among the top 100 until 1955, it's slowly faded to its current position. Particularly common as a middle name for both males and females. It's also the second most common Korean family name.

Leland   Rank: 342

Origin: Old English
Meaning: Meadowland
Alternate Spellings:
Leeland, Leighland, Leyland
Gender Variations: Leah, Leigh
Nickname: Lee
Similar Names: Leighton, Leonard, Lester, Lovell, Lyndon

➡ A surname that originated as a personal name for someone who lived by a low-lying grassy area. Namesakes include Leland Stanford, founder of Stanford University during the 19th century, and Charles Godfrey Leland, a 20th-century humorist. Steadily used until 1999, it reappeared in 2005 and shot up to its current position today.

Leo   Rank: 236

Origin: Greek
Meaning: Lion
Gender Variations:
Leona, Leone, Leonora, Leora, Leota
Nickname: Lee
Similar Names: Leon, Leonard, Leonardo, Leopold, Lionel, Lyon
Namesake: Leo Buscaglia (author)

➡ A variation of Leon that was popular during Roman times. It ranked among the top 100 from 1882 to 1937, most likely influenced by Russian novelist Leo Tolstoy, author of *War and Peace* and *Anna Karenina*. Also the name of a constellation and the fifth sign of the zodiac. Thirteen popes are among the namesakes.

Leon   Rank: 505

Origin: Greek
Meaning: Lion
Alternate Spelling: Leone
Gender Variations: Leona, Leonie, Leonora
Nickname: Leo
Similar Names: Leandro, Leo, Leoncio, Leonard, Leonardo, Lionel, Lyon
Namesakes: Leon Redbone (jazz/blues musician), Leon Spinks (boxer)

➡ The English, German, and Polish form of Leo first influenced during the early 20th century by Leon Trotsky, the Russian Communist revolutionary. Film and television actor Leon Ames, one of the founding members of the Screen Actors Guild,

brought attention to the name during the 1940s and 1950s. Listed among the top 100 names from 1893 to 1942. A chart topper in Germany.

Leonard   Rank: 614

Origin: Old German
Meaning: Strong as a lion
Alternate Spellings:
Lenard, Lennard, Leonerd, Leonhard
Gender Variations: Lena, Lenda, Lenette, Lenia
Nicknames: Len, Lenny
Similar Names: Leo, Leon, Leonardo, Lonny
Namesakes: Leonard Bernstein (composer), Leonard Nimoy (actor)

➡ The name of a 5th-century Frankish saint considered the patron saint of prisoners and horses. It was brought into Britain by the Normans and rarely used during the Middle Ages. It made a comeback during the 19th century, but has waned in popularity since Leonardo came into prominent use.

Leonardo   Rank: 184

Origin: Old German
Meaning: Strong as a lion
Gender Variations: Leona, Leonie, Leonora
Nicknames: Leo, Nardo
Similar Names: Lennox, Lenny, Leonard, Leopold, Lionel

➡ The Italian, Spanish, and Portuguese form of Leonard. A notable bearer was Leonardo da Vinci, the Italian Renaissance painter best known for the *Mona Lisa* and *The Last Supper*. It was brought back into vogue by actor Leonardo DiCaprio, who was named by his mother during pregnancy after she felt him kick while looking at a painting by da Vinci.

Leonel   Rank: 468

Origin: American
Gender Variations:
Leona, Leonie
Nicknames: Leon
Similar Names: Lemuel, Leon, Leopardo, Leopold, Leroy, Lionel

➡ A combination of the names Leon and Lionel used sporadically in the U.S. since 1939.

Leroy   Rank: 956
Origin: French
Meaning: The king
Alternate Spellings:
Leeroy, Leroi
Gender Variation: Leonora
Nicknames: Lee, Roy
Similar Names: Elroy, Delroy, Leo, Leon,
Lionel
Namesake: Leroy Robert "Satchel" Paige
(Baseball Hall of Famer)
➡ A French nickname derived from the
elements *le roi.* Associated with the 1973
No. 1 song "Bad, Bad Leroy Brown" by Jim
Croce. Professional wrestler Roland Daniels,
also known as Leroy Brown, entered the ring
during the 1980s while the Jim Croce song
played in the background.

Levi   Rank: 135
Origin: Hebrew
Meaning: Joined
Alternate Spelling: Levy
Gender Variations:
Levia, Levina
Similar Names: Leif, Leon, Lëvon, Lewin,
Lewis
Namesake: Levi Strauss (clothing
manufacturer)
➡ In the Old Testament, the third of Jacob's
12 sons and the namesake of the Levites, one
of the 12 tribes of the Israelites. In the New
Testament, Matthew's given name before he
changed it. Also noted for 19th-century
abolitionist Levi Coffin, often referred to as
the president of the Underground Railroad.
The name peaked in popularity prior to 1900.

Lewis   Rank: 678
Origin: German
Meaning: Famous warrior
Alternate Spellings:
Louis, Luis
Gender Variation: Lewella
Nicknames: Lew, Lewie
Similar Names: Lewin, Llewelyn, Lowie
Namesakes: Huey Lewis (musician), Sinclair
Lewis (novelist/playwright)
➡ The English form of Louis used during the
Middle Ages. Notable for English author
Lewis Carroll, the author of *Alice's Adventures
in Wonderland,* and the surname of Irish
author C. S. Lewis, known for the series
The Chronicles of Narnia.

Liam   Rank: 98
Origin: Old German
Meaning: Determined
protector
Alternate Spelling: Lyam
Gender Variations: Liane, Willa, Wilma
Similar Names: Bill, Wilhelm, Will, Willis, Wilmer
Namesake: Liam Gallagher (British musician)
➡ The Irish short form of William generally
found in Ireland but currently a chart topper
in Scotland and England. Irish actor Liam
Neeson is a namesake.

Lincoln   Rank: 300
Origin: Old English
Meaning: Lake colony
Gender Variations: Lin,
Lincoln
Nicknames: Lin, Link
Similar Names: Landon, Lindall, Linden,
Linnell, Lucius, Lyndon
Namesake: Lincoln Steffens (journalist)
➡ A surname taken from an early Roman
settlement in England. Abraham Lincoln, 16th
president of the U.S., brought much attention
to the surname from 1861 to 1865. Usage peaked
in 1895, but the name is on the rise again.

Logan   Rank: 19
Origin: Irish Gaelic
Meaning: Small cove
Alternate Spelling: Logen
Gender Variation: Logan
Similar Names: Landon, Lloyd, Lochlain,
Loman, Lorne
Namesake: Logan Fowler (*Baywatch* character)
➡ A surname that originated as a Scottish
place name and known for 20th-century
essayist and critic Logan Pearsall Smith.
The name was influenced during the
mid-1970s by the film *Logan's Run,* adapted
from the novel of the same name. Listed
among the top 500 names for girls.

London   Rank: 638
Origin: English
Meaning: Fierce ruler of
the world
Gender Variation: London
Nicknames: Lon, Lonnie
Similar Names: Landon, Langdon, Logan,
Lonato, Lonzo, Lyndon
➡ A place name for the capital of the United
Kingdom and one the oldest cities in the

world. Novelist Jack London, who wrote the *Call of the Wild*, is a famous bearer of the surname. It debuted in 1886, then promptly disappeared until 2000. Listed among the top 400 names for girls.

Lorenzo
Rank: 301

Origin: Latin
Meaning: Crowned with laurel
Alternate Spellings: Larenzo, Lorentzo
Gender Variations: Laurencia, Lorenza
Nicknames: Lorenz, Renzo
Similar Names: Laurence, Laurent, Leando, Leonardo, Loren
➡ The Italian and Spanish form of Laurentius, known for actor Lorenzo Lamas, who starred in the prime-time television soap opera *Falcon Crest* during the 1980s. Lorenzo Odone, whose medical treatment for adrenoleukodystrophy (ALD) was the inspiration for the 1992 film *Lorenzo's Oil*, is another notable bearer.

Louis
Rank: 326

Origin: German
Meaning: Famous warrior
Alternate Spellings: Lewes, Lewis, Luis, Luiz
Gender Variations: Louisa, Louise, Louiza
Nicknames: Lou, Louie
Similar Names: Louie, Ludwig, Luigi, Luigino, Lutz
Namesakes: Louis Armstrong (jazz musician), Louis L'Amour (author), Louis Pasteur (scientist), Robert Louis Stevenson (author)
➡ The French form of Ludwig and a common name among French royal and noble families. Louis XIV, also known as Louis the Great, ruled France for 72 years, the longest reign of any European monarch. Actor Lou Gossett Jr. uses a shortened form of the name. Lewis is the common spelling in England and tops the chart in Scotland.

Luca
Rank: 349

Origin: Greek
Meaning: From Lucania
Alternate Spelling: Luka
Gender Variations: Luce, Lucy
Nickname: Luc
Similar Names: Lucas, Lucian, Lucky, Luke
Namesake: Michael De Luca (producer)

➡ The Italian variation of Luke historically known for Luca Pacioli, a 15th-century Italian mathematician and Franciscan friar who published several books on mathematics. The name debuted in 2000 at No. 626.

Lucas
Rank: 59

Origin: Greek
Meaning: From Lucania
Alternate Spellings: Loucas, Loukas, Lukas, Luukas
Gender Variations: Lucero, Lucia
Nickname: Luc
Similar Names: Luca, Luce, Lucius, Lucky, Luke
Namesakes: Josh Lucas (actor)
➡ The Latin form of Luke that was first used as a surname. It took a huge jump in popularity during the 1980s. Producer, director, and screenwriter George Lucas, who rocketed to fame with the *Star Wars* and *Indiana Jones* films, is a bearer of the surname. Actor Lukas Haas uses an alternate spelling. Also a place name for a region in southern Italy.

Lucian
Rank: 824

Origin: Latin
Meaning: Illumination
Alternate Spelling: Lucien
Gender Variations: Lucile, Lucinda, Ludince
Nickname: Luc
Similar Names: Lucais, Lucan, Lucca, Lucas, Luciano, Lucio, Luken, Lukian
➡ Derived from the Roman family name Lucianus, which was taken from the name Lucius. Saint Lucian of Antioch, who was a noted scholar during the 4th century, is a famous bearer. Famed Italian opera singer Luciano Pavarotti uses the Italian, Portuguese, and Spanish form of the name. It recently made a comeback after losing favor with parents for more than 50 years.

Luis
Rank: 62

Origin: German
Meaning: Famous warrior
Alternate Spellings: Lewis, Louis, Luiz
Gender Variations: Luisa, Luise, Luiza
Nicknames: Lou, Louie
Similar Names: Leon, Lucas, Luce , Lucio
➡ The Spanish form of Louis and Lewis listed among the top 100 since 1980. A common name among Hispanic families.

Luke   Rank: 43

Origin: Greek
Meaning: From Lucania
Alternate Spelling: Luc
Gender Variations:
Luce, Lucille
Similar Names: Lucian, Lucio, Lucius,
Lucky, Luka, Lukas
Namesakes: Luke Duke (*The Dukes of Hazzard* TV character), Luke Perry (actor), Luke Spencer (*General Hospital* television character), Luke Wilson (actor)
⇒ A place name for Lucania, a region in Southern Italy now called Basilicata. In the New Testament, Luke is the author of the third Gospel and the Acts of the Apostles. During the Middle Ages, it was the basis for several surnames, such as Lucas and Luck. The name was influenced by Luke Skywalker, the character from the blockbuster *Star Wars* films.

Maddox   Rank: 235

Origin: Anglo-Welsh
Meaning: Benefactor's son
Alternate Spellings:
Maddocks, Maddux,
Madocks, Madox, Madux
Gender Variation: Madison
Nicknames: Mad, Maddy
Similar Names: Macsen, Maddock, Maddog
⇒ Surname derived from the personal name, Madoc, that's often used as a surname.
It gained international attention when actress Angelina Jolie adopted her first son from Cambodia in 2002 and renamed him Maddox, which led to its first popularity chart appearance in 2003 at No. 583.

Malachi   Rank: 150

Origin: Hebrew
Meaning: Messenger of God
Alternate Spellings:
Malachie, Malachy,
Malakai, Malaki, Malakie, Malechy
Gender Variations: Malicia, Mallory
Nickname: Mal
Similar Names: Malcolm, Malkah, Mallory
⇒ A minor prophet and the author of the book of Malachi in the Old Testament. Malachy was a 12th-century saint in Ireland. The name has seen a revival in popularity since 1987, favored by parents as part of a biblical trend.

Malcolm   Rank: 545

Origin: Scottish Gaelic
Meaning: Devotee of
Saint Columba
Alternate Spellings:
Malcom, Malkolm
Gender Variations: Malcolmina, Malina
Nicknames: Mal, Colm
Similar Names: Callum, Coleman, Colin, Malkah, Mallory
Namesakes: *Malcolm in the Middle* (TV series), Malcolm McDowell (English actor)
⇒ Form of the name Mael Coluim, which refers to Saint Columba, a 6th-century monk who is credited with Scotland's conversion to Christianity. Also the name of the prince of Scotland who became king after Macbeth murdered his father, which became the basis for Shakespeare's play *Macbeth*. African-American parents use the name in honor of civil rights activist Malcolm X. Actor Denzel Washington who appeared in the title role of the 1992 film, *Malcolm X*, gave his son this name. Actor Harrison Ford also has a son named Malcolm.

Malik   Rank: 290

Origin: Arabic/Hindu
Meaning: King, master
Alternate Spellings:
Malek, Malick, Melik
Gender Variations: Malika, Malikia
Nickname: Mal
Similar Names: Mahdi, Malachi, Malcus, Manute
⇒ First listed among the top 100 names in 1970 and peaked at No. 97 in 1996. The name was influenced by basketball player Malik Sealy, who was also an aspiring actor until his untimely death in 2000. A popular choice for African-American parents.

Manuel   Rank: 164

Origin: Hebrew
Meaning: God is with us
Gender Variations:
Manuela, Manuelita
Nickname: Manny
Similar Names: Emmanuel, Manases, Manolito, Manuelo
Namesake: Manny Ramirez (baseball player)
⇒ The short form of the Hebrew name Emmanuel and known for General Manuel Noriega, the military dictator of Panama

from 1983 to 1989. Also a place name for a municipality in Spain. Preferred by Hispanic families.

Marcel
Rank: 957

Origin: French
Meaning: Dedicated to Mars
Alternate Spellings: Marcell, Marcelle
Gender Variations: Marcella, Marcelyn, Marcy
Similar Names: Carmelo, Marc, Marcellino, Marcello, Marcellus, Marciano, Marco, Marcus
Namesakes: Marcel Dionne (Canadian hockey player), Marcel Pronovost (Canadian Hockey Hall of Famer)
➡ A form of the Latin name Marcellus and associated with Mars, the Roman god of war. The name is internationally known for French mime Marcel Marceau.

Marcelo
Rank: 890

Origin: Latin
Meaning: Dedicated to Mars
Alternate Spelling: Marcello
Gender Variations: Marcelina, Marcella, Marcelle, Marcelline, Marcelyn
Nicknames: Marcel
Similar Names: Carmelo, Marc, Marcas, Marcelino, Marcellus
Namesake: Marcelo Rios (Chilean tennis player)
➡ The Spanish and Portuguese variation of Marcellus that debuted on the popularity chart in 1971.

Marco
Rank: 206

Origin: Latin
Meaning: Dedicated to Mars
Alternate Spelling: Marko
Gender Variations: Marcelle, Marcia, Marcy
Nickname: Marc
Similar Names: Marcel, Marcos, Marcus, Marzio
Namesakes: Marco Andretti (Indy car driver), Marco Pantani (Italian cyclist)
➡ The Spanish, Portuguese, and Italian form of Mark. The most famous bearer is Marco Polo, the 13th-century Italian explorer. The name has gained popularity in recent years.

Marcos
Rank: 248

Origin: Latin
Meaning: Dedicated to Mars
Alternate Spelling: Markos
Gender Variations: Marcia, Marcie
Nickname: Marc
Similar Names: DeMarcos, Marco, Marcus, Marius, Marlon, Marzell
Namesake: Ferdinand Marcos (Philippines president)
➡ The Spanish and Portuguese form of Mark. Notable for Spanish explorer and Franciscan friar Marcos de Niza, who claimed to have seen the legendary Seven Cities of Cibola in 1539. A place name for the Texas city of San Marcos.

Marcus
Rank: 112

Origin: Latin
Meaning: Dedicated to Mars
Alternate Spellings: Markus, Marquus
Gender Variations: Marcia, Marga
Nickname: Marc
Similar Names: Demarcus, Jamarcus, Marcel, Marcellus, Markos, Marquis
Namesakes: Marcus Allen (football player), Marcus Aurelius (Roman Emperor), Marcus Tullius Cicero (Ancient Roman philosopher)
➡ Possibly associated with Mars, the god of war in Roman mythology. Shakespeare used the name for the brother of the title character in the play *Titus Andronicus*. It was influenced by the 1970s series *Marcus Welby, M.D.*, considered one of the most popular doctor shows in U.S. television history.

Mariano

Origin: Ancient Rome
Meaning: Manly
Gender Variation: Mariana
Similar Names: Marijan, Marijus, Marin, Marino, Marinus, Mario, Marion, Marius, Merrion
➡ The Italian form of the Roman family name Marianus and sporadically used in the U.S. since prior to the turn of the 20th century.

Ma ⇒ boys' names

Mario
Rank: 178

Origin: Latin
Meaning: Manly
Alternate Spelling: Mareo
Gender Variations:
Mariana, Marion
Similar Names: Mariano, Marianus, Marin, Marino, Marinus, Marius
Namesakes: Mario (R&B singer), Mario Batali (TV chef), Mario Cuomo (politician), Mario Lemieux (Hockey Hall of Famer), Mario Lopez (actor), Mario Puzo (novelist), Mario Vazquez (*American Idol* finalist)
⇒ The Italian and Spanish form of the Roman clan name, Marius, possibly influenced by Mars, the Roman god of war. Italian-American car-racing legend Mario Andretti brought much attention to the name during the 1960s and 1970s. A chart topper in Spain.

Mark
Rank: 129

Origin: Latin
Meaning: Dedicated to Mars
Alternate Spellings: Marc, Marke
Gender Variations: Marcella, Marcia
Similar Names: Marcel, Marcello, Marco, Marcos, Mario, Markham, Markey, Markus, Martin, Marx
Namesakes: Mark Hamill (actor), Mark Harmon (actor), Marc Jacobs (fashion designer), Mark McGwire (baseball player), Mark Ruffalo (actor), Mark Spitz (swimmer), Mark Wahlberg (actor)
⇒ From the Latin name Marcus, associated with the author of the second Gospel of the Bible that bears his name and known as a companion to disciples Peter and Paul. Marc Antony, the Roman general and lover of Cleopatra, is a historical namesake. Author Mark Twain, who was born Samuel Clemens, is another famous bearer. The name peaked during the 1960s at No. 6.

Markell
Origin: American
Alternate Spellings: Markel, Marquel
Gender Variation: Markie
Similar Names: Marek, Marko, Markos, Markus, Marx
⇒ A created elongated version of Mark occasionally used since 1994.

Marlon
Rank: 508

Origin: Old French
Meaning: Little hawk
Alternate Spellings: Marlan, Marlen, Marlyn
Gender Variations: Marla, Marlene
Similar Names: Marlin, Marlis, Martin, Marvin, Merle, Merlin
Namesake: Marlon Wayans (actor)
⇒ Possibly a form of Marc first used during the 1950s. It was greatly influenced by major motion picture star Marlon Brando, who was named after his father. He started his career on Broadway during the 1940s and was offered his first screen role in 1950 and his last in 2001. Comedian and political commentator Dennis Miller named his son Marlon.

Marquis
Rank: 553

Origin: Old French
Meaning: Nobleman, lord of the borderlands
Alternate Spellings: Markese, Markise, Marquece, Marqueese, Marques, Marquez, Marquise
Gender Variation: Marquita
Nickname: Mark
Similar Names: Marcus, Marley, Marlon, Martin, Marvin
Namesake: Marquis Daniels (basketball player)
⇒ Originally an aristocratic title derived from the word *marchis* and rarely used as a given name until 1970. A literary name for Monsieur de Marquis, a fictional character in the Charles Dickens novel *A Tale of Two Cities*.

Marshall
Rank: 417

Origin: Old German
Meaning: Horse servant
Alternate Spellings: Marchall, Marschall, Marshal, Marshell, Martial
Gender Variation: Marsha
Nickname: Marsh
Similar Names: Malcolm, Martin, Marvin, Maynard, Mitchell, Wendell
⇒ A Norman French occupational surname for someone who looked after horses derived from the Germanic *marah* and *scalc*. Used as a given name during the 19th century. Its early popularity is perhaps the influence of Marshall Field's department store.

Martin Rank: 200

Origin: Latin
Meaning: Warlike
Alternate Spellings:
Marten, Marton, Martyn
Gender Variations: Martina, Martine
Nicknames: Mart, Marty
Similar Names: Marden, Marnin,
Marston, Marvin
Namesakes: Martin Lawrence (actor),
Martin Scorsese (director), Martin Sheen
(actor), Ricky Martin (pop singer)
➡ Originated from the name Martinus which
relates to Mars, the Roman god of war. The
name was influenced early by Saint Martin
of Tours, a 4th-century bishop and patron of
France, who divided his cloak in two so he
could give half to a beggar. Famous bearers
include Martin Luther, the 16th-century
German priest whose teachings inspired the
Protestant Reformation, and Martin Luther
King Jr., the U.S. civil rights leader. The name
peaked before the turn of the 20th century.

Marvin Rank: 346

Origin: Welsh
Meaning: Sea friend
Alternate Spellings:
Marven, Marvyn
Gender Variations: Marva, Marvene
Nickname: Marv
Similar Names: Martin, Marvis, Marwin,
Mervin, Merwin
Namesakes: *Marvin* (comic strip), Marvin
Hagler (boxer/actor)
➡ The medieval form of Mervyn used as
a surname during the Middle Ages. Recently
associated with soul singer and songwriter
Marvin Gaye, who gained international fame
during the 1960s, 1970s, and 1980s.

Mason Rank: 39

Origin: German
Meaning: To make
Alternate Spelling: Mayson
Gender Variation: Maisie
Similar Names: Jason, Macon, Marvin, Miller
Namesakes: James Mason (actor), Perry
Mason (television attorney)
➡ A surname used during the Middle Ages
for a person who worked with stone
ultimately derived from *macian*. First used as
a given name during the 1840s, it shot into
the top 100 in 1997.

Mateo Rank: 274

Origin: Hebrew
Meaning: Gift of God
Alternate Spelling:
Matteo
Gender Variations: Mae, Mattea
Nicknames: Mat, Teo
Similar Names: Mateus, Matheo, Matheu,
Mathis, Matia, Matias, Matthias, Mattieu
➡ The Spanish form of Matthew derived
from Mattathias used popularly as
a given name since 1995. Popular today
with Hispanic families.

Mathias Rank: 741

Origin: Hebrew
Meaning: Gift of God
Alternate Spellings:
Matias, Matthias
Gender Variations: Mathia
Nicknames: Math, Matt,
Similar Names: Matai, Mateo, Mathieu,
Mathis, Matia, Matias, Mattan, Matthan
➡ A form of Matthias and the Greek
variation of the Biblical name Matthew
used in the Authorized Version of the
New Testament. The name was in use at
the turn of the 20th century, faded out in
1919, and suddenly reappeared in 2003.

Matthew Rank: 5

Origin: Hebrew
Meaning: Gift of God
Alternate Spellings:
Matheu, Mathew,
Mathieu, Matthieu
Gender Variation: Mattie
Nickname: Matt
Similar Names: Mateus, Mathis, Matias,
Mats, Matteo, Matthia, Matthias
Namesakes: Matthew Broderick (actor),
Matthew McConaughey (actor), Matt Damon
(actor), Matt LeBlanc (actor)
➡ A biblical name for one of the 12 apostles
and the author of the first Gospel in the
New Testament. Ranked among the top 10
since 1972 and is one of the most common
names found in English-speaking countries.
Matt is a popular shortened form. *Friends*
actor Matthew Perry has helped keep the
name current. Tennis star Mats Wilander
uses the Swedish and Norwegian variation.

Ma ⇒ boys' names

Maurice   Rank: 400

Origin: Late Latin
Meaning: Moorish, dark skinned
Alternate Spellings: Morice, Morrice
Gender Variation: Maura
Nickname: Mauri
Similar Names: Mauricio, Maury, Morris, Morrison, Moss, Murray
Namesakes: *Maurice* (1987 film), Maurice Gibb (musician), Maurice Sendak (writer/illustrator)
⇒ Derived from Mauricius, the name of a Byzantine Emperor who ruled until the turn of the 7th century. Brought into England by the Normans, which led to several surnames such as Morris and Morse. The name peaked prior to the turn of the 20th century. Belgian-French actor and entertainer Maurice Chevalier kept it in front of the public starting in 1929. Morris is more commonly used today.

Mauricio   Rank: 368

Origin: Latin
Meaning: Dark, swarthy
Gender Variations: Marisol, Maura
Nickname: Moe
Similar Names: Mario, Maurice, Mauro, Maurus, Morris
⇒ The Spanish form of Mauricius associated with the Moors, a Muslim people of mixed Arab, Spanish, and Berber origins who lived in northwest Africa. The name's meaning refers to their dark or swarthy coloring.

Maverick   Rank: 605

Origin: English
Meaning: Independent
Gender Variations: Mave, Mavis
Nickname: Mav
Similar Names: Dallas, Hunter, Maurice, Maxwell, Remington
Namesakes: *Maverick* (George Thorogood album), The Mavericks (country musicians)
⇒ A term that refers to an unbranded range animal that originated with Samuel Maverick, a 17th-century Texas lawyer and land baron. It's highly identified with Bret and Bart Maverick, gambling brothers from the 1957 to 1962 television series *Maverick*. Also the

call sign of Lt. Pete Mitchell, played by Tom Cruise in the 1986 film *Top Gun*. The name has been used sporadically since 1958.

Max   Rank: 160

Origin: Latin
Meaning: The greatest
Alternate Spellings: Maks, Maxx
Gender Variations: Maxie, Maxine
Similar Names: Maxim, Maximillian, Maximo, Maximus, Maxwell
Namesakes: *Max* (2002 film), Max Baer Jr. (actor), Max Lucado (Christian author), Max von Sydow (Swedish actor), Miracle Max (*Princess Bride* movie character)
⇒ The short form of names such as Maximilian and Maxwell and a favorite in Australia since the 1979 debut of the *Mad Max* film trilogy. Used as an independent name in the U.S. starting in the 1880s.

Maxim   Rank: 852

Origin: Latin
Meaning: The greatest
Alternate Spelling: Maksim
Gender Variation: Maxy
Nicknames: Max, Maxi
Similar Names: Maxime, Maximo, Maximos
⇒ A variation of Maximus associated with Russian author Aleksei Maksimovich Peshkov, better known as Maxim Gorky. Occasionally used as a boy's given name since 2000.

Maximilian   Rank: 348

Origin: Latin
Meaning: The greatest
Alternate Spellings: Maksymilian, Maximilien, Maximillian, Maximillien
Gender Variations: Maxene, Maximillienne
Nicknames: Max, Maxim
Similar Names: Maxfield, Maximiliano, Maximino, Maximus
⇒ A form of Maximilianus popular among royalty and saints. Academy Award-winning Austrian actor Maximilian Schell brought attention to the name when he made his Hollywood debut in 1958.

Maximo   Rank: 922

Origin: Latin
Meaning: The greatest
Alternate Spelling:
Maksimo
Gender Variations: Maxie, Maxima
Nickname: Max
Similar Names: Massimo, Maxim, Maxime,
Maximos, Maximus
➡ The Spanish form of Maximus
predominantly used since 2002.

Maximus   Rank: 374

Origin: Latin
Meaning: Greatest
Gender Variations:
Maxima, Maxine
Nickname: Max
Similar Names: Maxen, Maxim, Maximillian,
Maximino, Maximo, Maximos
➡ A Roman family name derived from
maximus that was popular among early
Roman leaders and saints. Its rise in
popularity began with Maximus Decimus
Meridius, the fictional character portrayed by
Russell Crowe in the 2000 film *Gladiator*.

Maxwell   Rank: 149

Origin: Scottish/Old English
Meaning: Stream of Maccus
Gender Variations: Maxine
Nickname: Max
Similar Names: Maxfield, Maxim, Maximillian
Namesakes: Maxwell Smart (*Get Smart*
TV character)
➡ A surname that originated from an English
place name also used as an elongated form
of Max. Sporadically popular throughout the
years, it's been listed among the top 200
names since 1990. Character Maxwell Q.
Klinger from the popular television series
MASH. comes to mind.

Mekhi   Rank: 443

Origin: American
Gender Variations:
Mecheka, Mechelle
Similar Names: Makai,
Makani, Makari, Mikel, Miki, Mikio
➡ A created name used mainly among
African-American parents that debuted on
the popularity chart in 1998. Television and
film actor Mekhi Phifer, the season-four winner
of *Celebrity Poker Showdown*, is a namesake.

Melvin   Rank: 425

Origin: Irish Gaelic
Meaning: Polished chief
Alternate Spellings:
Melvon, Melvyn, Melvynn
Gender Variations: Melva, Melvina, Melvine
Nickname: Mel
Similar Names: Malvin, Melville, Melwin,
Vinnie
Namesakes: Mel Gibson (actor), *Melvin and
Howard* (1980 film), The Melvins (rock band)
➡ A Scottish surname and form of the name,
Melville that achieved its highest popularity
ranking during the 1920s. Academy Award-
winning actor, writer, director, and producer
Mel Brooks, whose real name is Melvin
Kaminsky, is a namesake.

Memphis   Rank: 923

Origin: Arabic
Meaning: Good place to live
Gender Variations: Mercia, Mercy
Similar Names: Melbourne, Meldon, Melville,
Mendel, Mercer
➡ A place name for several cities and towns
in the U.S., including Memphis, Tennessee.
Associated with the wife of Epaphus in
Greek mythology who, according to legend,
founded Memphis, Egypt, the ancient city
located on the Nile. Also the name of a
character in the 2006 Academy Award-
winning animated film, *Happy Feet*. First
recognized as a boy's given name in 2006.

Messiah   Rank: 798

Origin: Hebrew
Meaning: Anointed
Gender Variation: Mesha
Similar Names: Christos, Immanuel, Isaiah,
Issiah, Moses, Mosiah
➡ Derived from the Hebrew Mashiah that
refers to the name of the expected king
and deliverer of the Jews. Also the title of
a famous oratorio composed by George
Frideric Handel in 1741. New to the chart in
2005, especially popular among parents
because of its biblical roots.

Micah   Rank: 148

Origin: Hebrew
Meaning: Who resembles God
Alternate Spellings: Mica, Micaiah, Micha, Michah, Mika, Mikah, Mikka, Myca, Mycah, Myka
Gender Variations: Micaela, Michalina, Michele, Michelle, Mikaya
Nickname: Mike
Similar Names: Makael, Michael, Mick, Miguel, Mishael, Mitchell
Namesakes: Micah Alberti (actor), *Micah Clarke* (novel by Sir Arthur Conan Doyle)
⇨ A variation of Michael with numerous namesakes found in the Bible. The most notable is a prophet who predicted the fall of Jerusalem and the coming of the Messiah. A book in the Old Testament bears his name. A latecomer to the popularity chart but becoming a prevalent name because of its strong Hebrew connection.

Michael   Rank: 2

Origin: Hebrew
Meaning: Who resembles God
Alternate Spellings: Mical, Micael, Micel, Michal, Micheal, Michel, Mikel, Mychael, Mychal
Gender Variations: Michaela, Michelle
Nicknames: Mick, Mickey, Mike, Mikey
Similar Names: Michail, Michiel, Miguel, Mikhail, Mitch, Mitchell
Namesakes: Michael Bolton (musician), Michael Douglas (actor), Michael J. Fox (actor), Michael Johnson (Olympic medalist), Michael Phelps (Olympic medalist), Michael Schumacher (German Formula One driver)
⇨ Michael has flirted among the 50 most popular names for more than 100 years. It climbed to No. 1 for the first time in 1954 and spent 38 years in the top spot. It was the name of one of the seven archangels and the leader of heaven's armies in the New Testament. Kings, saints, and emperors have also been given this name. Today most people think of musician Michael Jackson or basketball star Michael Jordan.

Miguel   Rank: 89

Origin: Hebrew
Meaning: Who resembles God
Gender Variations: Michelle, Miguela
Nickname: Mico
Similar Names: Michael, Mihail, Miko, Milo
Namesake: Miguel Sandoval (actor)
⇨ The Spanish and Portuguese variation of Michael and a place name for San Miguel, Mexico. Spanish novelist Don Miguel de Cervantes Saavedra, the author of *Don Quixote*, is a namesake.

Miles   Rank: 202

Origin: Latin/Old German
Meaning: A soldier, merciful
Alternate Spellings: Myles, Mylz
Gender Variations: Milessa, Milena, Mylie, Mylinda
Similar Names: Emile, Michael, Mick, Milan, Milo, Mitch
Namesakes: Miles O'Brien (*Star Trek: Deep Space Nine* TV character), Miles O'Keeffe (actor)
⇨ A possible variation of the Latin name Emil and sometimes associated with Michael. Myles is the English form, known historically for Myles Coverdale, who first translated the Bible into English during the 16th century. Other namesakes include Myles Standish, the English-born Pilgrim leader, and jazz great Miles Davis. Regularly used in the U.S. for more than 125 years.

Milo   Rank: 679

Origin: English
Meaning: Merciful
Alternate Spelling: Mylo
Gender Variation: Millie
Similar Names: Melvin, Mickey, Milan, Milford, Mills
Namesakes: Milo (*Bloom County* comic strip character), *Venus de Milo* (Greek statue)
⇨ A form of the name Miles currently associated with young Hollywood actor Milo Ventimiglia best-known for playing Jess Mariano on the television series *Gilmore Girls*. Motion picture actor, director, and producer Mel Gibson has a son by this name.

Milton
Rank: 845
Origin: Old English
Meaning: From the mill town
Alternate Spellings: Millton, Milten, Miltin, Mylton
Gender Variation: Millie
Nicknames: Milt, Milty
Similar Names: Melton, Milburn, Milford, Millard
➡ Originated as a surname and place name first associated with 17th-century English poet John Milton, who is best known for the epic poem, *Paradise Lost*. Comedian Milton Berle kept the name in front of the public during the golden age of television in the late 1940s and 1950s. Listed among the top 200 from 1880 to 1957, the name has declined in recent years.

Misael
Rank: 620
Origin: Aramaic
Meaning: Who is like God
Alternate Spelling: Missael
Gender Variation: Mikaela
Similar Names: Michael, Miguel, Mishael
➡ A form of the biblical name Mishael, one of the three men thrown into the fiery furnace by Nebuchadnezzar in the book of Daniel. The name was added to the popularity chart in 1990.

Mitchell
Rank: 275
Origin: Hebrew
Meaning: Who resembles God
Alternate Spelling: Mitchel, Mitchill
Gender Variation: Mitchelle
Nickname: Mitch
Similar Names: Michel, Mick, Mickey, Miko, Miles, Milo
Namesakes: Mitch Ryan (actor), Mitch Ryder (musician)
➡ Originated as a surname during the Middle Ages, derived from a medieval form of Michael. Recognized as a given name during the 19th century, usage peaked during the 1990s. Margaret Mitchell, author of the classic *Gone with the Wind*, is a bearer of the surname.

Mohamed
Rank: 467
Origin: Arabic
Meaning: Worthy of praise
Alternate Spellings: Mohamad, Mohamet, Mohammad, Mohammed, Muhamet, Muhammad, Muhammed
Nicknames: Amed, Hamad
Similar Names: Mahmoud, Mahmud, Mahomet, Mamduh, Mehmet
Namesake: Mohamed "Momo" Sissoko (French-Malian soccer player)
➡ Variation of Muhammad, the name of the 7th-century prophet and founder of the religion of Islam. In popular use in the U.S. since 1982.

Moises
Rank: 344
Origin: Hebrew/Egyptian
Meaning: Drawn out of the water
Gender Variation: Moriah
Nickname: Mo
Similar Names: Moisey, Moishe, Mose, Moses, Moshe, Moss
Namesakes: Moises Alou (Dominican baseball player), Moises Arias (actor)
➡ Originated from the Hebrew name Moshe, which is a variation of Moses. Rarely used in the U.S. until 1958, it's climbing slowly up the popularity chart as part of a biblical naming trend.

Morgan
Rank: 366
Origin: Welsh
Meaning: Borne from the sea
Alternate Spelling: Morgen
Gender Variations: Morgana, Morgance, Morganne
Similar Names: Monty, Mordecai, Morley, Morris, Mortimer, Morton
Namesakes: Harry Morgan (actor), J. P. Morgan (financier), Tracy Morgan (comedian/actor)
➡ A surname, place name, and variation of Morcana. Known for Morgan Earp, the younger brother of Wyatt, who was involved in the gunfight at the O.K. Corral. Actor and director Morgan Freeman is a more recent namesake. Traditionally a boy's name, but currently more popular for girls.

Moses
Rank: 445

Origin: Hebrew/Egyptian
Meaning: Drawn out of the water
Alternate Spelling: Mozes
Gender Variation: Moriah
Nickname: Mo
Similar Names: Moises, Moishe, Mose, Moshe, Moss
Namesake: Moses Malone (Basketball Hall of Famer)
⇨ Derived from the Hebrew name Moshe, the biblical name for the Jewish leader who delivered the Israelites from captivity in Egypt and was also the recipient of the 10 Commandments from God. An enduring name that's been popular among Jewish families and lately part of a biblical name revival. Singer Chris Martin and actress Gwyneth Paltrow have a son named Moses.

Moshe
Rank: 662

Origin: Hebrew/Egyptian
Meaning: Drawn out of the water
Gender Variation: Misha
Similar Names: Moisey, Moishe, Mose, Moss, Mozes
⇨ The Hebrew form of Moses and known for Moshe Katsav, the 8th president of Israel, and Moshe Dayan, the 20th-century Israeli military leader and politician. The name has been consistently used by parents since 1973.

Nash
Rank: 742

Origin: Middle English
Meaning: At the ash tree
Gender Variations: Nasha, Nasya
Similar Names: Nate, Nathan, Neal, Nick
Namesakes: Ogden Nash (poet), Steve Nash (Canadian basketball player)
⇨ A surname derived from the phrase atten ash. Known for mathematician John Forbes Nash, the recipient of the 1994 Nobel Prize in Economics and the inspiration for the 1998 film, A Beautiful Mind. The name debuted on the popularity chart in 1997.

Nasir
Rank: 418

Origin: Arabic
Meaning: Supporter
Alternate Spellings: Naseer, Naser, Nasr, Nasser, Nassor

Gender Variation: Nasira
Nickname: Nas
Similar Names: Mahir, Nadir, Nasim, Nizar, Qadir
⇨ A form of Nasara that debuted on the popularity chart in 1996.

Nathan
Rank: 23

Origin: Hebrew
Meaning: God has given
Alternate Spellings: Nathen, Nathon
Gender Variations: Naarah, Naomi, Nathalie
Nicknames: Nat, Nate, Natty
Similar Names: Jonathan, Lathan, Natan, Nathaniel, Neal, Nehemiah
Namesake: Nathan Lane (actor)
⇨ A biblical name for a prophet during the reigns of David and Solomon. American Revolutionary War hero Nathan Hale is a historical bearer. It's been listed among the top 50 since 1975.

Nathaniel
Rank: 69

Origin: Hebrew
Meaning: God has given
Alternate Spellings: Nathanael, Nathaneal, Nathanial, Nathanyal, Nathanyel, Nethaniel, Nethanyel
Gender Variation: Nathalie
Nicknames: Nat, Nate, Nathan, Natty, Thaniel
Similar Names: Nate, Nathan, Neal, Nehemiah, Nicholas, Nicodemus, Noah
Namesakes: Nathanael West (author/screenwriter), Nathaniel Hawthorne (novelist)
⇨ A biblical name for one of the apostles who was also called Bartholomew. Listed among the top 100 in 1978, peaking at No. 61 in 2000 and 2001. Musician Nat King Cole, born Nathaniel Coles, used a short form of the name.

Nehemiah
Rank: 362

Origin: Hebrew
Meaning: Comforted by God
Alternate Spellings: Nehemia, Nehemya, Nehemyah
Gender Variations: Neah, Neriah
Nicknames: Nemiah, Nemo
Similar Names: Nechemia, Nehmiah, Nereus, Nicanor, Nicodemus, Noah
⇨ The name of an Old Testament Jewish leader who reconstructed the walls of

Jerusalem after returning from captivity in Babylon. It was in popular use as a given name in 1886, then disappeared until 1998, climbing to its current position as part of a biblical name revival.

Neil
Rank: 604

Origin: Gaelic
Meaning: Champion
Alternate Spellings: Neal, Neale, Neel, Neill, Niel
Gender Variations: Neala, Neilina
Similar Names: Nels, Nelson, Niels, Nigel, Niles
Namesakes: Neil Cavuto (TV host), Neil Diamond (musician), Neil Patrick Harris (actor), Neil Young (Canadian musician)
➡ A variation of the Scottish name Niall that was popular in Ireland and Scotland during the Middle Ages. Astronaut Neil Armstrong gave the name worldwide attention when he became the first man to walk on the moon in 1969. It peaked in 1953 at No. 146.

Nelson
Rank: 447

Origin: Old English
Meaning: Son of Neil
Alternate Spelling: Nelsen
Gender Variation: Nell
Nickname: Nels
Similar Names: Neal, Neilson, Nigel, Niles, Nilsson, Nolan
Namesakes: Nelson Eddy (singer/actor), Nelson Rockefeller (former U.S. vice president), Judd Nelson (actor), Willie Nelson (country musician)
➡ A surname used as a first name historically and known for the 19th-century British admiral Lord Horatio Nelson, who defeated Napoleonic forces in the Battle of Trafalgar. It's more recently associated with anti-apartheid activist and former South African president Nelson Mandela. The name peaked during the late 1800s but has been used steadily since that time.

Nestor
Rank: 927

Origin: Greek
Meaning: Traveler
Alternate Spellings: Nester, Nestore
Gender Variation: Nesta
Nickname: Nest
Similar Names: Nestorio, Nicandro, Nicolas, Nicomedes

➡ The name of the king of Pylos in Homer's epic poems, the *Iliad* and the *Odyssey*. He is the oldest of the warriors at Troy and is known for his wisdom. The name peaked during the early 1890s and is preferred by Hispanic parents.

Nicholas
Rank: 17

Origin: Greek
Meaning: Victorious people
Alternate Spellings: Nicholaus, Nickolas, Nicolaas, Nicolas, Nicolaus, Nikkolas, Nikolas, Nikolaus
Gender Variations: Nicola, Nicole, Nikki
Nicknames: Colas, Cole, Nick, Nicky, Nico, Nicol, Nichols
Similar Names: Colin, Nick, Nico, Nicodemus, Nikos
Namesakes: *Nicholas Nickleby* (Charles Dickens novel), Nicolaus Copernicus (astronomer)
➡ Derived from the Greek name Nikolaos and known for the 5th-century patron saint of children, also known as Santa Claus. In the New Testament, Nicolaus is mentioned as a deacon. An enduring name in the U.S., it broke into the top 100 in 1972, peaking at No. 6. Actor Nicolas Cage uses the Spanish variation.

Nick
Rank: 820

Origin: Greek
Meaning: Victorious people
Alternate Spellings: Nic, Nik, Nyck, Nyk
Gender Variations: Nichole, Nicola, Nicole, Nicki
Nickname: Nicky
Similar Names: Colin, Dominic, Nels, Nichol, Nicolas, Nikita, Nikko, Nixon
Namesakes: Nick Carraway (*The Great Gatsby* character), Nick Faldo (English golfer), Nick Nolte (actor)
➡ The short form of Nicholas that's also used as an independent name. Best-known for Nick Charles, the fictional detective from *The Thin Man* mystery novel written by Dashiell Hammett in 1933, that was adapted into a successful film in 1934. The name is more recently associated with actor and pop singer Nick Carter, a member of the Grammy-nominated group, The Backstreet Boys. The name peaked in 1918 at No. 173 and has fallen to its current ranking.

Nico
Rank: 667
Origin: Greek
Meaning: Victorious people
Alternate Spelling: Niko
Gender Variations: Nicky, Nicola
Nickname: Nic
Similar Names: Niccolo, Nichol, Nick, Nicky, Niklas, Nikodem
⇒ The Italian and Dutch short form of Nicholas or Nicodemus used as a given name since 1988.

Nigel
Rank: 709
Origin: English
Meaning: Black
Alternate Spellings: Nigal, Nigiel, Nigil
Gender Variations: Negelia, Nigella
Similar Names: Neal, Neely, Nelson, Niall, Niles
⇒ From the Latin name Nigellus, which is a form of Neil. A common name in England and Wales during the 1960s and '70s. Fashionable in the U.S. since 1971. Most famous bearers are from United Kingdom, including renowned actor Nigel Hawthorne, who was knighted in 1999.

Noah
Rank: 15
Origin: Hebrew
Meaning: Rest, comfort
Alternate Spelling: Noa
Gender Variations: Nona, Nonie
Nickname: Noe
Similar Names: Noach, Noam, Noble, Noel, Nolan
Namesake: Noah Adams (National Public Radio host)
⇒ In the Old Testament, Noah built an ark which allowed his family and each species of animal to survive the Great Flood. Listed among the top 100 most popular names since 1995. Lexicographer Noah Webster, who finished the first American dictionary in 1828 when he was 70 is a historical namesake. Actor Noah Wyle, best known for his role as Dr. John Carter on the television drama *E.R.*, is a current bearer.

Noe
Rank: 450
Origin: Hebrew
Meaning: Rest, comfort
Gender Variations: Noella, Noelle

Similar Names: Noach, Noah, Noam, Noel
⇒ The French form of Noah. A good choice for trendsetting parents who prefer names with an international flavor and biblical roots.

Noel
Rank: 448
Origin: French
Meaning: Christmas
Alternate Spellings: Nowel, Nowell
Gender Variations: Noele, Noelia, Noella
Similar Names: Emile, Eugene, Henri, Leon, Nicolas, Renard
Namesake: Sir Noel Coward (playwright)
⇒ A vocabulary word for a Christmas carol that dates back to the Middle Ages when the common spelling was "Nowel" or "Nowell." Known for 20th-century British playwright and actor Sir Noel Coward. An enduring name that has never achieved a huge amount of popularity. A good choice for parents who are particularly fond of the holiday season.

Nolan
Rank: 145
Origin: Irish/English
Meaning: Champion
Alternate Spellings: Nolen, Nolin, Nollan, Nollin, Nolon, Nolun, Nolyn
Gender Variations: Nola, Nolene
Similar Names: Noland, Norman, Norris, Norton
⇒ Originates from the Irish surname Nuallan that's been more commonly used for boys but occasionally given to girls. Noted baseball pitcher Nolan Ryan has helped move the name up the popularity chart since the 1970s.

Norman
Rank: 145
Origin: Old German
Meaning: Northman
Gender Variations: Norma, Normina
Nickname: Norm
Similar Names: Noble, Norris, Norton, Norwood, Nowell
Namesakes: Norman Bates (*Psycho* movie character), Norman Fell (actor), Norman Mailer (writer), Norman Rockwell (artist), Norman Schwarzkopf (military general), Norman Vincent Peale (preacher/author)
⇒ Derived from *nord* and *man* referring to a Norseman or Viking. Historically the Normans were descendants of the Vikings who settled

in a part of northern France called Normandy. They conquered England at the Battle of Hastings during the 11th century. The name was favored in England before the conquest, and remained in use after, fading during the 14th century. In the U.S., the name became fashionable during the 19th century and was listed among the top 200 from 1880 to 1972.

Octavio
Rank: 669

Origin: Latin
Meaning: Eighth
Gender Variations: Octavia, Ottavia
Similar Names: Octavian, Otavio, Ottaviano
Namesake: Octavio Paz (Mexican writer/poet)
➨ The Spanish form of the Roman family name Octavius. A good choice for Hispanic parents.

Oliver
Rank: 173

Origin: Latin
Meaning: Olive tree
Alternate Spellings: Olivor, Olliver, Ollivor, Olyver
Gender Variations: Livia, Livvy, Olive, Olivia, Olivie
Nickname: Ollie
Similar Names: Olivier, Osbert, Osborne, Oscar, Osmond, Oswald
Namesakes: *Oliver!* (1968 award-winning musical)
➨ A variation of the French name Olivier, used in English-speaking countries since medieval times. Influenced by Oliver Cromwell, the 17th-century British military leader who was lord protector of England, Scotland, and Ireland. A literary name for the title character in Charles Dickens' novel *Oliver Twist*. The name peaked prior to 1900, but remains in steady use. Film director Oliver Stone is a current influence.

Omar
Rank: 131

Origin: Arabic/Hebrew
Meaning: Flourishing, eloquent
Alternate Spellings: Ommar, Omarr
Gender Variation: Oma
Similar Names: Amir, Ammar, Jamar, Omari, Omarion, Omri, Umar

Namesakes: Omar Bradley (military general), Omar Epps (actor), Omar Little (*The Wire* TV character), Omar Omidyar (eBay founder)
➨ The Old Testament name for Esau's grandson and the chieftain of an Edomite clan. Also linked with 12th-century Persian poet Omar Khayyam, best known for writing the *Rubaiyat of Omar Khayyam*. Egyptian-born actor and international bridge player Omar Sharif is another famous bearer. A top 200 name since 1988.

Omari
Rank: 715

Origin: Arabic/Hebrew
Meaning: Flourishing, eloquent
Gender Variation: Oma
Nickname: Omar
Similar Names: Amari, Amarion, Damarion, Jamarion, Omarion, Omri, Umar
➨ A variation of Omar that appeared on the popularity chart in 1978 and 1980 before disappearing until 1997.

Omarion
Rank: 728

Origin: Arabic/Hebrew
Meaning: Flourishing, eloquent
Gender Variation: Oma
Nicknames: Omar, Omari
Similar Names: Amari, Amarion, Damarion, Jamarion
➨ New to the popularity charts as of 2002, influenced by Omari "Omarion" Ishmael Grandberry, former lead singer of B2K, whose first album was released in 2002. After the group disbanded in 2004, he moved on to a solo career and then became an actor in 2004.

Orion
Rank: 529

Origin: Greek
Meaning: Hunter
Alternate Spelling: Oryon
Gender Variation: Oriana
Similar Names: Oren, Orlando, Orson, Orville
➨ A maverick name taken from Greek mythology for the son of Poseidon who became a mighty hunter. A constellation bears his name. Former actress Liberty Phoenix, sister of Joaquin, named one of her sons Indigo Orion.

Or ⇒ boys' names

Orlando
Rank: 356

Origin: German
Meaning: Bright sun
Gender Variation: Orla
Nicknames: Orly, Lando
Similar Names: Orson, Orville, Roland, Rolando, Rowland, Rollin, Rowe
Namesakes: Orlando Jones (actor), Tony Orlando (singer)
⇨ The Italian form of Roland and a literary name of one of the central characters in Shakespeare's play *As You Like It*. Hollywood leading man Orlando Bloom is a namesake. Also a popular tourist destination in Florida.

Oscar
Rank: 118

Origin: Old English
Meaning: Spear of the gods
Alternate Spelling: Oskar
Gender Variations: Orva, Osanna
Similar Names: Osbert, Osborn, Osmond, Oswald, Ozzy
Namesakes: *Oscar* (1991 film), Oscar de la Hoya (boxer), Oscar de la Renta (fashion designer), Oscar Hammerstein II (songwriter), Oscar Wilde (Irish writer)
⇨ Used by 18th-century Scottish poet James Macpherson in his *Poems of Ossian*. The poem was so highly regarded by Napoleon, he gave the name to his French godson, who ascended the throne of Sweden as Oscar I in 1844. Associated with the statuette given out each year for achievement in the motion picture industry at the Academy Awards. The name peaked in popularity prior to 1900 and is still a chart topper in Sweden.

Osvaldo
Rank: 491

Origin: Old English
Meaning: God rule
Alternate Spelling: Oswaldo
Gender Variation: Ovelia
Similar Names: Octavio, Odalis, Olegario, Oscar, Ozzie
⇨ The Italian, Portuguese, and Spanish form of Oswald, which is derived from os and *weald*. Saint Oswald was a 7th-century king of Northumbria who brought Christianity to northeast England. In popular use since 1961.

Owen
Rank: 58

Origin: Welsh
Meaning: Well born
Alternate Spellings: Owain, Owin, Owynn
Gender Variation: Owena
Similar Names: Eugene, Evan, Ewan, Ewen, Iwan, John
Namesake: Clive Owen (actor)
⇨ The Welsh form of Owain and the Greek form of Eugene that has suddenly become fashionable since 2000 with a little help from Academy Award-nominated actor and writer Owen Wilson.

Pablo
Rank: 292

Origin: Latin
Meaning: Small
Gender Variations: Paola, Paulina, Pavla
Similar Names: Pablos, Paol, Paulino, Paulo, Pavlo
⇨ The Spanish form of Paulus best-known for Spanish painter and sculptor Pablo Picasso, one of the most recognized figures in 20th-century art.

Parker
Rank: 116

Origin: Old English
Meaning: Keeper of the park
Gender Variation: Parker
Similar Names: Palmer, Parry, Pascal, Patrick, Porter
Namesake: Peter Parker (*Spider-Man* character)
⇨ An occupational surname for a gamekeeper that has steadily risen in popularity since the late 1970s, influenced by actor Parker Stevenson. Jazz saxophonist and composer Charlie "Bird" Parker is a famous bearer of the surname. Also used as a girl's name.

Patrick
Rank: 110

Origin: Latin
Meaning: Nobleman
Alternate Spellings: Patric, Patrik, Patryk
Gender Variations: Patty, Patrice, Patricia, Patsy, Tricia
Nicknames: Paddy, Pat
Similar Names: Fitzpatrick, Paden, Patricio, Patton

Namesakes: Patrick Duffy (actor), Patrick Ewing (basketball player), Patrick Swayze (actor), Patrick Stewart (English actor)

➥ Taken from the Roman name Patricius and widely known for Saint Patrick, a Christian missionary during the 5th century who became the patron saint of Ireland. His feast day is also known as Saint Patrick's Day. Also known for 18th-century U.S. statesman and orator Patrick Henry who is remembered for his speech "Give me liberty or give me death." Television and film actor Patrick Dempsey is a current influence.

Paul   Rank: 134

Origin: Latin
Meaning: Small
Gender Variations:
Paula, Pauletta, Paulette, Paulina, Pauline
Similar Names: Pablo, Paolo, Pasha, Paulos, Paulsen, Pavel, Pavlo
Namesakes: Paul Bunyan (folk hero), Paul Cezanne (19th-century painter), Paul Gauguin (19th-century painter), Paul McCartney (musician), Paul Simon (musician)

➥ Derived from the Latin family name Paulus that became common among the early Christians. Paul, originally known as Saul, converted to Christianity after seeing a vision of Christ. He became a missionary, authored 14 epistles in the New Testament, and is considered a saint in the Roman Catholic Church. Also the name of several kings and six popes. Paul Revere, whose famous ride in 1775 warned colonists of the arrival of British troops, influenced the name.

Pax

Origin: Latin
Meaning: Peaceful
Alternate Spelling: Paxx
Gender Variation: Paz
Similar Names: Jax, Max, Paxti, Paxton, Paz, Peace, Pei, Placido

➥ Pax is associated with Nemesis, the Roman goddess of peace, who was referred to as Pax-Nemesis in Rome. The name is internationally known for the adopted son of celebrity couple Angelina Jolie and Brad Pitt.

Paxton   Rank: 777

Origin: Old English
Meaning: Poecc's settlement
Alternate Spellings:
Paxten, Paxtin, Paxtyn
Gender Variation: Paxton
Similar Names: Paden, Palmer, Parker, Patrick, Patton, Payton

➥ A surname derived from an English place name of unknown meaning. Actor and film director Bill Paxton is a bearer of the surname. The name debuted in 1997 and is currently at its peak.

Pedro   Rank: 219

Origin: Greek
Meaning: Rock
Gender Variation: Petra
Similar Names: Pepe, Pete, Peter, Petros, Piedro
Namesakes: Pedro Almodovar (Spanish filmmaker), Pedro Delgado (Spanish Tour de France winner)

➥ The Spanish and Portuguese form of Peter and historically the name of two emperors of Brazil and two Spanish conquistadors. It peaked in 1992 at No. 188 but is still listed among the top 300.

Perry   Rank: 958

Origin: Old English
Meaning: Pear tree
Alternate Spellings:
Parry, Perrie
Gender Variations: Pera, Perrie
Nickname: Per
Similar Names: Percy, Peter, Peyton, Philbert, Philip, Pierce, Porter
Namesakes: Luke Perry (actor), Perry Ellis (fashion designer), Steve Perry (singer), William "The Fridge" Perry (football player)

➥ Derived from *pyrige* and possibly a pet form of Peregrine or a surname for someone who lives by a pear tree. Historically known for Matthew Calbraith Perry, the Navy commodore credited with opening Japan to the West in 1854. Actor Matthew Perry, best-known as Chandler Bing on the television sitcom *Friends*, is another famous bearer of the surname. The name peaked prior to the turn of the 20th century.

Peter
Rank: 167

Origin: Greek
Meaning: Rock
Alternate Spellings:
Peder, Petar, Peterr,
Petr, Petre, Pieter
Gender Variations: Petra, Petrina, Petula
Nickname: Pete
Similar Names: Patrick, Pearce, Petros,
Pierce, Pierre
Namesakes: Peter Cetera (musician), Peter
Gabriel (English musician), Peter Jackson
(producer), Peter Krause (actor), Peter O'Toole
(English actor), Pete Sampras (tennis player)
➡ A fisherman who became one of the
earliest disciples of Jesus, whose name
was changed from Simon to Peter, according
to the New Testament. He's considered a
saint in the Roman Catholic Church and the
first bishop of Rome. Peter the Great, the
18th-century czar of Russia is another notable
bearer. Often used in literature and nursery
rhymes, it peaked prior to 1900 but is still
in regular use.

Peyton
Rank: 154

Origin: Old English
Meaning: Village of the
warrior
Alternate Spellings: Paten,
Patin, Paton, Payton
Gender Variations: Peyton
Similar Names: Paden, Patrick, Patton, Paxton
Namesakes: Peyton Manning (football
player), Walter Payton (football player)
➡ A surname that originated from a place
name. Perhaps best known for the 1957 film
Peyton Place that was adapted for television
during the 1960s. Currently ranks at No. 138
as a girl's name.

Phillip
Rank: 285

Origin: Greek
Meaning: Lover of horses
Alternate Spellings: Fillip,
Philip, Philippe, Phillipe
Gender Variations: Phillippa,
Phillippina, Pippa
Nicknames: Phil, Pip
Similar Names: Felipe, Philbert, Philo, Phineas
Namesakes: John Philip Sousa (composer),
Phil Collins (musician), Philip Roth (novelist)
➡ A slightly shortened form of the surname
Phillips and the name of one of Christ's
apostles in the Bible. It spent more than
50 years ranked among the top 100, peaking
at No. 64 in 1950. Actor and Academy Award-
winner Philip Seymour Hoffman has brought
interest back to the name. It ranks highly
in several European countries, including
England where it's associated with Prince
Philip, Duke of Edinburgh, the husband and
consort of Queen Elizabeth II.

Phinnaeus

Origin: Hebrew/Egyptian
Meaning: Face of protection
Alternate Spellings: Phineas, Phinehas, Phineus
Gender Variation: Phenice
Nicknames: Phin, Phinny
Similar Names: Pinchas, Pincus, Pinhas,
Phelan, Philip
➡ A variation of Phinehas, the biblical name
for the grandson of Aaron who killed an
Israelite because he married a Midianite
woman and later succeeded his father as
high priest of the Israelites. Phineas "P. T."
Barnum, who founded the Ringling Brothers
and Barnum and Bailey Circus is another
notable bearer. Actress Julia Roberts and
Danny Moder named a son Phinnaeus.

Phoenix
Rank: 423

Origin: Greek
Meaning: Dark red
Alternate Spellings:
Fenix, Phenix, Phoenyx
Gender Variation: Phoenix
Similar Names: Philandros, Philip,
Philomenos, Pirro
Namesakes: *Phoenix* (1988 film), River
Phoenix (actor)
➡ A mythical Egyptian bird, a symbol of
immortality, with a bright red and gold
plumage that perishes in flames and is reborn
from the ashes every 500 years. A place
name for a major city in Arizona. Also
recognized as the surname of popular actor
Joaquin Phoenix. Occasionally used for girls.

Pierce
Rank: 549

Origin: English
Meaning: Rock
Alternate Spellings:
Pearce, Peerce
Gender Variations: Paris, Persia
Similar Names: Pearson, Percy, Peter,
Piercy, Pierre, Piers

Namesakes: David Hyde Pierce (actor), Hawkeye Pierce (*MASH* character)

➩ A surname that originated during the Middle Ages from Piers. Highly recognized for Irish actor Pierce Brosnan.

Porter
Rank: 476

Origin: Old French
Meaning: Doorkeeper
Alternate Spelling: Porteur
Gender Variation: Portia
Similar Names: Palmer, Parker, Potter
Namesakes: Cole Porter (composer), Kalan Porter (*Canadian Idol* winner)

➩ An occupational surname for someone who carried goods. Famed 19th-century short-story writer William Sydney Porter who used the pen name O. Henry, is a bearer of the surname. Mainly used during the 19th century but appears to be making a comeback.

Preston
Rank: 114

Origin: Old English
Meaning: Priest settlement
Alternate Spellings: Prestan, Presten, Prestin, Prestyn
Gender Variation: Presley
Similar Names: Porter, Prescott, Presley, Prestley, Price, Priestly
Namesake: Robert Preston (actor)

➩ An English surname that derives its meaning from land that was passed around between churches. A place name for a city in northwest England that became the 50th city during the 50th year of Queen Elizabeth's reign. Recently influenced by fictional character Dr. Preston Burke from the television medical drama *Grey's Anatomy*. The name has ranked among the top 200 since 1993.

Prince
Rank: 825

Origin: Latin
Meaning: Prince
Gender Variations: Prisca, Priscilla
Similar Names: Duke, Preston, Price, Prinz

➩ Derived from the Latin root princeps for a male member of a royal family. Associated with famed rock musician Prince, who changed his name to a symbol in 1993 and back again in 1999 because of a contract dispute. The name received its highest rankings prior to the turn of the 20th century. Entertainer and musician Michael Jackson has a son by this name.

Quentin
Rank: 347

Origin: Latin
Meaning: Fifth-born child
Alternate Spellings: Quenten, Quenton, Quinten, Quintin, Quinton
Gender Variations: Quinta, Quintina
Nicknames: Quent, Quinn
Similar Names: Quincy, Quintilian, Quinto, Quintus

➩ A derivative of the given name Quintus and a literary name for the hero of the 1823 historical novel *Quentin Durward* by Sir Walter Scott. Director and screenwriter Quentin Tarantino is a famous bearer of the name. Listed among the top 20 in France.

Quincy
Rank: 489

Origin: Old French
Meaning: Estate of the fifth son
Alternate Spellings: Quincey, Quinsy
Gender Variations: Quinn
Nicknames: Quin
Similar Names: Quentin, Quinn, Quintin, Quintus
Namesake: *Quincy, M.E.* (television show)

➩ A surname derived from the given name Quintus. John Quincy Adams, the 6th U.S. president who was born in Quincy, Massachusetts, is a famous bearer. Currently known for record producer Quincy Jones. A popular choice for African-American families.

Quinn
Rank: 282

Origin: Irish Gaelic
Meaning: Descendant of Conn
Alternate Spelling: Quin
Gender Variation: Quintessa
Similar Names: Quincy, Quintin, Quintus
Namesake: Aidan Quinn (actor)

➩ A surname used as a given name and also the short form of Quincy and Quintin. Influenced during the 1950s and 1960s by Academy Award-winner Anthony Quinn, who became known as a painter, sculptor, and writer in later years. His son Francesco Quinn became an actor in 1986.

Ra ⇒ boys' names

Rafael
Rank: 217

Origin: Hebrew
Meaning: God has healed
Alternate Spelling: Raphael
Gender Variations: Rafaela, Raquel
Similar Names: Rafaelo, Ramiro, Rapha, Ricardo, Roberto, Rodolpho
Namesake: Raphael Sanzio (Renaissance painter)
⇒ A variantion of Raphael who was known as an archangel in the Bible. The name peaked in 1985 at No. 195 but is still listed among the top 300. Spanish professional tennis player Rafael Nadal is a current namesake.

Ralph
Rank: 764

Origin: Old German
Meaning: Wolf counsel
Alternate Spelling: Ralf
Gender Variation: Ralphina
Nickname: Ralphie
Similar Names: Rafe, Ralston, Raoul, Raul, Rolph
Namesakes: Ralph Macchio (actor), Ralph Nader (activist)
⇒ The contracted form of Radulf derived from *rad* and *wulf* that led to other forms of the name during the Middle Ages, including Radulf, Raulf, and Raul. Ralf became popular during the 16th century, which gave way to Ralph in the 18th century. The name was influenced by poet Ralph Waldo Emerson during the 19th century. Listed among the top 100 names from 1880 to 1963, it has steadily declined since that time. English actor Ralph Fiennes is a current bearer.

Ramiro
Rank: 567

Origin: Latin
Meaning: Powerful in the army
Gender Variation: Ramona
Similar Names: Ramirez, Raul, Reinaldo, Remedio, Renato
⇒ A form of the popular surname Ramirez that dates back to the 16th century when children were given a surname that was adapted from their father's first name. Also the name of a popular saint from the 6th century and two Spanish kings. Listed among the top 600 names since 1944.

Ramon
Rank: 367

Origin: Old German
Meaning: Protecting hands
Alternate Spellings: Ramone, Raymon
Gender Variation: Ramona
Nickname: Ray
Similar Names: Ramiro, Raul, Raymundo, Reinaldo, Renato, Reyes
⇒ The Spanish form of Raymond influenced by Mexican actor Ramon Novarro, who achieved his greatest success after appearing in major box office films during the 1920s and early 1930s. The name peaked at No. 182 during that time but has diminished slightly in recent years.

Randall
Rank: 622

Origin: German
Meaning: Wolf, protector
Alternate Spellings: Randal, Randel, Randell
Gender Variations: Randa, Randi
Nicknames: Ran, Rand, Randy
Similar Names: Randolph, Ransford, Ransley, Roland, Ronald
⇒ The medieval form of Randolf derived from the elements *rand* and *wulf* that led to the use of the surname. Television and film actor Tony Randall, who's best known as neat freak Felix Unger in the 1970s television series *The Odd Couple*, is a famous bearer of the surname. It was listed among the top 100 names from 1948 to 1970.

Randy
Rank: 310

Origin: German
Meaning: Wolf, protector
Alternate Spelling: Randey
Gender Variations: Brandi, Randi
Nicknames: Ran, Rand
Similar Names: Rankin, Ransley, Ransom, Ray, Raymond, Rayner
Namesakes: Randy Newman (musician), Randy Travis (country musician), Randy Quaid (actor)
⇒ The short form of Randall and Randolph that debuted as a given name in 1935 and was listed among the top 100 from 1948 to 1984.

Rashad
Rank: 660

Origin: Arabic
Meaning: Good sense, good guidance

Alternate Spellings: Rashaad, Rashod
Gender Variations: Rasha, Rashida
Similar Names: Raghid, Rajab, Rashid, Rida, Riyad
➡ Associated with famed football player and sportscaster Ahmad Rashad. Born Bobby Moore, he changed his name in 1972 when he converted to the Islam. The name debuted on the popularity chart in 1974.

Raul   Rank: 255

Origin: German
Meaning: Wolf counsel
Alternate Spellings: Raol, Raoul
Gender Variations: Raoula, Rayla
Similar Names: Rafael, Rafe, Ralf, Rolf
➡ The Italian and Portuguese form of Radulf that became popular in the U.S. in 1904 and is preferred by Hispanic families.

Ray   Rank: 560

Origin: Old German
Meaning: Protecting hands
Alternate Spellings: Rae, Rai, Raye, Rey
Gender Variations: Raven, Ravenna
Similar Names: Rayner, Rene, Reyes, Rob, Roy
Namesakes: Ray Bolger (dancer/actor), Ray Krebbs (Dallas TV character), Ray Liotta (actor)
➡ The short form of Raymond that's also used as an independent name, but not to the extent of the popular, longer version. The name peaked prior to the turn of the century but is still in regular use. Singer Ray Charles and actor Ray Romano have kept the name in front of the public for decades.

Raymond   Rank: 194

Origin: Old German
Meaning: Protecting hands
Alternate Spellings: Raemond, Raimond, Raimund, Ramond, Raymund, Raymunde, Reimund, Reymond
Gender Variation: Ramona
Nickname: Ray
Similar Names: Ramon, Ray, Rayner, Reagan, Redmond
Namesake: Raymond Floyd (PGA golfer)
➡ Introduced to England by the Normans during the 11th century. Parents lost interest in the name until the mid-19th century and then it hit its stride during the early 20th century with a little help from Canadian actor Raymond Massey, whose film career started in 1927. Actor Raymond Burr, widely known as television attorney Perry Mason, kept the name in front of parents starting in the 1950s.

Reagan   Rank: 792

Origin: Irish Gaelic
Meaning: Descendant of the little king
Alternate Spellings: Reagen, Regan, Regen
Gender Variations: Reagan, Reenie
Similar Names: Aidan, Keegan, Rayan, Rearden, Reece, Reggie, Riordan, Ronan
➡ A form of Regan, derived from the surname O'Riagain, that's best known as the surname of Ronald Reagan, the 40th U.S. president. First charted for boys in 1996, it ranks among the top 150 names for girls.

Reece   Rank: 413

Origin: Welsh
Meaning: Ardor
Alternate Spellings: Riece, Reace, Rees, Reese, Rhys
Gender Variation: Reese
Similar Names: Regan, Reid, Reisel, Rene, Sean, Steffan
Namesake: Jonathan Rhys-Meyers (Irish actor)
➡ The anglicized form of Rhys most likely used as a transferred form of the surname. Sporadically used as a given name until 1986 when parents started using the name on a regular basis. Rhys and Reece rank highly in England, Scotland, and Wales.

Reginald   Rank: 516

Origin: Norman
Meaning: Powerful one
Gender Variation: Regina
Nicknames: Reg, Reggie
Similar Names: Reinald, Reinhold, Reynaldo, Reynold, Ronald, Ronaldo
➡ Derived from Reginaldus, the Latin form of Reynold, also influenced by the Latin regina. Often shortened to Reg or Reggie for a casual flair. Sports enthusiasts will associate the name with baseball player Reggie Jackson and football player Reggie White. Pop star Elton John, whose birth name is Reginald Dwight, is a namesake. It recently slipped out of the top 500.

Reid
Rank: 422

Origin: Scottish
Meaning: Red, red-haired
Alternate Spellings: Read, Reade, Reed, Reide, Reyd
Gender Variations: Reed, Reina
Similar Names: Reece, Reisel, Remus, Rene
⇨ A surname that originated as a nickname for someone with a ruddy complexion or red hair. Use as a given name. Predominantly found in the U.S. Famed actress Tara Reid has brought attention to the name within the past several years.

Reilly
Origin: Gaelic
Meaning: Outgoing people
Alternate Spellings: Reilley, Riley, Rylee, Rylie, Ryley
Gender Variations: Rilla, Rylee
Similar Names: Raul, Reid, Reisel, Ridley, Rowley, Royal
Namesakes: John C. Reilly (actor), *Mary Reilly* (1996 film)
⇨ A surname used as a given name that debuted in 1996. A variation of the top 200 name Riley.

Remington
Rank: 781

Origin: Old English
Meaning: From the raven's home
Gender Variations: Regina, Reina
Nickname: Remy
Similar Names: Reginald, Remy, Reymund, Reynard
⇨ Originated from a surname and place name that first became known for 20th-century U.S. painter, illustrator, and sculptor Frederic Remington. Its 1983 debut on the popularity chart as a boy's given name was possibly inspired by the 1980s television series *Remington Steele*.

Rene
Rank: 492

Origin: Latin
Meaning: Reborn
Alternate Spelling: Renee
Gender Variations: Rena, Renata, Renee
Nicknames: Ren, Rennie
Similar Names: Reginald, Regis, Remy, Renato, Romain
⇨ The French form of Renatus that was used by early Christians as a baptismal name in reference to the birth of Christ. Historically known for Rene Descartes, the 17th-century French philosopher and mathematician. Favored as a boy's name but occasionally used for girls since the 1940s. Canadian singer Celine Dion named her son Rene Charles.

Rex
Rank: 814

Origin: Latin
Meaning: King
Gender Variations: Regina, Rexana, Rexanne
Similar Names: Rafe, Reagan, Reed, Rexer, Rexford, Rhett, Rick
Namesakes: *Oedipus Rex* (Sophocles' play), Rex Reed (film critic)
⇨ Taken from the Latin vocabulary word that was adopted as a given name during the 19th and 20th centuries. It was popularized by English stage and film actor Rex Harrison, born Reginald Carey Harrison and who's best known for his portrayal of Professor Henry Higgins in the 1964 film *My Fair Lady*. The name peaked in 1951 at No. 171.

Reynaldo
Rank: 834

Origin: German
Meaning: He who rules with good judgment
Alternate Spelling: Reynaldo
Gender Variations: Regina, Ronalda
Nicknames: Naldo, Rey
Similar Names: Ramiro, Ranald, Reginaldo, Reinhold, Renato, Renaud, Reynaud, Rinaldo, Ronald, Ronaldo
Namesake: Reynaldo Rosales (actor)
⇨ The Spanish form of Reynold composed of the elements *ragin* and *wald*. The name has been used occasionally since 1921 and is a popular choice among Hispanic families.

Rhett
Rank: 683

Origin: Old Welsh
Meaning: Advice, counsel
Alternate Spellings: Rhet, Ret, Rett
Gender Variations: Rhea, Rhetta
Similar Names: Brett, Reece, Reg, Reid, Rex

⇨ A form of the Dutch surname de Roedt that was brought to the U.S. by Colonel William Rhett in 1698. Best known for fictional character Rhett Butler, the hero in Margaret Mitchell's 1936 classic novel *Gone with the Wind*. Motion picture actor Clark Gable received an Academy Award nomination for his role in the 1939 film. The name has been in popular use since 1955.

Ricardo
Rank: 152

Origin: Old German
Meaning: Powerful leader
Alternate Spelling: Riccardo
Gender Variations: Ricarda, Ricki
Nicknames: Rick, Ricky
Similar Names: Enrique, Richard, Rico, Rikard, Ritchie, Roberto
Namesake: Ricardo Montalban (Mexican actor)
➡ The Spanish form of Richard popularized by the surname of fictional characters Lucy and Ricky Ricardo in the 1950s television classic *I Love Lucy*. Also associated with a kind of conga drum used in Cuban music. Preferred by Hispanic families.

Richard
Rank: 99

Origin: Old German
Meaning: Powerful leader
Alternate Spellings: Richart, Richerd
Gender Variations: Richelle, Richondra, Ricki
Nicknames: Dick, Rich, Rick, Ricky, Ritchie, Ryker
Similar Names: Broderick, Ricard, Ricardo, Richmond, Roderick
Namesakes: Little Richard (musician), Richard Burton (actor), Richard Gere (actor), Richard Marx (musician), Richard Nixon (37th U.S. president), Richard Rodgers (composer)
➡ Derived from the elements *ric* and *hard* that were introduced by the Normans into Britain. Associated with three kings including England's King Richard I, also known as Richard the Lionhearted, who first influenced the name during the 12th century. Today the name is linked with several well-known actors, musicians, and one U.S. president. An enduring name that's been listed among the top 100 for over 100 years.

Ricky
Rank: 394

Origin: Old German
Meaning: Powerful leader
Alternate Spellings: Ricci, Rickey, Rikky
Gender Variation: Ricki
Similar Names: Aric, Dick, Dicky, Rich, Rick, Ritchie, Rocky
Namesakes: Ricky Martin (Puerto Rican singer), Ricky Nelson (singer/actor), Ricky Rudd (NASCAR driver), Ricky Schroeder (actor)
➡ The pet form of Richard that peaked during the 1950s when audiences tuned in to watch the antics of Ricky Ricardo and his wife, Lucy, on the popular television sitcom *I Love Lucy*.

Riley
Rank: 101

Origin: Old English
Meaning: Rye clearing
Alternate Spellings: Reilley, Reilly, Rylee, Ryley, Rylie
Gender Variation: Riley
Similar Names: Harley, Kiley, Raleigh, Richey, Ridley, Rigel, Ripley
Namesakes: Pat Riley (NBA coach), Riley "B.B." King (musician)
➡ A common surname that's also spelled Reilley or Reilly. Popular as a boy's name but predominantly used for girls since 2002.

River
Rank: 511

Origin: Anglo-Norman
Meaning: River
Gender Variations: Riva, Rivka
Similar Names: Rich, Ridley, Riley, Rio
➡ A vocabulary word for a natural stream of water that may have been influenced by the surname Rivers. Best known for River Phoenix, a highly regarded actor during the 1980s and 1990s whose life was cut short in 1993 by a drug overdose. The name debuted on the popularity chart in 1994 and is currently at its peak. Rarely used as a girl's name as well.

Robert   Rank: 47
Origin: Old German
Meaning: Bright fame
Gender Variations:
Bobbi, Roberta, Robertina,
Robyn, Ruperta
Nicknames: Bert, Bob, Bobby, Rob, Robby,
Robin
Similar Names: Roberto, Robin, Roderick,
Ruben, Rubert, Rupert
Namesakes: Robert DeNiro (actor), Robert
Downey Jr. (actor), Robert Duvall (actor),
Robert E. Lee (army general), Robert Redford
(actor)
⇒ The name of three Scottish kings including
Robert the I of Scotland, also known as
Robert the Bruce, who liberated Scotland
from England during the 14th century. His
popularity paved the way for a variety of
surnames including Roberts and Robertson.
Consistently listed among the top 40 names
for more than 100 years. Novelist Robert
Louis Stevenson and poets Robert Browning,
Robert Burns, and Robert Frost are literary
bearers of the name.

Roberto   Rank: 215
Origin: Old German
Meaning: Bright fame
Gender Variations:
Roberta, Robertina
Nicknames: Bob, Bobbie, Rob, Robbie
Similar Names: Robert, Robertino, Rodolfo,
Rolando, Ruberto, Rupert
Namesakes: Roberto Alomar (Puerto Rican
baseball player), Roberto Clemente
(Baseball Hall of Famer), Roberto Duran
(Panamanian boxer)
⇒ The Italian, Portuguese, and Spanish form
of Robert that peaked in 1980 at No. 145.
Academy Award-winning Italian film and
television actor and director Roberto Benigni
is a famous bearer. Preferred by Hispanic
families.

Rocco   Rank: 490
Origin: German
Meaning: To rest
Alternate Spelling:
Rocko
Gender Variation: Coco
Nickname: Roc
Similar Names: Rico, Roch, Rocky,
Rodrigo, Romano, Rosario

⇒ An Italian name known for a 14th-century
French saint who stopped to nurse plague
victims while on his way to Rome. He was
eventually stricken with the illness and
became the patron saint of the sick. The
name peaked during the 1920s and faded out
in 1996. Madonna brought attention back to
the name in 2000 when she named her son
Rocco, prompting its return to the popularity
chart in 2001.

Rocky   Rank: 973
Origin: German
Meaning: To rest
Alternate Spelling: Rockey
Gender Variation: Rochelle
Nickname: Rock
Similar Names: Renzo, Riccardo, Rico,
Rockford, Rockland, Rocklin
Namesakes: Rocky Dennis (*Mask* character),
Rocky Raccoon (Beatles song), Rocky the
Flying Squirrel (animated character)
⇒ A form of Rocco that debuted on the
popularity chart in 1942 and peaked in 1955.
The name was influenced by boxer Rocky
Marciano, born Rocco Francis Marchegiano,
who held the title of Heavyweight Champion
of the World from 1952 to 1956. Also the
name of a 1976 film about an amateur boxer
named Rocky Balboa who gets a shot at
the world heavyweight title. The winner of
three Academy Awards, the film generated
five sequels.

Roderick   Rank: 730

Origin: Old German
Meaning: Famous power
Alternate Spellings:
Roderic, Roderich, Rodric,
Rodrick
Gender Variations: Roderiga, Roderika
Nicknames: Rod, Roddy
Similar Names: Broderick, Rodman,
Rodmond, Rodney, Rodrigo, Rodrigue
⇒ A compound name derived from the
elements *hrod* and *ric*. Popularized in
literature by Sir Walter Scott in his 1811 poem
"The Vision of Don Roderick" and Edgar
Allen Poe for a character in his 1839 short
story "The Fall of the House of Usher." It was
also the name of the title character in
Roderick Hudson, a 1876 novel by Henry
James. British actor Roddy McDowall, born
Roderick McDowall, is a famous bearer.

Rodney
Rank: 449

Origin: Old English
Meaning: Fame, Hroda's island
Alternate Spellings: Rodnee, Rodnie
Gender Variation: Rodina
Nicknames: Rod, Roddy
Similar Names: Brodericck, Rodrick, Rodrigo, Rodman, Rory
Namesake: Rodney "Rod" Carew (Baseball Hall of Famer)
➡ A surname used as a given name since the 18th century. Inspired by George Brydges Rodney, 1st Baron, an 18th-century English admiral who won important naval battles against the French, Spanish, and Dutch. More recently known for comedian and actor Rodney Dangerfield, whose career peaked during the 1980s. Listed among the top 100 names from 1946 to 1977.

Rodolfo
Rank: 519

Origin: Old German
Meaning: Wolf
Alternate Spelling: Rodolpho
Gender Variation: Roderica
Similar Names: Raoul, Rolf, Rollin, Rollo, Rudolfo, Rudolph, Rudy
➡ The Italian, Spanish, and Portuguese form of Rudolf inspired by Italian film actor Rudolph Valentino, born Rodolfo Pietro Filiberto Raffaello Guglielmi, who was known as the "Great Lover" of the 1920s.

Rodrigo
Rank: 363

Origin: Old German
Meaning: Famous power
Gender Variation: Roderiga
Nicknames: Rod, Roddy
Similar Names: Broderick, Roberto, Roderick, Roderigo, Rodolfo, Rodrigue, Rogelio
➡ The Italian, Portuguese, and Spanish form of Roderick. Shakespeare used the name for one of the central characters in his play *Othello*.

Rogelio
Rank: 517

Origin: Late Latin
Meaning: Request
Gender Variation: Rogelia
Nickname: Rog
Similar Names: Ramiro, Ricardo, Rogerio, Rogerios, Rutger

➡ The Spanish form of the Late Latin name Rogelius ultimately derived from the Latin *rogatus* that has slowly climbed the popularity chart since its debut in 1929 at No. 983. A good choice for Hispanic families.

Roger
Rank: 453

Origin: Old German
Meaning: Famous spear
Alternate Spelling: Rodger
Gender Variation: Jorey
Nickname: Rodge
Similar Names: Rogerio, Rogers, Roland, Ruggero, Rupert, Rutger
Namesakes: Roger Clemens (baseball player), Roger Federer (Swiss tennis player), Roger Staubach (Football Hall of Famer)
➡ An Old French personal name derived from the elements *hrod* and *ger* that was brought into England by the Normans. The name grew in popularity during the Middle Ages, which led to several surnames, including Dodges, Hodges, and Rogers. Associated during the 13th century with English philosopher Roger Bacon. Influenced during the 1960s, 1970s, and 1980s by Roger Moore, star of the television series *The Saint* and known as the longest-running James Bond actor.

Roland
Rank: 787

Origin: Old German
Meaning: Famous land
Alternate Spellings: Roeland, Rolande, Rolland, Rowland
Gender Variations: Rolanda, Rolande
Nicknames: Rollie
Similar Names: Orlando, Rolan, Rolando, Rollo, Rowley
➡ Derived from an Old French personal name. that was introduced by the Normans into Britain. Influenced by the 12th-century epic poem, *The Song of Roland*, considered one of the oldest major works in French literature. The name's popularity during the Middle Ages led to the creation of several surnames, including Rowland, which became the preferred spelling during the 17th century. Shakespeare also used this form in four of his plays. Roland became the favorite in both the U.S. and United Kingdom during the 1920s. Orlando is the most widely used variation today.

Ro ⇒ boys' names

Rolando   Rank: 571

Origin: German
Meaning: Famous land
Alternate Spelling: Rollando
Gender Variation: Rolande
Nicknames: Lando, Rolan
Similar Names: Raimundo, Reinaldo, Roberto, Rodolfo, Rodrigo, Rogelio, Rolando
⇒ The Spanish form of Roland that debuted on the popularity chart in 1946 and is currently one of the most widely used forms of the name. Preferred by Hispanic families.

Roman   Rank: 209

Origin: Latin
Meaning: Citizen of Rome
Gender Variations: Roma, Romaine, Romana, Romina
Similar Names: Romain, Romano, Romanos, Romanus
Namesakes: Roman Dzindzichashvili (chess grandmaster), Roman Gabriel (football player)
⇒ A variation of Romanus that refers to a native of Rome and used by several early saints. Polish film director Roman Polanski influenced the name starting in the 1960s.

Romeo   Rank: 574

Origin: Latin
Meaning: Pilgrim to Rome
Gender Variations: Roma, Romana
Similar Names: Romain, Roman, Rome
Namesake: Lil' Romeo (rapper)
⇒ Italian form of Romaeus and best known for the hero in Shakespeare's tragedy *Romeo and Juliet*, which led to the name's general meaning for a young lover. Sporadically used in the U.S. until recently. Parents are starting to take another look at this moniker since soccer star David Beckham and wife, former Spice Girl Victoria Adams Beckham, named their son Romeo.

Ronald   Rank: 251

Origin: Old Norse
Meaning: Ruler's counselor
Gender Variations: Rhona, Ronalda
Nicknames: Ron, Ronnie
Similar Names: Reginald , Reinhold, Renaud, Reynold, Rheinallt, Rinaldo, Roald, Roland, Ronan

Namesake: Ronald McDonald (clown/spokesman)
⇒ The Scottish form of Rognvaldr primarily used in Scotland until the 19th century. The name received a surge of popularity during the 1940s influenced by English actor Ronald Colman. He started his career as a silent film star and won an Academy Award in 1948 after successfully making the transition to "talkies." Also associated with former U.S. president Ronald Reagan.

Ronan   Rank: 598

Origin: Celtic
Meaning: Little seal
Alternate Spellings: Ronen, Ronin, Ronyn
Gender Variation: Rona
Nickname: Ron
Similar Names: Reagan, Reilly, Riley, Rogan, Ronald, Ross, Rowan, Ryan
⇒ An enduring name based on legend in Ireland that's still widely used in Ireland today. The name made its U.S. debut in 2001.

Rory   Rank: 826

Origin: Galic
Meaning: Red King
Alternate Spellings: Rorey, Rorry
Gender Variation: Rori
Similar Names: Rick, Rodd, Roderick, Rodman, Rodney, Roric, Rurik
Namesakes: Rory Cochrane (actor), Rory Culkin (actor)
⇒ A form of the Gaelic name Ruaidhri and the Scottish name Ruairidh. Use was limited to Scotland until the 1940s when Rory Calhoun became known as a film star in the U.S. It debuted on the popularity chart in 1947. Former Microsoft CEO Bill Gates has a son named Rory. Also considered a nickname for Roderick.

Ross   Rank: 747

Origin: Scottish
Meaning: Cape, promontory
Alternate Spelling: Rosse
Gender Variation: Roslyn
Similar Names: Roscoe, Rossano, Rossiter, Roswald, Russ
⇒ A Scottish place name for someone who lived near a cape that became a favorite

among parents in the mid-1800s. The name has been recently inspired by television characters Ross Geller from *Friends* and Dr. Douglas Ross from *ER*.

Rowan
Rank: 426

Origin: Gaelic
Meaning: Little redhead
Alternate Spellings: Roan, Roane, Rohan, Rowen
Gender Variations: Roana, Rowanne, Rowena
Similar Names: Reagan, Riordan, Roland, Ronald, Rooney, Rowe, Ryan
Namesake: Rowan Atkinson (English actor)
➡ A variation of the medieval name Ruadhan and a surname with usage dating back to the 16th century. The name may also be associated with the small deciduous tree with clusters of bright red berries.

Roy
Rank: 458

Origin: Irish Gaelic
Meaning: Red
Alternate Spelling: Roi
Gender Variation: Roxy
Similar Names: Elroy, Leroy, Royal, Royce, Roydon, Royer, Royston
➡ Originally a Scottish nickname known for Rob Roy, an 18th-century Scottish outlaw. Also known for Roy Rogers, born Leonard Franklin Slye, who started his career as a singer and became a popular radio, film, and television star. He was nicknamed "King of the Cowboys" during a career that spanned several decades starting in the 1930s. The name was listed among the top 100 until 1968.

Royce
Rank: 901

Origin: Old German
Meaning: Famous
Alternate Spelling: Roice
Gender Variation: Rowan
Nickname: Roy
Similar Names: Reece, Rolf, Royle, Royston
➡ A surname derived from the medieval female name Rohesia. Popular usage may have been inspired by the luxury car company Rolls-Royce, founded by Henry Royce and C. S. Rolls in 1906.

Ruben
Rank: 227

Origin: Hebrew
Meaning: Behold a son
Alternate Spellings: Reuban, Reuben, Reubin, Rubin
Gender Variation: Ruby
Nickname: Rube
Similar Names: Ramon, Raul, Roberto, Rudy
Namesakes: John Reuben (Christian rapper), Reuben (British rock/metal band), Ruben Blades (Panamanian singer)
➡ German and Spanish variation of Reuben, and the name of one of the 12 sons of Jacob and Leah. Reuben was the preferred spelling until 1925. The name is currently inspired by Ruben Studdard who rose to fame in 2003 as the winner of the second season of *American Idol*.

Rudy
Rank: 628

Origin: Old German
Meaning: Fame, wolf
Alternate Spellings: Rudi, Rudie
Gender Variation: Ruby
Similar Names: Roffe, Rolf, Rollo, Ruben, Rufus, Rupert
➡ The short form of Rudolph and the title of a 1993 inspirational film about Daniel "Rudy" Ruettiger who dreams of playing football at the University of Notre Dame in spite of numerous obstacles. Former mayor of New York City Rudolph "Rudy" Giuliani is another famous bearer of the name.

Russell
Rank: 404

Origin: Old French
Meaning: Little red one
Alternate Spelling: Roussell, Russel
Gender Variation: Ruth
Nickname: Russ
Similar Names: Raymond, Richard, Robert, Roland, Rousseau, Rufus, Rusty
Namesakes: Bertrand Russell (British philosopher), Kurt Russell (actor)
➡ A surname that originated as a nickname for someone with red hair or a red face. The name enjoyed years of popularity before falling from favor in 1983. New Zealand actor Russell Crowe is a famous bearer of the name.

Ryan
Rank: 14
Origin: Irish Gaelic
Meaning: Little king
Alternate Spellings: Rayan, Rhyan, Rian, Rien, Rion, Ryane, Ryen, Ryon, Ryun
Gender Variations: Rhea, Ryana, Ryanne
Similar Names: Kian, Kieran, Kilroy, Riordan, Rory, Ryder, Ryne
Namesakes: Nolan Ryan (Baseball Hall of Famer), Ryan Cabrera (musician/actor), Ryan Gosling (actor), Ryan Newman (NASCAR driver), Ryan Phillippe (actor), Ryan Seacrest (television host)
⇒ Originated from the surname Riain that wasn't particularly well-known at the beginning of the 20th century, it slowly increased in usage during the 1940s and then gained popularity in 1970 when actor Ryan O'Neal starred in the film *Love Story*. Former baseball player Ryne Sandberg uses a variation of the name.

Ryder
Rank: 257
Origin: Old English
Meaning: Horseman
Alternate Spelling: Rider
Gender Variation: Ryanne
Similar Names: Ryan, Ryker, Ryland, Ryley
⇒ Originated as an English occupational surname for a messenger. It first hit the popularity chart in 1994 preferred by parents because of its "y" in the middle spelling. Actress Kate Hudson and rock and roll singer Chris Robinson have a son named Ryder.

Ryker
Rank: 624
Origin: Old German
Meaning: Powerful leader
Alternate Spelling: Riker
Gender Variation: Rylee
Similar Names: Rich, Rick, Ritchie, Ryan, Ryder, Ryland
⇒ A nickname for Richard that's been used as a boy's given name in its own right since 2003. It follows a current trend of names that use a "y" in the middle.

Rylan
Rank: 258
Origin: Old English
Meaning: Dweller in the rye land
Alternate Spelling: Ryland
Gender Variation: Ryleigh

Nicknames: Ry, Ryle
Similar Names: Ryan, Ryce, Rycroft, Ryder, Ryman
⇒ A variation of the ever-popular Ryan that joins several other contemporary names with the "ylan" ending, such as Dylan, Kylan, and Wylan. It made its debut on the popularity chart in 1992 at No. 844 and is currently at its peak.

Sage
Rank: 689
Origin: Latin
Meaning: To taste, have good taste, be wise
Gender Variation: Sage
Similar Names: Ash, Basil, Birch, Leaf, Sorrel
⇒ Taken from the vocabulary word for a mature, wise man. Also a nature name for a type of aromatic, light grayish-green leaf used as a spice. The name debuted on the popularity chart in 1991. Listed among the top 500 names for girls.

Salvador
Rank: 390
Origin: Latin
Meaning: Savior
Alternate Spellings: Salvadore, Salvatore
Gender Variation: Salvatrice
Nickname: Sal
Similar Names: Sancho, Santiago, Saturnino, Segundino, Sergio, Servacio, Silvestre
⇒ The Spanish form of Salvatore often given in honor or Jesus Christ's sacrifice for the salvation of mankind. Spanish surrealist painter and printmaker Salvador Dali is a famous bearer of the name.

Sam
Rank: 463
Origin: Hebrew
Meaning: Name of God
Alternate Spelling: Samm
Gender Variation: Sammi
Nickname: Sammy
Similar Names: Sage, Samson, Samuel, Sandford
Namesakes: Sam Malone (*Cheers* TV character), Sam Neill (New Zealand actor), Sam Spade (fictional detective), Sam Waterston (actor), Yosemite Sam (cartoon character)
⇒ The short form of Samuel and Samson that's also used independently. Also a patriotic name long associated with Uncle Sam, the popular symbol of the U.S. dating

back to the War of 1812. Actor and playwright Sam Shepard, who received the Pulitzer Prize for Drama in 1979, is a famous bearer.

Samir
Rank: 835
Origin: Arabic
Meaning: Entertaining companion
Alternate Spelling: Sameer
Gender Variation: Samira
Similar Names: Saad, Sabir, Salim, Salman, Shadi, Shakir, Siraj
➡ Occasionally used in the U.S. since its introduction in 1977. The name of a fictional character from the 1999 cult comedy *Office Space*.

Samson
Rank: 887
Origin: Hebrew
Meaning: Like the sun
Alternate Spelling: Sampson, Samsone
Gender Variation: Samsara
Nicknames: Sam, Sammie
Similar Names: Salome, Samppa, Samuel, Sansom, Saul, Shem
➡ A biblical name for the Jewish hero in the Old Testament who was known for his legendary strength derived from his uncut hair. His story is the source of an oratorio by Handel, an opera by Camille Saint-Saens, a painting by Rembrandt, a poem by John Milton, and a 1949 film by Cecil B. DeMille. The name has been used sporadically since prior to the turn of the 20th century.

Samuel
Rank: 25
Origin: Hebrew
Meaning: Name of God
Alternate Spellings: Samual, Samuele, Samuil
Gender Variations: Samanta, Samantha
Nicknames: Sam, Sammy
Similar Names: Samson, Simeon, Simon, Solomon
Namesakes: Samuel Goldwyn (movie mogul), Samuel L. Jackson (actor)
➡ Derived from Shemuel, the name of the prophet and judge who anointed Saul and David as kings of Israel in the Old Testament. Listed among the top 100 names for more than 125 years. Revolutionary leader Samuel Adams is a historical namesake. Novelist Samuel Clemens, who wrote under the pen name Mark Twain, also comes to mind.

Santana
Rank: 877
Origin: Spanish
Meaning: Gracious saint
Gender Variations: Sanjuana, Santana
Nickname: San
Similar Names: Salvador, Sancho, Santiago, Santino
➡ Possibly a blend of the elements "Saint" and "Ana" notable for the surname of Grammy Award-winning rock musician and guitarist Carlos Santana and rapper and producer Juelz Santana. Also recognized as a girl's name.

Santiago
Rank: 231
Origin: Latin
Meaning: Saint James
Alternate Spellings: Sandiago, Sandiego, Santeago, Santiaco
Gender Variation: Santana
Similar Names: Diego, Jaime, Salvador, Sancho
➡ Composed of the elements *san* and *Diego*, which is a pet form of James. Also a place name for cities in Chile and Spain.

Santos
Rank: 718
Origin: Spanish
Meaning: The saints
Gender Variation: Santana
Similar Names: Salvador, Sanchez, Santiago, Santo
➡ A surname used as a given name that's been listed among the top 800 since 1919.

Saul
Rank: 297
Origin: Hebrew
Meaning: Prayed for
Alternate Spelling: Sol
Gender Variation: Salome
Nickname: Sauly
Similar Names: Paul, Samuel, Seth, Shiloh, Silas, Simon
➡ Derived from the Hebrew Shaul, the name of the of the first king of Israel in the Old Testament. Also the Hebrew name for the apostle Paul before he converted to Christianity. It's climbed the popularity chart along with other biblical names considered trendy by parents today.

Sawyer   Rank: 247

Origin: Middle English
Meaning: Woodsman
Gender Variation: Sawyer
Similar Names: Darrien,
Davian, Lawyer, Rainier, Ryder, Sayer
Namesake: Sawyer Brown (country music band)
⇨ An occupational surname for a woodworker popularized by the fictional young boy who persuades his friends to white-wash a fence in the 1876 Mark Twain novel *The Adventures of Tom Sawyer*. Recently known for James "Sawyer" Ford, the fictional character played by Josh Holloway on the hit television series *Lost*. A unisex name.

Scott   Rank: 253

Origin: Old English
Meaning: Scotsman
Alternate Spellings:
Scot, Skot, Skott
Gender Variation: Scota
Nickname: Scotty
Similar Names: Escott, Scanlon, Schuyler, Scotto, Scully
Namesake: Scott Baio (actor)
⇨ Transferred use of the surname that denoted someone from Scotland. Parents still give the name today in honor of their Scottish heritage and ancestry. Notable bearers include actors George C. Scott and Scott Glenn. Also considered a literary name for short-story writer and novelist F. Scott Fitzgerald, author of *The Great Gatsby*.

Seamus   Rank: 842

Origin: Greek/Latin
Meaning: Supplanter
Alternate Spellings:
Seumas, Seumus
Gender Variations: Shaun, Shauna
Similar Names: Jacob, Jacobus, Jamie, Jamison, Sean, Seaton, Shamus
⇨ The Irish form of James that's known in the literary world for Irish poet and writer Seamus Heaney, who was awarded the Nobel Prize in Literature in 1995.

Sean   Rank: 68

Origin: Hebrew
Meaning: God is gracious
Alternate Spellings:
Shaughan, Shaun, Shawn, Shon

Gender Variation: Shawn
Similar Names: John, Shane, Shea, Spence
Namesakes: Sean Astin (actor), Sean "Diddy" Combs (rapper/actor), Sean Penn (actor), Shawn Wayans (actor/comedian)
⇨ The Irish form of John influenced by Scottish actor and producer Sean Connery, who starred in seven James Bond films during the 1960s and 1970s. A chart topper in Ireland and occasionally used as a girl's name.

Sebastian   Rank: 76

Origin: Latin
Meaning: Man from Sebaste
Alternate Spellings:
Sabastian, Sabastien, Sebastien, Sebastyen
Gender Variation: Sebastiana
Nickname: Seb
Similar Names: Septimus, Silvester, Stafford
Namesake: Johann Sebastian Bach (German composer)
⇨ From the Roman name Sebastianus, which was the name of a town in Asia Minor. Saint Sebastian was a 3rd-century Roman soldier who was martyred after he was discovered to be a Christian. First listed among the top 100 names in 2000. A literary name used by Shakespeare in the plays *Twelfth Night* and *The Tempest*. Also a character in *Brideshead Revisited* by novelist Evelyn Waugh.

Semaj   Rank: 693

Origin: American
Gender Variation: Selma
Similar Names: Seamus, Sean, Sebastian, Selwyn
⇨ The name James spelled backwards that was first discovered by parents in 1999.

Sergio   Rank: 195

Origin: Latin
Meaning: Servant
Gender Variation: Georgia
Nickname: Serge
Similar Names: Salvador, Serge, Sergei, Sergius
Namesake: Sergio Garcia (Spanish golfer)
⇨ The Italian, Spanish, and Portuguese form of Sergius and the name of 33 saints. It debuted in the U.S. in 1935 and peaked in 1992 but is still listed among the top 200. Serge is the French variation and Sergei is used in Russia.

Seth
Rank: 103

Origin: Hebrew
Meaning: Appointed
Gender Variation: Beth
Similar Names: Heath, Keith, Sean, Sheth, Wyeth
Namesake: Seth Green (actor)
➡ A biblical name for the third son of Adam and Eve, born after his brother Abel was murdered. The Puritans used it for the name of a child after the death of an elder sibling. Also known for the god of chaos in Egyptian mythology. A literary name for a fictional character in George Eliot's first novel, *Adam Bede*.

Shane
Rank: 179

Origin: Irish Gaelic
Meaning: God is gracious
Alternate Spellings: Shain, Shaine, Shayn, Shayne
Gender Variations: Shana, Shanee, Shania, Shayne
Similar Names: Evan, Hank, John, Sean, Shea
Namesakes: Shane Black (screenwriter/actor/director), Shane West (actor)
➡ The anglicized form of Sean that first hit the popularity chart in 1953, the same year that the classic western *Shane* was released. Used as a girl's name during the 1970s.

Shannon
Rank: 986

Origin: Gaelic
Meaning: Old, wise
Alternate Spellings: Shannan, Shannen, Shanon
Gender Variations: Shanna, Shannah, Shannon
Nickname: Shan
Similar Names: Shamus, Shane, Shawn, Shay, Sheamus
Namesake: Del Shannon (singer)
➡ Composed of the Gaelic elements *sean* and *abhann* and associated with the Shannon River, the longest river in Ireland. Used sporadically as a given name starting in the late 1800s, eventually peaking at No. 98 in 1976. Listed among the top 400 names for girls.

Shea

Origin: Gaelic
Meaning: Admirable
Alternate Spellings: Shae, Shai, Shay, Shaye
Gender Variations: Shea, Sheena, Sheila
Similar Names: Lashay, Shaun, Shaw, Shaylon
Namesake: John Shea (actor)
➡ A surname and Anglicized form of Seaghdha. It recently dropped off the top 1,000 as a boy's name but is listed among the top 900 for girls.

Sheldon
Rank: 843

Origin: Old England
Meaning: Steep valley
Alternate Spellings: Shelden, Sheldin
Gender Variation: Shelby
Nickname: Shel
Similar Names: Shelby, Shelton, Sherman, Sherwood
Namesakes: Sheldon Leonard (TV producer), Sheldon "Shel" Silverstein (poet/musician), Sydney Sheldon (novelist)
➡ Derived from a surname and place name for several locations in England. Used as a given name in the U.S. since 1881, it peaked during the 1930s and has faded since that time.

Sidney
Rank: 801

Origin: Old French/English
Meaning: Of Saint Denis or wide island
Alternate Spelling: Sydney
Gender Variations: Sidoney, Sydney
Nickname: Sid
Similar Names: Sigmund, Silas, Silver, Silvester, Simon, Sinclair
Namesakes: Dr. Sidney Freedman (*MASH.* character), Sidney Kingsley (playwright), Sidney Sheldon (novelist),
➡ A place name that derives from either Old French or Old English that was especially fashionable during the first half of the 20th century. A literary name for Sydney Carton, the hero in the 19th-century novel *A Tale of Two Cities*, by Charles Dickens. Known for Bahamian-American actor and film director Sidney Poitier, who became the first African-American male actor to win an Academy Award. Listed among the top 50 for girls.

Silas
Rank: 373
Origin: Greek/Latin
Meaning: Forest
Alternate Spelling: Sylas
Gender Variation: Sileas
Similar Names: Sylvain, Silvano, Sylvan, Silvanus, Silvio, Sylvester, Sylvestro
Namesake: Silas Carson (actor)
⇨ A variation of Silouanus and the name of a prophet who was a missionary companion of Paul in the New Testament. He's mentioned in several epistles by the name Silvanus. The 1861 novel *Silas Marner*, by George Eliot, possibly spurred the name to its peak during the late 1800s.

Simeon
Rank: 950
Origin: Hebrew
Meaning: God is listening
Alternate Spellings: Simion, Simyon, Symeon
Gender Variations: Simona, Simone, Simonetta, Simonette
Nickname: Simmie
Similar Names: Salome, Samson, Semyon, Shealtiel, Shem, Shimon, Simon, Solomon
Namesake: Simeon ten Holt (Dutch composer)
⇨ A common biblical name. In the Old Testament the name of a son of Jacob and Leah who founded one of the 12 tribes of Israel. In the New Testament Simeon greeted Mary and Joseph at the temple in Jerusalem and blessed the Christ child. A royal name in Bulgaria for a 10th-century tsar. The name peaked prior to the turn of the 20th century but is recently becoming more fashionable with other biblical names.

Simon
Rank: 246
Origin: Hebrew/Greek
Meaning: God is listening
Alternate Spellings: Simen, Simone, Symon
Gender Variations: Simona, Simone, Simonetta, Simonette
Similar Names: Siemen, Silas, Simeon, Solomon, Stephen
Namesakes: Paul Simon (musician), Simon Bolivar (Latin American revolutionary leader), Simon Legree (*Uncle Tom's Cabin* character)
⇨ A popular name in the Bible with several namesakes found in the New Testament. Best known is Simon Peter, one of Christ's original 12 disciples, whom Jesus named Peter. He became a leader in the early Christian Church. Simon the Zealot was also mentioned among the original disciples. Today most people think of British producer Simon Cowell, the blunt *American Idol* judge. The name has been in and out of popularity since it was first listed among the top 1,000.

Skyler
Rank: 270
Origin: Dutch
Meaning: Scholar
Alternate Spellings: Schuyler, Schylar, Schyler, Skuyler, Skylar, Skyller, Skylor
Gender Variation: Skylar
Nickname: Skye
Similar Names: Sawyer, Sinclair, Slater, Sloan, Starr, Sutton
⇨ A contemporary spelling of the surname Schuyler, brought to New York by 17th-century settlers, which led to its use as a given name by prominent New Yorkers. Schuyler Colfax, a native of New York City, was the 17th vice president of the U.S. More common as a boy's name but also used for girls.

Solomon
Rank: 486
Origin: Hebrew
Meaning: Peaceful
Alternate Spellings: Salomon, Salomone, Soloman
Gender Variation: Soloma
Nicknames: Sol, Solly
Similar Names: Samuel, Saul, Seth, Silas, Simeon
⇨ A biblical name known for the son of David and Bathsheba who succeeded his father as king of Israel. Known for his wisdom, he was the author of the book of Proverbs, Ecclesiastes, and the Song of Songs. The name grew in popularity during the Middle Ages and peaked prior to the turn of the 20th century. Also associated with the 1977 novel *Song of Solomon* by Toni Morrison.

Sonny
Rank: 883
Origin: English
Meaning: Son
Alternate Spelling: Sonnie
Gender Variation: Sunny
Nickname: Son
Similar Names: Santana, Santigo, Santo, Santos

➡ A nickname typically used for a young boy. Also the pet form of Santino, used by Mario Puzo for fictional character Santino "Sonny" Corleone in his 1969 novel *The Godfather*, adapted into a 1972 Academy Award-winning movie. Politician and entertainer Sonny Bono also comes to mind. Steadily used as a given name since 1927.

Spencer   Rank: 182
Origin: Old French
Meaning: Dispenser of provisions
Alternate Spelling: Spenser
Gender Variation: Spenser
Nickname: Spence
Similar Names: Sheldon, Sherman, Sorrel, Stafford, Stewart
Namesakes: John Spencer (actor), Spencer Haywood (basketball player), *Spenser: For Hire* (TV series)
➡ Originated as an occupational surname influenced in England by Sir Winston Leonard Spencer Churchill. Two-time Academy Award-winner Spencer Tracy kept the name in front of the public during a career that spanned 37 years.

Stanley   Rank: 600
Origin: Old English
Meaning: From the rocky meadow
Alternate Spellings: Stanlee, Stanleigh, Stanly
Gender Variation: Stacey
Nickname: Stan
Similar Names: Stanbury, Standish, Stanfield, Stanford, Stanhope, Stanmore, Stanton
Namesakes: Stanley Cup (NHL championship trophy), Stanley Kowalski (*A Streetcar Named Desire* character), Stanley Kubrick (film producer/director), Stanley Laurel (comedian), Stanley Roper (*Three's Company* TV character)
➡ A common place name for any number of English locals that led to the creation of several surnames, including Stanborough and Stancombe. The name was influenced during the 19th century by British explorer Sir Henry Morton Stanley, who was sent to Africa to provide aid to Scottish missionary and explorer Dr. David Livingstone. After finding his hero, he famously said, "Dr. Livingstone, I presume?" Hip-hop artist M. C. Hammer, born Stanley Kirk Burrell, named his son Stanley.

Sterling   Rank: 784

Origin: English
Meaning: Genuine, of high quality
Alternate Spelling: Stirling
Gender Variations: Starlena, Starling
Similar Names: Sinclair, Spencer, Stafford, Stanford, Stanley, Stewart
Namesake: Sterling Marlin (NASCAR driver)
➡ A surname used as a given name. influenced by actor Sterling Hayden, who played notable roles in several films during the 1940s, 1950s, 1960s, and 1970s. Stirling is occasionally used in the United Kingdom.

Steve   Rank: 532
Origin: Greek
Meaning: Crown, garland
Gender Variations: Stefana, Stephanie, Stevie
Nickname: Stevy
Similar Names: Esteban, Esteve, Stefan, Stephanos, Stevano, Steven
Namesakes: Steve Allen (entertainer), Steve Harvey (actor/comedian), Steve Martin (actor/comedian), Steve Perry (musician)
➡ The short form of Steven and Stephen, also used as an independent name. Influenced by actor Steve McQueen during the 1960s and 1970s.

Steven   Rank: 90
Origin: Greek
Meaning: Crown, garland
Alternate Spellings: Stefan, Steffen, Stefon, Stephan, Stephen, Stevan, Stevon, Stevyn
Gender Variations: Stephanie, Stevie
Nickname: Steve
Similar Names: Steffen, Stephanos, Stevenson, Stever, Stinson
Namesakes: Stephen Baldwin (actor), Stephen Sondheim (composer), Steven Seagal (actor), Steven Tyler (musician)
➡ A form of Stephen that reflects how the name is pronounced in the English-speaking world. A biblical name for Saint Stephen, an early Christian who was stoned to death and is considered the first Christian martyr. An enduringly popular name, which has been listed among the top 100 since 1941. Known in the literary world for novelists Stephen Crane and Stephen King. Film director and producer Steven Spielberg is another famous bearer.

Stone   Rank: 984

Origin: Old English
Meaning: Stone
Gender Variation: Aston
Similar Names: Clay, Cliff, Flint, Shad, Skye, Storm
⇨ A surname for someone who lived by a large rock or boulder. Also a contemporary nature name picked up directly from the vocabulary word. Occasionally used as a given name since 1995.

Sullivan   Rank: 916

Origin: Irish Gaelic
Meaning: Dark eyes
Alternate Spellings: Sullavan, Sullevan
Gender Variation: Sula
Nickname: Sully
Similar Names: Seamus, Sean, Seanan, Shamus, Shane, Shay, Sweeney
Namesake: Sullivan (alternative rock band)
⇨ An Irish surname derived from Suileabhan. Television host Ed Sullivan, whose variety series, *The Ed Sullivan Show*, aired from 1948 to 1971, is a bearer of the surname. In use prior to the turn of the century, the name is rarely picked up today.

Talan   Rank: 309

Origin: French
Meaning: Sharp
Alternate Spellings: Talen, Talin, Tallan, Tallen, Tallon, Talon
Gender Variations: Talia, Taline, Telma
Similar Names: Dalen, Dylan, Taneli, Taylan
⇨ Possibly a form of talon, which is a vocabulary word for the claw of an animal, especially a bird of prey. First used as a boy's given name in 2005 at No. 540, it's climbed among the top 400.

Tanner   Rank: 142

Origin: Old English
Meaning: Leather maker
Gender Variations: Tania, Tanner
Similar Names: Tarquin, Tate, Terrence, Treynor
Namesake: Henry Ossawa Tanner (painter)
⇨ An occupational surname for someone who tans hides, favored by parents starting in 1976. Occasionally used as a girl's name.

Tariq

Origin: Arabic
Meaning: Knocking one
Alternate Spellings: Tarek, Tarez, Taric, Tarik, Tarique
Gender Variation: Terika
Similar Names: Tahir, Tahmid, Taliba, Tamid, Tawfiq
Namesake: Tariq Ali (Pakistani writer/filmmaker)
⇨ The name of the morning star from the holy Koran, the religious text of Islam. Associated with Tariq Abdul-Wahad, born Olivier Michael Saint-Jean, the first NBA basketball player born and raised in France. He changed his name after converting to Islam in 1997. Also the name of the Muslim general who conquered Spain. Rarely used in the U.S.

Tate   Rank: 412

Origin: Old English
Meaning: Cheerful
Alternate Spellings: Tait, Taitt, Tayte
Gender Variation: Tatum
Similar Names: Tad, Taft, Thane, Toby, Todd, Tracy
Namesake: Larenz Tate (actor)
⇨ Taken from an English surname that's been used sporadically since 1971. A good choice for parents who are looking for a name with a positive meaning.

Taylor   Rank: 222

Origin: Middle English
Meaning: To cut
Alternate Spellings: Tailer, Tailor, Tayler
Gender Variations: Tayla, Taylor
Similar Names: Talbot, Tanner, Terrill, Tyler
Namesake: Jonathan Taylor Thomas (actor)
⇨ An occupational surname for a tailor that was first used as a given name during the 19th century. Zachary Taylor gave the name early recognition when he led troops to victory during the Mexican-American War. Musician James Taylor, whose career has flourished for many years, is a more recent namesake. Predominantly used as a girl's name.

Tayshaun

Origin: American
Alternate Spellings: Tashaun, Tashaun, Tayshawn
Gender Variations: Shauna, Shayne
Nickname: Shaun
Similar Names: Deshawn, Leshawn, Rayshawn, Tashawn
Namesake: Tayshaun Prince (basketball player)
➩ A modern combination of "tay" with the name Shaun. Most commonly preferred by African-American families.

Teagan
Rank: 827

Origin: Irish
Meaning: Poet
Alternate Spelling: Taegan
Gender Variations: Teagan
Similar Names: Regan, Taylor, Teague, Terrill, Terron, Tiarnan
➩ Derived from the Gaelic *tadhg* that debuted on the popularity chart in 2004. Parents may see this as another option for Reagan.

Terrance
Rank: 465

Origin: Latin
Alternate Spellings: Terance, Terence, Terrence
Gender Variation: Terrena
Nickname: Terry
Similar Names: Taylor, Terenzio, Terrell, Terry, Torrence, Tyrone
Namesakes: Terence Stamp (English actor), Terence Trent D'Arby (musician)
➩ A variation of the Roman family name Terence, that's been steadily used since 1932.

Terrell
Rank: 520

Origin: Old English
Meaning: Ruler of thunder
Alternate Spellings: Terrel, Terrill, Terryl
Gender Variations: Teresa, Terri, Teryl
Nickname: Terry
Similar Names: Terrance, Terron, Tyrell, Tyrone
➩ Originated as a surname and a variation of Tyrrell, a good choice for African-American parents who may prefer the trendier "y" in the suffix spelling.

Terry
Rank: 446

Origin: Old German
Meaning: Power of the tribe
Alternate Spellings: Terrey, Terri, Terrie, Thierry
Gender Variation: Teri
Similar Names: Derek, Derry, Terrence, Terrell, Terris, Torry
Namesakes: Terry Bradshaw (Football Hall of Famer), Terry Labonte (NASCAR driver)
➩ Originally a surname derived from the name Theodoric that became a nickname for Terrence after the turn of the 20th century. Listed among the top 50 during the 1940s, 1950s, and 1960s. Popularity slowed when it became a favorite for girls.

Thaddeus
Rank: 998

Origin: Aramaic
Meaning: Heart
Alternate Spellings: Thadaios, Thaddaos, Thaddaeus, Thaddaus, Thaddius, Thadeus
Gender Variations: Thalia, Thea
Nicknames: Tad, Thad
Similar Names: Tamar, Terah, Thomas, Timaeus, Timothy, Titus, Tobiah
➩ A Christian saint and one of Christ's 12 original apostles mentioned in the New Testament. He is also referred to as Judas Thaddaeus. Rarely used in the U.S., it peaked in 1918 at No. 308.

Theodore
Rank: 296

Origin: Greek
Meaning: Gift of God
Alternate Spelling: Theodor
Gender Variations: Thea, Theodora, Dora
Nicknames: Tad, Ted, Teddy, Theo
Similar Names: Teodoro, Thaddeus, Theobald, Theodorus
Namesake: Theodore Rousseau (French painter)
➩ A form of Theodorus that peaked during the presidency of Theodore Roosevelt. Also known for fictional character Theodore "Beaver" Cleaver on the late 1950s and early 1960s television show *Leave It to Beaver*. The name of several early saints and two popes. Recognized in literature for novelist Theodore Dreiser and children's author Theodore "Dr. Seuss" Geisel.

Thomas
Rank: 51

Origin: Greek/Aramaic
Meaning: Twin
Gender Variations: Tamsin, Thomasina, Thomasine, Tomina
Nicknames: Tom, Tommy
Similar Names: Thaddeus, Theodore, Thomason, Timothy, Tomas
Namesakes: Tom Clancy (author), Tom Cruise (actor), Tom Hanks (actor), Tom Petty (musician), Tom Selleck (actor)
⇒ In the New Testament, Thomas was the apostle who doubted the resurrection of Jesus, which coined the saying "doubting Thomas." Popularized during the 12th century by Saint Thomas Becket, Archbishop of Canterbury, which led to the development of several common surnames. The name has ranked among the top 40 for more than 125 years. A literary name for poet Thomas Stearns "T.S." Eliot and novelist Thomas Hardy. Other famous bearers include theologian Saint Thomas Aquinas, inventor Thomas Edison, and U.S. president Thomas Jefferson.

Timothy
Rank: 94

Origin: Greek
Meaning: To honor God
Alternate Spellings: Timmothy, Timothea, Timothee, Timothey, Tymmothy, Tymothy
Gender Variations: Timothea, Timaula
Nicknames: Tim, Timmy
Similar Names: Thaddeus, Theodore, Thomas
Namesakes: Tim Allen (actor), Tim Burton (director/producer), Tim McGraw (musician), Tim Robbins (actor), Timothy Dalton (English actor)
⇒ In the New Testament, the name of a young Christian who became an assistant to Paul and later a respected disciple of Jesus. A literary name for beloved character Tiny Tim from the Charles Dickens book *A Christmas Carol*. Listed among the top 100 names since 1943.

Titus
Rank: 550

Origin: Greek/Latin
Meaning: Pleasing
Alternate Spelling: Tytus
Gender Variations: Tiria, Tirzah

Nickname: Ty
Similar Names: Tiberius, Timothy, Tito, Tobias, Tyrus
Namesake: *Titus* 2000 (TV series)
⇒ The biblical name for a companion of Paul who assisted him with missionary work. Also known for Titus Flavius Vespasianus, the Roman Emperor who conquered Jerusalem during the 1st century. *Titus Andronicus* is one of Shakespeare's earliest tragedies. Preferred by parents who are looking for a trendy biblical name.

Tobias
Rank: 484

Origin: Hebrew
Meaning: God is good
Gender Variation: Tobi
Nickname: Toby
Similar Names: Tobiah, Tobey, Tobin, Tobit
Namesake: Tobias Wolff (author)
⇒ The Greek form of Tobiah and the name of several biblical figures in the Old Testament. In the *Harry Potter* book series, fictional character Tobias Snape is the father of Professor Severus Snape.

Toby
Rank: 509

Origin: Hebrew
Meaning: God is good
Alternate Spellings: Tobe, Tobee, Tobey, Tobi, Tobie
Gender Variation: Toby
Similar Names: Tobiah, Tobias, Tobin, Todd, Tom, Tony
Namesake: *Toby Tyler* (Walt Disney film)
⇒ The short form of the Hebrew name Tobias. Actor Tobey Maguire, star of the *Spider-Man* films, and country music singer and songwriter Toby Keith are famous bearers. Occasionally used as a girl's name.

Todd
Rank: 653

Origin: Middle English
Meaning: Fox
Alternate Spelling: Tod
Gender Variation: Tori
Similar Names: Tate, Ted, Thad, Troy
Namesakes: *Sweeney Todd* (2007 film), Todd Bodine (NASCAR driver), Todd Eldredge (figure skating champion), Todd Rundgren (musician)
⇒ A surname used as a first name derived from *todde* that possibly denotes a fox hunter. Fashionable in the United Kingdom

during the 1960s and listed among the top 100 names from 1959 to 1985 in the U.S.

Tomas
Rank: 488

Origin: Greek/Aramaic
Meaning: Twin
Alternate Spellings:
Thomas, Tomasz, Tomaz
Gender Variations: Tomasa, Tomasina
Nicknames: Tom, Tommy
Similar Names: Toma, Tomascio, Tomasa, Tome, Tomek, Tomito, Tommaso
➡ A form of Thomas in several languages, including Irish, Portuguese, Spanish, and Swedish. Ranked among the top 500 since 1990.

Tommy
Rank: 460

Origin: Greek/Aramaic
Meaning: Twin
Alternate Spellings: Tomey, Tomie, Tommey, Tommie
Gender Variation: Thomasina
Nickname: Tom
Similar Names: Timmy, Thomas, Tobey, Tomas, Tony, Tory
Namesakes: *Tommy* (rock opera), Tommy Lasorda (Baseball Hall of Famer), Tommy Lee (drummer), Tommy Lee Jones (actor)
➡ The pet form of Thomas that's also used as an independent name. It peaked during the 1940s when Tommy Dorsey introduced his first band during what came to be known as the "Swing Era." Fashion designer Tommy Hilfiger is a current bearer of the name.

Tony
Rank: 329

Origin: Latin
Meaning: Priceless, praiseworthy
Alternate Spellings:
Toney, Toni, Tonie
Gender Variations: Toni, Tonia
Nickname: Tone
Similar Names: Anthony, Antoine, Anton, Antonio, Antony, Tone, Tonio
Namesakes: Tony Danza (actor/talk show host), Tony Stewart (auto racing champion)
➡ The short form of Anthony whose use as an independent name peaked during the 1960s, which coincided with the commercial successes of singer Tony Bennett and actor Tony Curtis. A past favorite among African-American families.

Trace
Rank: 536

Origin: American
Gender Variation: Tracey
Similar Names: Tracy, Travis, Trevor, Trey, Troy, True, Tyce
➡ An invented name that's possibly a short form of Tracy. Influenced by country singer and songwriter Tracy "Trace" Adkins. Country singer and actor Billy Ray Cyrus has a son by this name.

Travis
Rank: 163

Origin: Old French
Meaning: Crossroads
Alternate Spellings:
Traviss, Travys
Gender Variations: Tracie, Trava
Nickname: Trav
Similar Names: Tracy, Travers, Traynor, Trenton, Trevor, Trey
Namesakes: Andy Travis (*WKRP* television character), Randy Travis (country singer)
➡ An occupational surname for someone who collected tolls at bridges. The name has drifted in and out of popularity, peaking in 1979 at No. 36.

Trent
Rank: 287

Origin: Latin
Meaning: Travel, journey
Gender Variation: Trena
Similar Names: Brent, Brenton, Trenton, Trevor, Trey, Troy
Namesake: Trent Reznor (musician)
➡ A surname for someone who lived by the Trent River in England. Also used as the short form of Trenton.

Trenton
Rank: 192

Origin: Old English
Meaning: Trent's town
Alternate Spellings:
Trenten, Trentin
Gender Variation: Trinity
Nickname: Trent
Similar Names: Brent, Brenton, Thornton, Travis, Traynor, Trevor
➡ A place name for a city in New Jersey that was established as a town by William Trent in the 18th century. During the American Revolution it was the site of an American victory over the British led by General George Washington. Trenton became the temporary capital of the U.S. and later the capital of New Jersey.

Trevon Rank: 530

Origin: American
Alternate Spellings:
Trevan, Treven, Trevin,
Trevonn, Treyvon
Gender Variations: Treva, Trevia
Similar Names: Trent, Trenton, Trevion,
Trevor, Trey, Troy
⇒ An invented name that might possibly be
a variation of Trevin or a new take on the
Welsh name Trevor. It made its debut as a
given name in 1989.

Trevor Rank: 125

Origin: Welsh
Meaning: Great settlement
Alternate Spellings:
Trefor, Trevar, Trever
Gender Variations: Treva, Trevina
Nickname: Trev
Similar Names: Travers, Travis, Trent, Trey
⇒ A form of Trefor that originated as a
Welsh surname and place name. English
actor Trevor Howard brought attention to the
name starting in the mid-1940s. Notable for
boxer Trevor Berbick, known as the last man
to fight Muhammad Ali, winning in 10 rounds
by a unanimous decision in 1981.

Trey Rank: 250

Origin: English
Meaning: Three
Alternate Spellings: Trai,
Tray, Traye, Tre, Treye
Gender Variation: Tracy
Similar Names: Tad, Tory, Trent, Troy, Ty
⇒ A variation of Troy and possibly a form of
the Irish name Traigh that's sometimes given
to the third son. The name has climbed the
popularity chart since 1962, influenced from
1998 to 2004 by fictional character Trey
MacDougal played by Kyle MacLachlan in
the series *Sex and the City*.

Tristan Rank: 86

Origin: Celtic/Latin
Meaning: Riot, sad
Alternate Spellings:
Tristen, Tristian, Tristin,
Triston, Trystan
Gender Variation: Trista
Nickname: Tris
Similar Names: Christian, Drystan,
Tristram, Tristrand
⇒ Derived from the Celtic name Drystan
and sometimes associated with the Latin
tristis. The name of the doomed hero in
the Celtic legend of Tristan and Isolde. The
story has been composed into an opera and
adapted into film several times. In the legend
of King Arthur, Tristan (also called Tristram)
was a knight of the Round Table. Listed
among the top 125 names since 1995, it broke
into the top 100 in 2006.

Troy Rank: 229

Origin: Irish Gaelic
Meaning: Foot soldier
Alternate Spellings: Troi,
Troye
Gender Variation: Tory
Similar Names: Terry, Todd, Tom, Torey,
Trent, Trey, Ty
⇒ A surname used for those people who
traveled from Troyes, France, to England
after the Norman Conquest. Best-known
for the ancient city in Asia Minor where the
Trojan War was fought that was made famous
in Homer's *The Iliad*. Also the title of a
2004 film starring Brad Pitt. Teen idol Troy
Donahue brought attention to the name
during the 1960s. Usage has declined slightly
since that time.

Truman Rank: 943

Origin: Old English
Meaning: Trusty man
Alternate Spellings:
Trueman, Trumaine, Trumann
Gender Variation: Trudy
Nickname: True
Similar Names: Thurman, Tremain, Turner
⇒ A surname that originated as a nickname
derived from *treowe*. The given name
was inspired by U.S. president Harry S.
Truman who held office from 1945 to 1952.
Truman Capote, the author of *Breakfast
at Tiffany's* and *In Cold Blood*, is another
famous bearer.

Tucker Rank: 260

Origin: Old English
Meaning: Tucker of cloth
Gender Variations: Tula,
Tulia
Nickname: Tuck
Similar Names: Tanner, Thatcher,
Tuckerman, Turner

Namesakes: Jonathan Tucker (actor), *Tucker: the Man and His Dream* (1988 film), Preston Tucker (automobile designer/entrepeneur)
➡️ Originated as an occupational surname for a fuller. Actor Chris Tucker, star of the successful *Rush Hour* films, keeps the surname in front of the public.

Ty
Rank: 210

Origin: Old English
Meaning: Tiler, roofer
Alternate Spelling: Tye
Gender Variation: Tyra
Similar Names: Tay, Theo, Trey, Tyler, Tyrone, Tyrus, Tyson
Namesakes: Ty Cobb (Baseball Hall of Famer), Ty Herndon (country music singer), Ty Law (football player)
➡️ The short form of Tyler and Tyson plus other names that begin with "Ty" that's been used independently as a given name since 1955. Carpenter and television personality Ty Pennington, born Tygert Burton Pennington, comes to mind.

Tyler
Rank: 18

Origin: Old English
Meaning: Tiler, roofer
Alternate Spellings: Tilar, Tylar, Tylor
Gender Variation: Taylor
Nickname: Ty
Similar Names: Taylor, Terence, Tyrone, Tyrus, Tyson
Namesakes: Steven Tyler (musician)
➡️ Originated as an occupational surname meaning "tiler of roofs." Tyler has been on the rise since 1955, breaking into the top 50 in 1984 and the top 10 in 1992. Popular in English-speaking countries.

Tyree
Rank: 700

Origin: American
Gender Variation: Tyra
Nickname: Ty
Similar Names: Trey, True, Tyre, Tyrell, Tyrone, Tyson
➡️ A place name for the second-highest mountain in Antarctica and for an island off of Scotland. May have been created from other names that begin with "Ty." Occasionally used since 1905.

Tyrell
Rank: 655

Origin: Old French
Meaning: Puller
Alternate Spellings: Tirell, Tirrell, Tyrel, Tyrelle, Tyrrel, Tyrrell
Gender Variation: Tyra
Nicknames: Ty, Rell
Similar Names: Terence, Terrill, Terris, Tyreece, Tyrone, Tyrus, Tyson
Namesake: Tyrell Biggs (Olympic boxer)
➡️ A surname that was possibly given to a stubborn person and a form of Tyrrell. Introduced on the popularity chart in 1979 and preferred by African-American families.

Tyrese
Rank: 621

Origin: American
Alternate Spelling: Tyreece
Gender Variation: Tyra
Nicknames: Ty, Tyree
Similar Names: Tydeus, Tyler, Tyree, Tyrell, Tyrone, Tyrus, Tyus
➡️ A modern blend of "Ty" with the suffix "rese" in popular use since 1998.

Tyrone
Rank: 575

Origin: Irish Gaelic
Meaning: Land of Owen
Alternate Spellings: Tirone, Tyron, Tyronne
Gender Variation: Tyra
Nickname: Ty
Similar Names: Tybalt, Tycho, Tyler, Tyrell, Tyrese, Tyson
➡️ A place name for a county in Northern Ireland. Influenced as a given name during the 20th century by father and son actors Tyrone Power and Tyrone Power Jr., known for their stage and screen presence.

Tyshawn
Rank: 902

Origin: American
Alternate Spelling: Tyshaun
Gender Variations: Lashawn, Shaun
Nickname: Shawn
Similar Names: Deshawn, Keyshawn, Tyrell, Tyrone, Tyson
➡️ An invented name that blends the prefix "Tay" with the popular name *Shawn*. The name debuted on the popularity chart in 1991 and is preferred by African-American parents.

Tyson   Rank: 276

Origin: Old French
Meaning: Firebrand
Alternate Spellings:
Tison, Tyeson, Tysin
Gender Variation: Tyra
Nickname: Ty
Similar Names: Tyler, Tyrell, Tyrese, Tyrone
Namesake: Tyson Beckford (actor/model)
⇒ A form of the surname Tison that's quickly gaining popularity as a given name. Also a nickname for someone who has a hot temper. World Heavyweight Champion Boxer Mike Tyson had an impact on the name during the 1980s.

Ulises   Rank: 525

Origin: Latin
Meaning: Angry one
Alternate Spellings: Ulisses, Ulyses, Ulysses
Gender Variations: Odessa, Ulyssa
Similar Names: Odysseus, Ulisse, Umberto, Uriah, Uriel
⇒ The Spanish form of Ulysses that is ultimately derived from Odysseus, the hero in Homer's epic *The Odyssey*. Ulysses S. Grant, the Union general during the Civil War and 18th president of the U.S. brought attention to the original form of the name.

Uriel   Rank: 403

Origin: Hebrew
Meaning: Light of God
Alternate Spelling: Uriell
Gender Variation: Ariel
Nickname: Uri
Similar Names: Ulrick, Ulrike, Uriah, Urias, Ursel, Uzziel
⇒ One of the seven archangels mentioned in the Apocrypha. Also regarded as a literary name for an angel in John Milton's *Paradise Lost* and the subject of a poem by Ralph Waldo Emerson. Steadily rising in popularity since 1985.

Valentin   Rank: 911

Origin: Latin
Meaning: Strong
Gender Variation: Valentina
Nickname: Val

Similar Names: Valente, Valentine, Valentino, Walenty
⇒ The Spanish form of Valentinus.

Valentino   Rank: 967

Origin: Latin
Meaning: Strong
Gender Variation: Valentina
Nicknames: Tino, Val, Vali
Similar Names: Valente, Valentin, Valentio, Valerio
⇒ The Italian form of Valentinus that first hit the popularity chart in the late 1920s. Influenced by the surname of Italian actor Rudolph Valentino. The name is also associated with the fashion brand founded by Italian designer Valentino Garavani. The name made a comeback in 2006.

Van   Rank: 904

Gender Variations: Vanna, Vanya
Similar Names: Val, Vaughn, Verne, Vin, Vince
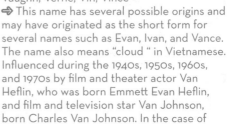
⇒ This name has several possible origins and may have originated as the short form for several names such as Evan, Ivan, and Vance. The name also means "cloud " in Vietnamese. Influenced during the 1940s, 1950s, 1960s, and 1970s by film and theater actor Van Heflin, who was born Emmett Evan Heflin, and film and television star Van Johnson, born Charles Van Johnson. In the case of Northern Ireland singer Van Morrison, the name is short for Ivan. It's rarely used today.

Vance   Rank: 719

Origin: Old English
Meaning: Dweller in a fen
Gender Variations: Fancy, Nancy, Yancy
Nickname: Van
Similar Names: Vaughan, Vere, Vergil, Vern, Vernon, Victor, Vince, Virgil
⇒ A surname used as a given name for someone who lived by a marsh or fen. Peaked during the 1960s at No. 373.

Vaughn   Rank: 734

Origin: Welsh
Meaning: Little
Alternate Spellings:
Vaughan, Von

Gender Variation: Faun
Similar Names: Van, Vance, Vern, Vernon, Victor, Vince, Virgil
Namesakes: Robert Vaughn (actor), Stevie Ray Vaughan (guitarist)

➡️ A surname that has been regularly used as a given name since the 1880s in both the U.S. and United Kingdom. Actor Vince Vaughn is a bearer of the surname. A variation of Vaughan.

Vicente   Rank: 599

Origin: Latin
Meaning: Prevailing
Gender Variations:
Vincenta, Vicentia
Similar Names: Vince, Vincent, Vinnie, Vinson
➡️ The Spanish and Portuguese variation of Vincent that's preferred by Hispanic parents.

Victor   Rank: 104

Origin: Latin
Meaning: Victor, conqueror
Alternate Spellings:
Victer, Viktor
Gender Variations: Tori, Vickie, Victoria
Nickname: Vic
Similar Names: Victorio, Vitor, Vittore, Vittorio, Vittorino
Namesake: Victor Garber (Canadian actor)
➡️ A name predominantly used by the early Christians. Popular among royalty, popes, and saints. Known in literature for French novelist Victor Hugo, author of *The Hunchback of Notre Dame* and *Les Miserables*. Listed among the top 125 names for more than 100 years.

Vincent   Rank: 108

Origin: Latin
Meaning: Prevailing
Gender Variations:
Vincentia, Vincetta
Nicknames: Vin, Vince, Vinnie
Similar Names: Vicente, Vincente, Vincentio
Namesakes: Vin Diesel (actor), Vince Lombardi (football coach), Vincent D'Onofrio (actor), Vincent Gardenia (actor)
➡️ An enduring name that started with the early Christians. Historically Dutch painter Vincent van Goh and French priest Saint Vincent de Paul come to mind. Actor Vince Vaughn uses the short form of the name.

Wade   Rank: 551

Origin: Old English
Meaning: Ford
Alternate Spelling:
Waide, Wayde
Gender Variations: Jada, Jade
Similar Names: Wadell, Wadley, Walter, Wasdworth, Watkin, Watt
Namesakes: Thomas Wade (poet/playwright), Wade Boggs (baseball player)
➡️ A surname taken from a shallow body of water where it's possible to cross by wading. In Margaret Mitchell's 1936 novel *Gone with the Wind*, Wade Hampton Hamilton was the son of Scarlet O'Hara and Charles Hamilton, named after his father's commanding officer, which was customary at the time. Listed among the top 500 names until 2001.

Walker   Rank: 414

Origin: Old English
Meaning: To walk, tread
Gender Variations: Willow
Similar Names: Wallace, Waller, Walter, Waters, Watkins, Watson
Namesakes: Herschel Walker (football player), Walker Percy (novelist)
➡️ An occupational surname for a cloth fuller used as a given name in the U.S. for at least 125 years. Chuck Norris brought attention to the name from 1993 to 2001 when he starred in the television series *Walker, Texas Ranger*.

Walter   Rank: 355

Origin: Old German
Meaning: Ruler of the army
Alternate Spelling:
Walther
Nicknames: Wally, Walt, Wat
Similar Names: Walden, Wally, Walton, Warner, Watkins, Watson
Namesakes: Walter Cronkite (anchorman), Walter "Walt" Disney (producer/director), Walter Payton (Football Hall of Famer), Walter "Walt" Whitman (poet)
➡️ Brought to England by the Normans, which led to the creation of several surnames. Popular in medieval England where it was pronounced "Water." In the U.S. it ranked among the top 100 from 1880 to 1972 but has declined since that time. Historically English writer and explorer Sir Walter Raleigh and Scottish poet Sir Walter Scott come to mind.

Warren   Rank: 506

Origin: Norman/Old German
Meaning: Enclosure
Alternate Spelling: Warrin
Gender Variations: Farron, Karen
Similar Names: Wallace, Waring, Wendell, Wilson, Winston
Namesakes: Warren Moon (Football Hall of Famer), Warren Zevon (musician)
⇨ A surname that originated from a place in Normandy called "La Varenne." The derivation has also been linked with the personal name Werner. It was popular during the 1920s in honor of President Warren G. Harding, the 6th U.S. president to die in office. More recently the name is associated with Warren Beatty, born Henry Warren Beaty, an Academy Award-winning actor, producer, director, and screenwriter.

Waylon   Rank: 547

Origin: Old English
Meaning: Near the footpath
Alternate Spellings: Walen, Walin, Walon, Waylen, Waylin, Weylin
Gender Variations: Jaylan, Kaylan
Nickname: Way
Similar Names: Waverly, Wayland, Wayne
⇨ A surname taken from an English place name and best known for country singer Waylon Jennings, who is considered one of the leaders of the outlaw country movement during the 1970s.

Wayne   Rank: 645

Origin: Old English
Meaning: Wagon maker
Alternate Spellings: Wain, Wayn
Gender Variations: Jayne, Jaynie
Similar Names: Dwayne, Swaine, Wayland, Waylon, Wynn
Namesakes: Bruce Wayne (Batman), Wayne Brady (comedian), Wayne Newton (entertainer), Wayne Rogers (actor), *Wayne's World* (1992 film)
⇨ An occupational surname for either a wagon driver or someone who built wagons. Film actor John Wayne brought much attention to the name starting in 1928. Born Marion Robert Morrison, he assumed the stage name "John Wayne" after Revolutionary War general Anthony Wayne. More recently Canadian Wayne Gretzky, one of hockey's greatest all-time players, comes to mind.

Wesley   Rank: 190

Origin: Old English
Meaning: Western meadow
Alternate Spellings: Weslee, Wesly, Wessley
Gender Variations: Chelsie, Lesley
Nickname: Wes
Similar Names: Wayland, Wendell, Westley, Weston, Willard, Winfield
Namesakes: Wesley Crusher (*Star Trek: The Next Generation* TV character), Wesley Snipes (actor)
⇨ An English place name popularized by John Wesley, the 18th-century Anglican clergyman who founded the Methodist Church with his brother Charles. In continuous use since that time in both the United Kingdom and the U.S. Westley, a variation of the name, caught on in the U.K. during the 1970s, although seldom used in the U.S.

Weston   Rank: 380

Origin: Old English
Meaning: Enclosure, settlement
Alternate Spellings: Westen, Westin
Gender Variation: Destiny
Nickname: Wes
Similar Names: Walton, Weldon, Westbrook, Westby, Westcott, Wilton
Namesake: Jack Weston (actor)
⇨ A surname and place name taken from any number of locations in England. Sporadically used until 1967, when it started moving up in rankings. Actor Nicolas Cage has a son named Weston.

William   Rank: 10

Origin: Old German
Meaning: Determined protector
Gender Variations: Billie, Velma, Wilma
Nicknames: Bill, Billy, Will, Willie, Wills
Similar Names: Walter, Werner, Wilhelm, Willard, Willem, Willis, Wilson
Namesakes: Bill Pullman (actor), Billy Crudup (actor)

➡ A royal name in the United Kingdom for nearly one thousand years starting with William the Conqueror. It declined steadily until 1982 when Prince Charles and Princess Diana named their first son William. In the U.S. William has remained among the top 10 for the past 125 years. Namesakes include four U.S. presidents and famed actor William Holden. Literary bearers include English playwright William Shakespeare and English poet William Blake. Actor Willem Dafoe uses the Dutch form of the name.

Wilson   Rank: 512

Origin: German
Meaning: Son of William
Alternate Spelling: Willson
Gender Variations:
Allison, Wilona
Nickname: Will
Similar Names: Wiley, Wilford, Wilhelm, Willard, Wilkie, Willem, William, Willis, Willy, Wilmer
➡ A surname used as a given name that peaked in 1913 during the presidency of Woodrow Wilson. More recently the surname of Beach Boy songwriter and lead singer, Brian Wilson. Known during the 1990s for fictional character Wilson K. Wilson Jr. from the television series *Home Improvement*.

Winston   Rank: 879

Origin: Old English
Meaning: Joyful stone
Alternate Spellings:
Winsten, Winstonn, Wynstan, Wynston
Gender Variation: Winona
Nickname: Win
Similar Names: Wilbur, Wilford, Willard, Wilmer, Wilson, Wilton, Windsor, Winslow, Winthrop, Winton
Namesake: George Winston (musician)
➡ A surname used as a given name that originated with the family of Winston Churchill, British prime minister during World War II. Also used in literature by George Orwell in his novel *1984*. The name peaked during the 1940s and was introduced as a brand of cigarettes in 1954 where clever advertising made it the #1 choice among smokers. The name is only used occasionally today.

Wyatt   Rank: 82

Origin: Old English
Meaning: Brave in war
Alternate Spellings:
Wiat, Wiatt, Wyat
Gender Variations: Wyanet, Wynne
Similar Names: Wade, Walker, Wiley, Willis, Woody, Wyeth, Wynn
➡ Derived from an English surname and best known for Wyatt Earp, the Wild West lawman who participated in the gunfight at the O.K. Corral in 1881.

Xander   Rank: 278

Origin: Greek
Meaning: Defender of mankind
Alternate Spelling: Zander
Gender Variation: Xandra
Nickname: Xan
Similar Names: Xandro, Xanthus, Xavier, Xenos
Namesake: Xander Berkeley (actor)
➡ The short form of Alexander that has rapidly climbed the popularity chart since its debut in 1999 at No. 925.

Xavier   Rank: 78

Origin: Basque
Meaning: New house
Alternate Spellings: Javier, Xaviar, Xavior, Xzavier, Zavier
Gender Variations: Xaviera, Zavia
Similar Names: Xabier, Xander, Xaver
➡ A Basque place name used during the Middle Ages that was influenced by Saint Francis Xavier, a 16th-century Jesuit priest and missionary who helped found the Society of Jesus (Jesuit Order). Best known for Spanish-Cuban bandleader Xavier Cugat, who introduced Latin-American dance music into the U.S. A popular name among Roman Catholic families.

Yahir   Rank: 387

Origin: American
Gender Variation: Yahaira
Similar Names: Yael, Yakov, Yara, Yoram, Yori, Yorick, Yuri
Namesake: Yahir Othon (Mexican singer/actor)
➡ A created name that made its debut on the popularity chart in 2002.

Yair   Rank: 712
Origin: Hebrew
Meaning: He shines
Gender Variation: Yaira
Similar Names: Jairus,
Yael, Yaffe, Yaniv, Yarden, Yaron
⇨ The Hebrew form of the biblical name
Jair that's been listed among the top 800
names since it debuted in 2003. A popular
choice for Jewish families.

Yandel   Rank: 674
Origin: American
Gender Variation: Yentl
Similar Names: Handel, Mandel, Randel,
Wendell
⇨ New to the popularity chart in 2006, the
name was inspired by the Grammy-nominated
Puerto Rican reggaeton duo Wisin and Yandel.
Possibly a twist on Handel.

Yosef   Rank: 944
Origin: Hebrew
Meaning: God will increase
Alternate Spellings: Yoseff, Yousef
Gender Variation: Yosefa
Nickname: Sef
Similar Names: Yehosef, Yoseif, Yosifya, Yusuf
⇨ The Hebrew form of Joseph mentioned in
the Bible as both the favorite son of Jacob
and Rachel and the husband of Mary, the
mother of Jesus. Occasionally used in the
U.S. since 1989.

Yusuf   Rank: 912
Origin: Hebrew
Meaning: God will increase
Alternate Spellings: Yousef, Youssef, Yusef,
Yusif, Yusuff
Gender Variation: Yuseffa
Similar Names: Jose, Joseph, Joses, Jozef,
Yosif, Yosup
⇨ The Arabic and Turkish form of Yosef
discovered by parents in 2001. Yusuf Islam
was known as English singer-songwriter Cat
Stevens from 1966 to 1978. He changed his
name when he converted to Islam.

Zachariah   Rank: 420
Origin: Hebrew
Meaning: God has
remembered
Alternate Spellings:
Zaccaria, Zaccariah, Zacharia,
Zacharyah, Zackariah, Zechariah,
Zecheriah, Zekariah, Zekeriah
Gender Variations: Zaharina, Zara
Nickname: Zach
Similar Names: Zaccheus, Zacharias, Zachary,
Zebadiah, Zedekiah, Zeke
⇨ A form of Zechariah and the name of 31
men in the Bible, including a minor prophet
who wrote the book of Zechariah. Rarely
used in the U.S. until 1972.

Zachary   Rank: 33
Origin: Hebrew
Meaning: God has
remembered
Alternate Spellings:
Zacary, Zacery, Zacharie, Zachery,
Zackary, Zackery, Zakari, Zakary
Gender Variation: Zahara
Nickname: Zach
Similar Names: Zachariah, Zacharias,
Zebulon, Zechariah, Zeke
⇨ The English form of Zechariah best known
for Zachary Taylor, the 12th U.S. president.
Fictional television character Doctor Zachary
Smith from *Lost in Space*, the 1960s series
released as a film in 1998, also comes to mind.

Zander   Rank: 306
Origin: Greek
Meaning: Defender of mankind
Alternate Spelling: Xander
Gender Variation: Zanna
Nickname: Zann
Similar Names: Alexander, Zandro, Zane,
Zandros
⇨ A surname and short form of Alexander
that's been used as a given name in its own
right since 2000 and peaked in 2004 at
No. 279. Xander was also a character from
Buffy the Vampire Slayer.

Zane   Rank: 243
Origin: American
Alternate Spellings:
Zain, Zaine, Zayne
Gender Variation: Zana
Similar Names: Buck, Bud, Gus, John,
Zachariah, Zack, Zeb, Zeke
⇨ A surname used as a given name that's
climbed the popularity chart since 1921.
Known for western novelist Zane Grey, born
Pearl Zane Gray, whose great-grandfather,
Ebenezer Zane founded Zanesville, Ohio.

making a list and checking it twice

Baby naming can be a challenging business. For most moms and dads, the process will start very humbly with a list of what you like and endless discussions of what you don't. To prepare you for the decision making ahead, the research has been gathered so you can focus on the important task of dreaming, choosing, and finding the perfect name.

The lists will help you sort and decide. Use these detailed compilations to spark conversation or begin a few lists of your own. You'll find hundreds of accessible, easy ideas and suggestions. Survey names across categories at a glance. Browse names by occupation, color, country, or state. Does choosing a name for your child leave you wide awake past your bedtime and into the hours of another time zone? Then turn the pages to find out what natives in other lands are naming their newborns.

You'll be able to compare the names of boxers to race-car drivers, British royalty to American presidents. If you find yourself stuck, ask yourself if you like one syllable or two, if you prefer the Old Testament or New. Do you like the sound of inventors and poets or kings and queens? Remember, just as there are different types of music, mythology, or sports, there are corresponding styles of names to go along with them.

⇒ **Athletes**
⇒ **Au Naturel**
⇒ **Religious**
⇒ **Celebrities**
⇒ **Cultural**
⇒ **Fictional Characters**
⇒ **Historical Leaders**
⇒ **Literary Figures**
⇒ **Musicians**
⇒ **Mythology**
⇒ **Invented & Unisex**
⇒ **Nicknames & Nickname-Proof Names**
⇒ **One Syllable & Two Syllable Names**
⇒ **Place Names**
⇒ **The Most Popular Names Around the Globe and Across the U.S.**

Lists ⇒ around the globe

Most Popular Names in Australia, New South Wales

BOYS	GIRLS
1. Jack	1. Chloe
2. Joshua	2. Charlotte
3. William	3. Ella
4. Lachlan	4. Emily
5. Thomas	5. Olivia
6. James	6. Jessica
7. Daniel	7. Isabella
8. Noah	8. Mia
9. Ryan	9. Sophie
10. Ethan	10. Sienna
11. Benjamin	11. Amelia
12. Samuel	12. Grace
13. Cooper	13. Hannah
14. Alexander	14. Lily
15. Liam	15. Georgia
Matthew	16. Sarah
17. Luke	17. Ava
18. Oliver	18. Zoe
19. Nicholas	19. Emma
20. Jacob	20. Jasmine
21. Riley	21. Ruby
22. Harrison	22. Hayley
23. Jake	23. Sophia
24. Lucas	24. Lucy
25. Jayden	25. Chelsea
26. Dylan	26. Matilda
27. Max	27. Jade
28. Bailey	28. Madison
29. Charlie	29. Caitlin
30. Isaac	30. Lara
31. Harry	31. Isabelle
32. Adam	32. Holly
33. Cameron	33. Alyssa
34. Christian	Maddison
35. Nathan	35. Angelina
36. Blake	36. Elizabeth
Jackson	37. Amy
Joseph	38. Imogen
39. Michael	39. Kayla
40. Tyler	Phoebe
41. Zachary	41. Alexandria
42. Jordan	Laura
Mitchell	43. Keira
44. Oscar	Samantha
45. Connor	45. Lauren
46. Angus	Molly
47. Hayden	47. Bella
48. Patrick	48. Tahlia
49. Jesse	49. Maya
50. Logan	50. Abbey

Most Popular Names in Australia, Northern Territory

BOYS	GIRLS
1. Jack	1. Emily
2. Joshua	2. Ella
3. James	3. Georgia
4. Thomas	Jessica
Ethan	5. Grace
6. Lachlan	Isabella
7. Michael	7. Chloe
8. William	Lily
9. Jacob	Mia
Xavier	10. Sarah
Jake	Amelia
12. Dylan	12. Sophie
Joseph	Ruby
Liam	14. Hayley
Luke	Ruby
16. Mitchell	Tahlia
Samuel	Matilda
Ryan	18. Emma
19. Jayden	Elizabeth
Daniel	Charlotte

KING OF THE HILL

Jack has climbed to the top of the charts in England (where he has reigned for more than a decade), Australia, Northern Ireland, Wales, and New Zealand. As boys' names go, he is the second most popular fellow in Ireland and Scotland.

Most Popular Names in Australia, South

BOYS	GIRLS
1. Jack	1. Ella
2. Lachlan	2. Chloe
3. Joshua	Charlotte
4. William	4. Emily
Thomas	5. Sophie
6. James	6. Olivia
7. Liam	7. Isabella
8. Riley	8. Jessica
9. Daniel	9. Zoe
Cooper	10. Hannah
11. Noah	11. Amelia
12. Alexander	12. Mia
13. Ethan	Lily
14. Samuel	14. Grace
Ryan	15. Sienna
Benjamin	Jasmine
17. Luke	17. Georgia
Jacob	Emma
19. Harrison	19. Caitlin
20. Nicholas	20. Lucy
21. Lucas	21. Ava
22. Connor	22. Madison
23. Bailey	23. Ruby
24. Tyler	24. Sarah
Oliver	25. Holly
26. Jackson	26. Chelsea
27. Cameron	27. Lauren
28. Jayden	28. Tahlia
Jake	Lilly
30. Matthew	Hayley
Brodie	Alyssa
Blake	32. Matilda
33. Mitchell	Imogen
Max	34. Amy
35. Jordan	35. Maddison
Dylan	36. Paige
Charlie	Amber
38. Michael	38. Jorja
39. Angus	Jade
40. Harry	Isabelle
41. Isaac	41. Brooke
Caleb	42. Zara
43. Tyson	43. Lara
44. Oscar	44. Summer
45. Seth	Alice
46. Nathan	46. Kayla
47. Henry	Abby
48. Zachary	48. Tayla
49. Cody	Kate
50. Hayden	Bella

Most Popular Names in Austria

BOYS	GIRLS
1. Lukas	1. Leonie
2. Tobias	2. Lena
3. David	3. Anna
4. Florian	4. Sarah
5. Alexander	5. Julia
6. Sebastian	6. Laura
7. Julian	7. Hannah
8. Fabian	8. Katharina
9. Simon	9. Sophie
10. Maximilian	10. Lea
11. Elias	11. Lisa
12. Philipp	12. Viktoria
13. Jakob	13. Lara
14. Felix	14. Selina
15. Jonas	15. Magdalena
16. Michael	16. Nina
17. Daniel	17. Elena
18. Paul	18. Johanna
19. Matthias	19. Sophia
20. Marcel	20. Vanessa
21. Dominik	21. Jana
22. Raphael	22. Jasmin
23. Moritz	23. Theresa
Nico	24. Alina
Stefan	25. Christina
26. Niklas	26. Emma
27. Leon	27. Emily
28. Thomas	28. Michelle
29. Manuel	29. Marie
30. Luca	30. Marlene
31. Benjamin	31. Melanie
32. Samuel	32. Chiara
33. Johannes	33. Angelina
34. Christoph	34. Amelie
35. Andreas	35. Valentina
36. Jan	36. Anja
Marco	37. Nadine
38. Kevin	38. Stefanie
39. Markus	39. Clara
40. Noah	Eva
41. Martin	41. Miriam
42. Patrick	42. Maria
43. Christian	43. Elisa
44. Lorenz	44. Anna-Lena
45. Oliver	45. Carina
46. Gabriel	Natalie
47. Clemens	47. Katrin
48. Kilian	Nicole
49. Pascal	49. Verena
50. Benedikt	50. Elisabeth

Lists ⇨ around the globe

Most Popular Names in Belgium

	BOYS		GIRLS
1.	Noah	1.	Emma
2.	Thomas	2.	Marie
3.	Nathan	3.	Laura
4.	Lucas	4.	Julie
5.	Louis	5.	Louise
6.	Arthur	6.	Clara
7.	Milan	7.	Manon
8.	Hugo	8.	Léa
9.	Maxime	9.	Sarah
10.	Mohamed	10.	Luna
11.	Nicolas	11.	Elise
12.	Simon	12.	Charlotte
13.	Théo		Lotte
14.	Tom	14.	Camille
15.	Victor		Lore
16.	Robbe	16.	Lisa
	Wout	17.	Chloé
18.	Alexandre	18.	Lucie
19.	Senne	19.	Amber
20.	Mathis	20.	Lola
21.	Lars	21.	Jade
	Matteo	22.	Lara
23.	Luca	23.	Hanne
24.	Romain	24.	Emilie
25.	Seppe	25.	Zoë
26.	Daan	26.	Juliette
27.	Mathias	27.	Lina
28.	Adam	28.	Eva
29.	Rune	29.	Sara
30.	Mathéo	30.	Amélie
31.	Gabriel		Zoé
32.	Jules	32.	Pauline
33.	Antoine	33.	Eline
34.	Arne	34.	Anaïs
35.	Kobe	35.	Nina
36.	Ethan	36.	Ella
37.	Alexander	37.	Nora
38.	Tristan	38.	Anna
39.	Xander	39.	Inès
40.	Jonas	40.	Noor
41.	Elias	41.	Victoria
42.	Samuel	42.	Elisa
43.	Loïc	43.	Célia
44.	Noa		Océan
45.	Robin	45.	Femke
46.	Sacha		Kato
47.	Raphaël	47.	Fleur
48.	Diego	48.	Kaat
	Liam	49.	Lena
50.	Julien	50.	Olivia

Most Popular Names in Brussels

	BOYS		GIRLS
1.	Mohamed	1.	Lina
2.	Adam	2.	Sarah
3.	Rayan	3.	Rania
4.	Ayoub	4.	Inès
5.	Mehdi	5.	Aya
6.	Amine	6.	Salma
	Hamza	7.	Yasmine
8.	Alexandre	8.	Imane
	Nathan	9.	Sara
10.	Gabriel	10.	Emma
	Noah	11.	Ines
12.	Lucas	12.	Laura
13.	Anas	13.	Clara
	Thomas	14.	Nora
15.	Samuel	15.	Léa
16.	Nicolas		Lucie
17.	Bilal	17.	Sofia
18.	Maxime	18.	Victoria
	Yanis	19.	Chloe
20.	Raphaël		Fatima
	Zakaria		Louise
22.	Hugo		Zoé
23.	Ilias	23.	Dina
24.	Romain	24.	Hajar
25.	Rayane	25.	Camille
	Yassine	26.	Alice
27.	David		Charlotte
28.	Antoine	28.	Marwa
	Victor		Sirine
30.	Ali	30.	Yousra
	Ayman	31.	Emilie
	Ibrahim	32.	Assia
33.	Arthur	33.	Anaïs
34.	Louis		Elise
	Yassin		Julia
36.	Martin		Juliette
	Walid		Lola
38.	Nassim		Manon
39.	Diego		Marie
40.	Simon	40.	Jeanne
41.	Ahmed		Olivia
	Julien	42.	Elisa
	Youssef		Hafsa
44.	Guillaume		Jade
	Ilyas	45.	Kawtar
	Mohammed		Maya
47.	Luca		Nina
48.	Matteo		Nour
	Sacha	49.	Farah
	Théo		Kenza

Most Popular Names in Canada, British Columbia

BOYS		GIRLS	
1.	Ethan	1.	Emma
2.	Jacob	2.	Emily
3.	Matthew	3.	Ava
4.	Joshua	4.	Olivia
5.	Nathan	5.	Hannah
6.	Liam	6.	Sarah
7.	Benjamin	7.	Sophia
8.	Ryan	8.	Ella
9.	Logan	9.	Isabella
10.	Daniel	10.	Madison
11.	Alexander	11.	Grace
12.	Noah	12.	Chloe
13.	Lucas	13.	Abigail
14.	James	14.	Samantha
15.	William	15.	Taylor
16.	Owen	16.	Brooklyn
17.	Nicholas	17.	Maya
18.	Samuel	18.	Sophie
19.	Tyler	19.	Julia
20.	Jack	20.	Lauren

In Brussels, often hailed as "the capital of Europe," Mohamed is already the No. 1 name for boys, joined by Adam, Ayoub, Rayan, and Mehdi in the top five. In Britain Muhammad would be the No. 2 name for boys if all 14 variant spellings were combined.

FOR RYAN OUT LOUD

Forget the Little Prince; the name Ryan means "little king." Among the royal Ryans holding court in the media are Canadian actors Ryan Gosling and Ryan Reynolds, American actor Ryan Phillippe, and American Idol host Ryan Seacrest.

Most Popular Names in Canada, Nova Scotia

BOYS		GIRLS	
1.	Ryan	1.	Emma
2.	Jacob	2.	Ava
3.	Ethan		Madison
4.	Noah		Olivia
5.	Liam	5.	Hannah
6.	Owen	6.	Abigail
7.	Alexander		Emily
	Matthew	8.	Sarah
9.	Jack	9.	Ella
10.	Benjamin	10.	Chloe
11.	Nathan	11.	Lily
12.	Evan	12.	Grace
13.	Cole	13.	Brooke
	William	14.	Sophia
15.	Joshua	15.	Faith
16.	Logan		Sophie
17.	Lucas	17.	Elizabeth
18.	Connor	18.	Brooklyn
19.	Cameron		Julia
	Nicholas		Rachel

Lists ⇨ around the globe

Most Popular Names in Canada, Quebec

	BOYS		GIRLS
1.	William	1.	Lea
2.	Samuel	2.	Jade
3.	Alexis	3.	Rosalie
4.	Nathan	4.	Florence
5.	Thomas	5.	Laurie
6.	Antoine	6.	Gabrielle
7.	Gabriel	7.	Sarah
8.	Justin	8.	Camille
9.	Olivier	9.	Oceane
10.	Felix	10.	Laurence
11.	Zachary	11.	Noemie
12.	Xavier	12.	Emma
13.	Jeremy	13.	Emilie
14.	Alexandre	14.	Juliette
15.	Mathis	15.	Maika
16.	Anthony	16.	Coralie
17.	Jacob	17.	Justine
18.	Raphael	18.	Megane
19.	Emile	19.	Ariane
20.	Vincent	20.	Emy
21.	Nicolas	21.	Chloe
22.	Benjamin	22.	Audrey
23.	Maxime	23.	Annabelle
24.	Tristan	24.	Marianne
25.	Noah	25.	Charlotte
26.	Simon	26.	Alicia
27.	Etienne	27.	Maya
28.	Charles	28.	Eve
29.	Adam	29.	Megan
30.	Mathieu	30.	Amelie
31.	Edouard	31.	Rose
32.	Loic	32.	Mia
33.	David	33.	Zoe
34.	Guillaume	34.	Elodie
35.	Lucas	35.	Alice
36.	Philippe	36.	Oceanne
37.	Alex	37.	Alexia
38.	Hugo	38.	Charlie
39.	Julien	39.	Leanne
40.	Victor	40.	Anais
41.	Tommy	41.	Victoria
42.	Louis	42.	Raphaelle
43.	Dylan	43.	Elizabeth
44.	Cedric	44.	Daphnee
45.	Michael	45.	Marilou
46.	Isaac	46.	Beatrice
47.	Christopher	47.	Maude
48.	Jonathan	48.	Melodie
49.	Liam	49.	Catherine
50.	Mathias	50.	Jasmine

Most Popular Names in Chile

	BOYS		GIRLS
1.	Benjamin	1.	Constanza
2.	Matias	2.	Catalina
3.	Vicente	3.	Valentina
4.	Martin	4.	Javiera
5.	Sebastian	5.	Martina
6.	Diego	6.	Sofia
7.	Nicolas	7.	Maria
8.	Juan	8.	Antonia
9.	Jose	9.	Fernanda
10.	Cristobal	10.	Francisca
11.	Joaquin	11.	Isidora
12.	Ignacio	12.	Camila
13.	Felipe	13.	Florencia
14.	Francisco	14.	Josefa
15.	Bastian	15.	Daniela
16.	Maximiliano	16.	Antonella
17.	Javier	17.	Millaray
18.	Gabriel	18.	Barbara
19.	Tomas	19.	Belen
20.	Luis	20.	Rocio
21.	Lucas	21.	Ignacia
22.	Franco	22.	Krishna
23.	Daniel	23.	Monserrat
24.	Pablo	24.	Gabriela
25.	Carlos	25.	Anais
26.	Cristian	26.	Carolina
27.	Rodrigo	27.	Natalia
28.	Fernando	28.	Pia
29.	Renato	29.	Victoria
30.	David	30.	Paula
31.	Jorge	31.	Emilia
32.	Agustin	32.	Renata
33.	Kevin	33.	Carla
34.	Fabian	34.	Alondra
35.	Esteban	35.	Genesis
36.	Victor	36.	Amanda
37.	Miguel	37.	Paz
38.	Alejandro	38.	Magdalena
39.	Manuel	39.	Alejandra
40.	Alonso	40.	Laura
41.	Eduardo	41.	Tamara
42.	Pedro	42.	Nicole
43.	Alvaro	43.	Karla
44.	Angel	44.	Trinidad
45.	Camilo	45.	Claudia
46.	Alexander	46.	Katalina
47.	Patricio	47.	Alexandra
48.	Marcelo	48.	Josefina
49.	Andres	49.	Maite
50.	Gonzalo	50.	Paloma

Most Popular Names in Czech Republic

BOYS	GIRLS
1. Jan	1. Tereza
2. Jakub	2. Eliška
3. Tomáš	3. Adéla
4. Adam	4. Natálie
5. Ondřej	5. Anna
6. Martin	6. Karolína
7. Filip	7. Kristýna
8. Lukáš	8. Aneta
9. Vojtěch	9. Nikola
10. Matěj	10. Kateřina

"For my daughter I had always loved the name Silvia—it means a "sylph of the woods," and Rea Silvia was the name of the she-wolf who raised Romulus and Remus, the twins who founded the city of Rome. For my son only two names felt right—Christopher and Nicholas. My husband and I liked the fact that Christopher was the patron saint of travelers."

–VERONIQUE C.

Most Popular Names in Denmark

BOYS	GIRLS
1. Lucas	1. Sofie
2. Mikkel	2. Laura
3. Magnus	3. Freja
4. Frederik	4. Mathilde
5. Mads	5. Caroline
6. Tobias	6. Emma
7. Oliver	7. Ida
8. Victor	8. Sara
9. Sebastian	9. Maja
10. Mathias	10. Julie
11. Emil	11. Anna
12. Noah	12. Clara
13. Christian	13. Signe
14. Marcus	14. Cecilie
15. Nikolaj	15. Emilie
16. Gustav	16. Josefine
17. Rasmus	17. Amalie
18. Alexander	18. Victoria
19. Jonas	19. Katrine
20. Kasper	20. Alberte
21. William	21. Isabella
22. Jacob	22. Lærke
23. Simon	23. Marie
24. Oscar	24. Nanna
25. Malthe	25. Andrea
26. Andreas	26. Frida
27. Benjamin	27. Sofia
28. Daniel	28. Liva
29. Anton	29. Frederikke
30. Nicklas	30. Camilla
31. Philip	31. Mille
32. Carl	32. Johanne
33. Christoffer	33. Maria
34. Lasse	34. Nicoline
35. Elias	35. Jasmin
36. Valdemar	36. Astrid
37. Jeppe	37. Lea
38. August	38. Tilde
39. Silas	39. Anne
40. Jonathan	40. Olivia
41. David	41. Mia
42. Marius	42. Filippa
43. Anders	43. Karla
44. Bertram	44. Rebecca
45. Villads	45. Alma
46. Laurits	46. Malou
47. Albert	47. Silje
48. Peter	48. Louise
49. Patrick	49. Line
50. Adam	50. Thea

Lists ⇒ around the globe

Most Popular Names in England/Wales

BOYS		GIRLS	
1.	Jack	1.	Olivia
2.	Thomas	2.	Grace
3.	Joshua	3.	Jessica
4.	Oliver	4.	Ruby
5.	Harry	5.	Emily
6.	James	6.	Sophie
7.	William	7.	Chloe
8.	Samuel	8.	Lucy
9.	Daniel	9.	Lily
10.	Charlie	10.	Ellie
11.	Benjamin	11.	Ella
12.	Joseph	12.	Charlotte
13.	Callum	13.	Katie
14.	George	14.	Mia
15.	Jake	15.	Hannah
16.	Alfie	16.	Amelia
17.	Luke	17.	Megan
18.	Matthew	18.	Amy
19.	Ethan	19.	Isabella
20.	Lewis	20.	Millie
21.	Jacob	21.	Evie
22.	Mohammed	22.	Abigail
23.	Dylan	23.	Freya
24.	Alexander	24.	Molly
25.	Ryan	25.	Daisy
26.	Adam	26.	Holly
27.	Tyler	27.	Emma
28.	Harvey	28.	Erin
29.	Max	29.	Isabelle
30.	Cameron	30.	Poppy
31.	Liam	31.	Jasmine
32.	Jamie	32.	Leah
33.	Leo	33.	Keira
34.	Owen	34.	Phoebe
35.	Connor	35.	Caitlin
36.	Harrison	36.	Rebecca
37.	Nathan	37.	Georgia
38.	Ben	38.	Lauren
39.	Henry	39.	Madison
40.	Archie	40.	Amber
41.	Edward	41.	Elizabeth
42.	Michael	42.	Eleanor
43.	Aaron	43.	Bethany
44.	Muhammad	44.	Isabel
45.	Kyle	45.	Paige
46.	Noah	46.	Scarlett
47.	Oscar	47.	Alice
48.	Lucas	48.	Imogen
49.	Rhys	49.	Sophia
50.	Bradley	50.	Anna

Most Popular Names in Finland

BOYS		GIRLS	
1.	Veeti	1.	Emma
2.	Eetu	2.	Ella
3.	Aleksi	3.	Siiri
4.	Joona	4.	Aino
5.	Elias	5.	Anni
6.	Juho	6.	Sara
7.	Lauri	7.	Venia
8.	Arttu	8.	Aada
9.	Leevi	9.	Emilia
10.	Matias	10.	Lida
11.	Niko	11.	Veera
12.	Onni	12.	Oona
13.	Ville	13.	Sofia
14.	Jesse	14.	Jenna
15.	Rasmus	15.	Vilma
16.	Aaro	16.	Julia
17.	Jimi	17.	Nea
18.	Juuso	18.	Milla
19.	Niklas	19.	Helmi
20.	Jere	20.	Laura
21.	Tuomas	21.	Vilvi
22.	Oskari	22.	Lotta
23.	Roope	23.	Pinja
24.	Valtteri	24.	Emmi
25.	Otto	25.	Sanni
26.	Miro	26.	Ronja
27.	Aapo	27.	Anna
28.	Antti	28.	Noora
29.	Joonas	29.	Inka
30.	Joel	30.	Lina
31.	Aatu	31.	Olivia
32.	Atte	32.	Saana
33.	Roni	33.	Neea
34.	Mikael	34.	Nella
35.	Santeri	35.	Roosa
36.	Kalle	36.	Ida
37.	Eero	37.	Pihla
38.	Daniel	38.	Elli
39.	Teemu	39.	Minttu
40.	Niilo	40.	Elina
41.	Jaakko	41.	Milja
42.	Anton	42.	Alisa
43.	Akseli	43.	Peppi
44.	Eemeli	44.	Saara
45.	Konsta	45.	Kiia
46.	Eeli	46.	Liris
47.	Julius	47.	Sonja
48.	Oliver	48.	Elsa
49.	Eelis	49.	Llona
50.	Joni	50.	Enni

Most Popular Names in France

BOYS	GIRLS
1. Enzo	1. Léa
2. Mathis	2. Emma
3. Lucas	3. Manon
4. Hugo	4. Camille
5. Nathan	5. Clara
6. Thomas	6. Lola
7. Théo	7. Jade
8. Clement	8. Chloé
9. Louis	9. Anais
10. Léo	10. Zoé
11. Tom	11. Océane
12. Maxime	12. Lilou
13. Raphael	13. Romane
14. Antoine	14. Lucie
15. Alexis	15. Sarah
16. Matheo	16. Julie
17. Ethan	17. Juliette
18. Alexandre	18. Marie
19. Baptiste	19. Eva
20. Jules	20. Ines

Enzo, an Italian derivation of Henry and a nickname for Vincenzo and Lorenzo, tops the list of boys' names in France. Vive la différence!

Most Popular Names in Germany

BOYS	GIRLS
1. Leon	1. Marie
2. Maximilian	2. Sophie/Sofie
3. Alexander	3. Maria
4. Lukas/Lucas	4. Anna/Anne
5. Paul	5. Leonie
6. Luca	6. Lena
7. Tim	7. Emily
8. Felix	8. Johanna
9. David	9. Laura
10. Elias	10. Lea/Leah

Most Popular Names in Iceland

BOYS	GIRLS
1. Jón	1. Guðrún
2. Sigurður	2. Anna
3. Guðmundur	3. Sigríður
4. Gunnar	4. Kristín
5. Ólafur	5. Margrét
6. Einar	6. Helga
7. Magnús	7. Sigrún
8. Kristján	8. Ingibjörg
9. Stefán	9. Jóhanna
10. Jóhann	10. María
11. Björn	11. Elín
12. Árni	12. Guðbjörg
13. Bjarni	13. Ásta
14. Helgi	14. Katrín
15. Halldór	15. Ragnheiður
16. Pétur	16. Hildur
17. Arnar	17. Erla
18. Kristinn	18. Guðný
19. Gísli	19. Ólöf
20. Ragnar	20. Lilja
21. Þorsteinn	21. Hulda
22. Guðjón	22. Elísabet
23. Páll	23. Steinunn
24. Daníel	24. Auður
25. Sveinn	25. Unnur
26. Birgir	26. Inga
27. Óskar	27. Eva
28. Davíð	28. Þórunn
29. Jóhannes	29. Sólveig
30. Karl	30. Þóra
31. Haukur	31. Berglind
32. Andri	32. Kolbrún
33. Haraldur	33. Bryndís
34. Ásgeir	34. Ásdís
35. Ágúst	35. Jóna
36. Kjartan	36. Halldóra
37. Sigurjón	37. Íris
38. Hörðu	38. Hrafnhildur
39. Þórður	39. Birna
40. Friðrik	40. Erna
41. Bjarki	41. Jónína
42. Jónas	42. Þórdís
43. Aron	43. Sara
44. Atli	44. Valgerður
45. Tómas	45. Guðlaug Sigurbjörg
46. Hilmar	
47. Baldur	47. Linda
48. Róbert	48. Rakel
49. Eiríkur	49. Edda
50. Rúnar	50. Hanna

Lists ⇒ around the globe

Most Popular Names in Ireland

BOYS		GIRLS	
1.	Sean	1.	Sarah
2.	Jack	2.	Emma
3.	Conor	3.	Katie
4.	Adam	4.	Aoife
5.	James	5.	Sophie
6.	Daniel	6.	Ava
7.	Luke	7.	Grace
8.	Cian	8.	Ella
9.	Michael	9.	Leah
10.	Jamie	10.	Ciara
11.	Aaron	11.	Amy
12.	Dylan	12.	Emily
13.	Thomas	13.	Lucy
14.	Ryan	14.	Chloe
15.	Darragh	15.	Caoimhe
16.	Oisin	16.	Hannah
17.	Matthew	17.	Rachel
18.	John	18.	Niamh
19.	Patrick	19.	Rebecca
20.	Ben	20.	Jessica
21.	David	21.	Anna
22.	Callum		Lauren
23.	Alex	23.	Kate
24.	Shane	24.	Laura
25.	Evan	25.	Mia
26.	Eoin		Molly
27.	Joshua	27.	Roisin
28.	Cillian	28.	Aisling
29.	Jake	29.	Saoirse
30.	Liam	30.	Ellie
31.	Mark	31.	Abbie
32.	Nathan	32.	Megan
33.	Ciaran	33.	Holly
34.	Samuel	34.	Ellen
35.	Cathal	35.	Erin
36.	Charlie	36.	Nicole
37.	Robert	37.	Aine
38.	Kyle	38.	Tara
39.	Fionn	39.	Shauna
40.	Joseph	40.	Clodagh
41.	Harry	41.	Ruby
42.	Cormac	42.	Lily
43.	Andrew	43.	Katelyn
44.	Calum	44.	Abigail
45.	Rory		Eva
46.	Stephen	46.	Caitlin
47.	Ronan	47.	Zoe
48.	Kevin	48.	Eimear
49.	Noah	49.	Shannon
50.	Eoghan	50.	Isabelle

Most Popular Names in Italy

BOYS		GIRLS	
1.	Francesco	1.	Giulia
2.	Alessandro	2.	Martina
3.	Andrea	3.	Chiara
4.	Matteo	4.	Sar
5.	Lorenzo	5.	Alessia
6.	Luca	6.	Francesca
7.	Mattia	7.	Sofia
8.	Simone	8.	Giorgia
9.	Davide	9.	Elisa
10.	Marco	10.	Alice
11.	Gabriele	11.	Aurora
12.	Giuseppe	12.	Anna
13.	Riccardo	13.	Giada
14.	Tommaso	14.	Gaia
15.	Antonio	15.	Federica
16.	Alessio	16.	Elena
17.	Federico	17.	Alessandra
18.	Giovanni	18.	Valentina
19.	Leonardo	19.	Ilaria
20.	Filippo	20.	Beatrice
21.	Samuele	21.	Arianna
22.	Daniele	22.	Camilla
23.	Michele	23.	Noemi
24.	Emanuele	24.	Eleonora
25.	Pietro	25.	Rebecca
26.	Giacomo	26.	Marta
27.	Edoardo	27.	Serena
28.	Stefano	28.	Laura
29.	Nicola	29.	Emma
30.	Vincenzo	30.	Maria

Most Popular Names in Japan

BOYS		GIRLS	
1.	Shun	1.	Misaki
2.	Takuni	2.	Aoi
3.	Sho	3.	Nanami
4.	Ren	4.	Miu
5.	Shota	5.	Riko
6.	Sota	6.	Miyu
7.	Kaito	7.	Moe
8.	Kenta	8.	Mitsuki
9.	Daiki	9.	Yuka
10.	Yu	10.	Rin

Most Popular Names in Lithuania

BOYS	GIRLS
1. Lukas	1. Kamile
2. Matas	2. Gabija
3. Nojus	3. Gabriele
4. Mantas	4. Austeja
5. Dominykas	5. Emilija
6. Nedas	6. Ugne
7. Dovydas	7. Auguste
8. Rokas	8. Viktorija
9. Titas	9. Rugile
10. Ignas	10. Deimante

Most Popular Names in Malta

BOYS	GIRLS
1. Matthew/Matthias/Matteo	1. Maria/Mariah
2. Luke/Luca	2. Martina
3. Michael/Michele	3. Amy
4. Aidan	4. Gulia/Julia
5. Jake Jamie/James	5. Shania
7. Andre/Andrea Isaac	6. Maia/Maya
9. Nathan/Nathaniel	7. Catherine/Katrina Emma/Emily Nicole
10. Zac	10. Michela
11. Nicholas	11. Yasmin/Jasmin
12. Kearon	12. Elisa/Eliza
13. Daniel	13. Hayley
14. Gabriel	14. Francesca
15. Jean	15. Elenia/Elena
16. Julian Neal	16. Sara/Sarah
18. Samuel	17. Kylie
19. Liam	18 Jade Thea
20. Thomas Sven	20. Kaya Kelsey
22. Carl Denzel	22. Christina
24. Kurt Ryan	23. Hannah Jessica Kimberly Lara
26. Alex	27. Aaliyah Kaylee Rachel

Most Popular Names in Netherlands

BOYS	GIRLS
1. Sem	1. Sanne
2. Ruben	2. Lotte
3. Daan	3. Sophie
4. Tim	4. Lieke
5. Thomas	5. Emma
6. Jesse	6. Fleur
7. Stijn	7. Eva
8. Thijs	8. Anna
9. Lucas	9. Noa
10. Milan	10. Julia
11. Sven	11. Iris
12. Lars	12. Lisa
13. Luuk	13. Anne
14. Bram	14. Sara
15. Jayden	15. Isa
16. Finn	16. Anouk
17. Max	17. Femke
18. Niels	18. Roos
19. Julian	19. Maud
20. Gijs	20. Britt

It is customary to address people by their first name in Iceland. Bjork (pronounced "Byirk") means "birch tree" in Icelandic. Even last names relate to the father's or mother's first name, as in the son of Jón (Jónsson) or the daughter of Jón (Jónsdóttir).

Lists ⇒ around the globe

New Zealand rejected the name 4Real for its use of numerals. The parents say, "Everyone knows what it means"—unlike the names found in baby-name books.

Most Popular Names in New Zealand

BOYS	GIRLS
1. Jack	1. Charlotte
2. Joshua	2. Ella
3. Daniel	3. Sophie
4. William	4. Emma
5. Samuel	5. Olivia
6. Jacob	6. Emily
7. Thomas	7. Grace
8. Benjamin	8. Jessica
9. Ryan	9. Hannah
10. Liam	10. Lily
11. Oliver	11. Isabella
12. Ethan	12. Lucy
13. James	13. Chloe
14. Luke	14. Ruby
15. Matthew	15. Georgia
16. Noah	16. Paige
17. Caleb	17. Amelia
18. Max	18. Maia
19. Jayden	19. Zoe
20. Logan	20. Madison
21. Dylan	21. Brooke
22. Connor	22. Holly
23. Alexander	23. Samantha
24. Blake	24. Sarah
25. Riley	25. Mia
26. Charlie	26. Ava
27. Nathan	27. Jasmine
28. Tyler	28. Kate
29. George	29. Caitlyn
30. Joseph	30. Hayley

Most Popular Names in Northern Ireland

BOYS	GIRLS
1. Jack	1. Katie
2. Matthew	2. Grace
3. Ryan	3. Emma
4. James	4. Sophie
5. Daniel	5. Ellie
6. Adam	6. Lucy
7. Joshua	7. Sarah
8. Callum	8. Hannah
9. Ben	9. Jessica
10. Ethan	10. Erin
11. Jamie	11. Niamh
12. Conor	12. Caitlin
Luke	13. Chloe
14. Thomas	14. Amy
15. Dylan	15. Leah
16. Sean	16. Aoife
17. Michael	Rebecca
18. Aaron	18. Emily
19. Jake	19. Aimee
20. Calum	Anna

Emma possesses universal appeal as a girl's name, reaching No. 1 in Finland, and Sweden, and No. 2 in France, Ireland, Scotland, the U.S., and Norway. Stateside Emma is the most popular girl's name in 17 states.

Most Popular Names in Norway

BOYS	GIRLS
1. Jonas	1. Thea
2. Mathias	2. Emma
3. Alexander	3. Sara
4. Andreas	4. Julie
5. Elias	5. Ida
6. Kristian	6. Hanna
7. Sebastian	7. Nora
8. Markus	8. Ingrid
9. Sander	9. Emilie
10. Tobias	10. Amalie
11. Martin	11. Maria
12. Henrik	12. Malin
13. Emil	13. Sofie
14. Lukas	14. Leah
Daniel	Anna
16. Adrian	16. Linnea
17. Magnus	17. Andrea
18. Kristoffer	18. Vilde
19. Oliver	19. Aurora
20. Noah	20. Hedda
21. Benjamin	21. Mathilde
22. Jakob	22. Tuva
23. Philip	23. Mia
Nikolai	24. Frida
25. Oskar	25 Marie
26. Fredrik	26. Oda
27. Marius	Elise
28. Sondre	28. Helene
29. William	29. Maja
30. Theodor	30. Karoline
31. Isak	31. Victoria
32. Thomas	Mina
33. Kasper	33. Marte
34. Hakon	34. Martine
Even	35. Selma
36. Eirik	36. Kaja
37. Johannes	37. Mari
38. Mats	38. Kristine
39. Erik	39. Maren
40. Ole	Jenny
41. Simen	41. Ella
42. Herman	42. Natalie
43. Joakim	Camilla
44. Jonathan	44. Eline
45. Lars	Celine
46. Sigurd	46. Ane
47. Jorgen	47. Madeleine
48. David	48. Mathea
49. Julian	49. Tiril
Aksel	Ingeborg

Most Popular Names in Poland

BOYS	GIRLS
1. Jakub	1. Julia
2. Mateusz	2. Aleksandra
3. Kacper	3. Wiktoria
4. Bartek	4. Zuzanna
5. Jan	5. Natalia
6. Michal	6. Oliwia
7. Maciej	7. Maja
8. Piotr	8. Zofia
9. Szymon	9. Karolina
10. Filip	10. Weronika
11. Mikolaj	11. Maria
12. Antoni	12. Anna
13. Aleksander	13. Gabriela
14. Igor	14. Magdalena
15. Adam	15. Amelia
16. Patryk	16. Alicja
17. Wiktor	17. Patrycja
18. Franciszek	18. Martyna
19. Krzysztof	19. Hanna
20. Maksymilian	20. Marta
21. Karol	21. Katarzyna
22. Dawid	22. Klaudia
23. Stanislaw	23. Dominika
24. Kamil	24. Emilia
25. Pawel	25. Agata
26. Oskar	26. Malgorzata
27. Dominik	27. Paulina
28. Tomasz	28. Joanna
29. Wojciech	29. Kinga
30. Lukasz	30. Barbara
31. Hubert	31. Antonina
32. Adrian	32. Lena
33. Damian	33. Nikola
34. Oliwier	34. Daria
35. Sebastian	35. Nina
36. Krystian	36. Izabela
37. Marcin	37. Kamila
38. Milosz	38. Milena
39. Konrad	39. Sandra
40. Ignacy	40. Iga
41. Daniel	41. Pola
42. Grzegorz	42. Laura
43. Kajetan	43. Justyna
44. Eryk	44. Monika
45. Przemyslaw	45. Jogoda
46. Rafal	46. Michalina
47. Tymon	47. Olga
48. Andrzej	48. Ewa
49. Julian	49. Urszula
50. Marcel	50. Lucja

Lists ⇒ around the globe

Most Popular Names in Scotland

BOYS		GIRLS	
1.	Lewis	1.	Sophie
2.	Jack	2.	Emma
3.	Callum	3.	Ellie
4.	James	4.	Amy
5.	Ryan	5.	Erin
6.	Cameron	6.	Lucy
7.	Kyle	7.	Katie
8.	Jamie	8.	Chloe
9.	Daniel	9.	Rebecca
10.	Matthew	10.	Emily
11.	Liam	11.	Hannah
12.	Ben	12.	Oliva
13.	Adam	13.	Rachel
14.	Dylan	14.	Leah
15.	Connor	15.	Megan
16.	Andrew	16.	Aimee
17.	Alexander		Holly
18.	Aidan	18.	Abbie
19.	Thomas	19.	Jessica
20.	Aiden	20.	Lauren
21.	Aaron	21.	Niamh
	Joshua	22.	Sarah
23.	Logan	23.	Anna
24.	Scott	24.	Caitlin
25.	Ross	25.	Eilidh
26.	Nathan		Isla
27.	David	27.	Eve
28.	Finlay	28.	Grace
29.	Euan	29.	Brooke
30.	John	30.	Mia
31.	Luke	31.	Molly
32.	Michael	32.	Charlotte
33.	Samuel	33.	Zoe
34.	Josh	34.	Eva
35.	Calum	35.	Keira
	William	36.	Morgan
37.	Kieran	37.	Cara
38.	Ethan		Millie
39.	Ewan	39.	Abigail
40.	Sean	40.	Nicole
41.	Sam	41.	Shannon
42.	Fraser	42.	Skye
43.	Owen	43.	Ruby
44.	Christopher	44.	Amber
45.	Jake		Paige
	Robert	46.	Kirsty
47.	Jay	47.	Kayla
	Joseph	48.	Ella
49.	Charlie	49.	Bethany
50.	Benjamin	50.	Beth

Most Popular Names in Republic of Slovenia

BOYS		GIRLS	
1.	Luka	1.	Nika
2.	Jan	2.	Eva
3.	Nejc	3.	Sara
4.	Ziga	4.	Lara
5.	Zan	5.	Ana
6.	Nik	6.	Lana
7.	Matic	7.	Maja
8.	Aljaz	8.	Masa
9.	David	9.	Ema
10.	Jaka	10.	Nina
11.	Miha	11.	Zala
12.	Jakob	12.	Ziva
13.	Tim	13.	Anja
14.	Gasper	14.	Neza
15.	Anze	15.	Klara
16.	Rok	16.	Tjasa
17.	Tilen	17.	Kaja
18.	Gal	18.	Spela
19.	Vid	19.	Hana
20.	Anej	20.	Pia

In Sweden, Elias Kai, a search engine expert, was granted permission to name his son Oliver Google Kai. Other names were not so lucky: Ikea and Veranda were rejected by authorities for being inappropriate, offensive, or just plain uncomfortable for the recipient.

Most Popular Names in Spain

	BOYS		GIRLS
1.	Alejandro	1.	Lucia
2.	Daniel	2.	Maria
3.	Pablo	3.	Paula
4.	David	4.	Laura
5.	Adrian	5.	Marta
6.	Javier	6.	Alba
7.	Alvaro	7.	Claudia
8.	Sergio	8.	Carla
9.	Carlos	9.	Andrea
10.	Marcos	10.	Sara
11.	Ivan	11.	Nerea
12.	Hugo	12.	Irene
13.	Diego	13.	Ana
14.	Jorge	14.	Natalia
15.	Miguel	15.	Julia
16.	Manuel	16.	Elena
17.	Mario	17.	Carmen
18.	Raul	18.	Sofia
19.	Antonio	19.	Marina
20.	Ruben	20.	Cristina
21.	Victor	21.	Ainhoa
22.	Marc	22.	Rocio
23.	Juan	23.	Daniela
24.	Iker	24.	Angela
25.	Samuel	25.	Alejandra
26.	Alex	26.	Aitana
27.	Alberto	27.	Nuria
28.	Jesus	28.	Sandra
29.	Angel	29.	Ines
30.	Nicolas	30.	Laia
31.	Francisco	31.	Alicia
32.	Oscar	32.	Candela
33.	Jaime	33.	Raquel
34.	Hector	34.	Patricia
35.	Jose	35.	Celia
36.	Pau	36.	Adriana
37.	Ismael	37.	Eva
38.	Guillermo	38.	Clara
39.	Pedro	39.	Ariadna
40.	Joel	40.	Noelia
41.	Ignacio	41.	Silvia
42.	Luis	42.	Martina
43.	Miguel Angel	43.	Carlota
44.	Gonzalo	44.	Carolina
45.	Izan	45.	Blanca
46.	Rafael	46.	Isabel
47.	Gabriel	47.	Miriam
48.	Aaron	48.	Lorena
49.	Andres	49.	Noa
50.	Fernando	50.	Ainara

Most Popular Names in Sweden

	BOYS		GIRLS
1.	Lucas	1.	Emma
2.	Oscar		Maja
3.	William	3.	Agnes
4.	Elias	4.	Julia
5.	Filip	5.	Alva
6.	Hugo	6.	Linnea
7.	Viktor	7.	Wilma
8.	Isak	8.	Ida
9.	Alexander	9.	Alice
10.	Emil	10.	Elin
11.	Anton	11.	Ella
12.	Erik	12.	Klara
13.	Axel	13.	Hanna
14.	Albin	14.	Ebba
15.	Simon	15.	Emilia
16.	Oliver	16.	Elsa
17.	Linus	17.	Moa
18.	Gustav	18.	Amanda
19.	Max	19.	Saga
20.	Leo	20.	Isabelle
21.	Liam	21.	Felicia
22.	Melvin		Nellie
23.	Ludvig	23.	Sara
24.	Jonathan	24.	Tindra
25.	Edvin	25.	Ellen
26.	Adam	26.	Matilda
27.	Felix	27.	Filippa
28.	Jakob	28.	Tilda
29.	Noah	29.	Olivia
30.	Kevin	30.	Lovisa
31.	Elliot	31.	Alma
32.	Theo	32.	Thea
33.	Viggo	33.	Tuva
34.	Rasmus	34.	Sofia
35.	Arvid	35.	Tyra
36.	Sebastian	36.	Nova
37.	Joel	37.	Alicia
38.	Carl	38.	Tilde
39.	David	39.	Stella
40.	Olle	40.	Nora
41.	Hampus	41.	Emelie
42.	Samuel	42.	Isabella
43.	Alvin	43.	Molly
44.	Casper	44.	Linn
45.	Gabriel	45.	Frida
46.	Benjamin	46.	Lisa
47.	Wilmer	47.	Anna
48.	Vincent	48.	Lova
49.	Marcus	49.	Selma
	Nils	50.	Cornelia

Lists ⇒ around the globe

Most Popular Names in Switzerland (German-Speakers)

	BOYS		GIRLS
1.	Luca	1.	Anna
2.	Noah	2.	Lena
3.	Leon	3.	Lara
4.	David	4.	Laura
5.	Joël	5.	Leonie
6.	Jan	6.	Julia
7.	Simon	7.	Lea
8.	Tim	8.	Sara
9.	Nico	9.	Nina
10.	Jonas	10.	Alina
11.	Lukas	11.	Elena
12.	Nils	12.	Sarah
13.	Leandro	13.	Chiara
14.	Fabian	14.	Mia
	Robin	15.	Jana
16.	Gian	16.	Selina
17.	Dario	17.	Vanessa
18.	Fabio	18.	Alessia
19.	Janis	19.	Jessica
20.	Julian	20.	Michelle
21.	Samuel	21.	Sophie
22.	Lars		Fiona
23.	Elias	23.	Lisa
24.	Florian	24.	Luana
25.	Timo		Céline
26.	Manuel	26.	Lorena
27.	Loris	27.	Livia
28.	Nicolas	28.	Angelina
29.	Andrin	29.	Jasmin
30.	Marco	30.	Anja
	Cédric	31.	Aline
	Levin		Zoé
33.	Matteo	33.	Larissa
34.	Livio	34.	Ladina
	Sven	35.	Fabienne
36.	Elia		Lia
37.	Tobias		Amelie
	Nevio	38.	Rahel
39.	Silvan	39.	Lynn
40.	Raphael	40.	Nora
41.	Marc	41.	Noemi
	Benjamin	42.	Melanie
43.	Daniel		Samira
44.	Pascal	44.	Lina
45.	Diego	45.	Emma
46.	Gabriel	46.	Svenja
	Michael	47.	Salomé
48.	Kevin	48.	Sarina
49.	Finn	49.	Sophia
		50.	Giulia

Most Popular Names in Turkey

	BOYS		GIRLS
1.	Arda	1.	Elif
2.	Yusuf	2.	Zeynep
3.	Mehmet	3.	Irem
4.	Mustafa	4.	Busra
5.	Emirhan	5.	Merve

Before 1868 Japanese surnames were bestowed only upon the emperor's favorites, nobility, and samurai as a symbol of privilege. They were not given to commoners. Today only the Japanese imperial family does not bear a surname.

Most Popular Names in Wales

	BOYS		GIRLS
1.	Jack	1.	Megan
2.	Dylan	2.	Jessica
3.	Joshua	3.	Olivia
4.	Thomas	4.	Ellie
5.	Rhys	5.	Emily
6.	Ethan	6.	Ruby
7.	Daniel	7.	Chloe
8.	Callum	8.	Sophie
9.	Oliver	9.	Grace
10.	Morgan	10.	Ffion
11.	James	11.	Ella
12.	William	12.	Seren
13.	Lewis	13.	Mia
14.	Benjamin	14.	Erin
15.	Samuel	15.	Lily
16.	Joseph	16.	Caitlin
17.	Jacob	17.	Lucy
18.	Cameron	18.	Katie
19.	Charlie	19.	Amelia
20.	Jake	20.	Cerys

Most Popular Names in Alabama

BOYS		GIRLS	
1.	William	1.	Madison
2.	Jacob	2.	Emma
3.	James	3.	Anna
4.	Joshua	4.	Emily
5.	John	5.	Hannah
6.	Michael	6.	Sarah
7.	Jackson	7.	Elizabeth
8.	Christopher	8.	Olivia
9.	Ethan	9.	Abigail
10.	Noah	10.	Ava
11.	Matthew	11.	Isabella
12.	Joseph	12.	Chloe
13.	Tyler	13.	Alexis
14.	Andrew	14.	Taylor
15.	Landon	15.	Savannah
16.	Caleb	16.	Ella
17.	Samuel	17.	Addison
18.	David	18.	Alyssa
19.	Austin	19.	Lauren
20.	Jordan	20.	Mary

Most Popular Names in Arizona

BOYS		GIRLS	
1.	Angel	1.	Mia
2.	Daniel	2.	Emily
3.	Jacob	3.	Isabella
4.	Anthony	4.	Ashley
5.	Jose	5.	Emma
6.	Jesus	6.	Madison
7.	Michael	7.	Ava
8.	Joshua	8.	Sophia
9.	Luis	9.	Samantha
10.	Gabriel	10.	Abigail
11.	David	11.	Alexis
12.	Christopher	12.	Alyssa
13.	Alexander	13.	Hannah
14.	Andrew	14.	Natalie
15.	Ethan	15.	Elizabeth
16.	Matthew	16.	Hailey
17.	Jonathan	17.	Alexa
18.	Joseph	18.	Brianna
19.	Juan	19.	Olivia
20.	Christian	20.	Victoria

Most Popular Names in Alaska

BOYS		GIRLS	
1.	James	1.	Emma
2.	Jacob	2.	Madison
3.	Michael	3.	Emily
4.	Andrew	4.	Isabella
5.	Ethan	5.	Ava
6.	Logan	6.	Hannah
7.	Benjamin	7.	Elizabeth
8.	Alexander	8.	Olivia
9.	Aiden	9.	Sophia
10.	John	10.	Abigail
11.	William	11.	Alyssa
12.	Joshua	12.	Kaylee
13.	Gabriel	13.	Jasmine
14.	Isaiah	14.	Kayla
15.	Samuel	15.	Lily
16.	Tyler	16.	Natalie
17.	Gavin	17.	Samantha
18.	Matthew	18.	Hailey
19.	David	19.	Ella
20.	Mason	20.	Grace

Most Popular Names in Arkansas

BOYS		GIRLS	
1.	William	1.	Madison
2.	Ethan	2.	Emily
3.	Jacob	3.	Emma
4.	Landon	4.	Abigail
5.	James	5.	Hannah
6.	Joshua	6.	Alexis
7.	Christopher	7.	Olivia
8.	Caleb	8.	Chloe
9.	Jackson	9.	Elizabeth
10.	Logan	10.	Anna
11.	Matthew	11.	Addison
12.	John	12.	Ava
13.	Michael	13.	Brooklyn
14.	Noah	14.	Isabella
15.	Andrew	15.	Alyssa
16.	Elijah	16.	Jasmine
17.	Mason	17.	Savannah
18.	Christian	18.	Taylor
19.	Hayden	19.	Hailey
20.	David	20.	Natalie

Lists ⇒ across the u.s.

Most Popular Names in California

BOYS	GIRLS
1. Daniel	1. Emily
2. Anthony	2. Isabella
3. Angel	3. Ashley
4. Jacob	4. Mia
5. David	5. Samantha
6. Andrew	6. Natalie
7. Jose	7. Sophia
8. Joshua	8. Emma
9. Christopher	9. Abigail
10. Matthew	10. Ava
11. Diego	11. Madison
12. Michael	12. Elizabeth
13. Jonathan	13. Alyssa
14. Alexander	14. Brianna
15. Nathan	15. Kimberly
16. Ethan	16. Jasmine
17. Joseph	17. Andrea
18. Christian	18. Jessica
19. Adrian	19. Alexa
20. Juan	20. Hannah

Most Popular Names in Connecticut

BOYS	GIRLS
1. Michael	1. Isabella
2. Matthew	2. Emily
3. Ryan	3. Ava
4. Nicholas	4. Olivia
5. Anthony	5. Emma
6. Alexander	6. Madison
7. Joseph	7. Grace
8. William	8. Julia
9. Jacob	9. Abigail
10. John	10. Sophia
11. Andrew	11. Samantha
12. Daniel	12. Hannah
13. Christopher	13. Mia
14. Joshua	14. Sarah
15. Tyler	15. Gabriella
16. Jack	16. Elizabeth
17. Benjamin	17. Ashley
18. James	18. Brianna
19. Ethan	19. Lauren
20. David	20. Katherine

Most Popular Names in Colorado

BOYS	GIRLS
1. Jacob	1. Isabella
2. Ethan	2. Emily
3. Alexander	3. Emma
4. Joshua	4. Hannah
5. Noah	5. Abigail
6. Andrew	6. Madison
7. Logan	7. Sophia
8. Michael	8. Ava
9. Daniel	9. Olivia
10. Benjamin	10. Samantha
11. Samuel	11. Grace
12. David	12. Ashley
13. Anthony	13. Mia
14. Christopher	14. Elizabeth
15. Joseph	15. Ella
16. Matthew	16. Addison
17. Tyler	17. Alexis
18. Gabriel	18. Nevaeh
19. Ryan	19. Natalie
20. Elijah	20. Chloe

Most Popular Names in Delaware

BOYS	GIRLS
1. Ryan	1. Madison
2. Michael	2. Emily
3. Jacob	3. Ava
4. John	4. Emma
5. Matthew	5. Olivia
6. Nicholas	6. Isabella
7. Christopher	7. Grace
8. Joshua	8. Kayla
9. Anthony	9. Elizabeth
10. James	10. Hannah
11. Ethan	11. Sophia
12. Alexander	12. Abigail
13. William	13. Alexis
14. Logan	14. Natalie
15. Andrew	15. Savannah
16. Nathan	16. Brianna
17. Isaiah	17. Alyssa
18. Christian	18. Mia
19. Joseph	19. Taylor
20. Cameron	20. Victoria

Most Popular Names in District of Columbia

BOYS	GIRLS
1. William	1. Katherine
2. Michael	2. Elizabeth
3. Christopher	3. Ashley
4. Alexander	4. Ava
5. Anthony	5. Sophia
6. Daniel	6. Olivia
7. John	7. Sofia
8. James	8. Caroline
9. Joshua	9. Abigail
10. Kevin	10. Hannah
11. Samuel	11. Anna
12. David	12. Emily
13. Jonathan	13. Madison
14. Nicholas	14. Maya
15. Matthew	15. Nevaeh
16. Jason	16. Kayla
17. Thomas	17. Morgan
18. Bryan	18. Sarah
19. Joseph	19. Taylor
20. Benjamin	20. Catherine

Most Popular Names in Georgia

BOYS	GIRLS
1. William	1. Madison
2. Joshua	2. Emily
3. Christopher	3. Emma
4. Jacob	4. Hannah
5. Michael	5. Ava
6. Andrew	6. Abigail
7. James	7. Olivia
8. Matthew	8. Ashley
9. Ethan	9. Isabella
10. David	10. Anna
11. Daniel	11. Sarah
12. John	12. Taylor
13. Christian	13. Elizabeth
14. Jonathan	14. Alexis
15. Brandon	15. Destiny
16. Alexander	16. Chloe
17. Joseph	17. Makayla
18. Noah	18. Brianna
19. Jackson	19. Lauren
20. Tyler	20. Sophia

Most Popular Names in Florida

BOYS	GIRLS
1. Joshua	1. Isabella
2. Michael	2. Emily
3. Anthony	3. Madison
4. Christopher	4. Sophia
5. Jacob	5. Emma
6. Daniel	6. Ava
7. Matthew	7. Olivia
8. David	8. Mia
9. Alexander	9. Hannah
10. Nicholas	10. Brianna
11. Christian	11. Abigail
12. Ethan	12. Ashley
13. Jonathan	13. Samantha
14. Tyler	14. Sarah
15. Joseph	15. Alyssa
16. William	16. Elizabeth
17. Gabriel	17. Kayla
18. James	18. Victoria
19. Logan	19. Alexis
20. Ryan	20. Jasmine

Most Popular Names in Hawaii

BOYS	GIRLS
1. Noah	1. Isabella
2. Joshua	2. Emma
3. Ethan	3. Madison
4. Dylan	4. Hailey
5. Elijah	5. Ava
6. Tyler	6. Kayla
7. Jacob	7. Malia
8. Logan	8. Mia
9. Isaiah	9. Taylor
10. Caleb	10. Jasmine
11. William	11. Sophia
12. James	12. Emily
13. Alexander	13. Alexis
14. Joseph	14. Chloe
15. Matthew	15. Alyssa
16. Christian	16. Maya
17. Jayden	17. Hannah
18. Michael	18. Kiana
19. Daniel	19. Samantha
20. David	20. Abigail

Lists ⇒ across the u.s.

Most Popular Names in Idaho

BOYS	GIRLS
1. Ethan	1. Emma
2. Jacob	2. Olivia
3. Joshua	3. Abigail
4. Noah	4. Hannah
5. Logan	5. Madison
6. Samuel	6. Emily
7. Andrew	7. Ava
8. Isaac	8. Taylor
9. Jackson	9. Hailey
10. Tyler	10. Elizabeth
11. Michael	11. Grace
12. William	12. Isabella
13. Matthew	13. Alexis
14. Austin	14. Chloe
15. Gabriel	15. Ella
16. Benjamin	16. Sophia
17. Carter	17. Brooklyn
18. Aiden	18. Sarah
19. Caleb	19. Alyssa
20. Daniel	20. Natalie

Most Popular Names in Indiana

BOYS	GIRLS
1. Jacob	1. Emma
2. Ethan	2. Ava
3. Andrew	3. Olivia
4. Michael	4. Madison
5. William	5. Emily
6. Logan	6. Abigail
7. Joshua	7. Hannah
8. Noah	8. Chloe
9. Elijah	9. Isabella
10. Matthew	10. Addison
11. Alexander	11. Elizabeth
12. Tyler	12. Grace
13. Gavin	13. Alexis
14. James	14. Lillian
15. Landon	15. Ella
16. Jackson	16. Sophia
17. Mason	17. Alyssa
18. Joseph	18. Anna
19. Benjamin	19. Nevaeh
20. David	20. Lauren

Most Popular Names in Illinois

BOYS	GIRLS
1. Daniel	1. Emily
2. Michael	2. Isabella
3. Jacob	3. Emma
4. Alexander	4. Olivia
5. Joshua	5. Ava
6. Anthony	6. Abigail
7. Matthew	7. Madison
8. Joseph	8. Grace
9. Andrew	9. Sophia
10. Ethan	10. Mia
11. Ryan	11. Samantha
12. Nicholas	12. Hannah
13. Christopher	13. Elizabeth
14. David	14. Ashley
15. William	15. Natalie
16. Nathan	16. Ella
17. John	17. Alexis
18. James	18. Sarah
19. Benjamin	19. Chloe
20. Jack	20. Addison

Most Popular Names in Iowa

BOYS	GIRLS
1. Ethan	1. Emma
2. Jacob	2. Ava
3. Noah	3. Olivia
4. Logan	4. Madison
5. Andrew	5. Hannah
6. Carter	6. Addison
7. William	7. Abigail
8. Jackson	8. Grace
9. Owen	9. Emily
10. Tyler	10. Elizabeth
11. Caleb	11. Alexis
12. Alexander	12. Ella
13. Mason	13. Isabella
14. Landon	14. Sophia
15. Hunter	15. Lauren
16. Samuel	16. Natalie
17. Benjamin	17. Anna
18. Joseph	18. Chloe
19. Austin	19. Hailey
20. Dylan	20. Taylor

Most Popular Names in Kansas

BOYS		GIRLS	
1.	Jacob	1.	Emma
2.	Ethan	2.	Emily
3.	Logan	3.	Abigail
4.	Alexander	4.	Madison
5.	William	5.	Ava
6.	Andrew	6.	Alexis
7.	Michael	7.	Addison
8.	Joshua	8.	Olivia
9.	Noah	9.	Hannah
10.	Gabriel	10.	Grace
11.	Joseph	11.	Sophia
12.	Tyler	12.	Isabella
13.	Landon	13.	Elizabeth
14.	Isaac	14.	Samantha
15.	Jackson	15.	Ella
16.	Anthony	16.	Lauren
17.	Luke	17.	Taylor
18.	Aiden	18.	Chloe
19.	Samuel	19.	Mia
20.	Benjamin	20.	Avery

Most Popular Names in Louisiana

BOYS		GIRLS	
1.	Landon	1.	Madison
2.	Ethan	2.	Emma
3.	Joshua	3.	Ava
4.	Jacob	4.	Emily
5.	Christopher	5.	Hannah
6.	Noah	6.	Abigail
7.	Michael	7.	Olivia
8.	John	8.	Isabella
9.	Christian	9.	Chloe
10.	William	10.	Alyssa
11.	Cameron	11.	Gabrielle
12.	Logan	12.	Taylor
13.	Tyler	13.	Sarah
14.	Dylan	14.	Mia
15.	Joseph	15.	Alexis
16.	James	16.	Anna
17.	Matthew	17.	Ella
18.	Caleb	18.	Elizabeth
19.	Mason	19.	Brianna
20.	Hunter	20.	Addison

Most Popular Names in Kentucky

BOYS		GIRLS	
1.	Jacob	1.	Madison
2.	William	2.	Emma
3.	Ethan	3.	Emily
4.	James	4.	Hannah
5.	Landon	5.	Abigail
6.	Logan	6.	Olivia
7.	Christopher	7.	Alexis
8.	Michael	8.	Chloe
9.	Austin	9.	Ava
10.	Andrew	10.	Addison
11.	Noah	11.	Isabella
12.	John	12.	Elizabeth
13.	Matthew	13.	Kaylee
14.	Joshua	14.	Brooklyn
15.	Joseph	15.	Alyssa
16.	Jackson	16.	Sarah
17.	Caleb	17.	Savannah
18.	Elijah	18.	Taylor
19.	Tyler	19.	Hailey
20.	Hunter	20.	Anna

Most Popular Names in Maine

BOYS		GIRLS	
1.	Jacob	1.	Emma
2.	Ethan	2.	Abigail
3.	Benjamin	3.	Emily
4.	Tyler	4.	Olivia
5.	Logan	5.	Madison
6.	Hunter	6.	Ava
7.	Owen	7.	Alexis
8.	Samuel	8.	Isabella
9.	Aiden	9.	Sophia
10.	Ryan	10.	Hannah
11.	Connor	11.	Grace
12.	Noah	12.	Ella
13.	Caleb	13.	Lily
14.	Dylan	14.	Elizabeth
15.	Matthew	15.	Natalie
16.	Jack	16.	Chloe
17.	Christopher	17.	Mackenzie
18.	Mason	18.	Sarah
19.	Nicholas	19.	Anna
20.	William	20.	Hailey

Lists ⇨ across the u.s.

Most Popular Names in Maryland

BOYS	GIRLS
1. Joshua	1. Madison
2. Michael	2. Emily
3. William	3. Abigail
4. Jacob	4. Emma
5. Matthew	5. Ava
6. Ryan	6. Isabella
7. Christopher	7. Sophia
8. Daniel	8. Olivia
9. Andrew	9. Hannah
10. Ethan	10. Sarah
11. Nicholas	11. Taylor
12. John	12. Ashley
13. Alexander	13. Samantha
14. Benjamin	14. Grace
15. James	15. Kayla
16. Anthony	16. Elizabeth
17. Noah	17. Alexis
18. Tyler	18. Alyssa
19. Joseph	19. Natalie
20. Christian	20. Chloe

Most Popular Names in Michigan

BOYS	GIRLS
1. Jacob	1. Ava
2. Ethan	2. Emma
3. Logan	3. Madison
4. Michael	4. Olivia
5. Andrew	5. Emily
6. Alexander	6. Isabella
7. Noah	7. Grace
8. Joshua	8. Hannah
9. Tyler	9. Sophia
10. Joseph	10. Abigail
11. Matthew	11. Alexis
12. Nicholas	12. Ella
13. Anthony	13. Elizabeth
14. William	14. Lauren
15. Nathan	15. Samantha
16. Benjamin	16. Chloe
17. Ryan	17. Natalie
18. James	18. Addison
19. Evan	19. Alyssa
20. Jack	20. Lillian

Most Popular Names in Massachusetts

BOYS	GIRLS
1. Matthew	1. Ava
2. Ryan	2. Isabella
3. Michael	3. Emma
4. Nicholas	4. Sophia
5. Andrew	5. Olivia
6. John	6. Emily
7. Joseph	7. Abigail
8. Jacob	8. Julia
9. William	9. Grace
10. Jack	10. Madison
11. Alexander	11. Sarah
12. Benjamin	12. Hannah
13. Anthony	13. Samantha
14. Daniel	14. Ella
15. James	15. Mia
16. Joshua	16. Elizabeth
17. Christopher	17. Lily
18. Nathan	18. Ashley
19. Tyler	19. Anna
20. Aidan	20. Chloe

Most Popular Names in Minnesota

BOYS	GIRLS
1. Ethan	1. Ava
2. Jacob	2. Grace
3. Logan	3. Olivia
4. Benjamin	4. Emma
5. Jack	5. Sophia
6. Noah	6. Ella
7. William	7. Abigail
8. Andrew	8. Emily
9. Samuel	9. Hannah
10. Joseph	10. Isabella
11. Mason	11. Elizabeth
12. Owen	12. Madison
13. Gavin	13. Anna
14. Alexander	14. Addison
15. Tyler	15. Lauren
16. Matthew	16. Natalie
17. Jackson	17. Hailey
18. Carter	18. Samantha
19. Nicholas	19. Isabelle
20. Dylan	20. Alexis

Most Popular Names in Mississippi

BOYS		GIRLS	
1.	William	1.	Madison
2.	James	2.	Anna
3.	Joshua	3.	Emma
4.	Christopher	4.	Hannah
5.	John	5.	Emily
6.	Michael	6.	Alexis
7.	Jacob	7.	Chloe
8.	Ethan	8.	Olivia
9.	Tyler	9.	Ava
10.	Jordan	10.	Isabella
11.	Landon	11.	Taylor
12.	Cameron	12.	Destiny
13.	Caleb	13.	Sarah
14.	Joseph	14.	Makayla
15.	Matthew	15.	Alyssa
16.	Elijah	16.	Abigail
17.	David	17.	Elizabeth
18.	Jonathan	18.	Trinity
19.	Christian	19.	Mary
20.	Robert	20.	Jada

Most Popular Names in Montana

BOYS		GIRLS	
1.	Jacob	1.	Emma
2.	Logan	2.	Abigail
3.	Michael	3.	Madison
4.	William	4.	Grace
5.	James	5.	Hannah
6.	Noah	6.	Ava
7.	Ethan	7.	Olivia
8.	Ryan	8.	Emily
9.	Alexander	9.	Elizabeth
10.	Wyatt	10.	Ella
11.	Aiden	11.	Alexis
12.	Joseph	12.	Hailey
13.	Tyler	13.	Isabella
14.	Samuel	14.	Morgan
15.	Austin	15.	Sophia
16.	Gabriel	16.	Chloe
17.	Mason	17.	Anna
18.	Andrew	18.	Samantha
19.	Dylan	19.	Taylor
20.	Benjamin	20.	Nevaeh

Most Popular Names in Missouri

BOYS		GIRLS	
1.	Jacob	1.	Emma
2.	Logan	2.	Madison
3.	Andrew	3.	Ava
4.	Ethan	4.	Abigail
5.	William	5.	Emily
6.	Michael	6.	Olivia
7.	Tyler	7.	Hannah
8.	Noah	8.	Isabella
9.	Alexander	9.	Alexis
10.	James	10.	Addison
11.	Joshua	11.	Elizabeth
12.	Jackson	12.	Sophia
13.	Landon	13.	Chloe
14.	Joseph	14.	Grace
15.	Gavin	15.	Anna
16.	Matthew	16.	Alyssa
17.	John	17.	Taylor
18.	Hunter	18.	Ella
19.	Caleb	19.	Lillian
20.	Mason	20.	Samantha

Most Popular Names in Nebraska

BOYS		GIRLS	
1.	Jacob	1.	Emma
2.	Alexander	2.	Ava
3.	Ethan	3.	Madison
4.	Andrew	4.	Addison
5.	Logan	5.	Emily
6.	Jackson	6.	Hannah
7.	William	7.	Abigail
8.	Noah	8.	Olivia
9.	Samuel	9.	Grace
10.	Michael	10.	Isabella
11.	Joseph	11.	Chloe
12.	Joshua	12.	Elizabeth
13.	Mason	13.	Alexis
14.	Tyler	14.	Sophia
15.	Zachary	15.	Ella
16.	Gavin	16.	Natalie
17.	Benjamin	17.	Anna
18.	Jack	18.	Samantha
19.	Caleb	19.	Avery
20.	Carter	20.	Lauren

Lists ⇨ across the u.s.

Most Popular Names in Nevada

BOYS	GIRLS
1. Anthony	1. Emily
2. Daniel	2. Isabella
3. Angel	3. Mia
4. Jacob	4. Emma
5. David	5. Ashley
6. Alexander	6. Samantha
7. Joshua	7. Ava
8. Michael	8. Madison
9. Joseph	9. Sophia
10. Christopher	10. Alexa
11. Christian	11. Natalie
12. Matthew	12. Alexis
13. Jose	13. Abigail
14. Jonathan	14. Jasmine
15. Tyler	15. Alyssa
16. Ethan	16. Elizabeth
17. Andrew	17. Hannah
18. Brandon	18. Brianna
19. Dylan	19. Kimberly
20. Diego	20. Angelina

Most Popular Names in New Jersey

BOYS	GIRLS
1. Michael	1. Isabella
2. Matthew	2. Ava
3. Daniel	3. Emily
4. Joseph	4. Sophia
5. Anthony	5. Olivia
6. Nicholas	6. Samantha
7. Ryan	7. Ashley
8. Christopher	8. Madison
9. Joshua	9. Mia
10. Alexander	10. Julia
11. John	11. Sarah
12. Andrew	12. Emma
13. David	13. Abigail
14. Jacob	14. Kayla
15. Tyler	15. Gianna
16. Justin	16. Grace
17. James	17. Brianna
18. Jack	18. Angelina
19. Brandon	19. Alyssa
20. Kevin	20. Victoria

Most Popular Names in New Hampshire

BOYS	GIRLS
1. Jacob	1. Emma
2. Ryan	2. Olivia
3. Benjamin	3. Emily
4. William	4. Ava
5. Andrew	5. Madison
6. Logan	6. Hannah
7. Owen	7. Abigail
8. Michael	8. Isabella
9. Tyler	9. Sarah
10. Cameron	10. Grace
11. Ethan	11. Sophia
12. Nicholas	12. Alexis
13. Matthew	13. Ella
14. Dylan	14. Samantha
15. Noah	15. Elizabeth
16. Samuel	16. Lily
17. Alexander	17. Chloe
18. Joseph	18. Hailey
19. Jack	19. Julia
20. Anthony	20. Lillian

Most Popular Names in New Mexico

BOYS	GIRLS
1. Isaiah	1. Isabella
2. Joshua	2. Alyssa
3. Gabriel	3. Emily
4. Daniel	4. Mia
5. Joseph	5. Madison
6. Jacob	6. Emma
7. Elijah	7. Nevaeh
8. Diego	8. Mariah
9. Michael	9. Samantha
10. Matthew	10. Abigail
11. Angel	11. Ashley
12. David	12. Elizabeth
13. Christopher	13. Jasmine
14. Ethan	14. Olivia
15. Anthony	15. Alexis
16. Jose	16. Ava
17. Noah	17. Angelina
18. Andrew	18. Destiny
19. Julian	19. Hannah
20. Isaac	20. Arianna

Most Popular Names in New York

BOYS		GIRLS	
1.	Michael	1.	Emily
2.	Matthew	2.	Isabella
3.	Joseph	3.	Ava
4.	Anthony	4.	Olivia
5.	Christopher	5.	Sophia
6.	Daniel	6.	Madison
7.	Nicholas	7.	Emma
8.	Ryan	8.	Ashley
9.	Joshua	9.	Samantha
10.	Alexander	10.	Sarah
11.	Jacob	11.	Mia
12.	Justin	12.	Kayla
13.	David	13.	Abigail
14.	Andrew	14.	Julia
15.	John	15.	Grace
16.	Ethan	16.	Brianna
17.	James	17.	Elizabeth
18.	Tyler	18.	Hannah
19.	William	19.	Alyssa
20.	Jayden	20.	Gabriella

Most Popular Names in North Dakota

BOYS		GIRLS	
1.	Logan	1.	Ava
2.	Ethan	2.	Emma
3.	Jacob	3.	Grace
4.	Carter	4.	Madison
5.	Noah	5.	Alexis
6.	Benjamin	6.	Ella
7.	Alexander	7.	Emily
8.	Hunter	8.	Olivia
9.	Jack	9.	Hannah
10.	Samuel	10.	Abigail
11.	Gavin	11.	Addison
12.	Wyatt	12.	Sydney
13.	Landon	13.	Sophia
14.	Mason	14.	Isabella
15.	Austin	15.	Avery
16.	Isaac	16.	Elizabeth
17.	Dylan	17.	Hailey
18.	Zachary	18.	Taylor
19.	Joseph	19.	Chloe
20.	Tyler	20.	Brooklyn

Most Popular Names in North Carolina

BOYS		GIRLS	
1.	William	1.	Madison
2.	Joshua	2.	Emily
3.	Jacob	3.	Emma
4.	Christopher	4.	Abigail
5.	Michael	5.	Hannah
6.	Ethan	6.	Ava
7.	James	7.	Olivia
8.	Matthew	8.	Sarah
9.	Andrew	9.	Elizabeth
10.	Noah	10.	Isabella
11.	John	11.	Ashley
12.	David	12.	Chloe
13.	Tyler	13.	Anna
14.	Alexander	14.	Savannah
15.	Caleb	15.	Alexis
16.	Daniel	16.	Taylor
17.	Joseph	17.	Hailey
18.	Christian	18.	Samantha
19.	Elijah	19.	Alyssa
20.	Jonathan	20.	Sophia

Most Popular Names in Ohio

BOYS		GIRLS	
1.	Jacob	1.	Emma
2.	Andrew	2.	Madison
3.	Ethan	3.	Ava
4.	Michael	4.	Olivia
5.	Noah	5.	Emily
6.	Joshua	6.	Abigail
7.	Logan	7.	Hannah
8.	Matthew	8.	Grace
9.	William	9.	Isabella
10.	Alexander	10.	Sophia
11.	Joseph	11.	Alexis
12.	Nicholas	12.	Elizabeth
13.	Tyler	13.	Chloe
14.	Ryan	14.	Samantha
15.	Nathan	15.	Sarah
16.	Anthony	16.	Lauren
17.	James	17.	Alyssa
18.	Benjamin	18.	Taylor
19.	Austin	19.	Ella
20.	Samuel	20.	Lillian

Lists ⇒ across the u.s.

Most Popular Names in Oklahoma

BOYS	GIRLS
1. Jacob	1. Emma
2. Ethan	2. Madison
3. Joshua	3. Emily
4. William	4. Abigail
5. Michael	5. Hannah
6. Logan	6. Addison
7. Landon	7. Chloe
8. James	8. Elizabeth
9. Caleb	9. Alexis
10. Christopher	10. Brooklyn
11. Matthew	11. Isabella
12. Mason	12. Ava
13. Jackson	13. Olivia
14. Noah	14. Avery
15. Tyler	15. Natalie
16. Christian	16. Alyssa
17. Joseph	17. Sarah
18. Andrew	18. Kaylee
19. Alexander	19. Samantha
20. Elijah	20. Trinity

Most Popular Names in Pennsylvania

BOYS	GIRLS
1. Jacob	1. Ava
2. Michael	2. Emily
3. Ryan	3. Madison
4. Joseph	4. Emma
5. Matthew	5. Olivia
6. Logan	6. Isabella
7. Anthony	7. Abigail
8. Ethan	8. Hannah
9. Joshua	9. Alexis
10. Nicholas	10. Sarah
11. Andrew	11. Sophia
12. John	12. Grace
13. Tyler	13. Elizabeth
14. Benjamin	14. Samantha
15. Alexander	15. Kayla
16. Daniel	16. Julia
17. Nathan	17. Alyssa
18. William	18. Ella
19. Noah	19. Lauren
20. Christopher	20. Anna

Most Popular Names in Oregon

BOYS	GIRLS
1. Jacob	1. Emma
2. Ethan	2. Emily
3. Alexander	3. Madison
4. Logan	4. Olivia
5. Noah	5. Abigail
6. Daniel	6. Isabella
7. Joshua	7. Ava
8. William	8. Hannah
9. Tyler	9. Sophia
10. Anthony	10. Samantha
11. Andrew	11. Elizabeth
12. Aiden	12. Grace
13. Gabriel	13. Natalie
14. Michael	14. Chloe
15. Isaac	15. Ella
16. Benjamin	16. Hailey
17. Dylan	17. Mia
18. Samuel	18. Alexis
19. Joseph	19. Taylor
20. James	20. Lily

Most Popular Names in Rhode Island

BOYS	GIRLS
1. Ryan	1. Isabella
2. Jacob	2. Olivia
3. Nicholas	3. Ava
4. Michael	4. Madison
5. Benjamin	5. Emily
6. Christopher	6. Emma
7. Alexander	7. Grace
8. Joshua	8. Abigail
9. Matthew	9. Hannah
10. Nathan	10. Sophia
11. Andrew	11. Ella
12. Ethan	12. Mia
13. John	13. Samantha
14. Anthony	14. Julia
15. Dylan	15. Elizabeth
16. Logan	16. Lily
17. Joseph	17. Alexis
18. Aidan	18. Sarah
19. Daniel	19. Angelina
20. Zachary	20. Ashley

Most Popular Names in South Carolina

BOYS	GIRLS
1. William	1. Madison
2. Christopher	2. Emma
3. James	3. Emily
4. Jacob	4. Hannah
5. Joshua	5. Olivia
6. John	6. Abigail
7. Ethan	7. Anna
8. Michael	8. Elizabeth
9. Noah	9. Isabella
10. Matthew	10. Sarah
11. Jackson	11. Taylor
12. Tyler	12. Ava
13. Andrew	13. Savannah
14. Joseph	14. Alexis
15. David	15. Destiny
16. Caleb	16. Brianna
17. Christian	17. Ella
18. Samuel	18. Jasmine
19. Daniel	19. Caroline
20. Landon	20. Ashley

Most Popular Names in Tennessee

BOYS	GIRLS
1. William	1. Madison
2. Jacob	2. Emma
3. Joshua	3. Emily
4. Ethan	4. Hannah
5. James	5. Abigail
6. Christopher	6. Olivia
7. Michael	7. Sarah
8. Noah	8. Chloe
9. Elijah	9. Alexis
10. Andrew	10. Anna
11. John	11. Ava
12. Jackson	12. Isabella
13. Matthew	13. Addison
14. Caleb	14. Elizabeth
15. Landon	15. Savannah
16. Tyler	16. Alyssa
17. Samuel	17. Brianna
18. Austin	18. Ella
19. David	19. Taylor
20. Logan	20. Lillian

Most Popular Names in South Dakota

BOYS	GIRLS
1. Jacob	1. Emma
2. Ethan	2. Hannah
3. Carter	3. Ava
4. Logan	4. Grace
5. Landon	5. Madison
6. Mason	6. Addison
7. Hunter	7. Emily
8. Joshua	8. Olivia
9. Jackson	9. Abigail
10. Samuel	10. Hailey
11. Noah	11. Alexis
12. Michael	12. Ella
13. Alexander	13. Taylor
14. Andrew	14. Chloe
15. Austin	15. Elizabeth
16. Aiden	16. Isabella
17. Benjamin	17. Brooklyn
18. Caleb	18. Avery
19. Carson	19. Sophia
20. Jack	20. Samantha

Most Popular Names in Texas

BOYS	GIRLS
1. Jose	1. Emily
2. Jacob	2. Mia
3. Joshua	3. Ashley
4. Daniel	4. Isabella
5. Christopher	5. Madison
6. Angel	6. Abigail
7. David	7. Emma
8. Juan	8. Natalie
9. Michael	9. Hannah
10. Ethan	10. Samantha
11. Christian	11. Ava
12. Anthony	12. Alyssa
13. Matthew	13. Brianna
14. Jonathan	14. Victoria
15. Andrew	15. Elizabeth
16. Diego	16. Sophia
17. Luis	17. Alexis
18. Joseph	18. Alexa
19. Alexander	19. Sarah
20. Noah	20. Chloe

Lists ⇒ across the u.s.

Most Popular Names in Utah

BOYS		GIRLS	
1.	Ethan	1.	Emma
2.	Joshua	2.	Abigail
3.	Jacob	3.	Olivia
4.	Samuel	4.	Elizabeth
5.	Benjamin	5.	Emily
6.	Jackson	6.	Brooklyn
7.	William	7.	Hannah
8.	Isaac	8.	Madison
9.	Mason	9.	Ava
10.	Logan	10.	Samantha
11.	Andrew	11.	Isabella
12.	Tyler	12.	Ella
13.	Nathan	13.	Grace
14.	James	14.	Sarah
15.	Alexander	15.	Hailey
16.	Matthew	16.	Alexis
17.	Joseph	17.	Lily
18.	Luke	18.	Sophia
19.	Daniel	19.	Chloe
20.	Noah	20.	Addison

Most Popular Names in Virginia

BOYS		GIRLS	
1.	William	1.	Madison
2.	Jacob	2.	Emily
3.	Michael	3.	Abigail
4.	Joshua	4.	Emma
5.	Christopher	5.	Hannah
6.	Ethan	6.	Sarah
7.	Andrew	7.	Ava
8.	Matthew	8.	Olivia
9.	James	9.	Elizabeth
10.	Joseph	10.	Isabella
11.	John	11.	Sophia
12.	Ryan	12.	Grace
13.	Daniel	13.	Taylor
14.	Alexander	14.	Ashley
15.	Tyler	15.	Katherine
16.	Noah	16.	Samantha
17.	Christian	17.	Alexis
18.	Anthony	18.	Natalie
19.	Benjamin	19.	Chloe
20.	David	20.	Anna

Most Popular Names in Vermont

BOYS		GIRLS	
1.	Jacob	1.	Emma
2.	Noah	2.	Ava
3.	William	3.	Abigail
4.	Owen	4.	Grace
5.	Aiden	5.	Olivia
6.	Nicholas	6.	Hannah
7.	Tyler	7.	Isabella
8.	Dylan	8.	Alexis
9.	Ryan	9.	Elizabeth
10.	Ethan	10.	Madison
11.	James	11.	Emily
12.	Benjamin	12.	Sophia
13.	Joshua	13.	Taylor
14.	Connor	14.	Hailey
15.	Evan	15.	Lily
16.	Hunter	16.	Chloe
17.	Logan	17.	Natalie
18.	Samuel	18.	Lillian
19.	Kyle	19.	Savannah
20.	Wyatt	20.	Sarah

Most Popular Names in Washington

BOYS		GIRLS	
1.	Jacob	1.	Emma
2.	Alexander	2.	Emily
3.	Ethan	3.	Ava
4.	Daniel	4.	Olivia
5.	Logan	5.	Isabella
6.	Andrew	6.	Madison
7.	Samuel	7.	Sophia
8.	Michael	8.	Abigail
9.	Nathan	9.	Hannah
10.	Benjamin	10.	Elizabeth
11.	William	11.	Natalie
12.	Ryan	12.	Grace
13.	Noah	13.	Samantha
14.	David	14.	Hailey
15.	Matthew	15.	Chloe
16.	Joshua	16.	Mia
17.	Anthony	17.	Ella
18.	James	18.	Alexis
19.	Tyler	19.	Sarah
20.	Joseph	20.	Anna

Most Popular Names in West Virginia

BOYS	GIRLS
1. Jacob	1. Madison
2. Ethan	2. Hannah
3. Logan	3. Emily
4. Landon	4. Abigail
5. Hunter	5. Alexis
6. James	6. Emma
7. Andrew	7. Olivia
8. Noah	8. Isabella
9. Michael	9. Chloe
10. William	10. Kaylee
11. Joshua	11. Sarah
12. Joseph	12. Ava
13. Caleb	13. Taylor
14. Tyler	14. Savannah
15. Austin	15. Elizabeth
16. Nicholas	16. Nevaeh
17. Brayden	17. Addison
18. Matthew	18. Grace
19. John	19. Alyssa
20. Isaiah	20. Brianna

Most Popular Names in Wyoming

BOYS	GIRLS
1. Ethan	1. Emily
2. Jacob	2. Emma
3. Logan	3. Madison
4. Ryan	4. Alexis
5. Hunter	5. Hannah
6. William	6. Abigail
7. Samuel	7. Hailey
8. Joshua	8. Grace
9. Michael	9. Taylor
10. Wyatt	10. Addison
11. Aiden	11. Ava
12. James	12. Elizabeth
13. Joseph	13. Avery
14. Aidan	14. Isabella
15. Mason	15. Nevaeh
16. Andrew	16. Kaylee
17. Landon	17. Olivia
18. Alexander	18. Sarah
19. Austin	19. Brooklyn
20. Caleb	20. Destiny

Most Popular Names in Wisconsin

BOYS	GIRLS
1. Ethan	1. Ava
2. Jacob	2. Emma
3. Logan	3. Emily
4. Mason	4. Olivia
5. Alexander	5. Isabella
6. Noah	6. Abigail
7. Benjamin	7. Hannah
8. Owen	8. Ella
9. Tyler	9. Grace
10. Michael	10. Sophia
11. Evan	11. Elizabeth
12. Jack	12. Addison
13. Andrew	13. Madison
14. Joseph	14. Alexis
15. Samuel	15. Hailey
16. Nathan	16. Samantha
17. William	17. Lauren
18. Joshua	18. Natalie
19. Matthew	19. Chloe
20. Ryan	20. Lily

Twenty-five of the 50 states bear names from indigenous languages. Hawaii and Connecticut are two examples. Eleven states are named after individuals, including Louisiana (after King Louis XIV), Delaware (for Lord de la Warr), and Maryland (in honor of Queen Maria, wife of King Charles).

Lists ⇒ athletes

Baseball Players

Alex (Rodriguez)
Babe (Ruth)
Barry (Bonds)
Bob (Gibson)
Cal (Ripken Jr.)
Cy (Young)
Derek (Jeter)
Frank (Robinson)
George (Brett)
Hank (Aaron)
Jackie (Robinson)
Joe (DiMaggio)
Kirby (Puckett)
Lou (Gehrig)
Mark (McGwire)
Mickey (Mantle)
Nolan (Ryan)
Orlando (Cepeda)
Pete (Rose)
Randy (Johnson)
Roberto (Clemente)
Rodney ("Rod" Carew)
Roger (Clemens)
Ryne (Sandberg)
Sammy (Sosa)
Steve (Carlton)
Ted (Williams)
Torii (Hunter)
Willie (Mays)

Basketball Players

Allen (Iverson)
Carmelo (Anthony)
Charles (Barkley)
Clyde (Drexler)
Dirk (Nowitzki)
Dominique (Wilkins)
Earvin ("Magic" Johnson)
Isiah (Thomas)
Jerry R. (Lucas)
Julius W. (Erving)
Kareem (Abdul-Jabbar)
Kevin (Garnett)
Kobe (Bryant)
Larry (Bird)
LeBron (James)
Michael (Jordan)
Moses (Malone)
Oscar (Robertson)
Patrick (Ewing)
Pete (Maravich)
Shaquille (O'Neal)
Tim (Duncan)
Tracy (McGrady)
Vernon ("Earl the Pearl" Monroe)
William ("Bill" Russell)
Wilt (Chamberlain)

Boxers

Aaron (Pryor)
Archie (Moore)
Carlos (Zarate)
Evander (Holyfield)
Fernando (Vargas)
Floyd (Patterson)
Gene (Tunney)
George (Foreman)
Jack (Dempsey)
Jake (LaMotta)
Jermain (Taylor)
Jerry (Quarry)
Joe (Louis)
John (Sullivan)
Ken (Norton)
Larry (Holmes)
Marvin (Hagler)
Max (Schmeling)
Mike (Tyson)
Muhammad (Ali)
Oscar (De La Hoya)
Pernell (Whitaker)
Ray ("Sugar Ray" Leonard)
Roberto (Duran)
Rocky (Marciano)
Roy (Jones)
Sonny (Liston)
Thomas (Hearns)
Wilfred (Benitez)

Football Players

Barry (Sanders)
Bart (Starr)
Bo (Jackson)
Brett (Favre)
Brian (Urlacher)
Carson (Palmer)
Dan (Marino)
Dante (Hall)
Emmitt (Smith)
Franco (Harris)
Jerry (Rice)
Joe (Namath)
John (Elway)
Johnny (Unitas)
Merlin (Olsen)
Michael (Irvin)
Peyton (Manning)
Randy (Moss)
Ray (Lewis)
Reggie (White)
Roy (Williams)
Steve (McNair)
Terry (Bradshaw)
Thurman (Thomas)
Tiki (Barber)
Tom (Brady)
Tony (Dorsett)
Troy (Aikman)
Vince (Lombardi)
Walter (Payton)

Golfers

BOYS

Arnold (Palmer)
Ben (Hogan)
Bernhard (Langer)
Bobby (Jones)
Byron (Nelson)
Calvin (Peete)
Cary (Middlecoff)
Chi Chi (Rodriguez)
David (Duval)
Davis (Love, III)
Ernie (Els)
Fred (Couples)
Gary (Player)
Gene (Sarazen)
Greg (Norman)
Hale (Irwin)
Isao (Aoki)
Jack (Nicklaus)
Jim (Thorpe)
John (Daly)
Johnny (Miller)
Julius (Boros)
Lee (Trevino)
Payne (Stewart)
Phil (Mickelson)
Raymond (Floyd)
Sam (Snead)
Sergio (Garcia)
Seve (Ballesteros)
Tiger (Woods)
Tom (Watson)
Vijay (Singh)
Walter (Hagen)

GIRLS

Amy (Alcott)
Angela (Park)
Annika (Sorenstam)
Beth (Daniel)
Betsy (King)
Carol (Mann)
Cristie (Kerr)
Donna (Caponi)
Dottie (Pepper)
Hee-Won (Han)
Jan (Stephenson)
Jeong (Jang)
Judy (Rankin)
Juli (Inkster)
Julieta (Granada)
Karrie (Webb)
Kathy (Whitworth)
Laura (Davies)
Lorena (Ochoa)
Louise (Suggs)
Marlene (Hagge)
Michelle (Wie)
Mickey (Wright)
Mildred ("Babe" Didrikson Zaharias)
Nancy (Lopez)
Pat (Bradley)
Patty (Sheehan)
Paula (Creamer)
Sally (Little)
Sandra (Haynie)
Sherri (Steinhauer)

Hockey Players

Bobby (Orr)
Brett (Hull)
Bryan (McCabe)
Cameron ("Cam" Neely)
Chris (Pronger)
Clark (Gillies)
Craig (Patrick)
Dany (Heatley)
Dominic (Hasek)
Eric (Lindros)
Gerry (Cheevers)
Gordie (Howe)
Grant (Fuhr)
Guy (LaPointe)
Joe (Thornton)
Mario (Lemieux)
Mark (Messier)
Martin (Brodeur)
Marty (Turco)
Patrick (Roy)
Paul (Coffey)
Phil (Esposito)
Raymond (Jean Bourque)
Roberto (Luongo)
Scott (Niedermayer)
Sergei (Gonchar)
Sidney (Crosby)
Wayne (Gretzky)

Race-Car Drivers

BOYS AND GIRLS
A.J. (Foyt)
Al (Unser)
Bobby (Allison)
Cale (Yarborough)
Craig (Breedlove)
Dale (Earnhardt)
Danica (Patrick)
Denny (Hamlin)
Gordon (Johncock)
Jackie (Stewart)
Janet (Guthrie)
Jeff (Burton)
Jimmie (Johnson)
Johnny (Rutherford)
Kasey (Kahne)
Kevin (Harvick)
Kurt (Busch)
Kyle (Busch)
Louise (Smith)
Mario (Andretti)
Mark (Martin)
Matt (Kenseth)
Parnelli (Jones)
Richard (Petty)
Rick (Mears)
Roger (Penske)
Shawna (Robinson)
Tony (Stewart)
Wendell (Scott)

Olympic Medalists

BOYS
Alberto (Tomba)
Aleksandr (Popov)
Apolo (Anton Ohno)
Bart (Conner)
Bjorn (Daehlie)
Brian (Boitano)
Cael (Sanderson)
Carl (Lewis)
Dan (Jansen)
Derek (Parra)
Edwin (Moses)
Elvis (Stojko)
Eric (Heiden)
Gary (Hall Jr.)
Greg (Louganis)
Hermann (Maier)
Ian (Thorpe)
Ingemar (Stenmark)
Ivar (Ballangrud)
Jesse (Owens)
Jonny (Moseley)
Justin (Gatlin)
Klete (Keller)
Kurt (Browning)
Lars (Riedel)
Mark (Spitz)
Matt (Biondi)
Michael (Phelps)
Paul (Hamm)
Rowdy (Gaines)
Scott (Hamilton)
Shaun (White)
Tamas (Darnyi)

GIRLS
Amanda (Beard)
Bonnie (Blair)
Brooke (Bennett)
Carly (Patterson)
Dorothy (Hamill)
Evelyn (Ashford)
Florence (Griffith-Joyner)
Inge (de Bruijn)
Jackie (Joyner-Kersee)
Janet (Evans)
Katarina (Witt)
Kerri (Strug)
Kristi (Yamaguchi)
Larisa (Latynina)
Lisa (Fernandez)
Ludmilla (Tourischeva)
Mary Lou (Retton)
Michelle (Kwan)
Monique (Henderson)
Nadia (Comaneci)
Nancy (Kerrigan)
Nellie (Kim)
Oksana (Baiul)
Olga (Korbut)
Peggy (Fleming)
Sarah (Hughes)
Shannon (Miller)
Summer (Sanders)
Tara (Lipinski)

Tennis Players

BOYS
Andre (Agassi)
Andy (Roddick)
Arthur (Ashe)
Bjorn (Borg)
Boris (Becker)
Carlos (Moya)
Greg (Rusedski)
Guillermo (Vilas)
Gustavo (Kuerten)
Ilie (Nastase)
Ivan (Lendl)
James (Blake)
Jim (Courier)
Jimmy (Connors)
John (McEnroe)
Ken (Rosewall)
Lleyton (Hewitt)
Mats (Wilander)
Michael (Chang)
Mikhail (Youzhny)
Nikolay (Davydenko)
Novak (Djokovic)
Patrick (Rafter)
Pete (Sampras)
Rafael (Nadal)
Robert (Hewitt)
Rod (Laver)
Roger (Federer)
Roy (Emerson)
Stan (Smith)
Stefan (Edberg)
Tommy (Haas)
Yannick (Noah)

GIRLS
Althea (Gibson)
Anastasia (Myskina)
Anna (Kournikova)
Arantxa (Sanchez-Vicario)
Billie Jean (King)
Chris (Evert)
Dorothy (Cheney)
Evonne (Goolagong)
Gabriela (Sabatini)
Hana (Mandlikova)
Helen (Wills Moody)
Jana (Novotna)
Jennifer (Capriati)
Justine (Henin)
Kim (Clijsters)
Lindsay (Davenport)
Margaret (Smith-Court)
Maria (Sharapova)
Martina (Navratilova)
Mary (Pierce)
Monica (Seles)
Nadia (Petrova)
Pam (Shriver)
Patty (Schnyder)
Serena (Williams)
Steffi (Graf)
Svetlana (Kuznetsova)
Tracy (Austin)
Venus (Williams)
Virginia (Wade)

Lists ⇨ au naturel

Animals & Birds

Avocet	Lark
Bear	Mallard
Birdy	Martin
Buck	Merlin
Bunny	Mynah
Cat	Otter
Colt	Phoenix
Drake	Puma
Fawn	Raven
Fox	Robin
Giselle	Sable
Hawk	Swan
Jay	Tiger
Joey	Wolf
Kitty	Wren

Colors

Amber	Magenta
Auburn	Mauve
Azure	Olive
Coral	Pink
Crimson	Roan
Ebony	Rose
Emerald	Royal
Fawn	Saffron
Fuchsia	Scarlet
Gray	Sienna
Hazel	Slate
Ivory	Sterling
Jade	Tawny
Kelly	Teal
Lilac	Violet

Gemstones & Minerals

Agate	Jade
Amber	Jasper
Amethyst	Lapis
Aqua	Malachite
Beryl	Mica
Cameo	Onyx
Coral	Opal
Crystal	Pearl
Diamond	Ruby
Emerald	Sapphire
Flint	Silver
Garnet	Slate
Gemma	Topaz
Goldie	Turquoise
Ivory	Zircon

Nature

BOYS	GIRLS
Alder	Acacia
Ash	Alyssum
Basil	Aura
Birch	Calla
Clay	Calyx
Cliff	Camillia
Cypress	Clover
Flint	Dahlia
Forrest	Echo
Heath	Forsythia
Larch	Freesia
Leaf	Indigo
Linden	Iris
Palm	Ivy
Pine	Lark
Quarry	Lily
River	Magnolia
Rock	Mahogany
Sage	Marigold
Shad	Meadow
Skye	Moon
Stone	Rain
Storm	Spring
Thorne	Summer
Zephyr	Willow

"I want those names to be their destiny, for my daughter to be honest and my son to be expansive."

—FOREST WHITAKER ON WHY HE NAMED HIS DAUGHTER TRUE AND HIS SON OCEAN

New Testament

BOYS	GIRLS
Andrew	Anna
Aquila	Bethany
Bartholomew	Candace
Cornelius	Chloe
Demetrius	Claudia
Gabriel	Damaris
James	Elizabeth
Jason	Eunice
Jesus	Herodias
Joachim	Joanna
John	Julia
Joseph	Lois
Luke	Lydia
Mark	Martha
Matthew	Mary
Matthias	Persis
Nathanael	Phoebe
Philip	Priscilla
Silas	Rhoda
Simon	Rhonda
Stephen	Salome
Thaddeus	Sapphira
Timothy	Susannah
Titus	Tabitha
Zacharias	Veronica

Old Testament

BOYS	GIRLS
Abel	Abigail
Adam	Delilah
Ammiel	Dinah
Amos	Elisheba
Asher	Esther
Azariah	Eve
Cain	Hannah
Caleb	Keturah
Cyrus	Keziah
Elam	Leah
Elijah	Mara
Elisha	Merab
Jadon	Michal
Jeriah	Miriam
Jesse	Naarah
Levi	Naomi
Kenan	Orpah
Malachi	Rachel
Micah	Rebekah
Phinehas	Ruth
Reuben	Sarah
Samson	Sherah
Simeon	Tamar
Tobias	Tirzah
Zebulon	Zibiah

Popes

Adeodatus	Gelasius	Pius
Adrian	Gregory	Pontian
Agapetus	Hilarius	Romanus
Agatho	Honorius	Sabinian
Alexander	Hyginus	Sergius
Anastasius	Innocent	Severinus
Anterus	John	Silverius
Benedict	Julius	Simplicius
Boniface	Lando	Siricius
Callistus	Leo	Sisinnius
Celestine	Liberius	Sixtus
Clement	Linus	Stephen
Constantine	Lucius	Sylvester
Cornelius	Marcellinus	Symmachus
Damasus	Marcellus	Telesphorus
Dionysius	Marinus	Theodore
Donus	Marcus	Urban
Eugene	Martin	Valentine
Eusebius	Miltiades	Victor
Eutychian	Nicholas	Vigilius
Evaristus	Paschal	Vitalian
Felix	Paul	Zephyrinus
Formosus	Pelagius	Zosimus

Saints

BOYS	GIRLS
Ambrose	Anne
Anthony	Agape
Bernard	Bernadette
Blaise	Brigid
Christopher	Candida
Dominic	Emma
Ferdinand	Faith
Francis	Fina
Hilary	Gertrude
Juan	Helena
Justus	Inez
Leo	Irmina
Maro	Jessica
Palladius	Margaret
Raphael	Monessa
Sebastian	Paula
Thomas	Pega
Titus	Prisca
Ulrich	Secundina
Urban	Tanca
Wilfrid	Ursulina
Zenobius	Veridiana

Lists ⇒ celebrities

Comedians

BOYS	GIRLS
Andy (Kaufman)	Amy (Poehler)
Bill (Cosby)	Carol (Burnett)
Billy (Crystal)	Caroline (Rhea)
Chevy (Chase)	Catherine (O'Hara)
Chris (Rock)	Ellen (DeGeneres)
Conan (O'Brien)	Gilda (Radner)
Dave (Chappelle)	Jane (Curtin)
Eddie (Murphy)	Janeane (Garofalo)
George (Carlin)	Julia (Louis-Dreyfus)
Jamie (Foxx)	Kathy (Griffin)
Jay (Leno)	Lily (Tomlin)
Jeff (Foxworthy)	Lucille (Ball)
Jerry (Seinfeld)	Margaret (Cho)
Jim (Carrey)	Maya (Rudolph)
Johnny (Carson)	Megan (Mullally)
Jon (Stewart)	Molly (Shannon)
Richard (Pryor)	Paula (Poundstone)
Robin (Williams)	Rachel (Dratch)
Rodney (Dangerfield)	Rita (Rudner)
Rowan (Atkinson)	Roseanne (Barr)
Sacha (Baron Cohen)	Rosie (O'Donnell)
Scott ("Carrot Top"	Sandra (Bernhardt)
Thompson)	Sarah (Silverman)
Steve (Martin)	Tina (Fey)
Will (Ferrell)	Whoopi (Goldberg)

GET SMART

Reality TV couple Trista and Ryan Sutter picked two smart-sounding surnames for their son, Maxwell Alston.

Models

Adriana (Lima)	Iman
Amber (Valletta)	Karen (Elson)
Andrew (Stetson)	Karolina (Kurkova)
Carolyn (Murphy)	Kate (Moss)
Cheryl (Tiegs)	Kathy (Ireland)
Christie (Brinkley)	Linda (Evangelista)
Christy (Turlington)	Marcus (Schenkenberg)
Cindy (Crawford)	Milla (Jovovich)
Claudia (Schiffer)	Naomi (Campbell)
Elle (Macpherson)	Shalom (Harlow)
Gisele (Bundchen)	Twiggy
Heidi (Klum)	Tyra (Banks)
Helena (Christensen)	Tyson (Beckford)

Movie Actors

BOYS	GIRLS
Al (Pacino)	Angelina (Jolie)
Ben (Affleck)	Audrey (Hepburn)
Brad (Pitt)	Charlize (Theron)
Bruce (Willis)	Demi (Moore)
Cary (Grant)	Diane (Keaton)
Denzel (Washington)	Drew (Barrymore)
Dustin (Hoffman)	Grace (Kelly)
Eddie (Murphy)	Gwyneth (Paltrow)
George (Clooney)	Halle (Berry)
Harrison (Ford)	Hilary (Swank)
Hugh (Jackman)	Jane (Fonda)
Jack (Nicholson)	Jessica (Lange)
Jimmy (Stewart)	Jodie (Foster)
Joe (Pesci)	Julia (Roberts)
John (Travolta)	Kate (Winslet)
Johnny (Depp)	Katharine (Hepburn)
Leonardo (DiCaprio)	Kirsten (Dunst)
Matt (Damon)	Marilyn (Monroe)
Morgan (Freeman)	Meg (Ryan)
Nicolas (Cage)	Meryl (Streep)
Orlando (Bloom)	Nicole (Kidman)
Robert (De Niro)	Reese (Witherspoon)
Samuel (L. Jackson)	Renee (Zellweger)
Sean (Connery)	Sophia (Loren)
Tom (Cruise)	Susan (Sarandon)

Television Actors

BOYS	GIRLS
Alan (Alda)	Alyssa (Milano)
Andy (Griffith)	Candice (Bergen)
Bill (Cosby)	Claire (Danes)
Carroll (O'Connor)	Courteney (Cox-Arquette)
David (Duchovny)	Ellen (Pompeo)
Don (Johnson)	Evangeline (Lily)
Dylan (McDermott)	Gillian (Anderson)
Fred (Savage)	Heather (Locklear)
Hank (Azaria)	Helen (Hunt)
Jason (Alexander)	Jane (Leeves)
John (Goodman)	Jean (Stapleton)
Kelsey (Grammer)	Jennifer (Aniston)
Matt (LeBlanc)	Lisa (Kudrow)
Matthew (Perry)	Mariska (Hargitay)
Michael (J. Fox)	Mary (Tyler Moore)
Neil (Patrick Harris)	Sally (Field)
Patrick (Dempsey)	Sandra (Oh)
Rob (Lowe)	Sarah (Jessica Parker)
Steve (Carell)	Teri (Hatcher)
Ted (Danson)	Tori (Spelling)
Tim (Allen)	Valerie (Bertinelli)
William (Peterson)	

cultural ← Lists

African-American

BOYS	GIRLS
Ashton	Aisha
Bryant	Bralyn
Calvin	Chellise
Danell	Dashay
DeAndre	Delicia
Elijah	Eleesha
Evander	Felita
Franklin	Gracelyn
Hakeem	Halle
Ibrahim	Iyanla
Ivory	Jalissa
Jamal	Jenise
Jaqwuan	Kania
Keandre	Latasha
Keshon	Latoya
LeVaughn	Maliaka
Marcus	Nikia
Nathaniel	Odessa
Priest	Roshawna
Quentin	Sharia
Rashon	Tyisha
Rondre	VeNay
Shawnel	Whitney
Tariq	Yolanda
Traveras	Zakia

Greek

BOYS	GIRLS
Alexander	Alexandra
Andrew	Alyssa
Christopher	Anastasia
Cyrano	Athena
Damon	Ava
Demetrius	Calista
Dennis	Callie
Hector	Cassandra
Hercules	Catherine
Homer	Chloe
Julius	Daphne
Karl	Diana
Linus	Evangeline
Napoleon	Helen
Nemo	Hillary
Nicholas	Kara
Peter	Kristina
Petros	Lydia
Socrates	Madeline
Spiro	Melissa
Stephen	Penelope
Thaddeus	Phoebe
Timothy	Sophie/Sophia
Titus	Teresa
Zeno	Zoe

Chinese

BOYS	GIRLS
Bo	An
Chan	Bik
Chen	Bo
Chung	Chin
Fai	Chow
Fu	Genji
Ho	Heng
Hong	Hua
Jin	Jin
Lei	Jun
Liang	Li
Lok	Lian
Long	Mei
Manchu	Mingmei
Shaiming	Ning
Shing	Peony
Sun	Shu
Tao	Sun
Wang	Tao
Wen	Yin
Yaun	Yu
Zian	Xhen

Hispanic

BOYS	GIRLS
Aciano	Alma
Alejandro	Beatrice
Berto	Carmen
Cesar	Dina
Diego	Elena
Ernesto	Estella
Francisco	Felicia
Geraldo	Gabriela
Hugo	Herminia
Isaac	Imelda
Jesus	Julia
Luis	Karmen
Miguel	Lucia
Nuncio	Maribel
Oscar	Noemi
Paulo	Olivia
Quinto	Pilar
Ricardo	Roxana
Sergio	Sofia
Tobias	Tulia
Urbano	Yolanda
Venturo	Zoe

Lists ⇨ cultural

Jewish

BOYS	GIRLS
Arion	Aaliyah
Barth	Abiah
Carmelo	Bethel
Chaim	Channah
Dannon	Chasya
Davin	Danica
Eder	Darice
Eliseo	Eden
Gersham	Eliana
Gilead	Gavra
Harrell	Hedya
Ira	Isha
Izaac	Joelle
Jadon	Katriel
Jakeem	Keziah
Kaleb	Liesbet
Levi	Marnina
Makis	Norah
Nissim	Orpah
Ozzie	Penina
Phineas	Rinnah
Ranon	Sari
Sameol	Thadine
Tobin	Urice
Yaron	Yachne

Native American

BOYS	GIRLS
Anoke	Aiyana
Cochise	Amitola
Delsin	Anatolia
Elu	Aponi
Jacy	Cheyenne
Kuruk	Dakota
Mandan	Elu
Mankya	Enola
Mohegan	Lakota
Motega	Mahala, Mahalia
Nodin	Nadie
Osage	Nituna
Patamon	Nokomis
Pawnee	Oneida
Pilan	Seneca
Sakima	Shasta
Shaman	Shawnee
Tadi	Shoshone
Takoda	Taima
Tyee	Talise
Wapiti	Tipper
Uncas	Vilhelmia
Yaholo	Wyanet
Yahto	Wynona
Yuma	Zuni

Muslim

BOYS	GIRLS
Abdul	Aliyyah
Ahamad	Adara
Ali	Adila
Ashraf	Almira
Habib	Amani
Hadi	Azhar
Hakeem, Hakim	Farah
Hamid	Fatinah
Jamal	Iman
Kadir	Jamilah
Karim	Kamilah
Malik	Latifah
Muhammed	Layla
Nadir	Lu'lu'
Nasser, Nassir	Malika
Omar	Muna
Qadir	Nadirah
Shakir	Noya
Sharif	Rashida
Talib	Rihana
Yusuf	Sakinah
Zuhair	Samira

Russian

BOYS	GIRLS
Akim	Anastasia
Avel	Cyzarine
Boris	Ekaterina
Demyan	Fayina
Egor	Feodora
Fyodor	Galina
Gavrie	Helina
Gavril	Irina
Ilya	Jelena
Kliment	Julya
Lesta	Katerina
Maksim	Kisa
Mikhail	Larissa
Naum	Lilia
Nikita	Natalya
Oleg	Oksana
Pavel	Olga
Rurik	Raisa
Sasha	Sasha
Uriah	Talia
Ustin	Vania
Yerik	Yeva

Film

BOYS

Ace (Ventura)
Austin (Powers)
Borat (Sagdiyev)
Bruce (Wayne)
Charles (Foster
    Kane)
Clark (Kent)
Forrest (Gump)
Fred (Dobbs)
George (Bailey)
Hannibal (Lecter)
Indiana (Jones)
Jack (Sparrow)
Jacques (Clouseau)
Jerry (Maguire)
John ("Bluto"
    Blutarsky)
Judah (Ben-Hur)
Luke (Skywalker)
Marty (McFly)
Napoleon (Dynamite)
Norman (Bates)
Peter (Parker)
Rocky (Balboa)
Roger (Rabbit)
Stanley (Kowalski)
Virgil (Tibbs)
Vito (Corleone)
Will (Scarlet)

GIRLS

Annie (Hall)
Ariel
Blanche (DuBois)
Bonnie (Parker)
Carrie (White)
Charlotte A.
    (Cavatica)
Clarice (Starling)
Eliza (Doolittle)
Elizabeth (Swann)
Ellen (Ripley)
Erin (Brockovich)
Ilsa (Lund)
Lara (Croft)
Leia (Organa)
Lois (Lane)
Louise (Sawyer)
Lucy (Honeychurch)
Maggie (Fitzgerald)
Marge (Gunderson)
Maria (von Trapp)
Marian (Paroo)
Mary (Poppins)
Mildred (Ratched)
Nellie (Forbush)
Norma Rae
    (Webster)
Sandy (Olsson)
Thelma (Dickerson)

Television

BOYS

Alex (P. Keaton)
Archie (Bunker)
Arthur (Fonzarelli)
Barney (Fife)
Ben (Cartwright)
Bret (Maverick)
Chandler (Bing)
Cliff (Huxtable)
Cordell (Walker)
Doug (Heffernan)
Dylan (McKay)
Frasier (Crane)
Gilbert ("Gil"
    Grissom)
Hank (Hill)
Homer (Simpson)
James (T. Kirk)
Jack (Bauer)
Jean-Luc (Picard)
Jerry (Seinfeld)
Joe (Friday)
John (Boy Walton)
Lincoln (Burrows)
Maynard (G. Krebs)
Peter (Petrelli)
Ricky (Ricardo)
Rob (Petrie)
Steve (Urkel)
Tony (Soprano)

GIRLS

Addison (Forbes
    Montgomery)
Ally (McBeal)
Carmela (Soprano)
Dana (Scully)
Edith (Bunker)
Elaine (Benes)
Eleanor (Frutt)
Grace (Adler)
Jessica (Fletcher)
Laura (Petrie)
Lucy (Ricardo)
Margaret (Hoolihan)
Mary (Richards)
Maude (Findlay)
Meredith (Grey)
Monica (Geller)
Morticia (Addams)
Murphy (Brown)
Niki (Sanders)
Rachel (Green)
Rhoda
    (Morgenstern)
Roseanne (Conner)
Samantha (Stevens)
Shirley (Schmidt)
Vanessa (Huxtable)
Veronica (Mars)
Xena

Literary

BOYS

Arjuna
Atticus (Finch)
Billy (Coleman)
Chia (Pao-yu)
Cyrano (de Bergerac)
Cyrus (Trask)
David (Copperfield)
Don (Quixote)
Ebenezer (Scrooge)
Ethan (Frome)
Fletcher (Christian)
Frodo (Baggins)
Hamlet
Harry (Potter)
Heathcliff
Holden (Caulfield)
Huckleberry (Finn)
Humbert (Humbert)

James (Bond)
Jay (Gatsby)
Jean (Valjean)
Nicholas (Nickleby)
Odysseus
Oliver (Twist)
Peter (Pan)
Rhett (Butler)
Robinson (Crusoe)
Romeo (Montague)
Sam (Spade)
Sherlock (Holmes)
Silas (Marner)
Tom (Sawyer)
Wilfred (of Ivanhoe)
Willie (Wonka)
Victor (Frankenstein)
Yuri (Zhivago)

GIRLS

Alice
Anna (Karenina)
Anne (Shirley)
Antonia (Shimerda)
Bridget (Jones)
Buttercup
Catherine
    (Earnshaw)
Clarissa (Dalloway)
Cleopatra
Cosette (Valjean)
Daisy (Buchanan)
Dorothy (Gale)
Elizabeth (Bennet)
Emma (Woodhouse)
Edna (Pontellier)
Hedda (Gabler)
Hermione (Granger)

Hester (Prynne)
Holly (Golightly)
Jane (Eyre)
Jean (Brodie)
Josephine (March)
Juliet (Capulet)
Katherina (Minola)
Lily (Bart)
Lolita
Mary (Lennox)
Medea
Moll (Flanders)
Natasha (Rostova)
Ophelia
Phoebe (Caulfield)
Scarlett (O'Hara)
Scout (Finch)
Tess (Durbeyfield)

Lists ⇒ fictional characters

Shakespearean Names

BOYS

Aaron (*Titus Andronicus*)
Antipholus (*Comedy of Errors*)
Antonio (*The Merchant of Venice, The Tempest*)
Apemantus (*Timon of Athens*)
Arthur (*King John*)
Benedick (*Much Ado About Nothing*)
Bertram (*All's Well That Ends Well*)
Berowne (*Love's Labour's Lost*)
Caius (*The Merry Wives of Windsor*)
Caliban (*The Tempest*)
Claudio (*Measure for Measure*)
Claudius (*Hamlet*)
Cloten (*Cymbeline*)
Cymbeline (*Cymbeline*)
Dromio (*Comedy of Errors*)
Edmund (*King Lear*)
Egeus (*A Midsummer Night's Dream*)
Escalus (*Measure for Measure*)
Florizel (*The Winter's Tale*)
Fluellen (*Henry V*)
Graziano (*Merchant of Venice, Othello*)
Hamlet (*Hamlet*)
Henry (*Henry V*)
Hugh (*The Merry Wives of Windsor*)
Iago (*Othello*)
Jaques (*As You Like It*)
John (*King John*)
Lafew (*All's Well That Ends Well*)
Leontes (*The Winter's Tale*)
Lucentio (*The Taming of the Shrew*)
Lysander (*A Midsummer Night's Dream*)
Mercutio (*Romeo and Juliet*)
Montano (*Othello*)
Orlando (*As You Like It*)
Orsino (*Twelfth Night*)
Othello (*Othello*)
Parolles (*All's Well That Ends Well*)
Petruchio (*The Taming of the Shrew*)
Polixenes (*The Winter's Tale*)
Polonius (*Hamlet*)
Prospero (*The Tempest*)
Proteus (*Two Gentlemen of Verona*)
Romeo (*Romeo and Juliet*)
Sebastian (*The Tempest, Twelfth Night*)
Shylock (*Merchant of Venice*)
Theseus (*A Midsummer Night's Dream*)
Timon (*Timon of Athens*)
Titus (*Titus Andronicus*)
Tybalt (*Romeo and Juliet*)
Valentine (*Two Gentlemen of Verona*)

GIRLS

Adriana (*The Comedy of Errors*)
Anne (*The Merry Wives of Windsor*)
Audrey (*As You Like It*)
Baptista (*The Taming of the Shrew*)
Beatrice (*Much Ado About Nothing*)
Bianca (*Othello, The Taming of the Shrew*)
Catherine (*Henry V*)
Celia (*As You Like It*)
Constance (*King John*)
Cordelia (*King Lear*)
Desdemona (*Othello*)
Diana (*All's Well That Ends Well*)
Eleanor (*King John*)
Gertrude (*Hamlet*)
Goneril (*King Lear*)
Helena (*All's Well That Ends Well*)
Hermia (*A Midsummer Night's Dream*)
Hermione (*The Winter's Tale*)
Hero (*Much Ado About Nothing*)
Hippolyta (*A Midsummer Night's Dream*)
Imogen (*Cymbeline*)
Isabella (*Measure for Measure*)
Jaquenetta (*Love's Labour's Lost*)
Jessica (*Merchant of Venice*)
Julia (*Two Gentlemen of Verona*)
Juliet (*Measure for Measure, Romeo and Juliet*)
Katherine (*Love's Labour's Lost, Taming of the Shrew*)
Lavinia (*Titus Andronicus*)
Luce (*The Comedy of Errors*)
Lucetta (*Two Gentlemen of Verona*)
Luciana (*The Comedy of Errors*)
Margaret (*Much Ado About Nothing*)
Maria (*Love's Labour's Lost, Twelfth Night*)
Mariana (*Measure for Measure*)
Miranda (*The Tempest*)
Nerissa (*The Merchant of Venice*)
Olivia (*Twelfth Night*)
Ophelia (*Hamlet*)
Paulina (*The Winter's Tale*)
Perdita (*The Winter's Tale*)
Phoebe (*As You Like It*)
Portia (*The Merchant of Venice*)
Regan (*King Lear*)
Rosalind (*As You Like It*)
Rosaline (*Love's Labour's Lost*)
Silvia (*Two Gentlemen of Verona*)
Tamora (*Titus Andronicus*)
Titania (*A Midsummer Night's Dream*)
Viola (*Twelfth Night*)

Explorers

Amelia (Earhart)	James (Cook)
Christopher (Columbus)	John (Smith)
	Juan (Ponce de Leon)
Daniel (Boone)	Leif (Ericsson)
David (Livingstone)	Marco (Polo)
Edmund (Hillary)	Meriwether (Lewis)
Ferdinand (Magellan)	Neil (Armstrong)
Francis (Drake)	Richard (Byrd)
Francisco (Coronado)	Robert (Peary)
Henry (Hudson)	Sacagawea
Hernando (Cortez)	Walter (Raleigh)
Ida (Pfeiffer)	William (Clark)
Jacques (Cousteau)	Zebulon (Pike)

Inventors

Alexander (Graham Bell)—Telephone
Alfred (Nobel)—Dynamite
Arthur (Schawlow)—Laser
Benjamin (Franklin)—Bifocals
Clarence (Birdseye)—Frozen food
Felix (Hoffman)—Aspirin
George (Eastman)—Photography film
Gideon (Sundback)—Modern Zipper
Harry (Coover)—Super Glue
Harvey (Firestone)—Air-filled rubber tires
Henry (Ford)—Automobile
John (Deere)—Cast steel plow
Josephine (Cochran)—Dishwasher
Lee (de Forest)—Radio
Louis (Parker)—Television
Milton (Bradley)—Game of Life
Nikola (Tesla)—Alternating current
Orville (Wright)—Airplane
Robert (Fulton)—Steamship
Samuel (Morse)—Morse code
Thomas (Edison)—Electric lamp, phonograph
Walter (Hunt)—Safety pin
Wilbur (Wright)—Airplane
William (Seward Burroughs)—Adding machine
Willis (Haviland Carrier)—Air-Conditioning

Nobel Prize Winners

Agnes ("Mother Teresa" Bojaxhiu)	Irene (Joliot-Curie)
	John (Steinbeck)
Albert (Einstein)	Marie (Curie)
Desmond (Tutu)	Niels (Bohr)
Ernest (Hemingway)	Norman (Borlaug)
Frederick (Sanger)	Samuel (Beckett)
Gao (Xingjian)	Toni (Morrison)
Henry (Kissinger)	Winston (Churchill)

Old-Fashioned

BOYS	GIRLS
Alan	Amanda
Alexander	Audrey
Anthony	Ava
Benjamin	Beatrice
Brett	Betty
Calvin	Bridget
Carter	Caroline
Charles	Catherine
Christopher	Celia
Cole	Dinah
Conrad	Dorothy
Daniel	Eleanor
Darren	Ella
David	Emily
Douglas	Emmeline
Edward	Eva
Edwin	Frances
Eric	Georgia
Ethan	Grace
Francis	Gretchen
Garrett	Hattie
George	Ida
Gerald	Irene
Graham	Isabel
Harry	Jacqueline
Henry	Janet
Hugh	Jeanette
Isaiah	Jennie
Jack	Joanna
Jefferson	Juliette
Joel	Kitty
Jonah	Leonora
Joshua	Lillian
Justin	Lola
Lewis	Louisa
Loren	Lucy
Maxwell	Maisie
Michael	Margaret
Nicholas	Martha
Oliver	Millie
Patrick	Natalie
Philip	Patience
Reginald	Priscilla
Robert	Rose
Samuel	Sadie
Thomas	Sophia
William	Sylvia
Wilson	Tallulah
Winston	Victoria
Wyatt	Violet
Zachary	Willa

Lists ⇒ leaders

British Royalty

Alexandra	Eugenie
Alfred	George
Alice	Harold
Andrew	Henry
Anne	James
Beatrice	Margaret
Camilla	Matilda
Charles	Michael
Diana	Philip
Edgar	Richard
Edmund	Robert
Edward	Victoria
Elizabeth	William

Truman (#943) recently joined Lincoln (#300) and Clinton (#844) in the top 1,000 boys' names.

Military

Alexander (the Great)
Bernhard (Montgomery)
Charlemagne (Charles the Great)
Chester (Nimitz)
Colin (Powell)
Douglas (MacArthur)
Eddie (Rickenbacker)
George (Patton)
Ghengis (Kahn)
James (Doolittle)
Joan (of Arc)
John ("Black Jack" Pershing)
Julius (Caesar)
Napoleon (Bonaparte)
Norman (Schwarzkopf)
Philip (of Macedonia)
Richard (the Lion-Hearted)
Robert (E. Lee)
Samuel (Houston)
Simon (Bolivar)
Sun (Tzu)
Thomas ("Stonewall" Jackson)
William (Wallace)

Kings & Queens

BOYS	GIRLS
Albert	Amina
Alexander	Anne
Amadeo	Beatrix
Carl	Candace
Charles	Catherine
Darius	Charlotte
David	Christina
Duncan	Cleopatra
Ferdinand	Eleanor
Frederick	Emma
George	Ingrid
Harold	Isabella
Henry	Jeanne
Ivan	Joanna
James	Juliana
John	Margaret
Juan	Maria
Louis	Mary
Malcolm	Matilda
Mohammed	Rania
Richard	Silvia
Roderick	Sofia
Umberto	Tamar
Vittorio	Victoria
William	Wilhelmina

U.S. Presidents

Abraham (Lincoln)
Andrew (Jackson)
Benjamin (Harrison)
Calvin (Coolidge)
Chester (A. Arthur)
Dwight (D. Eisenhower)
Franklin (D. Roosevelt)
George (Washington)
Gerald (Ford)
Grover (Cleveland)
Harry (S. Truman)
Herbert (Hoover)
James (Madison)
John (F. Kennedy)
Lyndon (B. Johnson)
Martin (Van Buren)
Millard (Fillmore)
Richard (Nixon)
Rutherford (B. Hayes)
Theodore (Roosevelt)
Thomas (Jefferson)
Ulysses (S. Grant)
Warren (G. Harding)
William (Taft)
Woodrow (Wilson)
Zachary (Taylor)

Authors

BOYS	GIRLS
Charles (Dickens)	Agatha (Christie)
Ernest (Hemingway)	Alice (Walker)
George (Orwell)	Amy (Tan)
Henry (James)	Anne (Frank)
Isaac (Asimov)	Beatrix (Potter)
Jack (Kerouac)	Charlotte (Bronte)
James (Joyce)	Edith (Wharton)
John (Steinbeck)	Esther (Forbes)
Jules (Verne)	Frances (Hodgson
Leo (Tolstoy)	Burnett)
Lewis (Carroll)	Harper (Lee)
Mario (Puzo)	Harriet (Beecher
Mark (Twain)	Stowe)
Nathaniel	Ida (Tarbell)
(Hawthorne)	Jane (Austen)
Nicholas (Sparks)	Jean (M. Auel)
Ray (Bradbury)	Joan (Didion)
Robert (Louis	Joyce (Carol Oates)
Stevenson)	Louisa (May Alcott)
Rudyard (Kipling)	Margaret (Mitchell)
Scott (Fitzgerald)	Mary (Shelley)
Sinclair (Lewis)	Maya (Angelou)
Stephen (King)	Pearl (S. Buck)
Tom (Clancy)	Selma (Lagerlof)
Truman (Capote)	Toni (Morrison)
Victor (Hugo)	Virginia (Woolf)
William (Faulkner)	Willa (Cather)

Playwrights

Anna (Deavere Smith)	Joyce (Carol Oates)
Anton (Chekhov)	Lillian (Hellman)
Arthur (Miller)	Margaret (Edson)
August (Wilson)	Neil (Simon)
Ayn (Rand)	Noel (Coward)
Ben (Johnson)	Oscar (Wilde)
Bertolt (Brecht)	Paula (Vogel)
Christopher (Marlowe)	Robert (Browning)
Clare Boothe Luce	Sam (Shepard)
David (Mamet)	Samuel (Beckett)
Edmond (Rostand)	Sinclair (Lewis)
Eugene (O'Neill)	Suzan-Lori (Parks)
George (Bernard Shaw)	Tennessee (Williams)
Harold (Pinter)	Thomas ("T. S." Eliot)
Henrik (Ibsen)	Thornton (Wilder)
Jean-Paul (Sartre)	Wendy (Wasserstein)
John (Patrick Shanley)	William (Shakespeare)

Poets

BOYS	GIRLS
Alfred (Lord Tennyson)	Adrienne (Rich)
Allen (Ginsberg)	Amy (Lowell)
Carl (Sandburg)	Anne (Bradstreet)
Dante (Alighieri)	Christina (Rossetti)
Dylan (Thomas)	Denise (Levertov)
Edgar (Allan Poe)	Dorothy (Parker)
Edward (Estlin Cummings)	Edith (Wharton)
Ezra (Pound)	Edna (St. Vincent Millay)
Henry (Wadsworth Longfellow)	Elizabeth (Barrett Browning)
Hermann (Hesse)	Emily (Dickinson)
Jack (Prelutsky)	Gabriela (Mistral)
James (Joyce)	Gertrude (Stein)
John (Keats)	Gwendolyn (Brooks)
Langston (Hughes)	Josephine (Miles)
Mark (Strand)	Joy (Harjo)
Omar (Khayyam)	Katherine (Anne Porter)
Pablo (Neruda)	Louise (Gluck)
Percy (Bysshe Shelley)	Lucille (Clifton)
Robert (Frost)	Margaret (Atwood)
Seamus (Heaney)	Marianne (Moore)
Shel (Silverstein)	Mary (Oliver)
Theodore (Roethke)	Maya (Angelou)
Thomas (Stearns Eliot)	Nikki (Giovanni)
Walt (Whitman)	Rita (Dove)
Walter (Raleigh)	Sara (Teasdale)
William (Wordsworth)	Sharon (Olds)
	Sylvia (Plath)
	Wislawa (Szymborska)

"What's in a name?
That which we
call a rose
by any other name
would smell as sweet."

–ROMEO AND JULIET

Lists ⇨ musicians

Country

BOYS	GIRLS
Alan (Jackson)	Brenda (Lee)
Billy Ray (Cyrus)	Carrie (Underwood)
Brad (Paisley)	Chely (Wright)
Buck (Owens)	Dolly (Parton)
Charley (Pride)	Emmylou (Harris)
Clint (Black)	Faith (Hill)
Conway (Twitty)	Gretchen (Wilson)
Garth (Brooks)	Jo Dee (Messina)
Gene (Autry)	Julie (Roberts)
George (Jones)	June (Carter Cash)
Hank (Williams)	Kitty (Wells)
Johnny (Cash)	LeAnn (Rimes)
Keith (Urban)	Loretta (Lynn)
Kenny (Chesney)	Lucinda (Williams)
Kris (Kristofferson)	Martina (McBride)
Lee (Greenwood)	Mary (Chapin
Marty (Robbins)	Carpenter)
Mel (Tillis)	Pam (Tillis)
Merle (Haggard)	Patsy (Cline)
Mickey (Gilley)	Patty (Loveless)
Randy (Travis)	Reba (McEntire)
Roy (Rogers)	Sara (Evans)
Tim (McGraw)	Shania (Twain)
Toby (Keith)	Tammy (Wynette)
Waylon (Jennings)	Tanya (Tucker)
Willie (Nelson)	Trisha (Yearwood)
Vince (Gill)	Wynonna (Judd)

Latin

BOYS	GIRLS
Cal (Tjader)	Ariadna ("Thalía"
Carlos (Vives)	Sodi Miranda)
Chayanne	Ana (Torroja)
Eddie (Palmieri)	Belinda (Peregrin
Elvis (Crespo)	Schull)
Emilio (Navaira)	Celia (Cruz)
Enrique (Iglesias)	Clare (Fischer)
Flaco (Jimenez)	Ednita (Nazario)
Freddy (Fender)	Elida (Y Avante)
Ibrahim (Ferrer)	Gloria (Estefan)
Israel (Lopez)	Jennifer (Lopez)
Jon (Secada)	Julieta (Venegas)
Jose (Feliciano)	Lani (Hall)
Juan (Luis Guerra)	Laura (Pausini)
Julio (Iglesias)	Linda (Ronstadt)
Luis (Miguel)	Mariana (Seoane)
Marc (Anthony)	Marta (Sanchez)
Mongo	Myriam
(Santamaria)	(Hernandez)
Pepe (Aguilar)	Nydia (Rojas)
Plácido (Domingo)	Olga (Tanon)
Ricardo (Morales)	Paulina (Rubio)
Ricky (Martin)	Selena (Quintanilla-
Roberto (Carlos)	Pérez)
Rubén (Blades)	Shakira
Ry (Cooder)	Sheena (Easton)
Tito (Puente)	Shelly (Lares)

Jazz

BOYS	GIRLS
Benny (Goodman)	Abbey (Lincoln)
Bill (Evans)	Anita (O'Day)
Cab (Calloway)	Betty (Carter)
Charlie (Parker)	Billie (Holiday)
Chick (Corea)	Carmen (McRae)
Coleman (Hawkins)	Dee Dee
Dizzy (Gillespie)	(Bridgewater)
Duke (Ellington)	Diana (Krall)
George (Russell)	Dinah (Washington)
Harry (Connick Jr.)	Ella (Fitzgerald)
Joe ("King" Oliver)	Ernestine
John (Coltrane)	(Anderson)
Lennie (Tristano)	Etta (Jones)
Louis (Armstrong)	Lena (Horne)
Mel (Tormé)	Nancy (Wilson)
Miles (Davis)	Nina (Simone)
Nat ("King" Cole)	Peggy (Lee)
Ornette (Coleman)	Rosemary (Clooney)
William ("Count"	Sarah (Vaughan)
Basie)	Shirley (Horn)

Pop

BOYS	GIRLS
Aaron (Neville)	Annie (Lennox)
Ben (Harper)	Britney (Spears)
Billy (Joel)	Carly (Simon)
Burt (Bacharach)	Celine (Dion)
Clay (Aiken)	Christina (Aguilera)
Corbin (Bleu)	Dionne (Warwick)
Dave (Matthews)	Janet (Jackson)
Elton (John)	Jessica (Simpson)
Elvis (Costello)	Kelly (Clarkson)
George (Harrison)	Linda (Ronstadt)
James (Taylor)	Macy (Gray)
Jim (Croce)	Madonna
John (Mayer)	Mariah (Carey)
Justin (Timberlake)	Nelly (Furtado)
Michael (Bolton)	Norah (Jones)
Paul (McCartney)	Paula (Abdul)
Phil (Collins)	Sarah (McLachlan)
Rod (Stewart)	Sheryl (Crow)
Stevie (Wonder)	Toni (Braxton)
Van (Morrison)	Whitney (Houston)

Rap/Hip-Hop

BOYS	GIRLS
Aliaune (Akon)	Aaliyah (Haughton)
André (Dr. Dre)	Cheryl (Salt-N-Pepa)
Antwan (Big Boi from Outkast)	Christine (Christina Milian)
Calvin (Snoop Dogg)	Ciara (Harris)
Carl (Twista)	Dana (Queen Latifah)
Carlton (Chuck D)	Deidra (DJ Spinderella of Salt-N-Pepa)
Christopher (Notorious B.I.G.)	
Clifford (Method Man)	Erica (Erykah Badu)
Cornell (Nelly)	Eve (Jeffers)
Curtis (50 Cent)	Faith (Evans)
Dante (Mos Def)	Inga (Foxy Brown)
Howard (Chingy)	Janet (Jackson)
James (LL Cool J)	Kimberly (Lil' Kim)
Jason (Jam Master Jay)	Lana (MC Lyte)
	Lauryn (Hill)
Jay (Young Jeezy)	Lisa (Left Eye of TLC)
Kanye (West)	
Lonnie (Common)	Louise (Lady Sovereign)
Marshall (Eminem)	
Mike (Jones)	Mariah (Carey)
Nasir (Nas)	Mary Jane (Mary J. Blige)
Nelust (Wyclef Jean)	
O'Shea (Ice Cube)	Melissa (Missy Elliott)
Robert (Vanilla Ice)	Nelly (Furtado)
Shawn (Jay-Z)	Rozonda ("Chilli" Thomas)
Sean (P. Diddy Combs)	
	Sandra (Salt-N-Pepa)
Trevor (Busta Rhymes)	Shawntae (Da Brat)
	Stacy Ann (Fergie of Black Eyed Peas)
Tupac (2Pac)	
Usher (Raymond)	Tionne (T-Boz of TLC)

Rock & Roll

Bob (Dylan)	Janis (Joplin)
Brenda (Lee)	Jerry (Garcia)
Brian (Wilson)	Jim (Morrison)
Bruce (Springsteen)	Jimi (Hendrix)
Buddy (Holly)	John (Lennon)
Carlos (Santana)	Joni (Mitchell)
Chuck (Berry)	Keith (Richards)
David (Lee Roth)	Linda (Ronstadt)
Diana (Ross)	Michael (Jackson)
Elvis (Presley)	Mick (Jagger)
Eric (Clapton)	Prince
Frankie (Valli)	Robert (Plant)
Jackson (Browne)	Roger (Daltrey)
James (Brown)	Stevie (Nicks)

Soul

BOYS	GIRLS
Antoine ("Fats" Domino Jr.)	Alicia (Keys)
	April (Hill)
Bill (Withers)	Aretha (Franklin)
Bobby (Brown)	Bettye (LaVette)
Brian (McKnight)	Beyoncé (Knowles)
Clarence (Carter)	Bonnie (Raitt)
Curtis (Mayfield)	Chaka (Khan)
David (Sanborn)	Dinah (Washington)
George (Benson)	Dionne (Warwick)
Ike (Turner)	Donna (Summer)
James (Ingram)	Eva (Cassidy)
John (Legend)	Faith (Evans)
Lionel (Richie)	Gladys (Knight)
Lou (Rawls)	Jennifer (Holliday)
Luther (Vandross)	Keyshia (Cole)
Marvin (Gaye)	Koko (Taylor)
Otis (Redding)	Mariah (Carey)
Percy (Sledge)	Mary (J. Blige)
Phillip (Walker)	Natalie (Cole)
Quincy (Jones)	Rory (Block)
Ray (Charles)	Stephanie (Mills)
Riley ("B.B." King)	Thelma (Houston)
Sam (Cooke)	Tina (Turner)
Solomon (Burke)	Toni (Lynn Washington)
Stevie (Wonder)	
William ("Smokey" Robinson)	Vanessa (Williams)
	Whitney (Houston)

The Red Hot Chili Peppers were originally known as Tony Flow and the Miraculous Masters of Mayhem.

Lists ⇒ mythology

Egyptian

Anubis (god of the dead)
Anuke (goddess of war)
Atum (god of creation)
Bastet (goddess of protection)
Bes (god who protects childbirth)
Chons (god of the moon)
Geb (god of the earth)
Hapy (god of the annual flood of the Nile)
Hathor (goddess of music, dance)
Horus (god of light)
Isis (goddess of nature)
Khepri (god of renewal, rebirth)
Maat (goddess of truth, justice)
Min (god of fertility)
Nephthys (goddess of the dead)
Nut (goddess of the sky, heavens)
Osiris (god of the underworld)
Ptah (god of craftsmen)
Ra (god of the sun)
Sekhmet (goddess of war)
Selket (goddess of scorpions, magic)
Seshat (goddess of writing)
Set (god of chaos, storms)
Shu (god of the air)
Tawaret (goddess who protects childbirth)
Tefnut (goddess of moisture)
Thoth (god of writing, knowledge)
Wepwawet (god of war)

"Everybody wasn't always too big on my mother having me. I believe at least probably my father. I don't think he wanted her to have the baby. So I really think that's what made her name me Faith. She had to keep the faith."

—FAITH EVANS

Greek

BOYS

Achilles (Greek warrior)
Apollo (god of the light, healing, music)
Ares (god of war)
Asclepius (god of medicine, healing)
Boreas (god of the north wind)
Cronos (father of Zeus)
Dionysus (god of wine, fertility)
Eros (god of love)
Eurus (god of the east wind)
Hades (god of the underworld)
Helios (god of the sun)
Hephaistos (god of metalwork)
Heracles (hero born with great strength)
Hermes (messenger of the gods)
Hypnos (god of sleep)
Morpheus (god of dreams)
Notus (god of the south wind)
Oceanus (father of rivers)
Pallas (father of the minor gods)
Pan (god of wild nature, shepherds)
Poseidon (god of the sea)
Thanatos (god of death)
Uranus (god of the sky)
Zephyrus (god of the west wind)
Zeus (king of the gods)

GIRLS

Aphrodite (goddess of love)
Artemis (goddess of hunting)
Atalanta (famous huntress)
Athena (goddess of war, wisdom)
Chloris (goddess of flowers)
Demeter (goddess of agriculture)
Eileithyia (goddess of birth)
Enyo (goddess of war)
Eos (goddess of dawn)
Eris (goddess of spite, quarrels)
Gaia (goddess of earth)
Hebe (goddess of youth)
Hecate (goddess of darkness, magic)
Hera (goddess of marriage, childbirth)
Hestia (goddess of hearth, home)
Irene (goddess of peace, wealth)
Iris (goddess of rainbows)
Nemesis (goddess of divine revenge)
Nyx (goddess of night)
Penelope (wife of Odysseus)
Persephone (goddess of the underworld)
Pheme (goddess of fame)
Selene (goddess of the moon)
Thetis (mother of Achilles)

Japanese

Amaterasu (Shinto sun goddess)
Amo-No-Minaka-Nushi (god of the Middle Heaven)
Benten (goddess of fortune)
Bimbogami (god of poverty)
Bishamon (good fortune god of war)
Gama (god of longevity)
Hamori (god who protects leaves)
Hoderi (god of fishing)
Hoori (god of hunting)
Inari (god of rice)
Izanagi (Shinto creator god)
Jurojin (good fortune god)
Kagutsuchi (god of fire)
Kannon (goddess of compassion, mercy)
Kojin (goddess of the kitchen)
Okuninushi (god of healing, sorcery)
Oho-Yama (great mountain god)
Raiden (god of lightning)
Ryujin (Dragon King of the sea)
Susanoo (god of the ocean)
Tsukiyomi (god of the moon)
Uzume (goddess of dancing)
Zenmyo (Shinto goddess)

Norse

Aegir (god of the sea)
Astrild (goddess of love)
Balder (god of the sun, peace)
Bragi (god of poetry)
Buri (ancestor of the gods)
Fjorgen (goddess of the earth, atmosphere)
Forseti (god of order and justice)
Frey (god of peace, fertility, prosperity)
Freya (goddess of fertility, love)
Heimdall (watchman of the gate of Asgard)
Hel (goddess of the dead)
Hermod (messenger of the gods)
Hoder (god of darkness and winter)
Idunn (goddess of spring, youth, immortality)
Kvasir (god of knowledge)
Loki (god of fire, magic)
Modi (god of battle)
Nerthus (goddess of fertility, mother earth)
Njord (god of the sea, winds)
Odin (father of the gods)
Saga (goddess of history)
Thor (god of thunder)
Tyr (god of war)
Ull (god of winter skiers)
Vidar (god of vengeance)

Roman

BOYS

Apollo (god of light, healing, music)
Aquilo (god of the north wind)
Auster (god of the south wind)
Bacchus (god of wine and fertility)
Cacus (god of fire)
Cupid (god of love)
Dis (god of the underworld)
Faunus (god of the countryside)
Favonius (god of the west wind)
Hercules (hero born with great strength)
Janus (god of doorways, beginnings)
Jupiter (god of the sky)
Mars (god of war)
Mercury (messenger god)
Neptune (god of the sea)
Pluto (god of the underworld)
Saturn (god of agriculture)
Silvanus (god of forests, groves, wild fields)
Sol (god of the sun)
Somnus (god of sleep)
Tiberinus (god of the river)
Veiovis (god of healing)
Vertumnus (patron of gardens and fruit trees)
Vulcan (god of metalwork)
Vulturnus (god of the east wind)

GIRLS

Aurora (goddess of dawn)
Bellona (goddess of war)
Carmenta (goddess of childbirth, prophesy)
Ceres (goddess of agriculture, motherly love)
Decima (goddess of childbirth)
Diana (goddess of nature, fertility, childbirth)
Flora (goddess of flowers, plants)
Fortuna (goddess of blessing, fertility)
Juno (goddess of light, birth)
Justitia (goddess of justice)
Juventas (goddess of youth)
Luna (goddess of the moon)
Matuta (goddess of the dawn)
Minerva (goddess of wisdom and arts)
Morta (goddess of death)
Necessitas (goddess of destiny)
Nona (goddess of pregnancy)
Pax (goddess of peace)
Pomona (goddess of fruit trees)
Salacia (goddess of the sea)
Salus (goddess of health, prosperity)
Tellus (goddess of the earth)
Venus (goddess of love, beauty)
Victoria (goddess of victory)

Lists ⇒ name game

Invented

BOYS	GIRLS
Blaise	Araminta
Braylon	Ayanna
Caden	Beyoncé
Coby	Brandy
Damarion	Brilliana
Danar	Christabel
Daquan	Clea
Darian	Cora
Darold	Gloria
Dewey	Janice
Dorian	Jessica
Jace	Kanisha
Jaden	Lucinda
Jaron	Malvina
Jasiah	Melba
Javon	Myra
Jaylen	Olivia
Kanye	Pamela
Kellen	Perdita
Keshawn	Stella
Markell	Thelma
Nebo	Tisa
Percival	Wendy
Tannon	Yuridiana
Villard	Zola

Unisex

Addison	Kennedy
Adrian	Kerry
Alex	Kyle
Alexis	London
Angel	Madison
Avery	Micah
Bailey	Morgan
Blair	Noel
Cameron	Parker
Carroll	Peyton
Casey	Presley
Chandler	Quinn
Chris	Reagan
Cody	Reese
Corey	Rene
Dakota	Riley
Darby	Rory
Daryl	Rowan
Dylan	Shane
Elisha	Shea
Jaime	Skylar
Jayden	Sydney
Jaylen	Taylor
Jean	Trinity
Jessie	Toby
Jordan	Tracy

Creative Spelling

BOYS

Aiden	Adan, Aedan, Aeden, Aidyn, Aydan
Antoine	Antwan
Brayden	Braden, Bradyn, Braeden, Braiden, Braydon
Caleb	Cayleb, Kaleb, Kayleb, Kaylob
Dion	Deion, Dejon, Deon, Deonne, Deyon, Dione
George	Jorge
Giovanni	Geovanni, Geovanny, Giovani, Giovonni
Isaiah	Isaia, Izaiah, Izayah
Malachi	Malachie, Malachy, Malakai, Malaki, Malechy
Reece	Reace, Rees, Reese, Rhys, Riece
Sean	Shaughan, Shaun, Shawn
Tristan	Tristen, Tristin, Triston, Trystan
Xavier	Xaviar, Xavior, Xzavier, Zavier

GIRLS

Aaliyah	Alia, Aliya, Aliyya, Aliyyah, Alya
Bailey	Bailee, Bailie, Baylee, Baylie
Caitlyn	Caetlin, Caitlin, Kaitlin, Kaitlyn, Kaitlynn
Cameron	Camren, Camryn, Kameron, Kamran
Diana	Dayana, Dianha, Dianna, Dijana, Dyana
Hailey	Hailee, Hailie, Haleigh, Haylee, Hayleigh, Hayley
Jasmine	Jasmyn, Jassmine, Jazmin, Jazmyn, Jazzmyn
Madison	Maddison, Madisen, Madissyn, Madisyn, Madyson
Makayla	Macaela, Makaila, McKayla, Micaela, Michaela, Michela, Mikaylah
Riley	Rilee, Rileigh, Rylee, Ryleigh, Ryley, Rylie
Tania	Tahnya, Taniyah, Tanja, Tannia, Tanya, Tonnya, Tonyah
Zoe	Zoey, Zoie

Last Names First

BOYS	GIRLS
Aaron	Ashley
Andrew	Avery
Barrett	Bailey
Boyd	Blair
Brady	Carey
Brennan	Casey
Brody	Cassidy
Bryson	Christie
Carson	Courtney
Carver	Darby
Chandler	Delaney
Chase	Gayle
Clay	Grace
Cody	Hadley
Coleman	Haley
Conner	Hanna
Cullen	Harper
Curtis	Hope
Dallas	Jewell
Fisher	Jordan
Gabriel	Kay
Gardner	Kelly
Gary	Kim
Glover	Kinsey
Greer	Lacey
Gunner	Lane
Hayden	Lara
Holden	Leslie
Jarrett	Lilly
Jaime	Lindsey
Jamison	Lynn
Jude	Madison
Keith	Marin
Landon	Mallory
Logan	Meredith
Lucas	Morgan
Maddox	Miley
Marcus	Paige
Mason	Piper
Merritt	Quinn
Mitchell	Reagan
Nicholas	Reese
Parker	Riley
Sampson	Rose
Spencer	Sierra
Tobias	Stacy
Travis	Talum
Wade	Taylor
Walker	Tracy
Willis	Whitley
Winfield	Whitney

Nickname Proof

BOYS	GIRLS
Aaron	Aida
Aidan	Amy
Arlo	April
Austin	Asia
Avery	Aubrey
Brayden	Autumn
Brent	Ava
Brian	Bailey
Bryce	Brooke
Carson	Carly
Chance	Casey
Chase	Celeste
Cody	Cheyenne
Cole	Daisy
Damian	Denise
Dane	Erika
Dylan	Erin
Ethan	Faith
Evan	Hailey
Gavin	Harmony
Grant	Heather
Hayden	Heaven
Henry	Heidi
Hunter	Hope
Ian	Iris
Ivan	Kara
Jake	Karen
Javier	Karla
Jesus	Keira
Jorge	Kennedy
Jose	Kiana
Killian	Kyra
Kyle	Leila
Landon	Lola
Liam	Marina
Mario	Maya
Mark	Mia
Max	Nina
Nolan	Nora
Omar	Paige
Oscar	Phoebe
Perry	Reagan
Preston	Reese
Roman	Riley
Ryan	Ruby
Sean	Scarlet
Seth	Sienna
Shane	Stella
Tanner	Summer
Trent	Tara
Wyatt	Zoe

Nicknames

BOYS

Abe	Abraham, Abram, Abel
Alec, Alex	Alexander
Andy	Anderson, Andre, Andreas, Andrew
Art	Arthur, Artis, Arturo
Ben	Benedict, Benjamin, Bennett, Benny
Bill, Billy, Will, Willie	Wilhelm, Willard, William, Willis, Wilson
Bob, Bobby, Rob	Robert, Roberto, Robin, Robinson
Charlie, Chuck	Charles, Charlton
Chris	Christian, Christopher
Cole	Colby, Colman, Nicholas
Dave	David, Davion, Davis
Denny	Dennis, Dennison, Denzel
Drew	Andrew
Ed, Eddie	Edgar, Edmund, Edward, Edwin
Eli	Elian, Elias, Elijah
Ernie	Ernest, Ernesto, Ernst
Fin, Finney	Phineas
Frank	Francis
Fred, Freddy	Alfred, Alfredo, Frederick
Gabe	Gabriel
Gene	Eugene
Gerry, Jerry	Gerald, Jeremiah, Jeremy
Greg	Gregor, Gregorio, Gregory
Hank	Henry
Harry	Harrison
Ike	Isaac
Jack	Jackson, John
Jake	Jacob, Jacobus
Jamie, Jim, Jimmy	James, Jameson
Jeff	Jeffery, Jefferson, Jeffry
Joe	Jonah Jonas, Joseph, Jovan, Jovani, Jovanny
Jude	Judah
Larry	Lawrence
Leo	Leonard, Leonardo, Leopold
Lou, Louie	Louis
Matt	Matthew, Matthias
Mel	Carmelo, Jamel, Melton, Melville, Melvin
Nat, Nate	Nathan, Nathaniel
Nick	Nicholas, Nicholson
Pat	Patrick, Patterson
Ray	Raymond, Raymundo, Rayner, Rayshawn
Rich, Rick	Ricardo, Richard
Sam, Sammy	Samson, Samuel
Shaq	Shaquille
Tad	Thaddeus
Ted, Teddy	Edmund, Edward, Theodore
Tom, Tommy	Thomas
Tony	Anthony, Anton, Antonio, Antony
Ty	Tyler, Tyrell, Tyrone, Tyshawn, Tyson
Wes	Wesley, Westley, Weston
Zach	Zachariah, Zacharias, Zachary

Nicknames

GIRLS

Nickname	Full Name(s)
Abbie	Abigail
Addie	Addison, Adela, Adelaide, Adeline
Alex	Alexa, Alexandra, Alexandria, Alexis
Allie, Ali	Alana, Alice, Alisa, Allison, Alyssa
Angie	Angel, Angela, Angelica, Angelina, Angelique
Annie	Angela, Angelica, Angelina, Ann, Anna, Annabella, Annabelle, Anne, Annette, Annika
Becca, Becky, Reba	Rebecca
Bella	Anabella, Arabella, Isabella, Izabella
Belle	Isabel, Isobel
Beth, Betsy, Betty, Liz, Lizzie	Elisabeth, Elizabeth
Bree	Breanna, Brianna, Brianne
Brit	Brittney, Brittany
Cassie	Cassandra, Cassidy, Catherine
Cate, Caty	Caitlin, Caitlyn, Catherine, Cathleen
Chris, Chrissy	Christa, Christiane, Christina, Christine, Cristal
Cindy	Cynthia, Lucinda
Elle, Ellie	Eleanor, Elena, Eleni, Elenora, Ella
Emmie, Emmy	Emma, Emmaline, Emily
Ginny	Genevieve, Ginger, Virginia
Gracie	Grace, Graciela
Hannah	Johanna
Hattie	Harriet, Henrietta
Jan	Janelle, Janessa, Janet, Janice, Janine
Jen, Jenny	Jenna, Jennifer
Jess, Jessie	Jessalyn, Jessica
Kate, Katie, Kay	Kaitlin, Katelyn, Katharine, Katherine, Kathleen
Laurie, Lori	Laura, Laurel, Lauren, Lorelei, Lorna
Lexie	Alexa, Alexis
Lisa	Melissa
Liv	Livia, Olivia, Olive
Lucy	Lucinda
Maddie	Madeline, Madison, Madonna
Maggie, Meg, Peg, Peggy	Margaret
Manda, Mandy	Amanda
Meg, Meggie	Megan
Mel	Melinda, Melanie, Melissa, Melody
Millie	Amelia, Emily, Mildred, Millicent
Nicky, Nikki	Nicola, Nicole
Pam, Pammie	Pamela
Pat, Patsy, Patty	Patience, Patrice, Patricia
Penny	Penelope
Sam, Sammie	Samantha
Sandy	Cassandra, Sandra
Sue, Susie	Susan, Suzannah, Suzanne, Suzette
Tammie, Tammy	Tamara, Tamar, Tamika, Tamsin
Tina	Christina
Toni	Antoinette, Antonia, Tonya
Tori	Victoria
Tricia, Trish	Beatrice, Patrice, Patricia
Val	Valencia, Valentina, Valeria, Valerie, Valery

Lists ⇒ name game

One Syllable

BOYS	GIRLS
Bill	Anne
Blake	Belle
Brett	Beth
Brice	Blair
Brock	Blythe
Cade	Brooke
Carl	Brynn
Chase	Claire
Chris	Dawn
Cole	Elle
Drake	Eve
Drew	Faith
Gage	Faye
Graham	Flor
Grant	Gayle
Heath	Grace
Jace	Hope
Jack	Jade
Jake	Jean
Jess	Joan
Joel	Joy
Kai	Joyce
Kyle	Kate
Lance	Laine
Mark	Leigh
Max	Lise
Miles	Lynn
Paul	Luz
Pierce	May
Prince	Nell
Quinn	Paige
Reid	Pearl
Rhett	Reese
Sam	Rose
Saul	Ruth
Sean	Saige
Seth	Scout
Trent	Shay
Troy	Skye
Ty	Spring
Wade	Tess

Seoul, South Korea, is the largest city in the world with a one-syllable name.

Two Syllables

BOYS	GIRLS
Aaron	Abby
Andrew	Allie
Barrett	Angie
Brady	Ashley
Brandon	Bailey
Brennan	Brandy
Brody	Carly
Bryson	Casey
Carson	Cheyenne
Carver	Christie
Chandler	Courtney
Cody	Daisy
Coleman	Darby
Colton	Dulce
Conner	Hadley
Cullen	Haley
Curtis	Hanna
Dallas	Harper
Dylan	Jewell
Fisher	Joelle
Gardner	Jordan
Gary	Julie
Glover	Kathy
Gunner	Kelly
Hayden	Kinsey
Holden	Kristen
Jaime	Lacey
Jarrett	Lara
Justin	Leslie
Kevin	Lilly
Landon	Lindsey
Liam	Lynnette
Logan	Maggie
Lucas	Marie
Maddox	Marin
Marcus	Michelle
Mason	Mindy
Merritt	Miley
Mitchell	Morgan
Pablo	Nicole
Parker	Noel
Quincy	Piper
Ryan	Reagan
Sampson	Renee
Spencer	Riley
Travis	Stacy
Tyson	Tatum
Walker	Taylor
Willis	Tracy
Winfield	Whitley
Xander	Whitney

Place Names

Abilene (city in Texas)
Aden (city in Yemen)
Africa (continent)
Ailsa (from Ailsa Craig, a Scottish island)
Ainsley (hotel in the United Kingdom)
Arcadia (mountainous region in Greece)
Arizona (U.S. state)
Arran (Scottish island)
Asia (the largest continent)
Barrie (Barry Islands, Wales)
Brie (region in France)
Capri (Italian island)
Carinthia (region in southern Austria)
Carmel (city in California, Indiana, and
    New York)
Carson (Carson City is the capital
    of Nevada)
China (located in East Asia)
Cimarron (city in western Kansas and a river
    in the U.S.)
Clodagh (river in Tipperary, Ireland)
Courtney (region in France)
Dacia (Roman province now called Romania)
Dakota (North and South Dakota)
Dallas (city in Texas)
Danna (biblical place)
Delancey (street in New York)
Denver (city in Colorado)
Deora (small town in Colorado)
Florence (city in Italy)
Gaetana (form of Gaeta, a region in
    southern Italy)
Galila (form of the biblical Galilee)
Geneva (city in Switzerland)
Harmony (city in California, Florida,
    and Minnesota)
Hibernia (Roman Latin name for Ireland)
Indiana (U.S. state)
Iona (island in the Hebrides)
Ionia (Ionian Sea and the Ionian Islands
    off Greece)
Ireland (second largest island in Europe)
Isla (from Isla Vista, California)
Jamaica (island in the West Indies)
Janoah (two biblical cities)
Jordan (country in the Middle East)
Kinneret (freshwater lake in northeast Israel)
Langley (Air Force base in Virginia)
Lantana (county in Florida)
Loire (river in France)
Lome (located on the Gulf of Guinea)
London (capital of the United Kingdom)

Lourdes (region in southern France)
Madeira (group of volcanic islands in the
    North Atlantic)
Madison (capital of Wisconsin)
Mallorca (island off Spain in
    the Mediterranean)
Marsala (city in Sicily)
Marseilles (city in France)
Martinique (West Indies island)
Meadow (a flat grassland)
Mecca (holy city of Islam)
Menemsha (town in Martha's Vineyard)
Messina (town in Sicily)
Montana (U.S. state)
Nairobi (capital of Kenya in East Africa)
Niagara (waterfall on the border between
    the U.S. and Canada)
Nevada (U.S. state)
Nicosia (capital city of Cyprus)
Odessa (fourth largest city in Ukraine)
Ophira (international airport in Egypt)
Orinda (town in California)
Osaka (third largest city in Japan)
Paris (capital of France)
Petaluma (town in northern California)
Petra (archaeological site in Jordan)
Provence (region in southeastern France)
Quintana (from Quintana Roo, a state
    in Mexico)
Radnor (Township in Pennsylvania)
Ravenna (city in Italy)
Regina (city in Canada)
Rochelle (taken from LaRochelle, a French
    fishing port)
Romney (oldest town in West Virginia)
Sahara (desert in north Africa)
Salamanca (city in western Spain)
Santiago (capital of Chile)
Sedona (city in Arizona)
Shannon (longest river in Ireland)
Skye (island in Scotland)
Sicily (island off Italy)
Siena (city in Tuscany)
Sitka (second oldest city in Alaska)
Sonora (state in north western Mexico)
Sydney (city in Australia)
Tiberia (from the Tiber River in Rome)
Tyne (English river)
Tyrol (Austrian alpine region)
Tyrone (county in Northern Ireland)
Valencia (city on the coast of Spain)
Valetta (city on the island of Malta)

Lists ⇨ by the decade

Most Popular Names from 1990–1999

BOYS		GIRLS	
1.	Michael	1.	Jessica
2.	Christopher	2.	Ashley
3.	Matthew	3.	Emily
4.	Joshua	4.	Sarah
5.	Jacob	5.	Samantha
6.	Nicholas	6.	Amanda
7.	Andrew	7.	Brittany
8.	Daniel	8.	Elizabeth
9.	Tyler	9.	Taylor
10.	Joseph	10.	Megan
11.	Brandon	11.	Hannah
12.	David	12.	Kayla
13.	James	13.	Lauren
14.	Ryan	14.	Stephanie
15.	John	15.	Rachel
16.	Zachary	16.	Jennifer
17.	Justin	17.	Nicole
18.	William	18.	Alexis
19.	Anthony	19.	Victoria
20.	Robert	20.	Amber

Most Popular Names from 1970–1979

BOYS		GIRLS	
1.	Michael	1.	Jennifer
2.	Christopher	2.	Amy
3.	Jason	3.	Melissa
4.	David	4.	Michelle
5.	James	5.	Kimberly
6.	John	6.	Lisa
7.	Robert	7.	Angela
8.	Brian	8.	Heather
9.	William	9.	Stephanie
10.	Matthew	10.	Nicole
11.	Joseph	11.	Jessica
12.	Daniel	12.	Elizabeth
13.	Kevin	13.	Rebecca
14.	Eric	14.	Kelly
15.	Richard	15.	Mary
16.	Jeffrey	16.	Christina
17.	Scott	17.	Amanda
18.	Mark	18.	Julie
19.	Steven	19.	Sarah
20.	Thomas	20.	Laura

Most Popular Names from 1980–1989

BOYS		GIRLS	
1.	Michael	1.	Jessica
2.	Christopher	2.	Jennifer
3.	Matthew	3.	Amanda
4.	Joshua	4.	Ashley
5.	David	5.	Sarah
6.	James	6.	Stephanie
7.	Daniel	7.	Melissa
8.	Robert	8.	Nicole
9.	John	9.	Elizabeth
10.	Joseph	10.	Heather
11.	Jason	11.	Tiffany
12.	Justin	12.	Michelle
13.	Andrew	13.	Amber
14.	Ryan	14.	Megan
15.	William	15.	Amy
16.	Brian	16.	Rachel
17.	Brandon	17.	Kimberly
18.	Jonathan	18.	Christina
19.	Nicholas	19.	Lauren
20.	Anthony	20.	Crystal

Most Popular Names from 1960–1969

BOYS		GIRLS	
1.	Michael	1.	Lisa
2.	David	2.	Mary
3.	John	3.	Susan
4.	James	4.	Karen
5.	Robert	5.	Kimberly
6.	Mark	6.	Patricia
7.	William	7.	Linda
8.	Richard	8.	Donna
9.	Thomas	9.	Michelle
10.	Jeffrey	10.	Cynthia
11.	Steven	11.	Sandra
12.	Joseph	12.	Deborah
13.	Timothy	13.	Tammy
14.	Kevin	14.	Pamela
15.	Scott	15.	Lori
16.	Brian	16.	Laura
17.	Charles	17.	Elizabeth
18.	Paul	18.	Julie
19.	Daniel	19.	Brenda
20.	Christopher	20.	Jennifer

Most Popular Names from 1950–1959

BOYS	GIRLS
1. James	1. Mary
2. Michael	2. Linda
3. Robert	3. Patricia
4. John	4. Susan
5. David	5. Deborah
6. William	6. Barbara
7. Richard	7. Debra
8. Thomas	8. Karen
9. Mark	9. Nancy
10. Charles	10. Donna
11. Steven	11. Cynthia
12. Gary	12. Sandra
13. Joseph	13. Pamela
14. Donald	14. Sharon
15. Ronald	15. Kathleen
16. Kenneth	16. Carol
17. Paul	17. Diane
18. Larry	18. Brenda
19. Daniel	19. Cheryl
20. Stephen	20. Janet

Most Popular Names from 1930–1939

BOYS	GIRLS
1. Robert	1. Mary
2. James	2. Betty
3. John	3. Barbara
4. William	4. Shirley
5. Richard	5. Patricia
6. Charles	6. Dorothy
7. Donald	7. Joan
8. George	8. Margaret
9. Thomas	9. Nancy
10. Joseph	10. Helen
11. David	11. Carol
12. Edward	12. Joyce
13. Ronald	13. Doris
14. Paul	14. Ruth
15. Kenneth	15. Virginia
16. Frank	16. Marilyn
17. Raymond	17. Elizabeth
18. Jack	18. Jean
19. Harold	19. Frances
20. Billy	20. Beverly

Most Popular Names from 1940–1949

BOYS	GIRLS
1. James	1. Mary
2. Robert	2. Linda
3. John	3. Barbara
4. William	4. Patricia
5. Richard	5. Carol
6. David	6. Sandra
7. Charles	7. Nancy
8. Thomas	8. Sharon
9. Michael	9. Judith
10. Ronald	10. Susan
11. Larry	11. Betty
12. Donald	12. Carolyn
13. Joseph	13. Margaret
14. Gary	14. Shirley
15. George	15. Judy
16. Kenneth	16. Karen
17. Paul	17. Donna
18. Edward	18. Kathleen
19. Jerry	19. Joyce
20. Dennis	20. Dorothy

Most Popular Names from 1920–1929

BOYS	GIRLS
1. Robert	1. Mary
2. John	2. Dorothy
3. James	3. Helen
4. William	4. Betty
5. Charles	5. Margaret
6. George	6. Ruth
7. Joseph	7. Virginia
8. Richard	8. Doris
9. Edward	9. Mildred
10. Donald	10. Frances
11. Thomas	11. Elizabeth
12. Frank	12. Evelyn
13. Harold	13. Anna
14. Paul	14. Marie
15. Raymond	15. Alice
16. Walter	16. Jean
17. Jack	17. Shirley
18. Henry	18. Barbara
19. Kenneth	19. Irene
20. Arthur	20. Marjorie

Lists ⇒ by the decade

Most Popular Names from 1910–1919

BOYS		GIRLS	
1.	John	1.	Mary
2.	William	2.	Helen
3.	James	3.	Dorothy
4.	Robert	4.	Margaret
5.	Joseph	5.	Ruth
6.	George	6.	Mildred
7.	Charles	7.	Anna
8.	Edward	8.	Elizabeth
9.	Frank	9.	Frances
10.	Thomas	10.	Virginia
11.	Walter	11.	Marie
12.	Harold	12.	Evelyn
13.	Henry	13.	Alice
14.	Paul	14.	Florence
15.	Richard	15.	Lillian
16.	Raymond	16.	Rose
17.	Albert	17.	Irene
18.	Arthur	18.	Louise
19.	Harry	19.	Edna
20.	Donald	20.	Catherine

Most Popular Names from 1890–1899

BOYS		GIRLS	
1.	John	1.	Mary
2.	William	2.	Anna
3.	James	3.	Margaret
4.	George	4.	Helen
5.	Charles	5.	Elizabeth
6.	Joseph	6.	Ruth
7.	Frank	7.	Florence
8.	Robert	8.	Ethel
9.	Edward	9.	Emma
10.	Henry	10.	Marie
11.	Harry	11.	Clara
12.	Thomas	12.	Bertha
13.	Walter	13.	Minnie
14.	Arthur	14.	Bessie
15.	Fred	15.	Alice
16.	Albert	16.	Lillian
17.	Clarence	17.	Edna
18.	Willie	18.	Grace
19.	Roy	19.	Annie
20.	Louis	20.	Mabel

Most Popular Names from 1900–1909

BOYS		GIRLS	
1.	John	1.	Mary
2.	William	2.	Helen
3.	James	3.	Margaret
4.	George	4.	Anna
5.	Charles	5.	Ruth
6.	Robert	6.	Elizabeth
7.	Joseph	7.	Dorothy
8.	Frank	8.	Marie
9.	Edward	9.	Florence
10.	Thomas	10.	Mildred
11.	Henry	11.	Alice
12.	Walter	12.	Ethel
13.	Harry	13.	Lillian
14.	Willie	14.	Gladys
15.	Arthur	15.	Edna
16.	Albert	16.	Frances
17.	Clarence	17.	Rose
18.	Fred	18.	Annie
19.	Harold	19.	Grace
20.	Paul	20.	Bertha

Most Popular Names from 1880–1889

BOYS		GIRLS	
1.	John	1.	Mary
2.	William	2.	Anna
3.	James	3.	Emma
4.	George	4.	Elizabeth
5.	Charles	5.	Margaret
6.	Frank	6.	Minnie
7.	Joseph	7.	Ida
8.	Henry	8.	Bertha
9.	Robert	9.	Clara
10.	Thomas	10.	Alice
11.	Edward	11.	Annie
12.	Harry	12.	Florence
13.	Walter	13.	Bessie
14.	Arthur	14.	Grace
15.	Fred	15.	Ethel
16.	Albert	16.	Sarah
17.	Samuel	17.	Ella
18.	Clarence	18.	Martha
19.	Louis	19.	Nellie
20.	David	20.	Mabel

Most Popular Twins' Names in 2006

1. Jacob, Joshua
2. Matthew, Michael
3. Daniel, David
4. Ella, Emma
5. Isaac, Isaiah
6. Madison, Morgan
7. Landon, Logan
8. Taylor, Tyler
9. Brandon, Bryan
10. Christian, Christopher
11. Gabriella, Isabella
12. Andrew, Matthew
13. Faith, Hope
14. Ethan, Evan
15. Jacob, Joseph
16. Joseph, Joshua
17. Mackenzie, Madison
18. Alexander, Benjamin
19. Hailey, Hannah
20. Madison, Matthew
21. Caleb, Joshua
22. Emily, Ethan
23. Isabella, Sophia
24. Joshua, Matthew
25. Nathan, Nicholas
26. Andrew, Anthony
27. Jayden, Jordan
28. Madison, Mason
29. Elijah, Isaiah
30. Jeremiah, Joshua
31. Alexander, Nicholas
32. Emma, Ethan
33. Olivia, Sophia
34. Ava, Emma
35. Hayden, Hunter
36. Logan, Luke
37. Natalie, Nathan
38. Christopher, Nicholas
39. Haley, Hannah
40. Jacob, Zachary
41. John, William
42. Nathan, Noah
43. Benjamin, Samuel
44. James, John
45. Jordan, Justin
46. Megan, Morgan
47. Alexander, Anthony
48. Isabella, Olivia
49. Jacob, Jordan
50. Joseph, Michael
51. Nicholas, Noah
52. Alexander, Andrew
53. Alexander, Christopher
54. Andrew, Jacob
55. Christopher, Matthew
56. Elijah, Ethan
57. Jacob, Samuel
58. James, Joseph
59. Matthew, Ryan
60. Ava, Olivia
61. Emma, Grace
62. Emma, Hannah
63. Jacob, Matthew
64. Jaden, Jordan
65. Jason, Justin
66. Jordan, Joshua
67. Makayla, Makenzie
68. Zachary, Zoe
69. Abigail, Emily
70. Andrew, William
71. Benjamin, Jacob
72. Emma, Olivia
73. Ethan, Nathan
74. Gabriel, Michael
75. Hannah, Sarah
76. Jacob, Justin
77. Jacob, Tyler
78. Jennifer, Jessica
79. Jonathan, Joshua
80. Jose, Juan
81. Mark, Matthew
82. Natalie, Nicole
83. Samuel, Sophia
84. Abigail, Emma
85. Alexander, William
86. Anna, Emma
87. Ashley, Emily
88. Ava, Sophia
89. Cameron, Christian
90. Emily, Sarah
91. Emma, Jacob
92. Grace, Hannah
93. Grace, Olivia
94. Jayden, Jaylen
95. Joseph, Nicholas
96. Joshua, Zachary
97. Logan, Lucas
98. Madison, Megan
99. Parker, Preston
100. Robert, William

resources

These resources were used to compile the Names Around the Globe lists.

Australia, New South Wales:
Birth, Death and Marriage top 50 baby name list is reproduced with the permission of the NSW Registry of Births Deaths & Marriages for and on behalf of the Crown in and for the State of New South Wales. It is subject to Crown copyright.
www.bdm.nsw.gov.au/births/popularBabyNames.htm

Australia, Northern Territory:
www.nt.gov.au/justice/graphpages/bdm/popnames.shtml

Australia, South:
www.ocba.sa.gov.au/bdm/

Austria:
www.statistik.at/fachbereich_03/bevoelkerung_vornamen.shtml

Belgium:
statbel.fgov.be/figures/d22a_nl.asp

Brussels:
statbel.fgov.be/figures/d22a_nl.asp?r=4

Canada, British Columbia:
vs.gov.bc.ca/babynames/baby2006.html#bnames
Copyright © 2007, Province of British Columbia

Canada, Nova Scotia:
www.gov.ns.ca/snsmr/vstat/intstat.asp

Canada, Quebec:
www.rrq.gouv.qc.ca/Interactif/PR2I121_Prenoms/PR2I121_Prenoms/PR2SPrenoms.
aspx?langue=frthttp://www.rrq.gouv.qc.ca/Interactif/PR2I121_Prenoms/PR2I121_Prenoms/PR2SPrenoms.aspx?langue=fr

Chile:
www.registrocivil.cl/Servicios/Estadisticas/Archivos/NombresComunes/2005.html

Czech Republic:
www.czso.cz/csu/redakce.nsf/i/nejcastejsi_jmena_deti_v_lednu_2005
© Český statistický úřad, 2007

Denmark:
dst.dk/Statistik/Navne/bestemt_aar/20061.aspx

England/Wales:
www.statistics.gov.uk/cci/nugget.asp?id=184
General Register Office for England and Wales

Finland:
www.vaestorekisterikeskus.fi/vrk/home.nsf/suomi/nimet

France:
Prenoms.com

Germany:
gfds.de/index.php?id=63

Iceland:
www.statice.is/?PageID=846

Ireland:
Published by the Central Statistics Office, Ireland and on the web at www.cso.ie

Ireland, Northern:
www.nisra.gov.uk/publications/default.asp?cmsid=1&cms=publications&pagesize=10&searchterm=&pageoffset=1&release=&pubtype=2

Italy:
www.istat.it/salastampa/comunicati/non_calendario/20060801_00/testointegrale.pdf

Lithuania:
www.stat.gov.lt/lt/pages/view/?id=1625&print=1&PHPSESSID=3c35b83663ef1ae5a0d0284af09c622f&PHPSESSID=3c35b83663ef1ae5a0d0284af09c622f

Malta:
www.nso.gov.mt/statdoc/document_file.aspx?id=1697

Netherlands:
www.svb.nl/internet/nl/regelingen/kinderbijslag/kindernamen/index.jsp

New Zealand:
www.dia.govt.nz/diawebsite.nsf/wpg_URL/Services-Births-Deaths-and-Marriages-Most-Popular-First-Names?OpenDocument

Norway:
www.ssb.no/english/subjects/00/navn_en/

Poland:
Poland Statistical Office

Republic of Slovenia:
www.stat.si/eng/novica_prikazi.aspx?ID=280

Scotland:
www.gro-scotland.gov.uk/statistics/library/pernames/popular-forenames-in-scotland-2005/index.html

Spain:
www.ine.es/en/daco/daco42/mnp/nomnac_en.htm

Sweden:
www.scb.se/templates/Product___30895.asp

Switzerland:
www.bfs.admin.ch/bfs/portal/de/index/themen/01/02/blank/dos/prenoms/01.html

Turkey:
www.nvi.gov.tr/11,Ana_Sayfa_Isim_Istatistikleri_Sun.html

Wales:
www.statistics.gov.uk/cci/nugget.asp?id=184

Ai ⇒ index

371

Ch ⇒ index

379

Da ⇨ index

381

Do ⇨ index

Es ⇒ index

Isaak, 250
Isabel, 5, 100, 120, 133, 238, 250,
   320, 327, 351, 361
Isabela, 133
Isabele, 133
Isabell, 133
Isabella, 5, 28, 30, 31, 33, 34, 45,
   67, 100, 133, 251, 314, 317, 319,
   320, 324, 327, 329, 341, 350,
   352, 361, 367
Isabelle, 5, 61, 62, 133, 314, 315,
   320, 327, 334
Isac, 250
Isadora, 251
Isai, 251
Isaia, 251, 358
Isaiah, 5, 250, 251, 277, 329, 331,
   336, 341, 351, 358, 367
Isaias, 251
Isak, 250, 325, 327
Isandro, 133
Isao, 342
Isay, 251
Isbel, 133
Isebella, 133
Iser, 250, 251
Isha, 348
Ishmael, 198, 251, 283
Ishmeil, 251
Isiah, 206, 251, 254, 260, 342
Isidora, 133, 134, 251, 318
Isidore, 134, 250
Isidoro, 133, 134
Isis, 10, 134, 356
Isla, 79, 134, 251, 326, 363
Ismael, 251, 327
Ismaela, 134
Ismail, 251
Isobel, 133, 251, 361
Isobelle, 133
Isolde, 134, 251, 306
Israel, 20, 141, 151, 183, 198, 206,
   214, 216, 227, 235, 244, 250,
   251, 253, 259, 261, 280, 297,
   300, 354, 363
Isreal, 251
Issa, 105, 112, 161
Issac, 250
Issiah, 277
Issur, 251
Issy, 134
Istar, 123
Itcel, 134
Itchel, 134
Itesel, 134
Ithamar, 250
Ithiel, 250
Itsel, 134
Itssel, 134
Itz, 134
Itza, 134, 196
Itzak, 134
Itzallana, 134
Itzayana, 134
Itzel, 134
Itzell, 134
Itzjac, 134
Itztli, 134
Iv, 85, 134, 251
Iva, 134, 251
Ivalyn, 134
Ivan, 134, 238, 250, 251, 258, 261,
   308, 323, 327, 343, 352, 359

Ivana, 132
Ivanna, 251
Ivar, 343
Ivee, 134
Ivett, 197
Ivette, 197
Ivey, 134
Ivia, 134
Ivianna, 134
Ivica, 251
Ivie, 134
Ivory, 263, 344, 347
Ivree, 134
Ivy, 79, 134, 344
Ivyanne, 134
Ivye, 134
Ivyie, 134
Iwan, 284
Ixchel, 134
Iyana, 99, 132
Iyanla, 347
Iyanna, 99
Izaac, 250, 348
Izaak, 250
Izabela, 133, 325
Izabele, 133
Izabella, 133, 361
Izabelle, 133
Izaiah, 251, 358
Izak, 250
Izanami, 357
Izayah, 251, 358
Izrael, 251
Izreal, 251
Izzie, 133
Izzy, 133, 251
J. C., 134
Jaakko, 320
Jabez, 253, 255
Jabin, 253
Jac, 252
Jacalynn, 134
Jace, 198, 252, 253, 358, 362
Jacelyn, 134, 135
Jacen, 254
Jacey, 134, 252, 253
Jaci, 134, 252
Jacie, 134, 140
Jacinda, 134
Jacine, 134
Jack, 5, 14, 27, 48, 49, 59, 134, 209,
   228, 239, 251, 253, 258, 271,
   310, 314, 315, 317, 320, 322, 324,
   326, 328, 330, 332, 337, 339,
   341, 342, 346, 349, 351, 353,
   360, 362, 365
Jackelyn, 134
Jacketta, 134
Jackie, 134, 165, 252, 253, 342, 343
Jacklyn, 252
Jacklynne, 134
Jackson, 5, 22, 30, 49, 57, 70, 134,
   136, 144, 200, 208, 252, 253,
   256, 257, 278, 286, 287, 289, 297,
   314, 315, 329, 331, 335, 338, 340,
   342, 346, 352, 354, 355, 360
Jacksyn, 252
Jaclyn, 17, 34, 134, 146
Jacob, 5, 8, 134, 151, 162, 174, 175,
   206, 208, 220, 251, 253, 255,
   259, 261, 270, 295, 298, 300,
   312, 314, 315, 317, 320, 324, 328,
   341, 360, 364, 367

Jacoba, 252
Jacobe, 252
Jacobina, 252
Jacobus, 252, 253, 298, 360
Jacoby, 252
Jacomus, 252, 253
Jacqualine, 134
Jacqualyn, 134
Jacquel, 134
Jacqueline, 59, 134, 252, 351
Jacquella, 134
Jacquelle, 134
Jacquelyn, 134
Jacquenetta, 134
Jacques, 134, 260, 349, 351
Jacquetta, 252
Jacquette, 134
Jacqui, 134
Jacquine, 134
Jacson, 252
Jaculine, 134
Jacy, 348
Jad, 134
Jada, 5, 134, 137, 252, 255, 309,
   335
Jadaryl, 134
Jade, 134, 135, 137, 252, 255, 309,
   314, 316, 318, 321, 323, 344, 362
Jadeana, 134
Jadeann, 137
Jadee, 134
Jaden, 5, 23, 103, 118, 134, 137, 145,
   214, 244, 252, 254, 255, 358,
   367
Jader, 134
Jadira, 134, 196
Jadira, 134, 196
Jadon, 137, 252, 255, 345, 348
Jadot, 134
Jadra, 134
Jadrienne, 134
Jadvyga, 323
Jadyn, 135, 137, 252, 255
Jae, 135, 137, 255
Jaeda, 134
Jaeden, 137, 252, 255
Jaedon, 137, 252, 255
Jael, 134, 135, 253
Jaelen, 135
Jaelyn, 134, 135, 137
Jaelynn, 135
Jaeyln, 134
Jahaira, 196
Jahara, 196
Jahleel, 253
Jahmal, 253
Jai, 255
Jaice, 252
Jaida, 134, 135
Jaide, 134
Jaiden, 137, 252, 253, 255, 262
Jaidon, 137, 252, 255
Jaidyn, 137, 252
Jailyn, 135, 137
Jaime, 64, 135, 174, 252, 253, 258,
   297, 327, 358, 359, 362
Jaimee, 135, 252
Jaimey, 135, 252
Jaimi, 135
Jaimie, 135, 252
Jaimison, 253
Jaimy, 135
Jaina, 134, 135

Jaine, 136
Jair, 253, 312
Jaira, 253
Jairo, 253
Jairus, 253, 312
Jaisen, 254
Jaison, 254
Jak, 252
Jaka, 326
Jakayla, 134, 135
Jake, 135, 252, 253, 255, 314, 315,
   320, 322, 324, 326, 328, 342,
   359, 360, 362
Jakeem, 348
Jakira, 196
Jaklyn, 134, 137
Jakub, 44, 252, 315, 325, 327
Jakson, 252
Jakub, 319, 325
Jala, 134
Jalani, 135
Jalen, 23, 134, 135, 252, 255
Jalena, 134
Jalene, 255
Jalia, 135
Jaliah, 135
Jalila, 134, 135
Jaline, 137
Jalissa, 142, 347
Jaliya, 135
Jaliyah, 84, 93, 135, 137, 143
Jalon, 255
Jalyn, 135
Jalynn, 135
Jamaal, 135, 253
Jamael, 253
Jamahl, 253
Jamaica, 266, 363
Jamal, 253, 347, 348
Jamall, 253
Jamar, 253, 283
Jamarcus, 253, 273
Jamari, 253
Jamarion, 224, 253, 283
Jamee, 135
Jamel, 360
Jamelia, 253
Jamell, 253
James, 5, 15, 18, 34, 47, 48, 55, 57,
   64, 67, 73, 75, 78, 100, 104, 112,
   116, 118, 124, 125, 133, 135, 139,
   143, 157, 210, 212, 215, 222, 223,
   227, 228, 231, 233, 235, 239,
   241, 243, 248, 250, 252, 253,
   257, 275, 284, 292, 293, 297,
   298, 302, 314, 315, 317, 320,
   322, 324, 326, 328, 343, 345,
   349, 351, 355, 360, 364, 367
Jamesina, 253
Jameson, 253, 257, 360
Jametta, 253
Jamey, 135
Jami, 135
Jamia, 135, 136
Jamie, 58, 135, 252, 253, 255, 257,
   298, 320, 322, 324, 326, 346,
   360
Jamiel, 135
Jamieson, 253
Jamila, 104, 253, 257
Jamilah, 348
Jamille, 104, 253
Jamin, 253

Jerrard, 256
Jerrauld, 256
Jerred, 254
Jerrelle, 256
Jerren, 254
Jerrett, 254
Jerri, 256, 257
Jerrick, 230
Jerrid, 254
Jerrie, 256
Jerrin, 254
Jerrod, 254
Jerron, 254
Jerrone, 256
Jerrot, 254
Jerry, 23, 28, 48, 52, 58, 242, 254, 256, 257, 342, 346, 349, 355, 360, 365
Jerry R., 342
Jervey, 254
Jervis, 254
Jesher, 261
Jesiah, 254
Jesica, 138
Jesous, 257
Jespar, 254
Jesper, 254
Jess, 138, 257, 278, 361, 362
Jessa, 138
Jessalyn, 138, 196, 257, 361
Jessamae, 138
Jessamine, 137, 138, 256, 257
Jessana, 138
Jessandra, 138
Jesse, 56, 57, 138, 221, 257, 314, 320, 323, 343, 345
Jessey, 257
Jessi, 138
Jessiah, 257
Jessica, 5, 49, 52, 67, 125, 138, 180, 257, 314, 315, 317, 320, 322, 324, 326, 328, 330, 345, 346, 349, 350, 354, 358, 361, 364, 367
Jessie, 55, 57, 75, 126, 138, 140, 257, 358, 361
Jessika, 138
Jesslyn, 138
Jessy, 138, 257
Jessye, 138
Jesus, 5, 94, 108, 157, 158, 162, 190, 193, 223, 237, 250, 253, 257, 261, 286, 296, 300, 304, 311, 312, 327, 329, 345, 347, 359
Jesusa, 257, 260
Jet, 257
Jethro, 257
Jett, 69, 257
Jetta, 257
Jette, 257
Jevan, 255
Jevon, 231, 255, 261
Jewel, 45, 135, 138, 139, 141, 142, 173
Jewell, 138, 359, 362
Jewelle, 138
Jiana, 127
Jiles, 257
Jilian, 139, 141
Jiliann, 139
Jilianna, 139
Jilianne, 139
Jilisa, 139
Jill, 17, 138, 139, 141

Jillana, 139
Jillayne, 139
Jillian, 37, 127, 137, 139, 142, 151, 153, 226
Jilliann, 139
Jillianne, 127
Jillion, 139
Jillissa, 139
Jillyn, 139
Jilly, 141
Jim, 34, 49, 198, 212, 223, 228, 253, 257, 270, 342, 343, 346, 354, 355, 360
Jimae, 139
Jimella, 139
Jimena, 139, 195
Jimenah, 139
Jimenez, 139, 354
Jimi, 139, 320, 355
Jimina, 139
Jiminah, 139
Jimisha, 139
Jimiyah, 139
Jimmee, 257
Jimmey, 257
Jimmie, 257, 343
Jimmy, 111, 217, 225, 233, 252, 253, 257, 343, 346, 360
Jin, 347
Jinia, 136
Jinny, 257
Jinya, 136
Jiselle, 128, 138
Jo, 139, 140, 175, 258, 260, 354
Jo Dee, 354
Joacheim, 258
Joachim, 258, 260, 345
Joahnna, 139
Joakim, 258
Joan, 27, 65, 112, 139, 151, 178, 258, 352, 354, 362, 365
Joana, 139, 251, 258
Joananna, 139
Joandra, 92, 139
Joanel, 139
Joanelle, 139
Joann, 139
Joanna, 107, 139, 258, 325, 345, 351, 352
Joannah, 139
Joannanette, 139
Joanne, 34, 139, 258
Joannie, 139
Joaquim, 223, 258
Joaquima, 258
Joaquin, 32, 34, 253, 257, 258, 283, 286, 318
Joash, 260, 261
Job, 50, 258
Jobeth, 258
Jocelin, 139
Joceline, 139
Jocelyn, 5, 13, 62, 139, 196
Jocelyne, 139
Jock, 252
Jodelle, 141
Jodene, 141
Jodie, 31, 346
Jody, 141, 257, 258
Joe, 14, 32, 44, 47, 49, 52, 69, 78, 258, 260, 342, 343, 346, 349, 354, 360
Joeanna, 139

Joel, 87, 138, 140, 209, 220, 258, 260, 320, 327, 328, 351, 354, 362
Joella, 258
Joelle, 78, 140, 258, 348
Joellen, 258
Joellyn, 135
Joely, 29, 43, 140
Joesiah, 260
Joetta, 258
Joey, 47, 145, 258, 260, 344
Jogoda, 325
Johan, 34, 139, 258
Johana, 139
Johann, 129, 255, 258, 261, 298
Jóhann, 321
Johanna, 60, 130, 131, 139, 255, 258, 321, 361
Jóhanna, 321
Johannah, 139
Johanne, 139, 258, 315, 319, 325
Johannes, 136, 139, 255, 258, 261, 315, 325
Johar, 196
John, 5, 8, 17, 27, 30, 37, 39, 41, 45, 47, 49, 52, 62, 69, 84, 100, 118, 120, 127, 136, 139, 140, 147, 148, 177, 200, 215, 217, 219, 222, 224, 230, 238, 244, 250, 253, 255, 257, 261, 264, 279, 280, 282, 284, 286, 287, 289, 290, 295, 297, 299, 301, 308, 310, 312, 322, 326, 329, 343, 345, 346, 349, 355, 360, 364, 367
Johnathan, 259
Johnathon, 259
Johnie, 259
Johnna, 139
Johnnie, 31, 62, 139, 259
Johnny, 31, 47, 74, 120, 127, 216, 217, 225, 244, 257, 259, 342, 343, 346, 354
Johnpaul, 259
Johnson, 17, 55, 100, 163, 208, 250, 252, 256, 258, 278, 308, 342, 343, 346, 352, 353
Johny, 259
Joi, 140
Joice, 141
Joie, 140, 141
JoJo, 258
Jolan, 140
Jolanda, 139
Jolee, 140
Joleigh, 140
Jolene, 137, 139, 259
Joley, 140
Joli, 140
Jolie, 17, 32, 34, 54, 73, 76, 93, 127, 138, 140, 150, 184, 197, 259, 272, 285, 346
Joliet, 140
Jolietta, 140
Joline, 140
Jolissa, 142
Joly, 140
Jon, 31, 57, 62, 258, 261, 346, 354
Jona, 259
Jóna, 321
Jonah, 139, 140, 258, 259, 351, 360
Jonah Jonas, 259, 360

Jonas, 258, 261, 315, 316, 319, 323, 325, 328, 360
Jónas, 321
Jonathan, 5, 52, 56, 60, 193, 259, 260, 280, 289, 307, 318, 319, 327, 329, 331, 335, 337, 339, 364, 367
Jonathen, 259
Jonathon, 259
Jonathyn, 259
Jonelle, 136, 139
Jones, 14, 17, 42, 47, 102, 116, 123, 128, 138, 170, 185, 217, 228, 233, 247, 259, 268, 271, 284, 287, 305, 342, 343, 349, 354, 355
Joni, 109, 259, 320, 355
Jonie, 259
Jonina, 259
Jónína, 321
Jonique, 192
Jonney, 259
Jonnie, 259
Jonny, 259, 343
Joona, 320
Joonas, 320
Joran, 140, 260, 261
Jordan, 5, 44, 61, 62, 139, 140, 198, 245, 254, 259, 260, 262, 278, 314, 315, 329, 335, 342, 358, 359, 362, 363, 367
Jordana, 140
Jordane, 140
Jordann, 140
Jordanne, 140
Jorden, 140, 259
Jordi, 259
Jordin, 140, 259
Jordon, 140, 259
Jordyn, 140, 259
Joren, 243
Jorene, 140
Jorey, 140, 293
Jorga, 126
Jorgan, 125
Jorge, 243, 260, 261, 318, 327, 358, 359
Jorgen, 243, 260
Jorgia, 126
Jori, 140, 243, 260
Jorja, 126, 315
Jorje, 260
Jorma, 256
Jory, 258, 259
Jos, 140
Josafata, 140
Josaffine, 140
Josann, 139
Josaphine, 140
Josceline, 139
Joscelyn, 139
Jose, 5, 140, 223, 258, 260, 261, 312, 318, 327, 329, 330, 336, 339, 354, 359, 367
Josee, 140
Josef, 260
Josefa, 161, 318
Josefina, 260, 318
Josefine, 140, 260, 319
Joselin, 139
Joselina, 196
Joselle, 128
Joselyn, 139, 141, 196
Josemar, 140

Ke ⇨ index

Me ⇒ index

405

Ri ⇨ index

411

Wy ⇨ index

This baby name book would not be complete without the names of the many talented collaborators who helped bring it to life. From the beginning, Michelle Shinseki was a graceful and fearless advocate, who saw the true potential of this project both on the page and online. Writing this book was an adventure, and I'd like to thank my brilliant editor, Alrica Goldstein, for her perseverance and passion in shaping and shepherding this book. I am indebted to Cathy Long for her meticulous research, indefatigable work ethic, and early-morning and late-night insights. Angie Hoogensen made designing a book with so many disparate elements and voices look easy, and even better, she made us look good! A first-time author needs plenty of sources of encouragement and knowledge and there were many folks at Meredith Books who generously shared their expertise and experience, including Jim Blume, Linda Cunningham, Lisa Berkowitz, Gregory Kayko, Matt Strelecki, Larry Erickson, Ken Carlson, Steve Rogers, Phil Morgan, Mark Mooberry, Toye Cody, Eddie Friend, Amy Tincher-Durik, Terri Fredrickson, Amy Nichols, Susan Soriano, and John O'Bannon. I am personally grateful for the support and nurturing of my family and friends, especially Deirdre Cossman, Natalie Danford, Cheryl Dury, Rhett Hall, James Hannaham, Maria Kleinman, Bruce Kluger, Amy Lee, Julie Malork, Teddy Moy, Christian Moy, Anne Sartori, Jonathan Parker, Lexi Walters, and Karr Wei Tan. Without their help and introductory assistance, I would not have been able to reach many of the parents and individuals interviewed for this book. And lastly, I would like to express thanks to all the families who agreed to appear on these pages and share their stories. They are the true pioneers, and they have inspired me with their tales of love and hope.